THE GROTOWSKI SO

WORLDS OF PERFORMANCE

What is a "performance"? Where does it take place? Who are the participants? Not so long ago these were settled questions, but today such orthodox answers are unsatisfactory, misleading, and limiting. "Performance" as a theoretical category and as a practice has expanded explosively. It now comprises a panoply of genres ranging from play, to popular entertainments, to theatre, dance, and music, to secular and religious rituals, to "performance in everyday life," to intercultural experiments, and more.

For more than forty years, *The Drama Review* (*TDR*), the journal of performance studies, has been at the cutting edge of exploring these questions. The Worlds of Performance Series is designed to mine the extraordinary riches and diversity of *TDR*'s decades of excellence, bringing back into print important essays, interviews, artists' notes, and photographs. New materials and introductions bring the volumes up to date. Each Worlds of Performance book is a complete anthology, arranged around a specific theme or topic. Each Worlds of Performance book is an indispensable resource for the scholar, a textbook for the student, and an exciting eye-opener for the general reader.

Richard Schechner
Editor, *TDR*
Series Editor

Titles in the series:

THE GROTOWSKI SOURCEBOOK

Edited by Lisa Wolford & Richard Schechner

London and New York

First published 1997
by Routledge
11 New Fetter Lane, London EC4P 4EE

Simultaneously published in the USA and Canada
by Routledge
29 West 35th Street, New York, NY 10001

Paperback edition published 2001 by Routledge

Routledge is an imprint of the Taylor & Francis Group

Typeset in Times by Solidus (Bristol) Limited
Printed and bound in India by
Thomson Press (India) Ltd

British Library Cataloguing in Publication Data
A catalogue record for this book is available from the British Library

Library of Congress Cataloging in Publication Data
Grotowski sourcebook / edited by Lisa Wolford & Richard Schechner.
        p. cm. — (Worlds of performance)
    Includes bibliographical references and index.
    1. Grotowski, Jerzy, 1933— —Criticism and interpretation.
    I. Wolford, Lisa. II. Schechner, Richard, 1934— . III. Series
    PN2859.P66G73   1997   96—53490
    792'.0233'092—dc21   CIP

ISBN 0 415 13111 1

For my moms,
Selma Sophia Schwarz Schechner
Artis Martin
RS

For Bos,
with abiding gratitude for what was given to me,
and infinite regret for my rebellious nature.
I remain always
your Nivedita.
LW

Grotowski, drawn by Marilyn Church

CONTENTS

PART III: OBJECTIVE DRAMA, 1983—86

PART IV: ART AS VEHICLE, 1986—

CONTENTS

ILLUSTRATIONS

CONTRIBUTORS

J. Ndukaku Amankulor taught in the Department of Performance Studies at New York University until his death in 1994. He was a director and had published articles on traditional African performance and comparative traditional performance in African and American journals, including *Performing Arts Journal, Exchange*, and *TDR*.

Eugenio Barba was born in southern Italy in 1936 and emigrated to Norway in 1954. From 1960—64 he studied theatre in Poland, spending three years with Jerzy Grotowski and writing the first book about him. He founded Odin Teatret in Oslo in 1964 and moved with it to Denmark in 1966. In 1979 he founded ISTA, the International School of Theatre Anthropology, and was awarded Ph.D. honoris causa in philosophy from the University of Arhus, Denmark in 1988. He has directed the following productions with the Odin Teatret: *The Birdlovers* (1965), *Kaspariana* (1967), *Ferai* (1969), *My Father's House* (1972), *Come! And the Day Will Be Ours* (1976), *Anabasis* (1977), *The Million* (1979), *Brecht's Ashes* (1982), *The Oedipus Story* (1984), *Marriage with God* (1984), *The Gospel According to Oxyrinchus* (1985), *Judith* (1987), *Talabot* (1988), *The Castle of Holstebro* (1990), *Kaosmos* (1994). Of the books he has published, the following have been translated into English: *Beyond the Floating Islands* (PAJ Publications 1986), *The Paper Canoe* (Routledge 1995) and, in collaboration with Nicola Savarese, *The Secret Art of the Performer* (Routledge 1991).

Eric Bentley, one of America's foremost drama critics, is the author of numerous works, including *The Playwright as Thinker, The Dramatic Event, The Life of the Drama* and *The Theatre of War*. Widely known for his translations of the plays of Bertolt Brecht, he is also a playwright and director.

Stefan Brecht is the author of numerous works, including an exhaustive two-volume study of Peter Schumann's Bread and Puppet Theatre. His other writings including *Queer Theatre* and *The Theatre of Visions: Robert Wilson*.

Peter Brook was born in London and educated at Oxford, where he founded the Oxford University Film Society. He is an advisory director of the Royal Shakespeare Company and heads the International Centre of Theatre Research based at Theatre des Bouffes du Nord in Paris. He has directed over fifty productions since 1946. These include *Love's*

Labours Lost and *Titus Andronicus* (with Laurence Olivier), *The Tempest* and *King Lear* (with Paul Scofield); and his celebrated stagings for the RSC of *Marat/Sade* in 1964 and *A Midsummer Night's Dream* in 1970. The same year, he moved to Paris to set up his own experimental theatre company. His productions since then include *Timon of Athens, The Ik, Ubu, The Conference of the Birds, The Cherry Orchard, Measure for Measure, The Mahabharata, Woza Albert!, The Tempest, The Man Who, Qui est la*, and most recently, *Happy Days*. His publications include *The Empty Space, The Shifting Point, There Are No Secrets*, and *The Open Door*.

Harold Clurman, founder of the Group Theatre, was a highly respected director and critic. He was theatre critic for *The New Republic, The Nation* and *The Observer*, and published numerous works, including *The Divine Pastime, On Directing*, and *The Fervent Years*. His contributions were recognized with four honorary doctorates, a George Jean Nathan Award, and La Croix de Chavalier de la Legion d'Honneur.

Margaret Croyden is a theatre critic, commentator and journalist whose pieces on the arts have appeared in the *New York Times* for over fifteen years. She has also written for the *Village Voice, American Theatre*, the *Nation, TDR, Antioch Review*, the *Texas Quarterly*, the *Transatlantic Review, Vogue*, and *Theatre Work* magazine. She is the author of *Lunatics Lovers and Poets: The Contemporary Experimental Theatre*, and a memoir, *In the Shadow of the Flame: Three Journeys* (Continuum Press 1993).

Halina Filipowicz, Associate Professor of Polish Literature, is affiliated with the Women's Studies Program at the University of Wisconsin-Madison. She is the author of *A Laboratory of Impure forms: The Plays of Tadeusz Rozewicz* (1991). Her articles on Polish theatre and drama have been published in numerous anthologies and journals, including *Engendering Slavic Literatures, Slavic Drama: The Question of Innovation, Poland under Jaruzelski, Themes in Drama, TDR, Theatre Journal, Theatre Quarterly*, and *Modern Drama*. She has edited special issues of *Slavic and East European Journal* and *Renascence*.

Robert Findlay is a professor in the Department of Theatre and Film at the University of Kansas. Over the years, he has written extensively about Grotowski's work in such journals as *Modern Drama, Theatre Journal, TDR, Slavic and East European Performance, Journal of Dramatic Theory and Criticism, Odra*, and *Poland*. He is also the translator (with Lillian Vallee) of Zbigniew Osinski's *Grotowski and His Laboratory*.

Ludwik Flaszen was literary adviser and co-founder, with Grotowski, of the Theatre of 13 Rows in Opole, Poland. His writings include *Cyrograf* and *Teatr skazany na magie*.

Marc Fumaroli is a noted scholar of theatre, literature and visual arts, and a member of the Academie Francaise. His writings include *L'Age de l'eloquence: rhetorique et "res literaria" de la Renaissance au seuil de l'epoque classique* and *L'Ecole du silence: le sentiment des images au XVIIe siècle*.

Ronald Grimes is one of the founding editors of the *Journal of Ritual Studies* and Professor of Religion and Culture at Wilfrid Laurier University at Waterloo, Canada. His writings include *Beginnings in Ritual Studies*, *Reading, Writing and Ritualizing: Ritual in Fictive, Liturgical and Public Places*, and *Ritual Criticism*.

Theodore Hoffman, formerly head of the theatre departrment at Carnegie Mellon University and of the professional theatre training program at NYU's Tisch School of the Arts, was also for a time associate editor of *TDR*.

Francois Kahn was an important collaborator in Grotowski's Paratheatrical and Theatre of Sources projects. He was a member of the group Theatre de l'Experience in Paris from 1971 to 1975, and of the Gruppo Internazionale l'Avventura in Volterra, Italy, from 1982 to 1985. Since 1986, he has worked as an actor, director and dramaturge at the Centro per la Sperimentazione e la Ricerca Teatrale in Pontedera, Italy. He has taught at the Ecole d'Art Dramatique in Milan, at C.S.R.T. in Pontedera, and in Londrina, Sao Paulo and Bahia, Brazil, in addition to conducting workshops with young actors in Russia and Israel.

Walter Kerr, who died in 1996, was best known for his work as theatre critic of the *New York Times*. He was also a playwright, teacher, and director. His works include *The Decline of Pleasure*, *The Theatre in Spite of Itself*, and *Journey to the Centre of the Theatre*. Kerr won a Pulitzer Prize for Dramatic Criticism in 1978.

Jan Kott was born in Warsaw, Poland, in 1914. He is Professor Emeritus of Comparative Literature and English at the State University of New York, Stony Brook. Kott is the author of the landmark work *Shakespeare, Our Contemporary*, and of numerous books, essays, and journal articles. His most recent publications include *The Memory of the Body* and *Still Alive: An Autobiographical Essay*.

Jenna Kumiega was born in England. She first visited Poland and saw the work of the Laboratory Theatre in 1972, while studying drama at Manchester University. She worked occasionally with the Laboratory Theatre in Poland and Italy between 1975 and 1981, while conducting research for an M. Litt (Bristol University) on the work of Grotowski. In 1982 she became involved with arts development in England, first in London and then in the rural counties of Herefordshire and Shropshire. She is the author of *The Theatre of Jerzy Grotowski* (Methuen 1985). Since 1991, she has been working as the Head of Arts Service for Shropshire County Council, England.

I Wayan Lendra is a Ph.D. candidate in the Department of Theatre and Dance at the University of Hawaii. He has spent thirty years as an actor—dancer, working in both kebyar and topeng dance-theatre. He was one of Jerzy Grotwoski's technical specialists in the Objective Drama Program at the University of California-Irvine.

Charles Ludlam, actor, director, and playwright, was founder and artistic director of the Ridiculous Theatre Company. His noted performances include *Bluebeard, Camille, Medea*, and *The Mystery of Irma Vep*. He died in 1987.

Charles Marowitz is a director, critic, and playwright who now writes a regular column for *Theatre Week* magazine. He is the artistic director of the Malibu Stage Company and currently Visiting Guest Artist at Cal Rep, a professional company attached to Cal State University, Long Beach. His most recent books include *Alarums & Excursions: Our Theatre in the 90s* (Applause 1996) and *The Other Way: An Alternative Approach to Acting and Directing* (Applause 1997).

Zbigniew Osinski was born in Poznan, Poland, in 1939. A theatre historian and theorist, he taught at the Adam Mickiewicz University in Poznan from 1962 to 1970. Since 1970, he has been employed by the Department of Polish Philology of Warsaw University. In 1990 he was appointed director of the Centre of Studies on Jerzy Grotowski's Work and of Cultural and Theatrical Research. He is the author of numerous books, including *Laboratorium Grotowskiego* (in collaboration with Tadeusz Burzynski), *Grotowski i jego Laboratorium*, and, most recently, *Grotowski wytycza trasy: Studia i szkice*. He has published edited volumes of texts by Grotowski, Juliusz Osterwa, Konrad Swinarski, Waclaw Radulski, and Mieczyslaw Limanowski.

Konstanty Puzyna was one of Poland's foremost theatre scholars. In addition to having edited the works of Stanislaw Ignacy Witkiewicz, he was the author of numerous works, including *Burzliwa pogoda*, *Felietony teatralne*, *Szkola dramaturgow i inne szkice*, and *Polmrok: Felietony teatralne i szkice*.

Thomas Richards, a performing artist, earned a degree in Music and Theatre Studies from Yale University as an undergraduate and also holds a Master's Degree in Art, Music and Performance from the University of Bologna. He became Jerzy Grotowski's assistant in 1986, when the Workcenter of Jerzy Grotowski was founded in Pontedera, Italy, and is now Grotowski's essential collaborator. He is the author of *At Work with Grotowski on Physical Actions* (Routledge 1995).

Donald Richie, the author of many books on film, was also a specialist on Japanese art and culture, and was particularly known for his studies of the work of filmmaker Akira Kurosawa.

Richard Schechner is the editor of *TDR* and the author of numerous books, including *The Future of Ritual* (Routledge 1993), *Performance Theory* (Routledge 1988), *Environmental Theater* (reissued by Applause 1994), and *Between Theater and Anthropology* (University of Pennsylvania Press 1985). He was the founding director of The Performance Group and is the founding artistic director of East Coast Artists. With these companies and elsewhere, Schechner has directed many productions including *Dionysus in 69*, *The Tooth of Crime*, *Mother Courage and her Children*, *Faust/gastronome*, and *Three Sisters*. Schechner is University Professor and Professor of Performance Studies, Tisch School of the Arts, NYU.

Ferdinando Taviani, born in Italy in 1942, is a prominent expert on Commedia dell'Arte. His books on the subject include *The Fascination of Theatre: Commedia dell'Arte and the Baroque Age* and (in collaboration with Mirella Schino) *The Secret of Commedia dell'Arte*. He specializes in the study of the social and cultural conditions affecting the European actor from the sixteenth to the nineteenth century and the problems of contemporary group theatre. In addition to his work as a historian, he has been active as adviser, dramaturg, and playwright for both traditional and group theatre. He has closely followed the activities of Odin Teatret since 1969, writing *The Book of Odin* in 1975. His more recent work includes *Uomini di scena, uomini di libro: Introduzione alla letteratura teatrale italiana del Novecento* (Il Mulino 1995).

Lisa Wolford is Assistant Professor of Theatre at Bowling Green State University. She has worked recurrently with Grotowski since 1989, and is the author of *Grotowski's Objective Drama Research* (University Press of Mississippi 1996). Her writings have appeared in various journals, including *TDR*, *New Theatre Quarterly*, *Slavic and East European Performance*, *Contemporary Theatre Review*, and *Canadian Theatre Review*. She is resident dramaturg for Theatre Labyrinth, an experimental performance company based in Cleveland, Ohio.

ACKNOWLEDGMENTS

A substantial portion of the work involved in preparing this collection took place in the summer and fall of 1995 while Lisa Wolford was in residence at the Workcenter of Jerzy Grotowski in Pontadera, Italy. Wolford thanks Carla Pollastrelli and Luca Dini of the Centro per la Sperimentazione e la Ricerca Teatrale for their invaluable assistance, as well as Roberto Bacci for allowing her to make use of the Centro's computer and communication facilities. She also thanks Jerzy Grotowski and Thomas Richards for their hospitality in inviting her to the Workcenter, as well as for the meticulous attention they devoted to editing, translating, and revising texts for inclusion in this collection. She also thanks members of the Workcenter community, most especially Mario Biagini, Luca Bolero, Walter Carreri, and Ian Morgan. She wishes to acknowledge her gratitude to Tracy Davis for her mentorship and sage counsel, to Paul Edwards and Dwight Conquergood for their input on various aspects of the project, and to Talia Rodgers for having the patience to see it through. She is profoundly indebted to McDonald and Ann Smith for their love and unquestioning support. Many thanks to John Wylam for his help in indexing the book, as well as for being such a patient and loving partner and devoted cat parent during the many research trips. Thanks also to Raymond Bobgan and Holly Holsinger of Theatre Labyrinth for the inestimable gift of their friendship and the joy of ongoing collaboration in their work, and to Brett Keyser, an extraordinary performer whose beautiful energy has brightened her days.

Richard Schechner thanks the *TDR* editors and assistants, most especially Mariellen Sandford, Marta Ulvaeus, Julia Whitworth, Anna Bean, Stephanie Haber-Hirsch, and Christine Dotterweich. Also he gratefully acknowledges the strong intellectual and emotional support he got from his colleagues in the Department of Performance Studies, especially from Peggy Phelan and Barbara Kirshenblatt-Gimblett. He deeply thanks Carol Martin for her patience, advice, love, and guidance. For his dear children Sam MacIntosh Schechner and Sophia Martin Schechner he offers gratitude for their conversations, insights, laughter, and love.

Portions of Chapter 1 and Chapter 29 appeared in earlier versions in *Grotowski's Objective Drama Research* by Lisa Wolford, University Press of Mississippi, 1996.

Chapter 8, "I Said Yes to the Past," an interview with Grotowski by

Margaret Croyden, was originally published in the *Village Voice*, 23 January 1969: 41—42, and is reprinted by permission of the author.

Chapter 16, "Is Grotowski Right — Did the Word Come Last?" by Walter Kerr was originally published in the Arts and Entertainment section of the *New York Times*, 30 November 1969: 1, 8, and is reprinted here by permission of the publisher.

Chapter 17, "Polish Laboratory Theatre: Towards Jerzy Grotowski," by Richard Schechner was originally published in the *Village Voice*, 8 January 1970: 45, and is reprinted by permission of the author.

Chapter 18 was originally published as a chapter titled "Jerzy Grotowski" in *The Divine Pastime* by Harold Clurman, New York: Macmillan, 1974: 221—226.

Chapter 19, "An Open Letter to Grotowski" by Eric Bentley was originally published in the Arts and Entertainment section of the *New York Times*, 30 November 1969: 1, 7, and subsequently apeared in *Theatre of War: Comments of 32 Occasions*, New York: Viking Press, 1972: 379—84. It is reprinted by permission of the author.

Chapter 21, "In Memory of Ryszard Cieslak," by Ferdinando Taviani was originally published in an English translation by Susan Bassnett in *New Theatre Quarterly* 8, 31: 249—260, 1992, and is reprinted by permission of the author.

Chapter 25, "Grotowski/The Mountain Project," by Jenna Kumiega was originally published by the *Dartington Theatre Papers*, series 2, number 9, Dartington Hall, 1978, and is reprinted by permission of the author.

Chapter 26, "Route to the Mountain: A prose meditation on Grotowski as pilgrim," by Ronald Grimes was originally published in *New Directions in Performing Arts*, Hamilton, December 1976, and is reprinted by permission of the author.

Portions of Chapter 27, "Theatre of Sources," by Jerzy Grotowski, were published in *The Theatre of Grotowski* by Jenna Kumiega, London: Methuen, 1985: 231—235. The current English version was translated and revised by Grotowski on the basis of various earlier publications, and is published here by permission of the author.

Chapter 31, "Grotowski, or the Limit," by Jan Kott was originally published in *New Theatre Quarterly*, 6, 23: 203—206, 1991, and subsequently appeared in *The Memory of the Body*, Evanston, Ill.: Northwestern University Press, 1992: 61—68. It is reprinted by permission of the author.

Chapter 34, "Grotowski in Irvine: Breaking the silence," by Charles Marowitz was originally published in *Alarums and Excursions*, Spring 1988: 3—6, and is reprinted here by permission of the author and the publisher.

Chapter 37, "Performer," by Jerzy Grotowski was originally published in the *Workcenter of Jerzy Grotowski*, Pontedera, Italy: Centro per la Sperimentazione e la Ricerca Teatrale, 1988: 36—41, and is reprinted here by permission of the author.

Chapter 42, "The Edge-point of Performance," an interview with Thomas Richards by Lisa Wolford, was originally published as *Book 1*, in the Documentation Series of the Workcenter of Jerzy Grotowski, Pontedera, Italy, Fall 1996. The extract printed in this collection constitutes approximately half of the longer version, and is included by permission of Thomas Richards.

The following essays were previously published in *The Drama Review* and are reprinted by permission of MIT Press and/or the authors:

Chapter 3, "Towards a Poor Theatre," by Jerzy Grotowski, 12, 1: 60—65, 1967.

Chapter 4, "Interview with Jerzy Grotowski by Richard Schechner and Theodore Hoffman," 13, 1: 29—45, 1968.

Chapter 5, "Doctor Faustus in Poland," by Eugenio Barba, 8, 4: 120—133, 1964.

Chapter 6, "Wyspianski's *Akropolis*," by Ludwik Flaszen, under the title "A Theatre of Magic and Sacrilege," 9, 3: 172—189, 1965.

Chapter 7, "Theatre Laboratory 13 Rzedow," by Eugenio Barba, 9, 3: 153—171, 1965.

Chapter 9, "A Myth Vivisected: Grotowski's *Apocalypsis*" by Konstanty Puzyna, 15, 4: 36—45, 1971.

Chapter 10, "External Order, Internal Intimacy," an interview with Grotowski by Marc Fumaroli, 14, 1: 172—177, 1969.

Chapters 12, 13, 14 and 15 were originally published under the title "On Grotowski: A Series of Critiques," 14, 2: 178—211, 1970. Chapter 13, Jan Kott's essay, "Why Should I Take Part in the Sacred Dance," subsequently appeared in the collection *Theatre of Essence*, Evanston, Ill,: Northwestern University Press, 1984: 139—145. It is reprinted here by permission of the author and publisher.

Chapter 20, "Grotowski's Laboratory Theatre: Dissolution and diaspora," by Robert Findlay, 30, 3: 201—225, 1986. The original version of the text was co-authored with Halina Filipowicz, and has been subsequently revised by Findlay and condensed by Lisa Wolford for publication in this volume.

Chapter 23, "Holiday," by Jerzy Grotowski, 17, 2: 113—135, 1973.

Chapter 28, "The Theatre of Sources," by Ronald Grimes, 35, 3: 67—74, 1981.

Chapter 30, "Tu es le fils de quelqu'un [You are someone's son]," by Jerzy Grotowski, 31, 3: 30—41, 1987. The current version of the text was revised by Jerzy Grotowski and translated by James Slowiak.

Chapter 32, "Bali and Grotowski: Some parallels in the training process," by I Wayan Lendra, 35, 1: 113—128, 1991.

Chapter 33, "Subjective Reflections on Objective Work," by Lisa Wolford, 35, 1: 165—189, 1991.

Chapter 35, "Jerzy Grotowski's Divination Consultation," by J. Ndukaku Amankulor, 35, 1: 155—163, 1991.

Chapter 38, "Grotowski, Art as a Vehicle," by Peter Brook, 35, 1: 92—94, 1991. The current version of the text has been edited and revised by Brook on the basis of an earlier English translation.

Chapter 39, "Grotowski Blazes the Trails," by Zbigniew Osinski, 35, 1: 95—112, 1991.

Chapter 40, "Where is Gurutowski?" by Halina Filipowicz, 35, 1: 181—186, 1991. The current version of the text has been edited and revised by Filipowicz.

Chapter 41, "Action: The unrepresentable origin," by Lisa Wolford, 40, 4: 134—153, 1996.

PREFACE

"I do not put on a play in order to teach others what I already know" Jerzy Grotowski, 1933—1999

Richard Schechner

On 14 January 1999, Jerzy Grotowski passed from activity into history. He was sixty-five. For more than twenty years he had worked nearly in secret. He died at the Grotowski Workcenter in Pontedera, Italy, far from the arenas where he had won his fame.

Since the mid-1980s, Grotowski appeared from time to time, made pronouncements, and offered interviews. Frequently his interviews and talks were published. He was well known and obscure simultaneously. His fame did not project him into the public eye but actually masked him. His presence was shadowy to those not in immediate contact.

Those making the pilgrimage to the Workcenter were admitted to witness the ongoing research of the Grotowski group, led by Thomas Richards and Mario Biagini. What was shown was *Action* ("not a performance, not a theatre piece," Richards and Biagini insist). Richards — the son of American director and educator, Lloyd Richards — is Grotowski's designated inheritor. Long ago, in the early 1970s, Grotowski "left the theatre" — a domain roughly bounded by the Wooster Group, Robert Lepage, and Pina Bausch on the one side, Peter Brook, Robert Wilson, and Ariane Mnouchkine in the middle, and Broadway, the Boulevard, and the West End on the other. Grotowski was no longer a part of that theatre.

Most young people interested in theatre, in the United States and the United Kingdom at least, don't know much about Grotowski, have never seen or participated firsthand in his work, and cannot directly study his methods. Still, Grotowski's influence and importance is deep, wide, abiding, and growing. How can that be?

To answer that question, I need to speak with two voices: one scholarly, the other personal.

Grotowski is one of four great directors of Western twentieth-century theatre. Stanislavsky systematized a method he felt would help directors to be respectful of plays, and actors to be truthful with regard to playing "life" onstage. Meyerhold thought through theoretically and demonstrated practically how to make actions just for the stage, how to give the theatre (as Artaud later said) "its own language to speak." Brecht, a poet-playwright-director, joined authorship, staging, and social purpose. After Stanislavsky, acting changed; after Meyerhold, directing; after Brecht, playwriting. But after Grotowski?

Around 1970, in the midst of a spectacular career making plays for the public, Grotowski decided to work either one-on-one or with very small groups. (There was an exception to this, which I will discuss shortly.) Even the public productions were for very limited audiences, usually no more than forty to eighty spectators. In such intimate settings, a performance was more an encounter than a distanced viewing. When he stopped making productions for the public, I was among those who complained that a great director was abandoning ship. But over time, I changed my mind. I now believe Grotowski never "left theatre" because he was never in it. Let me explain.

From childhood, Grotowski was attracted by Eastern philosophies and spiritual life. When he was barely twenty, at a time when such travel was difficult (Grotowski came of age in Poland under a repressive regime in the depths of the Cold War), he journeyed to central Asia. Later he made trips to China and India. When he returned to Poland after his first Asian sojourn, there were few options open for him with regard to his interests. He told me he selected theatre because during the workshop and rehearsal period — which he extended for months, even years — he and his small group of similarly minded people freely explored and expressed their thoughts, feelings, and beliefs. "Process, not product" was more than a slogan in Opole and Wroclaw. When the censor finally arrived, it was mostly to examine texts, not mise-en-scène.

And what texts did Grotowski put into their hands? During his Poor Theatre phase, Grotowski made text-collages from Polish and Greek classics and from the Bible; or he used works such as Christopher Marlowe's *Dr Faustus* or Calderon de la Barca's *The Constant Prince*. Oh, but how he treated those texts! He deconstructed them, interrogated them, rearranged them, used them as materials rather than as finalities. No one has made "performance texts" with any greater care, detail, wholeness, and complexity than Grotowski and his Laboratory Theatre colleagues. His stagings were, as he himself put it, scalpels with which to operate on and dissect both the souls of the performers and the condition of European society and culture. The censors had no option but to approve the words — of the actions they had hardly a clue. That the Poor Theatre phase produced great works of art is roughly parallel to saying that the stained-glass windows at Chartres or a Yoruban Gelede mask, like many other religious or ritual objects and performances, are great works of art: they are, but fundamentally as part of spiritual processes.

Grotowski's effects on the theatre will not be through the establishment of a method of actor training, an approach to mise-en-scène, or an insistence on a dramaturgy of political purpose. Grotowski will affect theatre through the influence he had on the people with whom he interacted on a personal, even intimate, level. Such an encounter might extend over years or it might last only a scintillation of time. Relating face-to-face with Grotowski could change the way a person experienced and understood the ground from which theatre grows. In other words, Grotowski changed lives and therefore changed the theatre. The tradition he comes from is that of the seer-shaman. His work was "technical" in the sense that Mircea Eliade identified shamans as "technicians of the sacred."

I was one who felt the heat of Grotowski's gaze, and who will miss his presence most dearly. He was one of my teachers, most especially so at the moment I was forming The Performance Group in 1967. For many who met Grotowski, encountering him was special. His presence hit like a Zen master's slap on the face. I always approached him carefully, with an almost Biblical fear born of respect. Not that he wasn't also playful and ironic, generous and sympathetic. He could go from support to icy sarcasm in a flash. It was hard to look deeply into his eyes, the conventional "mirror of the soul," because either you gazed at eyes reduced in appearance by thick glasses or when he took them off, a squint. His health was frail yet he didn't take care of himself. He smoked, he ate erratically. Once, in a California restaurant, he ordered a very large steak, asked it to be singed only, and tore into the raw meat. "I am a wolf!" he exclaimed.

Of what matter are these personal details? I know that others will have very different descriptions and experiences. We are all blind men giving opinions about the elephant. Grotowski shaped himself to suit his encounters with individuals. In his work one-on-one he had an unparalleled gift to enter into what Martin Buber called the "Ich—du," the I—you, relationship. His shape-shifting was not trickery or avoidance, but meant to drill to the core of the matter. His appearance was liable to change radically, as when in the early 1970s he morphed from being a chubby smooth-faced man in a dark suit and sunglasses to a skinny long-haired type in a blue-jean jacket toting a backpack — a cross between a hippy and a martial arts master. He slept God knows when, certainly not at night when he exulted in his work.

Grotowski's influence operates the way a rock dropped into a pond causes concentric waves to expand outwards in ever-widening circles. One can find Grotowski everywhere in today's theatre. Sometimes the mark is clear, as with Eugenio Barba's Odin Teatret in Denmark, Vladimir Staniewski's Gardzienice in Poland, James Slowiak's and Jairo Cuesta's New World Performance Laboratory of Cleveland, or Nicolas Nuñez and Helena Guardia's work in Mexico. Sometimes the influence is not discernible on the surface, as with The Performance Group and through it to the Wooster Group, or Joseph Chaikin, Peter Brook, and André Gregory, and many more.

But, ironically, a wide-ranging indirect influence is probably not what Grotowski wanted. For him, such an outward movement of effects is too haphazard, too risky, too fraught with misuses and misinterpretations. That is why he picked who was to have his most secret secrets, who would transmit the work to the next generation. As in the families of noh theatre in Japan (and Grotowski in key ways is like Zeami — the fourteenth-century playwright and actor, a founder and key theorist of noh drama), Grotowski found his "son" in Richards, in whose presence the master died.

Grotowski's influences on the theatre flow from three ideas that he identified, and attempted to systematize. First, that powerful acting occurs at a meeting place of the personal and the archetypal — in this he continued and deepened the work of Stanislavsky. Second, that the most effective theatre is the "poor theatre" — one with a minimum of accoutrements beyond the presence of the actors. Third, that theatre is intercultural, differentiating and relating performance "truths" in and from many cultures. He explored these ideas over a lifetime of scrupulous work that was precise, detailed, systematic, physical: a set of practices more than a colloquium of beliefs. His writings can appear inspirational or opaque. But actually working with him was another matter altogether. He belongs to oral tradition.

He was artistic and spiritual integrity incarnate.

The last time I saw him was in Copenhagen in 1996. We sat in the corner of crowded room drinking coffee. Though nearly his age, I felt like his son. When I learned of his death, I wept.

GENERAL INTRODUCTION

Ariadne's Thread:
Grotowski's journey through the theatre

Lisa Wolford

The long and multifaceted creative journey of stage director and performance researcher Jerzy Grotowski stands out as one of the most original and eccentric careers in the annals of theatre history. Beginning his professional work in 1959 as artistic director of a sparsely subsidized theatre in the small Polish city of Opole, Grotowski rose to international prominence within ten years, and was hailed as one of the most influential figures in twentieth-century theatre.[1] An early pioneer in the field of environmental theatre, Grotowski's contributions to contemporary performance include a reconceptualization of the physical basis of the actor's art and an emphasis on the performer's obligation to daily training, as well as the exploration and refinement of a performance technique rooted in the principles of Stanislavsky's Method of Physical Actions.[2] The group Grotowski founded, the Teatr Laboratorium, developed in a distinctive performance style that emphasized the encounter between actor and spectator as the core of the theatrical exchange, stripping away extraneous elements of costume and scenery in order to focus on the actor's ability to create transformation by means of her/his art alone (Grotowski 1968).

Grotowski rejected the notion of theatre as entertainment, seeking instead to revitalize the ritualistic function of performance as a site of communion (with others, with transcendent forces), a function he attributes to the ritual performance traditions of tribal cultures and to the archaic roots of Western theatre (see Kumiega 1985:128–143). Drawing on the sacred images of Catholicism, as well as on Jung's theory of archetypes and Durkheim's cross-cultural study of religious behaviors (see Ch. 2, this volume), Grotowski's productions sought to challenge the audience by confronting the central myths of Polish culture, provoking spectators into a re-evaluation of their most deeply held beliefs. The productions of the Laboratory Theatre were characterized by a transgressive and at times blasphemous treatment of sacred

Plate 1.1   Jerzy Grotowski in the late 1960s. (Photo: Nordisk Teaterlaboratorium.)

cultural symbols. Grotowski realized that identification with myth was impossible in an era no longer united by a "'common sky' of belief" and that confrontation with myth was the only means to penetrate beyond superficial acceptance of religious beliefs; by means of such confrontation he invited the individual (both actor and spectator) to explore his or her own sense of truth in light of the values encoded in the myth (see Ch. 2). Grotowski's productions were ritualistic, not in the exoticized or Orientalist sense of imitating or appropriating elements from the rituals of other cultures, but rather in terms of their reliance on Christian themes and imagery, a consistent focus on martyrdom as a heroic act, and an emphasis on music, chant and poetry rather than naturalistic speech.

One element of Grotowski's work that remained consistent from the beginning was his emphasis on sustained and methodical research involving the fundamental principles of the actor's art. In *Towards a Poor Theatre*, Grotowski articulates the need for a type of performance laboratory modeled after the Bohr Institute (1968:127–31), a forum for investigation of the principles governing artistic creativity. While he rejects any possibility of discovering "recipes" or formulae for creation, which he asserts would inevitably be sterile, Grotowski voices a desire to demystify the creative process, seeking to define a methodology of performance training that would free the actor to accomplish his or her work without obstruction and also without waiting for random inspiration. This notion that the actor's craft, while by no means scientific, is governed by certain "objective laws" (Grotowski 1968:128) foreshadows later developments in Grotowski's lifework.

In 1970, when he was thirty-seven years old, Grotowski startled the international theatre community by announcing that he no longer intended to develop new productions, having arrived at the conclusion that it was impossible for theatre to facilitate the type of communion between actor and spectator that he sought to realize within the frame of performance (see Kumiega 1985:144–156). "My work as a director, in the classical sense, was something beautiful. But a certain automatism had begun to encroach. What are you doing? *Othello*. And after? After, I. . . . One can become mechanical" (Thibaudat 1989:35). Rather than repeating his prior achievements, Grotowski preferred to shift his professional activity toward hitherto unexplored areas at the intersection of performance, anthropology, and ritual studies.

Robert Findlay estimates that the world-wide bibliography on Grotowski stands at approximately 20,000 entries (in Wolford 1996a:xv). Limitations of length for this volume make it unfeasible even to include all the texts on Grotowski's work originally published in *The Drama Review*, despite the fact that the journal played a fundamental role in introducing Grotowski's work to Western audiences. Richard Schechner and I have tried to make a representative selection of texts from each of the recognized periods of Grotowski's research, though our collection undeniably privileges English-language materials and previously translated articles. In addition to the predictable abundance of Polish documents, significant works continue to appear in French, Italian, and Mexican books and journals, as well as in Middle Eastern, Asian, and Russian publications.

The record this volume presents is incomplete from another perspective as well. The question of what gets recorded and whose voice is authorized to speak becomes particularly complex in relation to writings detailing the work of Grotowski's post-theatrical period. Both Theatre of

Participation and Theatre of Sources have been documented almost exclusively by occasional or outside participants; long-term practitioners and workleaders in these projects have tended to be silent about the precise details of the activities with which they were involved. Seen from the vantage of the practitioner, it is easy to understand how premature translation of nonverbal processes can threaten the life of a creative work (particularly one premised on disruption of the internal discursive voice), as the practitioner then falls prey to the temptation to reduce the new experience to the category of what is already known, imposing familiar formulas that fit badly or not at all. But from the viewpoint of scholarship, of performance history, the scarcity of documentation from the work of the paratheatrical and Theatre of Sources periods of Grotowski's research presents enormous complexities. Most available accounts of activities conducted in these years are written by persons who arrived for brief and at times relatively unstructured periods of work. Such documents can be extremely valuable, especially when inflected with the conscious artistry of a skilled writer such as Jennifer Kumiega or the embedded theory of an anthropologist as knowledgeable of ritual practice as Ronald Grimes. But the silence of those who were systematically present, working day after day for a number of years, makes it easy for the reader to overlook the fact that there is other knowledge to which we simply do not have access. A substantial portion of the paratheatrical work in fact involved no outside participants, but was conducted under closed conditions with a small team of skilled practitioners. The fact that none of these people have documented their experience creates a skewed image, emphasizing the more loosely structured, large-group experiments over the focused work of the resident team. The people who know aren't talking – at least not openly, at least not now, and possibly not ever. And so the rest of the story, which reveals a great deal about the question of conscious structure in works that highlighted spontaneity, about strategies deployed by the leaders in participatory work, about the intensive preparation conducted behind closed doors – all this remains unwritten.

OUT OF THE LABYRINTH

Performance theorists who examine the development of Grotowski's research emphasize the implications and significance of his decision at the initiation of the paratheatrical phase of his activity to abandon the formal structure of theatre production, eliminating the distinction between actors and spectators. Bonnie Marranca, with a discernible note of political ambivalence, comments on Grotowski's "distaste for theatre as representation" and suggests that his post-theatrical work provides "the most extreme example of the contemporary urge to turn away from spectacle, spectatorship, and by extension, aesthetics" (in Marranca and Dasgupta 1991:16). Even Eugenio Barba, who has always been among Grotowski's most steadfast and visible supporters and who began his own theatrical career assisting Grotowski in Opole during the poor theatre phase of Grotowski's work, finds himself at a loss when attempting to categorize the Polish researcher's work in the field of Art as vehicle. "I have been told that this is not a performance," wrote Barba in response to a rare public session held at Grotowski's Pontedera Workcenter in 1990, "yet I see 'people who are acting.' If what is happening here is only for them, then why am I here? Why was I invited and why did I come?" (1995:99)

The question of how to situate Grotowski's post-theatrical research remains contested, at times explosively so. Although he did not premiere any new productions after 1968, Grotowski remained active in a multi-faceted role as creative artist, performance theorist, artistic teacher, and pioneer of innovative performance genres. Figures as diverse as Jan Kott, Robert Brustein, and Charles Marowitz have questioned the validity of his post-theatrical work on the grounds that it offers little that can be put to practical use in more conventional forms of theatre practice. Such criticism reflects a common, almost pervasive thread of negative response to Grotowski's post-theatrical activity, focusing on the dubious legiti-macy of work that utilizes artistic means but is not mounted for public view. How is the value of such work to be judged if it is not assessed by spectators and critics? What and whom does it serve, if its primary purpose is not to communicate with an audience? What is the use of the actor's talent if the work does not culminate in a publicly accessible production?

Indeed, despite Grotowski's division of his work into five separate phases, from an outside perspective the relevant distinction appears to boil down to only two: his work in the theatre, which received an enormous amount of international recognition, and the work he began after "leaving theatre behind," which has been perceived as becoming progressively more isolated and obscure. People of the theatre have tended, by and large, to (mis)interpret the post-theatrical phase(s) of Grotowski's work as somewhat suspect, self-indulgent, and elitist, having more to do with therapy or alternative spiritualities than with art. Kazimierz Braun, as summarized by Filipowicz, depicts Grotowski as "a has-been who left no trace in the collective cultural memory or the current theatre practice," (Ch. 40:402) while Marowitz suggests that "As an 'influence,' Grotowski's dynamic corporeality came and went within a period of about ten years" (Ch. 34:351). The possibility that Gro-towski's post-theatrical research might have value in itself, quite apart from the question of its usefulness for theatre (or in most evaluations, its lack thereof), has received serious consideration only from a small circle of respected European theatrologues and an even smaller group of American scholars.

Grotowski himself found nothing shocking or self-contradictory in the unusual course of his creative journey:

> In appearance, and for some people in a scandalous or incomprehensible manner, I passed through very contradictory periods; but in truth [. . .] the line is quite direct. I have always sought to prolong the investigation, but when one arrives at a certain point, in order to take a step forward, one must enlarge the field. The emphases shift. [. . .] Some historians speak of cuts in my itinerary, but I have more the impression of a thread which I have followed, like Ariadne's thread in the labyrinth, one sole thread. And I am still catching clusters of interests that I had also before doing theatre, as if everything must rejoin.
>
> (Thibaudat 1995:29)

Grotowski saw the various phases of his work as being unified by certain consistent desires and questions, underlying interests that fascinated him since childhood, long before he ever thought of pursuing work in the field of theatre. Indeed, Grotowski claimed that it was almost by chance that he chose a career in theatre at all. When the time arrived for him to enroll for university studies, he considered three different fields which he thought offered more or less equal opportunities to pursue his primary interests: theatre, Sanskrit studies, and psychology. The entrance examination for the theatre school was scheduled first among the three, and when Grotowski (contrary to his own expectations), was accepted into the theatre program he chose to enroll.[3] Grotowski suggested that the underlying impulses of his work would have remained much the same even if he had chosen to pursue a career in another field.

Writing to Grotowski in the form of a published letter, Barba meditates on the enormous separation between his own work and that of his first teacher:

> You once said that you were like Aramis, who, when he was a musketeer always talked about becoming a monk, and when he then began his religious career always talked about his life as a soldier. Nowadays you often analyze your productions of twenty and thirty years ago. For a long time, you haven't wanted to make any more productions. Those who have seen your work know that you could make marvelous ones.
>
> You, however, are weaving other threads. You have fulfilled – you say – the task which was entrusted to you. [. . .]
>
> You often explained your choice. But you owe us no explanation. You ask new questions. Do you still ask *my* questions? [. . .]

What did we believe in so many years ago, when you were weaving your productions and I imagined that I was learning about theatre and, instead, was discovering myself while discovering you? You probably already believed in what you believe in today.

Is there, then, something which is steadfast and absolute? If so, it is found in the depths of a labyrinth. The thread thus becomes sacred because it does not bind us but connects us to someone or to something which keeps us alive.

(Barba 1995:136)

Barba's imagery of weaving and threads resonates strongly with Grotowski's own evocation of his lifework as being unified by "one sole thread." I suspect that Grotowski would have answered the question of belief which Barba raises in the affirmative – saying that yes, when he worked as a stage director, he already believed in much of what he believed in during the period when his life and work were drawing to a close.

The thread that leads out of the labyrinth, Ariadne's golden skein, marks the trace of an unbroken journey toward elsewhere.

THE MANIFESTATIONS OF PROTEUS

In his most celebrated manifestation, Grotowski was a stage director, founder of the Theatre of 13 Rows in Opole, Poland. This coincides with the "Theatre of Productions" or first period of Grotowski's work, which Zbigniew Osinski dates from 1959–1969. It is the Grotowski of this manifestation that Findlay describes as "[having] done more than anyone else to bring about a re-evaluation of the theatre and the premises upon which theatre has stood, not simply in the twentieth century, but for all time" (in Osinski 1986:9). Considering the impact of the Laboratory Theatre's work on performance theory and presentational styles, it is startling to remember that the ensemble mounted new productions for only ten years of its history, and was the object of critical attention for only half that time.

Even during the explicitly theatrical phase of his work, Grotowski problematized the relation between *pretense* and performance, leading his actors toward the accomplishment of a "total act," an absolute disarmament by means of which the actor "reveals [. . .] and sacrifices the innermost part of himself [. . .] that which is not intended for the eyes of the world" (Grotowski 1968:35). Actors in the Laboratory Theatre were not concerned with questions of character or with placing themselves in the given circumstances of a fictional role. Rather, their task was to construct a form of testimony drawing on deeply meaningful and secret experiences from their own lives, articulated in such a way that this act of revelation could serve as a provocation for the spectator. As Philip Auslander notes, "Grotowski privileges the self over the role in that the role is primarily a tool for self-exposure" (1995:64).

In *Towards a Poor Theatre*, Grotowski cited the "relationship of perceptual, direct, 'live' communion" between actor and spectator as the core element of the theatrical exchange. "At least one spectator is needed to make it a performance. [. . .] We can thus define the theatre as 'what takes place between spectator and actor'" (1968:32). According to Kumiega,

> Grotowski believed that the actor's gift of self-sacrifice had the potential to realize some of the fundamental aspects of ritual, for which he was searching in the theatrical experience: i.e. an act of revelation and communion between those present which would consequently permit deeper knowledge and experience of self and others (and hence change).
>
> (1985:143)

Underlying Grotowski's work during this period was a conviction regarding the capacities of performance to catalyse inner transformational processes, a function he linked to archaic performative forms, historically prior (in Western culture, at any rate) to the division between sacred and aesthetic aspects of art. Grotowski sought to reclaim and revitalize this affective capacity of performance, yet with full awareness that identification with conventional religious forms could no longer serve to invoke profound change on individual or communal levels in a world which lacked a "common sky" of belief.

From the earliest phases of his research, throughout each of his various forms and manifestations, Grotowski's investigations have been motivated by certain elusive but strangely consistent desires: a longing for communion and for the possibility of lasting transformation of the actor/doer as human being. Ludwik Flaszen describes the underlying goal of Laboratory Theatre performances using a rhetoric that is strangely resonant with that adopted by Grotowski in later phases of work:

> Grotowski's productions aim to bring back a utopia of those elementary experiences provoked by collective ritual, in which the community dreamed ecstatically of its own essence, of its place in a total, undifferentiated reality, where Beauty did not differ from Truth, emotion from intellect, spirit from body, joy from pain; where the individual seemed to feel a connection with the Whole of Being.
>
> (Flaszen in Kumiega 1985:156)

At a certain point in his research, Growtowski discovered that the conventional structure of performance could neither foster nor contain the type of communion he hoped to create. Kumiega suggests that the impossibility of systematically educating the spectator and the passivity of his or her conventionally assigned role were factors that obstructed the possibility for authentic encounter within a theatrical context (1985:150). "If Grotowski was really searching for the same level of authenticity as could be experienced in archaic pre-theatrical forms," Kumiega suggests, "then perhaps the search within theatre and art was self-defeating" (1985:156). Similarly, Johannes Birringer observes that

> [w]hen it became clear that [. . .] an act of *directed* spontaneous presence (i.e. [. . .] prepared for performance in front of an audience) could not break the divisive play of mirrors within the theatrical structure of performance, abandoning performance itself was only logical.
>
> (1991:219)

ABANDONING MIMESIS

Paratheatre or Theatre of Participation, which constituted the second period of Grotowski's research, involved an (attempted) "extermination of the mimetic" (Blau 1990b:255) and of the "mask of representation" (Birringer 1991:219). Paratheatre de-emphasized artistic criteria and questions of technique; the conventional structure of dramatic perform-ance was replaced by improvised activities involving spontaneous contact between a team of experienced workleaders and a number of outside participants.

Renata Molinari suggests that despite efforts in a range of contempo-rary theatrical experiments to bridge the division between actors and spectators, the boundary remains more or less fixed so long as performance is contextualized in a framework of organized representa-tion. She asserts that what is necessary to overcome this division is the elimination of "the possibility of being a spectator, creating, thus, a situation in a designated place and time [. . .] in which, on the basis of techniques of the actor, a meeting among persons can occur" (1982:19). Molinari describes Grotowski's paratheatrical experiments, in which she recurrently participated, as "a work of meeting" in which participants are no longer spectators, but are repositioned as co-actants "in the presence of persons who have greater theatrical knowledge, more refined tech-niques, different abilities, and who use all this on a level of non-representation" (1982:20). Daphna Ben Chaim, like Molinari, focuses on "meeting" as a key element of the paratheatrical work, as well as on Grotowski's disruption of the representational frame. Ben Chaim remarks that the Grotowski of the paratheatrical period had "given up all notion of representation" (1984:48); instead, he was "concerned with approaching reality head-on – by *presenting* it" (1984:49).

Ben Chaim is one of many scholars who, focusing on Grotowski's rejection of the mimetic aspects of performance, positions the director's work as an extension of the project of Artaud, a designation Grotowski would have adamantly contested. While Grotowski had great admiration for Artaud, whom he described as a "poet of the possibilities of the theatre" (1968:125), he resisted the pervasive tendency to view his work as part of an Artaudian lineage, a habit of thought Grotowski argued is distortive in so far as it misrepresents the technical and ideological basis of his own practice in the work of Stanislavsky, by whose direct successors he was trained.[4] Artaud, Grotowski maintained, had extra-ordinary visions of what the theatre could be, but never articulated a clear methodology by means of which to realize these visions (see Grotowski 1968:117–25). Yet the principles of the Theatre of Cruelty, particularly as expounded by Jacques Derrida (1978) and Herbert Blau (1990), problematize the boundaries of representation in a manner that casts interesting light on the dynamics of Grotowski's post-theatrical research. According to Blau, "the boundary of performance is a *specular* boundary" (Blau 1990b:256). "If there were nobody there to see it," he asks, "would it be another matter?" (1990a:253). Grotowski's paratheatrical experiments, which attempted to create concrete and authentic instances of communion among co-actants engaged in spontaneous activity, volatilized this boundary by eradicating the distinction between performers and spectators. If, as Grotowski does in *Towards a Poor Theatre*, one defines theatre as "what takes place between spectator and actor," and if "at least one spectator is needed to make it a performance" (1968:32), then what precisely are we left with when the spectator's role is erased – or more accurately, recast in the form of co-participant? What is being represented in a paratheatrical event, which abandons text and structure in search of an improvised dramaturgy of the real? Ben Chaim observes that the paratheatrical experiments, rather than being framed as fictional events, were "scene[s] in the real lives of the participants' (1984:70). Individuals were "free to respond with 'active or passive reactions,'" but were "no longer invited to imagine – to do so would be inappropriate" (1984:49). Like the Theatre of Cruelty as evoked by Derrida, paratheatre attempted to position itself in a realm outside the "infinite chain of representations" in which "the irrepresentability of the living present is dissimulated or dissolved, suppressed or deported" (Derrida 1978:235). Grotowski's participatory experiments attempted to access unmediated experience/perception, striving to create events that were "not a representation," but "rather life itself, in the extent to which life is unrepresentable" (Derrida 1978:234).

Susan Bennett, in a book on theatrical reception which opens with an epigram from *Towards a Poor Theatre*, is dubious regarding Grotowski's attempts to situate his work outside the conventional structure of performance, suggesting that the idea of theatre will inevitably remain – as a haunting trace, indissoluble double of the elusive "Real" that Grotowski seeks to address. "With the name of Grotowski attached to any project, the audience is provided with a particular set of *theatrical* expectations" (1990:16). Kumiega likewise comments on the tendency of participants in the early paratheatrical work to perceive events through a theatrical frame, interpreting objects and activities as symbols rather than actuals (1985:185). On one hand, I would suggest that the horizon of expectations with which individuals approached Grotowski's work altered over time, and that persons familiar with the latter stages of his activity (either through direct exposure or by report) were likely to have acquired a very different set of expectations from those Bennett suggests, expectations that presuppose a disruption/interrogation of theatrical structure. As Bennett acknowledges, the cultural markers that determine what constitutes performance have been repositioned again and again, usually in ways that provoke anxiety and resistance (1990:104). This level of anxiety is further intensified in regard to Grotowski's work, partly as a result of the relative inaccessibility of the post-theatrical projects, and partly in response to the esoteric aspects of his agenda, both real and imagined. Grotowski's post-theatrical work explicitly shifts the locus of meaning away from its conventional place in the perception of the spectator, relocating it (and it is precisely in this aspect that his later work most closely corresponds to ritual or initiatory practices) in the experience of those who do. The basic impulse of the work is autotelic, concerned with performative elements as a tool by means of which the human being can undertake a work on her/himself.

THE OLD HEAVY BURDEN OF DISCIPLINE AND PRECISION

In the early 1980s, Grotowski abandoned participatory work, finding it no more suitable than conventional theatre to facilitate his goals of creating authentic communion or rediscovering the ritual efficacy attributed to performance in the ancient Mystery schools. "There are banalities of work on improvisation, just as there are banalities of work on forms and structures," he warns (Ch. 30:294). He discovered that unstructured contact among random groups of individuals frequently remained at the level of personal and/or cultural cliché – performing "intimacy" or spontaneity rather than accomplishing an act of disarmament. Grotowski's experiments in paratheatre convinced him of the necessity for participants to demonstrate a level of "nondilettantism" or artistic competence in order to transcend such behavioral clichés and create a structure within which an authentic meeting could occur. He noted that during his research in Theatre of Sources he encountered, in the living ritual traditions of various cultures, a form of participatory theatre without banality. Yet in this instance as well, the problem of dilettantism emerged; imprecise execution obstructed the affective capacity of traditional songs and dance-forms. "Theatre of Sources revealed real possibilities. But it was clear that we could not realize them *in toto* if we did not pass beyond a somewhat 'impromptu' level" (1995:121). Beginning with Objective Drama Research, which can be viewed as a dialectic with the participatory experiments, Grotowski paid ever greater attention to issues of technical competence. Although both Theatre of Sources and the early stages of Objective Drama were structured to accommodate active participation by outside visitors, Grotowski increasingly distanced himself from the participatory model, taking up again the "old, heavy burden of detail and precision" that was the legacy of his work with the Laboratory Theatre (Grotowski 1990).

Grotowski's final work, Art as vehicle, developed since 1986 at the Workcenter of Jerzy Grotowski and Thomas Richards in Pontedera, Italy, fundamentally challenges contemporary, secular notions of performance as entertainment, with the attendant expectation that the value of such work can be determined only in the context of its reception by outside observers. This work centers on an exploration of very special vibratory songs connected to Afro-Caribbean ritual practice, and on a process of energy transformation that can occur within the doer as a result of working with these tools.[5] Thomas Richards, leader of the day-to-day work at the Pontedera research centre, suggests that the songs facilitate a "journey from one quality of energy, dense and vital, up and up toward a very subtle quality of energy, and then that subtle something descending back into the basic physicality. [. . .] It's as if these songs were made or discovered hundreds or thousands of years ago for waking up some kind of energy (or energies) in the human being and for dealing with it" (Ch. 42:435). Although witnesses are periodically invited to view the performance structures developed at the Workcenter, the reception of the work by spectators is neither Grotowski's nor Richards' primary goal.

Peter Brook, in a 1987 conference, focused on introducing and contextualizing the work of the Pontedera research center, directly raises a recurrent and at times explosive question: '[W]hat precise, concrete relationship exists between Grotowski's work – and the theatre?" (Ch. 38:379). Like Grotowski, Brook seems to conceptualize the post-theatrical work as a continuation rather than a contradiction of what came before. "If you look at this new work closely, you ran see that it was the old direction that continued to develop, to evolve, to become richer and richer, both important and necessary" (p. 380). Brook examines the question of how to evaluate Grotowski's later research first from the perspective of theatre, asserting "that there is a living, permanent relationship between research work without a public and the nourishment that this can give to public performance" (p. 381). Brook then shifts to a different register, suggesting that "in another epoch, this work would have been like the natural evolution of a spiritual opening" (p. 381). "It seems to me that Grotowski is showing us something which existed in the past but has been forgotten over the centuries. That is that one of the vehicles which allows man to have access to another level of perception is to be found in the art of performance" (p. 381).

In considering the question of the relationship between the investigations conducted at the Workcenter and the wider spectrum of theatre practice, Brook suggests an analogy to the relation between the monastery and the church, an analogy at one point appropriated and extended by Grotowski (see Tiezzi 1988 and this volume, Ch. 34), though he later distanced himself from such ecclesiastical metaphors (see Thibaudat 1995:30). Brook attests that the hidden work of closed research exerts a profound influence on other forms of theatre work, even if this influence appears indirect.

To approach the question of what the impeccable craft employed by Grotowski's collaborators might signify if public audiences are not granted access to the work, there are two distinct vantage points from which one can formulate a response – or else, like Brook himself, one may choose to take each in turn. If one insists on evaluating Grotowski's recent research primarily in regard to its tangible and immediate contributions to contemporary theatre, one might begin with a detailed consideration of how, concretely, the activities of the Pontedera Workcenter have fed back into more recognizable forms of artistic work. Both Grotowski and Richards emphasized that the foundational elements of their work are the same as those of the actor's craft. Indeed, a majority of practitioners in residence at the Workcenter over the past fifteen years come from theatrical backgrounds and have eventually gone on to pursue careers in public theatre performance. In addition, by 1996 more than 150 theatre companies had witnessed the Workcenter's activities in a format of work exchange, a dynamic based on peer critique and reciprocal presentation of the separate groups' creative work; the fact that the Workcenter's practice is made accessible in this way belies the supposed isolation of Grotowski's final research. A number of scholars and other individuals affiliated with the arts, whether as practitioners, administrators, or in some other capacity, have also witnessed the creative activities of the Workcenter. It is reasonable to assume that a fair proportion of these people have been influenced by what they witnessed in Pontedera, either on a level of artistic craft or less tangibly, in terms of an expanded vision of the range and potential of performance phenomena, and that this influence might somehow be reflected in their independent work.

But to judge Grotowski's later practice solely from the viewpoint of its impact on theatrical production is to impose a set of criteria very different from that which the creators of this work have articulated for themselves. Perhaps it is also necessary to examine Art as vehicle from a different vantage, accepting that the transformational effects of the performative material on the doers is sufficient as an end unto itself, without reference to other justifications or benefits. Filipowicz seems to take this point of view when she suggests that Brook's emphasis on the value of Grotowski's work for other forms of performance practice "decenters the claim about the spiritual search" (Ch. 40:404). "If Grotowski's new work indeed falls within the long tradition of mysticism – and this is what Brook seems to imply – then its potential for serving the theatre's practical needs of the moment is really beside the point" (p. 404).

Filipowicz touches on a central issue, as it seems to be precisely the ambiguous positioning of Grotowski's work at the intersection of performative and esoteric practices which has always given rise to the most intense controversy. During his Theatre of Productions phase, Grotowski used the structure of theatre to address sacred issues and themes; such a strategy is by no means unique, and the work remained consistently (if subversively) within the framework of Polish Catholicism. In Art as vehicle, Grotowski's aim was far more radical; he (re)appropriated the means and structure of performance to serve an explicitly esoteric goal, establishing a type of performance practice that attempted to reconstitute certain elements associated with Orphic and Eleusinian Mysteries (see Ch. 39:394). This particular transgression of boundaries is not an issue of experimentation with form or genre, but rather problematizes a fundamental division between sacred and secular (within which realm performance is generally positioned in contemporary Western culture). Grotowski's later research is even more suspect in that it corresponds to no recognizable orthodoxy, drawing from various North African and Near Eastern traditions, both in terms of its subject materials and its creators' understanding of energetic and ritual processes.

Richards relates the work of Art as vehicle to that of the Bauls, yoginbards of India whose spiritual practice takes the form of songs and dances that can be appreciated on an aesthetic level. He suggests that the Bauls, by means of their ritual songs, accomplished "something that was like performing, but it's not just that they were doing theatre [. . .] what they were doing really was related to the work with their teacher, to this something 'inner'" (Ch. 42:445). Speaking at a semi-public meeting held at the Workcenter in August 1995, Grotowski also referred to the tradition of the Bauls as an analogy for the practice of Art as vehicle. This comparison highlights the ambivalent nature of spectatorship in relation to Grotowski's current work. When Richards spoke to me about the Bauls, he noted that they would often travel from village to village to sing for the people they met. If the presence of outside witnesses was truly perceived as irrelevant to their work, then why did the Bauls bother travelling from one place to another to sing in the villages? Conversely, why would the villagers bother to come and see, if the work did not touch them in some way? Of course what the Bauls were doing was not, as Richards suggests, "*like* performing"; it *was performance*, whether or not it required the presence of anyone except for their guru (and presumably God) to attain its full meaning. The yogin-bards may well have been, as Richards claims, more concerned with some type of internal work related to self-transformation than they were with how the villagers interpreted their songs, but I venture that those people standing around the village square found their own way of coming to terms with what they saw. From where they stood, it was performance, which is not to say that it was not simultaneously another matter, something that might also be described as meditation or prayer.

Seen in light of a desire to separate their work from conventional notions of performance-as-mimesis, claiming for their practice an efficacy and objective impact associated more with ritual than with theatre as it is normally understood, comparisons such as those advanced by Richards and Grotowski in their attempts to peripheralize the spectator's role reveal a certain logic. The assumption that performance exists *for* the spectator, that it is a consumable product, the value of which can be assessed only in terms of its effect on an outside observer, is sufficiently prevalent in Euro-American theatre culture that Grotowski needed to articulate a different set of criteria for the evaluation of his work. Perhaps I must finally concede that Bennett is right in sug-gesting that Grotowski's work will always be shadowed by a particular set of "*theatrical* expectations," which is not to say that Grotowski himself was resigned to the inevitability of such projections, or that he did anything to accommodate them. Theatre, for the aging Grotowski, was something pertaining to his past, a practice with which he had not occupied himself for nearly thirty years. Art as vehicle is not a mimetic enactment of ritual performance; *it is ritual*, even if it is possible to discern the seams where Grotowski's practice is grafted on to the roots of ancient tradition. Even if one can argue that those roots seem to have been tampered with: transplanted, excavated, hybridized, perhaps even partly imagined. For the performer, the inner process (if, by an act of grace, it should appear) is actual. It is a manifestation of Grace.

Auslander, in a critique of performance theories rooted in a metaphysics of presence, elaborates on an assertion by Derrida that there are two responses to the realization that all is difference. "Having lost what we still suspect was the only valid theatre, the theatre of communal ritual, we either rhapsodize about theatres of other times and places or attempt to ground theatrical activity in versions of presence which bear the stamp of secularism, psychology or political analysis in the place of religion" (1995:66). I would suggest that Grotowski's post-theatrical research, most particularly Art as vehicle, skewed the terms of Auslander's equation through its attempt to *actualize*, to create – rather than "rhapsodize about" – a type of performance practice which reconstitutes the efficacy of traditional ritual, albeit within a highly controlled and limited setting, acknowledging rather than attempting to disguise or sublimate the metaphysical impulse that remains intransigently, if unfashionably, at its center. Which is not to suggest that Grotowski was fully successful in escaping the unnegotiable limit of representation, or that this was even, finally, a primary aspect of his goal; rather, it might be more accurate to suggest that participants in later stages of his work arrive at the sort of paradoxical perception that Barbara Myerhoff describes as characteristic of ritual practice: "[W]e make magic, believe in it and do not, at once, we make ourselves anew, yet remain familiar to ourselves, are capable of being carried away, changed, yet know fully and freely exactly what we are doing and why" (1990:249).

Throughout the final years of his life, Grotowski was preoccupied with what he described as the "process of transmission," saying that a deep and systematic research cannot be accomplished in the span of a single lifetime, but is rather the matter of many generations. Grotowski spoke of his lifelong investigation as "a tangible thread and a practice" that he himself received from other hands: "It's as if my heritage comes from distant generations. It passes through many generations and even several races. And, at the same time, it's not a question of syncretism, or a melange, but of the objectivity of the impact of certain practical approaches, even if they've appeared in different contexts" (Thibaudat 1995:30). Grotowski seemed deeply concerned that this practice (of which he did not consider himself the originator or sole fabricator) should neither disappear nor become frozen at the moment of his death, but rather should continue to develop under the guidance of others. A posthumously published text that appeared in the summer 1999 issue of *TDR* explicitly poses these questions:

What can one transmit? How and to whom to transmit? These are
questions that every person who has inherited from the tradition asks
himself, because he inherits at the same time a kind of duty: to transmit
that which he himself received. What part has research in a tradition? To
what extent should a tradition of a work on oneself or, to speak by
analogy, of a yoga or of an inner life be at the same time an investigation,
a research that takes with each new generation a step ahead? In a branch
of Tibetan Buddhism it is said that a tradition can live if the new
generation goes a fifth ahead in respect to the preceding generation,
without forgetting or destroying its discoveries. [. . .] In the field of Art
as vehicle, if I consider the work of Thomas Richards on *Action,* on the
ancient vibratory songs and on all this vast terrain linked to the tradition
[. . .] I observe that the new generation has already advanced in respect to
the preceding one.

By foregrounding the relation between tradition and research, Grotowski
articulated a notion of tradition-as-process that is in keeping with recent
paradigms of ethnographic scholarship, a conceptualization that fore-
grounds agency in the transmission and production of ritual practices
and allows for adaptation, invention and change, even as it sidesteps
politically-charged issues of cultural ownership and intervention.

As Eric Hobsbawm and Terence Ranger have suggested (1983), it is
the nature of an invented tradition to find its genealogy in the past, to
suture itself on to a base of purportedly ancient custom in order to
legitimize its efficacy and importance. Ideally, if a tradition perpetuates
itself over an extended period of time, the aspect of "invention" may
become so naturalized as to be nearly invisible, and the acts of
hybridization and transplantation involved in its creation recede from
view, perhaps giving an illusion that the invented practice is the result
of an uninterrupted transmission through the ages. Hobsbawm theorizes
that the process by which a tradition comes to be "invented" is most
clearly exemplified and most visible in those instances where a particular practice is "deliberately constructed by a single initiator"
(1983:5). While this is not quite the case with Art as vehicle, given the
important contributions made by Grotowski's collaborators, it is possible
to extend this construct to an analysis of the final stage of Grotowski's
work. Drawing on a background of extensive fieldwork and practical
research, Grotowski created a distinctive form of ritual performance
practice that functions in accordance with principles that can be traced
to recognized systems of esoteric discipline. The tradition of which
Grotowski was in a sense both creator and keeper was not transmitted
to him whole, not given to him, complete, in the framework of master
and disciple, but rather assembled through long years of practical
research and collaboration with ritual specialists of various traditions.

Grotowski did not seek out these specialists in order to create a melange of their disparate practices, but rather to investigate principles of psychophysiological impact that could be seen to recur as the result of different embodied techniques. This tradition finds its "home," its site of embodiment, in a dislocated interculture that is not African, Indian or Polish, and most certainly not Italian, despite the fact that the physical building where this work is done is located in a rural Tuscan village. To borrow a phrase from Joseph Roach, the practice of Art as vehicle constitutes a type of "displaced transmission," assembled from fragments of living tradition surviving in diverse locations and cultural milieux.

The last time I saw Grotowski was in 1996 at a symposium in Sao Paolo, Brazil, which focused on research conducted at the Pontedera Workcenter. The symposium was part of a month-long program of events that included presentations of *Action*, the performance structure developed by Richards and his colleagues under Grotowski's supervision, along with screenings of a film by Mercedes Gregory of an earlier performance piece created at the Workcenter, *Downstairs Action*. The final phase of the event consisted of a three-day conference with presentations by Grotowski, Richards, and Mario Biagini, another important figure in the research conducted at the Workcenter, along with scholars, artists, and arts organizers who had supported Grotowski's work during different phases. Among the speakers, there was a pronounced generational divide between the scholars and curators whose primary point of reference in relation to Grotowski was the work of the Laboratory Theatre, and those who became involved with Grotowski's work in later years.

Grotowski was always a very careful organizer, and he structured the conference in such a way that Russian director Anatoliy Vassiliev was the final speaker. This came at the end of a very long night, when everyone's attention was a little frayed after having been crammed together in a smoke-filled auditorium for three days, with all discussion mediated by translators. From the moment Vassiliev began to speak, the quality of attention among the 3,000 or so participants seated in the room became more focused, more electric.[6] He spoke in a straightforward, unpretentious manner, clearly from the perspective of a stage director, but also with a strong appreciation for the more ineffable aspects of Grotowski's work. Describing his first encounter with the research conducted in Pontedera, Vassiliev spoke about the experience of having come upon a door that seemed, from the outside, to be closed, but through which he was allowed to enter. He talked about what he saw in that special place, watching Thomas Richards and the other doers in their work. He spoke about his hunger, after having been admitted, to return there, to pass through the doorway again – and, with much humor and irony, he related the different tactics and machinations he employed to be allowed to see the work again, and the ways in which his desires were thwarted. Vassiliev described Grotowski's work as "the realization of a non-narrative theatre." The best actors, he said, are *transparent*, as if the body of the actor is something compact that cannot be penetrated. Such transparency, he cautioned, is extraordinarily difficult to achieve, although numerous methods exist to facilitate this return to the transparent body. In Grotowski's work, Vassiliev observed, it is possible to discern the precision and discipline that enable the actor to realize this quality of psychic transparency. When the actor works in this way, Vassiliev elaborated, nothing is methodical; he becomes entirely open, a channel for the divine. If the channel of transparency is opened, he continued, and the actor starts to gather forces that are linked to that spirit, at that moment theatre changes its essence. It stops being a narrative theatre. At that moment, he concluded, what we are faced with is something entirely different – something almost unknown in the modern world.

On the final evening of the conference, a woman in the audience spoke about the perceived isolation of the Workcenter. What is the significance, she asked, of the fact that all this knowledge, all this theory, ends up in the hands of a few actors for eight or ten years? I cannot fully recall who replied to her question or everything that was said, but it seemed to me that the true answer came in the words of Vassiliev. "Even if there's a small group, two people – Thomas and Mario – that's enough so that we may direct our thoughts towards a secret. [. . .] We are in front of a door. We must go through that door."

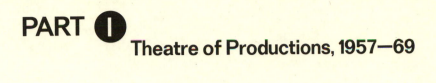

PART I

Theatre of Productions, 1957—69

2

INTRODUCTION

Theatre of Productions, 1957—69

Richard Schechner

Every Grotowski fan knows the story. At the Warsaw 1963 International Theatre Institute meeting, Eugenio Barba[1] (following Grotowski's instigation) insisted that delegates travel to Lodz to see the Polish Laboratory Theatre's version of Christopher Marlowe's *Dr. Faustus*. Barba arranged and paid for the illegal trip. Many of the international visitors were blown away, launching Grotowski's reputation in Europe and beyond. And a pattern was set: Grotowski would always be better received outside Poland than within. The indifference, or was it hostility, was mutual. Grotowski established his centers and undertook his performance research mostly outside Poland.[2] *Dr. Faustus* was in Lodz that day, but the Lab's home was Opole, a provincial backwater midway between Wroclaw and Krakow, where the theatre was struggling to survive.

What the delegates saw was the Lab's textual and theatrical montage of Marlowe's play, described by Barba in Chapter 5. *Dr. Faustus* was far from Grotowski's first production. After graduating in June 1955 with a diploma in acting from the Krakow Theatre School, he enrolled for a year's course in directing at the State Institute of Theatre Arts (GITIS) in Moscow. While at GITIS, he directed several plays under the supervision of Yuri Zavadsky, while studying the work of Stanislavsky, Vakhtangov, Meyerhold, and Tairov. He was drawn to Stanislavsky's work on the actor's process, a high regard that he has maintained his whole life. Grotowski began his professional directing career in Krakow in April 1957 with a production of Eugene Ionesco's *The Chairs*, co-directed with Aleksandra Mianowska. During the 1957–58 season, he directed two stage works and three radio plays, including Kalidasa's *Shakuntala*. During the 1958-59 season, Grotowski directed Jerzy Krysztof's *The Ill-Fated* and Chekhov's *Uncle Vanya*. Critics began noticing the young man, barely twenty-five years old. According to Osinski (1986:27–30), *Vanya* presaged some of Grotowski's more famous works. In his program note, the young director revealed an attitude towards text that marks his Theatre of Productions phase: "The creative theatre [. . .] does not want merely to illustrate the dramatic text mechanically and slavishly. The theatre wants to be a creative art using dramatic theme as its basis [*sic*]."

In 1959 Grotowski accepted Ludwik Flaszen's invitation to become the stage director of the tiny Theatre of 13 Rows in Opole. Flaszen (b. 1930), by then a well-known critic and theorist, was destined to play Danchenko to Grotowski's Stanislavsky. For their inaugural season in 1959, the two men proposed a slate of works by Cocteau, Mayakovsky, Eliot, Shakespeare, Byron, and Kalidasa – and one Polish play. The censors forbade only Eliot's *The Cocktail Party*. It was at the Theatre of 13 Rows that Grotowski became himself. But not immediately or completely, if published photographs of the early works are taken as evidence. The 1960 productions of *Cain*, *Mystery-Bouffe*, *Sakuntala*, and Goethe's *Faust* (Grotowski directed it for Poznan's Polski Theatre) look derivative of bio-mechanics and expressionism, a kind of forced "avant-gardism." The young director's Moscow education was transparent. The mugging and straining bodies showed that Grotowski's actors were not yet well trained in what was to become his rigorous system.

The big change occurred sometime before the June 1961 premiere of Adam Mickiewicz's *Forefather's Eve*. Not only was this the first Polish classic that Grotowski restored, but it was Grotowski's first wholly environmental theatre staging, bringing actors face-to-face with specta-tors deployed throughout the performance space. Gone were the thirteen rows; instead spectators were seated in small clumps of movable chairs with the actors performing amidst them. In writing about *Forefather's Eve*, Grotowski sounds like the man represented in *Towards a Poor Theatre*.

> If *Forefather's Eve* is a ritual drama, then we draw very literal conclusions: we arrange the collectivity, which is not divided into viewers and actors but rather into participants of the first and second order. [. . .] Gustav-Konrad's monologue was made similar to the Stations of the Cross. He moves from viewer to viewer, like Christ. [. . .] His pain is supposed to be authentic, his mission of salvation sincere, even full of tragedy; but his reactions are naive, close to a childish drama of incapacity. The point is to construct a specific theatrical dialect; of ritual and play, the tragic and the grotesque.
>
> (in Osinski 1986:54)

Photos show actors who are relaxed, into their bodies. Gone is the neo-constructivist feel. Even the poster advertising *Forefather's Eve* looks like what the world came to know from Wroclaw's Polish Laboratory Theatre.

Indeed a metamorphosis was taking place. In March 1962, the Theatre of 13 Rows changed its name to the Laboratory Theatre of 13 Rows. Grotowski told me in 1996 that he wanted his theatre to be like the lab of Neils Bohr that his older brother Kazimierz once worked in, a place of continuous exploration. *Forefather's Eve* was followed in February 1962 by Grotowski's reconstruction of another classic Romantic Polish text, Juliusz Slowacki's *Kordian*. From that point on, the new work was classic Grotowski, work that was exemplary of "poor theatre." During long months of workshop and rehearsals, the "work on the self" intensified; productions opened, were worked on still, went through many versions. *Akropolis* first opened in September 1962 but by 1965 had gone through five versions. *Dr. Faustus* opened in 1963, *The Constant Prince* in 1965. *Apocalypsis cum figuris* premiered in February 1969, after being seen in several "open rehearsals" during 1968. Dates for these productions are fluid, signalling more a kind of official recognition than any sense of artistic finality. Often enough, Grotowski opened a production more than once, showing it and then withdrawing it in order to rework. Sometimes a production would be worked on for months, even years, and never open. *Apocalypsis* was a later version of *The Gospels* which was never publicly performed.

From the mid-1960s on, Grotowski found it more and more difficult to do theatre as such. Performances drew closer to a direct involvement with spectators even as the work of the actors on themselves concerned intimate materials about themselves. But this material was not expressed in a personal or psychologically naturalistic way (as in some of the actor training exercises of Lee Strasberg). Rather Grotowski and his colleagues moved closer and closer to archetype and ritual. *Apocalypsis* came at the very conclusion of the Theatre of Productions phase. In 1969 and 1970 it segued into paratheatre, although it continued to be performed, in one guise or another, until 1981 (see Osinski 1986:161).

In January 1965 the Laboratory Theatre had relocated from Opole to Wroclaw, a large, important cultural and economic center in southern Poland with strong historical ties to Germany and Western Europe. Even as the theatre settled into its new digs near the old town central square, the Theatre of Productions was coming to its climax and shortly thereafter its conclusion. The Wroclaw theatre – an intimate space, a single brick-faced room, with a fairly low vaulted ceiling and magnificent acoustics – was initiated on 10 January 1965 with a showing of *Akropolis*, perhaps Grotowski's best-known production – maybe because it is the only one with a widely distributed videotape, filmed in the Twickenham Studios, London, not in Wroclaw.[3] *Akropolis* also shows the strong input of Jozef Szajna who in the New York program is given credit for "co-realization, properties, and costumes."[4] Grotowski is credited with "staging" the production.

The *Sourcebook* contains key texts detailing and explaining Grotowski's Theatre of Productions. Grotowski lays out his basic approach to theatre and acting, his treatment of sources, his textual montages and *mise-en-scenes*, and his work with actors. One ought to be careful not to confuse or conflate Grotowski's work with actors with his *mise-en-scenes* with his method of textual montage. The three are in conversation with each other, but are distinct. Grotowski is rare because he is a master of all three: actor training, *mise-en-scene*, and textual montage. Grotowski himself made the textual montage and depended on the actors to find specific gestures and vocal tones to express feelings and open new interpretations of the literary texts. Flaszen's role was to serve as Devil's advocate and in-house critic, challenging and querying what he saw. Most directors are not so widely skilled as Grotowski. Peter Brook is a master of *mise-en-scene*, one of the century's most important directors, but he has not developed a transmittable method of actor training nor has he done much textual montage. Conversely, Lee Strasberg was a terribly influential trainer of actors (and as his film appearances prove, a fine performer), but a lousy director. Strasberg didn't adapt texts at all. Brecht was a significant playwright, often piecing his works together from various sources, who also enunciated an acting theory and put together a company at the Berlin Ensemble that included great actors. But Brecht did not teach acting separately from trying to find out what worked for this or that particular production. In the European theatre of this century, only Stanislavsky, Meyerhold, and Grotowski have been master teachers of acting as well as great directors. And only Grotowski–Flaszen and Brecht have made new plays or original textual montages.

Over the twelve years of the Theatre of Productions, Grotowski evolved a way of actor training, a style of *mise-en-scene*, and a method of textual montage. These can be summarized.

1   Extremely detailed psychophysical acting, surpassing even Meyerhold's bio-mechanics. Grotowski's work with actors synthesized Stanislavsky's "work on the self," Meyerhold's bio-mechanics, French and Polish mime, yoga, tai chi chuan, and original movements devised by Grotowski and his actors during long hours and months of workshop research. Alongside the highly developed psychophysical exercises was an equally developed vocal technique. Actors learned to resonate different parts of their bodies, sing and utter sounds of a depth and intensity rarely if ever heard in the theatre before. It seems to me that much of this vocal work has its source in Grotowski's wide travels and studies in interior central Asia, India, and China.

2   A constructivist, then environmental theatre approach to space, bringing spectators and performers into very close contact with each other. The performance spaces expressed the themes of the productions. The spaces were not simply arranged for seeing or experiencing, but they acted strongly as signs. However, for the most part, Grotowski avoided "audience participation" as it was practiced by the Performance Group or the Living Theatre. Spectators were more like witnesses, the barely visible eyes peering over the fence to look down on the actions of *The Constant Prince*. Or, as in *Akropolis*, the spectators were the living observing the dead or soon-to-be-dead prisoners of Auschwitz.

3   Textual montage that took various literary or dramatic texts as material rather than as the original or ultimate source of the performance. In this practice, Grotowski (though he has never acknowledged any debt), did very much what Happeners were doing or, closer to home, what Tadeusz Kantor was accomplishing. Even in using the term "montage," Grotowski refers to the theories and practices of Sergei Eisenstein and his myriad descendants in cinema: the assembling of a rapid set of images that taken together lead the spectator to certain themes that are intelligible only in the whole sequence, not in any of its parts experienced separately. Grotowski developed this principle powerfully for theatre. To be effective, he needed highly trained and responsive performers. They were the actual bodies of the montage, the makers of the images, gestures, and sounds.

4   The development of a method of actor training combining the most rigorous physical work with psychological–spiritual practices. The underlying theory proposes that what is most intimate and hidden in each individual, what is core or deep or secret, is the same as what is most archetypal or universal. In other words, to search out the "intimate, most personal self" is to find the Universal Self. In this work, too, Grotowski found sources in his journeys to Asia. The training itself, however, was in no way mystical. Like yoga or martial arts, the techniques were precise, exact, disciplined, learnable. The results were indescribable, and would vary from person to person, event to event, moment to moment. In his actor training work during the Theatre of Productions phase, Grotowski added his own approach to materials he took from Stanislavsky, Meyerhold, and Osterwa[5].

3

TOWARDS A POOR THEATRE

Jerzy Grotowski

I am a bit impatient when asked, "What is the origin of your experimental theatre productions?" The assumption seems to be that "experimental" work is tangential (toying with some "new" technique each time) and tributary. The result is supposed to be a contribution to modern staging – scenography using current sculptural or electronic ideas, contemporary music, actors independently projecting clownish or cabaret stereotypes. I know that scene: I used to be part of it. Our Theatre Laboratory productions are going in another direction. In the first place, we are trying to avoid eclecticism, trying to resist thinking of theatre as a composite of disciplines. We are seeking to define what is distinctively theatre, what separates this activity from other categories of performance and spectacle. Secondly, our productions are detailed investigations of the actor–audience relationship. That is, *we consider the personal and scenic technique of the actor as the core of theatre art.*

It is difficult to locate the exact sources of this approach, but I can speak of its tradition. I was brought up on Stanislavsky; his persistent study, his systematic renewal of the methods of observation, and his dialectical relationship to his own earlier work make him my personal ideal. Stanislavsky asked the key methodological questions. Our solutions, however, differ widely from his – sometimes we reach opposite conclusions.

I have studied all the major actor-training methods of Europe and beyond. Most important for my purposes are Dullin's rhythm exercises, Delsarte's investigations of extroversive and introversive reactions, Stanislavsky's work on "physical actions," Meyerhold's bio-mechanical training, Vakhtangov's synthesis. Also particularly stimulating to me are the training techniques of Asian theatre – specifically the Peking Opera, Indian Kathakali, and Japanese Noh theatre. I could cite other theatrical systems, but the method which we are developing is not a combination of techniques borrowed from these sources (although we sometimes adapt elements for our use). We do not want to teach the actor a

Plate 3.1 Training at the Theatre Laboratory in Poland, early 1960s. (Photo: Fredi Graedel.)

predetermined set of skills or give him a "bag of tricks." Ours is not a deductive method of collecting skills. Here everything is concentrated on the "ripening" of the actor which is expressed by a tension towards the extreme, by a complete stripping down, by the laying bare of one's own intimacy – all this without the least trace of egotism or self-enjoyment. The actor makes a total gift of himself. This is a technique of the "trance" and of the integration of all the actor's psychic and bodily powers which emerge from the most intimate layers of his being

Plate 3.3   Training exercises at the Theatre Laboatory, early 1960s.
(Photo: Ryszard Cieslak.)

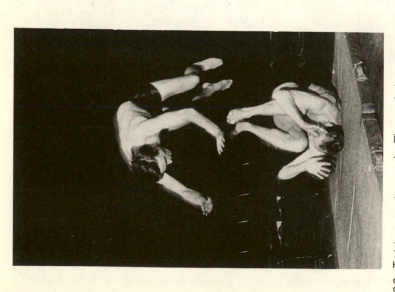

Plate 3.2   Training exercises at the Theatre Laboratory, early 1960s.
(Photo: Ryszard Cieslak.)

and his instinct, springing forth in a sort of "translumination."

The education of an actor in our theatre is not a matter of teaching him something; we attempt to eliminate his organism's resistance to this psychic process. The result is freedom from the time-lapse between inner impulse and outer reaction in such a way that the impulse is already an outer reaction. Impulse and action are concurrent: the body vanishes, burns, and the spectator sees only a series of visible impulses. Ours then is a *via negativa* – not a collection of skills but an eradication of blocks.

Years of work and of specifically composed exercises (which, by means of physical, plastic, and vocal training attempt to guide the actor towards the right kind of concentration) sometimes permit the discovery of the beginning of this road. Then it is possible to carefully cultivate what has been awakened. The process itself, though to some extent dependent upon concentration, confidence, exposure, and almost disappearance into the acting craft, is not voluntary. The requisite state of mind is a passive readiness to realize an active role, a state in which one does not "want to do that" but rather "resigns from not doing it."

Most of the actors at the Theatre Laboratory are just beginning to work toward the possibility of making such a process visible. In their daily work they do not concentrate on the spiritual technique but on the composition of the role, on the construction of form, on the expression of signs – i.e., on artifice. There is no contradiction between inner technique and artifice (articulation of a role by signs). We believe that a personal process which is not supported and expressed by a formal articulation and disciplined structuring of the role is not a release and will collapse in shapelessness.

We find that artificial composition not only does not limit the spiritual but actually leads to it. (The tropistic tension between the inner process and the form strengthens both. The form is like a baited trap, to which the spiritual process responds spontaneously and against which it struggles.) The forms of common "natural" behavior obscure the truth; we compose a role as a system of signs which demonstrate what is behind the mask of common vision: the dialectics of human behavior. At a moment of psychic shock, a moment of terror, of mortal danger or tremendous joy, a man does not behave "naturally." A man in an elevated spiritual state uses rhythmically articulated signs, begins to dance, to sing. A *sign*, not a common gesture, is the elementary integer of expression for us.

In terms of formal technique, we do not work by proliferation of signs, or by the accumulation of signs (as in the formal repetitions of Asian theatre). Rather, we subtract, seeking *distillation* of signs by eliminating those elements of "natural" behavior which obscure pure impulse. Another technique which illuminates the hidden structure of signs is *contradiction* (between gesture and voice, voice and word, word and thought, will and action, etc.) – here, too, we take the *via negativa*.

It is difficult to say precisely what elements in our productions result from a consciously formulated program and what derive from the structure of our imagination. I am frequently asked whether certain "medieval" effects indicate an intentional return to "ritual roots." There is no single answer. At our present point of artistic awareness, the problem of mythic "roots," of the elementary human situation, has definite meaning. However, this is not a product of a "philosophy of art" but comes from the practical discovery and use of the rules of theatre. That is, the productions do not spring from *a priori* aesthetic postulates; rather, as Sartre has said: "Each technique leads to metaphysics."

For several years, I vacillated between practice-born impulses and the application of *a priori* principles, without seeing the contradiction. My friend and colleague Ludwik Flaszen was the first to point out this confusion in my work: the material and techniques which came spontaneously in preparing the production, from the very nature of the work, were revealing and promising; but what I had taken to be applications of theoretical assumptions were actually more functions of my personality than of my intellect. I realized that the production led to awareness rather than being the product of awareness. Since 1960, my emphasis has been on methodology. Through practical experimentation I sought to answer the questions with which I had begun: What is the theatre? What is unique about it? What can it do that film and television cannot? Two concrete conceptions crystallized: the poor theatre, and performance as an act of transgression.

By gradually eliminating whatever proved superfluous, we found that there can exist theatre without make-up, without autonomic costume and scenography, without a separate performance area (stage), without lighting and sound effects, etc. It cannot exist without the actor–spectator relationship of perceptual, direct, "live" communion. This is an ancient theoretical truth, of course, but when rigorously tested in practice it undermines most of our usual ideas about theatre. It challenges the notion of theatre as a synthesis of disparate creative disciplines – literature, sculpture, painting, architecture, lighting, acting (under the direction of a *metteur-en-scene*). The "synthetic theatre" is the contemporary theatre, which we readily call the Rich Theatre – rich in flaws.

The Rich Theatre depends on artistic kleptomania, drawing from other disciplines, constructing hybrid-spectacles, conglomerates without back-bone or integrity, yet presented as an organic artwork. By multiplying assimilated elements, the Rich Theatre tries to escape the impasse presented by movies and television. Since film and TV excel in the area of mechanical functions (montage, instantaneous change of place, etc.), the Rich Theatre countered with a blatantly compensatory call for "total theatre." The integration of borrowed mechanisms (movie screens onstage, for example) means a sophisticated technical plant, permitting great mobility and dynamism. And if the stage and/or auditorium were mobile, constantly changing perspective would be possible. This is all nonsense.

No matter how much theatre expands and exploits its mechanical resources, it will remain technologically inferior to film and television. Consequently, I propose poverty in the theatre. We have resigned from the stage-and-auditorium plant: for each production, a new space is designed for the actors and spectators. Thus, infinite variation of performer–audience relationships is possible. The actors can play among the spectators, directly contacting the audience and giving it a passive role in the drama (e.g. our productions of Byron's *Cain* and Kalidasa's *Shakuntala*). Or the actors may build structures among the spectators and thus include them in the architecture of action, subjecting them to a sense of the pressure and congestion and limitation of space (Wyspianski's *Akropolis*). Or the actors may play among the spectators and ignore them, looking through them. The spectators may be separated from the actors – for example, by a high fence, over which only their heads protrude (*The Constant Prince*, from Calderon): from this radically slanted perspective, they look down on the actors as if watching animals in a ring, or like medical students watching an operation (also, this detached, downward viewing gives the action a sense of moral transgression). Or the entire hall is used as a concrete place: Faustus's "last supper" in a monastery refectory, where Faustus entertains the spectators, who are guests at a baroque feast served on huge tables, offering episodes from his life. The elimination of stage/auditorium dichotomy is not the important thing – that simply creates a bare laboratory situation, an appropriate area for investigation. The essential concern is finding the proper spectator/actor relationship for each type of performance and embodying the decision in physical arrangements.

We forsook lighting effects, and this revealed a wide range of possibilities for the actor's use of stationary light-sources by deliberate work with shadows, bright spots, etc. It is particularly significant that once a spectator is placed in an illuminated zone, or in other words becomes visible, he too begins to play a part in the performance. It also became evident that the actors, like figures in El Greco's paintings, can "illuminate" through personal technique, becoming a source of "spiritual light."

We abandoned make-up, fake noses, pillow-stuffed bellies – everything that the actor puts on in the dressing room before performance. We found that it was consummately theatrical for the actor to transform from type to type, character to character, silhouette to silhouette – while the audience watched – in a *poor* manner, using only his own body and craft. The composition of a fixed facial expression by using the actor's own muscles and inner impulses achieves the effect of a strikingly theatrical transubstantiation, while the mask prepared by a make-up artist is only a trick.

Similarly, a costume with no autonomous value, existing only in connection with a particular character and his activities, can be transformed before the audience, contrasted with the actor's functions, etc. Elimination of plastic elements which have a life of their own (i.e., represent something independent of the actor's activities) led to the creation by the actor of the most elementary and obvious objects. By his controlled use of gesture the actor transforms the floor into a sea, a table into a confessional, a piece of iron into an animate partner, etc. Elimination of music (live or recorded) not produced by the actors enables the performance itself to become music through the orchestration of voices and clashing objects. We know that the text *per se* is not theatre, that it becomes theatre only through the actors' use of it – that is to say, thanks to intonations, to the association of sounds, to the musicality of the language.

The acceptance of poverty in the theatre, stripped of all that is not essential to it, revealed to us not only the backbone of the medium, but the deep riches which lie in the very nature of the art-form.

Why are we concerned with art? To cross our frontiers, exceed our limitations, fill our emptiness – fulfil ourselves. This is not a condition but a process in which what is dark in us slowly becomes transparent. In this struggle with one's own truth, this effort to peel off the life-mask, the theatre, with its full-fleshed perceptivity, has always seemed to me a place of provocation. It is capable of challenging itself and its audience by violating accepted stereotypes of vision, feeling, and judgment – more jarring because it is imaged in the human organism's breath, body, and inner impulses. This defiance of taboo, this transgression, provides the shock which rips off the mask, enabling us to give ourselves nakedly to something which is impossible to define but which contains *Eros* and *Caritas*.

In my work as a producer, I have therefore been tempted to make use of archaic situations sanctified by tradition, situations (within the realms of religion and tradition) which are taboo. I felt a need to confront myself with these values. They fascinated me, filling me with a sense of interior restlessness, while at the same time I was obeying a temptation to blaspheme: I wanted to attack them, go beyond them, or rather confront them with my own experience, which is itself determined by the collective experience of our time. This element of our productions has been variously called "collision with the roots," "the dialectics of mockery and apotheosis," or even "religion expressed through blasphemy; love speaking out through hate."

As soon as my practical awareness became conscious and when experiment led to a method, I was compelled to take a fresh look at the history of theatre in relation to other branches of knowledge, especially psychology and cultural anthropology. A rational review of the problem of myth was called for. Then I clearly saw that myth was both a primeval situation, and a complex model with an independent existence in the psychology of social groups, inspiring group behavior and tendencies.

The theatre, when it was still part of religion, was already theatre. It liberated the spiritual energy of the congregation or tribe by incorporating myth and profaning or rather transcending it. The spectator thus had a renewed awareness of his personal truth in the truth of the myth, and through fright and a sense of the sacred he came to catharsis. It was not by chance that the Middle Ages produced the idea of "sacral parody."

But today's situation is much different. As social groupings are less and less defined by religion, traditional mythic forms are in flux, disappearing and being reincarnated. The spectators are more and more individuated in their relation to the myth as corporate truth or group model, and belief is often a matter of intellectual conviction. This means that it is much more difficult to elicit the sort of shock needed to get at those psychic layers behind the life-mask. Group identification with myth – the equation of personal, individual truth with universal truth – is virtually impossible today.

What is possible? First, *confrontation* with myth rather than identification. In other words, while retaining our private experiences, we can attempt to incarnate myth, putting on its ill-fitting skin to perceive the relativity of our problems, their connection to the "roots," and the relativity of the "roots" in the light of today's experience. If the situation is brutal, if we strip ourselves and touch an extraordinarily intimate layer, exposing it, the life-mask cracks and falls away.

Secondly, even with the loss of a "common sky" of belief and the loss of impregnable boundaries, the perceptivity of the human organism remains. Only myth – incarnate in the fact of the actor, in his living organism – can function as a taboo. The violation of the living organism, the exposure carried to outrageous excess, returns us to a concrete mythical situation, an experience of common human truth.

Again, the rational sources of our terminology cannot be cited precisely. I am often asked about Artaud when I speak of "cruelty," though his formulations were based on different premises and took a different tack. Artaud was an extraordinary visionary, but his writings have little methodological meaning because they are not the product of long-term practical investigations. They are an astounding prophecy, not a program. When I speak of "roots" or "mythical soul," I am asked about Nietzsche; if I call it "group imagination," Durkheim comes up; if I call it "archetypes," Jung. But my formulations are not derived from humanistic disciplines, though I may use them for analysis. When I speak of the actor's expression of signs, I am asked about Asian theatre, particularly classical Chinese theatre (especially when it is known that I studied there). But the hieroglyphic signs of the Asian theatre are inflexible, like an alphabet, whereas the signs we use are the skeletal forms of human action, a crystallization of a role, an articulation of the particular psycho-physiology of the actor.

I do not claim that everything we do is entirely new. We are bound, consciously or unconsciously, to be influenced by the traditions, science and art, even by the superstitions and presentiments peculiar to the civilization which has molded us, just as we breathe the air of the particular continent which has given us life. All this influences our undertaking, though sometimes we may deny it. Even when we arrive at certain theoretic formulas and compare our ideas with those of our predecessors, we are forced to resort to certain retrospective corrections which themselves enable us to see more clearly the possibilities opened up before us.

When we confront the general tradition of the Great Reform of the Theatre from Stanislavsky to Dullin and from Meyerhold to Artaud, we realize that we have not started from scratch but are operating in a defined and special atmosphere. When our investigation reveals and confirms someone else's flash of intuition, we are filled with humility. We realize that theatre has certain objective laws and that fulfilment is possible only within them, or, as Thomas Mann said, through a kind of "higher obedience," to which we give our "dignified attention."

I hold a peculiar position of leadership in the Polish Theatre Laboratory. I am not simply the director or producer or "spiritual instructor." In the first place, my relation to the work is certainly not one-way or didactic. If my suggestions are reflected in the spatial compositions of our architect Gurawski, it must be understood that my vision has been formed by years of collaboration with him.

There is something incomparably intimate and productive in the work with the actor entrusted to me. He must be attentive and confident and free, for our labor is to explore his possibilities to the utmost. His growth is/attended by observation, astonishment, and desire to help; my growth is projected onto him, or, rather, is *found in him* – and our common growth becomes revelation. This is not instruction of a pupil but utter opening to another person, in which the phenomenon of "shared or double birth" becomes possible. The actor is reborn – not only as an actor but as a man – and with him, I am reborn. It is a clumsy way of expressing it, but what is achieved is a total acceptance of one human being by another.

Translated by T.K. Wiewiorowski.
© 1967 Jerzy Grotowski

INTERVIEW WITH GROTOWSKI

Richard Schechner and Theodore Hoffman

SCHECHNER: You often talk about the "artistic ethic," what it means to live the artistic life.

GROTOWSKI: During the course I did not use the word "ethic," but nevertheless at the heart of what I said there was an ethical attitude. Why didn't I use the word "ethic"? People who talk about ethics usually want to impose a certain kind of hypocrisy on others, a system of gestures and behavior that serves as an ethic. Jesus Christ suggested ethical duties, but despite the fact that he had miracles at his disposal, he did not succeed in improving mankind. Then why renew his effort?

Perhaps we should ask ourselves only which actions get in the way of artistic creativity. For example, if during creation we hide the things that function in our personal lives, you may be sure that our creativity will fall. We present an unreal image of ourselves; we do not express ourselves and we begin a kind of intellectual or philosophical flirtation – we use tricks, and creativity is impossible.

We cannot hide our personal, essential things – even if they are sins. On the contrary, if these sins are very deeply rooted – perhaps not even sins, but temptations – we must open the door to the cycle of associations. The creative process consists, however, in not only revealing ourselves, but in structuring what is revealed. If we reveal ourselves with all these temptations, we transcend them, we master them through our consciousness.

That is really the kernel of the ethical problem: do not hide that which is basic. It makes no difference whether the material is moral or immoral; our first obligation in art is to express ourselves through our own most personal motives.

Another thing which is part of the creative ethic is taking risks. In order to create one must, each time, take all the risks of failure. That means we cannot repeat an old or familiar route. The first time we take a route there is a penetration into the unknown, a solemn process of searching, studying, and confronting which evokes a special "radiation" resulting from contradiction. This contradiction consists of mastering the unknown – which is nothing other than a lock of self-knowledge – and finding the techniques for forming, structuring, and recognizing it. The process of getting self-knowledge gives strength to one's work.

The second time we come to the same material, if we take the old route we no longer have this unknown within us to refer to; only tricks are left – stereotypes that may be philosophical, moral, or technical. You see, it's not an ethical question. I'm not talking about the "great values." Self-research is simply the right of our profession, our first duty. You may call it ethical, but personally I prefer to treat it as part of the technique because that way there is no sense of its being sweet or hypocritical.

The third thing one could consider "ethical" is the problem of process and result. When I work – either during a course or while directing – what I say is never an objective truth. Whatever I say are stimuli which give the actor a chance to be creative. I say, "fix your attention on this," search for this solemn and recognizable process. You must not think of the result. But, at the same time, finally, you can't ignore the result because from the objective point of view the deciding factor in art is the result. In that way, art is immoral. He is right who has the result. That's the way it is. But in order to get the result – and this is the paradox – you must not look for it. If you look for it you will block the natural creative process. In looking only the brain works; the mind imposes solutions it already knows and you begin juggling known things. That is why we must look without fixing our attention on the result. What do we look for? What, for example, are my associations, my key memories – recognizing these not in thought but through my body's impulses; to become conscious of them, mastering and organizing them, and finding out whether they are stronger now than when they were unformed. Do they reveal more to us or less? If less, then we have not structured them well.

One must not think of the result and the result will come; there will be a moment when the fight for the result will be fully conscious and inevitable, engaging our entire mental machinery. The only problem is when.

It is the moment when our living creative material is concretely present. At that point one can use one's mind to structure the associations and to study the relationship with the audience. Things which were prohibited earlier are inevitable here. And, of course, there are individual variations. There is the possibility that someone will begin with the play of the mind and then later leave it for a time and still later come back to it. If this is your way, still do not think of the result but of the process of recognizing the living material.

Another problem called "ethics." If one formulates what I am about to formulate, one thinks of it as being very ethical; but I have found at the base of it a completely objective and technical problem. The principle is that the actor, in order to fulfil himself, must not work for himself. Through penetrating his relationship with others – studying the elements of contact – the actor will discover what is in him. He must give himself totally.

But there is a problem. The actor has two possibilities. Either, one, he plays for the audience – which is completely natural if we think of the theatre's function – which leads him to a kind of flirtation that means that he is playing for himself, for the satisfaction of being accepted, loved, affirmed – and the result is narcissism; or, two, he works directly for himself. That means he observes his emotions, looks for the richness of his psychic states – and this is the shortest way to hypocrisy and hysteria. Why hypocrisy? Because all psychic states observed are no longer lived, because emotion observed is no longer emotion. And there is always the pressure to pump up great emotions within oneself. But emotions do not depend upon our wills. We begin to imitate emotions within ourselves, and that is pure hypocrisy. Then the actor looks for something concrete in himself and the easiest thing is hysteria. He hides within hysterical reactions – formless improvisations with wild gestures and screams. This, too, is narcissism. But if acting is not for the audience and not for oneself, what is left?

The answer is a difficult one. One begins by finding those scenes that give the actor a chance to research his relationship with others. He penetrates the elements of contact in the body. He concretely searches for those memories and associations which have decisively con-ditioned the form of contact. He must give himself totally to his research. In that sense it is like authentic love, deep love. But there is no answer to the question, "Love for whom?" Not for God, who no longer functions for our generation. And not for nature or pantheism. These are smoky mysteries. Man always needs another human being who can absolutely fulfil and understand him. But that is like loving the Absolute or the Ideal, loving someone who understands you but whom you've never met.

Someone you are searching for. There is no single, simple answer. One thing is clear: the actor must give himself and not play for himself or for the spectator. His search must be directed from within himself *to* the outside, but not *for* the outside.

When the actor begins to work through contact, when he begins to live in relation to someone – not his stage partner but the partner of his own biography – when he begins to penetrate through a study of his body's impulses, the relationship of this contact, this process of exchange, there is always a rebirth in the actor. Afterwards he begins to use the other actors as screens for his life's partner, he begins to project things onto the characters in the play. And this is his second rebirth.

Finally the actor discovers what I call the "secure partner," this special being in front of whom he does everything, in front of whom he plays with the other characters and to whom he reveals his most personal problems and experiences. This human being – this "secure partner" – cannot be defined. But at the moment when the actor discovers his "secure partner" the third and strongest rebirth occurs, a visible change in the actor's behavior. It is during this third rebirth that the actor finds solutions to the most difficult problems: how to create while one is controlled by others, how to create without the security of creation, how to find a security which is inevitable if we want to express *ourselves* despite the fact that theatre is a *collective* creation in which we are controlled by many people and working during hours that are imposed on us.

One need not define this "secure partner" to the actor, one need only say "you must give yourself absolutely" and many actors understand. Each actor has his own chance of making this discovery, and it's a completely different chance for each. This third rebirth is neither for oneself nor for the spectator. It is most paradoxical. It gives the actor his greatest range of possibilities. One can think of it as ethical, but truly it is technical – despite the fact that it is also mysterious.

SCHECHNER: Two related questions. Several times you told students – particularly during the *exercises plastiques* (which I will describe later) – to "surpass yourselves," "have courage," "go beyond." And you also said that one must resign oneself "not to do." First question: What is the relationship between surpassing oneself and resigning oneself? Second question – and I ask them together because I feel they are related, though I don't know why: Several times when we were working with scenes from Shakespeare you said, "Don't play the text, you are not Juliet, you didn't write the text." What did you mean?

GROTOWSKI: Without a doubt your questions are related, your impul–ses are very precise. But it is very difficult to explain. I know what the relationship is but it is difficult for me to express it in logical terms. I accept that. At a certain point, traditional logic does not function. There was a period during my career when I wanted to find the logical explanation for everything. I made formulas that were abstract so that they could encompass two divergent processes. But these abstract formulas were not real; I made pretty sentences which gave the impression that everything was logical. This was cheating, and I decided never again. When I don't know why, I don't try to devise formulas. But often it's a problem of different logical systems. In life we have both formal and paradoxical logic. The paradoxical logical system is strange to our civilization but quite common to Asian or medieval thought. It will be difficult for me to explain the relationship you sensed in your questions, but I think I can explain the consequences of that relationship.

When I say "go beyond yourself," I am asking for an insupportable effort. One is obliged not to stop despite fatigue and to do things that we know well we cannot do. That means one is also obliged to be courageous. What does this lead to? There are certain points of fatigue which break the control of the mind, a control that blocks us. When we find the courage to do things that are impossible, we make the discovery that our body does not block us. We do the impossible and the division within us between conception and the body's ability disappears. This attitude, this determination, is a training for how to go beyond our limits. These are not the limits of our nature, but those of our discomfort. These are the limits we impose upon ourselves that block the creative process, because creativity is never comfortable. If we begin really to work with association during the *exercises plastiques*, transforming the body movements into a cycle of personal impulses – at that moment we must prolong our determination and not look for the easy. We can "act it" in the bad sense, calculating a move, a look, and thoughts. This is simply pumping.

What will unblock the natural and integral possibilities? To act – that is to react – not to conduct the process but to refer it to personal experiences and to be conducted. The process must take us. At these moments one must be internally passive but externally active. The formula of resigning oneself "not to do" is a stimulus. But if the actor says, "Now I must decide to find my experiences and my intimate associations, I must find my 'secure partner,'" he will be very active, but he will be like somebody confessing who has already written everything out in pretty sentences. He confesses, but it's nothing. But if he resigns himself "not to do" this difficult thing and refers himself to things that are truly personal and externalizes these, he would find a very difficult truth. This internal passivity gives the actor the chance to be taken. If one begins too early to conduct the work, then the process is blocked.

SCHECHNER: So that's why you said, "Don't play the text." It wasn't time yet.

GROTOWSKI: Yes. If the actor wants to play the text, he's doing what's easiest. The text has been written; he says it with feeling and he frees himself from the obligation of doing anything himself. But if, as we did during the last days of the course, he works with a silent score – saying the text only in his thoughts – he unmasks this lack of personal action and reaction. Then the actor is obliged to refer to himself within his own context and to find his own line of impulses. One can either not say the text at all or one can "recite" it as a quotation. The actor thinks he is quoting, but he finds the cycle of thought which is revealed in the words. There are many possibilities. In the Desdemona murder scene we worked on in the course her text functioned as erotic love-play. Those words became the actress's – it didn't matter that she didn't write them. The problem is always the same: stop the cheating, find the authentic impulses. The goal is to find a meeting between the text and the actor.

HOFFMAN: When the students were doing private work you demanded absolute silence. This was hard to get because it runs against our tradition where we are all "sympathetic collaborators" responding with "love" to our fellow actor. A few words on this.

GROTOWSKI: Lack of tact is my specialty. In this country I have observed a certain external friendliness which is part of your daily mask. People are very 'friendly," but it is terribly difficult for them to make authentic contact; basically they are very lonely. If we fraternize too easily, without etiquette or ceremony, natural contact is impossible. If you are sincere with another, the other treats that as part of the daily mask.

I find that people here function and behave like instruments or objects. For example – and this has happened to me frequently – I am invited out by people who are not my friends. After a few drinks they begin hysterically to confess themselves and they put me in the position of a judge. It's a role that is imposed on me, as if I were a chair to be sat on. I am as much a judge as a consumer who goes into a store; at the base of it the store is not there for him – he exists for the store.

There are qualities of behavior in every country that one must break through in order to create. Creativity does not mean using our daily masks but rather to make exceptional situations where our daily masks do not function. Take the actor. He works in front of others, he must confess his most personal motives, he must express things he always hides. He must do this consciously, in a structured way, because an inarticulate confession is no confession at all. What blocks him most are his fellow actors and the director. If he listens to the reactions of others he will close himself. He wonders if his confession is funny. He thinks he may become the object of a behind-the-back discussion, and he cannot reveal himself. Every actor who privately discusses the intimate associations of another actor knows that when he expresses his own personal motives he, too, will be the subject of someone else's jokes. Thus one must impose on the actors and the director a rigid obligation to be discreet. It's not an ethical problem, but a professional obligation – like those we impose on doctors and lawyers.

Silence is something else. The actor is always tempted into publicotropism. This blocks the deep processes and results in that flirtation I talked about before. For example, the actor does something that one may call funny in the positive sense; his colleagues laugh. Then he begins pumping to make them laugh more. And what was at first a natural reaction becomes artificial.

There is also the problem of creative passivity. It's difficult to express, but the actor must begin by doing nothing. Silence. Full silence. This includes his thoughts. External silence works as a stimulus. If there is absolute silence and if, for several moments, the actor does absolutely nothing, this internal silence begins and it turns his entire nature toward its sources.

SCHECHNER: I would like now to move into a related area. A lot of work in the course and, as I understand it, in your troupe is concerned with the *exercises plastiques*. I don't want to translate this term because the work is not exactly what we understand in English as "body movement." Your exercises are psycho-physical; there is an absolute unity between the psychical and the physical, the associations of the body are also the associations of the feelings. How did you develop these exercises and how do they function in the training and in the *mise-en-scene*?

GROTOWSKI: All the movement exercises had, at first, a completely different function. Their development is the result of a great deal of experimentation. For example, we began by doing yoga directed toward absolute concentration. Is it true, we asked, that yoga can give actors the power of concentration? We observed that despite all our hopes the opposite happened. There was a certain concentration, but it was introverted. This concentration destroys all expression; it's an internal sleep, an inexpressive equilibrium: a great rest which ends all actions. This should have been obvious because the goal of yoga is to stop three processes: thought, breathing, and ejaculation. That means all life processes are stopped and one finds fullness and fulfilment in conscious death, autonomy enclosed in our own kernel. I don't attack it, but it's not for actors.

But we also observed that certain yoga positions help very much the natural reactions of the spinal column; they lead to a sureness of one's body, a natural adaptation to space. So why get rid of them? Just change all their currents. We began to search, to look for different types of contact in these exercises. How could we transform the physical elements into elements of human contact? By playing with one's partner. A living dialogue with the body, with the partner we have evoked in our imagination, or perhaps between the parts of the body, where the hand speaks to the leg without putting this dialogue into words or thought. These almost paradoxical positions go beyond the limits of naturalism.

We also began to work with the Delsarte system. I was very interested in Delsarte's thesis that there are introverted and extroverted reactions in human contact. At the same time, I found his thesis very stereotyped; it was really very funny as actor training, but there was something to it, so I studied it. We began searching through Delsarte's program for those elements which are not stereotyped. Afterwards we had to find new elements of our own in order to realize the goal of our program. Then the personality of the actor working as instructor became instrumental. The physical exercises were largely developed by the actors. I only asked the questions, the actors searched. One question was followed by another. Some of the exercises were conditioned by an actress who had great difficulty with them. For that reason I made her an instructor. She was ambitious and now she is a great master of these exercises – but we searched together.

Later we found that if one treats the exercises as purely physical, an emotive hypocrisy, beautiful gestures with the emotions of a fairy-dance develop. So we gave that up and began to look for personal justification in small details: by playing with colleagues with a sense of surprise, of the unexpected – real justifications which are unexpected – how to fight, how to make unkind gestures, how to parody oneself, and so on. At that moment, the exercises took life.

With these exercises we looked for a conjunction between the structure of an element and the associations which transform it into the mode of each particular actor. How can one conserve the objective elements and still go beyond them toward a purely subjective work? This is the contradiction of acting. It's the kernel of the training.

There are different kinds of exercises. The program is always open. When we are working on a production we do not use the exercises in a play. If we did, it would be stereotyped. But for certain plays, certain scenes, we may have to do special exercises. Sometimes something is left from these for the basic program.

There have been periods – up to eight months – when we have done no exercises at all. We found that we were doing the exercises for their own sake and we gave them up. The actors began to approach perfection, they did impossible things. It was like the tiger who ate his own tail. At that point we stopped the exercises for eight months. When we resumed them they were completely different. The body developed new resistances. The people were the same but they had changed. And we resumed with a great deal more personalization.

HOFFMAN: You told us that you use these exercises as tests. What do you look for?

GROTOWSKI: They do function as tests. If an actor has blocks, the underdeveloped parts of his body are very visible. One can also observe the blocks in the work on associations. For example, in a physical exercise it is necessary to evoke a partner, to live for him, take the stimulus from him – all the functions of dialogue. Blocks in this process are clearly visible during the exercises. In the somersaults, the actor who hesitates, who will not take risks, will also hesitate at the culminating moment of his role.

SCHECHNER: I want to move now into another area, *mise-en-scene*. I don't know how to begin here. Many people I respect have seen your work and have spoken of it as absolutely extraordinary. But I would be lying if I said I thought so myself. I haven't seen any of your productions. I don't know precisely how I would feel about them. Therefore I cannot ask the same kind of specific questions I asked before. I'm interested in finding out how you construct a *mise-en-scene*, the relationship between it and the space in which it is done, its "environmental" aspects.

GROTOWSKI: I don't work alone. Perhaps I should say a few words about the structure of the troupe. There is Ludwik Flaszen, a well-known writer, and literary and theatre critic. Officially he is our dramaturg. But this is not really exact because I look for plays myself, plays which are necessary for certain actors. And the actors work together with me in making the textual montage.

But two points of view are necessary. A number of the intellectual positions taken by Ludwik are different from mine, although we agree on aesthetics. He is very analytical and he looks for intellectual precision. He seeks to clarify explanations and looks for coherence. He is our Devil's advocate. I invite him to a rehearsal and I ask him to attack it, find all the points that are incoherent, find the weak spots. Afterwards, I may or may not agree, but nevertheless, I am obliged to be more coherent. Ludwik has often pointed out very important things.

Many of the principles that I have explained today have been working since the beginning, but I was not fully aware of them. Later I understood them better. There were moments when Ludwik asked me, "How does it happen? How does it function?" I didn't know why it functioned, but I saw that it did and through Ludwik's questions I had a chance to make things conscious.

There are two important principles that have worked since the beginning, but step-by-step, more consciously. The first is the truth word-for-word. I take a play because I am fascinated by it. Sometimes things fascinate me which I do not like, just as there are parts of my nature that are contradictory. Don't hide them. Don't illustrate the play, but meet it. Everything I don't like in Poles (in me) I must not like in the work; everything I want to attack I must really attack. Everything must be developed to its nth degree, to its last consequence.

The second principle is the question, "Is this possible?" You begin, the project has in it essential things that are not possible. For example, in order to do this the actor must be able to fly, to be invisible, things that are against nature. But to be really truthful, one must do it. How do you make the impossible possible? In some ways it is a technical question. One finds some analogy and when the technical thing is found one finds also the justifications and the context of personal associations.

The result is that the initial project changes because we've penetrated something within us. It is difficult for me to know what was mine and what was the actors'. The work is tangible, but the possibilities inside the frame of work we keep completely. If something works, we are ready to change all our first plans. One day we began work on a play. After some time in rehearsal we noticed that the themes changed and so we took the text of another play that was more in keeping with the evolution of rehearsals.

Be open and look on your work as a great expedition, full of surprises, of the unexpected. Be faithful to your temptations. We have temptations, why? They are stupid, but then why are they necessary to us? Work, and often we discover that the temptation was not stupid at all; within, it was a very significant thing for us.

At the beginning, when I worked in the more classical theatre, I thought that the most important thing was to avoid the rivalry between theatre and film. So I asked myself: How can we have a meeting between actors and spectators which is a real one, an exchange, something that cannot be done in film or on TV?

That was not concrete enough, so I began with completely naive things. Actors spoke directly to spectators, or actors played in the entire hall including where the audience was supposed to be. Then it became necessary to change everything. I found a young theatre architect, Gurawski, who was also possessed by the idea of transformation of the theatre space and the spatial relationship between actors and spectators. In the Laboratory Theatre people are in collaboration. We agree that if one has a problem, one seeks an associate; the theatre is always group work. I can't do everything in this group, but I can stimulate each member and be stimulated in return.

How did we make these transformations in the actor–spectator relationship? At first I was tempted to treat the spectators as actors. That means the theatre has eaten the audience. In the good sense it is another tiger that has eaten his tail. All right, but how do you do this? After many experiments I discovered certain consequences. The action of the production takes place at the same time as that of the performance. The theatre is literally where it happens. For example, in *Kordian*, a play full of glory, individuality, and romanticism, we transformed the space into an insane asylum (this was before *Marat/Sade*, in 1960). In the original play – written in the time of Russian domination in the 19th century – one scene was set in a mental hospital, where Kordian was put because he made an attempt against the Tsar (afterwards he was condemned to death). We made this scene the frame for the totality of Kordian's story, and the entire space became a big room in a mental hospital, with hospital beds and so on. The actors were on the beds along with the spectators. The actors were either doctors or patients, the most interesting cases. The Chief Doctor sometimes provoked the patients, pretending to be Pope or Satan. He treated some of the spectators also as patients. Those spectators who were treated as patients were sometimes furious; it happened also that others were proud because they had been judged "normal."

After a few minutes the audience understood that this was not a joke: the greatest myths of Poland were analysed as the myths of craziness. Kordian decides to give his blood for the motherland. In the original play he decides this on Mont Blanc, before God and all Europe. But in our performance the related text was said by a man in a straitjacket with doctors bleeding him as they did in the 18th century. Kordian's motivation – to give his blood for the nation – was the kind of motivation that was real to everyone. At that moment, there happened hysterical cries among the spectators – certain very deep national values were attacked in order to revalue them.

I think that it might be difficult for a foreigner to understand the associative mechanism which operated in *Kordian*. My nation has been faced for centuries with the question of heroism and sacrifice. Our production of *Kordian* was a perverse counter-case to the arguments about the uselessness of sacrifice. Kordian gives his blood for the motherland – literally – but his act is alienated and without collective backing. A cynic would say in such a situation, "This must undoubtedly be a madman," therefore the whole action was located where Kordian really is a madman: in a madhouse. We were emphasizing that Kordian's attitude is crazy to the extent that he is out of a realistic perspective. At the same time, we believed that Kordian's action was obviously and deeply human – not his alienation but his capacity for sacrifice. So we thought: Let us confront Kordian with the Chief Doctor, who will represent common sense in its cynical, egoistic form – i.e., an individual is "normal" when he gives his whole mind to his own narrow interests. The doctor was a "normal" man, but his "normality" was vulgar and dirty; it was lower-minded than Kordian's craziness, and this was the second plane of the perform-ance. For, in the final settlement, Kordian was wrong because he wanted to act in alienation, or isolation if you prefer, but he was right in wanting to do something of higher value, to sacrifice his life and his blood. When the spectators left the theatre, they judged Kordian morally right, even though his act took place in a madhouse. They expressed this opinion in an unambiguous manner. The contradictions of Kordian's attitude were brought to light, and the performance, through apparent negation of Kordian's behavior, aimed to affirm it.

When I talk of unity of action that is the kind of unity I am thinking of. But the action must go beyond this. It must open into life, the unexpected in life. It is cruel because it is true. We did a lot of experiments like that; plays where the actors encircled the spectators, where they asked the spectators questions, where they touched the spectators. But we saw there was always cheating and trickery on our side. And at the same time, we were looking for a kind of spontaneity from the audience that is impossible in our society. We looked for common reactions which are possible only if people all have the same faith-references, if they "know the liturgy" well. Today there are many half-faiths – a Tower of Babel – so it is impossible to find this kind of ritual. One can stimulate external phenomena and make the audience sing with the actors – often out of tune, and sometimes feeling a certain rhythm as when they are listening to jazz – but it's not a deep, authentic participation. It's only the participation of the common mask.

On the other hand, we ignored the obvious fact that the spectators are anyway playing the role of spectators – they are observers! And when we put them in the role of madmen, we simply disturbed their natural function as observers – or, in the best case – as witnesses; in consequence their reactions were not natural. The unity of place, time, and action was not accomplished.

We solved this problem when we did Marlowe's *Doctor Faustus*. For the first time we found a direct word-for-word situation. The dramatic function of the spectators and the function of the spectator as spectator were the same. For the first time we saw authentic spontaneity. The audience was treated as Faustus's invited guests, people whom Faustus seeks so that he can make an analysis of his own life. The spectators are around a long table and Faustus, with other people from his life, arranges for them a flashback. It was absolutely tangible. If, for example, he were to say, "now you will see the scene of when I first met the devil. I was sitting in a chair like this, and I was listening to a song." Then there is the song and in front of the spectators someone comes in. The confession was authentic because the actor really mobilized the associations of his life. At the same time he made Faustus's confession with the text, he accomplished his own very drastic but disciplined confession.

There were waves of movement in the room. Faustus never waited for answers from the spectators, but he observed their eyes and we saw in them some physical symptoms of the impact, and also one could hear their breathing; something real was happening.

Before *Faustus* we staged Wyspianski's *Akropolis*, where we got the same thing but weren't fully aware that we were doing this. *Akropolis* is a classical play organized around a Polish sanctuary, the Royal Palace of Krakow. During the night of the Resurrection, the figures on the royal tapestries come to life and play out episodes from old Greek and Hebrew history. At the end there is the resurrection of Christ (he is Apollo at the same time) and a triumphant procession forms.

All very good, we said. But the Royal Palace is not a sanctuary any more; it is not what it was for Wyspianski in the 19th century: the cemetery of our civilization. That's why Wyspianski called the Royal Palace the Akropolis: it was Europe's ruined past. We asked ourselves painful and paradoxical questions. What is the cemetery of our civilization? Perhaps a battleground from the war. One day I knew that without a doubt it was Auschwitz. In the play of Wyspianski, at the end the Savior arrives. But in Auschwitz the savior never came for those who were killed.

We organized it all into the rhythm of work in the extermination camp, with certain breaks in the rhythm where the characters refer themselves to the traditions of their youth, the dreams of their people –

the dream of freedom, of normal life which for them was impossible. Each dream was broken, each act was a paradox. Helen and Paris were two male homosexuals (a common occurrence in prisons) and their love scene was watched by the mocking and laughing prisoners. The final procession was the march to the crematorium. The prisoners took a corpse and they began to sing, "Here is our Savior." All the procession disappears into the hole during the song of triumph.

We cannot play prisoners, we cannot create such images in the theatre. Any documentary film is stronger. We looked for something else. What is Auschwitz? Is it something we could play today? Auschwitz is a world which functions inside us. In the performance the SS men were not visible, only prisoners. We did not show victims but the rules of the game: in order not to be a victim one must accept that the other is sacrificed. At that moment we touched something essential in the structure of the extermination camps. For example, the scene between Jacob and the Angel: Prisoner "Jacob," kneeling, carries the wheelbarrow on his back and in it is the prisoner "Angel." The Angel must lie there, but Jacob will die if he does not rid himself of his burden. During the fight Jacob says the words with a very beautiful, elevated melody – all the stereotypes of the meeting between Jacob and the Angel. At certain moments throughout the text there were authentic incantations of agony, lack of air, screaming, hate.

No realistic illusions, no prisoners' costumes. We used plain costumes made from potato sacks, and wooden shoes. These were close to reality, a reality that is too strong to be expressed theatrically. How did we cope with this danger? The rhythm of the actors' steps functioned as music, every moment was organized in tempo and volume so that the shoes became a paradoxical musical instrument which, in that situation, was harsher than a direct image.

The prisoners worked all the time. They took metal pipes that were piled in the center of the room and built something. At the start, the room was empty except for the pile of pipes and the spectators were disseminated through all the space. By the end of the production the entire room was filled by the metal. The construction was made of heating pipes. We didn't illustrate a crematorium but we gave the spectators the association of fire. It was indirect; nevertheless, afterwards the spectators said that we had built a crematorium.

Certain scenes typified the kind of unity I am talking about. The marriage of Jacob and Rachel, for example. A prisoner takes a piece of pipe, there is nothing else, and he begins to look for a woman. He touches the pipe as if it were a woman. To the other prisoners it becomes reality and some of them answer, with proper text, as if the pipe were a woman. For the first prisoner it is the pipe that has answered. The marriage procession is that of tragic farce. A man and a woman – a man and a pipe – and they begin to sing songs of marriage that are very well known in Poland. At that moment an authentic process begins in the actor, a return to the memory of life – no more buffoonery. Then the marriage procession, laughter and songs, and the rhythm of the wooden shoes.

These scenic elements – pipes, shoes, wheelbarrows, costumes – were very intentionally found. It's no accident that the famous Polish designer, Szajna, who spent years at Auschwitz, picked these elements. He has always been called abstract. The scenic elements of *Akropolis* were not abstract, but neither were they realistic. These elements were concrete objects, things from bad dreams, but all completely "untheatrical." Szajna found these objects in flea markets and junk shops.

The actors did not play prisoners, they played what they were doing – people plunged into absurd, detailed routine. They referred back to their memories and their personal contacts with happier days and, at the culminating moments, these associations were broken by this absurd work.

Each actor kept a particular facial expression, a defensive tick, without make-up. It was personal for each, but as a group it was agonizing – the image of humanity destroyed.

The spectators sat throughout the room. They were treated as people of another world, either as ghosts which only got in the way or as air. The actors spoke through them. The personal situation of the spectators was totally different from that of the characters. The spectators functioned both as spectators and within the context of the play. They are in the middle and at the same time they are totally irrelevant, incomprehensible to the actors – as the living cannot understand the dead.

Finally, *The Constant Prince*. The entire production was based on the motives of the Prince. It was an attempt to realize through Ryszard Cieslak, the actor who played the Prince, something impossible: a psycho-physical peak like ecstasy but at the same time reached and held consciously. That means that if Cieslak treated his profession as the Prince treated his fate, the result would be a similar kind of fullness. This makes the spectator uncomfortable, it's too much. So we put the spectators in a voyeuristic relationship to the production. The room was constructed so that the audience was almost hidden behind a wall. They watched something much lower down – as medical students observe an operation, a surgery – and there was no relation whatsoever between the actors and spectators. None. They were watching something prohibited.

One could see over the wall the heads of the audience, and one could observe the rhythm of these heads and, at certain points, the rhythm of breathing. Some of my foreign students were deceived. They said, "You are a traitor to the idea of osmosis between the spectator and the actor." I am always ready to be a traitor to any exclusive rule. It is not essential that actors and spectators be mixed. The important thing is that the relation between the actors and the spectators in space be a significant one.

If the spectator and the actor are very close in the space, a strong psychic curtain falls between them. It's the opposite of what one might expect. But if the spectators play the role of spectators and that role has a function within the production, the psychic curtain vanishes.

SCHECHNER: My question about textual montage is really one about your attitude toward the text. I think you know the question I want to ask.

GROTOWSKI: The initial montage is done before rehearsals begin. But during rehearsals we do additional montage all the time. The principle is the following – it is very clear if one understands the creative situation of the actor – one asks the actor who plays Hamlet to recreate his own Hamlet. That is, do the same thing that Shakespeare did with the traditional *Hamlet*.

Every great creator builds bridges between the past and himself, between his roots and his being. That is the only sense in which the artist is a priest: *pontifex* in Latin, he who builds bridges. It is no accident that Joyce wrote *Ulysses* or that Thomas Mann wrote *Doctor Faustus*. It is rather easy to take a myth and to form one's work around it. If that is all you do, it is either an illustration or a travesty. What I prefer are new works which are eternal – I may not even know what objects are being referred to (did Joyce really want to write his own *Odyssey*?). But clearly many things in *Ulysses* are important to him, and ancient. *Ulysses* is not an illustration or travesty. I am conscious of Joyce in his work, and his work is part of our world. At the same time something archaic exists in the book and in that sense it is eternal.

It's the same with the creativity of the actor. He must not illustrate Hamlet, he must meet Hamlet. The actor must create within the context of his own life and being. And the same for the director. I didn't do Wyspianski's *Akropolis*, I met it. I didn't illustrate Auschwitz from the outside; it's this thing in me which is something I didn't know directly, but indirectly I knew.

One structures the montage so that this confrontation can take place. We eliminate those parts of the text which have no importance for us, those parts with which we can neither agree nor disagree. Within the montage one finds words that function *vis-à-vis* our own experience. The result is that we cannot say whether it is Wyspianski's *Akropolis*. Yes, it is. But at the same time it is our *Akropolis*. One cannot say that this is Marlowe's *Faustus* or Calderon's or Slowacki's *Constant Prince*. It is also our *Faustus*, our *Constant Prince*. All the fragments of the text which were unnecessary were eliminated, but we did not interpolate. We did not want to write a new play; we wanted to *confront*.

It's an encounter, a confrontation. That's why interpolations were not needed. But there is rearrangement of words, scenes. We organize the event according to the logic of our cues. But the essential parts of the text – those which carry the sense of the literary work – remain intact and are treated with great respect. Otherwise there could be no encounter.

SCHECHNER: Is there anything you would like to add?

GROTOWSKI: I want to underline certain points. What is unity of action in a production? Unity of action is not unity of action of the play. The audience knows that they are not seeing the real Hamlet in Denmark. One must always look for the word-for-word truth. The audience can watch the process of confrontation – the story and its motives meeting the stories and motives in our lives. If there is this contradictory action, this meeting, if the audience sees all these small details which lift the confrontation into flight, if they, as spectators, become part of this confrontation, we have the unity of action.

Next, the problem of ethics. There is only one thing that can be considered as ethics, everything else is technique. And even this one thing can be related to technique. I do not believe that one can really create if one is not condemned to create. It must be for us the only thing possible in life, the essential task. But one cannot accomplish one's life-task and be in disaccord with it. If, at certain moments, we do things that are in complete disaccord with our artistic task, something creative in us will be destroyed. Do not take this as a kind of sermon. This question must be treated with a great deal of healthy reasoning and with a sense of humor.

Finally, creativity in theatre does not exist if there is no score, a line of fixed elements. Without this there is only amateurism. One can esteem amateurism as one esteems a lovely rock that one has found at the beach, but it's not a work of art. What is an acting score? That is the essential question. The acting score is the elements of contact.

To take and to give the reactions and impulses of contact. If you fix these, then you will have fixed all the contexts of your associations. Without a fixed score a work of mature art cannot exist. That's why a search for discipline and structure is as inevitable as a search for spontaneity. Searching for spontaneity without order always leads to chaos, a lost confession because an inarticulate voice cannot confess.

One cannot achieve spontaneity in art without structuring of detail. Without this one searches but never finds because total freedom gives a lack of freedom. If we lack structured details we are like someone who loves all humanity, and that means he loves no one.

Edited by Richard Schechner and Jacques Chwat.

5

DOCTOR FAUSTUS: TEXTUAL MONTAGE

Eugenio Barba

Faustus has one hour to live before his martyrdom of hell and eternal damnation. He invites his friends to a last supper, a public confession where he offers them episodes from his life as Christ offered his body and blood. Faustus welcomes his guests – the audience – as they arrive and asks them to sit at two long tables on the side of the room. Faustus takes his place at a third, smaller table like the prior in a refectory. The feeling is that of a medieval monastery, and the story apparently concerns only monks and their guests. This is the underlying archetype of the text. Faustus and the other characters are dressed in the habits of different orders. Faustus is in white; Mephistopheles is in black, played simultaneously by a man and a woman; other characters are dressed as Franciscans. There are also two actors seated at the tables with the audience, dressed in everyday clothes. More about them later.

This is a play based on a religious theme. God and the Devil intrigue with the protagonists – that is why the play is set in a monastery. There is a dialectic between mockery and apotheosis. Faustus is a saint and his saintliness shows itself as an absolute desire for pure truth. If the saint is to become one with his sainthood, he must rebel against God, Creator of the world, because the laws of the world are traps contradicting morality and truth.

> *Stipendium peccati mors est*. Hal Stipendium, etc.
> The reward of sin is death. That's hard.
> *Si peccasse negamus, fallimur*
> *Et nulla est in nobis veritas*.
> If we say we have no sin,
> We deceive ourselves, and there's no truth in us.
> Why then belike we must sin.
> And so consequently die.
> Ay, we must die an everlasting death.
>
> (I, i, 39–47)

Plate 5.1   Scenic arrangement for the Theatre Laboratory's *Doctor Faustus* by Christopher Marlowe. Design by Jerzy Grotowski. (Photo: Opiola-Moskwiak.)

Whatever we do – good or bad – we are damned. The saint is not able to accept as his model this God who ambushes man. God's laws are lies. He spies on the dishonor in our souls the better to damn us. Therefore, if one wants sainthood, one must be against God.

But what must the saint care for? His soul, of course. To use a modern expression, his own self-consciousness. Faustus, then, is not interested in philosophy or theology. He must reject this kind of knowledge and look for something else. His research begins precisely in his rebellion against God. But how does he rebel? By signing his pact with the Devil. In fact, Faustus is not only a saint but a martyr – even more so than the Christian saints and martyrs, because Faustus expects no reward. On the contrary, he knows that his due will be eternal damnation.

Here we have the archetype of the saint. The role is played by an actor who looks young and innocent – his psycho-physical characteristics resemble St. Sebastian's. But this St. Sebastian is anti-religious, fighting God.

The dialectic of mockery and apotheosis consists then of a conflict between lay sainthood and religious sainthood, deriding our usual ideas of a saint. But at the same time this struggle appeals to our contemporary "spiritual" commitment, and in this we have the apotheosis. In the production, Faustus's actions are a grotesque paraphrase of a saint's acts;

and yet, he reveals at the same time the poignant pathos of a martyr.

The text is rearranged in such a way that Act V, scene two of Marlowe's script – where Faustus argues with the three scholars – opens the production. Faustus, full of humility, his eyes empty, lost in the imminence of his martyrdom, greets his guests while he begins his confession. What we usually call virtues, he calls sin – his theological and scientific studies; and what we call sin, he calls virtue – his pact with the Devil. During this confession, Faustus's face glows with an inner light.

When Faustus begins to talk about the Devil and his first magic tricks, he enters into the second reality (flashbacks). The action then shifts to the two tables where Faustus evokes the episodes of his life, a kind of biographical travelogue.

Scene 1. Faustus greets his guests.

Scene 2. Wagner announces that his master is soon to die.

Scene 3. A monologue in which Faustus publicly confesses as sins his studies and exalts as a virtue his pact with the Devil.

Scene 4. In a flashback, Faustus begins to tell the story of his life. First there is a monologue recalling the moment when he decided to renounce theology and take up magic. This interior struggle is represented by a conflict between an owl, who symbolizes the erudite personality, and a donkey, whose stubborn inertia is opposed to the owl's learning.

Scene 5. Faustus talks to Cornelius and Valdes, who come to initiate him in magic. Cornelius turns a table into a confessional booth. As he confesses Faustus, granting him absolution, Faustus begins his new life. The spoken text often contradicts its interpretation; for example, these lines describe the pleasures of magic. Then Cornelius reveals the magic ceremonies to Faustus and teaches him an occult formula, which is nothing other than a well-known Polish religious hymn.

Scene 6. Faustus in the forest. By imitating a gust of wind, the tumbling of leaves, the noises of the night, the cries of nocturnal animals. Faustus finds himself singing the same religious hymn invoking Mephistopheles.

Scene 7. The appearance of Mephistopheles (the Annunciation). Faustus is on his knees in a humble pose. Mephistopheles, on one leg, a soaring angel, sings his lines accompanied by an angelic choir. Faustus tells him that he is ready to give his soul to the Devil in exchange for twenty-four years of life against God.

Scene 8. The mortification of Faustus. A masochistic scene provoked by the arguments of the Good and Bad Angels. Faustus rubs his own spit in his face, knocks his head against his knees, rips at his genitals

– all while reciting his lines in a calm voice.

Scene 9. During a walk Faustus tells Mephistopheles of his decision to give him his soul.

Scene 10. Faustus's baptism. Before signing the contract, Faustus is almost drowned in a river (the space between the tables). Thus he is purified and ready for his new life. Then the female Mephistopheles promises to grant all his wishes. She comforts Faustus by rocking him in her lap (the Pieta).

Scene 11. Signing the pact. Faustus reads his contract with Mephistopheles in a commercial tone. But his gestures reveal a struggle to suppress the anguish which torments him. Finally, overcoming his hesitation, he tears his clothes off in a kind of self-rape.

Scene 12. The double Mephistopheles, using liturgical gestures, shows Faustus his new vestments.

Plate 5.2 Zbigniew Cynkutis and Rena Mirecka in *Doctor Faustus*. (Photo: Opiola-Moskwiak.)

Plate 5.3   The Double Mephistopheles, Antoni Jaholkowski and Rena Mirecka, carries Faustus to Hell. (Photo: Opiola-Moskwiak.)

Scene 13. Scene with his "devil-wife." Faustus treats her as if she were a book which held all the secrets of nature.

> Now would I have a book where I might see all
> Characters and planets of the heavens, that I might know
> Their motions and dispositions.[. . .]
> Wherein I might see all plants, herbs, and trees that
> Grow upon the earth.
>
> (1604 Quarto, I, v, 618–620, 634–635)

The saint examines the slut as if he were carefully reading a book. He touches all parts of her body and reads them as "planets," "plants," etc.

Scene 14. Mephistopheles tempts Faustus. In Scene 13 the young saint has begun to suspect that the Devil is also in God's service. Scene 14 corresponds to a real break in reality. Mephistopheles, at this point in the production, is like a police informer. He takes three roles: Mephistopheles himself, the Good Angel, and the Bad Angel. It is not by accident that the double Mephistopheles is dressed as a Jesuit who tempts Faustus to act sinfully. But when Faustus begins to understand the consequences, he calmly evaluates the Good Angel's words. In this scene, Mephistopheles, as the Good Angel, offers Faustus a meeting with God. They act as if it were late at night in a monastery, and two dissatisfied monks were talking quietly out of everyone's hearing. But Faustus refuses to repent anything.

Scene 15. Astrological discussions. Mephistopheles plays the role of a loyal servant exalting the harmony and perfection of his master's creation in duplicating the sound of the celestial spheres. The conversation is interrupted by two guests who talk of beer and whores. These are the two actors who have been sitting for the whole performance among the spectators. They have played all the farce roles (Robin, Vintner, Dick, Carter, Scholars, Old Man, etc.). In their scenes they represent the banality that marks our everyday life. One of these comic scenes (with the Horse Courser) is acted right after Faustus asks Mephistopheles, "Now tell me who made the world?" Our daily platitudes are themselves arguments against God. Our saint demands to know who is responsible for the creation of such a world. Mephistopheles, servant of God's evil urge, falls into a real panic and refuses to answer: "I will not."

Scene 16. One by one Lucifer shows the Seven Deadly Sins to Faustus. Faustus absolves them as Christ absolved Mary Magdalene. The Seven Deadly Sins are played by the same persons: the double Mephistopheles.

Scene 17. Faustus is transported to the Vatican by two dragons, the double Mephistopheles.

Scene 18. Faustus, invisible at the feet of the Pope, is present at a banquet in St. Peter's. The banquet table is made of the bodies of the double Mephistopheles, who recites the Ten Commandments. Faustus slaps the Pope, breaking him of his pride and vanity. He transforms the Pope into a humble man – this is Faustus's miracle.

Scene 19. At the palace of Emperor Charles V, Faustus performs miracles in the tradition of the popular legends. He splits the earth and brings forth Alexander the Great. Then Faustus outwits Benvolio, a courtier who wants to kill him: Benvolio's rage is directed against the tables – he actually dismantles the table-tops, and turns sections of the tables over, all the while thinking he is dismembering Faustus. Then Faustus turns Benvolio into a little child.

Scene 20. Return to the present – Faustus's last supper. Faustus picks up his conversation with his guests. Upon the urging of a friend he conjures up Helen of Troy, unmasking by comic allusions the female biological functions. Helen begins to make love to him – immediately she gives birth to a baby. Then, while in this erotic position, she becomes the wailing infant. Finally she is transformed into a greedy baby at suck.

Scene 21: The double Mephistopheles shows Paradise to Faustus. This would have been his had he followed God's precepts: a good, calm, and pious death. Then they show him the hell that awaits him: a convulsive and violent death.

Scene 22: The final scene. Faustus has but a few minutes to live. A long monologue which represents his last, and most outrageous, provocation of God.

> Ah Faustus,
> Now hast thou but one bare hour to live,
> And then thou must be damned perpetually!
>
>   (V, ii, 130–131)

In the original text, this monologue expresses Faustus's regret for having sold his soul to the Devil; he offers to return to God. In the production, this is an open struggle, the great encounter between the saint and God. Faustus, using gestures to argue with Heaven, and invoking the audience as his witness, makes suggestions that would save his soul, if God willed it, if He were truly merciful and all-powerful enough to rescue a soul at the instant of its damnation. First Faustus proposes that God stop the celestial spheres – time – but in vain.

> Stand still, you ever-moving spheres of heaven,
> That time may cease and midnight never come.
>
>   (V, ii, 133–134)

He addresses God, but answers himself, "Oh, I'll leap up to my God! Who pulls me down?" (V, ii, 142). Faustus observes an interesting phenomenon: the sky is covered with the blood of Christ, and just one half-drop would save him. He demands salvation:

> See, see, where Christ's blood streams in the firmament!
> One drop would save my soul, half a drop!
>
>   (V, ii, 143–144)

But Christ vanishes, even as Faustus implores him, and this prompts Faustus to say to his guests, "Where is it now? 'Tis gone." (V, ii, 147). Then God's angry face appears, and Faustus is frightened:

> . . . And see where God
> Stretcheth out his arm and bends his ireful brows!
>
>   (V, ii, 147–148)

Faustus wants the earth to open and swallow him, and he throws himself to the ground.

> Mountains and hills, come, come, and fall on me,
> And hide me from the heavy wrath of God.
>
>   (V, ii, 149–150)

But the earth is deaf to his prayers and he rises crying, "O no, it will not harbor me!" (V, ii, 153). The sky then resonates with the Word and in all the corners of the room the hidden actors, reciting like monks, chant prayers like the Ave Maria and the Pater Noster. Midnight sounds. Faustus's ecstasy is transformed into his Passion. The moment has come when the saint – after having shown his guests the guilty indifference, yes, even the sin of God – is ready for his martyrdom: eternal damnation. He is in a rapture, his body is shaken by spasms. The ecstatic failure of his voice becomes at the moment of his Passion a series of inarticulate cries – the piercing, pitiable shrieks of an animal caught in a trap. His body shudders, and then all is silence. The double Mephistopheles, dressed as two priests, enters and takes Faustus to hell.

Mephistopheles lugs Faustus away on his back, holding him by the feet, the saint's head down near the ground, his hands trailing on the floor. Thus he goes to his eternal damnation, as a sacrificial animal is carried, as one is dragged to the Cross.

The female Mephistopheles follows humming a sad march which becomes a melancholy religious song (the Mother of Sorrows following her Son to Calvary). From the saint's mouth come raucous cries; these inarticulate sounds are not human. Faustus is no longer a man, but a panting animal, an unclaimed, once-human wreck moaning without dignity. The saint against God has attained his "summit," he has lived God's cruelty. He is the victor – morally. But he has paid the full price of that victory: eternal martyrdom in hell where all is taken from him, even his dignity.

Translated by Richard Schechner.

6

WYSPIANSKI'S *AKROPOLIS*

Ludwik Flaszen

Wyspianski's drama has been modified in parts to adjust to the purpose of the director. The few interpolations and changes in the original text do not, however, detract from the style of the poet. The balance of the text has been somewhat altered by the deliberately obsessive repetition of certain phrases such as "our Akropolis" or "the cemetery of the tribes." This liberty is justified because these phrases are the motifs around which the play revolves. The prologue is an excerpt from one of Wyspianski's letters, referring to the "Akropolis" as the symbol of the highest point of any specific civilization.

Of all the plays Grotowski directed, *Akropolis* is the least faithful to its literary original. The poetic style is the only thing which belongs to the author. The play was transposed for stage conditions totally different from those planned by the poet. In a sort of counterpoint pattern, it has been enriched with associations of ideas which bring out, as a secondary result of the enterprise, a specific concept of the technique: the verbal flesh of the work had to be translated and grafted on the viscera of foreign stage setting. The transplant had to be done with such skill that the words would seem to grow spontaneously from the circumstances imposed by the theatre.

The author conceived his work as a panoramic view of the Mediterranean culture whose main currents are represented in the Polish Akropolis. In this idea of the "cemetery of the tribes," to quote Wyspianski, the concept of the director and that of the poet coincide. They both want to represent the sum total of a civilization and test its values on the touchstone of contemporary experience. To Grotowski, contemporary means the second half of the twentieth century. Hence his experience is infinitely more cruel than Wyspianski's and the century-old values of European culture are put to a severe test. Their merging point is no longer the peaceful resting place of the old cathedral where the poet dreamed and meditated in solitude on the history of the world. They clash in the din of an extreme world in the midst of the polyglot confusion where our century has projected them: in an extermination camp. The characters re-enact the great moments of our cultural history, but they bring to life not the figures immortalized in the monuments of the past, but the fumes and emanations from Auschwitz.

It is indeed a "cemetery of the tribes," but not the same as the one where the old Galician poet wandered and dreamed. It is literally a "cemetery," complete, perfect, paradoxical; one which transforms the most daring poetic figures into realities. "Our Akropolis," blind with hope, will not see the Resurrection of Christ–Apollo: he has been left behind in the mysterious outer reaches of collective experience. The drama formulates a question: what happens to human nature when it faces total violence? The struggle of Jacob with the Angel and the backbreaking labor of the inmates, Paris' and Helen's love duet and the derisive screams of the prisoners, the Resurrection of Christ and the ovens – a civilization of contrast and corruption.

Trapped at its roots, this image of the human race gives rise to horror and pity. The tragicomedy of rotten values has been substituted for the luminous apotheosis which concluded the philosophic-historic drama of the old poet. The director has shown that suffering is both horrible and ugly. Humanity has been reduced to elemental animal reflexes. In a maudlin intimacy, murderer and victim appear as twins.

All the luminous points are deliberately snuffed out in the stage presentation. The ultimate vision of hope is squashed with blasphemous irony. The play as it is presented can be interpreted as a call to the ethical memory of the spectator, to his moral unconscious. What would become of him if he were submitted to the supreme test? Would he turn into an empty human shell? Would he become the victim of those collective myths created for mutual consolation?

The play is conceived as a poetic paraphrase of an extermination camp. Literal interpretation and metaphor are mixed as in a daydream. The rule of the Theatre Laboratory is to distribute the action all over the theatre and among the spectators. These, however, are not expected to take part in the action. For *Akropolis*, it was decided that there would be no direct contact between actors and spectators: the actors represent those who have been initiated in the ultimate experience, they are the dead; the spectators represent those who are outside of the circle of initiates, they remain in the stream of everyday life, they are the living. This separation, combined with the proximity of the spectators, con-tributes to the impression that the dead are born from a dream of the living. The inmates belong in a nightmare and seem to move in on the sleeping spectators from all sides. They appear in different places, simultaneously or consecutively, creating a feeling of vertigo and threatening ubiquity.

In the middle of the room stands a huge box. Metallic junk is heaped on top of it: stovepipes of various lengths and widths, a wheelbarrow, a bathtub, nails, hammers. Everything is old, rusty, and looks as if it had been picked up from a junkyard. The reality of the props is rust and metal. From them, as the action progresses, the actors will build an absurd civilization; a civilization of gas chambers, advertised by stovepipes which will decorate the whole room as the actors hang them from strings or nail them to the floor. Thus one passes from fact to metaphor.

The costumes are bags full of holes covering naked bodies. The holes are lined with material which suggests torn flesh; through the holes one looks directly into a torn body. Heavy wooden shoes for the feet; for the heads, anonymous berets. This is a poetic version of the camp uniform. Through their similarity the costumes rob individuals of their personality, erase the distinctive signs which indicate sex, age, and social class. The actors become completely identical beings. They are nothing but tortured bodies.

The inmates are the protagonists and, in the name of a higher, unwritten law, they are their own torturers. The merciless conditions of the extermination camp constitute the milieu of their lives. Their work crushes them with its size and its futility; rhythmical signals are given by the guards; the inmates call out in screams. But the struggle for the right to vegetate and to love goes on at its everyday pace. At each command the human wrecks, barely alive, stand up erect like well-disciplined soldiers. The throbbing rhythm of the play underscores the building of the new civilization; the work expresses the inmates' stubborn will to live, which is constantly reaffirmed in every one of their actions.

There is no hero, no character set apart from the others by his own individuality. There is only the community, which is the image of the whole species in an extreme situation. In the fortissimos, the rhythm is broken into a climax of words, chants, screams, and noises. The whole thing seems multishaped and misshapen; it dissolves, then reforms itself into a shivering unity. It is reminiscent of a drop of water under a microscope.

During the pauses in the work, the fantastic community indulges in daydreams. The wretches take the names of biblical and Homeric heroes. They identify with them and act, within their limitations, their own versions of the legends. It is transmutation through the dream, a phenomenon known to communities of prisoners who, when acting, live a reality different from their own. They give a degree of reality to their dreams of dignity, nobility, and happiness. It is a cruel and bitter game which derides the prisoners' own aspirations as they are betrayed by reality.

Jacob tramples his future father-in-law to death while asking for

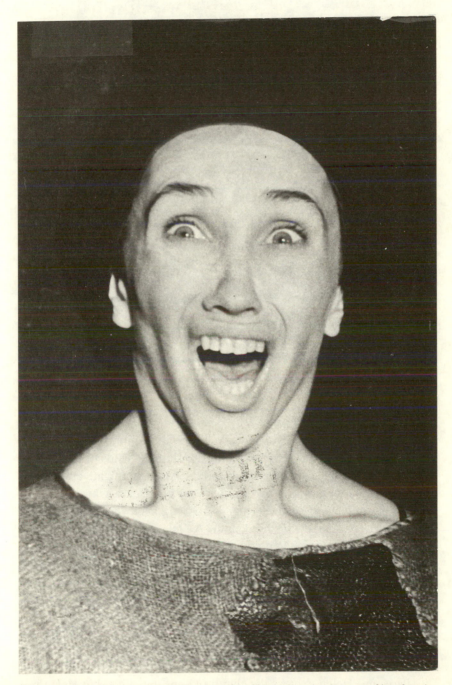

Plate 6.1 Rena Mirecka creates a mask for *Akropolis* soley by use of her facial muscles. (Photo: Theatre Laboratory.)

Plate 6.2   Jacob, Zygmunt Molik, courts Rachel, Rena Mirecka. (Photo: Theatre Laboratory.)

Rachel's hand in marriage. Indeed, his relationship to Laban is not governed by patriarchal law but by the absolute demands of the right to survive. The struggle between Jacob and the Angel is a fight between two prisoners: one is kneeling and supports on his back a wheelbarrow in which the other lies, head down and dropping backward. The kneeling Jacob tries to shake off his burden, the Angel, who bangs his own head on the floor. In his turn the Angel tries to crush Jacob by hitting his head with his feet. But his feet hit, instead, the edge of the wheelbarrow. And Jacob struggles with all his might to control his burden. The protagonists cannot escape from each other. Each is nailed to his tool; their torture is more intense because they cannot give vent to their mounting anger. The famous scene from the Old Testament is interpreted as that of two victims torturing each other under the pressure of necessity, the anonymous power mentioned in their argument.

Paris and Helen express the charm of sensuous love, but Helen is a man. Their love duet is conducted to the accompaniment of the

Plate 6.3   The struggle between Jacob, Zygmunt Molik, and the Angel,
Zbigniew Cynkutis. (Photo: Theatre Laboratory.)

snickering laughter of the assembled prisoners. A degraded eroticism
rules this world where privacy is impossible. Their sexual sensitivity has
become that of any monosexual community, the army for example.
Similarly, Jacob directs his expression of tenderness toward compensatory objects: his bride is a stovepipe wrapped into a piece of rag for a veil.
Thus equipped, he leads the nuptial procession, solemnly followed by all
the prisoners singing a folksong. At the high point of this improvised
ceremony, the clear sound of the altar bell is heard, suggesting naively
and somewhat ironically a dream of simple happiness.

The despair of men condemned without hope of reprieve is revealed:
four prisoners press their bodies against the walls of the theatre like
martyrs. They recite the prayer of hope in the help of God pronounced
by the Angel in Jacob's dream. One detects in the recitation the ritual
grief and the traditional lament of the Bible. They suggest the Jews in
front of the Wall of Lamentation. There is, too, the aggressive despair of
the condemned who rebel against their fate. Cassandra, one of the
prisoners, a female, walks out of the ranks at roll call. Her body wriggles,
her voice is vulgar, sensuous, and raucous; she expresses the torments of
a self-centered soul. Shifting suddenly to a tone of soft complaint, she
announces with obvious relish what fate holds in store for the community. Her monologue is interrupted by the harsh and guttural voices of the
prisoners in the ranks who count themselves. The clipped sounds of the
roll call replace the cawing of crows called for in Wyspianski's text.

Plate 6.4   The marriage procession of Jacob and Rachel. (Photo: Theatre L:aboratory.)

As for hope, the group of human wrecks, led by the Singer, finds its Savior. The Savior is a headless, bluish, badly mauled corpse, horribly reminiscent of the miserable skeletons of the concentration camps. The Singer lifts his hands in a lyrical gesture, like a priest lifting the chalice. The crowd stares religiously and follows the leader in a procession. They begin to sing a Christmas hymn to honor the Savior. The singing becomes louder, turns into an ecstatic lament torn by screams and hysterical laughter. The procession circles around the huge box in the center of the room; hands stretch toward the Savior, eyes gaze adoringly. Some stumble, fall, stagger back to their feet and press forward around the Singer. The procession evokes the religious crowds of the Middle Ages, the flagellants, the haunting beggars. Theirs is the ecstasy of a religious dance. Intermittently, the procession stops and the crowd is quiet. Suddenly, the silence is shattered by the devout litanies of the Singer, and the crowd answers. In a supreme ecstasy, the procession reaches the end of its peregrination. The Singer lets out a pious yell, opens a hole in the box, and crawls into it, dragging after him the corpse of the Savior. The inmates follow him one by one, singing fanatically. They seem to throw themselves out of the world. When the last shout of the condemned prisoners has disappeared, the lid of the box slams shut. The silence is very sudden; then after a while a calm, matter-of-fact voice is heard. It says simply, "They are gone, and the smoke rises in spirals."

The joyful delirium has found its fulfilment in the crematorium. The end.

The strictest independence from props is one of the main principles of the Theatre Laboratory. It is absolutely forbidden to introduce in the play anything which is not already there at the very beginning. A certain number of people and objects are gathered in the theatre. They must be sufficient to handle any of the play's situations.

There are no "sets" in the usual sense of the word. They have been reduced to the objects which are indispensable to the dramatic action. Each object must contribute not to the meaning but to the dynamics of the play; its value resides in its various uses. The stovepipes and the metallic junk are used as settings and as a concrete, three-dimensional metaphor which contributes to the expression of the poet's vision. But the metaphor originates in the function of the stovepipes; it stems from the activity which it later supersedes as the action progresses. When the actors leave the theatre, they leave behind the pipes which have supplied a concrete motivation for the play.

Each object has multiple uses. The bathtub is a very pedestrian bathtub; on the other hand, it is a symbolic bathtub: it represents all the bathtubs in which human bodies were processed for the making of soap and leather. Turned upside down, the same bathtub becomes the altar in front of which an inmate chants a prayer. Set up in a high place, it

Plate 6.5   The fional action, prisoners descending into the crematorium. (Photo: Theatre Laboratory.)

becomes Jacob's nuptial bed. The wheelbarrows are tools for daily work; they become strange hearses for the transportation of the corpses; propped against the wall they are Priam's and Hecuba's thrones.

The musical instruments are important accessories. They play the monotonous cacophony of death and senseless suffering: metal grating against metal, clanging of the hammers, creaking of the stovepipes through which echoes a human voice; a few nails rattled by an inmate evoke the altar bell. There is only one real musical instrument, a violin. Its leitmotif is used as a lyrical and melancholy background to a brutal scene, or as a rhythmic echo of the guards' whistles and commands. The visual image is almost always accompanied by an acoustic one. The number of props is extremely limited; each one has multiple functions. Worlds are created with very ordinary objects, as in children's play and improvised games. We are dealing with a theatre caught in its embryonic stage, in the middle of the creative processes when the awakened instinct chooses spontaneously the tools of its magic transformation. A living being, the actor, is the creative force behind it all.

All the actors use gestures, positions, and rhythm borrowed from pantomime. Each has its own silhouette irrevocably fixed. The result is a depersonalization of the characters. When the individual traits are removed, the actors become stereotypes of the species.

The means of verbal expression have been considerably enlarged because all means of vocal expression are used, starting from the confused babbling of the very small child and including the most sophisticated oratorical recitation. Inarticulate groans, animal roars, tender folksongs, liturgical chants, dialects, declamation of poetry: everything is there. The sounds are interwoven in a complex score which brings back fleetingly the memory of all the forms of language. They are mixed in this new Tower of Babel, in the clash of foreign people and foreign languages meeting just before their extermination.

The mixture of incomparable elements, combined with the warping of language, brings out elementary reflexes. Remnants of sophistication are juxtaposed to animal behavior. Means of expression literally "biological" are linked to very conventional compositions. In *Akropolis* humanity is forced through a very·fine sieve: its texture comes out much refined.

7

THEATRE LABORATORY 13 RZEDOW

Eugenio Barba

What has been called "the intellectual adventure of the twentieth century" is a sudden awareness of the unexploited possibility of the arts. It is more than a lucid hubris, more than a deliberate effort to transcend the limits imposed by tradition and prudence. It is a deep conviction that art must change its structure and even its function. All the arts have purified themselves, eliminating the intrusions of other arts; they have rejected everything that was not necessary and vital to their own intentions.

Only the theatre has not done this. Several times it has tried to destroy itself so that new forms could arise. The period of great reform with Appia, Craig, Meyerhold, Vakhtangov, and Piscator was the most serious of these attempts. Its results were negligible. Theatres still are antiquated buildings where classical and contemporary texts are recited in a routine and conventional style. There is no creative act on stage – only the sterile repetition of worn-out formulas and hybrid styles which try to look "modern" by exploiting the discoveries of other art forms. There is no purification, no effort to develop (or rediscover) the essence of theatre. There is no new means of expression suited to our century. Acting, diction, contact between actor and public, architecture – everything is still meant to satisfy the *Gentiluomini* of the Renaissance or the *Honnetes Gens* of the seventeenth century. In the midst of this dead end several voices called for reforms, for a return to primitive spontaneity or popular forms. They called for laboratory theatres in which to explore the means of theatrical production. But their cries remained silent: paper revolutions. Witkacy and Artaud, both great visionaries, belong to literary history.

Then in 1959, in a small provincial Polish town, Opole, a young director, accompanied by a young critic, opened a small theatre which from the very start had a specific character: a laboratory in which Jerzy Grotowski and Ludwik Flaszen experimented with actors and audiences. They were trying to build a new aesthetic for the theatre and thus to purify the art.

Grotowski wished to create a modern secular ritual, knowing that ancient rituals are the first form of drama. Through their total participation "primitive" men were liberated from accumulated unconscious material. The rituals were repetitions of archetypal acts, a collective confession which sealed the solidarity of the tribe. Often ritual was the only way to break a taboo. The shamans were masters of the sacred ceremonies, in which every member of the community had a part to play. Some of the elements of "primitive" ritual are: fascination, suggestion, psychic stimulation, magic words and signs, and acrobatics which compel the body to go beyond its natural, biological limitations.

It would have been difficult, of course, to revive these ceremonies in our day. New means had to be found to force the spectator into an active collaboration. Grotowski preserves the essence of "primitive" theatre by making the audience participate, but he leaves out the religious elements and substitutes secular stimuli for them. Grotowski uses archetypal images and actions to unleash his attack on the audience. He breaks through the defenses of the spectator's mind and forces him to react to what is going on in the theatre.

The archetypes must be found in the play's text. And, in this context, archetype means symbol, myth, image, leitmotif – something deeply rooted in a civilization's culture.[1] It is a metaphor and model of the human condition. For example, Prometheus and the Sacrificial Lamb correspond to the archetype of the individual sacrificed for the community. Faustus and Einstein (in the imagination of the masses) correspond to the archetype of the Shaman who has surrendered to the Devil and in exchange has received a special knowledge of the universe. The essential task is to give life to an archetype through the staging of a play. It is what the poet Broieski called "the expression by the voice and body of the very substance of man's destiny." Several examples from Grotowski's work illustrate this.

> *The Ancestors* by Mickiewicz has been treated as a ritual drama. The audience is a collective group participating in the action. Spectators and actors are scattered through the whole room. The actors speak to everyone who is there. They treat the audience as fellow actors and even invite them to become active participants. The last scene of the play tells the story of Gustav-Konrad, who, from a Czarist jail, rebels against the established order. He is the rebel with whom Poland, torn and conquered, identifies. Ordinarily this scene is presented as a metaphysical revolt and played with great pathos. In the Laboratory Theatre it demonstrates the naivete of the individual who believes himself to be a savior. The long soliloquy has been changed into the Stations of the Cross. Gustav-Konrad moves among the spectators. On his back he carries a broom, as Christ carried his cross.

His grief is genuine and his belief in his mission sincere. But his naive reactions are shown to be those of a child who is not aware of his limitations. Here the director used a specific dialectic: entertainment versus ritual, Christ versus Don Quixote. The meaning of the production becomes clear in the final scene, where the individual revolt aimed at effecting a radical change is shown as hopeless.

(Grotowski 1961: n.p.)

Kordian, by Slowacki, is another example of Grotowski's methods. It is a Polish classic, as well known to Poles as *Peer Gynt* is to Norwegians. It takes place in the divided Poland of the nineteenth century. A young aristocrat, Kordian, wants to sacrifice himself for his country and free it from Russian rule. An attempt against the Tsar's life fails and, after being committed to a lunatic asylum, Kordian is judged sane and condemned to death. Grotowski considers the scene in the hospital the key to the play. Hence, the entire play is set in the hospital. All of Kordian's experiences, the people he meets, the plots he organizes, the women he loves, are presented as hallucinations. An evil doctor who turns into the Pope, then the Tsar, and finally an old sailor, brings about the hallucinatory crises. In the original text, Kordian recites a solemn soliloquy on top of Mont Blanc. There he offers his blood to Poland and Europe. In Grotowski's production, the doctor takes a blood sample: dialectic of derision and apotheosis. The sufferings of Kordian are real, but the reasons for his suffering are imaginary. His sacrifice is noble, but naive.

"It is not the first time that our Laboratory presented a heroic personality obsessed with the idea of saving mankind," said Flaszen. "The director analyzed the meaning of an individual act in an era where collective action and organization are the guarantees of success. Today, the man who tries to save the world alone is either a child or a madman, and I am not sure that in our world he could even claim the charm of Don Quixote" (Flaszen 1962).

Or, as Grotowski said:

> No rule is sacred, not even the rule that a single archetype must be represented. Ordinarily there are several archetypes in a text. They branch out and intermingle. One is chosen as the pivot of a play. But there are other possibilities. One could, for example, present a set of archetypes all of which would have the same value in the play. It is by means of the archetype that the dialectic of derision and apotheosis attacks a system of taboos, conventions, and accepted values. In this way, each production has a "multifaceted mirror" effect. All the facets of the archetype are successively destroyed; new taboos rise from the destruction and are, in turn, destroyed.

(Grotowski 1961: n.p.)

Five years of work and experimentation have brought success to Grotowski's theatre. The point is no longer to present convincing characters, but to use the text as a catalyst setting off a violent reaction in the spectator. "Not to show the world as separated from the spectator, but, within the limits of the theatre, to create with him a new world" (Flaszen n.d.). The main problem of the Laboratory was to find new means of expression. "Many people are surprised that our productions have nothing in common with literary theatre," Grotowski said.

> Faithful recitation of the text and illustration of the author's ideas are the goals of the traditional theatre. We, on the contrary, believe in the value of a theatre that some have called "autonomous." For us the text is only one of the play's elements, though not the least important. The "peripeteia" of the plays (as we do them) do not correspond to the text. They are expressed through purely theatrical means. The director takes liberties with the text. He cuts, he transposes. But he never indulges in personal interpolation. He lovingly preserves the charm of the words and watches carefully to see that they are spoken. The text is artificial and composed, but it is the author's text.
>
> (Flaszen n.d.)

This free treatment of the text is the first decisive step in liberating the theatre from literary servitude. The director uses the playwright's text as the painter uses landscape motifs and as the poet uses semantic material accumulated by his civilization. As a text undergoes transpositions and scoring, it acquires new interpretive possibilities. It becomes the experimental ground on which the creative director works. Of course, the reborn text has only limited powers if it is not supported by a completely new acting technique.

Grotowski begins with the assumption that "everything which is art is artificial." Pushing this to its extreme expression, he has come up with the following:

> No technique is sacred. Any means of expression is permitted, provided that:
>
> 1   It is functional, justified by the logic of the production. Walking on one's feet demands the same justification as walking on one's hands. The logic of life cannot be substituted for the logic of art.
> 2.   It has been deliberately chosen. It can no longer be changed, except in certain scenes where limited improvisation is permitted.
> 3.   It is "built," composed. Theatrical techniques form a structure whose parts cannot be altered.

> We are especially interested in an aspect of acting which has seldom
> been studied: the association of the gesture and intonation with a definite
> image. For example, the actor stops in the middle of a race and takes the
> stance of a cavalry soldier charging, as in the old popular drawings. This
> method of acting evokes by association images deeply rooted in the
> collective imagination.
>
> (Grotowski 1961: n.p.)

According to Grotowski, there are three kinds of actor. First, there is the
"elementary actor," as in the academic theatre. Then there is the
"artificial actor" – one who composes and builds a structure of vocal and
physical stage effects. Thirdly, there is the "archetypal actor" – that is,
an artificial actor who can enlarge on the images taken from the
collective unconscious. Grotowski trains this third type of actor. In
developing his actors, Grotowski instills in them certain principles which
are characteristic of the Theatre Laboratory:

> *The deficiencies of the actor are used, not hidden*. An actor's
> handicaps are as important as his qualities. An old actor can play
> Romeo if he emphasizes his limitations. That is, if he situates his part
> within a definite composition. The part then becomes that of Romeo
> in his old age reminiscing with Juliet.
>
> *Costumes and props are the actors' partners or they are "artificial
> extensions of the actor."* The actor gives life to the prop by treating
> it as a living thing. It is friendly or hostile to him. The "partner" may
> be a costume – in that case there is a contrast between the two: the
> actor is young and handsome and the costume is ugly; or the
> situation is poetic and the costume is vulgar and coarse. When used
> as extensions of the actor, costumes and props accentuate the
> gestures by inhibiting them. For example, a sleeveless costume
> prevents the actor from using his arms. In any case, the accessories
> must not be used as ornaments. Their only function is to increase the
> actor's power of expression. In *Kordian*, for example, the hospital
> beds are used as acrobatic parallel bars.
>
> *Each character is depicted most purely by vocal or physical effects*.
> The actor gives concrete expression to his desires, passions,
> thoughts, etc., by a physical action (gymnastics, acrobatics, or
> pantomime) or a vocal action (incantation, production of associated
> sounds, etc.) To make the effect properly suggestive, it must be done
> in a trance (concentrating all the psychic energies). To achieve
> communication, it must be a sign which awakens associations buried
> in the audience's unconscious. The sign must be a revelation which
> starts a train of reactions and brings to consciousness latent feelings
> linked to individual or collective experiences. These experiences will

be related to the culture, history, and folklore of the country.

There must be direct contact between actors and audience. There is no stage. The actor speaks directly to the spectator, touches him, is around him all the time, startles him by frequent surprise effects. There is individual contact between one actor and the whole audience and there is collective contact between a team of actors and the audience. There are several forms of collective contact. In Byron's *Cain* the spectators are descendants of Cain. They are present but remote and difficult to approach. In Kalidasa's *Shakuntala*, they are just a crowd of monks and courtiers. In Mickiewicz's *The Ancestors*, they are made to participate in the crop and harvest ritual. An actor becomes the Chorus Leader and the audience the Chorus. In *Kordian* the spectators are patients in the asylum; as such they are the doctor's enemies. In Wyspianski's *Akropolis* they are completely ignored, because they represent the living while the actors are ghosts. The actors speak while gliding between the

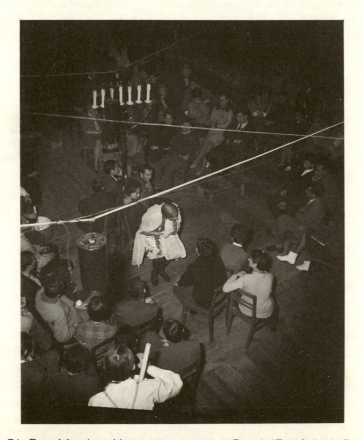

Plate 7.1 Rena Mirecka addresses spectators in *Dziady* (*Forefather's Eve*) by Mickliewics. (Photo: Mozer Zdzislaw.)

Plate 7.2   Kordian by Juliusz Slowacki. (Photo: Edward Weglowski.)

spectators, but there can be no contact.

Theatrical magic consists in doing publicly that which is considered impossible. For example, the actor transforms himself into another man in full view of everyone. Or else he becomes an animal or an object. Acrobatics liberate the actor from the laws of gravity.

Plate 7.3   In *Kordian*, a demonic doctor, Zygmunt Molik, transforms himself into a solider as another doctor, Antoni Jaholkowski, watches. (Photo: Edward Weglowski.)

Make-up is unnecessary. Make-up does not accentuate the physical characteristics of the actors. The actor can change the expression on his face through control of facial muscles. Lighting, sweat, and breathing transform his muscles into a mask.

The spectator's unconscious is deliberately attacked. The actor does not give a visual representation of the archetype – this would be familiar and banal. Through his technique he evokes and attacks a collective image. In the improvisation in *The Ancestors*, Gustav-Konrad does not look like Christ and he does not carry a cross. But with his ridiculous broom and quixotic outbursts he collides with the popular representation of Christ: hence his shock value. A faithful reconstruction of either Gustav-Konrad or Christ would have been familiar and boring.

The artificiality which Grotowski strives for must stem from reality, from the organic necessity of the movement or the intentions. Deformation must have a value as form, or else everything becomes a frivolous puzzle or, even worse, pathology. Artificiality is tied to life by an unbreakable umbilical cord. A few examples will help to show what is meant:

Every gesture must be composed. A short series of motions is a micro-pantomime which must illuminate the character. There can be no complication for its own sake. The actor must be able to shift the spectator's attention from the visual to the auditory, from the auditory to the visual, from one part of the body to the other, etc. This is the skill of magicians.

There must be theatrical contrast. This can be between any two elements: music and the actor, the actor and the text, actor and costume, two or more parts of the body (the hands say yes, the legs say no), etc.

Parts are exchanged during performance. Romeo becomes Juliet and Juliet becomes Romeo.

The actor metamorphoses. An actress is a secretary, then a mistress, then the boss, then a telephone, typewriter, table, sofa, etc. This was done in Mayakovsky's *Mystere-Bouffe*.

Characters are built on several levels. A doctor is in fact the Devil who becomes the Pope, then the Tsar, and then an old sailor (*Kordian*).

Styles change rapidly. The same scene is played by the same actor in artificial, naturalistic, pantomimic, improvisational, and other styles.

Physiological manifestations are used. In the improvisation of *The Ancestors*, for example, Gustav-Konrad is exhausted and drips with sweat. He does not try to hide it. His gestures suggest that it is the blood that Christ sweated.

The word is more than a means of intellectual communication. Its pure sound is used to bring spontaneous associations to the spectator's mind (incantation).

Each day the actors work their way through a series of exercises:

1. Diction, vocal work, artificial pronunciation (incantation). They shift from one timbre to another, chant, whisper. These exercises are always accompanied by breathing exercises. The secret of good diction is breathing. The experiments at the Laboratory investigated the part played by the brain in the formation of sound; the importance of the throat muscles for an appropriate opening of the larynx; how to determine the proper pause for a specific role; harmony between breathing and the rhythm of a sentence; breathing as a dramatic effect (where it is not a physiological necessity); complete breathing from the abdomen *and* chest (usually only the abdomen is considered necessary); simultaneous use of the cranial and thoracic sounding boards; loss of voice as a result of psycho-logical problems or faulty breathing.
2. Plastic motion following the Delsarte method and others. Simultane-ous activity of different parts of the body, each at a different rhythm (the arms move fast, the legs slowly, the actors speak at different speeds); muscle control; instant relaxation of the muscles not engaged in motion.
3. Study of mime, both artificial and naturalistic.

This training results in a decidedly anti-naturalistic style in which rhythm and dynamism are as strictly fixed as in a musical score. The actor must be highly skilled and rigorously trained to control a technique which governs each gesture, each breath, each voice tone, and which uses acrobatics and gymnastics. This actor must provoke and fascinate the audience. To do so he must play his score correctly – but in a trance of concentration – while deliberately attempting to subjugate the spectator. As a shaman, he must create a magic action and prod the spectator into participation. He must force the audience to drop its social mask and face a world in which old values are destroyed without offering in their place any metaphysical solutions.

A struggle therefore ensues between performer and spectator. The one tries to fascinate the other and overcome all defenses; the other fights against the spell of gestures and words, grasping at old logic and seeking shelter in a social shell. According to Grotowski, the director shapes the two groups, actors and spectators. They both must become aware of being part of the ritual–spectacle. It is this very awareness that distinguishes theatre from film. The future of the theatre depends upon this close contact between spectator and actor, which makes possible an act of collective introspection. Of course, putting the audience on stage (there is no "stage," but the action takes place in the space where the audience sits) presents problems. A new theatre architecture is needed. From the moment when Grotowski eliminated the stage, he was involved in architectural problems. A young architect, Jerzy Gurawski, has joined the company to help with these investigations.

The Laboratory Theatre rejects the eclecticism which has cancerously eaten away at the modern theatre. It is foolish to try to "modernize" the theatre by using electronic music, abstract settings, and clownish makeup. These are only superficial copies of what an audience can see at a concert, art exhibition, or circus. These elements are not essential to the theatre, which needs only the physical and vocal expressions of the actors. Theatricality could be defined as a deformation and/or reformation of life with its own autonomous aesthetic. Movies and television have taken over the social function of the theatre and the only way for the theatre to survive is for it to exploit its unique characteristic: the direct contact between actor and audience. The actor, each night, faces the live critical audience; he recites his part *at* a public eager to note his slightest mistake. Every night he must find new ways to fascinate and control his audience; and every night it is a different audience challenging him. The Theatre Laboratory is looking for new forms of theatrical magic, for new alphabets to be used by the actor–shaman. Much is written, but little is done because directors and actors must make money. What madman would dare finance an experiment so eccentric, so shocking by its aggressiveness, and demanding so much skill from its actors? The Polish government has understood the necessity and has proven its goodwill by supporting Grotowski's experiments. Will others follow suit in other countries?

"I SAID YES TO THE PAST"
Interview with Grotowski

Margaret Croyden

CROYDEN: What do you mean by "poor theatre"?

GROTOWSKI: "Poor theatre" gives up the trappings used in the other visual arts. It is a theatre that concentrates on human actions only, and the relationship between the actors and the audience. It gives up all conventional stage effects like lights, music, scenery, makeup, props, and spectacular effects because they are not essential. These effects are mechanical and often autonomous and can be used separately outside the metier. Make-up, for instance, is unnecessary because the actors are trained to use their facial muscles like masks and, thus, actors have a variety of masks to choose from. We do not need elaborate and expensive props either. In *Akropolis* we use pieces of scrap iron, two wheelbarrows, a bathtub, and a rag doll. We use these props in any way we choose; we make of them what we wish. Material things prevent our real confrontation with art. We wish to confront our art without costly devices or commercial accoutrements. We want to use ourselves only; we want to work through our own impulses and instincts, through our own inner beings and through our own individual responses. To be poor in the biblical sense is to abandon all externals. And that is why we call our theatre "poor theatre."

CROYDEN: Why do you consider the actors and not the playwright the core of your theatre?

GROTOWSKI: The actor is the creator because he brings the literature of the theatre to life. He must be like a magician and entrance the audience. Of course, I don't want to overlook the importance of dramatic literature, but it exists in itself; each one of us can buy the dramas of Shakespeare and study them. We don't want to illustrate these dramas on the stage. We want to confront the text, which is an entirely different matter. To confront the text means to test it, to struggle with it, to come to grips with its meaning in terms of our own modern experiences, and then to give our own answers. Since we use mostly the classics as our texts, it means we must also confront the past. If we really want to be creative, each of us must be a bridge between the past and the present, between our own individual roots and the archetypal roots of the past. It is the actors who, during the performance, ultimately experience this confrontation. And that is what is really decisive.

CROYDEN: Your production of *Akropolis* juxtaposes classical myth with Auschwitz. What are you trying to convey?

GROTOWSKI: *Akropolis* is based on a classical Polish play. I reworked it to analyze not only the great myths of the past but the biblical and historical traditions as well. It dramatized the past from the point of view of heroic values. Since World War II we have noticed that the great lofty values of Western civilization remain abstract. We mouth heroic values, but real life proves to be different. We must confront the great values of the past and ask some questions. Do these values remain abstract, or do they really exist for us? To discover the answer we must look at the most bitter and ultimate trial: Auschwitz. Auschwitz is the darkest reality of our contemporary history. Auschwitz is the trial of humankind. What has been our goal in this play? To put two opposite views on the stage, to create brutal confrontations in order to see if these past dreams are concrete and strong, or only abstractions. In other words, we wanted to confront our ancestral experiences in a situation where all values were destroyed, and that is why we chose Auschwitz. What was the reaction to this play? The audience watches the confrontation; they observe the dreams of the prisoners, and the dreams of the great people of our past. Past dreams appear annihilated by the reality of Auschwitz. But in another sense, the dreams survive because they give weight and depth to the prisoners, for they feel themselves part of the collective past. Man in that situation is being tested, pitted against past ideals. Does he survive the test? The audience will decide.

CROYDEN: Your production of *Akropolis* is stunning but very bitter. Not only Auschwitz but the whole world appears to be a concentration camp. People kill each other swiftly and smoothly; very few seem to help each other. Does this represent your world view?

GROTOWSKI: It is true that in the extermination camps many who survived found solidarity. For many, this produced a sense of absolution and nobility. But if we really want to confront the Auschwitz experience, we must confront its darkest aspects: the mechanics of the camp. For instance, the air itself was limited. Where three people were together there was only enough air for one. To live meant to breathe the air that another one lacked. If we want the truth, we must show Auschwitz as a giant mechanism with all its cruelty. The mechanics of the camp were arranged for a specific goal and they worked. We cannot avoid this reality. It is a choice we made: the mechanism of Auschwitz in confrontation with past values.

CROYDEN: Is confrontation with myth the key to the avant-garde theatre?

GROTOWSKI: I don't know what avant-garde theatre is today. For example, people say that the avant-garde theatre is "total theatre," the use of every mechanical or technical apparatus available: film, circus effects, electronics, and so forth. But I don't think so. People think that to be avant-garde one must present plays that are essentially ambiguous. But I am looking for other values. I feel that one must not look for avant garde art but for art. . . It is impossible to create if we destroy the bridge to the past. Myth or archetype links us to the past. The past is the source of our creative efforts. To be sure, our life is individual and personal; we live in the present, but we are the result of something larger – a greater history than our own personal one – an interindividual and interpersonal history. When we produced *Akropolis* I was forced to confront my own roots and, at first, I discovered that I wanted to crush the mirror of the past. I knew it was impossible; my image was reflected in that mirror. Consciously I said "yes" to the past, and realized the past was not annihilated but reinforced.

CROYDEN: Do you favor a theatre of very little verbalization?

GROTOWSKI: Yes. But what does verbalization mean? Many actors transform any language into a verbal one, that is, they themselves have no life, there is no process of organicity in them. They do not perform "the total act" of the actor. By that I mean, the actor must use all of his biological and physical forces toward conjuring up his creative consciousness in order to illuminate his vision. Many actors have no cycle of living impulses inside their bodies that lead to creativity. But when an actor does externalize his biological or physical impulses, the last phase of it, the apex of it, is expressed through the text – through words. I ask actors for total expression of this process of physical and biological impulses. "The total act" is total self-revelation in a moment of extreme honesty. When that happens, there is room for words. At that point, words are unavoidable; what is produced then is a supra-language, the base of which is derived from the biological and the physical. We cannot say, therefore, that we are for or against language, just as in life, we are not for or against language. We live with language, but not only with language.

CROYDEN: What is the relationship in your theatre between spontaneity and formal technique?

GROTOWSKI: Structure or form is a discipline; it is significant because it is a process of signs that stimulates the spectators' associations. This discipline is organized and structured; without it we have chaos and pure dilettantism; this is the first thing. The second thing: if you have structure which stimulates the audience, and if the actor does not express "the total act," if he does not reveal all of himself (I mean his instinctive and biological roots), action is prevalent, but it is not a living action. It is significant, but it is not alive. A great work is an expression of contradiction, of opposites. Discipline is obtained through spontaneity, but it always remains a discipline. Spontaneity is curbed by discipline, and yet there is always spontaneity. These two opposites curb and stimulate each other and give radiance to the action. Our work is neither abstract nor naturalistic; at the same time, it is both abstract and naturalistic. It is natural and structured, spontaneous and disciplined.

CROYDEN: Do you believe that the naturalist theatre is irrelevant?

GROTOWSKI: I don't believe that aesthetic genres are decisive in art. One cannot say that there is a naturalistic style, or an avant-garde style, and that these styles are the only means of expression. Each person is different, and must find his own mode of creative expression; there is no rigid course. The question is, which style is best suited to release our innermost feelings and to find a great rapport with the audience. And we do not know beforehand which style will succeed. One thing is sure: we must avoid stereotypes. We must discover our own answers and we can only do this by confronting our own sources. People say that our acting technique is anti-naturalistic. I don't think so. I think we use elements of the naturalistic and the physiological as well as pantomimic, improvisational, and so forth. We try to mix styles, and we do not decide for or against any one style beforehand. Perhaps today we are far from naturalism, but tomorrow we may be closer to it because the questions that life presents will be different, the answers will be different, and I myself will be different.

CROYDEN: What is the role of the audience in your theatre?

GROTOWSKI: As far as the spectator is concerned, he is not watching a story unfold, nor is he listening to an anecdote. The audience is confronted with a human act, and he is invited to react totally, even at the moment of the performance. We do not care to assault or provoke the audience, nor do we wish to do all kinds of stupid things to get a rise out of the audience. What is important is to confront the spectator and that is something quite different. One can use many stimuli to provoke, but we prefer to use only common aspects of our common experiences, polarize these aspects, and then involve the audience in such confrontations. Sometimes the audience sits in a semicircle quite near to the action; sometimes the actors perform in between the audience's seats. In *Akropolis* the audience represents the living watching the "dead" inmates in their nightmare dreams. Ultimately the audience must give its own answer. Will humankind retrieve its past dreams? Can they survive the greatest brutality of the century? Is there hope? The answers are left to the audience.

Translated from French by Helen Klibbe.

A MYTH VIVISECTED: GROTOWSKI'S *APOCALYPSIS*

Konstanty Puzyna

An account of *Apocalypsis cum Figuris* has long been overdue. It is total theatre, collectively created, no sooner thought through than orchestrated for the proper instruments, for the specific members of the company. It is the most mature fruit so far produced by the ascetic labors of the Wroclaw Theatre Laboratory. In any case, it is an event, one of more than local interest, and we don't get those every day of the week. It needs, therefore, to be recorded as accurately as possible before it slips out of focus. Fair enough, only how? Seldom does something so straightforward prove so baffling.

Ordinarily in describing a play we can always fall back on the script, on the lines and the plot. In *Apocalypsis* there are only the bare bones of a scenario. In the reading, the text is a haphazard jumble of quotations from the Bible, liturgical chants, Dostoevsky, T.S. Eliot, Simone Weil. On the face of it there appears to be no linking thread whatsoever. Vague associations flicker dimly through the collage; it dawns on you eventually that Simon Peter in his denunciation is speaking the words of the Grand Inquisitor from *The Brothers Karamazov* and that when the Simpleton defends himself, bitterly and pathetically, he is quoting from Eliot. But these texts have not been stitched together into anything resembling a plot; they are simply stand-bys, one of the props. The whole fabric of Grotowski's stage poem has been woven entirely from what his actors do and experience; the story and the subject of *Apocalypsis* is spun from their interplay alone.

Both one and the other are oblique, snarled and enigmatic. It is the laws of poetry, not prose, which hold sway here: distant associations, overlapping metaphors, tableaux, actions and meanings continually fading into each other. Once again the imagery is all in the actors. It is embodied in gesture and mime, movement and intonation, groupings and place-changes, inward reactions and counter-reactions. They hint at biblical scenes and village customs, liturgical symbols and drunken brawls, a back-street con man and David before the Ark. Meanings are

Plate 9.1 Poster for *Apocalypsis cum figuris*.

multiplied and telescoped; an actor's face will express one thing, the motion of his hand another, the response of his partner something else again; his voice growls threateningly, his eyes sparkle elatedly, his body twitches with pain. The virtuosity of the representation is breath-taking, the etching of each sign marvelously precise, but it is all run together and gone in a flash. Half the business we can only just register out of the corner of our eye, and, though it lodges in our consciousness, we would have to watch each sequence several times over if we wanted to describe it in detail, and even then it would take up two columns of print – just like a close analysis of all the sense in a line of good poetry.

It is only the sum of these meanings that gives them import, and it is a many-layered one, a whorl of references full of deliberately pointed contradictions, enacted with absolute logic and clarity to the point where they dissolve into opacity. To borrow a term from painting, each scene in *Apocalypsis* employs broken color. Or, putting it another way, it has an arresting density, both of imagery and thought, which is the height of simplicity. It is much easier to understand this poem than to explain it rationally.

I can just see this admission bringing a smirk to the faces of the numerous skeptics in the critical and theatre world, though it is true that they have grown more chary of rushing forward with words like "gibberish," "quackery," and the like. The trouble is that these people have many more barriers to overcome than normal audiences, especially the youngest ones, brought up in a different world and weaned on different books, different films, different styles of art, who are less prone to getting hung up over ambiguities and shock effects; open-minded and alert, they often enough can, as Artaud wanted, "soak up metaphysics through the pores." This gathering tide among the young and their (sociologically noteworthy) fascination with Grotowski has begun to worry many a pundit; it has also taken some of the wind out of his opponents' sails, and the world-wide acclaim lavished on the Wroclaw troupe has knocked them even further off-balance. Indeed, one can now even hear grudging mumbles of "really rather interesting." It does one's heart good to see such a climb-down. But, to get back to *Apocalypsis*, even a condescending smile is not quite as canny a reaction as they seem to imagine: try to sum up in one sentence what *The Waste Land* or even Galczynski's *Solomon's Ball*, is about. Well?

Insofar as it has one, the storyline of *Apocalypsis* has to do with the return of Christ, a Second Coming, here and now, in our midst. The Christ is one so designated purely for a lark – but is he a false one? This Christ retravels the whole of his gospel journey and ends up defeated. Yet does he in fact lose? How can we be sure? The emotional and intellectual power of *Apocalypsis* is condensed in these questions. If Grotowski was merely trying to say that God is dead, he would be echoing Dostoevski and rehashing what is now a platitude and no longer worth repeating. He might tread on a few touchy Catholic toes; the rest of his audience would be left cold. But to ask *whether* God is dead is to stir up a nest of problems which are far from trite. All the more so since, in the metaphoric language of *Apocalypsis*, God or Christ need not necessarily mean the Judaeo-Christian personal deity. It may signify a great many, very different, human concerns.

For instance, it could denote a certain unconscious psychic need, collective as well as individual, for parental care, or universal human love, or higher justice, or expiation of guilt. It may, in other words, be a matter of archetypes. Archetype has become a vogue-word in criticism today, and Grotowski himself was fond of using it to distraction. In fact, it is none too clear in the Jungian sense of the collective unconscious. More accurate, I think, is the interpretation that sees the archetype as the need itself, common to various cultures and ages, and expressed in certain motives; on the whole, however, it has become customary to give the term "archetypes" simply to these motives, or as they have been described by Levi-Strauss, by no means an enthusiast on this point, "certain mythological themes with which, Jung thought, specific meanings seemed to be connected." Undoubtedly one such theme is Christ, as a Christian myth of course, not a historical figure. To ask whether Christ is dead is, therefore, to perform a vivisection on a theme which has shaped the whole of our European culture, and through this vivisection to probe the continuing vitality of a certain nexus of archetypes. Do they still live on in us as an inward need or have they died out?

The vivisection is a ferocious one. The Christ myth is subjected to the test of blasphemy, the test of cynicism, and the test of verbal argumentation, the most acute ever made, since it comes from *The Brothers Karamazov*. The object is to strip the myth of all the rich finery in which it has been decked out by religion, tradition and habit: to have it stand naked before us and try to defend itself.

The stage is equally bare. Not that there is a stage really. Just an empty windowless room with dark walls. From a corner of the floor two spotlights slant upward. Four rough benches stand untidily against the walls. These are for the audience and can seat just thirty: will we be spectators or is it perhaps witnesses we are about to become? Sprawled all in a heap on the floor lie the actors, deadbeats who seem to have passed out from too much to drink. They are dressed in white, modern clothes, fairly nondescript, with just an occasional distinguishing touch: the man who will be Judas (Zygmunt Molik) has a look of cheap elegance, but his shirt-tails have come drunkenly loose, and the

Plate 9.2 Apocolypsis cum figuris: The Simpleton, Ryszard Cieslak; Mary Magdalene, Elizabeth Albahaca. (Photo: *TDR*.)

prospective Simon Peter (Antoni Jaholkowski) is slumped over, swaddled in a sort of white poncho that will take on the significance of a priest's robes when he becomes the master of ceremonies and Christ's chief antagonist.

The girl (Elizabeth Albahaca) rises to her feet and begins to murmur softly, her voice rising until we hear she is singing something in Spanish. The words are repeated in Polish by John (Stanislaw Scierski):

> Verily, verily I say unto you, except ye eat the flesh of the Son of Man, and drink his blood, ye have no life in you.

And later: "For my flesh is meat indeed and my blood is drink indeed."

These early lines contain the clue to many of the specific shocks that follow: flesh is eaten and blood is drunk "indeed," that is, literally. By extension, love, too – a key concept in the Christian story – is treated literally: as sex. The eroticism, of course, is mystical, as in the writings of John of the Cross where mysticism and eroticism are fused and the results even take on a very strange flavor: God is the lover (He), John the mistress (She, the soul). This tradition goes back to the *Song of Solomon*, the most sensuous religious poem we know. *Apocalypsis* has in fact helped itself to a handful of the juicier passages: "my beloved put in his hand by the hole" is a sample. Of course, in this context, sex also becomes the antithesis of love: hate. This is the suggestive backcloth on which is threaded the whole dialectic of challenge and blasphemy, on the one hand, and fascination and yearning on the other. The whole vivisection of the myth.

So they are lying there, spent and numb, spiritually as well as physically. The world is empty; there is no point in waiting for Godot.

Plate 9.3 *Apocolypsis cum figuris*: left to right — Mary Magdalene, Elizabeth Albahaca; Simon Peter, Antoni Jaholkowski; The Simpleton, Ruszard Cieslak; Judas, Zygmunt Molik; Lazarus, Zbigniew Cynkutis. (Photo: *TDR.*)

Something does stir, however: the girl who had been singing. She darts uncertainly back and forth among the recumbent figures, pressing a loaf of bread to her breast like an infant. They come to at last. John runs over, spreads a white towel on the floor, the girl puts the loaf down and wraps it up. John pulls something halfway out of his waistband; the girl ducks down, slurping loudly at what may or may not be a hipflask, then John bends down and does the same. The girl thrusts a knife into his hand. John strikes the floor with it, seizes the loaf, places it beneath his body and lies down, performing jerky, unmistakable movements. The girl scurries around agitatedly. The man leaps to his feet, runs off with the bread; she catches him and tries to retrieve the loaf. They struggle, and the man flings her to the floor. He lies down on his back, presses the loaf to his belly; the hip movements are repeated until, taut and arched, he collapses in orgasm on the floor. He lies there panting. The girl snatches the loaf from him, steps away, lays it on the ground and strikes it twice with the knife, each blow drawing a groan from the prostrate man as though she were stabbing him.

Here is one brief actors' sequence, and it is passages like this that carry forward and build up the performance. It is also an example of acting metaphor. Bread here stands for food, a child, the Host, while a primitive, improvised snack in some station waiting room passes into a profane, sexual outburst culminating in the implicit murder of – the baby, the man, God?

The profanation of the Host brings the gathering to life. They start looking for some new kicks and hit on the idea of summoning up the Savior – or rather re-designating one, since that is the best they can do – and seeing what happens.

"Rise," says Simon Peter, and begins distributing roles, gesturing: "Mary Magdalene," "Judas, indicate him." The man cast as Judas points to Lazarus (Zbigniew Cynkutis). But that won't do at all; Simon Peter steps across to a corner of the room and out of the shadows pulls a figure we had not noticed before: a startled witless yokel. This is the Simpleton (Ryszard Cieslak). He cowers there in a black, slightly large overcoat. His feet are bare, and he is carrying a white stick, though he is not blind. His Polish name *Ciemny* means literally "the Dark One"; here it denotes the only man in dark clothes, but also suggests other things: "sightless" – incapable of seeing the real world; or "benighted" – unable to comprehend life as the "enlightened" can. He is contrasted with the others by everything, from color to the role's "innards." He has a different scale of values, good and evil are simple and spontaneous instincts, he is "undefiled." Perhaps he is also one of those "touched" village idiots, or even Satan himself. Cieslak acts and hints at all these meanings. It is a great performance, probably more brilliant than his Constant Prince, though apparently less graphic.

From the start he is the butt of a taunting attack. Guffaws of derision lash him at each sentence in Simon Peter's "nominating speech": "You

Plate 9.4   Apocalypsis cum figuris: The Simpleton, Ryszard Cieslak. (Photo: TDR.)

were born in Nazareth," "You are a child," "You died for them on the Cross," "You are God," "You died for them," "But they failed to recognize you." A choir chants a well-known hymn, "He is Hanging on the Cross." All of them have now got into the swing of the masquerade, but beneath the horseplay we can feel an edge of tension: what if. . . . The Simpleton seems also to have caught the mood, or perhaps he just wants to join in, even at his own expense. But it is not that simple. He is man-handled, shooed off, ignored, as they ostentatiously keep to themselves. He circles them gingerly, stopping in front of one or another, gazing into his eyes and whistling softly, beseechingly. It gets him nowhere; he remains an *outsider*; he even keeps physically to the edge of the circle. All the time he is treated to an incessant stream of provocation, tantalization, clowning, ogling, and gibes. Eventually Simon Peter leaps on his back and frantically spurs him on, his white cape flowing, amid the wild cries of the others. "The horseman of the Apocalypse is the Pope, galloping on the back of the Apostle," a Polish critic commented. Not an apostle actually, but Christ, and in any case this interpretation, though admissible, is not the only one. What is more important is the literal, colloquial sense of "taking Christ for a ride." And of goading and whipping him into a frenzy.

Sure enough, the Simpleton goes berserk. He tosses Simon Peter to the ground and careens off on his own, writhing and twitching with ecstasy, his bare feet thudding out a syncopated rhythm, as though his cavortings were some kind of dance, both Dionysian and despairing. It is a dance; and he is Dionysus, and also David before the Ark of the Covenant, and all the time Christ; I remember Grotowski telling me that one of the New Testament apocrypha referred to Jesus dancing.

The dance suddenly breaks off. The Simpleton collapses. Something stirred in him after all, he was close to believing. The antics now fall apart, into disjointed, loose-knit episodes, which look as though every-one is a little stymied by the game they have started and is desperately casting around for some way of getting it moving again. The action, which had so far been flowing briskly, if erratically and confusedly, now spills off into separate pools and backwaters, falters and splits up. Judas launches off on some incoherent, inconclusive, leering, slightly absurd anecdote about the wise and foolish virgins; odd tags from the Bible are trotted out; bits of nursery games appear; all of them suddenly begin singing "Guantanamera," a Spanish hit tune of the late 1960s played almost nightly by the band in Wroclaw's Hotel Monopol, and they burst into a frenetic, orgiastic dance. There are also moments of total enervation when nothing happens whatsoever. But the combined effect is to generate a mood and to pace the emotional climaxes of each successive acting sequence. Here and there these are interspersed with gospel "figures," acting as chronologically random reminders of actual events in the Christ story.

Reminders for the audience, but chiefly, and increasingly in earnest, for the Simpleton. For instance, Simon Peter calls up the scene of the piercing of Christ's side on the Cross by suddenly exclaiming: "And I saw water flowing from the right side of the temple, hallelujah!" Whereupon all of them elbow their way to the Simpleton, expose his ribs and, one after the other, put their mouths to his side, gulping noisily. As they drink, they seem to swell grotesquely like leeches. The last of them slumps to the ground gurgling as though he were rinsing with a mouthful of some phlegmy slop: "It's liquor in his veins, not blood." The raising of Lazarus is an intricate take-off on a wake complete with Eastern-style lamentations. The Simpleton watches it spellbound, hooked. Eventually he says emphatically and gravely: "Lazarus, I say unto thee, arise." Lazarus gets up and swaggers toward him menacingly like a hooligan picking a fight. He delivers a long passage from the *Book of Job*, and his words ring with resentment at the interruption of as natural a process as death through the meddling of an imbecile. As he speaks, he clutches the loaf that had earlier been lanced. He breaks it in two, scoops at one half as though he were digging a pit, gouges out the dough, rolls it in his fingers and hurls two pellets into the Simpleton's face. He is stoning him with bread, but with his own corpse as well, with a gray, shapeless, sticky pulp. His eyes light up as though his retaliation for an idiotic infraction of the human right to burial were a relief.

The next argument against Christ and the Simpleton comes in the encounter with Mary Magdalene. Here, however, the case unexpectedly falters. At a certain moment John (and for the equivocal eroticism of the scene it is important that it should be John) pairs him off with a prostitute. He shows him the girl:

> Come hither, I will show unto thee the judgment of the great whore that sitteth upon many waters with whom they have committed fornication and have been made drunk with the wine of her fornication.

The Simpleton walks over, and they gaze into each other's eyes. They embrace gently and move off into the corner of the room where the two spotlights on the floor cast their slanting beams upward. They stand just in front of them, illuminated and radiant from their light, and the room suddenly turns dark. Their movements are now deliberate and languid as though they were rediscovering their bodies, surprised, abashed, voiceless. They might be a mobile sculpture. John strips off his tunic, stands in the middle of the room half-naked and then advances toward them, taut, expectant, alert, spring-heeled. The Simpleton and Mary Magdalene slowly bend backward. Her body arches into a bow, John quickens his

Plate 9.5   Apocalypsis cum figuris: John, Stanislaw Scierski. (Photo: *TDR.*)

stride, running ever faster; you can hear his panting breath, the soft patter of his feet, and the faint wailing of the wind. Somewhere in the distance, dogs are howling; the world is vast and still. In the darkness it is impossible to see which of the actors are creating these background sounds. Mary Magdalene's body suddenly crumples. Both of them sink limply to the ground, and at that moment John lurches and pulls up short as though shot. He moves to the other end of the room and again starts running toward the lovers, who once more slowly arch their bodies backward. Now the Simpleton is the bow, she the arrow, both of them inwardly tense, wreathed in light, radiant, almost mystical. What is so remarkable about this sequence is not so much its pointing of the age-old associations between hunting and sex, but the tremulous *purity* that

Plate 9.6   Apocalypsis cum figuris: Mary Magdalene, Elizabeth Albahaca. (Photo: *TDR.*)

shines through all the suggestiveness. This is, I think, the most daring and lyrical love scene I have ever seen in the theatre.

From this scene onward the Simpleton imperceptibly begins to get the upper hand, through his innocence, purity, meekness, goodness. He is impregnable. The main theme now returns to the foreground, that is Simon Peter's challenge, taunting and recriminatory. Odd lines and then whole passages from the Grand Inquisitor's speech appear:

> Twenty years have passed since he promised to come and found his kingdom. Twenty years have passed since his prophet wrote that he would come soon but that not even he knew the hour and day of his coming, only his father in heaven. But mankind has been expecting him with unchanging faith and with the old emotion. No, with greater perhaps, because the communion of man with heaven has ended.

The attack is pressed: "Man was born a rebel, but can a rebel be happy?" And again: "Damn you for coming to trouble us." The Simpleton defends himself listlessly and stoically:

> Because I do not hope to turn again
> Because I do not hope
> Because I do not hope to turn
> I no longer strive to strive towards such things
> (Why should the aged eagle stretch its wings?)

That is Eliot. The Simpleton is beginning to speak like Christ, but he is still the Simpleton: he refuses, inwardly shrinks from, the challenge. His reply is not even delivered directly after the onslaught but held over for several intervening scenes. In relating Grotowski's poem I have over-simplified its dramatic structure, and yet even then my account tends to run on impossibly.

It can't be helped. Some points have to be labored. Seeing that so many obviously intelligent people cannot make head or tail of the language of the Theatre Laboratory there is nothing for it but to keep illustrating its syntax and its stage vocabulary. Some examples, however piecemeal, need to be shown of the acting imagery which gives muscle to *Apocalypsis*. No other company in Europe has explored this kind of metaphor. Nor could it, if it tried. It is simple enough to grope around in a piece of bread; it is far more difficult to conjure up associations as remote as the grave. In any case who would care to pour so much corporate effort, thought and imagination into every "bread and butter" production? Our everyday diet is hackneyed: we prefer it that way.

There is also in *Apocalypsis* a vibrancy in the acting that is uncanny and of a very special nature. The point is that what has been written about the supremacy of gesture, situation, and bodily expression over the spoken word might be taken to imply mime techniques. But in mime the technique is in a sense external, a detached sequence of signs where sheer proficiency is more important really than depth of feeling. In Grotowski's company on the other hand, it is an article of faith that the actors' experiencing, incredibly intense as it is, should center on their own genuine and intimate concerns. Of course we do not actually discover their personalities, but even so their behavior is not far short, some say, of exhibitionism. Is this true, though? After all, the self-exposure of the actor is not in effect much greater than that of many writers and is to no less a degree controlled by rigorous rules of composition. It is, however, taken much farther than in the case of ordinary actors where experiencing is more a matter of imaginatively feeling their way into a role than a conscious process of release from hidden complexes, memories, bygone experiences, and inhibitions. But this is the reason why the power and *truthfulness* of expression is so immense in Grotowski's actors, why there is so much genuine creativeness – though of a special kind: the behavior of the actor all but resembles

Plate 9.7 ·Apocalypsis cum figuris. The Simpleton, Ryszard Cieslak. (Photo: *TDR.*)

psychoanalytical transference. Perhaps this explains the strongly erotic temper of the performance, the impression it gives of a continuous interaction of aggression and surrender, sadism and masochism, sacrifice and revenge. The whole of *Apocalypsis* pulsates with this dialectic.

It is dusk. Simon Peter has sat down near one of the spotlights and masked the other with his coat. They have gone out. We are plunged into darkness. Someone is moving, there is the sound of footsteps and humming, and then silence again. A long pause follows. Then we see a flicker of candles, and a big, blazing set of them is brought in and set down before the Simpleton. The rest of the performance continues by candlelight. Before we can grasp the point of this change and that caesura of darkness, we hear the words: "Behold thy beloved cometh, go out and meet him," and the Simpleton answers in the manner of Christ. But now he *is* Christ; the incarnation is complete. "One of you shall betray me," says the Simpleton. At Simon Peter's bidding John asks: "Who is it, Christ?" and the Simpleton pinches the flame of a candle in his finger and with a quick movement makes a mark on Simon Peter's forehead. "Lord," shouts Judas. "What of me?" and Simon Peter replies: "Judas, son of Iscariot, we are together." For it is Simon Peter, the accuser-priest, who is the betrayer; Judas the hustler is simply a stooge. "Lord, where goest thou?" asks Simon Peter. Golgotha begins.

Plate 9.8 *Apocalypsis cum figuris*: The Simpleton, Ryszard Cieslak. (Photo: TDR.)

Golgotha unfolds first through the singing of hymns ("Glory be to the Great and Just One," "Lamp of God") and then through a mighty lament from the Simpleton. In fact it is really the Agony in the Garden. The elegy is propelled by long, choking gulps of Eliot: "If the word is lost, lost," "people, my people," "this is not the time nor place," "I come in vain." Candles, removed from the main set, twinkle around the room. One stands by itself on the floor, and when he has finished his lament the Simpleton flings himself down on the ground in an ecstasy of pain with his arms outstretched and his head just by it. The others crowd around his feet, staring, holding their blazing candles, with that solitary one at his head. . . . They have crucified him at last.

The singing starts again, solemn and ritualistic, the gathering stepping softly, respectfully. But a note of jubilation soon creeps in: "Kyrie Eleison," "Sursum Corda." Since they have crucified him, they have won: they have come into possession of not only God and a rite, but a temple; it's only natural to do a spot of huckstering in it. We hear snatches of street traders' pitches: "a belly for sale," "a praying mother for sale," "myself for sale," "God's flesh for sale," "fresh meat for sale." Life makes sense again; things are looking up.

But now that he believes, the Simpleton cannot let them get away with it. He leaps to his feet in rage, lashes them with a rolled up towel, frantic with pain and grief. With his scourge, he drives the money-lenders from the temple, and they slink out one after the other. Only John suddenly turns at bay, and the Simpleton's arm is checked in mid-movement. John's impassioned account, taken from Simone Weil, of a little garret on whose door a lover once knocked is a rejection of the Simpleton's love. And of Christ's love, of course: mysticism and sex are still one and the same. In a new fit of frenzy the Simpleton drives John out and sinks helplessly to the ground. The candles are burning in front of him, and one by one they will eventually disappear. At the other end of the room, also with a candlestick in front of him, sits Simon Peter. Only he is left. They eye each other. The final duel is about to take place.

Once again Dostoevsky returns, the most bitter of his accusations:

> Instead of the old stern law, man was himself to decide in the freedom of his heart what is good and what is evil, with your image and your likeness before him. But did it never occur to you that he would eventually reject your image and your truth if you laid on him so terrible a burden as freedom of choice?

The Simpleton does not answer, staring at Simon Peter, while into the space between them steps a bizarre procession. It is made up of John and Mary Magdalene. They are carrying a basin, which they fill with water, and then step into it barefoot, one after the other, wash their feet, dry them, wrap themselves in black shawls, remove the bowl and walk off singing: "He knows what torment is, he knows the sadness of tears." Two country women, setting off for a funeral, homely, resolute, sullen. There is silence. Simon Peter returns to the attack: "Hear me then: we are not with you, but with another; that is our secret. We have been not with you, but with another for a long, long time, for many centuries." Now the Simpleton breaks into his second great dirge from Eliot, even more tragic and despairing than the first. History "gives too late what's not believed in." The return of Christ can only be a dream. It will never come true.

Simon Peter begins putting out the candles one by one, when the Simpleton suddenly begins to sing: "Cogitavit Dominus dissipare . . ." The last candle goes out in the middle of the chant. His voice rises and amplifies, filling the darkness, clear-toned, reverberating with Job's groans on the ruins: "Jerusalem, Jerusalem, convertere ad Dominum, Deum tuum." He is silent. Now from the darkness there rings out Simon Peter's stern, cold command: "Go and come no more." The lights go up. The room is empty: only the audience remains.

To my mind this is the first time, probably, that Grotowski has touched a raw contemporary nerve. As long as he was searching for his beloved archetypes in Auschwitz (*Akropolis*) or in the story of Kordian, he was clearly off the mark. For me personally, even the version of Marlowe's *Faustus*, one of Grotowski's theatrically most accomplished early productions, rang hollow. I was unmoved. It was not until *Apocalypsis* that I found myself riveted, watching with a fascination far beyond the line of duty, even though Catholicism and Christianity are matters I can take or leave alone. This time I cared, and deeply.

The audience slowly gets to its feet. They pick their way across the stearin-sprinkled floor, through the little puddles of water, among the scattered chunks of bread. There is no conversation, no discussion, no joking, only complete silence. As though this was not a theatre that would go through the same motions the next night. As though here, in this small dark room, something had really happened.

AN APPENDIX TO *APOCALYPSIS*

Grotowski's acting poem has too many levels and too many meanings to be dealt with in one analysis. There is always something left out, as in analysing Joyce's *Ulysses*. *Ulysses* is a certain mental model for all structures of the *Apocalypsis* type. To encompass the whole history of mankind in a small contemporary event; to transpose the history of Christ on to a drunken foolishness and timelessness and spacelessness on to the concrete of everyday life; to interweave with allusions to various cultures and epochs; to bind with analogies everything with everything; to change

Plate 9.9   *Apocalypsis cum figuris*: The Simpleton, Ryszard Cieslak. (Photo: TDR.)

the river of time into simultaneity; to create an associational field almost infinite but not arbitrary, to the contrary – rigorously organized by the matter of the work – it is precisely in this that the relationship and similar aims lie. In contemporary prose or poetry it is nothing new, but in the theatre? Especially when the matter in *Apocalypsis* consists almost entirely of acting, not the word?

When writing about *Apocalypsis* before, I dealt mainly with the plot and the dramaturgy of the performance – the collective dramaturgy created on stage by actors and the director out of the actors' actions. First of all I connected the motive of Ciemny and the "apostles." But it is a little like telling the motives of Bloom, Dedalus and Molly from *Ulysses*, adding how the Homeric myth is transposed on to them. This is but a skeleton of a work or a scenario of *Apocalypsis* reconstructed from a finished performance.

A critic writing about an ordinary performance does not summarize the play, because he assumes that the reader knows it or can read it. Now I can proceed in a similar way: I can refer to my own description of the performance. Let us do a vertical cross-section of *Apocalypsis* and look at its three specific characteristics: multiplicity of meanings, simultaneity, and "the law of universal analogy."

Let us go back to the dramaturgy for a while. Six characters. One of them, called Simon Peter, later on, for fun "creates" Ciemny as Christ. When Ciemny becomes convinced, he is attacked and rejected. But Ciemny really becomes Christ. However, it is not clear whether he is a true Christ or a false one. If he is a false Christ, then Simon Peter represents the arguments of the Church, its rightful alertness in unmasking false Messiahs. If he is a true Christ, there are two possibilities. Simon Peter represents the Church as an institution, a complex mechanism of earthly power, for which a return of Christ and his evangelical principles would mean ruin. Or Simon Peter – especially because he uses lay arguments from Dostoevski rather than theological ones – represents simply a lay world, hostile towards Christ's teaching. In *Apocalypsis*, these three possibilities – plus some other lesser ones – are not given the spectator to choose from. We must trace them simultaneously and receive them collectively. Only then do they make sense. Even though they are contradictory. In *Apocalypsis*, there is no "or – or," there is only "and – and."

This principle "and – and" is also present in the structure of situations and in the actors' work. The love scene is a good example. I described it well earlier, but I did not analyze its elements. It contains a comparison between sex and hunting, and its participants are Ciemny, Mary Magdalene and John. On the plane of movement and gesture John plays the game (a stag or a fawn), while Ciemny and Magdalene play alternately a bow and a bowstring. On the "psychological" plane, Ciemny and Magdalene act simply a sexual act, while John – in his breathless running *towards* the lovers – plays their libido in a sense. On the plane of plot, John, who had let in a half-idiot on a prostitute, now encounters them, excited and jealous at the same time. On the plane of a biblical story, the three characters are John, Magdalene and Christ immersed in a complex eroticism. Its violence is strengthened – but also alleviated – by the other planes. And again, in the performance those planes are simultaneously related; only in a description do they appear in a linear fashion.

Acting metaphors. In an early part of the performance, Ciemny, running nervously around the others, suddenly raises on his toes and becomes almost immobile in the air with his arms spread apart, head hidden between the shoulders, and palms softly hanging down. It is a moment, a flash: an image of a bird climbing up in the air and an image of the crucified Christ. Seemingly the image does not serve anything here. The crucifixion will occur later, the image of a bird may be remembered when Ciemny says after Eliot, "Why should the aged eagle spread its wings?" But this also comes later. But that poetic figure reveals to us not only the simultaneity of two distant meanings suddenly linked by means of the actor's gesture, as well as their remote relationship with other parts of the performance. That poetic figure also shows how the river of time is changed into simultaneity. At that point Ciemny is not Christ yet, but he is already crucified. Events occur in time, but they are always present, outside time, before time, after centuries.

They are present as poetic images, seemingly disconnected. Those images do not move the action, but constantly they interweave it with a shimmering net of remote analogies. A spectator often only notices the images in *Apocalypsis*, but he does not see them; it is only after several weeks that they emerge from memory, strangely clear and precise. Therefore analysing one scene only, it is difficult to grasp all its meanings and associations. There is Simon Peter mounting Ciemny and galloping on him as if he were a horse. Partially, I explained this scene earlier, but I overlooked a certain earlier image, when Ciemny jumps on Simon's back and hangs on his shoulder, with his head on Simon's chest. It is another image-moment: the Good Shepherd with a lamb. And the whole scene of "making a horse out of Ciemny" (a Polish idiom meaning to make a fool out of someone) is structurally related with this image: it is its reversed reminder. Reversed and scoffing.

Through such metaphors Grotowski illustrates the "law of universal analogy." All world phenomena reflect in one another, but we usually overlook those connections. Time passes, there is history and the contemporary world, nature and culture, psychological and physical facts, but hidden analogies unite them in a full and essentially immobile whole. A constant process of uniting remote images into an integrated system of analogies is, of course, the basis of all poetic thinking; after all, metaphors are based on analogies. But sometimes this kind of thinking becomes especially important, when it refers not only to the work itself, but to the world outside it. The principle of "universal analogy" comes from Swedenborg, but we also find it in the esoteric tradition which comes later, in surrealists, Breton and Artaud. Also in Joyce.

The throng of acting images – sharp and momentary – revealed by the company of the Laboratorium – comes not only from the joy of creating and associating. It is probably something more: a dream of the mysterious logic of the world, of the "unity in plurality" which we have tried to find for centuries. Unsuccessfully, but is this important?

EXTERNAL ORDER, INTERNAL INTIMACY

Interview with Grotowski

Marc Fumaroli

FUMAROLI: During the recent seminar in Holstebro, Denmark, important questions were raised about the proper role of the theatre artist in relation to society. Several of the American participants strongly felt the need for a more direct involvement in contemporary social problems than your theatre seems to represent.

GROTOWSKI: This need exists for many artists throughout the world today. I am not so much questioning the assumption behind this desire as the works which are used as proof of its validity. There are two temptations which could make me abandon my own path and lead me to regard theatre as an act of life. The first of these temptations is to devalue certain sociopolitical attitudes by reducing them to simple generic and verbal affirmations. I could indulge my ego by juggling with grand words such as "humanism," "solidarity with the oppressed," "the rights of my own personality," but this would serve nothing but my own sentimental and intellectual comfort.

Our rights as men should begin with our acts rather than with declarations or testimonials to ourselves. We are like trees: we don't have to worry in which direction destiny, climate, the winds, and the tempest are veering, or to know whether the earth will be fertile or sterile; the very fact of our birth obliges us to respond to the challenge of life, and to answer it in the manner of nature itself, which never hurries and never hesitates. If our seeds fall upon stone, so much the worse. Even this does not free us from our duty; if we refuse, on whatever pretext, to perform the acts required of us, we shall be like a tree thrown into a fire and destroyed. And that will be right. This fire is not of a social order; it flames inside me as soon as I betray, in one way or another, my duty as a living man, the duty to perform acts. The worst threat to man's survival lies in my own sterility; and this sterility is nothing but an escape from creation.

The second temptation is that of confusing my comfort with the free development of my nature. If, as an actor, comfort became my main care, I would forget that rehearsals are for the creation of scenic facts, and that all my work should be determined by the necessity of arriving at those facts. I would be too filled with flattering affirmations which hold out the promise, to myself and all others, of turning on the green light for my own spontaneity. These noble affirmations aim at assuring me the most agreeable comfort – of not working in the very place I am supposed to work, namely, in the rehearsal hall. My efforts or, rather, the byproducts of my inertia, would have only one end – to identify what is personal and what is private. I would spend my time creating the so-called working atmosphere instead of really getting down to work. The rehearsals would be transformed into chatty sessions devoted to noble and exalted topics. Then, at last, I would begin to work. This is called "improvisation." Once, perhaps, this word meant something. Today it is no more than a pretentious word serving as a substitute for work.

In conformity with the ideals I wanted to maintain, I could only improvise in keeping with my nature. Thanks to the "working atmosphere," I would already feel as though I were immersed in the warm waters of family relations with the other members of the group – delivered of all responsibility. It is the group that creates instead of me. I would find myself interesting. It would suffice me to be who I am. Whatever I might do – walk, howl, shout – I would feel absolved by the group. If I wished to show myself human, I would seek contact: touch the hands of my partners, look them straight in the eyes. I'd see nothing at all there, but no matter, the essential thing is to be human and do improvisations; it is not difficult, so I would do it. To demonstrate that I am also an animal, I would crawl on four feet and utter inarticulate cries. That is biological, that is spontaneous. In brief, I would express myself, and still call this "improvisation." If I felt tired, then I'd lie down, that's one of the rights of man, and I'd leave my colleagues on the stage to follow the evangelical precept, "Let the dead bury their dead." Thus, I would lie down and rest; it is relaxation once more. I live in a nervous world: outside, there is the money I must earn, or which I have earned thanks to my brave statements about the development of mankind. I must dance like a dog around the all-powerful opinion-makers.

But each of us knows the difference between real work and pretended work; and in the secret of my interior conscience, I would be perfectly well aware if the basis upon which my life is founded were infertile or sterile, if this basis were a substitute which prevented me from giving myself seriously. Allow that one may lie with words, but to make a falsehood of one's entire life, that is a far greater disaster; for this falsehood, carefully cultivated, poisons the whole being. This is a strange way to eliminate the division between theatre and life!

If I really wish to do this, then I must turn toward the experience of my own life, toward my own life in person, flesh and blood, external and internal intimacy, where I am called upon to create in the capacity of an actor on the stage, to make my own life entirely visible. I am obliged to create very precise sketches which have surged up from the concrete facts of my personal experience rather than to do improvisations. These sketches are the direct opposite of improvisations – which protect me from the act of truth, from the act which really abolishes the frontier between life and the theatre – and what I must show in this act is precisely what I prefer to hide, because it is so essential to me that I cannot allow myself even to talk about it with friends. If I boast about being a man in search of his own dignity, then I am obliged to be conscious not in words, but in acts and facts. I am obliged to be precise in my work. Now, what reveals the presence of a consciousness is structure, clarity, the precise line of the work. The absence of precision in work, the lack of structure in a work, are so many sins against consciousness, and, therefore, against that human dignity for which I pretend to struggle.

If I boast of questing for a reconciliation with myself, and of seeking a totality which would put an end to my division into body and soul, sex and intellect, it amounts to saying that I refuse any longer to feel apart from my own body, my own instinct, my own unconscious, that is, from my own spontaneity. The trouble is that spontaneity could end in a lying spectacle, a trivial vision of false savages in a forest or of human four-legged beasts howling and biting the rumps of their partners. Spontaneity, to be truly spontaneous, is to allow free rein to the profound flux which rises from my whole experience, even physical, but related to my consciousness, for how could I cut myself off from my consciousness even in order to rediscover my spontaneity? I am as I am, as far away from mechanics as from chaos: between the two shores of my precision, I allow the river, which comes out of the authenticity of my experience, to advance, slowly or rapidly. Every performance is as hazardous, as risky, as a rehearsal. Whatever the subjective riches I have succeeded in mobilizing from the depths of my being to fill this road, nothing protects me from the risk of losing, during a performance, all I have obtained. Such are the conditions under which my spontaneity and my totality may appear in all their authenticity.

It is true that, for such an act, human relations in the course of work

count for much. But you do not play at family life, at friendship. You work, and in the work you esteem and respect the time and effort of your colleagues. You respect the discipline of working in common, according to the rules which each one has accepted and which, therefore, obligate one. Order is the necessary condition which allows me to concentrate upon creation. You have a mutual respect for each other because, in a creative community, each has a right to create, but his duty is to do so in his role, as a responsible individual. There is a meeting ground, mutual exchange, but this meeting and this exchange burn on the hearth of the act of creation. It has nothing to do with the much touted "working atmosphere."

FUMAROLI: You have insisted on the duties and responsibility of the actors as professionals. What is the role of the director in the theatre as an act of life?

GROTOWSKI: As a stage director, I could have the choice of fraternizing with all the members of the group to an extreme extent, to the point of tears and exhibitionist confessions. In this I could imagine that I have established another dimension of comfort in work, and have accorded the actor a fraternal acceptance which, by virtue of confidence and security, makes possible the creative act. In this I would be wrong. Can I truly grant this actor such acceptance without knowing his whole being, his whole nature, his whole experience of life? What value can that warmth emanating from me have for him, if, in every circumstance, whether important or futile, I give as much of myself to no matter whom? How is an actor able to distinguish between the moments when I am unreservedly fraternal toward him and the moments when I am satisfied with mere fraternal gestures? No, what I must do is to create between him and myself a field of creative communication. This is evident when we mutually go out toward each other, without a word or almost none, and, in any case, without any conventional gesticulation that mimes fraternity. This is evident when I forget I am a director in his presence, and not because I wish to multiply, relative to him, the external manifestations of fraternization, which would merely disguise the lack of deep interest I feel toward him. Inversely, this feeling of belonging to a creative community rather than to a family bathed in comfort can tempt me to exaggerate my private authority as a director. Doubtless it is very true that work relations should be recorded inside a freely accepted order, an objective order which obligates the director as well as the actors; but it is not normal for the director to reserve for himself all the privileges of this order and for the actors all the obligations of work. Instead of a hypocritically fraternal director, there is at the other extreme what I would call the director as tamer. By what signs does one recognize him? By these: he neither appeals to the actors nor defies them nor bestows on them a quality of attention which is like a luminous and pure consciousness, a consciousness that identifies itself with presence, a consciousness devoid of all calculation, but at the same time attentive and generous. The director as tamer wishes, on the contrary, to extract all the creative elements by force from the actors. He does not respect germination; it is he who always knows in advance what to do. There are actors who love this kind of director. He frees them from the responsibility of creating.

FUMAROLI: Recently in the United States there has been great controversy over the artistic and ethical validity of nudity on the stage. What reactions do you have to this?

GROTOWSKI: Nudity and sex are what I call man's external intimacy; there is nothing about this intimacy that is suspect, doubtful, or wretched. I believe the contrary. But when anything is truly precious, there is nothing more deplorable and disastrous than to see it transformed into merchandise and become an object of commerce. Where does pornography begin? It begins as soon as we are confronted with the external intimacy of a man deprived of his internal intimacy. That is to say, when the intimacy is not total. Take pornographic photographs: you have there all the intimate aspects of the human being, but they are only appearances. You have an abstraction, for the other side of human intimacy is absent, because this side could not manifest itself in the commercial conditions under which such photographs are taken. Nudity here, as in the theatre, functioning on the same principle, is only publicity intended to attract more consumers – here one sells and buys human intimacy.

In our epoch, when religious values are almost totally exhausted, human intimacy is perhaps the single value which has any chance of surviving, perhaps because it is of earthly rather than heavenly origin. Man in his intimacy: such is the last of our temples. We must scourge the peddlers and chase them out of the temple.

I believe deeply in the actor's work; a complete disarmament and stripping, in the old and noble sense of the word, play an essential role. Through this stripping the actor can rise to a summit which is objective and even corporeal, but this is something that cannot be sold. If the actor should know and practice this stripping both in the old, noble sense and in the objective and palpable one, flesh and blood, he may then confront the public even if clothed from head to foot: the vital impulses emanating from him and revealing him will make him a more naked man than the actor who undresses in public in order to cover up his lack of sincerity as an actor, which means as a human being. If one is against the return to the hypocritical morality of a Tartuffe, all the more must one demand a little more esteem for what is holy, more honesty, more dignity, and less diminishing of the values of sex and nudity.

FUMAROLI: The number of spectators for individual performances of your plays is extremely limited. Does this create the danger that your audience will be elitist? Beyond what point do you feel it is impossible to have a true confrontation between actors and spectators? Do you believe that the confrontation between actors and spectators demands direct audience participation?

GROTOWSKI: Each spectator has different needs and, in the course of his life, his needs may even change. Our task as artists is to find spectators for whom the kind of work we create is truly necessary. What has been in the past the privilege of certain social groups should be recognized as the privilege of the man in the street: the right to choose and, in particular, the right to choose a type of theatre, a type of creation, as necessary to him. I also believe that, if one seeks, as we do, to meet each spectator rather than an undifferentiated public, it is perhaps preferable that the audience not be monstrous. Our productions are therefore designed for the number of spectators they can truly contain. It is quite another problem that in Wroclaw our hall is small and, consequently, this affects the structure of our performances. Certain musical works are meant only for a small number of instruments rather than for a symphony orchestra. Spectators are not instruments, but we have created our productions in terms of a small audience. In Wroclaw we perform for a public which oscillates between forty and a hundred spectators. If one takes into account the difference in population between New York and Wroclaw, in a similar theatre in New York we would be playing to an audience of between one thousand and sixteen hundred. Can one call that an elite theatre? And then, what kind of elite? In our town we have spectators of different ages, different classes, different backgrounds. There are university professors who are very responsive, and there are others who never come to our theatre or, if they do, remain indifferent. There are workers who are very responsive and receptive, and others who ignore us. As for the problem of space, we seek in each of our performances a certain type of spatial relation between the actors and the spectators, between the playing area and the place where the observers are located. This problem's importance in theatrical art has been much exaggerated. In particular, direct audience participation has become a new myth, a miraculous solution, and it is probable that our theatre has unconsciously contributed to giving sanction to it. In fact, spatial relations are only important if they form an integral part of the structure of the production. If this internal coherence is nonexistent, all explorations into the space of the production reduce themselves to pretexts to liberate us from our true duties. One has no right to juggle with ideas instead of assuming one's professional responsibilities. As if by mingling the actors and the spectators, we could bring about direct participation! Experience proves that by putting a distance between the actors and the spectators in space, one often rediscovers a proximity between them; and, inversely, the best means of creating a sort of abyss between them is to have them mingle in space.

Together with Jerzy Gurawski, my chief collaborator in this area, we have studied this problem over many years. After so many explorations, experiences, and reflections, I still doubt the possibility of direct participation in today's theatre, in an age when neither a communal faith exists, nor any liturgy rooted in the collective psyche as an axis for ritual.

All I can say with certainty is that in the theatre of our civilization I have never come across direct participation. The Theatre Laboratory seeks a spectator/witness, but the spectator's testimony is only possible if the actor achieves an authentic act. If there is no authentic act, what is there to testify to?

Translated from French by George Reavey.
© 1969 Jerzy Grotowski

INTRODUCTION: THE LABORATORY THEATRE IN NEW YORK, 1969

Richard Schechner

Presented at this point in the *Sourcebook* are several responses to the Laboratory Theatre's 1969 presentations in New York. These responses are not reviews, although Walter Kerr was the senior reviewer for the *New York Times* and Harold Clurman, a director of great authority, and a former member of the Group Theatre, also wrote reviews. These selections are reactions by a cross-section of thinkers to the productions of the Laboratory Theatre. They also include questions directed toward Grotowski.

Although by 1969, Grotowski had already set sail for paratheatre, his Theatre of Productions work was new to the American theatre. The Laboratory Theatre was scheduled to perform in the U.S.A. in 1968. But in the aftermath of the Soviet invasion of Czechoslovakia, visas were denied. Only after a year would Grotowski's productions be seen in New York. Until that time, the work was known mostly through publications in *TDR* and by word of mouth spreading from the four-week workshop Grotowski and Cieslak led at New York University's School of the Arts in November 1967. I was in that workshop and can attest to its rigor, seriousness, and intensity. We did exercises both physical and psycho-physical – starting with stuff based to some degree on yoga and moving on to the "plastiques" (free-flowing movements) and "association exercises" that mark the Theatre of Productions phase of Grotowski's work.[1] Grotowski concentrated much of his attention on vocal work, on identifying and enlivening resonators in various parts of the body. Without referring to Martin Buber's "ich und du" (I and you) directly, Grotowski spoke a great deal, and with commitment and passion, about finding a "secure partner," a being – not necessarily another human person – with whom one could communicate. He insisted that theatre was not possible without this intimate and no-holds-barred communication. For myself, this need for another, for a partner one could trust, related also to work being done in group therapy. I felt that the therapeutic work was extremely useful for theatre because it helped people relate to each other, it recognized that the irreducible human unit of existence was two. The movement work was led mostly by Cieslak. He instructed, he laid on hands, he cajoled, he participated. Grotowski spoke in French and we got what he said through translators. Cieslak spoke less often, and then mostly in Polish to Grotowski who, when he felt it necessary, translated. But words of instruction were not very necessary for Cieslak, whose body was a book we all could plainly read, and whose movements were clear instruction as to what we were trying to accomplish. Needless to say, none or at best very few persons in that workshop were able to match the excellence of Cieslak or the intense dedication of Grotowski, and then only for brief flashes. But in that workshop the seeds of several important groups were planted, including The Performance Group and André Gregory's Manhattan Project (best-known production, *Alice in Wonderland*, 1970).

But a workshop for a dozen actors and directors is one thing, public performances another. On 16 October 1969, a year later than originally planned, the Laboratory Theatre culminated its fifth foreign tour by opening its three-play repertory in Greenwich Village's Washington Square Methodist Church. *The Constant Prince* was shown 23 times, *Akropolis* 11, and *Apocalypsis* 14. All told, 48 performances were offered. These had a great impact both on professional theatre artists and on the press. When *Time* selected the most important events of the decade 1960–69, the Laboratory Theatre's productions were awarded first place in the theatre field.

The reactions of the New York press were electric, mostly positive but sometimes acidly against, as a brief selection demonstrates. Jerry Talmer in the *New York Post* (17 October) on *Prince*:

> the Grotowski company is indeed extraordinary, and far superior in discipline and sheer poetic brilliance to groups in the U.S. and abroad (i.e., the latter-day Living Theater) claiming common origins. [. . .] This company is as trained, as unified, as crackfire as a football team or ballet troupe. It starts on a dime, stops on a dime, and seems to have access to everything: chanting, whispering-chanting, birdcalls, seagull cries, the Kyrie eleison of liturgical ritual, instant switches from terrible sobbing to natural conversational tones.

Clive Barnes in the *New York Times* (5 November) on *Akropolis*:

> Grotowski's purpose in *Akropolis* is to challenge the audience to see itself in the context of Auschwitz. To accept some iota, a scintilla of that horror, to be involved in that web of human choices and squalid heroism. [. . .T]he Laboratory Theatre has devised both this environmental setting, with actors responding antiphonally to one another, across the audience, and a

stylized playing style in which simple sculptural-like objects, or even day-to-day things like wheelbarrows, involve the spectator by familiarity into a sense of participation. The style of acting is singular. The actors use their face muscles to provide masklike images of misery and acceptance, their voices are dehumanized, their entire manner represents humanity in such a condition of degradation that the humanity itself is flickering like a guttering candle. [. . .] Grotowski's actors are all dazzling technicians, with masterly discipline and control. They aim in technique to remove the shadow line between appearance and reality, and to take us with them on a new theatrical journey. It is a fascinating experience. It has changed my basic thinking about the theatre.

Even the negative reactions were very strong. For example, Ross Wetzsteon in the *Village Voice* (27 November):

A Grotowski production is a mass in worship of its own devotion. Thus his company's impulse is less religious than pietistic, finding self-satisfaction in submission, and submitting only to self-chosen disciplines. And this air of self-celebrating piety – the aggrandizing sacrifices, the smug humility – combines with the fashionable, even superciliously elitist ambiance of the company's New York performances to produce that most noxious of attitudes, chic spirituality. The middle European fairy-tale grotesquerie of the imagination behind these plays, their passionately disciplined cliches and rigorously formalized awkwardness, are merely intensely disappointing – but the showy gestures of self-sacrifice, the nobility-on-tour tone, and the victimized-by-superiority themes are nothing less than loathsome.

Yes, the Laboratory Theatre made its mark.

Grotowski, reacting against the attention paid to him at the expense of his company, distributed a mimeographed statement that contains one of the clearest outlines of the Laboratory's way of working during the Theatre of Productions phase. The statement reads, in part:

I am anxious to dispel a certain misunderstanding which is liable to arise from the tendency in discussion and analysis of the Theatre Laboratory to feature my name and my name alone. Without in any way wishing to give an impression of mock modesty, I must stress that in the end I am not the author of our productions, or at any rate not the only one. [. . .] "Grotowski" is not a one-man band. [. . .]

My name is, in fact, only there as a symbol of a group and its work in which are fused all the efforts of my associates. And these efforts are not a matter of collaboration pure and simple: they amount to creation.

In our productions next to nothing is dictated by the director. His role in the preparatory stages is to stimulate the creative associations for which the impulse comes from the actors and to organize the final structure in which they assume a specific shape. It is one of the basic principles of our method of creation to have this kind of interplay in which director and actors give as much as they take, ceaselessly exchanging. [. . .] This exchange does not take place at the level of discussion either; it is in essence an exchange of our life experience, a reciprocal offering of the signs of our biographies [. . .].

But despite his demurring, people saw the work of the Laboratory as mainly Grotowski's. Were they wrong? Even as the productions of the Laboratory were being performed in New York, Grotowski himself was moving from the Theatre of Productions to Paratheatre and from there to Theatre of Sources. Were these moves a group decision, discussed either verbally or in the whole-life manner suggested by Grotowski in his handout? If the move was fully collaborative, why did most Laboratory Theatre members not also move from productions to paratheatre? The fact is, Grotowski had a change of direction, or perhaps, more accurately, a return to his fundamental life drive: the search for spiritual knowledge. The Theatre of Productions was for more than a decade his means towards that end. But by the late 1960s, Grotowski knew (even if his colleagues did not) that something else was needed, another path was to be taken – one leading out of the theatre toward using theatrical or rather performance techniques and performative ways of knowledge in pursuit of something outside of theatre.

If the New York tour marked one of the final moments of Theatre of Productions, the Laboratory did not formally cease to exist until years later, in 1984, long after Grotowski left it. Throughout the 1970s and into the 1980s, the Lab remained an organizational shell, providing services to its members. "I did not close it," Grotowski told me, "because it protected those who remained in Poland." In the mid-1980s, Zbigniew Cynkutis, one of Grotowski's earliest collaborators, the Faust of *Dr. Faustus*, inhabited the Polish Laboratory Theatre space in Wroclaw at Ratusz Rynek 27, where he tried to start up again. Cynkutis dubbed his theatre Drugie Studio Wroclawskie (Second Studio, Wroclaw). No need to ask what was the First. Cynkutis's effort failed, it had to: the Laboratory Theatre, space and spirit, was Grotowski's. Others could share in the work, could contribute to it, but no other could be it. What came after Grotowski in Wroclaw was not another theatre, after-image or inheritance, but the Laboratory Theatre archives, curated by Zbigniew Osinski.

THE LABORATORY THEATRE IN NEW YORK, 1969: A SET OF CRITIQUES

Stefan Brecht

DO MEN GATHER GRAPES OF THORNS, OR FIGS OF THISTLES?

Calderon's *Constant Prince* is a devotion to absolute monarchy, the Christian knight, and Christianity. These three are what the Prince is constant to. The first is still the degradation of nations; the second, thirty years after Cervantes' exposition, was worn-out camouflage for the *auri sacra fames* of colonial adventurers; and Christianity, in the conscious motivations of the play's characters, appears as what it was: Europe's claim to world empire – with specific reference to the white man's first action on this claim, fifteenth-century Portuguese colonialism in Africa. But the cunning of genius distills their inward truth from these vile fictions and presents it as the virtue and wisdom of the Prince. A captain, generous, cool. A Franciscan knight. A noble man.

Calderon's play glorifies nobility. He presents it as *character*, expressed in and by a whole life. His poetry defines the noble life as able use of the body, in an intelligent commitment to responsible leadership and in a spirit of unbounded spontaneous generosity. A willing but above all a noble expenditure of the flesh. He makes us feel that a noble life is not only happy quite independently of suffering, but fortunate independently of happiness in that it realizes the spirit. Spiritual fulfilment appears as transcendence of temporality. The reader feels that nobility, though extraordinary, is not a gift, but achievable or at least worth trying for. This impression is strengthened by the other characters: good, even loving, but not noble, and thus unhappy in spite of pleasures, unfortunate in spite of happiness, their lives wasted, failures. The play generates a notion of life: an opportunity for spiritual realization by nobility. Or: an opportunity to transcend the flesh and the world by the use of the flesh and by help to the world. A corollary notion: time (and thus the temporal) is an illusion. Seize the time!

Calderon and the Prince presumably believe in virtue's reward by

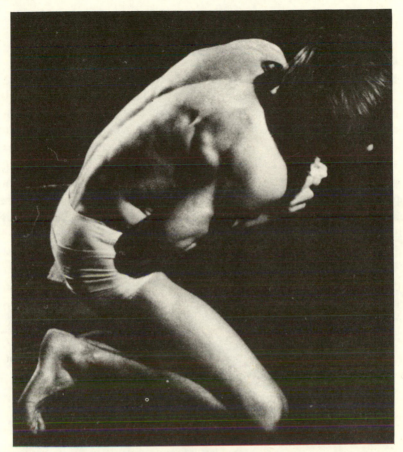

Plate 12.1 The Constant Prince. (Photo: Max Waldman.)

happiness in an afterlife. But the play opens no perspectives onto eternal bliss. The Prince's concern (nominally out of fealty to Our Lady, really by a generous interpretation of his charge of captaincy) is to save souls. His virtue is that his responsibility for the welfare of others is constant. He lives for it. In the laboratory situation Calderon sets up, this life turns out a protracted dying. The protagonist acquiesces.

Like most plays, this play became the story of one person, the achievement of a destiny. The antagonist is the hero's straightman; the busy-ness of the others sets up his fixed destiny, which, friends and foes, they do not affect but only execute. The Princess's horror of wedding a corpse makes her the Prince's metaphysical negative. Wedded to life, her name is Phenix. From the fury of plot and the sound of monologues arises that faint quality that makes an event live in experience: the others by their diverse distractions destroy the hero. Nobody is wicked.

The sensitive Phenix is a bitch, but Calderon makes that her girlish privilege – sky and ocean are her gardens (Mirecka's acting withers her flowers). Bitro is a turncoat, Muey a defaulter, the king himself not a bad guy, just a bit greedy, a little rigid. They are normally weak people.

The play is a frame for the hero's life, a prolonged decline in misery, not stayed by the others. For the welfare of his fellow men, voluntarily and without resistance, he suffers his chosen fate. There is no voluptuousness in his sufferings (he is no masochist) – when he wishes he had more time left to endure them, in part this is the Christian atavism that sufferings are a pleasing offering to God, in part Calderon is momentarily confusing the Prince and the Jesus of theology, but in the main it is an appreciation of life not subject to the calculus of pleasures. Nor does he enjoy dying. (St. Francis is said to have apologized to his body, calling it his ass, for the excessive burdens he imposed on it.)

His flesh is for him the tool of his spirit, which grows as his flesh withers and declines. This inverse correlation is because of the circumstances and might not hold under others: Calderon has arranged the circumstances so that this correlation will dramatically illustrate cool virtue, the noble spirit's freedom. For the Prince is a proud man and loves God's sunshinely world.

Beyond this trite but elevated theme of virtue there is the shadow of a theme of wisdom:

> That the cradle and the coffin
> Are so like each other wrought [. . .]
> That when we are born, together
> We our first and last bed see.

Life is unbecoming. Leaving coolly is to live well.

The beauty of the play is not the protagonist's virtue but his way of slipping into death. His decline demonstrates beautiful detachment from life, virtuous motivation connected with wisdom, but (though this is a matter of poetic suggestion, of an emergent Gestalt) the beauty of the play is its picture of life. The man's clock runs down, but instead of diminishing, he expands. He eats time, and whatever time remains is valuable to him because he can use it for further substantial nourishment. The illusion of a future life would not only cheapen the act, it would destroy it.

The Prince hates neither himself nor his flesh: he is not running away, is not fending off. Just as he in a grandiose little scene advances into Africa without stumbling, he advances into the night without stumbling. The very term "death" becomes inappropriate before our eyes. Life is the flower of death, death the plant. A spirit at one with its withering shares the life of the plant.

It is not a sad play.

Plate 12.2   The Constance Prince. (Photo: Max Waldman.)

Grotowski trains his audience on the action like a telescope. The protagonist is at the focal point. What to him seem tall walls, to them is the geometry of bare outline. He coughs up his ghost on a shallow alter, expedited by an inner ring of gaily bureaucratic demon torturers – but actually on the indifferent wondering lens of the spectators, his real cause of death. We witness the rehearsal of an execution.

An introductory seance prepares us. Too weak to die, its victim rises and joins the orgy in the office.

The tortures are delicately right. We are satisfied that they suffice to achieve the subject. They are conventionally brutal gestures of humiliation, abruptly torn out of the lives of the operating team. The Prince is K. on trial, but he is handsome. The impression is that they have finished him off on schedule. A law of just proportions applicable only to the finite rules this theatre's time (as visibly it rules its space, a vortex not spiraling upward into infinity but funneling down into a point). A life is something to be done with.

The theatre group is demonstrating something to its own satisfaction. The operation: to distill heartbeat into spirit.

The victim is in charge, but victims usually are. With the obscene openness of a happy young pretty initiate into prison life, secretly counting the augmentations to his vanity, the "Prince" conducts his vivisection. His spirit is that of passive buggery – being fucked in the arse – rather than of masochism: for he is enjoying not particular pains but the attack on his core, the central violence done himself, and he does not lose himself in pain; it fuses with adoration of the dominator. Such passion arises from vanity and self-hatred: the possession certifies that he is pretty, the brutality cleanses him of the dross. The withdrawal of the centurion's lance gives this pretty skin full of shit that all too momentary feeling of purity – really just emptiness, I would say. He is voluble.

But so are the others. The spectacle is in black and white. He is in white, the others are in black. What you see is white, the verbal gesticulation is impenetrable black. The sound is severed from the movement of the bodies. The motions hang on it. *Their* words are quite insincere, *his* are beside the point. We would not understand them if we did. The elegant screw of his rib cage bears up the black and thorny crown of his cogent argument, its cogency tautened by his passion. His fellow men applaud him (at one point Jaholkowski as the King for quite a while keeps his hands in readiness for further applause, illustrating a prime function of public approval: the obliteration of performance). The Prince's ululations pump out the ballast of his pain. He is the officiant at a millenalist penitential.

The heart of the Prince is the center. Its beat is an itch to him. It jars his beauty. To the others, his life is precious. It's what they have to work with. His pulse is their time beat as they slowly reduce him to zero.

Grotowski has ejected into the phantom life of the words two of the three virtues held up to us by Calderon: generosity and leadership. Rummaging in its Christian reminiscences, he has perverted the third one, coolness, into spirituality. Grotowski's Prince rages against his flesh, his servants visiting his rage on it to clear his mind for the anguishing purification of his spirit. He is not detached: he screams for detachment. His life is his intimate enemy.

Grotowski has converted the Christian knight into a martyr-mad saint by concentrating on the Prince's personal life at the moment, as prisoner. He encapsulates Calderon's unbounded empire. In this intimate ambience, he discerns the paradox of destructive fondness. He sees it, and makes us see it, as fond destructiveness. He thus plunges us into a universe of malevolence. In such a universe, withdrawal of the spirit is a clever move. But in such a world also, living is *only dying* (whereas in

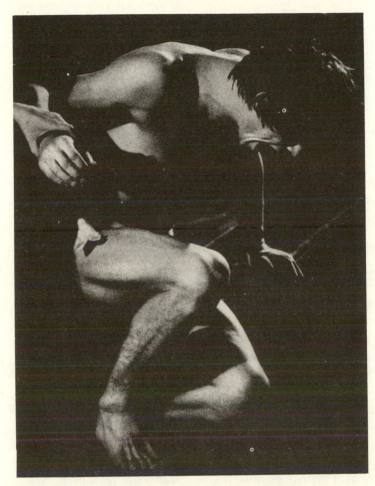

Plate 12.3 The Constant Prince. (Photo: Max Waldman.)

Calderon's world, living *is* dying and none the worse for it). Calderon's Prince chooses to relate to the others as servant. Grotowski subverts this courtly gesture of a noble man into the contemptible stratagem of a saint – which (contrary to what Grotowski seems to think) will avail him nothing. It will not gain him even *his* freedom.

The production focuses on life. It presents it as evil movement. The stillness of absence emerges as ideal; life as diminution; the good life as rendition of time. The best is negative. Grotowski has invited us to a celebration of death.

The production is a hard-headed adoration of saintliness – hard-headed in facing its inconveniences, risks, and uncertainties. Grotowski presents saintliness as expressed in a certain manner of death: death as the tour de force of slavish servility to murderous humanity – as a willing and eager, though very difficult, acquiescence in the evil men naturally do. He makes us feel that a saintly death is glorious because it achieves beatitude. Beatitude appears as the beauty of pure soul, of spirit divorced from flesh. Spirit's divorce from flesh appears as loss of the temporal, through voluntarily giving it away. In truth: an annihilation. One receives the impression that saintliness is a unique beauty of the personality. This impression is strengthened by Grotowski's presentation of the generality of men (exemplified by the other characters) as gaily and routinely engaged in the natural exercise of malice and as fervently attached to the flesh – their own poisonous flesh and the flesh of those they mortify. A notion of the human condition emerges: as not only beastly but ugly servitude to the (fortunately mortal) flesh, with the only alternatives the murderous adoration of it or the saintly flight from it into death. A corollary notion: *le temps des assassins* is all we have.

The hero's project is strictly egoist – his own salvation. It is loveless, for his subservience to the will of the others is for his own sake and abets their evil-doing, thus it is not for their good. And though it is entirely spiritualist, conceived in enmity to the flesh and indifference to life, it is worldly and in the carnal mode, for the beatitude desired is a beauty one can be vain of, like the beauty of the body.

This egoism is the essence of the Christianity preached in the Gospels, and their chief likeness to the Old Testament. It contrasts sharply with the life of Jesus the Christ: the first-born son of God, consubstantial with God, sacrificed by God out of love for man, Who with only occasional slight hesitations acquiesces in His own immolation – for the sake of mankind.

Whereas Calderon's play is illuminated by the life of the sweet Jesus (or of St. Frances), Grotowski's production has been instructed by His mean word.

It endeavors not only to give meaning to the terms of this project but to show that it can be done – if only by an exceptional personality. Furthermore, it endorses the project, though neither recommending it to everyone nor even setting it up as ideal exemplar to approach, but spitefully telling us evil-doers what we are missing.

Its undertaking is threefold: to render openness to injury, self-abnegation, mortification, beatitude meaningful; to give such words specific/emotional/volitional denotation by theatrical experience and show that they refer to spiritual possibilities (realities); to show that the road to beatitude indicated leads to it and that beatitude is good.

The performance is quite finished. The gestures are the international theatrical gestures of Occidental theatre which actors have copied from one another since at least the early nineteenth century, the Romantic vocabulary of motivation and character of ego-psychology, which was given a new lease on life by the silent movies. In this theatre they seem out of a world of dreams, surprised out of the corner of an eye as they change into something else, essentially quite familiar but odd in their context. Apart from Cieslak's, the hero's, repertory of egotism, they are melodramatic and comic, those of the bad guys and tortured spirits of vulgar commercial provincial theatre and film, posed as though for a hidden camera one is mocking. Unlike most artistically ambitious Western theatre since the 1920s, Grotowski has apparently found this vocabulary largely adequate for his purposes. He has increased the precision of the gestures and thus their intensity – giving them considerable hieroglyphic power. He has made a grisly selection within the gesticulary of ego-psychology theatre by imposing a metaphysics: "Men are piteously evil, may God save their souls." He has stressed and generalized a pathology of waiting and impatience (greed for response), the tensions of a predatory social sensitivity. This is the opposite of the Method's little reform. The overall result: black and white Daguerre stills in the strobe motion of the early flicks.

It is hard to imagine these actors' gestures used for affection. When the agents of the Prince's dying kiss him, they are sucking his life's blood. Their caresses are ghoulish. Genitals are for castration. When the characters skip, storm, or dance in concert, it is a celebration of evil, but not a convivial one. Their typical gestures hide their faces – behind crooked arms, coattails, umbrellas, hats, by a bent back or by a turn. They are lone; they refuse communication. Their gestures are tricky. Peter Schumann pointed out, regarding another play of Grotowski's, that often apparently benign gestures turn into taunts: bread offered is dropped.

The severance of discourse from life seems one of the designs of the actors' verbal training. They have much breath left from their vigorous mimicry, giving their speech independent power. (Slowacki's poetry may enhance this effect abnormally.) Even the hero's precious life breath, fading way, magically seems something else than the breath he spends on his lengthy loud monologues. The vocal and the body-gestures are coordinated but self-contained wholes, suggesting a body-spirit duality, the sounded breath representing only the mind. Thus even if the text's words and tonalities, timbres, inflections, changes of pitch, conveyed affection (as they do not in this production), this affection would be purely mental, no matter how great the passion (which is consistently great in this production). It would be mere momentary meaning, detached from the person voicing it, part of a dialectical sequence in mind. I suspect that the persistent tone of insincerity in the production characterizes speech in Grotowski's other productions as well. But Grotowski's style of vocal gesture seems to preclude even the sincerity of sobriety, even that of broken, divided passion. (Part of my impression may be due simply to his adaptation and interpretation of

Plate 12.4   *The Constant Prince.* (Photo: Max Waldman.)

Calderon's logic of flowery metaphor.) Social life conducted from off
the top of an inner air-reservoir is grim.

The glory, power, and innovation of Grotowski's theatre, however,
seem to me to be that it is spiritualist and experimental. Spiritualist
theatre is concerned with the spirit of man transcending and underlying
the individual's ego. Grotowski's particular spiritualism seems transcendentalist and Christian, viewing spirit as individuated substance or soul,
real independently of the body and of other souls, capable of relating to
both, but diminished in its association with them.

This is not the only spiritualism. The immanentist spiritualism of
humanist communism views spirit as the form of human bodies insofar
as they relate to one another. This suggests a different theatre.

Grotowski aims to present spirit theatrically and to demonstrate his
own view of spirit. This inspires his message and his technique. His

brand of spiritualism transforms intercourse into a means of self-realization. The spiritual man emerges as a loner at war with his flesh, relating passively to others. His gestures are those of solitude, solicitude for himself, submission to others. The gestures of the (loving/evil) flesh and other-bound spirit are aggressive, other-directed, negatively carnal (sadistic), cooperative in evil only, conspiratorial, self-hiding. Generic spiritualism on the other hand furnished a manner of gesture that sublimates the body.

Cieslak's movements, facial expressions, tones do not express thoughts or external sensations but only emotional and volitional states of the spirit. They express these states naturally (as though the body were just the organ of spirit throughout): unformed by communicative function, undistorted by the resistances of a physical body, not hedged in by gestures of using the body. His communications of submission to and acquiescence in humiliation were shaped to express the spirit behind such communications, not their function of address and effect. His expressions of bodily states (e.g., physical pain) paint the feeling of pain. There were no gestures *of* a body, only gestures *by* a body: corporeal monologue of spirit itself. An incarnation.

The others' gestures demonstrate agile malevolences cooperating distrustfully in the destruction of a person, in an emotion of solicitous fondness of him (approaching adoration). They express destructiveness and love complementing one another not by the fortuity of individual character but by the logic of the human spirit. Their clever calculation and cunning trickery do not evoke, however, the spirit's external adaptation to the material and socially structured reality of an alien world, but rather its own native well-being in this world, its spiritual duality and indirection, its free delight in it. The gestures do not show possessed souls nor bondage of spirit, but a devilish spirit at play in a world which is that negative spirit's own, its extension.

Some peculiarities of this acting style: the gymnastic involvement of the whole body (not just a physical carrier of expressive limbs and face, as in most theatre), reduced here to spiritual symbol; the use of language as gesticulating sound; some exaggeration and definition of movement to stand for attitudes; the virtual elimination of non-expressive instrumentally functional movements, and of movement-components not carrying expressive meaning, and of inanimate stances expressing only corporality; the suffusion of any remaining instrumental gestures with expressive content; the virtual elimination of gestures indicating social conditioning or denoting individuality; the transposition of conventional gestures into direct person-to-person gestures showing present emotional intent or attitude; the consistent transformation of gestures of accommodation to another into gestures expressive of emotional intent (the other simply functioning as occasion). These peculiarities serve Grotowski's persistent focusing on the spirit's life.

It is a significant consequence of this style that the spectator does not ask himself whether the performer really feels the emotion portrayed. The use of the body as symbol relates us to the spiritual states symbolized. It displaces both the body as body and the performer as person. It's not that Cieslak vanishes into Don Fernando, but that Cieslak creates such an intense focus on his physical being as to channel attention to an ideal compounded of emotions and intents.

The acting by its intense physicality makes an intense spirituality arise for us, divorced from it and seeming solely real. The Grotowskian actor actualizes spirit for us by diffusing his ego through his body. However shitty its nuance, this approach is a theatrical revolution. It opposes ego-theatre.

Most theatre since the Age of Reformation directs the spectator's attention to specific individuals: to this individual and to that individual. It imputes to others a self. Following the practice of modern real life, it construes the he or she on the model of the I. It conceives the ego as being of a particular motivating character, but as being in itself unique, no matter how like other egos. Two perfectly alike persons would still be thought of as having different egos.

The ego *has* a body: the unique individual is the ego *with* that body. Its stance proclaims its occupancy of a unique location as the radiating fact of its presence, its gestures proclaim the precarious command of ego over body. Stance and gestures are addressed to other unique individuals who respond in kind, each one formally acknowledging the unique identity of the others by asserting his own. This ballet of social intercourse evokes the metaphysical monstrosity of a "social order" whose values govern conduct. The ego-theatre's repertory of gestures is ruled by the paradoxes of bourgeois life: unique individuals intrinsically relative to their bodies and one another; their free action intrinsically relative to an objective order. On its stages the unique individual is forever struggling to emerge from a body and from its fixed tenure in a social web. Thus, though the ego-theatre's sole concern is to show its spectators the particular individual, its spectacles forever tragically reduce to a show of physical atoms and ideal forces.

The ego-theatre's acting is designed to evoke the character or personality of *this* person, not spiritual realities (attitudes, emotions, inclinations) *per se*, but qualities characterizing individuals in whom, *per se*, it is solely interested. Its gestures are not designed to illuminate the nature of these realities (what one feels or wants) but to affirm their inherence. The nature of love, etc., is presumed known: conventional abbreviations of gestures will do for expressing it, but the actor works his

Plate 12.5   The Constant Prince. (Photo: Max Waldman.)

arse off to make us believe that the character loves, to suggest that he loves differently from others, why he loves, or what he, given the emotion, is apt to do. Moreover, the ego being a faculty of containment, its squeezing of its own spiritual essences is what this theatre works on expressing. To evoke the mystical unity of what is called "this person," its actors try to create characters they think might work, and so they systematically cast their imagination and recalls only onto the skimpy versions of spiritual life that people think they can afford.

Grotowski's theatre works on the assumption that the limitations of ego-psychology can be transcended. It is intensely individualist, but its concern is not with an individual but with individuality. Its actors select and fashion their gestures not to bring out what one person would be apt to do but what the spirit of man can and must do. This shatters the nominalism of the bourgeois fiction. Portraying a saint in the midst of evil humanity, they are not concerned with characterization or motivation but with the essence of saintliness and evil. Concerning the problem of turning the other cheek, most other theatre would ask: what kind of person would have this attitude? What would motivate him? Could there possibly be a character who fully achieves this? How could he express it with others? Grotowski's theatre asks: What does it consist of? What is its place in the reality of spirit? How can we most fully express its essence?

One attends this theatre with the intensity of awaiting an important result. Not the standard tension of what-will-happen? but the strain of grasping its meaning – a difficulty, one quickly realizes, not relating to foreign language or Grand Guignol manner, not of telling what they are doing down there or why, but in grasping the meaning for life of this theatrical metaphor, its real import for us. One then realizes that one's tension is caused by the performance's indications that they may not come up with a meaning, though they are trying to, and that they are concerned with it being the right meaning and emerging as such. It's a risk venture and a feat. The air of experiment (stimulated externally by Grotowski's shepherding of his audience) does not arise from an attempt to validate a non-theatrical (verbal) thesis, nor from the play's content, but from the style of the presentation. *The content consists of experiments.* The characters seem bent on achieving something difficult, the Prince by an exercise of self-discipline, the others by a delicately adjusted handling of him. Both parties are fairly sure of the result they hope for and of their means being of the right sort, but not quite sure it will work. Yet the spiritualist manner of performance makes these experiments seem neither those of individuals enacted by performers nor just those of performers trying to achieve plausibility in enacting individuals, but experiments in spiritual process carried on by gestures. The production is not merely a presentation of an experiment but the experiment itself.

The experimental air is supported by the abstract simplicity of the setting and of the correlative spiritual forces, and by the apparent contingency of what eventuates at each moment on what each force previously attained.

Will the staging enable the actors to generate the spiritual states aimed at, with sufficient precision and intensity to make their sequence self-inductive, each state naturally yielding the next? The acting tests a truth to which it gives meaning and the meaningfulness of which it also tests – by its success in evocation.

Confronted with the requirements for beatitude posed by the Sermon on the Mount, we may ask: (1) What do the words mean? What is "turning the other cheek" *really*, i.e., inwardly as reality of the spirit? What is "beatitude"? (2) Is the fulfillment of the requirements apt to lead to beatitude? (3) Do we want beatitude? Is it good? (4) Is it humanly possible to fulfil the requirements (or to be beatific)?

Only the fourth is the kind of question dealt with by ego-theatre. Historically, Christianity has answered it in the negative by doctrines of grace, absolution, and beatitude after death. Grotowski, by theatrical enactment, tries to answer 1–3, setting aside the question of secular feasibility. He gives theatrical images in answer to 1, and theatrically answers 2 and 3, in the sense of those images, by yes.

If persistent theatrical questioning in the sense of question 1 yields no meanings, no intuition of states that other terms do not cover better, we will have that much justification for concluding that the sermon is mere verbiage. If persistent theatrical experimentation on question 2 always comes out negative, persons in search of beatitude will be smart to forget the sermon. If persistent theatrical presentation of beatitude does not succeed in investing it with an aura of value, does not obtain for it our emotional approbation, then even if experiments on 2 came out positive, the inductively wiser part would again be an unchristian life.

Assume the requirements are unfulfillable, the result unattainable. If we can't do it, the problem arises: how can an actor show us with his body what it would be like? But the actor does not have to be a true Christian to show us: he has only to come up with body configurations expressing the spirit that achieves the result. He is limited to humanly possible gestures carrying this meaning: but he may hit on them without this requiring the corresponding spirituality to be psychologically (or socially) possible. Bodily expressiveness radiating beyond a core of habitual usage may transcend human possibility. Of course, the audience must be able to get the actor's meaning. But the paradox of men being able to show others that something humanly impossible is spiritually possible is resolved if it be true that we can be aware of modes of spirituality that we cannot live either outwardly or inwardly.

An experimental theatre does not have to go beyond the humanly possible. I mention that assumption and that paradox and its problematical solution because Grotowski's theatre may be understood to tell us that while we partake in spirituality, life cannot exhaust the potentials of our spirituality – but that theatre can reflect into the regions we inhabit an image even of those we cannot live in, by its fuller knowledge of the geography of this larger world: illuminating our paths within the inhabitable regions, defining their directions. In any event, to an experimental theatre confessing transcendentalist spiritualism, the question of human feasibility is secondary. It is primary for immanent spiritualism, which limits itself to the humanly possible, whether so far ever actual or not.

As a spiritualist experiment, Grotowski's spectacle is successful but dishonest. It is successful in that its searching technique faithfully reports not only the negative result but the negative premises. It is dishonest in that it borrows from Calderon to give the impression that the experiment was successful (in the sense of positive results from positive premises).

Plate 12.6   The Constant Prince. (Photo: Max Waldman.)

It is perhaps not so much a simulated experiment or a mendacious report on an experiment, as a rigged experiment.

The premises are negative in that the Prince effectively comes across as just such an egoist as Jesus expected even the best of men to be. The production shows him as loving at most only his tormentors, and even them at most only with that passive accommodation required by his use of them for his own ends (which are spiritual but egoist). Like the sermon, the production dispenses with "love thy neighbor" as negligible routine, so that "love your enemies" comes across to mean love them *as* your enemies and *because* they are your enemies. In short: the hero is loveless. (The non-resister cannot manage to love his enemies: his submission certifies to his lack of love for their other victims.)

The result is negative: spiritual and physical death as the wages of loveless submission to evil; and the satisfaction of self-loving vanity as the reward for active self-hatred.

But this truth – that egoistic spirituality is self-defeating because it kills the spirit, emptying it rather than purifying it – is incompletely presented, and hidden. It is incompletely presented because the Prince's lack of love, his egoism (concern for his own salvation), his vanity, are not accentuated but merely emerge due to the power of an experimental approach. It is hidden by investing the hero with some of the loveliness of Calderon's noble man – the Prince's purloined mask of unassuming modesty masks defeat, his fatal moment of serenity derives from the tranquil pride of Calderon's Don Fernando.

The production clearly credits the hero with a final achievement –

something like beatitude. It gives three images of this state: the beauty of a pure soul, the willing anticipation of non-being, the state of non-being. But none of them is an achievement. Desired beauty is marred by vanity and by the meanness of the wish to be superior. Purity of soul is negative, metaphor for death. Death may be a relative good, but only when achievement is impossible. Its willing anticipation is an achievement only as transcendence of the illusions of an agreeable world, not as flight from an evil world.

Not only is odious humility dressed up to impress us as the nobility of a man calmly accepting death out of a concern for others, but it is presented as achieving what might be achieved only by a nobility not seeking it: because of the spirit. The beatitude of saintliness is a byproduct of nobility about which the noble man could not care less. It is the goal only of a perverted egoist – whose spiritual ugliness will show.

By its experimental form, the production advances the claim that it is not just a bravura statement of personal preference (which would be fine) but an objective investigation of the exigencies and possibilities of spirit. That it does in fact turn out such (to the extent that it reveals the negative results of negative premises) is to the credit of its method: the production demonstrates that spiritualist experimentalism is a feasible and valuable way of working in the theatre. But the attempt to dress up personal preference as objective investigation is unsavory. The result is an impression that this theatre is up to no good.

Grotowski in his black glasses, in black and white, a philistine *à la* Kierkegaard, was leaning there as though hiding in the shadow of the high scaffolding, streaks of light from the projectors on him, but weakly, having filtered through the benches. He is watching as the last touch is put on his performance, the installation of the audience.

There was something ribald about the incantations. Perhaps Grotowski identifies with the evil spirit of the tormentors.

The light of the body is the eye: if therefore thine eye is single, thy whole body shall be full of light.

But if thine eye be evil, thy whole body shall be full of darkness. If therefore the light that is in thee be darkness, how great is that darkness!

WHY SHOULD I TAKE PART IN THE SACRED DANCE?

Jan Kott

I saw Grotowski's Laboratory Theatre for the first time in the early 1960s in Opole, a small town in Silesia. The audience was restricted to twenty-five, but that evening only four or perhaps five guests from Warsaw and two young girls from the local school came to the performance of *Akropolis*. I saw Grotowski's theatre for the second time three years later. He had already moved to Wroclaw, where he was given space in the old town hall. I came then to a festival of contemporary Polish plays and some sort of symposium, for which critics from the entire country had gathered. The forum was boring, the plays mediocre, the productions uninteresting, but all the theatres were filled to capacity. At Grotowski's theatre the audience was again restricted to thirty or forty, but at that performance of Calderon's *The Constant Prince* there were no more than a dozen or so. Grotowski already at that time had his enthusiasts and his enemies, but the number in both camps could be counted on one's fingers. During all those years Grotowski's theatre did not enter into Poland's theatrical life; it did not attract even the young. It was in Poland, but really did not exist in Poland.

Grotowski's theatre was subsidized by the government from the very beginning. Poland is probably the only country in the world to permit itself the luxury of financing a theatre laboratory and sufficiently poor that this allocation fell short of even providing sustenance for the members of the ensemble. During the first two or even three years, Grotowski and his actors starved – and not by any means in the figurative sense of the word. Poverty was at first a practice of this theatre; only later was it raised to the dignity of aesthetics. I don't know whether the members of the group made their triple vows as monks and nuns, but this theatre was modeled along the strict lines of a cloister. Grotowski demanded from his followers seclusion, obedience, and physical training almost beyond the limits of human endurance. The renunciation of material goods, given conditions in Poland, was probably the easiest decision. Far more difficult was the renunciation of the theatre of politics.

The theatre in Poland in the second half of the fifties was perhaps the most political in the world. Even the Western Theatre of the Absurd transferred to the Vistula became unequivocally, or one might even say, desperately political. Grotowski's theatre developed at an historical moment of prolonged political unrest. The Prague Spring lasted a month; the Polish Apocalypse of freedom in October 1956 lasted three days. The awakening from an apocalypse is bitter: in Poland the realization of a hopeless situation, and later, resignation to the dread this hopelessness provoked lasted for years. In conditions of arbitrary and unlimited political repression every public activity is a compromise. In the theatre a political compromise is always ultimately an artistic compromise. Grotowski took the heroic decision to be uncompromising. But under the conditions of repression, such a decision exacts the price of supplanting politics with metaphysics.

After Grotowski's appearance in England and the United States, a couple of nimble-witted critics noticed with a certain astonishment that the greatest artistic success of a country which considered itself "socialist" was the mystic theatre of obscure religious experiences. Grotowski, especially in his early period, asserted that the task of the actor, the "holy" actor in his terminology, was to experience and incarnate archetypes. I doubt whether the return to "archetypes" is possible in contemporary theatre, but I know with complete certainty that "archetypes" are politically harmless; they are, in any case, ambiguous and hard to make out. Julien Sorel in Stendahl's *The Red and the Black* learned very early in his seminary days that gestures are safer than words. The most important questions remain: what do these gestures mean? What does the excellence of Grotowski's theatre signify?

Even a theatre that wishes to reach back to archetypes must feed on living ceremony, ritual, and liturgy, which stem from its own country. *Akropolis* and *The Constant Prince*, which I saw years ago in Poland, seemed to me contrived and very distant. *Apocalypsis cum Figuris*, which I saw in New York, struck me at once with its Polishness.

The pilgrims to the miraculous shrine of Our Lady at Kalwaria Zebrzydowska climb on their hands and knees up steep stairs ornamented with figures of Christ's Passion, bruising their knees on the sharp rocks. Czestochowa, where there is another holy image of the Black Madonna, the Queen of Poland, is transformed in May, the month of the cult of the Virgin Mary, into a huge campsite. A few streets away from the monastery one finds market stalls, which sell beads and scapulars, all kinds of worthless religious baubles, and rolls with sausages. But the pilgrims generally arrive with their own supplies. The village women unfold large colored kerchiefs right on the marketplace, on which they set great loaves of home-baked bread. The men pull flat bottles of vodka out of their pockets, drink straight from them, and then pass them on to the women. The action of *Apocalypsis* begins with this scene. A woman places a loaf of bread on a white kerchief. A man reaches with his hand above his belt and offers the half-closed hand to the woman. He then raises it to his lips. His Adam's apple moves up and down – he pours the vodka straight down his throat in the time-honored Polish way.

Along the main street of Czestochowa pass processions led by priests and little boys in white cassocks. The men sing with hoarse voices as in *Apocalypsis*: "Glory to the Highest and Most Just." The women with squeaky and tearful voices wail: "Lamb of God." The religious songs are mixed with drunken hiccups and the squeals of young girls. The men squatting in the square are already drunk. One barely hears the hymn from the monastery: "And I saw the water flowing from the right side of the temple. Alleluia!" Nearby is a figure of the crucified Christ with a pierced side. The artisan did not spare the red paint. In *Apocalypsis* a man with a white coat thrown over his shoulders bares the side of a barefoot beggar in a black jacket which reaches to his knees, and sucks his wounds. Again his Adam's apple moves rhythmically up and down; the liquid gurgles in his throat. But others have already pushed him aside. They want to drink too. One after another, like leeches, they suck the blood transformed into vodka.

Czestochowa is full of beggars. It is as though all the country's blind, lame, and crippled, shaking their wooden stumps, had agreed to a vast meeting or mating here. The most numerous are the village idiots. Peasants from Eastern Poland consider them sanctified. They are afflicted, but no one knows why. They mumble, lisp, gabble; perhaps God wants to say something through them. They look into space with tear-filled eyes; perhaps they have seen something. Ryszard Cieslak, the main actor, "Ciemny" in the play, raises himself from the ground; he has a white stick in his hand and he looks over the heads of the drunken men. Now he runs up to them and looks in their faces and smiles half-wittedly. A man puts his hand into a chunk of bread, crushes it into a hard ball, and throws it, as if it were a lump of earth, into Cieslak's face. The village idiot runs away, skipping across the square in leaps and bounds. But another man catches up with him, jumps on his back, and spurs him on like a horse. Curses and profanities are scattered about. A woman recites the Litany. In profanities and litanies the names of God and Mary are repeated. In the American program *Ciemny* was translated as "Simpleton." Some critics saw in him the medieval Everyman. However, this village idiot, transformed by the prostitute and drunkards into Christ, stems rather from Aleksandr Blok's *The Twelve*. But he is not the Christ of any revolution.

At night, Czestochowa is dark. Candles have burned out; street lamps are extinguished. A woman carries out a bucket of water. She soaks her feet, tired from walking. Under the monastery wall the drunkards sleep wrapped up in their coats. Even in their dreams they mumble profanities or prayers. In the darkness someone struggles with a girl. The whores are also pilgrims. The sour smell of equine and human urine is mixed with the sweet smell of incense burners and the odor of vomit. "Go and return no more," says Simon Peter to the village idiot, tormented beyond human endurance. But if this is beyond human endurance, does this mean it is sacred? If this were Christ, He really had no reason to come. Thus ends Grotowski's *Apocalypsis*, the Polish "Walpurgisnacht."

Grotowski brought a Method and metaphysics with him to the West. His Method is precise and verifiable; his metaphysics is obscure and ambiguous. Cieslak was a young man without experience when he surrendered himself to Grotowski's Method. He became one of the greatest actors in the world. Peter Brook told me that after Stanislavsky, no one knew as much about acting as Cieslak and Grotowski. The corporality of the Laboratory Theatre, the ultimate precision of gesture, faces transformed into masks by a simple contraction of muscle, the sounds as language – these can only be compared with the Japanese Noh, in which the actor's art is handed down from generation to generation. Even Kabuki, in comparison with the Laboratory Theatre, seems to be too loose. But recognition of the external perfection of this theatre in effect diminishes Grotowski, just as the recognition only of a magnificent ballet of war in Brecht's *Coriolanus* diminishes the Berliner Ensemble.

There remain only two serious questions: What is the final meaning of Grotowski's metaphysics? And is it possible to separate his Method from his murky mysticism and apply it in a theatre with other goals and a profane vision? Or to put it bluntly: Can one apply his Method in a theatre which seeks to replace metaphysics with a refusal to cooperate with the establishment and its values? Grotowski's teaching, like Brecht's, has the ambition to be a total system: from the theology of initiation to semantics, from the ethics of acting to the technology of lighting. But in practice, these two Scriptures contradict each other. Brecht wrote:

> Give us light on the stage, lighting engineer! How can we,
> Playwrights and actors, present our images of the world
> In semi-darkness? Nebulous twilight
> Lulls to sleep. But we need the spectators'
> Wakefulness, even watchfulness. Let them dream
> In blazing clarity!

The last scenes of Grotowski's *Apocalypsis* are played in darkness. Grotowski returns to the old rites of purification, the only difference being that the catharsis is to be introduced by violent means as by flagellation in some medieval code for monks. The actors offer to the audience a physical humiliation of their bodies. And this to Grotowski represents the holiness and the sacrilege/sacrifice of the actor. For Brecht everything sacred within the system of repression and exploitation was morally suspect. He despised the actor's trance and any aesthetic satisfaction from human suffering. Brecht's famous opposition between the "epic" and "dramatic" theatres, when quoted today, could be directed against Grotowski; it implies a rejection of his Method and the metaphysics which goes with it:

> The spectator of the *dramatic* theatre says: "Yes, I have felt the same – I am just like this. – This is only natural. – It will always be like this. – This human being's suffering moves me, because there is no way out for him. – This is great art: it bears the mark of the inevitable. – I am weeping with those who weep on the stage, laughing with those who laugh."
>
> The spectator of the *epic* theatre says: "I should never have thought so. – That is not the way to do it. – This is most surprising, hardly credible. – This will have to stop. – This human being's suffering moves me, because there would have been a way out for him. This is great art: nothing here seems inevitable. – "I am laughing about those who weep on the stage, weeping about those who laugh."

For the theatres of the Contestation, which evolved from the school of the Absurd and discovered almost a half-century later the old Dada and surrealism as a new nourishment, Brecht seems old-fashioned with his rationalism, flat and bourgeois with his optimistic didacticism, dry and limited because of his respect for literary tradition and discourse. Grotowski was welcomed by these theatres as the guru from Poland. He taught the techniques of shock. The languages of praxis and imagination, social and sexual revolution, of Marx and Freud, of Herbert Marcuse and of Timothy Leary became fatally intermixed. The theatre of the counter-culture felt that revolution could enter the mind only through the skin, as formulated in the gospel of Artaud.

Marcuse, in his *Essay on Liberation* (1969), the coldest analysis of the impossibility of revolution in sated consumer societies, argues that when a radical revolutionary tactic does not exist, Utopian thought recovers its lost attraction and dignity. If revolution is impossible, rebellion could always be acted out. Rebellion is an instant revolutionary Utopia. But in an objectively non-revolutionary situation, a revolutionary Utopia which could be realized instantly can only be acted out. Sit-in, teach-in, love-in, these are forms of instant liberation. Utopias acted out, and thus theatre.

The Woodstock Festival was a real *Paradise Now*. It was also an *Apocalypsis cum Figuris*, but the figures in it were not exactly the same. One can accept one of these apocalypses or reject both, but one cannot accept both of them at the same time.

When the village idiot, cast as Christ, has already passed through all the stages of his Passion, when he has been spat upon and ridiculed, and disowned by all, Cieslak's face changes: for a moment he becomes beautiful, as if illumined by an inner light. When *The Constant Prince* is only a tortured body, the same unearthly smile lights up on Cieslak's face. When in the last scene of *Akropolis* the prisoners go down into the depths of the crematorium, the same light illumines their faces. In Grotowski's theatre liberation comes only through death, the torture of the body, and the humiliation of the spirit. I am not sure whether, to accept Grotowski's metaphysics, one must believe that there is a God. But I am certain that one must give up hope and renounce the possibility of revolt.

In Sophocles' *Oedipus the King*, when it seems for a moment that the mysterious Oracle of Delphi could have made a mistake and that Oedipus

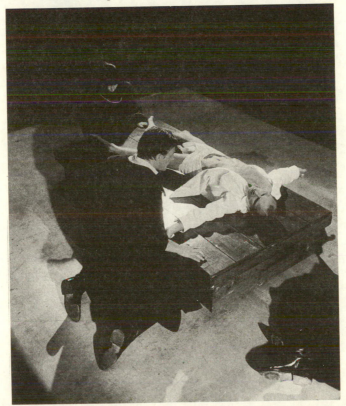

Plate 13.1 The torture of the first prisoner in *The Constant Prince*. (Photo: Odeon Theatre, Paris.)

Plate 13.2 Ryszard Cieslak and Rena Mirecka in *The Constant Prince*.
(Photo: *TDR.*)

did not kill Laius, the Chorus rebels. Suddenly the tragic world in which
the son is predestined to kill his father and sleep with his mother
collapses. If man is stronger than the wrath of God, the Chorus shouts,
"Why should I take part in the sacred dance?"

Why should I take part in the sacred dance?

(Translated by E.J. Czerwinski.)

14

LET GROTOWSKI SACRIFICE MASCULINITY TOO

Charles Ludlam

In his production of Calderon's *The Constant Prince*, Grotowski has chosen to eschew the play's prophecy, and what I believe to be its focal image:

> Trade darkest death for woman's woe,
> Despite thy flame-like beauty's glow,
> The deed cannot thy beauty see,
> A corpse's ransome thou must be!
> (*The Constant Prince*, Act II, Scene I)

Of the six characters Grotowski preserves from the original, the Phenix is the only woman. It is she, a living treasure, who will be the ransom of the dead Prince. In Grotowski's production all six characters are of equal strength. The Prince's ordeal, although exquisite in conception, lacks dimension without the earthly beauty of this woman to counterpoint his spiritual perfection. The Phenix might as well be a man.

Without a feminine motif the essence of the play becomes physical exertion. The stage is a pit with wooden sides and linoleum floor. The audience, squeezed together on backless wooden benches, perches around the oblong periphery as though to watch a cockfight. There is nothing of particular visual beauty except Stanislaw Scierski's belly. For about an hour and a quarter the audience sits, in extreme discomfort, watching and listening to the actors make images (some banal and some unclear) with their voices and their bodily movements, all the while suffering a generalized anguish. Here the Prince, like a holy man, awakens and develops the higher nature of men by his power to endure.

How is a victim, captive and enslaved, able to overcome his tormentors? Calderon's Prince is constant:

> KING: Is it not a well-known precept,
> That a slave in all things must
> Be obedient to his master?

> Be so now.
> THE PRINCE: In all things just,
> Heaven, no doubt, commands obedience,
> And no slave should fail therein;
> But, if it should chance, the master
> Should command the slave to sin,
> Then there is no obligation
> To obey him; he who sins
> When commanded, no less sinneth.
> KING: Thou must die.
> THE PRINCE: Then life begins.
> KING: That this blessing may not happen,
> Rather dying live! Thou'lt see
> I can be cruel.
> PRINCE: And I patient.

The King tests the Prince's modesty by torturing him. But the Prince does not regard his life as his exclusive personal property. He places it at the disposal of the people at large. In so doing he endures. His sacrifice immortalizes him. A petty man is harmed by his possessions because instead of sacrificing them he would keep them for himself. The Prince is the Fool, for, like the image of the unnumbered Arcanum of the Tarot, he stands on the mountain high above his fellow men. His eyes are on heaven and as he moves he steps off the precipice.

In contrast, Grotowski's Prince is under the oppression of faceless totalitarianism, both of the Polish state and of Grotowski's direction; his character is flattened by unrelieved tension and in this he merely epitomizes the other actors. Anguish expresses itself involuntarily in bursts of song, in dance, and rhythmic movements of the body. The actors speak (Polish) so fast and change pitch in such a premeditated way that we must say they sing. From time immemorial, music from within has inspired slaves to dance. It is in this way that joy and relief make themselves felt.

But theatre is more than the casting off of shackles. We must find harmony with the order of the universe. The celebrations of sacrificial feasts and sacred rites are the means employed by great rulers to unite men. They give expression to the interrelation of the family and its social articulation in the state. Sacred music and splendid ceremony arouse a tide of emotion shared by all hearts in unison. The spectacle must go down to the very foundations of life, awakening a consciousness of the common origin of all creatures.

Grotowski's theatre treats us as consumers of a useless luxury item because it invites us to sacrifice, but not to partake. When audience empathy (pity, terror, and impotent rage) for a superior man serves the purpose of tragedy, this Totalitarian Theatre of Energy collapses and a metaphysical theatre is born. In any event, the disunion of playmakers and their audience must be overcome at the outset. Mutual mis-understandings and distrust must be dispersed.

Grotowski is a modern artist. He reduces form and strips way the glamour of the baroque, leaving nothing but the orgiastic miasmas of barbarity. If he must sacrifice femininity let him sacrifice masculinity too. For we have crossed the threshold of the post-modern period and a phantasmagoria born of ecstasy transcending all earthly bliss plays on our mental horizon.

15

ASIAN THEATRE AND GROTOWSKI

Donald Richie

Though Grotowski's Laboratory Theatre actually owes little to Asian theatres, one is nonetheless surprised by its apparent resemblance to those of India, China, Japan. Surprised, that is, until one realizes that Grotowski, deliberately refining theatre to its two salient parts – actor and spectator – has, at the same time, returned to ritual theatre. Although Grotowski has listed some influences of the Indian Kathakali, of the Peking Opera, of the Noh, on his work, more important than any such is that in seeking to define what is distinctively theatre, what separates this activity from other categories of performance and spectacle, he and his actors have rediscovered ritual theatre for the West. It was, of course, never lost in the East. The aims of the Polish Laboratory and the classic theatres of Asia are consequently the same.

Up to a point. When Grotowski writes that, "the theatre, when it was still part of religion, was already theatre," he is describing classical Asian drama as well as his own. The Catholic confession – an archetype which, one guesses, would now best fulfil a definition of theatre which included only actor and spectator – has its Asian forms, as does any other kind of religious drama one cares to mention. Certainly, the audience in ritual theatre is in the position to judge; and, certainly, whatever was originally meant by catharsis, it included the idea of absolution. When he continues, however, by saying that, "it liberated the spiritual energy of the congregation or the tribe by incorporating myth and profaning or rather transcending it," he is speaking, not of Asia, not of early Western ritual theatre, but of the Polish Laboratory Theatre.

The ritual, in ordinary definition, is the repetition of an archetypal act. It is, in itself, a collective convention and its re-enactment has a social purpose – the rituals of the Catholic Church, for example. The Western theatre has forgotten this, or, more precisely, has not until this chaotic and unassured century had need for remembering it. Asian classical theatre, on the other hand, continues to need the ritual.

One of the results of this is that the Polish Lab Theatre wants confrontation with ritual rather than identification through it. Grotowski uses ritual to attack, and Asia uses it to reassure. He uses force: forcing his audience to "drop its social mask." The Asian ritual drama, on the other hand, assumes that the social mask is the face itself.

The differences are enormous, since they are differences of intent. With purposes so at variance one would expect the Polish Lab to be less like the Asian theatre with which it seems to share so much. These differences are interesting because, in examining them, it may be possible to define more completely Grotowski's theatre and the obviously important role it is playing during this decade. Following then are some contrasts, using as a particular example the classical theatre of Japan.

THE TEXT

In Asian classical theatre the text is known. The audience appears with certainly the story and often whole sections of dialogue firmly in mind. This is sometimes necessary. The contemporary Japanese cannot understand the language of Noh. He either familiarizes himself with the play he is going to see or else brings along the book – as one might bring along a score to a chamber music concert. Even if he knows the language he cannot understand it when he's at the Noh because of the separation of the vowels, the deliberate pace of the delivery. He understands no more and probably less than we understand of the language at the opera or – it has been said – than Poles can understand the delivery of the text of Grotowski's plays.

The Noh spectator looks forward not to what is done but to how it is done. This is our attitude upon seeing *Lucia* or *Carmen*. Surprise, an emotion as unwelcome in the East as it is prized in the West, is thus successfully avoided. The Polish Laboratory Theatre, of course, consciously seeks to surprise – and succeeds admirably – and this is the difference which, indeed, one might expect between a theatre which seeks to reassure and one which seeks to unsettle, despite the theatrical ideas they share. In both, certainly, the text is mainly a pretext. Since the text is known in Asian theatre, there is no need to pay much attention to it. It is as much a vehicle in the Noh as it is in Grotowski's work. The text of the Noh is a collage of Chinese poetry, songs and catches of the day, etc., all crafted with the greatest and most transparent skill by Zeami and his contemporaries, whose original contribution was the very large one of seamlessly welding disparate parts. Grotowski's method is very similar. For example: sections of the Wyspianski play make up *Akropolis*; one scene of the original encloses all of *Kordian*. The Polish example is certainly less eclectic in that everything in a play comes from a single source, while in the Noh everything is a potpourri, and we fail to recognize this fact only because of the aesthetic and temporal distance involved.

In none of these theatres – Asian or Polish – is the text treated with any degree of respect. During the New York Kabuki performances of the late 1950s, Kanzaburo was continually changing the ending of *Kagosturube* – his reasons being a combination of personal whim and genuine concern that the foreign audience might not understand the sword mystique which concludes the drama. At one point he killed both the faithful maid and the faithless courtesan, at another he killed merely the courtesan, yet again he killed only the maid – willingly departing from conventions which he plainly regarded as only incidental to his performance. Grotowski too has scant respect for text – as in his *Doctor Faustus*, an example we know. The difference is that once a play has been recast by the Polish Lab Theatre it is fixed absolutely; if a change is made that change is followed consistently in all subsequent productions. The Kabuki's changes are not invariably consistent.

To be sure, the Japanese actor's freedom does not allow him to invent whole sections as he proceeds. Kanzaburo was picking and choosing among alternate versions which he and the rest of the cast knew. The point, however, is that the Japanese actor allows himself a kind of freedom which the Polish actor does not. Grotowski's actors need the text as pretext, and without it are no longer able best to make the gift of themselves, of which their director speaks. The Japanese actor, in theory at any rate, can change at will among known alternatives. The implication is that his technique – and there seems no other word for it – is so assured that he is able to continue to present himself no matter what he is saying or doing. And again, this indicates a difference in these theatres. Grotowski, attacking, keeps his forces in very close order. The Japanese, reassuring, in part at any rate, suffers no such compulsion. He allows himself a freedom which, one suspects, the Polish actor would not know how to contain. His theatre can reassure because he is free. The Polish actors are under constraint; their performances appear compulsive, learned by rote, magnificently learned, but learned none the less. The Japanese gives the illusion, at least, of spontaneity.

The Japanese feels, perhaps consequently, very free to rearrange. The New York performances of *Chushingura*, for example, contained only four scenes – an hour or so – from the twelve-hour original. Grotowski also obviously feels free to arrange, but the differences are interesting. He will expand the insane-asylum scene from *Kordian* into the entire play, but he will not perform only the asylum scene. Yet something like this is, in effect, what the Japanese do when in New York they make the hari-kiri scene from *Chushingura* all of *Chushingura* – suicide prefaced and followed by a few minor scenes. The Japanese seemed quite happy to suggest that *Chushingura* is about a suicide when, actually, it is about revenge. Grotowski is saying something quite different: *Kordian* is about many things but they might just as well happen in the insane asylum, and it so happens that the original had such a scene. Therefore, it may be stretched as a kind of dramatic rubric over the entire drama.

MUSIC

Music is a part of the ritual drama. In fact, most surviving ritual drama inclines more toward what we would call opera than what we would call theatre. To think of Chinese theatre is to think of Chinese opera.

Grotowski uses music in several ways, a few of which coincide with its uses in ritual drama. He knows, for example, that in moments of emotional stress – sorrow, for example – the voice rises, and words turn to song, as in various kinds of crooning and keening. This is one of the precepts of the Noh, music which, if we listen with an empty ear, sounds like lament. In the Bunraku, the narrator breaks into song at moments of greatest emotional stress. There is a beautiful example in *Akropolis*. Jacob says, ". . . tear me from the hand of my brother Esau for I fear him very much lest having come to beat me . . ." and his words turn into song, his account becomes a melisma. Likewise, when the Harpist says, "You ordered me to wait and persevere in my strength, although you beat me with a burden . . ." his voice changes, rises – the effect is the same as the upward and questioning turn of a strophe ending in the Noh. It is the aural equivalent of the posed Kabuki stance called the *mie*. Again, when Jacob and Rachel are on the platform sorting the plastic "hair" their talk becomes chant – a real imitation of Ambrosian chant, as in the more openly liturgical of the Noh drama where the Chorus consciously imitates Buddhist chant.

Here musical resemblances end, however. Both use music as a form of incantation but this is only one of the musical categories which Grotowski uses. His other uses require an intellectual response from his audience rather than an emotional one. Continually attacking, he makes his music comment upon the action as well as interpret. The solo violin in *Akropolis* is an example. He deliberately uses a hapless and tawdry little tune, redolent of vapid popular music. He does this knowing it will accentuate the horror and pathos of his concentration-camp setting. At the end of the play he uses a well-known Polish anthem: "hey, laugh day, hey, play harp/Wind, carrying the playing into the field," sings the marching cast, and the pathos of the situation is that they are singing a patriotic anthem set to new and optimistic words as they go off to their gas chamber. Perhaps Kabuki very occasionally does something like this – Sukeroku remembers and sings a song he knew when he was happier

than he finds himself in the middle of the play which bears his name – but again, the intent is simpler and, more important, makes no intellectual demands of the audience, and certainly no demands outside the context of the play. Grotowski's aims are such that he needs this kind of going against the grain, though, it must be added, his use of irony is perhaps not so straightforward as I have made it seem. The violin piece, for example, might be heard as being ironical about irony. The whole point of Asian theatre, however, is that it goes so smoothly with the grain that the question of grain, of there even being something to go against, never comes up.

SET, COSTUMES, PROPS

If only actor and spectator are truly necessary, if even text is dispensable, naturally, sets, costumes, props, etc., are not necessary at all. Yet almost all theatres use them. The Noh quite openly suggests that Noh is boring and that the gorgeous brocade costumes give you something to look at. The actors are finely dressed in Kabuki not because the plays are historical but because actors love to dress up, the Kabuki above all else being an actor's theatre.

Grotowski's use of these unnecessary elements, however, is different from that in the East. As in his use of music, his manipulation of these elements is based upon an assumption. The wheelbarrow in *Akropolis*, the naked body in *The Constant Prince*: these are both props, in a way, and they are used because they might-have-been-there. It is proper for people in concentration camps to use wheelbarrows and it is proper for martyrs to be unclothed. At the same time, both the wheelbarrow and the body are used for other purposes as well. Jacob and the Angel wrestle and the wheelbarrow becomes a kind of burning bush – if we know the context in which Grotowski is working.

This means there is a double meaning. As with the music, we must look under the ostensible meaning to find the actual. Asian theatre, however, is singularly innocent of this. A piece of cloth waved is a sea in Peking but it is not anything else unless it changes its character entirely and becomes a cloak or a table. Things do not have two meanings in Asia. They have only – and this is important – their ostensible meaning. There is no more irony, consequently, in Asian theatre than there is in Asia. The ostensible meaning is the only meaning. The social mask is the face.

THE MASK

The Asian knows perfectly well that there is no such thing as personality, that there is barely any such thing as person. The use of masks – real ones in the Noh, painted ones in Kabuki and in China, use of muscles to simulate masks as in Kathakali or Malayan theatre – is indicative of the need to fabricate personality in the theatre. "I am the kind of person who . . ." is not a common concept in Asia. The emphasis is so entirely upon being that becoming, in the sense of having a coherent personality to become, is not a thought widely encountered. Personality is identified with a mask. Grotowski and his actors come from the other side of the world, where the idea of personality is insisted upon by Greeks and Christians alike. His ideas of personality, at its fullest, is that one person may play several parts or that the muscular "masks" may be changed in accordance with a part or with an emotion to be expressed.

The difference is striking. In the Noh, for example, when the *shite* retires and returns again with a different mask, it is a magical moment because an idea is received which is shocking for an Asian: that things are not always what they seem. We, used to this, adept indeed in digging out what we then please to call the truth, would be equally surprised if what is ostensibly offered turned out to be the real. Grotowski, like the rest of us in the West, lives in a relative world where it is possible for us to entertain the idea of one person being several simply because we are so certain about the core, the personality, the identity of this person.

Or were. One of the reasons that Grotowski's theatre has become so suddenly meaningful is that we now commonly doubt our identities, at the same time finding that we have nothing else to believe in. Thus, just as the Noh creates a frisson by its suggestion that there are several levels, Grotowski creates his – one which Asia has long lived with – that there might not be any.

ACTOR AND SPECTATOR

Perhaps the most basic of the differences here is that Asian classical theatre has no director. Tradition gives the actors their roles, their lines, the way they speak, the way they move. To see a "rehearsal" of the Kabuki is to see a roomful of men moving about, beginning, ending speeches in conversational tones. There is no need for rehearsals, which occur only when one of the many variations within a play are to be used and the actors want to make sure they all remember it – just as members of a string quartet might play through a Mozart quartet movement if they intend to repeat and want to make certain they all know the first ending, since they've usually used only the second.

Grotowski's theatre is, of course, very much a director's theatre. He had leaflets passed during the New York performances denying this – or, rather, insisting that he and the actors shared the responsibility. Nonetheless, the theatre is in his image – which is what would be expected since neither he nor his actors have any tradition, since they have not trained since childhood, and since they have no context, social, aesthetic, or otherwise, for what they are doing. Perhaps this is the reason they create one. Of help to them in this is the casting of the audience in the play. In *Cain* we are the descendants of Cain; in *The Ancestors* we are courtiers; in *Doctor Faustus* we are the guests; in *Akropolis* we are the living.

All of this is no help to us. And, indeed, we do not feel ourselves to be any of these things. But it is of enormous help to the actor. He needs a context badly and we are it.

The Asian actor finds his context in his culture. The audience, therefore, is not given a role. It is, however, assigned a quality. We are judges. This works two ways. In the first place we are given information (from the Chorus in the Noh, from the reciters in Bunraku and some Kabuki) and know more than the actors do. We judge what is happening and how they react in light of our knowledge, not theirs. In the second place, we judge as we judge when we go to the opera – we judge the performance and find it winning or wanting. Neither of these qualities is either called for or necessary in the performances of the Polish Lab Theatre. We know no more than they do – sometimes less in that the text is purposely rendered unintelligible – and we have few standards by which to judge the excellences. We therefore, and rightly, judge ensemble acting when we see his plays. And we are most impressed.

We are impressed for many of the reasons that we are in Asian theatre. Absolute dedication to doing this one thing an actor can do – present himself to his audience. To be sure, all theatre is about the direct contact between actor and audience. This is true of *Cactus Flower* as it is of *Kagotsurube* or *Akropolis*. The difference is that the latter two know it. For this reason one cannot film Japanese theatre and one cannot film Grotowski. One can, however, film *Cactus Flower* with no loss at all. No matter how fine the films of, say, *Akropolis* and *Hagoromo* – and they are excellent – they are never enough, because the actor has something in mind which film does not by its nature capture. Grotowski spoke of this when he said that the one element of theatre which film and television cannot better is the closeness of the actor.

Therefore, Grotowski decided that he must break down the distance separating actor from spectator. This is one solution, but the Asian is another. The Noh puts its actors out on an apron extending into the audience but is careful to place them on a much higher level than the spectators. The Kabuki has a runway leading through the audience but, again, it is not *of* the audience, and the actor ends up behind a proscenium in any event. Grotowski feels that the core of the theatre is an encounter between actor and spectator and that the man who makes the act of self-revelation – and this is the actor's task – is making contact with himself through his audience. This is quite so, but Asia would point out that the way to contrive this is not by putting him physically closer to the spectators, let alone among them, but by making him move further away.

Why are so many moving plays written about kings and queens and other nobility? Why do plays about the common man so commonly fail to move? It is because an aesthetic distance is being observed. We feel free to go toward and we do so willingly. In contemporary Western theatre, however, and Grotowski is but a single example, we are not treated with such tact. The actor is shoved at us, "Here he is, now feel!" is the command. Is anyone moved by this? Does one feel? I was much intrigued by the Polish Lab Theatre, much interested, but not moved. I am very moved by *Matsukaze*, however, when I can go of my own volition to the old man playing the old man in the Noh drama. He makes me want to feel, he makes it necessary for me to.

Grotowski says, "I think the essential thing is that the actor must not act *for* his audience, he must act in confrontation with the spectators, in their presence." Which is right, but he might have added further that it was necessary that the confrontation be more than physical – that it be also, and more importantly, psychological, metaphysical, philosophical, and religious. And this is something that physical proximity inhibits. At the same time, it is interesting that this has not yet occurred to Grotowski – and certainly to none of the directors busily confronting their audiences in, say, New York – but one would not expect it to. His ritual theatre wishes to attack and to unsettle. He does not want to make you come to him. He wants to go out aggressively to you. The ritual is the same, its uses are different. He is right for his time and his place.

It is interesting that Grotowski feels the need for a ritual theatre. Perhaps it is that solidarity of any sort is imperative in our fragmented times. Certainly, his way is different and far more direct than the ritualizing of *Hair* and the rest of that sentimental tribe which would equate protest with pleasure. He feels that he must confront, must shock, because our precarious social health demands it. And this is something which Asia, still spiritually healthy, does not as yet need.

IS GROTOWSKI RIGHT —
DID THE WORD COME LAST?

Walter Kerr

I have been searching back through my notes and my random memories of the three performances Jerzy Grotowski and his Polish Laboratory Theatre have given here, to see if I could say whether any one moment was more representative for me of the company's special qualities than all the others I'd been exposed to. I think I have found one. It occurred during *Akropolis*, the piece in which Jewish and Greek legend run together like a blood puddle at Auschwitz.

The center of the stage, a construction of gas pipes, bathtubs, and wheelbarrows gone rusty, was for the moment emptied of actors. We, sitting directly on the stage, were closer to the core of things than the performers were. We were aware of one another and in separation. The performers were all behind us, scattered in the unidentified dark, making rushed, whispering sounds that felt as though the walls of a room were hurrying to meet at a corner.

A sudden sibilant raked my ear; the speaker was near my shoulder. I didn't turn to see who it might be. A body was thrust violently past and above me, to land with a thud in the wheelbarrow an inch from my head; I didn't shy, or think I was going to be struck. I looked at the audience's faces, opposite and to the left. Almost all were open-mouthed as the actors emerged into light again, wooden soles stomping, eyes heavy-lidded and vacant white, shoulders thrust forward to jab at other bodies in erratic rhythm; otherwise, those faces were entirely composed.

That is to say, Mr. Grotowski has entirely succeeded in achieving at least three of his promised effects:

He has put the audience and the actors together in an extraordinarily close relationship without insisting upon that false intimacy, that overbearing directness of contact, that marks and mars the work, say, of the Living Theater. The actors are next to you. But they never invade or so much as threaten to invade your public privacy. You are you, they are they, our functions are distinct, even if our bodies should touch. We tumble together like so many checkers in a glass, without dissolving into one another and ending up mud. Atoms interplay, but retain their stability.

He has arrived at a discipline in performing that breeds confidence in the performers and in the occasion. Though all protective forms have apparently broken down and we are absolutely exposed to the violence of performers manhandling properties where we sit, we are not fearful that performer or prop is going to lurch out of control and do us damage. To play our parts we need only be still; the action will wash over us but leave us intact. In honoring his own skill, the actor honors us. We trust him.

Grotowski has created composure, rest, openness, ease. In his audience. This is established, a bit mysteriously, even before the performance begins. The auditorium doors are kept locked until a few minutes before performance time. The audience gathers on the steps, standing, seated, smoking, chatting – and waits. By all the laws of logic, this should be irritating. Instead, the mood becomes docile, patient, bemused, friendly.

Once inside, the interior quiet continues. One may be seated onstage in a very sharp white light without being made to feel self-conscious. Woolgathering during the performance, one may catch another pair of eyes across the way woolgathering in just the same way. There is no guilt in this, nor is there sly humor. Both pairs of eyes are apt to redirect themselves to the action, as if by common consent and with the tacit acknowledgment that they'll be woolgathering again a little later.

Cruelty or suffering within the action does not agitate anyone looking on; the cruelty, the suffering, is studied, passively, reflectively, without engagement. The audience remains throughout the performance in repose, and afterward leaves with a psyche as unruffled as the actors' faces. The effect is that of time out from living. Apprehension has been outlawed for an hour or so. If this is a theatre of "trance" for the actors, to use one of Grotowski's words, it is nearly that for the spectators, too.

Control in the performing, trust in the watching, detachment in the close relationship, finally a kind of peace for both actor and spectator – for the actor because he has completed his act, for the spectator because he has let himself be calm and undemanding – these are good things to have, in and for themselves. It should be stressed that, in Grotowski's theatre, they exist in and for themselves. They are not meant to lead us on toward any other value, to play servant to any other thing. They are the end of it, except for whatever indirect private therapy can be read into the qualities themselves. The experience is a closed one.

The actor's function, for instance, has been entirely altered. He has ceased being an instrument and has become an object. Normally the actor is thought of as an interpreter of what someone else has prepared, an instrument of the playwright, a servant of the public, a tool used by the director in bringing playwright and public together. Here he is forbidden to "play to" the public or show it the least concern. In Grotowski's "poor theatre" everything that might interfere with the actor's concentration upon himself is pared away; costumes that might make him pretend to be another person, lighting that might shelter him in atmosphere, a text that might demand he serve another man's psychology. He is his own man now, and alone. He is alone with his own body, his own capacity for making sounds, his own personal stripped-down truth.

For Grotowski only the art of the actor dare be regarded as "theatre." Brushing everything else aside, the actor trains himself to be responsive to whatever impulses stir at the "innermost core" of his being, taking care that his reflexes work so quickly that "thought has no time to intervene." The face, normally expressive of thought, becomes a mask. Words, which "are always pretexts," are to be subordinated to preliterary sound. And, since the actor must forge his "score" out of his own body and out of nothing else, the text written by another (the play proper in our usual understanding) either vanishes altogether or is treated as a malleable plaything with no authority of its own.

Work without a text, Grotowski asks? And answers, "Yes; the history of the theatre confirms this. In the evolution of the theatrical art the text was one of the last elements to be added. If we place some people on a stage with a scenario they themselves have put together and let them improvise their parts as in commedia dell'arte, the performance will be equally good even if the words are not articulated but simply muttered." Grotowski's special bogey is literature. "Faced with literature," he says, "we can take up one of two positions: either we can illustrate the text through the interpretation of the actors . . . in that case, the result is not theatre and the only living element in such a performance is the literature. Or, we can virtually ignore the text . . . reducing it to nothing."

Here we come upon a problem, a serious one. In closing off the performed act as he does, closing it off particularly to the intrusion of the dramatist, Grotowski forces us into the paradox that what is good for theatre is bad for drama. The two are not bedmates but mortal enemies, unrelated, mutually corrupting. With this either/or fiat, Grotowski declares theatre to be – always and in all ways – a simple thing, not a complex one, much as Elizabeth Hardwicke does to opposite effect when she declares that drama is first and last literature and nothing else.

Is the interplay between drama and theatre that we have come to call casually by either name actually capable of being reduced to this simplicity? At this late date in time I rather doubt it, since the evolutionary process has been at work. Mr. Grotowski, perhaps a shade disingenuously, claims that theatrical history proves his point because in the evolutionary process words came out last. Does that mean that they don't belong? Or could it mean that they are an organic extension of the original impulse arriving through increased complexity at a new richness? The evolutionary movement is always toward complexity. To most cases the new complexity achieves a higher order of existence, of perception and the capacity for action.

It is impossible to prove now what the commedia dell'arte, with its improvised performances, was or was not for the simple reason that no one wrote it down. Such descriptive fragments as survive do not suggest that it was superior, *as theatre*, to Molière, who did write it down. Molière worked on a commedia base; the time and intelligence he spent on writing it down most probably constituted an improvement. I do not really suppose that the first playwright, or any playwright thereafter, marched in upon the actors and took over, stealing the form they had developed. I think the actors asked for help, begging the playwright to come in because they didn't know what to say or didn't feel they were saying it all or saying it well enough.

This process, subliminally and ironically, is already repeating itself in the Laboratory Theatre. The third of the pieces shown here, *Apocalypsis cum figuris*, was improvised subverbally by the performers. When the entire "score" was worked out in terms of movement and sound, the program notes tell us, Mr. Grotowski turned aside to the library and, helping himself to substantial passages from Dostoevsky, T.S. Eliot, Job and St. John, substituted "literary" materials for what the actors had been saying on impulse. Why, if not to increase the profundity and power of the sounds coming from the actors?

It isn't possible for someone who does not understand Polish to say exactly how these insertions affect the experience. And they are in any case used impressionistically, not for narrative purposes. Nevertheless, and quite plainly, in this particular case it is the director who is taking on the task of the writer, as in the case of Shakespeare and Molière it was the actor who did; he is here selecting what is to be said, consciously structuring it if not actually inventing the words. I suspect that it is how the complex organism of the "play" (theatre and drama simultaneously) came into being so long as the evolutionary impulse continues to press us forward.

I found myself content with all three performances of the company, content to be there, content to experience this much, content to go away contented after the hour or so of playing time. I did, however, find myself less interested in the third than in the first. I did not become bored; I simply found myself thinking my own thoughts oftener. The closed experience is a real experience (as it always has been with a clown or a serious mime) but it is not, by definition, an expanding one. It is capable of infinite variation but not much advancement.

I wondered, as I sat on a bench with my back to a radiator watching a black-clad simpleton carry an apostle in flaring white robes about the open floor on his twisted shoulders, whether my attentiveness might not be diminishing simply because it was being given nothing more complex to feed on. The human mind, whether on its way to the moon or to the Washington Square Methodist Church, says more, more. That's the way of it.

A POLISH CATHOLIC HASID

Richard Schechner

These are notes, they are tentative. Grant Grotowski and his actors a superb craft, possibly the best in the world today. A distinct craft amply expounded in *Towards a Poor Theatre, TDR,* and elsewhere. Grant Grotowski and his actors a focus and intensity hardly, if ever, seen, heard, or felt in a theatre. A duplicate reality, the "double" Artaud insisted lay in the heart of the theatrical experience. Wasn't Cieslak signaling through his own personal flames during those moments in *The Constant Prince* when sound issued from his back as if he were himself the burning sacrificial wood? Grant Grotowski and his actors a singular (and peculiar) triumph over the New York theatre reviewers, John Simon excepted, but no one enters Simon's world, not even John Simon. The journalistic and theatrical tribute laid humbly before the man in the dark suit and shaded glasses is touching. Those who, previously, had not even thought seriously once about the theatre are now "thinking through again" the "meaning" of the theatre; people are starting to "speculate" and "wonder," old "values" are called into "question," new values are "revealed."

Grotowski receives his visitors, who approach him at parties, sometimes jauntily, but still with underlying delicacy; those who come close to Grotowski gesture to him as if from a distance. Homage to an icon. Grant Grotowski uniqueness, a spectacle in himself as compelling and complicated as any of his performers. He is distant and then suddenly a sharp-toothed narrow smile, a felt warmth in his voice, and he is an utterly disarming little boy. He speaks as Catholics with their prelates would speak, and in tongues not unknown to Hasidic Jews. Grotowski is somewhat otherworldly – but I am not certain from which other world he comes as emissary. He is a man ghettoized in the old sense, not struggling to get out, or to burn down the structures that torment him, but to find endurance and truth within the walls.

Somewhere in the work of the Polish Lab is its political harmlessness. Harmless to the authorities in both Warsaw and Washington. (When the troupe was denied entrance into the U.S. in 1968, the State Department was frank in declaring that they had nothing against Grotowski or his actors, but that visas were not being issued to Polish nationals as a gesture protesting the Soviet invasion of Czechoslovakia. Once the heat was off, the Committee to Welcome Grotowski was told, visas would be issued.) Harmless to reactionary reviewers like Walter Kerr. The immunity runs in both directions: the Polish Lab was not harmed (or seemed not to be) by the $10 price tag fixed to seats, the brutalizing treatment of spectators by Brooklyn Academy house managers, or the super elite quality of the audience admitted to "share" the ceremonies.

Deeper in the work is what Jan Kott calls a "homosexual Mont Blanc" – a rich image suggesting (to me) a difficult climb, successful and yet vain; a Moby Dick purity; monolithic, beautiful, inscrutable, irrelevant; a sexual provocation never completed and essentially turned in against itself. Several qualities are shared by all three productions seen here: (1) the absolute scoring of the pieces; (2) the sadomasochistic quality of the behavior within the pieces; (3) the impenetrable membrane separating the performers and between the troupe as a whole and the audience; (4) extraordinary rapidity of movement and speech; (5) facial and particularly eye expressions that suggest an inward look, not a communication with others; the self-epiphany of the sacrificed. Grotowski carefully warns performers against self-indulgence, narcissism, audience-tropism; the search for truth is absolute. He denies that his theatre is mysterious in the religious sense. But obviously his speech, interviews, writing, and the writing of those close to him is larded with religious terminology of a very particular kind. For example: "offering," "spiritual act," "only a great sinner can become a saint," "holiness," "profanation," "sacrilege," "if he does not exhibit his body, but annihilates it, burns it, frees it from every resistance to any psychic impulse, then he does not sell his body but sacrifices it," "atonement," "holy actor," "self-sacrifice," "self-penetration," "excess," "a mobilization of all the physical and spiritual forces of the actor who is in a state of readiness, a passive availability, which makes possible an active acting score," "humility," "spiritual predisposition," "the actor must act in a state of trance." These quotations (and they are not wrenched out of context) all come from five pages of Grotowski's 1964 dialogue with Eugenio Barba, "The Theatre's New Testament" (Grotowski 1968:33–37).

We are face to face with a medieval cosmology, intensity, belief, and (perhaps) practice. A sexually charged world that is blocked from active completion (or active political involvement); a world driven inwards toward perfection through renunciation, flagellation, active and ruthlessly persistent introspection; a world in which the individual is asked to renounce his everyday human claims to redirect his unstaunchable drives, turning them from others into himself. I am not making judgments, but trying to locate the center of Grotowski's work. Images emerge of whipping, throwing, spitting, of "coming forth," and spewing. Excitement becomes (literally) circular; there is much pressing down and crushing, laying out and dissecting. Speech becomes more than incantatory; it breaks apart and is redistributed among the physical attributes of self-abnegation. Talking becomes singing (hosannahs and praises, either positively or negatively rendered), or spewing, or in-breathing where the words are taken back and ingested; or plaintive cries (not for help) insistently proclaim the immolation that is taking place before our eyes. The actors are there but absolutely beyond the reach of the spectators, who watch just outside the physical space (as in *The Constant Prince* and *Apocalypsis*) or immobilized within it (as in *Akropolis*). The "sacred" act that is the felt intention of the Polish Lab Theatre is, in truth, a bottomless longing – the middle term of a process that begins with sucking and ends with weaning. Psychoanalyst Donald Kaplan suggests that this middle term is "renunciation." One wishes to "go back to the source" and to "go on to the end." The two wishes pull in opposite directions with equal force. The performer is (literally) stretched out between them, dissected and rendered.

Grotowski's genius is to find the physical objective correlatives for this double tension, to cast it in exquisitely balanced and counterpointed spatial and spiritual processions. The dominating images of the Laboratory Theatre are those of Pieta; the dominating tones are longing and questing, a double pull back and forth. Literally the performances go "back and forth" until (again literally) the performers "give up." This is Grotowski's celebrated *via negativa*. It is definitely a "way," a physical movement, and it is negative – resignation, renunciation, giving up. The actors go on by not going back and by needing less and less support. Thus the "poor theatre" is an appropriate description of the process.

I do not know very much about Poland, its present situation or history. But I would guess that Grotowski's theatre rises out of a crisis and turning point in Polish awareness, a crisis that stimulates the deepest Catholic longings and provokes the strongest "Marxist" anticipations (and disappointments). Ludwik Flaszen said this week (December 1969) that the audiences in Poland for the Laboratory Theatre were mostly students and intelligentsia. These people would be most aware of the contradictions and countertugs between Catholicism and Marxism, and of the utter failure (in Poland) of both systems. I see also in Grotowski a species of Hasidic Judaism once so strong in Eastern Europe and particularly Poland. A strain of Judaism now all but extinct after Auschwitz. It was a celebratory medievalism, one full of contradictory worship, influenced as it was both by intensive Talmudic scholarship and introspection and medieval Christian rites. The heart of this Hasidism was its overwhelming sense of parable, the active sensibility of its theology. These two elements in Grotowski's work need further, and extensive, investigation.

I am not surprised that an essentially bourgeois culture in turmoil, such as ours today, is so swept away by Grotowski's work. (I know that most Americans are unaware of Grotowski; but the theatre has been deeply touched, and across the board, from the radicals to the reactionaries. Only the black theatre has been unmoved, and understandably so.) There is in these performances and the well-articulated theories underlying them a promise of salvation. And, if intellectuals in America are hungry for anything, it is salvation. Burdened by guilt and unenlightened, no theatre piece could be more aptly titled for the American theatre than *Apocalypsis*. I am afraid, however, that the apocalypse is not around the corner, and that Grotowski is right when he suspects that next year there will be another savior slouching (or sailing or flying) toward New York to be born.

JERZY GROTOWSKI

Harold Clurman

In one of his occasional writings Jean Cocteau cites a Chinese proverb: "Genius creates hospitals." Whenever a towering personality appears, a host of lesser men become warped in imitation of the greater one.

Jerzy Grotowski is a genius, but I shudder to think how many misbegotten "Grotowskis" his Polish Laboratory Theatre will spawn. To be influenced by a master is natural, but for the most part the result is dilettantism or disaster. The reason for all such unfortunate developments is that the superficial characteristics of the original model are mistaken for their meaning and value. The artist's inner history, his basic sources, the social and emotional circumstances of his growth, are very rarely operative in his disciples. Thus a new "manner" is contrived, a fashion sold by the insensitive to the ignorant.

I am sure that Grotowski's methods of training, chiefly designed as preparation for his productions, may prove stimulating and constructive for student actors and other professionals, but they do not constitute the essence of his art. For its better understanding one must turn from the theories and formal techniques to the works themselves. Three of Grotowski's productions (none of them more than an hour long) were staged at the Washington Square Methodist Church in New York from October 16 to November 26 (1969), for limited audiences: one hundred at most; in one case, only forty.

The first one of these was based on a Grotowski scenario which he made from a romantically baroque adaptation of Calderon's *The Constant Prince*. The second was *Akropolis*, no more than an extract from a play by the nineteenth-century Polish dramatist Wyspianski; the locale and stress were entirely altered. *Apocalypsis cum figuris*, the third production, was "evolved by its performers under the guidance of the director by means of acting exercises and sketches." The spoken text was culled from brief passages of the Bible, *The Brothers Karamazov*, one of T.S. Eliot's poems, and from something by Simone Weil.

Grotowski is all paroxysm. Thus his is the most contemporary of all theatres, for it can no longer be denied that we live in a time of cataclysm.

Our very entertainments mask the face of agony. In the internal and outer upheaval, forms disintegrate, language decays, communication is conducted in jerks. Electric circuses serve as temples. Flesh is macerated. What is left of the soul goes into hiding or cries out in howls in which the difference between mirth and sorrow can hardly be distinguished. Even the gayest expressions contain the infernal.

These tendencies were already discernible in the expressionist theatre after the First World War. But at that time there was an element of journalism and propaganda (especially in Germany) in the outcries of horror. With the end of the Second World War – in the work of Beckett, Pinter, Genet and others – an element of private anguish became apparent, of withdrawal into secret chambers of consciousness where mainly grotesque (sometimes muted) signs of agony were displayed as if more overt declarations were somehow indecently sentimental.

As we ordinarily understand the terms, story or plot does not exist in Grotowski's plays. There is only a design of fantastically contorted bodies and symbolically violent relationships hardly congruous with realistically purposive action. The figures move in space which with one exception (*Akropolis*) does not resemble any identifiable environment. We are in a fearsomely imagined Gehenna where laws of time, gravity, and natural logic have been suspended.

Grotowski's theatre (I speak of it as a unit because he does not consider himself to be its sole creator) is distinct from its predecessors in the vein of modern martyrdom. The tone and inspiration of his theatre derive from the extermination camp. His productions bring us into the realm of the Last Judgment. *Akropolis* takes place on the threshold of mass extinction. The figures are last seen descending into a hole beneath the floor and when they have disappeared under its stovelike cover there flows back a final murmur, "Now we die."

Akropolis may not be the "best" of Grotowski's productions, but it is the most representative. Here the prisoners re-enact moments of the mythical past – Hebrew and Greek – distorting them by the use of the props at hand – metal pipes, rags – so that a wedding ceremony is made hideous and the cohabitation of Paris and Helen is performed by two men. The lines spoken at incredible speed are not dialogue; they are tortured exclamations projected in the direction of another being, but with no shape as personal address. (It has been said that a knowledge of Polish does not make the lines readily intelligible, but it is evident in *Apocalypsis cum figuris* that they are not meant to be taken as are the lines of an ordinary play; solemn and poetic passages are delivered in a mode which brutally contradicts and virtually obliterates their initial intent.)

In *Akropolis* the executioners and their victims become nearly identical: they are kin. The rhythm of the meaningless tasks assigned them is set by one of the prisoners who plays a violin while their labors are accented by the drumlike tread of their rough boots. This vision has nothing in common with the factual exposé of the Nazi crimes in Peter Weiss's *The Investigation*. There is no redemption here and except for the closing moment – the march to the Holocaust – very little pathos.

What we have seen is the tragic farce of civilization's values utterly despoiled. The prisoners themselves have been reduced to savage blasphemy. They are no longer individuals but the debris of humanity. If pity and terror are evoked in the spectator, if his moral sensibility is affected, it is through a kind of impersonal revulsion, from which he recovers as if from an anxiety dream he remembers as something intolerably spectral. One cannot normally sustain or assimilate such experiences.

Still, there is nothing chaotic in the spectacle. The names of Breughel, Bosch, Grunewald are frequently invoked for purposes of comparison; but that is misleading, for there was a sumptuousness in those artists. Grotowski's stage, architecture, costuming are bare. Everything has been stripped to the bone. (It is in this regard that his is a "poor theatre.") The structure of the playing area changes with each new play, so that the spectators are always in a different relation to the actors. Sometimes they look down as into an enclosed pit, sometimes they surround the action at stage level, sometimes they are ranged in a tierlike elevation slightly above. The actors are always very close, but they never move into or mingle with the audience.

Much has been made by various commentators of the company's extraordinary technical achievements in the use of voice and body. They are certainly striking and display training, prowess, and command of a most remarkable sort. The voices unfalteringly emit sounds which remind one of the strange leaps of the twelve-tone system, with startling crescendos followed by crushed whisperings that do not resemble ordinary speech. They convey an otherworldly sphere *in extremis*. The lament of the Constant Prince (the play itself might be called the slaughter of innocence) is so desperate and prolonged as to exceed the bounds of human grief. We have arrived at the point of doomsday.

Yet all this has been given precise form. The exercises of Grotowski are intended to make the actor surmount his supposed breaking point, to stretch him vocally and bodily so that he can hold nothing back; to remove his restraints, those "blocks" imposed by his usual social comportment. He is wracked so that he becomes nothing but his id and thus releases what he primally is. Whether he actually succeeds in this, or whether it is altogether desirable that he do so, is another matter which I have no desire to question or capacity to determine at this juncture. One may say that in this respect the outstanding actor is Ryszard Cieslak, as the Constant Prince and as the Simpleton in *Apocalypsis*.

To understand Grotowski's form and content as a single process one must consider certain other elements which have gone into his creation. Grotowski is an intensely cultivated theatre artist. He has absorbed Stanislavsky's lessons in regard to acting; he has responded to the impulse in Artaud; he has learned from Meyerhold's precepts on movement, and has felt the impact of the apocalyptic artists already mentioned. In addition and not unlike Brecht, he seeks to establish a certain space between the spectator and the spectacle so that for all their ferocity his plays may be appreciated contemplatively.

Grotowski's art is imbued with strains from Catholic and other litanies and rituals. In *Akropolis*, especially, one hears echoes of Roman and Jewish services, as well as Slavic melodies. It is inescapable that while Grotowski is not a "believer," his is a ritualistic, indeed a religious art. (He has said that he wished his productions to be received in strict silence.) He seeks purification through the inhuman. We are to be redeemed through hellfire.

Goethe has said that no man can thoroughly capture the meaning of an art form who fails in some knowledge of the land and people of the art's provenance. Grotowski is a citizen of Poland which was razed and decimated through the Nazi invasion and by the concentration camps which were its concomitants. Born in 1933, he is the witness and heir – as are most of his actors – of his country's devastation. The mark of that carnage is on their work. It is an abstract monument to the spiritual consequences of that horrendous event.

And that is why most productions done *à la* Grotowski must be largely fraudulent. His theatre has its roots in a specific native experience. It is organic with a lived tradition which was shattered and defamed by unimaginable inequity and boundless shame. Where an art lacks the foundation of corresponding realities it is ornament, entertainment, or more pretense.

Countless times I have been asked apropos these performances of the Polish Laboratory Theatre whether I *liked* them. My answer: It doesn't matter whether any of us "likes" them. This troupe is what I have repeatedly called true *theatre*. It may always remain a theatre for the few (I do not refer to snobs), even a cult. Its "message" is well-nigh intolerable and its fanaticism forbidding. But its dedication to its vision of life and art is unparalleled in any theatre of our day.

DEAR GROTOWSKI

An open letter

Eric Bentley

Dear Jerzy Grotowski:

I won't say I know exactly what theatre is but I know that it is something in the whole community's network of communications. What is your theatre? How does it relate to your environment, the Poland of 1969? There is little of Karl Marx in your theatre, but then there isn't all that much Karl Marx in your Communist Party, is there? So is your theatre a retreat to old Catholic Poland? Your published disclaimer of belief in God doesn't prove it isn't. The Church has reality for you, whether God does or not; a disproportionate degree of reality, even. Your slogan as a director would seem to be: when in doubt, fall back on ritual. And even the Church never went so far as to believe that in ritual there was salvation.

I am saying that what comes through from your theatre to a radical spectator – and in America very many of your spectators will be radicals – is a certain conservatism. Conversely, it will be our conservative press that will most readily call you avant-garde. Are you a reactionary? And, if not, does your work lend itself to reactionary interpretation and use? What attracted you to Calderon's play, *The Constant Prince*? The tacit assumption that Spain is entitled to a chunk of Africa because its princes are such devout Catholics? A nice retort to Peter Weiss's "Song of the Lusitanian Bogey"!

I'm kidding, but only just. Christianity without belief has a tradition, but an ugly one, one that, for my generation, recalls certain Frenchmen who supported Hitler. Even when not fascistic, that kind of Christianity was snobbish. T.S. Eliot, for example, whom you draw upon, sometimes seemed to suppose that Christianity was a religion for cultivated, superior chaps only. For Pharisees, not for publicans, whores and sinners, let alone fishermen. And such was the spirit breathed by your *Constant Prince*, I thought. Not by Calderon's, though judged in our unhistorical way, he was an imperialist. For Calderon believed in a Jesus who, though divine, was no superior chap.

Your Constant Prince might equally be called the Good Boy with a Slight Case of Masochism.

Conservatism in art, as is well known, often brings a certain formalism in its train. Your version of Auschwitz in *Akropolis* is over-aesthetic and therefore distressingly abstract. Mythological analogies indeed! When the curtain goes up on Peter Weiss's *The Investigation*, we see young Auschwitz guards dressed up, as by that time they were in real life, in senility and business suits. For dramatic truth and expressivity, that moment is worth any fifteen minutes of your *Akropolis*. And in it we forget Peter Weiss as we seldom, if ever, forget you in *Akropolis*. Which means that in that moment *The Investigation* is art and not cult of personality. Those who disliked Weiss's show complained that its subject was too unpleasant. Those who liked yours praised various technical devices. In New York, thousands of whose families lost relatives in the extermination camps, you show us an Auschwitz that is of technical interest to theatre students! If that isn't an example of a deplorable formalism, what would be?

Am I too ideological? Very well, let's just speak of your tone, the tone of your book, *Towards a Poor Theatre*, the tone of your program notes, and the tone, apparently taken from you, of all other persons connected with your shows, right down (or up) to the ushers. Not that the ushers are all of one kind. They are of two kinds. Only one is hostile, snippety, peremptory, quasi-military. The other is a little unctuous, mealy-mouthed, and very reverential. Why the absence of humor? Why can no one relax? You have been a traumatic experience for New York and while this might do New York a lot of good, it would certainly seem that our city had a lot to put up with. Have you any idea how many people have suffered rebuff, if not insult, in their attempts to see the Polish Laboratory Theatre? I seem to have spent most of October and November visiting the wounded. Their cries still ring in my ears. Church doors have not suffered such blows since Martin Luther drove great nails into them – rumor has it that Theodore Mann, for one, went on pounding on yours all through the night and never did get in – though he had tickets. Other luminaries of our benighted American theatre (no irony) got in and roundly declared your theatre was no good anyway. They were so miffed.

And so on. And so forth. A book could be written, and probably will be, on the mess around your performances. May it be a better one than yours! Do you realize that the Anglo-American version of your book isn't even in good English? And this was what, for many of us, heralded your visit. Mind you, we could have penetrated bad prose, if that was the only problem, but this, surely, must be a bad book in any language. If there is a new theatre, it deserves a properly articulated description, if not a grandly conceived theory. You have made the mistake of publishing a bundle of scraps and pretending that it is a worthy manifesto. A book that oscillates between the trivial and the grandiose.

In short, for many of us, your work got the worst conceivable send-off, and don't reply that so many have swooned over you, fawned on you, etc., etc., because we know that is true, and it only made the whole thing all the harder to take. It was not till the evening of your third show that I recovered from the trauma. During the show, *Apocalypsis*, something happened to me. I put it this personally because it was something very personal that happened. About halfway through the play I had a quite specific illumination. A message came to me – from nowhere, as they say – about my private life and self. This message must stay private, to be true to itself, but the fact that it arrived has public relevance, I think, and I should publicly add that I don't recall this sort of thing happening to me in the theatre before – or even in revivalist meetings, though maybe I haven't attended enough of the latter.

Do I digress? Say so at your peril, for your theatre is redeemed, it seems to me, by just this peculiar intimacy. Peculiar: not the "intimacy" of our own Off Off (off, off, off . . .) Broadway efforts, one part ineffectual goodwill, two parts clumsy aggression. A man shows you his penis, a woman clouts you over the ear, while the whole acting company shouts four-letter denunciations at you – that's our intimacy, our charming "audience involvement." When I see your theatre, and now that I've even got to the detraumatized point were I *can* see it, I note that your work, in this respect as in others, is a corrective to everything that happens here in your name. Any rudeness stops in the lobby. In your theatre a spectator is a person and is allowed to keep his dignity, i.e. his individual separateness. Sometimes your actors come within inches of us, but they never lay hands on us, nor whisper in an individual ear. In the space our body occupies, we are inviolate. Now if the closeness to the actor brings us something extra, the fact that it is not a complete merger like sexual intercourse seems to me equally important, embodying a dialectical law of art according to which, if there is closeness, it must be balanced and, as it were, canceled by distance.

Dignity is involved too. In your conservatism, you aren't afraid of being bourgeois when what is bourgeois is rather nice. Chairs are rather nice. The floor is, well, rather uncomfortable and, in New York, extremely dirty. The bourgeoisie's case against discomfort and dirt is definitive. Besides, a third of the American people have bad backs: they need a chair to prop them up. Although you sometimes use uncomfortable benches,

I noticed that you had chairs for spectators right next to the ovens of Auschwitz at *Akropolis*. Actually, one could have wished they were less near, for it was too comical to see a mustachioed man in mod clothes leaning against a gas oven. That is where I am even more conservative than you, and want my spectators "off stage." But I am glad you sometimes hold on to chairs: make your American disciples buy some.

Apocalypsis is a very beautiful thing. It vindicates your idea of a theatre, and since only thirty-nine other readers of *The Times* (or some small multiple of forty) will have seen it, I should perhaps tell what it is about: Jesus. Who else? He's your man, if not your Man, and this time, you were, in his phrase, a fisher of men and caught him in your net. Him or someone else by the same name. Yes, there was a slight feeling of *déjà vu* and your program notes spelled out for us the word "Dostoyevski." Who was it said you are anti-literary? You are too literary by half. You have read all European literature, and haven't forgotten nearly enough of it. But, literary though it is in inspiration, your image of Jesus becomes theatrical in its incarnation. That's how it becomes yours and, through the performance, ours.

Yours is a Jesus *sui generis*, a small young Pole, wearing an unbuttoned raincoat over just a pair of black shorts, and carrying a white stick. His eyes protrude. His mouth tends to hang open. He tends to run, to be "on the run." He has a strange, loping way of running, and when other characters stand in his way so he will collide with them, he is as much confused as frightened. Now possibly, as far as this description goes, there is nothing that could not be projected, say, by Marcel Marceau from the stage of a very large theatre. You insist on a very small theatre. Correction. You insist on *no* theatre. What you insisted on in New York was the Washington Square Methodist Church. And when I saw *Apocalypsis* I saw, too, *why* you had been so fussy. Fussiness is the name given to perfectionism by those who see no need of perfectionism. You needed it because, in addition to clear outline, you wished your image to have many delicate, shifting details which would get lost in a larger place. Your non-theatre is so small, it has many of the advantages of movie close-ups. One watches the play of wrinkle and muscle on your actors' bodies.

Here's an aspect of your conservatism that I would call positive: you have created the conditions in which you can achieve a theatrical equivalent of modern poetry. I call this conservative because the kind of modern poetry your work evokes, and was suggested by, is that of the great, and now long past, generations, the poetry of the Symbolists| and (again the name!) T.S. Eliot. Perhaps one would have the right perspective if one were sweepingly to say that the theatre tends to be out of date and that at last, with you, it arrives where poetry was some fifty years ago.

There is a question in my mind whether your work is dramatic. It's certainly lyric. You're a poet. And, as I say, it's theatrical. So it's poetry of the theatre. Drama comes about as a culmination, a kind of grand synthesis, late in any historical sequence (fifth-century Athens, Elizabethan England). You, it seems to me, are going back to the beginning, scraping back, as Stark Young once put it (he was a painter) to the design. Stark Young was speaking of Martha Graham, for in America this return to the beginning, the rock bottom, of theatre has chiefly been undertaken by dancers. But you, too, are a choreographer.

Apocalypsis presents Jesus and his disciples by the means of choreography, and, looking back, I now see much more clearly than I did at the time how *The Constant Prince* and *Akropolis* were put together and how they present themselves to us. I would call your Poor Theatre *elemental theatre* to avoid jokes about poor theatre at $200 a seat, which is what your tickets were selling for on the black market. Poor Theatre is theatre reduced to its elements, and this is not as an economy in the money sense, but as an attempt to discover the necessary by removing anything that might prove superfluous.

In your notes on *The Constant Prince* you congratulate yourself on catching the "inner meaning of the play." Cool it. The inner meaning of a three-act masterpiece cannot be translated into any one-act dance drama. Its meaning is tied indissolubly to its three-act structure: otherwise Calderon himself would have reduced it to one act – he was a master of the one act. What you caught in *The Constant Prince* was the meaning, outer, inner, as you will, of another play, your own, which is vastly simpler and cruder than Calderon's and would probably bore his audience if it could return to life, but which for us is valid and therefore not boring. In retrospect, I very much admire the way in which each of your evenings was a separate exploration. I understand "environmental theatre" now, just as I now see what intimacy means. In *The Constant Prince*, we were medical students looking down on an operating table or a bullfight crowd looking down on the fight. In *Akropolis*, we were inside the world of the play and the players – within the electrified barbed wire of an extermination camp. In *Apocalypsis*, we were a small group of onlookers, small enough to feel ourselves disciples of the disciples. The decision to limit the number of "customers" to 90 or 100 at the first two plays, and to 40 at the last, may be arbitrary, but, now that we know what you were after, we will grant that *some* arbitrary figure must inevitably be named. These events are planned as a whole: such and such actors to be seen by so and so many spectators from such and such an angle at such and such a distance.

If I have indicated my initial revulsion from (some aspects of) the first two shows, I should add that I now think of them with much more satisfaction. Can an experience change after the fact? Clearly not, but one can realize after the fact that one had more fun than one has been admitting to. Irritation tends to make one forget, or disregard, non-irritating elements. And you came to us attended by more irritants than anyone in the whole history of the American theatre. The few of us who were lucky enough to see all of your work learned to be grateful for all three shows.

I do not withdraw the criticisms offered above. For one of my temperament and my views, those objections remain, but I can attest that the longer one stays with your work the more one finds to engage attention and even win admiration. More than that: one perceives, finally, that the irritating things (other than those for which you bear no responsibility) are the defects of a quality, the negative aspects of a fanaticism which is your main source of energy. "Fanaticism" is perhaps too strong an expression, but "enthusiasm" would be too weak a one. In uncharitable moments, one thinks of you as self-important. That is the note you sound in your published pronouncements, not least when you tell us you're not as important as all that: when you asked critics to pay attention to the rest of the company, it was as if you wouldn't settle for rave reviews for yourself, you would demand rave reviews for all your pals. But behind your self-importance is your importance.

If, on the one hand, you are conservative and at points even reactionary, you are, on the other, radical in the most radical sense of the word: you are digging for the roots, all the time for the roots of your art, and intermittently for the roots of the unprecedented sufferings of our time, man's unremitting inhumanity to man. Politically, your theatre would help, I think, to undermine a bad regime or to bolster a good one. Salud!

Fraternally yours,
Eric Bentley

TEATR LABORATORIUM HAS DECIDED TO BREAK UP

It Has Been 25 Years

Yesterday we received a communication from the Wroclaw Teatr Laboratorium. We quote it in full:

For some time, the company has ceased to exist practically as a cohesive creative group. It has become a cooperative of individuals conducting independent works in a variety of directions.

That's in the very nature of things. We believe that, as the Laboratorium, we've accomplished what we set out to accomplish. We ourselves are astounded that we persisted as a group for a quarter of a century — constantly changing, inspiring one another, radiating our common energy onto others.

The creative age of a company is not the same as the creative age of an individual. Some of us will take up the risk of a fully independent artistic life; others — perhaps — will want to continue their work together, in some other, new, institutional framework.

Each of us remembers that our origins lie in the common source whose name is Jerzy Grotowski, Grotowski's theatre.

We are saddened that in the last few years we have lost in their prime Antoni Jaholkowski, Jacek Zmyslowski, and Stanislaw Scierski.

After twenty-five years, we still feel close to one another, just as it was in the beginning, regardless of where we are now — but we have also changed. From now on each of us has to meet alone the challenge of his/her own creative biography and the times in which we live.

As of 31 August 1984, the Theatre of 13 Rows, the Institute of the Actor's Method, Institute of the Actor — in other words the company of the Teatr Laboratorium, after exactly twenty-five years, has decided to dissolve.

We want to express our gratitude to all those who during those years helped us, accompanied us, and trusted us, in Opole, in Wroclaw, in Poland, and throughout the world.

Founding members:

Ludwik Flaszen

Rena Mirecka

Zygmunt Molik

Ryszard Cieslak

and the company

(*Gazeta Robotnicza*, 28 January 1984, Wroclaw, Poland)

GROTOWSKI'S LABORATORY THEATRE

Dissolution and diaspora

Robert Findlay

The passing of Jerzy Grotowski's Polish Laboratory Theatre on 31 August 1984, after twenty-five years of operation, went generally unnoticed here in the United States. There had been, of course, the 28 January 1984 statement presaging the official closure signed by members of the group still in Wroclaw, which appeared in the Wroclaw daily newspaper *Gazeta Robotnicza*, later to be republished by such Polish journals as *Dialog* and *Odra*. But the official closing and dissolution in August 1984 sparked no extensive response either in the international press or in English-language journals and magazines devoted to theatre practice. There were no immediate tributes in praise of what had been a truly unique operation.

One might ask why. After all, this was an experimental theatre company which, at least in the period of the late 1960s and early 1970s, had inspired internationally the highest forms of praise. Grotowski was lauded as the most significant theatrical innovator since Stanislavsky and Brecht and his company acclaimed as the most disciplined and inspired group of performers to grace the twentieth century. Simply as a point of theatre history, one would suppose the closing of Grotowski's operation to be a major event. If, for example, the Moscow Art Theatre had closed its doors permanently after twenty-five years, one might assume that some considerable notice would be taken. (The Moscow Art Theatre, by the way, still officially exists today as an institution.) Or if tomorrow the Berliner Ensemble suddenly, for whatever reason, decided to disband, one might hope that the word would get out immediately.

THE AESTHETIC DILEMMA

In 1959, the unknown twenty-six-year-old theatre director Jerzy Grotowski (b. 1933) and the youthful but even at that time established critic Ludwik Flaszen (b. 1930) founded in the provincial town of Opole,

Poland, a small experimental theatre group (the Theatre of 13 Rows) that eventually would be called the Laboratory Theatre and would become world famous. Of the founding group of actors whom Grotowski first directed in such productions as Cocteau's *Orphee* and Byron's *Cain*, two – Zygmunt Molik (b. 1930) and Rena Mirecka (b. 1934) – remained with the company until its official closing and dissolution twenty-five years later. A third founding member, Antoni Jaholkowski (b. 1931), remained with the company until his death from cancer on 1 September 1982. In 1961, two other important members, Zbigniew Cynkutis (b. 1938) and Ryszard Cieslak (b. 1937), joined the group and were to stay with it until the closing in August 1984. Later, in the mid-1960s, Stanislaw Scierski (b. 1939) and Elizabeth Albahaca joined the company. Scierski was with the group until his death by his own hand in July 1983, while Albahaca remained until the closing of the Laboratory Theatre in 1984.

From its very inception, Grotowski's group was devoted to research and experimentation. While its earliest productions seem fairly conventional by standards later developed by the group, there can be little doubt of the intention to found a laboratory dealing with theatrical questions. This was not a company that would produce plays for a general or mass audience. It was not a group that would have one eye on its art and the other on the box office. Rather, it would be an artistic laboratory in which experimental research would be conducted. Though Grotowski understood the vast difference between scientific and artistic research, he was nonetheless fascinated by the model of the Bohr Institute for advanced physicists in Copenhagen, about which he spoke in 1968:

> Bohr and his team founded an institution of quite extraordinary nature. It is a meeting place where physicists from different countries experiment and take their first steps into the "no man's land" of their profession. Here they compare their theories and draw from the "collective memory" of the Institute. This "memory" keeps a detailed inventory of all the research done, including even the most audacious, and is continually enriched with new hypotheses and results obtained by the physicists.
>
> (1968:127)

The Laboratory Theatre operated at first in relative isolation and obscurity. But after 1965 word of the group's disciplined and richly artistic productions spread throughout experimental circles both in Europe and America. In 1965 as well, the group moved from the provincial town of Opole to the large metropolitan city of Wroclaw and began to perform and conduct workshops outside Poland – in France, England, Sweden, Denmark, and eventually by late 1967 in the United States. By the 1970s, the group was known throughout the world, visiting Asia, Australia, Central and South America, Africa and the Middle East.

Perhaps the most significant event in the dissemination of Grotowski's beliefs and methods was the publication in 1968 of *Towards a Poor Theatre*, a collection of essays by him and about his work, edited by Eugenio Barba. While seeming at times to be equally as visionary a manifesto as Antonin Artaud's *The Theatre and Its Double* (1938), Grotowski's perceptions in *Towards a Poor Theatre* were nonetheless tied closely to the practical and disciplined solving of specific theatrical problems. While Artaud was able to articulate theoretically the possibility of a contemporary theatre based on ceremony and myth that would psychically confront the spectator, Grotowski clarified, extended, and put into practice such a theatre.

In 1968, the Laboratory Theatre performed for the first time *Apocalypsis cum figuris*, critically recognized as Grotowski's masterpiece. *Apocalypsis* was performed with six actors (five men and a woman) in a totally bare space, surrounded on four sides by the audience, with only two spotlights aimed obliquely at the ceiling, and a minimum of properties: a loaf of bread, a knife, and some candles. Although *Apocalypsis* continued to be performed numerous times throughout the world for the next thirteen years (until 1981 and the death of Antoni Jaholkowski, who played Simon Peter), by 1970 Grotowski and his people were moving into a new though connected realm of research and experimentation, what Grotowski referred to as "paratheatrical experiences." At the same time, the entire organization of the Laboratory Institute was reconstituted. In addition to those performing *Apocalypsis* on a regular basis, Grotowski added a group of new, younger members in their twenties: Teo Spychalski (who actually had joined the group in the late 1960s), Irena Rycyk, Teresa Nawrot, Zbigniew Koslowski, Jacek Zmyslowski, and Wlodzimierz Staniewski, among others. Thus emerged a number of paratheatrical projects in the 1970s which included members of the Laboratory Institute but also a vast number of individuals from outside the group and from all over the world (musicians, painters, actors, psychologists, psychiatrists, sociologists, anthropologists, college and university students, etc.).

Typically, such projects were structured events lasting for days and sometimes weeks, sometimes occurring in closely confined spaces, sometimes in the forest or mountains. Grotowski insisted that such projects were not to be considered as actor training, as psychotherapy, as secular mysticism, or necessarily as art *per se*. He said the experiments simply presented a means of allowing creative individuals the possibility of "meeting" in an atmosphere that had been carefully structured for such encounters. (Some of Grotowski's earliest public attitudes on these new directions may be found in Josef Kelera's report, "Grotowski w mowie pozornie zaleznej.")

Spurred by the success of the group's various paratheatrical experiments, Grotowski, in the late 1970s and early 1980s, embarked on a new series of experiments that came under the general title Theatre of Sources. Over a period of approximately five years, from 1977 through 1982, Grotowski worked with a multinational group of people representing such diverse cultures as India, Colombia, Bengal, Haiti, Japan, Poland, France, Germany, Mexico, and the United States. While members of this primary group at various times spent a number of months at a field base near Wroclaw, there were innumerable expeditions in various parts of the world to study what Grotowski called "source techniques." While certainly a number of people in the 1970s had questioned the pertinence of the so-called paratheatrical experiments to traditional theatrical work, perhaps with some reason, the directions taken by Grotowski in Theatre of Sources seemed even more remote from usual conceptions of theatre. In the mid-1970s, Grotowski, partly in an attempt to avert such criticisms, had announced his so-called "exit" from the theatre (Burzynski 1975). In an extended interview with Andrzej Bonarski, he had said:

> If someone claims that I ought to be putting on productions, then he probably assumes I was not a bad director. [. . .] Now, when I have entered another domain which I have called paratheatrical experiment, I need that credit. [. . .] I was a producer, a former director, and now I don't know how to describe it – or perhaps just a little [. . .] some say a scientist. Maybe not really a scientist, but some man who has had a theatrical adventure, yes, somewhere along the line, a theatrical one.
>
> (1975:13)

While certainly it was Grotowski who provided the major artistic inspiration for the Laboratory Theatre during its so-called theatrical period, even some of his closest colleagues such as Zbigniew Cynkutis and Ryszard Cieslak had difficulty at first trying to fathom what he was about when he first began the paratheatrical experiments and hence his so-called "exit" from the theatre. Something of the beginnings of this artistic dilemma of the Laboratory Theatre are noted in Cynkutis's and Cieslak's statements to a group of young Italians in Milan in February 1979. The two actors, seated on the floor of a makeshift platform, speaking in English and translated into Italian by Carla Pollastrelli, had just been asked from the audience about the period shortly after the first performances of *Apocalypsis cum figuris* in the late 1960s when Grotowski was changing the fundamental direction of the Laboratory Theatre from theatrical toward paratheatrical work:

Cieslak answers by speaking first of the period prior to the development of *Apocalypsis*, of the years in which each production from the earliest to *Kordian* to *Akropolis* to *Tragical History of Doctor Faustus* to *The Constant Prince* had served as the creative groundwork for each successive experiment. For Grotowski, each production was always considered to be his last. With *Apocalypsis*, this fact became apparent very early in its development. "Ten or eleven years ago," says Cieslak, "Grotowski had the vision of where he was going with the paratheatrical work – but no one in the company really comprehended. He knew, but we didn't." Cynkutis picks it up from here. "In the period 1970 to 1973, we seemed to be wasting a lot of time because of a lack of understanding. Grotowski had the sense of where he wanted to take us, but at first we didn't understand. Now . . . today" – he smiles – "we understand better."

(Findlay 1982:47)

Perhaps the aesthetic dilemma of the Laboratory Theatre – and one of the major reasons for the group's dissolution in August 1984 – is best summarized by noting what happened to the company with each new step forward into "no man's land." In the theatrical period, the experiments of the group had called for a small, tightly knit company of actors, designers, a director, and a literary adviser or dramaturg. This streamlined production organization performed frequently at the home base in Wroclaw and traveled all over the world doing performances and holding workshops and meetings. It was a remarkably mobile unit: few props, no big settings, no complex costumes.

With the paratheatrical work, the company had been extended by the addition of members and the inclusion of vast numbers of outsiders for brief periods. While there seemed to have been few noticeable tensions arising between the members of the acting company and the newcomers, the reconstitution of the Laboratory Theatre in the early 1970s nonetheless produced a much different structure from the simple, tight, cohesive acting group formed by Grotowski and Flaszen in 1959. Though all company members, new and old, were part of most paratheatrical projects, Grotowski himself, owing to his own continuing research, in the 1970s became progressively less central in the day-to-day operations of the group, though it should be remembered that Grotowski was frequently a presence and a participant in these projects. And then too it should be remembered that one of the major sources of cohesiveness during this period was the continuing performance of *Apocalypsis cum figuris* by the members of the acting company.

When in the late 1970s Grotowski took another step into "no man's land" to develop Theatre of Sources with a multinational group, he was further separating himself from the ongoing day-to-day operations of the others. Cynkutis was named vice-director of the Laboratory Theatre and came to function largely as an actor–manager of the company still performing *Apocalypsis cum figuris* on a somewhat less regular basis than before. It was at this time, as well, that various members of the acting company and even some of the others began to travel abroad conducting workshops and directing productions on their own. Cieslak was in demand all over the world (Ronen 1978). Cynkutis was abroad frequently; in West Berlin in 1981, for example, he directed a production based on Thomas Mann's *Doctor Faustus* at the Theaterhaus. In 1980 Elizabeth Albahaca went to Italy for a short period to work with another company. And Rena Mirecka, Zygmunt Molik, and Stanislaw Scierski traveled abroad with some regularity to conduct workshops.

Still, performances of *Apocalypsis* continued. In addition, in 1980–81, during the period of Solidarity, there was an attempt by some members of the group still in Wroclaw (under the direction of Cieslak) to develop another performance, eventually titled *Thanatos Polski*. This work, however, was hardly comparable artistically to the theatrical work that had gone before under Grotowski's direction (Kumiega 1985:208–212).

Eventually it was no longer possible for Antoni Jaholkowski to perform, owing to his illness. Perhaps it was his death in September 1981, more than anything else, which signaled the eventual dissolution in 1984. Without Jaholkowski, there could be no performances of *Apocalypsis*, and without performances of *Apocalypsis*, there was no longer the artistic need of a cohesive acting unit. With members of the Laboratory Theatre in far-flung parts of the world, with no real point of artistic focus in Wroclaw, the resolution was to dissolve the company.

THE POLITICAL DILEMMA

When the Laboratory Theatre was founded in 1959, it was at a unique point in Polish history and political life, a period commonly referred to as the Thaw or the Polish October. Stalin had died in 1953, and eventually Khrushchev had come to power in the Soviet Union. By 1956 he had denounced Stalin as a tyrant. The effects of that pronouncement were of course significant in the Soviet Union, but there were also profound effects in the whole Eastern Bloc, particularly in Poland, where the old Stalinists in power were immediately undermined. Thus after 1956, when Wladyslaw Gomulka came to power as First Secretary, Poland experienced a period of relative liberalization in which the arts were allowed to flourish. Almost immediately, there emerged a new group of playwrights, influenced by Beckett, but nonetheless indige-nously Polish in their imaginative and experimental treatments of dramatic subjects. The tired, ideological dramas of socialist realism

Plate 20.1   The funeral of Antoni Jaholkowski, September 1981. Pallbearers at left are Ryszard Cieslak and Zbigniew Cynkutis; Jaholkowski's father, wife, and son are at centre; Rena Mirecka carries flowers with ribbon at right. (Photo: Zbigniew Cynkutis.)

became a thing of the past. The most important of these playwrights were Slawomir Mrozek and Tadeusz Rozewicz. This is the period, as well, in which student and cabaret theatres began to develop in Poland. It is also the time when significant work by Polish film directors such as Andrzej Wajda began to appear. This, then, was the social and political context in which Grotowski and Flaszen, together with a small company of actors, were given the opportunity, with a modest government subsidy, to begin their experimental operation in Opole.

It is significant that Grotowski, as a student in the Theatre School in Krakow in the mid-1950s, was deeply involved with the political currents of his time. Indeed, he gained some notoriety as an anti-Stalinist youth activist long before he gained fame as a theatrical director. In 1957, for example, he was a member of the governing body, the Secretariat, of the Provisional Central Committee of the Union of Socialist Youth. Although he, with others, eventually withdrew in protest from the Secretariat, he was instrumental in founding, as part of the Union of Socialist Youth, the Political Center of the Academic Left (POLA ZMS). He seems to have been an articulate spokesperson, since his views frequently were reported in various publications. Many years later in an interview with Bonarski, he said:

> I wanted to be a political guru, and a very dogmatic one at that. I was so fascinated by Gandhi that I wanted to be like him. But I found out that's impossible for objective reasons, and besides it would be against my

nature, which is capable of fair play but cannot fully believe that everyone has good intentions.

(1975:12)

The early years in Opole were extremely difficult ones for members of the group. There was no room in the theatre for administrative offices or a scene shop; in the dressing room there was no hot water; the living quarters were unheated. Although there was a firm core of young people and Party activists who supported the theatre, as Bogdan Loebl reported in *Odra* in 1962, there were many in Opole and throughout Poland with a much more conservative leaning, both artistically and politically, who would have been happy to see the Theatre of 13 Rows go out of existence. Just as the Thaw after 1956 had produced an atmosphere of liberalization, and hence artistic experimentation, there were many by the mid-1960s who believed that "democratization" had gone too far. Although there was little in the early productions of the Theatre of 13 Rows that could be labeled overtly political, the times were such that anything which seemed obviously "radical" or "elitist" – terms applied frequently in this period to Grotowski's group – tended to generate suspicion politically. In addition, there were many who labeled the theatre's work as "gibberish," "sham," and "charlatanism" (Osinski 1986:53). And, indeed, despite growing recognition abroad, by the season 1963–64, it looked as if the Theatre of 13 Rows would lose its subsidy and go out of existence.

Typical of the concerted opposition to the group at this time was the article, tinged with sarcasm, by Jan Alfred Szczepanski published in *Trybuna Ludu*, the official organ of the Central Committee of the Party:

> Perhaps the Theatre of 13 Rows is known throughout the world, but it certainly is not known in Warsaw. [. . .] How is it [. . .] that such an excellent prize-studded theatre like 13 Rows has been carefully avoiding the capital for five years? We would certainly like to get acquainted with it, at least so we could believe the praise of such a learned periodical as *Pamietnik Teatralny* [an allusion to articles about the group by both Flaszen and Zbigniew Raszewski, which had just appeared].

(Osinski 1986:18)

Ultimately, the group was to gain a reprieve. A special governmental commission in Warsaw decided that Opole was not the proper setting for Grotowski's theatre. The large metropolitan city of Wroclaw (pop. 600,000) might provide a more appropriate environment. This is not to suggest that opposition to the group, political or otherwise, immediately ceased at the moment that the move from Opole to Wroclaw was complete. But the atmosphere surrounding the group did change. By

1965, when the move was made, the group's artistic accomplishments and growing international reputation could hardly be ignored. While some of the more vociferous critics were silenced as a result, occasionally "the old game," as Grotowski refers to these attacks, would occur again.

Those who recall Grotowski's frequent denials during the 1960s and 1970s that his work was political – indeed, he called it "apolitical" – may be surprised by what he says today. "I had to say I was not political in order to be political. *The Constant Prince*, for example, was a very political work" (from a discussion in New York, 30 August 1984). *The Constant Prince* was, of course, the first performance to be developed after the move to Wroclaw. A "political" reading of that performance certainly is not inappropriate. *The Constant Prince* presented the fundamental situation of a noble individual (Don Fernando, played by Cieslak) who seemingly accedes to his torturers, even accepting ecstatically their cruel punishments, but whose spirit remains true and indomitable. Ultimately, though the Prince dies, he wins out over his torturers. The situation of the Prince is not unlike that of Grotowski and his group in 1965 in the face of numerous vituperative attacks, political and otherwise, in the Polish press. And if, as Grotowski says, *The Constant Prince* was political, what of *Tragical History of Doctor Faustus* and, finally, what of *Apocalypsis cum figuris*?

The predominance of religious imagery in Grotowski's work always allowed the possibility of the disclaimer that his work was not political. For the Polish authorities, the ultimate image of a tortured Christ the rebel, the revolutionary, must have been satisfactory, particularly if the image of the crucified Christ was an atheistic, existential one: Kordian in a psychiatric ward; Don Fernando in the grips of cruel torturers; Ciemny – the Simpleton, childlike, naive, the perpetual lover of human beings – cruelly ridiculed then tantalized with mock friendship and sexually abused by a group of woozy drunks as they are gradually sobering up.

If Grotowski's theatrical statement was at least partially a political one, as he now suggests, it used one of the most apolitical images possible: a crucified Christ figure. Yet this is an image that has extremely strong reverberations in Catholic Poland. In a discussion in Long Beach, California, 10–11 March 1985, Grotowski talked of the difference between the priests, the purveyors of information, and the visionaries, always the rebels. He said: "The example of Christ, as a living human being only, is very important to me." And then, jokingly, not wistful or self-indulgent, but ironic, smiling, laughing, almost self-deprecatory, telling a funny story: "Jesus Christ had only three years; I had twenty-three with the Laboratorium."

By the close of the 1960s, the Laboratory Theatre had reached the apex of its theatrical fame, specifically through its world-wide performances of *Akropolis*, *The Constant Prince*, and *Apocalypsis cum figuris*. This period in Poland, as elsewhere in the world, was one of political unrest. In January 1968, students in Warsaw applauded all the anti-Russian speeches in Kazimierz Dejmek's production of the Polish classic *Forefather's Eve* by Adam Mickiewicz. Growing from this incident were continued demonstrations against censorship throughout Poland not only by students but professors and intellectuals. The police dealt harshly with the demonstrations, and governmental repressive measures followed. Unrest was further fueled by economic stagnation and the raising of food prices. The latter action caused strikes in Gdansk. It is this period of Polish history with which Wajda deals in his film *Man of Marble*. Eventually, by December 1970, Gomulka was forced to resign for "reasons of health." He was replaced as First Secretary by Edward Gierek, known for his popularity among workers. Gierek for a time was able to bring some resolution to the unrest by once again lowering food prices.

By 1976, however, a similar economic crisis occurred. Poland had come to be totally dependent upon foreign credit. Gierek sought to project the image of Poland as the Japan of Europe – an utter and absurd fantasy. While in the mid-1970s there was the illusion in Poland of some stability owing to foreign credits, by August 1980, with the strike of shipyard workers in Gdansk and the founding of Solidarity, all of Gierek's illusions for Poland dissolved. He, like Gomulka, resigned for "reasons of health."

During the Gierek years, the Laboratory Theatre went abroad for extended periods but still continued to perform *Apocalypsis* in Poland on a fairly regular basis, partly as a means of making contact with those people who might have been interested in participating directly in paratheatrical experiments such as *The Mountain Project* and *Tree of People*. Typical of the notices distributed throughout Poland in this period is the poster of Cieslak against the background of a rugged mountain, which said in part:

> We meet with people who are looking for us whom we are looking for because they are like us. We meet for several days outside the city without division into the active ones and spectators. All of us are looking for one another in the great field of human activity. If you want to participate in our adventure, write a few words about what you're doing, what you're looking for, and what you expect from such a meeting with us and others. Send all this information with your correct address to Ryszard Cieslak, Instytut Laboratorium, Rynek Ratusz 27, 50–101 Wroclaw, Poland.

There is nothing overtly political or seditious in such an invitation. Its appeal is chiefly to the young and adventuresome, who tended to flock to Wroclaw in large numbers in order to participate in such projects. Cieslak's appeal was to those who wished to make connections with one another in an open and spontaneous way. Certainly there were some who came, as Teresa Nawrot once suggested in a conversation in Wroclaw (8 January 1980), because they were "interested in simply meeting people of the opposite sex," but generally the appeal was to those, particularly in Poland, who believed in the possibility of an open, non-repressive engagement with other people: what Grotowski came to call at this time "active culture."

While it has been habitual not to see the work of the Laboratory Theatre as political, Grotowski's present attitude – that his work was always political – necessitates a potentially political reading of everything occurring during the twenty-five-year life of his group. Indeed the basis of "active culture," if not the means, is found in some of Grotowski's earliest statements as a political activist during the Thaw after 1956. In the founding of the ZMS Political Center of the Academic Left in March 1957, for example, the young Grotowski, twenty-four years old, together with Adam Ogorzalek, issued the following statement, published in *Gazeta Krakowska*:

> We want an organization that will teach people to think politically, to understand their interests, to fight for bread and democracy and for justice and truth in everyday life. We must fight for people to live like humans and be masters of their fate. We must fight for young people's right to work, learn, and to have a career. We must fight for workers' universities, against employment of minors in hard and demanding jobs, for fair allocation of summer leaves, apartments, and bonuses, for equal rights for blue and white collar workers, for fair work standards, for the primacy of specialists. We must fight for young people to live a better and more satisfying life. We must fight for people to speak their minds without fear of being harassed. We must fight so that stupid and corrupt individuals won't hold positions of responsibility.
>
> (Osinski 1986:19)

In a statement the next month, April 1957, at a ZMS congress in Warsaw, Grotowski called for a commitment of young people to "join in the life of the country, and to work for the common cause":

> No one can give us bread, civilization and freedom. We must make bread, just as we must make freedom and civilization happen. It's not true that one can hide away in one's private little world and go on living. [. . .] In our country, young people look forward to civilization, to a decent

standard of living, to justice, to decision-making about their own lives, to technological progress. Ours is a road to civilization and freedom.

(*Walka Mlodych*, June 1957, quoted in Osinski 1986:20)

The Solidarity period in Poland lasted from August 1980 until December 1981. While it was a period of relative freedom in Poland, it was also one of persistent uncertainty and fear. There was always the possibility that the Soviet Union would invade – that with each new governmental concession to the people eventually a price would have to be paid. The bill came due on 13 December 1981 when martial law was declared by General Wojciech Jaruzelski, who had come to power a month earlier. The Polish phrase *stan wojenny* or "state of war" is a much stronger indication of the realities of the Polish state in this period than the phrase "martial law." For a time, Polish communications with the rest of the world were totally cut off. Cynkutis, scheduled to teach the spring 1982 semester at the University of Kansas, did not arrive on schedule. Eventually by the end of January 1982 he was able to leave Poland legally and officially and arrive with his family – his wife Jolanta and two daughters. Grotowski later in 1982 was able to go to Denmark for a period of time, visiting Barba in Holstebro, still pursuing his work with Theatre of Sources. But eventually, during the period of martial law, all members of the Laboratory Theatre were able to go abroad individually, many of them to Paris. Cieslak went to Scandinavia. Grotowski himself left for the United States, first teaching at the University of California-Irvine. At the point that he requested political asylum in the United States, he told his colleagues either to seek political asylum for themselves or to go back to Poland together, as a group, thereby avoiding persecution for Grotowski's absence. The members of the group thus returned to Poland by choice and the Laboratory Theatre remained formally intact under the acting directorship of Ludwik Flaszen. But by agreement, the group did no public performances and no large projects in Poland. Individual members continued to work outside Poland, doing workshops, directing productions, and taking teaching engagements, all under the institutional name of the Laboratory Theatre. The political dilemma was not resolved; it was only held in abeyance. While the dissolution of the Laboratory Theatre may have provided a resolution to the members' artistic dilemma, the eventual dissolution was simply an acquiescence to the political powers then operative in Poland.

THE PERSONAL DILEMMA

Sitting in a brightly lit, all-night restaurant on upper Broadway in New York City on 31 August 1984, the date of the official closing, Grotowski is amused as he speaks about what it was like in fall 1959 when the group that would become the Laboratory Theatre first came together. He says there had been a bus chartered in Krakow to take members of the new company to Opole. He smiles as he tells how Jaholkowski had arrived on that first day: "Antek showed up for the bus ride to Opole with his bag of makeup supplies – false beard, false mustache, spirit gum." Then later: "Everyone was asking me what we were going to do in Opole. I said we were going to form an ashram." He laughs a little and his eyes crinkle slightly: "Since nobody knew at that time what an ashram was, I was okay. . . ."

If it was not exactly an ashram nor quite a religious order that Grotowski founded in Opole in 1959, it was nonetheless an organization that called for extreme personal commitment and discipline from its members. As guest lecturer in a graduate seminar in contemporary theatre at the University of Kansas on 13 April 1982, Cynkutis talked about the willingness of the people in the group to stretch themselves, to go beyond what they believed possible:

> I remember there was a time in Opole when we tried to fly – literally "to fly." We stopped thinking the way we always had thought – that we are human beings, that we cannot fly. Who says we cannot fly? What does that mean? So – we tried to fly. Yes, we kept falling, of course, but we did not accept that we could not fly. Sometimes it hurt to fall. But we kept on trying anyway, since we believed that nothing was impossible.

On another occasion, 26 May 1982, in an interview in Lawrence, Kansas, Cynkutis spoke very personally of the kinds of strains and demands he felt placed upon him by his involvement with Grotowski and the Laboratory Theatre:

> There was the time up to 1970 or 1971, the time of performances, of plays, the time of heavy work, sweat given to the profession, blood. Broken knee. The price. Broken [first] marriage. Broken life. A loss of privacy. The devotion to this profession: but such a heavy life, heavy work against myself; yes, it was necessary to work against myself in order to be better, to achieve better quality. And this way of thinking made me feel that I was a very average actor. Not someone very talented. Not someone who had a calling. Let's say this profession happened to me, and because I met a man, Grotowski, of great seriousness working in the theatre, I devoted myself to him. And something came out of this work. It helped me to understand the life of others, my own life, the world. Maybe it was not a very well-selected job, but it was done honestly. But this job came to be like a scalpel in the hands of a surgeon. A lot of pain.

Leaving Poland and coming to the United States in January 1982 during the period of martial law, Cynkutis and his family remained until August 1984. Slightly more than a year before his return, on 22 July 1983, the order of martial law had been rescinded in Poland. But it was in the same month Cynkutis returned to Poland that the Laboratory Theatre officially closed its doors and dissolved. Cynkutis formed what became known as the Drugie Studio Wroclawski (Second Studio of Wroclaw). The Polish government gave him the space formerly occupied by the Laboratory Theatre, 27 Rynek Ratusz, in addition to the task of overseeing all historical records, photographs, films, and videotapes, etc., of the Laboratory Theatre.

Cynkutis, of course, was in the United States when the members in Wroclaw signed the notice officially closing and dissolving the Laboratory Theatre. When asked by telephone how he felt about that action, he said he was not really in favor of it. He wishes his former colleagues had not closed the theatre, but he says he understands why they did it. He says he also wishes Grotowski had not left Poland, but he understands why he did that too.

Cieslak was contacted by telephone on 1 April 1986 around midnight Paris time. Cieslak had been outside Poland for quite some time, working with Peter Brook in Paris, and performing in Brook's production of the *Mahabharata*. The production is about ready to close, says Cieslak, and he does not really know what he will do next. He may or may not stay with Brook. There is some possibility he will come to the United States. When asked about why the Laboratory Theatre closed, he says it was too complicated a matter to discuss very well by telephone.

Those from the outside who have been involved with the Laboratory Theatre for any length of time over the years know that the members possess great respect for one another. To say they all love one another is probably not quite accurate, but the respect they feel verges on what might be called love – a love that grows of professional ties, being together a long time, the knowledge that one has been through hell and back with another person, the awareness of artistic accomplishment with that other person. Perhaps it is more a matter of sisterhood and brotherhood. That is not to say that tensions have not existed at times among members of the group. The situations of Cynkutis and Cieslak are probably not unique.

Cynkutis and Cieslak both joined the company at approximately the same time (Cynkutis arrived on 1 June 1961, Cieslak on 1 October 1961). At first, though Grotowski always stressed the idea of ensemble, it seemed that Cynkutis would be the designated "star" of the operation; it was he, for example, who played the title roles of Kordian in the play by Slowacki (1962) and Faustus (1963). There is even some possibility that he was the one originally indicated to play Don Fernando in *The Constant Prince*. But Cynkutis and Zygmunt Molik both left the company for approximately a year in 1965–66. By the time of their return (according to Cynkutis, they were invited back), Cieslak had developed his awesome performance in *The Constant Prince*. It was this performance that was being declared by critics internationally as the most luminous and gifted of the twentieth century.

Cynkutis talked of Cieslak's performance during a graduate seminar at the University of Kansas on 20 April 1982:

> Grotowski's decision to do *The Constant Prince* was influenced by the work on *Doctor Faustus*. The next step was to find "the total actor," one who is giving of himself totally. [. . .] Grotowski wanted to discover how such a "total act" can create real feeling here and now. He wanted to break down the conventional separation between the fictional and factual worlds. Grotowski gave up on "tricks"; instead it was to be done by the actor. If the actor is extremely true, intensive during performance, if his body is open like that of a patient during an operation, then it will happen. In *The Constant Prince* it occurred. The performance by Ryszard Cieslak was unbelievable. He was able to risk everything totally, to give up his own personality to Grotowski. Cieslak became an extension of Grotowski; he was recreated by Grotowski.

In the performance of *Apocalypsis cum figuris*, which dealt with the myth of the Second Coming, there was an ironic moment early in the performance when Simon Peter (Jaholkowski) first designates the character playing Lazarus (Cynkutis) to be the returned Savior. A little later, the Lazarus figure is rejected and the village idiot, the Simpleton (Cieslak), is dragged from the shadows of the audience and mockingly indicated as the Christ figure. In New York City on 31 August 1984, Grotowski acknowledged that something of the tensions between Cynkutis and Cieslak had played into that theatrical moment but that it had been Jaholkowski in a rehearsal who had mistakenly indicated Cynkutis. "I was happy with Antek's mistake," said Grotowski, "and we kept it in the performance."

While it is best not to make too much of personal tensions among group members, it is only humanly natural that such tensions would play some part in the decision to disband. People who have worked together for so many years, who have suffered together but who have also known the heights together, eventually come to need a breath of fresh air from one another. Inevitably there is simply the need for independence from one another. In many respects, it was probably Grotowski, among group members, who first began to exercise that need for independence. Maybe he was trying to tell the group something. Maybe the healthy thing is to submit to one's need to follow one's own impulse as an artist and researcher and, ultimately, to work with new people, to get a new perspective.

LEGACY OF THE LABORATORY THEATRE

In Richard Schechner's essay, "The Decline and Fall of the (American) Avant-Garde," he discusses in detail six specific reasons why, after flourishing between 1950 and 1975, the American avant-garde theatre declined. Such groups as the Living Theater, the Open Theater, the Performance Group and others failed to develop any sense of ongoing tradition: their texts were "performance texts" rather than "dramatic texts" and could only be performed by the groups that developed them. But perhaps more importantly, the avant-garde failed to develop "any adequate way of transmitting performance knowledge from one generation of theatre workers to another" (1982:29). Schechner continues:

> Grotowski was a pioneer of performance texts and performance knowledge. He had been among the most successful in getting his ideas across. This is because he emphasized "process," specifically in the training methods he developed. These methods can be acquired only person-to-person, face-to-face. During each phase of his career [. . .] Grotowski has involved people from his own Theatre Laboratory and people from the outside. From Eugenio Barba to the latest follower of Grotowski, people have come to his work, stayed variable lengths of time, and left; taking with them their own versions of what Grotowski and his associates were doing. In his writing Grotowski proclaims a rhetoric of closedness, privacy, and intimacy – but in fact he has been extremely open and sharing. The intimacy is within the work itself, not closing off the work as a whole. [. . .] Grotowski understands that only by means of body-to-body training can these new means of theatrical production be transmitted.
>
> (1982:33–34)

Perhaps the dissolution of the Laboratory Theatre and the diaspora, or scattering, of its former members is a good thing, for whatever complex reasons the official closing occurred. Rather than staying home and simply resting on their fame in Wroclaw, former members of the group, widely dispersed throughout Europe and North America, are training a whole new generation of theatre practitioners directly, face-to-face, body-to-body. Like the group that first rode the chartered bus from Krakow to Opole in 1959, many are starting anew on their own: as workshop leaders, directors, theatre managers, etc. Each brings her/his own particular experience with Grotowski and the Laboratory Theatre to bear in the confrontation with the new generation.

And Grotowski – the instigator of this whole thing, the investigator, the researcher – is still "on the way," still following the model of the Bohr Institute for advanced physicists in Copenhagen, taking steps into "no man's land."

AFTERWORD (JUNE 1996)

What appears above is a shortened and revised version of the original essay published in *TDR* ten years ago. Some matters discussed in the original are more extensively covered in other portions of this book. But ten years ago, Grotowski had only recently begun work at his Centro di Lavoro di Jerzy Grotowski in Pontedera, Italy. Since that time, of course, he has received numerous international recognitions for his work, plus honorary doctorates and a substantial unsolicited grant from the Mac-Arthur Foundation in 1991.

Sadly, Zbigniew Cynkutis died in an automobile accident just outside Wroclaw in January 1987, only months after the original version of this essay appeared in *TDR*. With his death, the promising work of the Drugie Studio essentially collapsed. Also sadly, Ryszard Cieslak died of lung cancer in July 1990, during a short tenure teaching and directing at New York University. Though I have not seen Zygmunt Molik or Rena Mirecka since June 1987, I'm told they both continue to live in Wroclaw and do occasional workshops in various parts of the world. Elizabeth Albahaca is in Montreal working with her husband Teo Spychalski, who directs his own Theatre of the Awakening [*Le Groupe de la Veillee*].

But the diaspora continues, most noticeably for me at least among a number of young Americans who never saw directly the performances of the Laboratory Theatre, but worked either with Grotowski or with former members of the company: namely long-term collaborators of Grotowski such as Thomas Richards and James Slowiak, along with students who worked with Grotowski for shorter periods of time. Some of that diaspora is well-documented in such recent books as Thomas Richards' *At Work with Grotowski on Physical Actions* (Routledge 1995) and Lisa Wolford's *Grotowski's Objective Drama Research* (University Press of Mississippi 1996). Although ten years ago in 1986, it seemed fairly clear that various elements of the so-called Grotowski "methods" would continue to exert influence, with this most recent generation of practitioners, the ongoing survival of these approaches seems a virtual certainty.

IN MEMORY OF RYSZARD CIESLAK

Ferdinando Taviani

THE DEATH

When Ryszard Cieslak died, almost nothing was reported in the papers, the announcement confined in most to a couple of lines. After his work on *The Constant Prince* and *Apocalypsis cum figuris*, Cieslak had ceased to be newsworthy.

Anyone wanting to explain precisely what Cieslak was would have to be able to extend the meaning of the word "miracle" and say it without fear of exaggeration. For Cieslak really was the miracle actor of the twentieth century. This kind of language is open to different interpretations, but it does have the advantage of making us reflect on some of the more unusual characters of twentieth-century theatre.

The following unsigned piece appeared among the obituaries in the *New York Times* on Saturday, 16 June 1990:

> Ryszard Cieslak, an actor and a central figure in the Polish Laboratory Theatre, died Thursday at the Burzynski Research Institute in Houston. He was 53 years old and lived in Manhattan.
>
> Dr. Stan Burzynski said that Mr. Cieslak had been admitted to the Institute 5 June, and that he died of lung cancer. Mr. Cieslak joined the Laboratory Theatre, which Jerzy Grotowski founded in 1959 in Poland as a vehicle for experimental drama, in 1962. After its dissolution in 1977, Mr. Cieslak and Mr. Grotowski worked together in numerous dramatic projects.
>
> Theatre critics cited Mr. Cieslak in 1969 as Off Broadway's most outstanding creator and the actor with the greatest promise. For the last four years, Mr. Cieslak taught acting to advanced students at the Tisch School of the Arts at New York University. He is survived by a daughter, who lives in Poland.

There seems to be a mistake here, and also one curious omission. The matter of a few months difference, between autumn 1961 when Cieslak effectively joined Grotowski's company, and 1962 as indicated in the

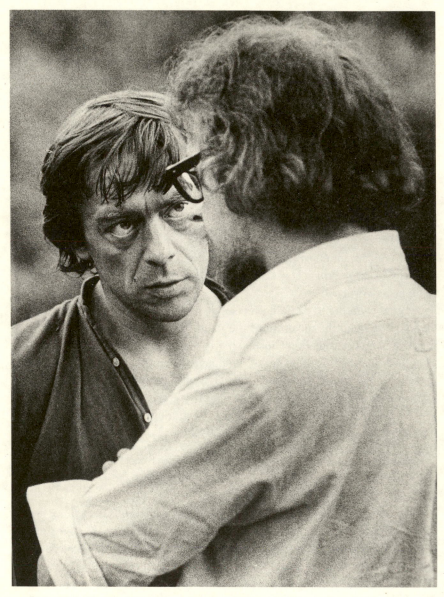

Plate 21.1 Ryszard Cieslak and Jerzy Grotowski. (Photo: Tony D'Urso.)

New York Times is insignificant. But the reference to 1977 is completely out of key. And that is symptomatic: it is as though this obituary wanted to stress the image of Cieslak orphaned by his own theatre, prefiguring what would happen to him later on.

Popular myth makes Cieslak out to be a victim. It suggests that in the sixties and seventies he was one of the greatest actors in the world, but that he blossomed and faded in *The Constant Prince*, and then repeated the same process in *Apocalypsis cum figuris*, though on a lesser scale, after which he was finished as an actor. According to this myth, he was destroyed by a double bind: he could only be capable as an actor with Grotowski, but he had to stop being an actor if he wanted to stay with Grotowski.

In fact, after *Apocalypsis*, Grotowski gave up directing. Cieslak followed him beyond the boundaries of performance theatre, and ventured into the territory that came later to be termed paratheatre. Nor was it a compromise: he transformed his presence as an actor into that of a stalker.

The myth says that he started talking about himself as an actor in the past tense, that when the windmills started to grind more strongly and the path to paratheatrical work seemed too exposed, perhaps even too repetitive, and when later still his professional isolation increased – when Grotowski distanced himself, some of his fellow actors died, and the company broke up – then Cieslak often began to consider a new performance, but that each time he did he would answer his own questions with another question: "Go on acting? But who with?"

It is curious that the *New York Times* obituary omitted to mention Cieslak's recent work with Brook and Carriere in *The Mahabharata*. However, that was just one episode, not the answer to the problem. The problem was still isolation.

THE ENCLAVE

Popular myth does not have the tools to comprehend the meaning of this impasse, so typical of theatre at the close of the twentieth century, where quite apart from the great theatrical systems (with their avant-gardes, their fringes, their bits and pieces from beyond the boundaries), real, true microsystems have also come into being.

These present critical opinion with some logistical problems: they are the size of a company or an ensemble, but they have all the features and the appearance of a tradition, of one of those styles or schools that we usually think of as self-contained systems, like ballet or dramatic theatre or opera or Kabuki. Popular myth can only assess these microsystems in terms of size, ignoring what they are, because it does not know how to evaluate the behavior of those actors who have problems moving through the marketplace once they are outside their own group.

Let's examine a few more assumptions. Twentieth-century theatre has assumed almost world-wide unity in terms of critical and commercial considerations, and at the same time has acquired the ability to split and reform itself here and there in cellular traditions. These subdivisions into types, cultures, traditions, styles, and schools, which were once great heathlands linked together by their own boundaries, now have boundaries within boundaries, and islands and fortified outposts. The vast territories are studded with countless enclaves, and nowadays, in most cases, it is the enclaves that are making history.

Although it may seem strange, that which determines a theatre culture or tradition has nothing to do with size or with age. It has to do with a certain wholeness in how it functions, with the fullness of a history, an awareness of difference, a heritage of practical knowledge. The first issue for a tradition or a culture is how to distinguish clearly between what is inside and what is outside. In cultures as in biology, the first step towards a living organism in the outer shape, the surround.

For Cieslak to take part in a production by Peter Brook was every bit as strange and difficult (and therefore every bit as significant) as it would have been for Henry Irving to take part in a ballet or for Nijinsky to have performed in Kabuki. There are such things as radical migrations, which are not impossible, nor against nature (the Centre founded by Brook in Paris creates theatre that starts from this sort of migration).

It would not be sensible to say that parcelling up cultures and traditions is a sign of impoverishment. Rather, this increases the expression of ideas and theatre practice by increasing the number of differences that generate meanings. This can result in a dispersion of ideas, or on the contrary in the growth of information and a recovery of the foreign dimension just when the whole world of theatre is intending to become a single place. In certain rare cases, work of great value can emerge that would formerly have been unthinkable for the theatre to accomplish.

THE TOUCHSTONE

Enclave theatre constantly tries to go beyond itself, for narrow boundaries lead outwards. In all this, the name of Ryszard Cieslak was synonymous with that of actor. His basic impulse was not to succeed, but to go beyond. It was *The Constant Prince* that made Cieslak Cieslak. Does that mean that he was a great actor in just one production?

The history of actors contains the names of many people who have disappeared, who achieved surprising results and did not know how to do it again or how to hold on to what they had done. Like fire in straw or will o' the wisps, actors can burn out quickly. But how can we measure continuity in the work of an actor like Cieslak?

When he performed *The Constant Prince*, he touched the heights, he was the first man to scale a theatrical Everest. But his progress as an actor cannot be sought in repeating similar undertakings, just as a great climber does not show his skill by going up and down eighteen thousand foot peaks: he leaves that to cable cars and ski lifts.

The way in which some great actors demonstrate their development is by moving from one show to another, from one role to another, occasionally touching the heights and sometimes shining light on ever changing characters. That was not Cieslak's way. For Cieslak, development in his work came from those acting skills that had both led to the creation of *The Constant Prince* and had enabled him to do it – work that could stand on its own, as a form of personal training, or be transformed into paratheatrical actions that were not fixed, or even serve to flesh out new characters.

At the start of this essay, I used the term "miracle actor." Yet what an inappropriate adjective that is! As though some invisible force had lifted Cieslak to those heights rather than his own meticulous preparation. The idea of a "miracle actor," whatever term one chooses, is linked to the notion of the one-off actor, and both these things belong to popular myth, not to serious views about theatre.

How many ways are there for an actor to show his or her professional skills? Can they only do so through performance? Even from the complex point of view of theatre culture, *The Constant Prince* was extraordinary. What the audience saw, what they talked about later and argued over, even the photographs of Cieslak in that production: all helped to transform current thinking about the possibilities of the actor's work. What it did was to change the way in which our culture conceives of the actor.

The humility of those photographs is symptomatic. For once, they were not pretentious, parasitical, or self-publicizing, but somehow part of the mystique of the whole production, which was played in different revised versions over the period from 1965 to 1969. It was certainly not an unrepeatable experience. Without so meaning, the photos of Cieslak in that performance acquired a different value from normal stage photos, and became historically significant – part of the memory system of the production, something on the edge of theatre. For "something had happened" and the photos testified to that happening, bearing witness rather than documenting. Because of *The Constant Prince*, what Grotowski had to say about actors became believable.

Today, nearly thirty years later, a long way away from anything like productions, Grotowski finds himself in a similar position, faced with the need for a similar kind of touchstone. If he does not have an audience, he must have people to bear witness, because only through the tangible actions of some of his co-workers can what he means by words like "ritual" and "performer" become "real things" – repositories of technical precision – for other people too.

Many members of the audience of *The Constant Prince* realized that they were seeing an actor able to do things no actor had done before. But what was there "to do"?

THE PERSONA

Following the established conventions of naming, we should say "Cieslak." But if we consider how the working process happened, we ought to say "Grotowski–Cieslak" instead. And if we think about the unadorned facts of how illusions are projected, we should do away with names altogether.

Thinking in the theatre still has trouble familiarizing itself with the simple reality through which two heads can form a single mind. The idea of such a "mind" seems illusory, metaphorical, something abstract. But it is illusory to separate the different heads of people who collaborate in a single creative process. If the process is "creative," that means that either by chance or by technique a structure of relationships has been set up that does not derive from a mechanical division of labor: a flow of events, passing through that structure with all the weight of its own causality, is subjected to a selective process that is by no means random.

Some of those "casual" components come into prominence or become fixed.[1] The true author in the process of creating relationships is the structure – the "in-between," linking the actions of the component parts.

When one talks about these things, it seems very abstract: in practice, it isn't at all, but part of the normal circumstances of those actors who work in a theatrical microsystem and who, because of the appropriately small dimensions of that world and its history, can easily see with the naked eye how the ecology of the creative process works.

Zbigniew Cynkutis, an actor with Grotowski from the start of the Theatre of 13 Rows, which then became Teatr Laboratorium, describes his experiences like this:

> Everything that we did that was any good was not even made by Grotowski, but was born between me and Grotowski, Grotowski and me; Cieslak and Grotowski, Grotowski and Cieslak. It was the strong, direct relationship between Grotowski and each actor that enabled that actor to express something – something that right from the start could not belong to the actor, but which in time became truly his.
>
> (Kumiega 1985:51)

A very different kind of actor, but someone who also has her roots in a fortified enclave, is Iben Nagel Rasmussen, who says something similar in a more animated way: "What you feel as a member of the audience doesn't come from the director, not even from the actor. It is the child speaking. [. . .] We need to discover silence if we want to understand what the child is saying" (Rasmussen 1979:49).

Is silence also about one's real self, the self that has a name? There is something slightly disturbing at the end of the quotation from Cynkutis, when he says "something that right from the start could not belong to the actor, but which in time came to be truly his." He goes on:

> That is why there is such a huge valley between Cynkutis the man, with a 42-year-old mind, when we take away everything that I got from the work with Grotowski – and Cynkutis after the work with Grotowski. Because so many things, thoughts, experiences, which to begin with were even strange to me and didn't belong, after long practice and investigation found their place in my bloodstream, in my respiratory system, in my muscles.
>
> (Kumiega 1985:51–52)

Here we have the optimistic idea of theatre work that becomes working on oneself, changing and improving oneself. But this idea also casts a shadow. There is a sense of becoming too attached to that which flows through oneself, the illusion of being a channel through which a (high-minded) message is transmitted. This illusion is reinforced by the audience, which projects onto the persona of the actor that image of him which they carry inside their heads.

In all probability, despite what legends say, no actor has ever seen his own personality dissolve because of the characters he plays. On the other hand, a great many actors have run the risk of believing that what they were able to do on stage revealed aspects of their inner being. And if we use Iben Nagel Rasmussen's terminology, in that case the "child" is straitjacketed and falls down the well.

THE SHADOW

Sometime in 1982, André Gregory, Grotowski's American friend, began to devise *Six Characters in Search of an Author*. One of the characters was to have been Cieslak.

Let's go back a bit. Let's go back to 1977, that erroneous date in the *New York Times* obituary. At that time there were still performances of *Apocalypsis cum Figuris*, which stayed in the repertoire in different versions for more than ten years, from 1969 to the last performances, which were probably the ones in Genoa in January 1980. At the same time, starting somewhere in 1974, paratheatrical events were starting to happen in the Teatr Laboratorium – *Vigil, The Tree of People*. . . . Cieslak facilitated *Acting Search*. These details, and what follows, were important to the genesis of *Six Characters*, and then developed, improbably, in the character of Dhritarastra.

After *Apocalypsis*, Grotowski ceased to be a director, but stayed on as leader. In 1981 Cieslak directed some of the actors from *Apocalypsis* and some new members of the group linked to paratheatrical activities. Together they produced *Thanatos Polski*, a non-performance with a precise division of texts, songs, and actions, but predetermined to include within it the actions of those members of the audience who accepted the invitation to step out of that role.

The context should not be forgotten. The dates we are discussing coincided with the cruel months and years of the Polish catastrophe. Here is a calendar of events:

On October 1978, Karol Wojtyla becomes Pope. In June 1979 he goes back to Poland. December is a month of protests and dissidents are arrested. On 20 May 1980, an unprecedented decree dismisses at one stroke 150 directors, senior civil servants from state enterprises, mayors, people responsible for waste and delays in production. In August the workers' protests explode and paralyse the shipyards on the Baltic coast. The steelworks of Nowa Huta in Krakow shut down. The Pope sends messages of solidarity to the workers. The government, through Tass, denounces "the activities of anti-socialist elements in Poland." This could have been the prelude to an invasion, as had happened in Hungary and Czechoslovakia.

On 5 September, Gierek, First Secretary of the Communist Party, has a stroke. His place is taken by Kania, deemed to be a liberal. Meanwhile the independent trade union movement, led by Walesa, begins calling itself Solidarnosc. The Warsaw Pact countries begin to isolate Poland and start closing their frontiers. With great difficulty (because it does not recognize the guiding role of the Communist Party) the statutes of Solidarnosc are officially registered in November 1980. On 16 December, in Gdansk, 600,000 people along with the highest political and religious authorities unveil the monument to the victims of anti-working-class oppression in 1970.

On 14 January 1980, Walesa goes to the Vatican. On 4 March, General Jaruzelski, who had become Prime Minister in February, goes to Moscow. Thirteen days later the Warsaw Pact troops start exercises in Poland, which go on longer than anyone anticipated. Many people think this is the gradual start of an occupation, and talk fairly openly about armed resistance and guerrilla warfare in the mountains. The Warsaw Pact troop exercises end on 7 April. On 10 April, Jaruzelski and the Diet ban all forms of strike action for a two-month period. On 1 May flour and rice are rationed along with sugar and meat. The pro-Soviet wing of the Communist Party are anti-Kania. On 18 October, Jaruzelski also takes on the duties of First Secretary. He sends special army units to different parts of the country. He pulls them out on 22 November, after discussions in Warsaw with Cardinal Glemp and Walesa. But on 12 December, at five in the morning, Jaruzelski proclaims martial law.

Walesa is arrested. Many supporters of Solidarnosc end up in prison. Trade union activity is banned and constitutional rights are suspended. Workers in social services are called up. Some 800 civil servants are fired. Riots break out all over the country. On 3 January 1982 the zloty is devalued by 100 per cent against the dollar. In May and June there are clashes in Warsaw and Wroclaw, and many are arrested or wounded.

The atmosphere in Poland is polluted and charged with mixed emotions: for rebellion, heroism, compromise with dictatorship, betrayal can all coexist in a single person. The dictatorship tries to compromise significant people in its favor. Solidarnosc quietly blacklists anyone who has had any dealings with the dictatorship. Walesa is freed in November. On 30 December, martial law is suspended (it will be revoked definitively in July 1983).

On 19 May 1983, 200,000 people in Warsaw attend the funeral of young Grzegorz Przemyk, who had been beaten to death by the police. The Pope visits Poland again, and in October the Catholic Church again clashes with the government. On 17 November, the authorities issue a list of the names of sixteen "extremist" priests. Meanwhile, Walesa receives the Nobel Peace Prize and the Polish government makes a verbal protest to the Swedish authorities.

In October 1984 a priest, Jerzy Popiluszko, is kidnapped and murdered by a volunteer group linked to the police force. His funeral provokes an enormous demonstration of popular outrage. In January 1984, price increases of staple foods range from 10 to 45 per cent. There is a further increase, of 20 to 70 per cent, in March 1985. Electricity, gas, and coal all go up. . . .

Thanatos Polski toured Poland, then went on to Italy and Sicily from March to May 1981. It contained clear allusions of the dangers of an invasion and internal oppression: a bloodstained garment was torn to pieces.

During the crisis months, when there was a threat of invasion, Grotowski traveled extensively in Poland, a sort of traveling writer cum traveling salesman, anonymous, alone, and active. He slept in trains and on floors. He talked to people. Professionally, he focused his energies on the longstanding Theatre of Sources, for which he was directing an international youth group. In September 1981, Antoni Jaholkowski, a friend from the old days, died.

THE COURAGE

In the early months of 1982, Grotowski left Poland definitively and went into exile abroad, taking pains to ensure that his co-workers would be all right. But soon Teatr Laboratorium ceased to exist: to avoid surviving as an empty institution lending its good name to the dictatorship, the group officially dissolved itself in the summer of 1984. This was first announced in Italy by *Il Manifesto*, then, after several months' delay, in the Polish press and elsewhere.

Cieslak worked in theatres around the world. His destiny began to resemble that of many solitary actors who had left important groups, who do a one-man show or seem to vanish altogether. He directed some productions that came out of intensive laboratory work: *Aleph*, in 1983, with the Centro per la Sperimentazione e Ricerca Teatrale in Pontedera, in Italy; *Vargtid* in the same year, with the Kimbri Ensemble at Aarhus, in Denmark; N*oche Obscura*, in 1984, with the Tema group in Albacete in Spain; *Peer Gynt* in 1986, again with the Kimbri Ensemble; Dostoevski's *Mon pauvre Fedia*, with the Labyrinth group in Paris, in 1987; and *Ash Wednesday*, in 1989, from Gorky's *The Lower Depths*, at New York University.

Some of these productions, particularly *Peer Gynt* and *Ash Wednesday*, were greatly admired, but the different languages and the different places in which he worked reveal the range of situations that filled Cieslak's solitude. Some of the young people who worked with him say that he was able to transmit the "meaning" of making theatre. Others explain that Ryszard was not only capable of teaching them technique, but could teach them about courage.

There is no point in hiding it: during this period, Cieslak was drinking even more than usual. Periodically he had to dry out. He smoked several packets of cigarettes a day. Yet they still say he taught them about courage. He was not so much an actor with great talent as an actor with great courage. Jan Kott, writing about what he calls "Grotowski's method," says: "Cieslak was a young man without experience when he surrendered himself to Grotowski's Method. He became one of the greatest actors in the world." And he goes on to add: "Peter Brook told me that after Stanislavsky, no one knew as much about acting as Cieslak and Grotowski" (Ch. 13:135). Yet when that young, inexperienced actor threw himself into the enterprise, surrendering to Grotowski's Method meant giving everything, holding nothing back, following another young man down a road where nothing was certain.

Eugenio Barba, who was there when Grotowski started to develop his own theatre, complains when he hears people talk about him starting with a company of highly qualified actors. The only actors who went to work

at Opole with Grotowski were those who were considered third-raters –
actors who stood next to no chance in the big theatres, and for whom it
was thus convenient to appear in a strange little provincial theatre. Unless
I am mistaken, Cieslak came from acting school, but he had a puppet
maker's diploma in his pocket, because he had been assessed as
physically inadequate to be a good actor.

Cieslak's courage did not only show itself when he went into an
undertaking without any guarantees. There was also the courage required
to break with his own self-image. Eugenio Barba hinted at that, when he
wrote in 1975:

> When I left Grotowski's theatre, Ryszard Cieslak was already a good
> actor, but he wanted to be an intellectual. It was as though a great brain
> were getting tangled up with that body that was so full of life, and
> flattening it out somehow, reducing that life to two dimensions. I saw him
> again two years later, when he came to Oslow with *The Constant Prince*.
> Right from the start, it was as though everything I remembered, everything
> I had based my ideas on, was disappearing beneath my feet. I saw another
> being, I saw a man who had discovered his own completeness, his own
> destiny, his own vulnerability.

And he adds:

> It was as though that brain which had been a sort of filter that clouded his
> actions had released itself and impregnated his whole body with phosphor-
> escent cells. He had the strength of a clear-thinking hurricane. "I cannot
> go on." Yet it was as though another greater, higher, greener wave were
> rising out of his body and breaking around him.

(Barba 1978:253)

THE ODYSSEY

If we move on to 1982, when the group actually broke up, Poland seemed
like a huge trap. Cieslak was on his own, and Andre Gregory, the
American friend, was considering *Six Characters*. It was only an idea,
and it never actually happened, but it is worthy of record, because in it
there is the sense of a theatrical Odyssey.[2]

Gregory was thinking about using actors who had been "abandoned"
by directors, such as the actors from his own Manhattan Project,
Chaikin's actors, some of the Living Theater actors – and above all the
Teatr Laboratorium actors. Those were the actors who would have played
Pirandello's characters. They would have come to a theatre in search of
an author, and would have found other actors already there. Gregory
thought that this second group, the actors in the play, could be made up

of good Off-Broadway performers. Cieslak was to have been one of the characters, and maybe Flaszen would have played the Father.

It was a simple idea that translated Pirandello quite literally. What had happened was that the end of the twentieth century had produced flesh-and-blood counterparts of those characters Pirandello had imagined in his head. Some actors, exiles from the enclaves, from the fortified outposts, sharing a history known to very few people, could actually appear in the foyer of a theatre, on the boundary line between the stage and the laboratory, looking for an author who could give some public meaning to the skills they carried with them. Each one could present some of the raw material of their own stage life, the basic matter (*mater*, mother) of possible stories – that which is commonly termed "individual training."

The basic situation that Pirandello devised could be staged by each of the actors bringing their own particular theatre culture and trying to convey its basic elements to other actors who were trained to be both more neutral and more flexible. The former were stronger and yet more fragile – they were migrants, truly in search of an author because in their outposts directors really were "authors" in the way Pirandello meant: they wove stories together, combining meaningful threads, and were able to distill a general sense of the vicissitudes of personal histories. The second group were weaker, and yet more resistant: they were actors who could be interchangeable on the ground.

It was a good, straightforward project: but it never happened, because the characters had to be certain particular people, and they had to be brought together despite the thousand and one other commitments they had in order to survive. Cieslak was not one of the wandering characters in Pirandello's mold, yet, despite that, he managed to do something that Pirandello's characters could not do: he brought his own stage life to an author and let him adapt it to his drama. That is exactly what he did. In July 1985, Cieslak reappeared in Avignon, as Dhritarastra in Brook and Carriere's *Mahabharata*. He was the blind king, who has lost his way, the father of the warring sons.

THE BLIND KING

At the start of the production, there was the suspicion that Brook had used him only for his face, as they do in the cinema. His was a magnificent, devastated face, with great hollow eyes the color of air, filled with soul and lost, like a Tiresias suddenly deprived even of his inner vision. But as the performance went on, Cieslak the actor, not the star, revealed the intelligence of his profession. This king has been blind from birth: he is an old man, yet he behaves as though he has only just lost his sight, living each moment like the first. Cieslak showed us a father who was doubly blind. He was not so much playing a blind man as the way in which a blind man experiences his own blindness. He seemed to be leaning over a dark, empty lake within himself, from which voices kept coming that would vanish straight away and become confused.

Some members of the audience felt sadness. They said that in that character they could not find a single trace of the theatrical marvels of *The Constant Prince* or *Apocalypsis*. They said Cieslak was a shadow of his former self. But others were struck by him, enraptured by the intimate inner life of that secondary character.

Yet others said that, following tradition, Cieslak's should have been listed as a "guest appearance." It is true that Cieslak resembled one of those great actors who make fleeting appearances playing character parts in productions. He was not old at all. But it was as though he had laid aside all his charisma, that precious manifestation of Narcissus' flower.

A few members of the audience who watched him closely even at those times when he was a long way away from the main action, at the back of the stage, noted with astonishment that as he played the role of Dhritarastra, Cieslak was going back to his old training, repeating the sequences in a small way, so that what had once been acrobatics and "dance" now becomes realism. The dimensions had changed, but the form the action took was still the same: it was training given to an author to use, it was high-quality work. And so Cieslak was not the shadow of himself, he was playing the shadow. He was an actor in search of an author.

THE RISK

You can see Cieslak's training program in black and white in a film made in 1972, *Training in the Wroclaw Laboratory Theatre*.[3] It consists of exercises by Rena Mirecka and Ryszard Cieslak supervised by Grotowski. You can follow a physical exercise into an organic flow that is thought. You can see how posture generates an image which in turn creates an idea, a line of thought, a situation, a fragment of a possible story.

People who still use the inadequate expression "theatre of the body" ought to sit down and watch this film, until they realize that what is going on is the exact opposite: this is "theatre of the mind" – mental processes made visible and tangible. Sometimes, like fish in a river, "content" rises to the surface, but what we are seeing is the rhythm of thought. That which is "body" and protection in everyday life, in the extraordinary life of Cieslak's training, become thoughts from the heart, courage. "When the performance is over," wrote Richard Schechner, "Cieslak 'cools down.' Often he drinks vodka, talks, smokes a lot of cigarettes. Getting out of the role is sometimes harder than getting into it" (Schechner 1983:97).

While Cieslak recorded *The Mahabharata* and his Dhritarastra for film and television, a new generation of young people was, with Grotowski, exploring pathways around the ones that Cieslak and his companions had opened up. That work did not lead to a performance. But the rare few who were allowed to take part and watch him could see exactly what Schechner felt was missing when he said, immediately after the passage quoted above, that Cieslak knew how "to prepare and be ready to flow with his role" but that he "hardly has an inkling of what to do afterwards." What they saw was a gradual passage, through a series of slight shifts of coloration, from the compressed time of the "ritual" to everyday time – a seamless grafting of extraordinary behavior onto everyday behavior and vice versa.

If dropping to your knees time and time again, day after day, risks damaging the meniscus, does repeatedly lurching from the compressed time of performance to the everyday time afterwards – the time of cigarettes and booze – risk bruising or straining something intimate and personal? We may not know anything for certain, but I do feel we should ask that question.

THE RED MARK

There is a film of *The Constant Prince*, too, in black and white, shot with an unseen camera, reconstructed with care and intelligence.[4] But the final touch of perfection is a red mark in just the right place, introduced between the black and the white like the final banner in the first print of Potemkin.

Let's look again at Cieslak in *The Constant Prince*. It is one of the fundamental performances of this century. Countless lives, in theatre and outside it, have changed direction after encountering that production. If the film is shown to a large audience of people, we cannot escape a slight sense of uneasiness, as though something rather improper were taking place. Cieslak's outer self, his "body," looks transparent. His actions are extreme, but controlled like a musical score. His agonies, torture, despair, and death are as precise as a dance. Grotowski's staging gave the audience the experience of watching something secret and forbidden. In the film, that intended embarrassment of watching is lost, hence the situation can even appear to be slightly awkward.

But let's watch Cieslak. Stefan Brecht was right when he suggested that Cieslak's movements, facial expressions, and tones did "not express thoughts or external sensations but only emotional and volitional states of the spirit," and that he expressed these states naturally, "as though the body were just the organ of spirit throughout" (Ch. 12:125). Perhaps this is another aspect of the courage that is part of such artistry: he could stand on the edge of a situation in which, for technical and professional reasons, he could risk seeing that the "I," the hole in the doughnut, was consistently a void.

Listen to Cieslak telling Schechner what was going on:

> The score is like a glass inside which a candle is burning. The glass is solid; it is there, you can depend on it. It contains and guides the flame. But it is not the flame. The flame is my inner process each night. The flame is what illuminates the score, what the spectators see through the score. The flame is alive. Just as the flame in the glass moves, flutters, rises, falls, almost goes out, suddenly glows brightly, responds to each breath of wind – so my inner life varies from night to night, from moment to moment. . . . I begin each night without anticipations: this is the hardest thing to learn. I do not prepare myself to feel anything. I do not say, "Last night this scene was extraordinary, I will try to do that again." I want only to be receptive to what will happen. And I am ready to take what happens if I am secure in my score, knowing that even if I feel a minimum, the glass will not break, the objective structure worked out over the months will help me through. But when a night comes that I can glow, shine, live, reveal – I am ready for it by not anticipating it. The score remains the same, but everything is different because I am different.
>
> (Schechner 1973:295)

Who is the author and who is the performer? These are not the kinds of work that can be signed by a single name. Grotowski and Cieslak can be seen as collaborators only by understanding their names as a unit. In reality, there is no such thing as collaboration between parts: there is interaction, a process of becoming, a profound and well-thought-out shape, a channel that is necessary and yet insignificant in its own right. And within that, something that flows.

The outer shape belongs neither to Grotowski nor to Cieslak. The flow is not Cieslak or Grotowski. For the member of the audience, and for the camera, the Prince exists, he is a definable character because he is defined and his name is fixed. But once again, let us remember that behind that paper fixity there is no torture and no death.

Grotowski has said on various occasions that none of the work he did with Cieslak on *The Constant Prince* began with the text. From details of lived experience, a score with physical actions and sounds was shaped that they tried to make objective, and which was related to memories of adolescence, none of which were painful. The actions that comprised

Cieslak's score came one after another out of his past, out of his first experience of love, in that age when the erotic is a no man's land between sexuality and prayer, where biological impulses are confused with spiritual urges. It was a meticulous labor of physical recollection and patient reconstruction.

When the score was shaped, when it had a clear, stable form – and therefore an objective form – references to the character of the Constant Prince were very carefully inserted within it. The words of the text were placed into the vocal score. And all those signs which the audience recognized as hope, bitterness, despair, torment, ice in the soul, pain, and death were interwoven through the physical score. The context was established: the relationship between the Prince and the other characters – that is, the plot, that which gives shape to the dramatic meaning – all of this was the careful crafting of an illusion. But it was not unimportant. It was also a glass container, something that the audience could rely on through the performance.

Let's come back to Cieslak. We can imagine him acting, knowing coldly and perfectly the details of the cruel story in which he was taking part. And yet he was lit by memories of past love. That is the ubiquity of the actor. It is neither utopian nor dystopian. It is a-topian. And perhaps that is why Grotowski, as a professional observer of actors and also as an observer of the audience, but one who knew all the intricacies of the illusion-weaving process, seemed to some people to be wearing a devious smile (see ch. 12).

Does all this seem like philosophizing? Well, if so, it's the sort of philosophizing that making theatre carries within itself.

What about the red mark we mentioned earlier? It was a red cloak, used in different ways through the performance – as a whip, a shroud, a blanket, a wrap. . . . Even the actual performance gave the impression of being in black and white. In the charcoal sketches of the key scenes of the reconstruction of *The Constant Prince* in the first volume of *Les Voies de la creation theatrale*, black and white were significantly interrupted by the red mark of the cloak, like an emblem of the fundamental color of the performance. It would be wonderful if a similar effect could be produced on film.

At the end, when the Prince was dead and the actor could relax, his body was covered by that same red cloak.

Translated by Susan Bassnett.

PART 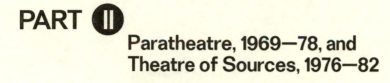 II

Paratheatre, 1969—78, and
Theatre of Sources, 1976—82

22

INTRODUCTION TO PART II

Paratheatre, 1969—78, and Theatre of Sources, 1976—82

Richard Schechner

The Paratheatre and Theatre of Sources phases of Grotowski's work overlap. They indicate two different but related efforts, Paratheatre being the logical extension of the Theatre of Productions and Theatre of Sources pointing to Objective Drama and Art as vehicle. Paratheatre emerged almost seamlessly from *Apocalypsis cum figuris*. That production had a hard time emerging as a public performance because its underlying action tended toward self-examination and the kind of "meeting" characterizing the Paratheatrical work. *Apocalypsis* was a production theatre piece desiring to be a paratheatrical work. It went through many months of workshop and a continuous metamorphosis from *The Gospels* based on the New Testament, to a work incorporating the Grand Inquisitor section of Dostoevsky's *The Brothers Karamazov* and on to what it finally became. During some performances of *Apocalypsis*, Grotowski selected a few members of the audience to stay behind – to engage in direct "meetings" with the members of the Laboratory Theatre. These meetings – direct interactions between members of the Laboratory Theatre and former spectators, now participants – were the kernel of what was to become Paratheatre.

Shortly after the end of the Laboratory's 1969 American tour, Grotowski took his second trip to India, returning to Poland in February 1970. Upon returning to Wroclaw, Grotowski mapped his road from theatre to his next destination. "We live in a post-theatrical epoch. What follows is not a new wave of theatre but rather something that will replace it. [. . .] I feel that *Apocalypsis cum figuris* is a new stage for me in my research. We have crossed a certain barrier" (Osinski 1986:120). Throughout 1970, Grotowski was extremely restless. In the summer he made his third trip to India and Kurdistan. "When he later met the Theatre Laboratory company at Shiraz [Iran] airport, even his closest associates did not recognize him – so much had he changed in that short time: he looked quite a different person from the one whom they had

Plate 22.1 Grotowski and Peter Brook in the 1970s. (Photo: Tony D'Urso.)

known under that name before" (Burzynski and Osinski 1979:95).
Grotowski was skinny, almost gaunt, with a scraggly beard: a persona
somewhere between Hippy and Guru. His dark suit and sunglasses were
gone. Instead, he was dressed in an American style, with blue jean jacket
and shoulder bag, his eyes glistening through clear lenses. His excursion
and transformation was in a manner reminiscent of G.I. Gurdjieff's
classic treks through interior central Asia. Grotowski aimed "his
wanderings far from the crowded centers of cultural life. It was, quite
literally, a ramble through the continents involving direct meetings with
people and places. Also, in a different sense, it was a journey away from

Plate 22.2 Grotowski and Eugenio Barba, Wroclaw, 1975. (Photo: Tony D'Urso.)

the theatre to the roots of culture; to essential communication and perception" (Kolankiewicz 1979:1).

In "Holiday" (Ch.23), a text collaged and adapted largely from his New York lectures in December 1970, Grotowski speaks of parallels between his own time and the epoch of Jesus when "some men walked in the wilderness and searched for truth." He goes on to say that if one is looking for truth then there are certain "things one cannot do with a clear conscience: for instance, mount a rostrum and pretend, perform a tragedy or a comedy in order to be applauded." The move away from theatre appeared definitive.

Out of theatre, but to where? The most comprehensive account of this phase of Grotowski's work – combining first-hand accounts with an historical overview – is a booklet assembled by Leszek Kolankiewicz, "Excerpts from *On the Road to Active Culture*," issued for a 1978 symposium held in Poland on Grotowski's work:

> Around 1969–70 Grotowski and his company overstepped the boundaries of theatre, in both meanings. [. . .] In 1970 Grotowski spoke about the death of certain words such as theatre, performance, spectator, and actor. He was talking about himself. In the period of a strikingly low phase in the life of world theatre, he spoke of a perspective he had envisaged for himself.
>
> (1978:4–5)

> [Quoting Tadeusz Burzynski] Grotowski is interested exclusively in creativity, he rejects at the outset any imitation, resists the temptation to duplicate himself. He is motivated by the passion of an explorer to such an extent that he treads only virgin tracks. [. . .] And the goal of these explorations is [. . .] the search for and try-out in practice of the conditions in which a man acting in unison with others could act sincerely and with his whole self, thus liberating the potential of his personality and realizing his creative needs; the searching for and practical exploration of what we would call the paratheatrical fact, and which would be another, hitherto unknown, form of art beyond the traditional division of onlooker and active person, man and his product, creator and recipient.
>
> (1978:6–7)

> [Quoting Leszek Kolodziejczyk] A para-theatrical experiment. What does it consist of? It consists of a common isolation by a group of people in a place far removed from the outside world, and an attempt to build a kind of genuine meeting among human beings. [. . .] This is not a performance, however, because it does not contain in it the elements of theatre such as plot or action. There is nothing to see for the audience either, because there is no audience. It is, on the other hand, a cycle of meetings between people who do not know one another at first, but gradually upon getting accustomed to one another, rid themselves of mutual fears and distrust; this, in the course of time, causes them to release in themselves the simplest, most elementary inter-human expression.
>
> (1978:8)

> As a theatre artist Grotowski was interested in the problem of contact: on the one hand between the director and the actor, on the other, between the actor and the spectator. [. . .] Transcending theatre was the next step on the road. It meant a break with meditation through playing a role [. . .] and with the one-sidedness of contact, caused by the duality of the actor and spectator.
>
> (1978:97–98)

For the paratheatrical work, the eleven more established members of the Laboratory were joined by younger people including (among the core group of seven), Wlodzimierz Staniewski – later to found the Gardzienice Theatre Association – and Jacek Zymslowski, deviser of *Vigil*. Paratheatre took place in Wroclaw and nearby forests; in the United States, France, Italy, and Australia. Grotowski describes the underlying theme of Paratheatre in "Holiday." The intense and intimate "work on the self" that characterized poor theatre, work seen in the passionate and transparent performances of Cynkutis, Molik, Mirecka, Cieslak, and the others, now had a new impetus: to dissolve the masks of imposture most people wear as their ordinary social selves and, in a spiritually vulnerable mode, to communicate directly face-to-face. Buber's *ich und du* informs and maybe guides the paratheatrical work. But there are other influences as well. Paratheatre often took place in pastoral settings – forests, meadows, hilltops – a quasi-Arcadian or Rousseauian world asserting the purity of "nature" as opposed to the "falseness" of "society," including the theatre of roles and pretended emotions. Paratheatre welcomed any and all of good will who could act on their desire to become "open." Given Grotowski's iron intellect, this sentimental program was not destined to endure long.

But while the experiment lasted, it was extraordinary. At a certain point in the work, around 1974, Grotowski stopped being the only leader. Members of the Laboratory set out on their own journeys. Zygmunt Molik and Antoni Jaholkowsi worked on "Acting Therapy" whereby performers could rid themselves of various blockages. Ludwik Flaszen led "Meditations Aloud," an attempt to get rid of the static of daily life and listen instead to the quieter, intimate inner voices, or even silence. Stanislaw Scierski led "Workshop Meetings," starting with actor training but going beyond in the direction of more unstructured meetings between individuals. Zbigniew Spychalski devised "Song of Myself," mostly working with non-Poles in Poland[1]. Zbigniew Cynkutis and Rena Mirecka remained closest to theatre with their "Event" project. But the program that drew the most attention was "Special Project," led by Ryszard Cieslak collaborating with eight others.[2] "Special Project" had two phases. The first and longest was the work of a few persons to "find [in themselves. . .] milestones-situations releasing activity, a simple act of life; and to join these situations in a kind of cycle" which a larger group did (dare I say "performed"?) in the second phase.

> Special Project enables man to tear himself from cliches. [. . .]It gives man a chance to find himself in the ever opening, embracing, variable world; it is as if every glance were here the first and the last, both at the same time. It is a call: we see, as in a mirror, darkly; let us see face to face.
>
> (Kolankiewicz 1978:23)

Margaret Croyden's *In the Shadow of the Flame* (1993) offers a strong, personal account of the Special Project.

Steadily in the early 1970s, Paratheatre developed – first involving a few dozen persons, then hundreds, then thousands. The work culminated in June–July 1974 in Wroclaw with the "University of Research" of the Theatre of Nations in which over 4500 people participated. In a way, it was a climax of the "'60s feeling," arriving tardily to Poland. Attending the gathering in Wroclaw were not only a multitude of ordinary persons, but an honor role of theatre including Eugenio Barba, Peter Brook, Jean-Louis Barrault, Joseph Chaikin, André Gregory, and Luca Ronconi. These luminaries offered lectures, workshops, "experiences." For that month, at least, they were all Grotowski-ites, all engaged in paratheatre. Gregory, in an interview, summed up the activities and aspirations of that period:

> What has been done in Wroclaw has the dimension of Woodstock – but I hope *this* will not perish. [. . .] It seems to me that this is a kind of revolution – not political, but creative. A kind of revolution because it says "yes" to life and "no" to death.
>
> (in Kolankiewicz 1978:45)

What is astonishing is that Grotowski's work, which in the 1960s seemed so esoteric and hermetic, offered in small rooms before tiny audiences, became during Paratheatre wide-open events attracting multitudes not to witness but to participate. The rigorous physical and psychophysical labor of the Theatre of Productions gave way to easy inclusivity. The *Uls* or "beehives" were

> Open for everyone who declared the willingness to actively participate, without any additional criteria for selection. They took place every evening and night on the premises of the Laboratory. They were programmed in turn by members of Grotowski's company and also by other participants of the University [of Research]. [. . .] In all, 21 "Beehives" took place, attended by 1842 people.
>
> (Kolankiewicz 1978:46)

During the late 1970s, Paratheatre continued to develop new aspects, even as Theatre of Sources was preparing to replace it. Some of the later paratheatrical events, *Vigil* (1976-77), *The Mountain of Flame* (1977), and *Tree of People* (1979), already took on a different tack. These were participatory events, but their focus began to shift from "meetings" and face-to-face encounters to attempting to uncover what was abiding, archetypal, old: the "sources" of performativity. Movements affined to Sufi dancing began to appear; song and chanting augmented the movements. In 1975, Tadeusz Buski not only described

Paratheatre but foresaw Theatre of Sources and even the work beyond it:

> How to become oneself, having rejected games and everyday pretence? How to go beyond the routine of professionalism? How is it possible to be spontaneous between the routine of professionalism and the temptation of chaos? What are man's capacities in action, when confronted face to face with another man? What is creative in man in the face of the living presence of others, in a mutual communion? How is it possible – while respecting differences between people – to achieve human understanding above the differences of race, culture, tradition, upbringing, language? In what conditions is it possible to achieve interhuman fullness? Is it possible to create a form of art other than those hitherto known – outside the division into the one who watches and the one who acts, man and his product, the recipient and the creator?
>
> (in Burzynski and Osinski 1979:109)

Work on oneself led from theatre to Paratheatre; searching for what is transcultural and essential led from Paratheatre to Theatre of Sources; distilling those sources into patterned behavior led to Objective Drama and Art as vehicle.

While members of the Laboratory continued in the last phases of Paratheatre, Grotowski himself was working on Theatre of Sources.

> Over a period of three years, from 1977 to 1980, Grotowski worked with a multi-national group of 36 people representing such diverse cultures as India, Colombia, Bangladesh, Haiti, Africa [sic], Japan, Poland, France, Germany, and the United States. While members of this primary group at various times spent a number of months at a field base near Wroclaw, there were also expeditions to study specific source techniques in the voodoo culture of Haiti, in the Yoruba area of Africa [Nigeria], among the Huichol Indians of Mexico, and with yogis in India.
>
> (Findlay in Osinski 1986:171)

Possibly Grotowski was reinforced in moving in this direction by his reading of and meeting with Carlos Castaneda. Certainly, there was a growing interest among inhabitants of the "new age" in the wisdom of "native peoples." This must have resonated with Grotowski's long-standing research into various ritual, shamanic, Sufic, and yogic practices.

At a June 1978 symposium on the "Art of the Beginner" organized in Warsaw by the Polish center of the International Theatre Institute (ITI), Grotowski, after listing many things the Theatre of Sources was not, read a description of what he intended it to be:[3]

The participants in the Theatre of Sources would be people from various continents, with different backgrounds of cultures and traditions. The Theatre of Sources will deal with the phenomenon of source techniques, archaic or nascent, that bring us back to the sources of life, to direct, so we say, primeval perception, to organic primary experience of life. Existence-presence. The theme will be original, i.e. primary dramatic phenomenon seen in terms of human experience. The Theatre of Sources is destined to cover the period between 1978 and 1980, with intensive activities during the three summers and a final production in 1980." In fact, it is not only in summer, but all year round and it is not the final production, but it is a kind of final opening, after a complete closing, en-closing, that is to say two years. I will go and close myself up with very few people. After two years, in 1980, there will be a period of opening which will include a greater number of people. [. . .] *The most important thing, I think, is the meeting between the old one and the young one.* When I say "the old," I mean this in the two senses: the representatives of an old tradition, of a source technique of an old tradition, and in the sense also of age, because most often, it is the old ones who make us understand how old age can be the fulfilment of the being. Does it mean only the "old people" from outside Europe? No. Happily, in Europe, there are also quite a few "beautiful old people." The "young" also from two points of view, a representative of the modern civilization which to tell the truth is quite young. [. . .] So *the young and the old* in the two senses – metaphoric and literal. [. . .] After having been in the period of performance theatre, we were in the period of para-theatre which ended in 1978, and now we enter into another stage.

(Grotowski 1978:9–11)

During Theatre of Sources, Grotowski began what was to be a very fruitful and long collaboration with Maud Robart, one of the leaders in the community of San Soleil, the Haitian group Ron Grimes discusses in Chapter 28. The Haitian ritual songs are an element of work that has remained important to Grotowski to the present day.

Theatre of Sources never became all Grotowski intended. Martial Law was imposed on Poland in 1981. Grotowski has not returned to Poland since, except for brief visits, even after the collapse of Communism in 1989. The work in Theatre of Sources with master teachers from different cultures became the basis for Objective Drama which led, in turn, to Art as vehicle. One thing can be said definitively. Once Grotowski left the Theatre of Productions, he never returned. No guest directing, no formation of a second Theatre Laboratory.

23

HOLIDAY [*SWIETO*]

The day that is holy

Jerzy Grotowski

These fragments are from Grotowski's texts from 1972, based in part on a shorthand record of his conferences at Town Hall, New York City, 12 December 1970 and New York University, 13 December 1970. Brief passages were also taken from Grotowski's statement at the Polish/ French seminar in Royaumont, France, on 11 October 1972, and from his lecture in Wroclaw on 23 October 1971. The order of the paragraphs was dictated by the order of questions received from the audience.

Holiday: *the Polish word* swieto, *in the ancient sense utilized by Grotowski, does not have a precise English equivalent. It has no connotation whatsoever of vacation or of a day free from work, but is directly related to the word "sacrum," or "holy." In its sound, it is very similar to the Polish word* swiatlo, *which means "light," but there is no direct etymological relationship.* Swieto *is not necessarily related to any particular religion, and even if it has strongly sacral connotations, it is also used in a secular sense. In any case, it indicates something special, exceptional, extra-quotidian.*

Some words are dead, even though we are still using them. Among such words are: show, spectacle, theatre, audience, etc. But what is alive? Adventure and meeting: not just anyone; but that what we want to happen to us would happen, and then, that it would also happen to others among us. For this, what do we need? First of all, a place and *our own kind*; and then that *our kind*, whom we do not know, should come, too. So, what matters is that, in this, first I should not be alone, then – we should not be alone. But what does *our kind* mean? They are those who breathe "the same air" and – one might say – share our senses. What is possible together? Holiday.

•

The first question that has been asked here is an actor's question. The questioner has said that what prevents him from really disarming himself is the reason why one engages in acting. He also has said that it is the need for approval from others that contributes to the fact that the actor remains armed. Yes, indeed, I believe that the motives which have led us to engage in theatre are not pure. Some want to pursue theatre as a commercial enterprise, others want to be acclaimed by the public or gain a certain status, or receive gifts from high society. Somehow we know that not only is there something dishonest about this, but also barren. A man [*czlowiek*] who gives his bodily presence in return for material gain – in one sense or another – by this very fact puts himself in a false position; today even more so than in the past when it was a profession clear in its ambiguity, approaching that of a buffoon. For that matter, the life around seemed simpler, too, more stabilized; atrocities were being committed then as ever, but they seemed far away. Everyone could build up in himself a feeling that he occupied a lasting position in the world. The world also took itself as more or less permanent – fallacious though this was – and thought that there existed more or less permanent rules of the game, more or less permanent beliefs. But time is different, even if we look at a certain singular phenomenon which occurred two thousand years ago in the peripheries of the huge empire encompassing the entire Western world, as it then was: some men walked in the wilderness and searched for truth. They searched in accord with the character of those times, which, unlike that of ours, was religious. But if there is a similarity between that time and ours, it consists in the need to find a meaning. If one does not possess that meaning, one lives in constant fear. One thinks that the fear is caused by external events, and no doubt it is they that release it, but that something we cannot cope with flows from ourselves, it is our own weakness and the weakness is the lack of meaning. This is why there is a direct connection between courage and meaning. The men who walked the vicinity of Nazareth two thousand years ago – they were rather young, which has been forgotten, and they are traditionally represented as old from the start – talked about strange things and sometimes behaved imprudently, but in the air there was a need to abandon force, to abandon the prevailing values and search for other values on which one could build life without a lie. If I have presumed to refer to that moment, it is to stress that – with all the differences – what is happening in our century is not happening for the first time and that we are not the first who are in the quest. And if one is in the quest, there are things one cannot do with a clear conscience: for instance, mount a rostrum and pretend, perform a tragedy or a comedy in order to be applauded, day after day fervently to exert oneself in order not to lose one's employ, push oneself into the limelight, hold tight to someone who is going to launch us . . . If we feel this to be futile, this is already not bad, because the situation becomes less false. But a thousand chances of escape are lying in wait for us; escape from life, in effect. For instance, if instead of occupying oneself with politics, one makes politics in the theatre, then this is obvious escape; if instead of revealing oneself as one is, to the end – one makes use of nudity and sex as a decorative element, or almost as in pornography, then this is worse than escape. One could multiply these examples. One could invent a new philosophy, call up new names, proclaim new methods, practice some kind of exercises and some sort of macrobiotic diet, i.e., always find something new for oneself, in appearance.

•

In the fear which is connected with the lack of meaning, we give up living and begin diligently to die. Routine takes the place of life, and the senses – resigned – get accustomed to nullity. Every now and then we rebel, but this is only for the sake of appearances. We make a big row, create a scandal – not too violent, as a rule, so that it will not threaten our position, something sufficiently banal that it could be accepted by others with sympathy. For instance, we drink ourselves unconscious. This shell, this sheath under which we fossilize, becomes our very existence – we set and become hardened, and we begin to hate everyone in whom a little spark of life is still flickering. It envelops all our tissues and the fear of someone's touch, or of exposing oneself, is ever greater. Shame of naked skin, of naked life, of ourselves, and at the same time, often, complete shamelessness when it comes to putting it all on the market, selling it all. We do not love ourselves, our own selves anymore; hating others we try to cure that lack of love.

With great agility, through hiding our gloom, we busy ourselves about our own funeral. How many functions are needed here, what effort, what ritual. And what is this death? The dressing, covering, possessing, escaping, canonizing of one's burden. And what remains, what lives? The forest. We have a saying in Poland: *We were not there – the forest was there; we shan't be there – the forest will be there*. And so, how to be, how to live, how to give birth as the forest does? I can also say to myself: I am water, pure, which flows, living water; and then the source is *he, she*, not *I*: he whom I am going forward to meet, before whom I do not defend myself. Only if *he* is the source can *I* be the living water.

And now a few words about the, so to speak, final dying. Some people say that man in a moment of dying sees his entire life in a flash, all that was essential in it – a kind of film. I do not know if this is true, but let's believe that it is. What do you think we are going to see at such a moment? What is important, what will return? The moment when you bought a car, when your boss praised you, or when a trick you played came off and you felt you were better than others because you were more clever?

•

I am sitting opposite someone who is like me and like many of you. I feel a need, so tangible that it seems one could touch it with one's fingers, and yet we cannot find words which could define it. I ask him question after question – the questions which I really ask myself: he replies and when I feel I cannot tell whether it is his reply or mine, I note down what he says. And in this way, there gradually emerges the description of our need:

To be "looked at" (yes, "looked at," and not "seen"); to be looked at, like a tree, a flower, a river, the fish in that river.

Life in falsehood, pulling wool over people's eyes, pretending: how long can one go on? To give up "what I can expect"; to come down to earth and to give one's hand – it is not a clean hand, it does not matter, what matters is the warmth of the body. To take off one's clothes and spectacles and to dip into the source.

•

I know that now I am supposed to reply in a more "technical" manner, for such a question has been asked. Do the things I am talking about transcend the psychophysical contact, as Stanislavsky saw it? Do you want me to say I have transcended him? I have too much respect for Stanislavsky to say this. I considered him once to be my father.

Stanislavsky was concerned with producing written drama, how to stage plays, remaining in agreement with the writer's intentions and the human experience of the actor. If an actor performs Hamlet, he ought to conceive everything that happens in the drama as assumed circumstances: that there are countries which are like prisons; that the atmosphere in such countries is exceptionally tense; that the crown prince loves his mother very much, but maybe he loves his father even more; that his father died murdered, etc. All these are circumstances. Stanislavsky asked the actor the question: what would you do *if* you found yourself in that situation? In the first – let us call it psychological – period, Stanislavsky stressed rather the question: what are you going to experience, what are you going to feel? In the second period – that of physical actions – he stressed rather the question: what would you do? How would you behave? One could say that the actor ought to have built of the material of his own nature the image of a role, its vision, shape. I think that in Stanislavsky, theatre – as the art of the actor – received its apogee. Wasn't a man divided in this kind of work? Yes, he was, and Stanislavsky seemed to assume this. He said, for instance, that the actor ought to have two perspectives: the purpose of his work (what it will give the spectator), and what the character he creates is doing and thinking. There are, however, different interpretations of this: for instance, the first perspective was also described by Stanislavsky as a kind of creative strategy. The actor already knows that the character will die in the finale of the play – this is the actor's perspective – so how is he to prepare the death?

What, for example, distinguishes what we are aiming at from Stanislavsky's wisdom, that genuine wisdom of craft? For us the question is: what do you want to do with your life; and so – do you want to hide, or to reveal yourself? There is a word which, in many languages, has a double meaning: the word *discover/uncover*. To discover oneself means to find oneself, and at the same time uncover what has been covered: to unveil. If we want to discover ourselves (like the hitherto unknown earth), we have to uncover ourselves (unveil, reveal ourselves). "Find out – unveil." There is something exceptionally precise about this double meaning.

It is not essential whether you feel that personally, for you, some written play is indispensable as a point of departure. Okay. Maybe yes, maybe no. But if Hamlet is for you a living area, you can also measure yourself with him; not as with a character, but a ray of light, falling on your own existence, which illuminates you so that you will not lie, will not play.

What did Stanislavsky understand by physical actions? He saw them as ordinary, everyday behavior: I am looking, I see you, I am wondering what to say, I withdraw into myself, I think again, again I look at you, I check the way you react – they are the most essential of physical actions, but they include also sitting down, walking, listening, various doings. Stanislavsky demanded of the actor to look for a logic in them, the logic of actions, continuity of behavior, and why at a given moment he should do this and not the other.

But are the everyday actions important in what is close to me, in that towards which we are aiming? Sometimes, perhaps, yes; at other times, no, not at all. On the whole, however, the ordinary, everyday actions, which for Stanislavsky were something essential, and in his case rightly so, from our perspective are rather means by which we hide or arm ourselves in life. Do you regard the way you behave with your friends in a café as disarmament? Every one of you must have experienced that, when he was sincere to the end – what was happening with him was not ordinary, and was not happening when he was talking, or when he only talked, but when he was totally naked, as in real love, which is not just gymnastics, but embraces us as whole, up to the loss of self before another person. Is it ordinary what we are doing then? Certainly, there are actions resulting from habit, but the most important of them are not such. Why is this not ordinary? Because in this case, when we touch, we touch with our own self, and when we touch in everyday life, we already think about something else.

●

Perhaps, everything I am talking to you about just now, you take to be metaphors. They are not metaphors. This is tangible and practical. It is not a philosophy but something one does; and if someone thinks that this is a way of formulating thoughts, he is mistaken. This has to be taken literally, this is experience. That these are metaphors . . . this is where the difference begins and it is the core of the difficulty. It is enough to understand that I am attempting here – in as much as I can – to touch on the experience of meeting – meeting with man [*czlowiek*]; then reject this word: metaphor . . . Am I talking about a kind of existence rather than about theatre?

•

Does the behavior of those people in the wilderness I mentioned at the outset, or the practices of yoga or Buddhism, belong to other epochs? It happened in another epoch and so belongs to another epoch. We can understand them because we have reached a similar point, but we are unable to formulate an answer in words. An analysis of this could take us too far from the theme of our conversation. May I be allowed to say, however, that there is something which remains the same in all epochs, or at least in those when people are aware of their human condition – this is the quest. The quest for what is the most essential in life. Different names have been invented to call it. I do not think it possible for myself to invent religious names; what's more I do not feel any need at all for inventing words. But the question of what is the most essential in life, which some of you can think abstract, really is of great import. Many people do reject it; they feel obliged to smile as if they were advertising toothpaste. But why are they so sad? Maybe they have missed something in life? Maybe they never asked themselves the only question they ought to have asked. It must be asked. And the answer? One can't formulate it, one can only do it.

•

We do a great deal in order to not find a reply to this question. We want to learn means: how to play? How best to pretend to be something or someone? How to play classical plays and modern plays? How to play tragic plays and comic plays? But if one learns *how to do*, one does not reveal oneself; one only reveals the skill for doing. And if someone looks for means resulting from our alleged method, or some other method, he does it not to disarm himself, but to find asylum, a safe haven, where he could avoid the act which would be the answer. This is the most difficult point. For years one works and wants to know more, to acquire more skills, but in the end has not to learn but to unlearn, not to know how to do, but how not to do, and always face doing; to risk total defeat; not a defeat in the eyes of others, which is less important, but the defeat of a missed gift, that is to say an unsuccessful meeting with oneself.

•

Does a man arm himself again, after he has fulfilled the act of carnal sincerity – disarmed himself in the meeting I am talking about – and when he, so to speak, is returning into everyday life? In order to approach the "impossible," one must somehow be a realist. In life, can one not hide? It is better if we do not hide, but let us imagine a situation in which you will reject all means of concealment, but others will not . . . maybe one must begin with some particular places. Yes, I think that there is an urgent need for a place where we do not hide ourselves and simply are as we are, in all the possible senses of the word. Does it mean that we remain in a vicious circle – that life is different here, and different there? No, I think that this will come out outside the place I have been talking about, will come out through a small opening, gap, window, door, penetrate outside.

•

There is in it also something like cleansing of our life. And it even makes me think very literally, tangibly, as an action: *cleansing*. This, too, is *swieto* [holiday], to be in *swieto*, to be *swieto*. There is no other way out here, but one must talk by associations: for some it will seem abstract, even embarrassing or ridiculous, for others it will be as concrete as it is for me. This, too, is something we can recognize one another by. And so, I am taking that risk and I will tell you about associations. Here they are, only some of them, there are very many:

games, frolics, life, our kind, ducking, flight; man-bird, man-colt, man-wind, man-sun, man-brother.

And here the most essential, central: brother. This contains "the likeness of God," giving and man [*czlowiek*]. But also the brother of earth, the brother of senses, the brother of sun, the brother of touch, the brother of Milky Way, the brother of grass, the brother of river.

•

A question has been asked about the concept of gesture as sign. In other words, that there exists something like gesture and what does it mean. . . . But do the contents, and the means to express it, exist separately? Must one have a conception of something and then look for means to put it into practice? It is commonly thought that this is the only way. I must confess that I regard it as altogether false. Entering on such a course, one is from the start divided into thinking and acting, intention and life; one deals with certain "ideas," which one assumes from the start, and then one looks for a way to illustrate them. One can, of course, construct in this way, and it will be logical; one can explain ideas, but this product will never fully encompass him who has made it, or him who encounters it, for it is not possible to achieve fullness walking the road of divisions. This is, let us add, only a small aspect of a wider problem, the perennial, rigidly fixed division between body and soul, a split which, in a more modern fashion, has been called the difference between mind and body, or the distinction between the psychic and physical. Someone here mentioned "the psychic act," which I allegedly looked for, as if the act we are looking for could be only psychic. In it, or rather towards it, man [*czlowiek*] acts with his living presence.

What perspective is opening here? A perspective which transcends acting, with all pretending, with all "playing." It is the fullness of man that is thrown onto the scale. A human being in his totality – that is to say what is sensory and at the same time shining through, as it were.

It can happen, however, that when we have achieved something which reveals our own life, we will sell it to others. But in that case, we are sure to give it up for destruction: while, on the face of it, remaining the same, it will be utterly destroyed. Slavery does not leave room for truth. What matters is not how to secure the audience's approval. One must not look for the audience's acceptance, but accept himself. The very word audience, for that matter, is "theatrical," dead. It excludes meeting, it excludes the relation: man–man [*czlowiek–czlowiek*]. Our courage to discover ourselves, to uncover ourselves, has another difficulty to overcome, caused by the eyes of the stranger. It is not enough to accomplish that which reveals us; one must do more: effect this, in as much as it is possible, in full light, not furtively, but overtly. Then, perhaps, this is a "sign," or becomes one?

•

What does it mean: not to hide oneself? Simply to be whole – "I am as I am" – then our experience and life are opening themselves. And every essential experience of our life is being realized through the fact that there is someone with us. And it does not matter whether that other person is present now, at this moment, or was present once, or will only be; that person either is actually, tangibly there, or exists as a need actualizing itself – he, she, that other who is coming, is emerging from the shadows, is pervading our life – is incarnated, of flesh and blood. We are like a big book, where the presence of other human beings is registered, thanks to which every essential experience becomes tangible. In the fulfilling of essential experiences we know: something is happening with me. And is happening in a most concrete way: in the senses, in the skin, in the tissues. We are not taking possession of it, but it takes possession of us, and then all our being quivers and vibrates. We are a living stream, a river of reactions, a torrent of impulses, which embraces our senses and the entire body. And this is the "creative material" you are asking about.

•

It is easy to give way to temptation for striving after a miraculous key to creativity; one easily assumes that there are ideas which are fertile and can easily be taught to others. This is how many people see the function of our exercises; the same exercises which we have considered only as kinds of tests to discover the points of resistance of our organisms. Or rather: a certain meaning of these exercises consisted in that on their basis we could occasionally recover trust for our organisms – lack of trust being a frequent cause of division. This then, let me repeat, is an area where we have wrestled with the mistrust of our own bodies – of ourselves – or, if you like, where we have confronted certain obstacles which offered us the greatest resistance. I am rather afraid that this latter possibility is too conceptual by now, though there is some truth in it. Anyway, the exercises are not even an introduction, not even a point of departure. They can prepare us for the proper *se*arch, give a certain discipline, a certain morale, I would say, in approaching one's resistances. They are like a prayer before something which is to be done; but if someone prays all his life, instead of doing things, he will not have achieved much.

•

When one talks about method, about a method of someone who was psychologically as shrewd as Stanislavsky was, as logical in his order of thinking as Brecht was, as technically precise as Meyerhold in his biomechanics, one usually wishes to find those miraculous cases which would exempt one from revealing oneself, from giving testimony, from the act. And when they talk about any method, "my" method for instance, the problem boils down to the same thing: nearly always they see it in the categories of "to know how to do." When they say that Grotowski's method exists as a system, the implication is that it is a false method. If it is a system, and if I myself have pushed it in this direction, I have contributed to a misunderstanding; it follows that I made a mistake and one must not go along that road, because it instructs "how to do," that is to say, it shows how to arm oneself. We arm ourselves in order to conceal ourselves; sincerity begins where we are defenseless. Sincerity is not possible if we are hiding ourselves behind clothes, ideas, signs, production effects, intellectual concepts, gymnastics, noise, chaos. If a method has any sense at all, it is as a way to disarmament, not as a system. On the way to disarmament it is not possible to foresee any result in advance, to know what and how it will happen, because this depends exclusively on the existence of him who fulfils the deed. One cannot possibly foresee the forms we shall arrive at, "themes" to whose temptation we shall fall, facts which will follow next. For this will depend on everyone personally. There is no answer which should be taken as a formula that should be adhered to.

•

It is not theatre that is indispensable but: to cross the frontiers between you and me; to come forward to meet you, so that we do not get lost in the crowd – or among words, or in declarations, or among the beautifully precise thoughts.

Everywhere in the professional theatre, one can see symptoms of its agony, and at the same time a convulsive battle to regain faith in something which does not excite us anymore. And when we fall prey to profound doubts, we want to defend them with noise, with the chatter of forms – or through the appeasing of our conscience by means of a new method. But the doubts remain.

•

If someone wishes to be sincere with regard to his own life, giving it a pledge with his own flesh and blood, one might assume that what he reveals will be exclusively personal, individual. It is not the whole truth, however; there is a certain paradox about it. If one carries one's sincerity to the limit, crossing the barriers of the possible, or admissible, and if that sincerity does not confine itself to words, but reveals the human being totally, it – paradoxically – becomes the incarnation of the total man [*czlowiek zupelny*] with all his past and future history. It is then superfluous to go to the trouble of analysing whether – and how – there exists a collective area of myth, an archetype. That area exists naturally, when our revelation, our act, reaches far enough, and if it is concrete.

•

A particular question has been asked here regarding responsibility, that is to say the extent of the respective rights and duties of the director and the actor, and about "collective creation." The idea of a group as a collective person must have been a reaction to the dictatorship of the director, i.e., someone who dictates to others what they are to do, despoiling them of themselves. Hence the idea of "collective creation." However, "collective creation" is nothing but a collective director; that is to say, dictatorship exercised by the group. And there is no essential difference whether an actor cannot reveal himself – as he is – through the fault of the individual director, or the group director. For if the group directs, it interferes with the work of every one of its members, in a barren, fruitless way – it oscillates between caprices, chance and compromise of different tendencies and results in half-measures.

•

If one assumes that at rehearsals the actor ought to construct his part outside himself, as it were, if he is merely its material, man is not free. But ask him to uncover himself, to reveal himself with the courage to cross the barrier, to be sincere beyond words and above the admissible measure, then his own freedom will find expression; it is not a freedom to do any random thing, but the freedom to be as one is. *The "order" still remains, however, as a bed of the stream: what is that which we have found and what one must not abandon in order to go on doing?* And: How not to defend oneself against doing, which seems an impossibility? This is very difficult to define precisely. It begins really to exist if the "director" exists towards the "actor," if he ceases to be "director" and ceases to exist; on the other hand, where the "actor" does not hide before him and his own partner, and so does not think about himself, about his fear. And is not an "actor" anymore. There can be no talk about a method here. The most essential in this intimate affair is he who is standing, facing the thing he is to fulfil, and no one can stand in for him, no one can undertake to do it for him.

•

In spite of all professional experience – that which is the germ, that act which determines all, that *unveiling*, could not be found through technical perfection, by means of training. It is something that is done directly, here and now, or one gives it up. It can happen that someone who has turned up from outside and is spending the first day in our group, who has never done anything in the theatre, thanks to his human determination will, right away, achieve the thing which we have been searching for for years. But another day a new problem will arise when that someone will want to repeat the act in a situational, "external" way, as a trick, as an effect, and there will lose everything. And we, with our experience of failure, should know that it is impossible for the thing ever to be "reconstructed" as an effect, as a trick. But it is not quite certain whether we are aware of it: our "professional life" still tempts us to exchange everything for effects.

•

What do I think about talent? But what is talent? It is certain only that there exists something like lack of talent. A case of that arises when someone occupies a place which – in a natural, manifest way – does not belong to him. Talent as such does not exist, only its absence.

•

What part does the audience play? Why worry about what the audience's part ought to be? And what does it really mean, "the audience"? We are doing something, and there are others who want to meet us. This is not audience, they are concrete human beings; some are opening their doors, others come to the meeting, there is something that will happen. This is more important than having an idea about the "audience" and its role. What is it that we are to do and what people do we want to meet? And what is that something that will happen to us and among us? These are the questions that we ask ourselves over and over again, every time; and if so – the place of those who have come to us will emerge of itself.

•

A slogan has been uttered here: The theatre and the Church are dying. I am coming back once more to this problem because to me it is very important. Bear with me if I repeat certain examples, which I find closest. Men shared bread and felt they shared God. They shared God. And we feel the need to share life, share ourselves, as we are, whole, share brother – and if one is brother – share not like brioche, but as bread. One must be like bread, which does not recommend itself, which is as it is and does not defend itself. How to know, how to refer to brother as to God? And then – how to become brother? Where is my nativity – as brother?

© 1972 Jerzy Grotowski

THE VIGIL [CZUWANIE]

for Ania Zmyslowska

Francois Kahn

> In traditional Polish culture, "czuwanie" means something between people
> that happens on the occasion of the death or birth of someone. "Czuwanie"
> is an old word, little used, which means: to be attentive in front of . . . to
> take care of . . . to be present before something.
>
> Jacek Zmyslowski

Czuwanie [*The Vigil*], a project directed by Jacek Zmyslowski (on which
I worked from the spring of 1977 in Poland until its final development
in the winter of 1981/82 in New York) is a work that has disappeared
together with its creator. The few analyses and testimonials dedicated to
it cannot, by reason of their small number, reflect the great importance
this work had for those who, either closely or from a distance, have
followed the research of the Teatr Laboratorium. To remedy this lack
partially and to attempt to clarify this essential phase of the Laboratory
Theatre, I refer to two sources: on one hand to the conference Jerzy
Grotowski dedicated to *Czuwanie* at Hunter College, New York, in May
1981, and on the other to the interview with the members of the guide
group of *Czuwanie* (and in particular Zmyslowski) made in Milan in
1979 by André Gregory for the documentary directed by Mercedes
Gregory and produced by Atlas Theatre Company. To simplify this
article and to avoid repetition, I made a montage of these two texts,
numbering the citations (1) for Grotowski and (2) for Zmyslowski.

(1) "At the beginning of the year 1970 the Teatr Laboratorium profoundly changed the direction of its research. From this moment its work
was no longer strictly theatrical. New experiences, which were opposed
to the traditionally passive role of the spectator, opened the possibility of
active participation in the creative process for those who wanted to take
part. At the beginning, only small groups of people, very carefully
selected, could participate in the proposed projects. In 1975, the work of
the Teatr Laboratorium was opened for the first time to a larger number

of people. During the "University of Research" which took place in Poland, people coming from all over the world were able to participate without any preliminary selection in one or another of the activities. In 1979, Jacek Zmyslowski, one of the youngest members of the Laboratory, created an international group with a view to work on a very complex project, the *Mountain Project*, which was envisioned in three phases: *Night Vigil* (*Nocne Czuwanie*), *The Way* (*Droga*), and the final event, which lasted for two weeks, *The Mountain of Flame* (*Gora Plomienia*). *The Vigil* (*Czuwanie*) was conceived as a work in itself only at the end of this complex project.

"The different possibilities of this action, like the number of participants or the duration of the event, were explored, but always keeping certain rules as a base: no selection of participants, no verbal communication, no spectators or passive observers."

(2) "Until this moment we had been in the habit of always meeting the people to talk to them and then trying to select the small groups. But there was something that wasn't working, at least this is what I think now, in this way of selecting the people. Because the only possible way to know one another, to see each other, is to make some work together and not simply to have a conversation.

"In this action there is only an empty space, the people who arrive, and nothing else. Very simple things happen in this time, but simple in the sense that everyone has the capacity to do something in this space, in this room. Seen from the outside it can seem simply that they are moving, sometimes in a way so delicate that even old people are able to do it. But it is very different from everything that we are in the habit of doing in our daily lives.

"When we don't move in our daily way, we communicate at a completely different level. I mean to say that normally we have the habit of speaking, we use words, but in *Czuwanie* we don't use the voice at all. In fact it is an action completely without noise. For someone who enters the space for the first time, the silence is something strange, because outside there is no silence; the absence of verbal communication is something strange. This creates a different situation, different relations among the people who didn't know each other before (even if I have already had a meeting with some of the people, I don't know anything about them). But because it is so simple, sometimes it is very difficult to take the first step. I think that one of the things we should do is to help make this first step so that no one will be afraid to move. By the fact that there is no judge, we are not wanting to judge the people who come. I don't want to be judged by the others."

(1) "Now I want to speak about the structure of *Czuwanie*, or more about the kind of strategy toward the participants and among the members of the group itself. When Jacek brought the people in and seated them in the room, he always used all the space, leaving a passage around and among the people. This gave the possibility for the guides to move around and among the participants, to create a type of net spun through movement. The secret of this movement consisted in the fact that it was not directed toward the participants, but that it existed among the members of the guiding group through their reciprocal contact. This net of movement that was spun around the participants created in a certain way the field, or we should say the runway that allowed them to enter in the action. Starting from the moment when the participants began to move, they themselves suggested to the guiding group the rhythm of the action. This rhythm was faster or slower according to the capacity of the participants taken as a totality, according to the energies or inertia of this totality. It was as if to say that the guiding group in a subtle way stimulated much more the space than the persons. Finally, they were left to themselves; sooner or later they would enter into the action *without being forced*. The first phase of the action thus had an open structure, where the type of positions or movements were never fixed, where the rhythm changed in relation to the group of participants. The second phase of the action began when the guiding group had "trapped" the participants inside the movement, in the "net" of the movement.

"This phase was much more open and connected to what was happening. In general there were two types of situation: if the movement of the participants were becoming, let us say, false, or if the action started to become chaotic, in this moment the guides returned to the earlier phase and they proceeded among themselves, keeping a certain distance in the space. But if the participants let themselves take the movement among the guides, the guides immediately reacted in relation to the movement of the participants. Here was operating the principle of *personalization* that was very important for Jacek. It is impossible to concentrate one's attention on everybody. There were one, two or three participants that found themselves in a certain moment really in a state of grace. Thus it was needed to adapt everything to function with these participants; the others found themselves simply in relation with those. This strategy of privileged rapport with someone, which leaves the others in a certain way as they like, does not imply loss of control of the action, but makes it possible to concentrate on the people more alive – not necessarily the most active but, we can say, the most organic . . . The question for the person doing is to find the spark, some energy. Often, to find this spark, it is necessary to make great physical effort. In this work, visions or miracles are not accepted; one's own limits are accepted; the space where one is is accepted; the other is accepted: as a mirror, as the place where one finds his own image, but not in a narcissistic sense. One accepts the space as a lake where one can swim. The reality that is born among the participants is a simple reality – of energy; it is in this reality that one swims and takes the energy. The persons in the room are as they are; the room is as it is, a space.

"These are the clear points. In this simple reality created by the persons is a flow of movement and not a flow of images . . . The end of the action was never structured beforehand, but always was in silence. It was not a "spiritual" silence, not silence simply in the sense of not talking – but from the intensity of the movement always the action arrived to a point of saturation. Here existed the strategy of the guides, because if it finished too late, the silence would be broken. They were finishing in the moment when everything was saturated. No one in this silence waited for the arrival of a sound. In this silence some energy was passing. One can say that it was the silence of intensity. In that moment Jacek would take the first person and lead him out of the space."

(2) "By the fact that it is a simple meeting – I feel – it is important to wait for the moment of "clear reality" and then to separate. I think it is an honest situation because every person who comes has the possibility to work with us again. It is a completely open work and if someone takes as a point of departure not the beginning of the action but the point where the previous one ended, then there is always the possibility of finding new things in this work."

From my personal experience I want to underline certain facts. Jacek, during all the work, never theorized the practice of *Czuwanie*. During the preparatory work the action was directed toward the mode of finding an alive contact among the guides, not as a group but as individuals. During *Czuwanie*, it was the evidence that was guiding us, in the sense that if the action arrived to the moments of evidence or of "clear reality," we were never speaking about this. Only if the contact or the courage was lacking among us, then Jacek would speak to us individually, and always in a very tangible way.

When Jacek used the word "simple," this reflected an essential choice in his work, that it was much more ethical than aesthetic. The simplicity consisted in the fact of refusal, for himself and the members of the group, of all objects, all ornaments, rites, everything behind which it is possible to hide, all the false justifications. This choice of reality (the time, the space, the real persons), the absence of discourse (also among the members of the group), the non-selection of the participants, this return to the most simple point, to this situation of interhuman relations stripped of everything that is aesthetic (but I don't say deprived of beauty) gave the basis for a work of research that is developing, in a manner visible or invisible, until today.

(1) "Jacek always insisted on the fact that what counts in the work are the extremely simple things: the movement and the space – the body and the space – the body and the movement. Nothing more, really nothing more, no miracle, no mystery, no metaphysics, no spirits, only the most simple things. In his explanations to his collaborators he always underlined the fact that it is necessary to accept certain limits and especially physical limits; for example we know that we cannot fly, so we don't speak about how to fly."

Translated by Lisa Wolford.

LABORATORY THEATRE/ GROTOWSKI/THE MOUNTAIN PROJECT

Jenna Kumiega

A LETTER FROM HOME

For Nick Janni

Do not come here if you wish
to be certain of returning.
There are many ways here, as many
as the tunes a piano will play,
and the way you choose or chooses
you will alter what you find here.
Not everyone who comes comes
here because he wished to, nor
do all the brave travellers arrive.
Do not come here if you wish
to be certain of returning.

At the frontier you are to
deposit the habit that you have
of describing the world, as it seems
to you. Nothing will seem here.
Instead, you must wear the habit
of knowing, without knowing
what it is you know, of meeting
someone who, unprecedentedly,
is not yourself. Do not come
here if you wish to be certain.

A.C.H. Smith

In December 1970, during a conference at New York University, Jerzy Grotowski made a definitive statement concerning his present position *vis-à-vis* theatre and the pursuit of art, the text of which has subsequently become known as "Holiday":

> Am I talking about a way of life, a kind of existence, rather than about
> theatre? Without a doubt. I think that at this point we are faced with a
> choice. . . . The quest for what is most essential in life. Different names
> have been invented for it; in the past these names usually had a religious
> sound. I do not think it possible for myself to invent religious names;
> furthermore I do not feel any need for inventing words.
>
> (Ch. 23:217, 218)

Despite distrust, disbelief, cynicism, and a general lack of comprehension, Grotowski was to repeat and expand this message in future public
debate. Perfectly willing, as always in discussion, to participate in
polemic concerning the Laboratory Theatre's former theatrical experiments, he was constantly at pains to emphasize that this was past history
for them, a closed chapter. They were now concerned primarily with "the
quest." The activity which encapsulated this quest became known as
paratheatre: formally, this relates to an activity which has its roots in
drama, but which specifically does not result in a theatrical presentation
before an audience. The terms "spectator" and "actor" lose their divisive
significance and both the action and the creation become a collective
responsibility.

In the early seventies, the members of the Laboratory Theatre
continued their search among themselves. Finally in the autumn of 1973
in Pennsylvania and France, they extended their experiments to include
selected outside participants. In this development *Apocalypsis cum
figuris* played a new role – it became, apart from a theatrical presentation,
a direct invitation to members of the public to participate in the
exploration. During the cycle of performances, Grotowski and the
members of the company met hundreds of hopeful participants, eventually selecting small groups of maybe six or seven. The process was
repeated in Australia, in the spring of 1974. And they had begun to search
in Wroclaw also, their home town, for young Polish people to join in the
work. In the entrance hall to the Laboratory Theatre, a notice was
prominently displayed to incoming members of the audience: "To
anyone interested: If you wish to meet us in paratheatrical work remain
in the auditorium after the performance of *Apocalypsis* and write down
in a few words what you seek from us. ACTING AMBITION IS NOT
REQUIRED."

Finally, in July 1975, the Laboratory Theatre opened its doors wide for
the first time to a curious public and expectant theatrical world. Under
the auspices of the Theatre des Nations Festival being held in Warsaw at
that time, Grotowski organized a "University of Research" in Wroclaw.
Within this framework diverse activities took place – press conferences
with Peter Brook, Jean-Louis Barrault, Joseph Chaikin, André Gregory;

showings of old Laboratory Theatre films; open classes in theatre technique led by Eugenio Barba and the Odin Teatret; the world premiere of films recording experimental work by Eugenio Barba in southern Italy and Peter Brook in Africa; a closed workshop for professional Polish actors conducted by Peter Brook; and even specialized psychiatric and medical consultations.

But the focal point of the interest of most participants was undoubtedly the program of paratheatrical projects led by members of the Laboratory Theatre. From the multitude which attended the "University of Research" – professional actors, journalists, students and ordinary members of the public – participants were selected to join in the closed work sessions. Twice during the course of the proceedings Grotowski held an unpublicized gathering in the evening of all the active participants, openly to discuss the work they had done and find out their reactions. On both occasions this was followed by a talk by Grotowski, and individual consultations between him and each participant; in these he sought to discover the participant's personal area of "quest" and gave advice on which project they should join. These events inevitably lasted until the early hours of the morning. But more significantly, "open" work sessions (called "Beehives") were held nightly at the theatre, in which all participants of the Research University could join. The only reservation was that there were to be no observers.

> *July 24, 1977, 11:00 a.m.*
> *Entering the room carries an element of surrender.*
> *Surrender of self. It is a familiar room:*
> *stone-edged, candlelit, the walls shrugging*
> *off sound, danger in the corners.*
> *The muscles tauten like rising hackles in*
> *a primal ritual of preparation and caution.*
> *There is the cold of ancient shadowed stone.*
> *And the quality of stillness that sound pierces*
> *tangibly, like a needle through flesh.*
> *The room breathes in the long silences. These are*
> *broken by occasional whispered instruction.*
> *No unnecessary elaboration. Already the face*
> *of the clock blurs in the long, primed waiting.*
> *Breathless, soon spinning in the vortex of*
> *random impulses. Bursts of meaningless electric*
> *charge along disordered nerve passages.*
> *Static charge builds up in immobility.*
> *There is a slow surrender of the control pattern.*

The origins of the progression from theatre to paratheatre may be seen to lie in one or two particular areas of preoccupation from Grotowski's early theatrical theory. These are (i) the actor/audience relationship and (ii) the manipulative actor/director relationship. What remains from the body of Laboratory Theatre theory now belongs in the history of theatre research: Grotowski's concept of "poor theatre," the experiments in architectural scenic arrangements, the development of the training of the actor's body and voice.

In formulating his theory of a "poor theatre," Grotowski eventually arrived at his definition of theatre as "what takes place between spectator and actor." He acknowledged that since he could not systematically educate the former, his preoccupation had to be "the personal and scenic technique of the actor." This he elevated to the level of "secular holiness." "One must give oneself totally, in one's deepest intimacy, with confidence, as when one gives oneself in love. Here lies the key. Self-penetration, trance, *excess*, the formal discipline itself" (Grotowski 1968: 38). But Grotowski has never really been content to renounce fully an investigation into the possibilities inherent in the psychic presence of an audience: "The performance engages a sort of psychic conflict with the spectator. It is a challenge and an excess" (1968:47).

This preoccupation may be detected in his constant exploration of spatial concepts and relationships: he inaugurated a procedure of staging in which each production became an experiment *per se* in some aspect of the actor/audience relationship. The spectators in turn became active participants in ritual (*Dziady* 1961), patients in a psychiatric ward (*Kordian* 1962), guests at a last supper (*Doctor Faustus* 1963), and voyeurs at acts of persecution and sadism (*The Constant Prince* 1965). "The essential concern is finding the proper spectator/actor relationship for each type of performance and embodying the decision in physical arrangements."

But in the years following the premiere of *The Constant Prince* – which was generally acknowledged to be a remarkable realization of the Laboratory Theatre acting technique – a change of emphasis became apparent in Grotowski's approach to the actor/spectator relationship. In an interview given in Montreal in June 1967, Grotowski states: "The core of the theatre is an encounter." But what he is referring to here, as he explains at length, is essentially the encounter between the actor and the text, the actor and director, and the actor and his own self. The spectator, at this stage, is not directly referred to at all. And it seems apparent from the next production, *Apocalypsis cum figuris*, that Grotowski was prepared at last to abandon the earlier charades, in which he had pursued the ideal of a reciprocally satisfactory actor/spectator relationship. In *Apocalypsis cum figuris* (1968), actors and audience, without pretence and on equal footing, enter together the playing area – a large empty room: the ones to give and present, the others to receive and witness. It is the furthest Grotowski could proceed in his obsessive manipulation of that elusive relationship and still remain within the bounds of theatre.

In *Apocalypsis cum figuris* the scenic space is created entirely by the actions of the actors, and the constantly shifting relative positions of actor/actor/spectator. When at one point the central persecuted character encircles the tight-knit group of the other actors, who are placed in the centre of the room, he is not only excluded from their group conscious-ness, he is trapped in the narrow channel between their active rejection and the passive refusal of the surrounding witnesses to intervene. By their own awareness of the roles which they have accepted for the duration of an hour, and their inability to cast off these roles, all present force the cycle of events nightly to its preordained conclusions.

Just as there is no previously constructed scenic arrangement, so for this production the audience cannot retreat into a specified role. They are witnesses, yes, but it is not possible to seek security in this fact. To maintain that position, unassailed, throughout *Apocalypsis cum figuris* is to maintain that position in regard to life. As the main character, nearing the end of his torment, raises himself slowly to his knees from where he has been slumped in exhaustion and searches the faces of those spectators sitting only inches from him, it is they who choose their position and response. Of course, the choice is unfairly balanced, since the weight of convention rests on the side of the status quo. The only just way in which the spectator may be liberated from his stultifying role of silent witness is to lift the weight of theatrical convention, which is what the Laboratory Theatre finally decided to do.

> *July 24, 1977, 6:00 p.m.*
> *We follow moist paths through the woods.*
> *We are skittish – soon sensitized to the*
> *communal presence, a move from any direction*
> *bringing a ripple of response.*
> *Already there is a testing: of each against*
> *the other, against any inference of a*
> *structure, against those who know the way.*
> *Even finally against the way: against the*
> *multiple shades of green and all its textures,*
> *against another acceptance of the horizon.*
> *Until we come up against ourselves.*
> *Our bodies.*

The second area of Laboratory Theatre interest, which eventually led to the abandonment of theatrical convention, is that of the actor/director relationship. Central to this are two related factors: Grotowski's attitude to theatrical text; and the Laboratory Theatre process of role-realization. Grotowski's response to theatrical text is clearly stated: for him it serves as a springboard, a challenge to respond to the writer's gesture with his own creative act. This finally led, through increasingly manipulative use of text, to the creation of *Apocalypsis cum figuris* from an improvisational basis. As a play it contains no intrinsic life of its own – there was no original dramatic text to which the actors were able to respond creatively, as with previous productions. Action was improvised, and speech also where absolutely essential. It was not until the action was finally crystallized that the actors were asked to make a personal and individual search through literature for the texts to which they and their creation responded. The text as it now stands contains mingled passages from Dostoevsky, T.S. Eliot, the Bible and Simone Weil.

There is no room in Grotowski's theatre for the Stanislavskian dual actor/observer. For Stanislavsky, in *Building a Character*, there was no middle road between the uncontrolled spontaneity of reading an unfamiliar book aloud for the first time, and the manipulative "perspective of the actor." For Grotowski, there is a middle road, but it is dependent on the close working relationship of the actor and director. For it is the director alone who is able, if he is in fine tune with his actors, to select the visually effective moments of truth, the moments of untruth, to encourage the journey to and beyond the actor's physical barriers. And, most importantly, to select, use and manipulate these moments to build up a creatively cohesive score.

Because of the convention of their respective positions, both the director and spectator crucially affect the validity of the "total act" of Grotowski's actor. He is not performing in the vacuum of an ethical concept, but is performing both in front of his director and the audience. And if the one is judging his "total acts" and using them to construct an artistic framework, and the other is manacled by the conventions of that framework and incapable of response – what then becomes of the giving, the gift?

> *July 24, 1977, 7:30 p.m.*
> *We halt atop a massive bump on the earth.*
> *It is very uncomfortable – grey bristles on*
> *grey skin. Dusty earth and spiky weeds.*
> *Already a grey sky.*
> *Finally we are led away like children to find*
> *some lying place of our own.*
> *I feel nothing. I want to lie down until*
> *the blurred fringe of dried grass blots out*
> *nearly everything except a circle of grey*

above me.
In sporadic bursts I burrow myself deeper
into that space. The long time alone is
interspersed: with sounds of other animals
moving nearby, gentle rustlings, and crazy
frenzied gallopings down the slope and
crashings in the wood.
The pleasurable primitive body reactions are
still tentative.
For a time the first, feathered rain starts.

Finally, within the context of Grotowski's gradually evolving philosophical model, it had to be accepted that "art," with all its formal criteria, would have to be abandoned in the ongoing exploration. This would serve to change only the context, not the essence of Grotowski's stated aim: "To cross our frontiers, exceed our limitations, fill our emptiness – fulfil ourselves" (1968:21). The search had been taken to the outer boundaries delineated by theatrical art, and since it is not in the nature of the Institute or its members to remain static, they had simply stepped beyond.

One aspect of art is its power to awaken knowledge by presenting shadows of reality which the spectator may never normally come face to face with, or may shun. In this lies both its potential strength and weakness. Its strength lies in its capacity to mobilize forces through reaction that could lead to positive action and change. But within the delicate balance of formalized reality lies the potential also for safe and easy evasion. Art may be apprehended increasingly as a formal structure, in which the system of signs and symbols may be exclusively credited with intrinsic value. We relate cerebrally and aesthetically to the structure, robbing the underlying reality element of its penetrating potentiality for change. The skull loses its death message and becomes an insignia – we too easily achieve a state of illusory cognizance with the world. As Peter Brook says: "The audience follows down those dark alleys, calm and confident. Culture is a talisman protecting them from anything that could nastily swing back into their own lives" (Brook 1968:11).

The spectator wards off the experience of reality itself by means of the cathartic properties of the artistic ethos – in so doing, not only does she rob the experience of reality, but she erects a totally superfluous barrier between it and herself. There is contained in this process an element of the scientific fantasy of the impartial, totally objective observer – constructing an unwieldy formal framework within which to assess, identify and analyse.

Grotowski's departure from theatre may also be seen as a reaction to the threat of this process. In this way he can be seen to be abandoning the general artistic ethic, rather than specifically theatre – seeking to tear aside the veil obscuring vision and interrelation, to reach out and be burned by the flames. It was this aspect precisely of Artaud's vision which originally appealed to Grotowski: "Actors should be like martyrs burned alive, still signalling to us from their stakes." But however often Grotowski denies the artistic ethos, the commentators continue to apply cultural criteria to the paratheatrical activities which only serve to confuse unnecessarily the profoundly simple precepts underlying the work. Grotowski, in stepping outside the confines of theatre, is assessed as having taken the accoutrements of art with him – the magnificent sets (the mountain curled about with mist, the forest dark and lambent) and the most dramatic of props (candle-flame, fire, water, stone, and earth).

It is not uncommon even for sympathetic participants in the para-theatrical activities to hold the same misconception. Consider the following, which is taken from the description by one participant in a 24-hour sojourn in the Polish countryside with the Special Project of Ryszard Cieslak:

> During the course of the night, it became clear that a metaphysical system, *theatrically translated* into stunning visual configuration, was at work. Its leading theme was the human drama [. . .] The series of events were designed like a long poem with *material symbols actually there*, not imagined. [. . .] Each was "staged" against a simple but deliberately chosen background – a lagoon, a tree, a windmill. [. . .] Fire was perhaps the most impressive image – fascinating in its flickering self and *symbolizing* as it does enlightenment, *warmth* and life.
>
> (Croyden 1975: 196–97, my emphasis)

July 24, 1977, 10:00 p.m.
We are being led by a Frenchman and a Pole.
The preparation, the buildup, all conditions
have led us as a group to a cowed docility
before them – a herd-like, restless acquiescence.
In any case there is no feedback from them.
Their body language is negative, toned down.
And above all we are led by curiosity; to
see where the next step takes us and how the
technicalities of survival will be achieved.

On a rough and open stretch of grey land
we stop to eat. The grey had started soaking
into the landscape long before. Suddenly, as

we crouch and squat above our clumsy preparations,
it is already nearing that stage of blackness
where vision begins to crumble if the
concentration is too intense. The only way
really to see is to retreat back behind vision,
to switch off the seeing apparatus, and permit
the alternative perceptive equipment to operate.

There are elements in the paratheatrical work which have recognizable parallels in the earlier theatrical theory; these relate either physiologically to the workings of the body, or metaphysically to the impulse for action, and do not derive from the artistic structure of signs characteristic of the early theatrical work. Among these, for example, is the concept termed by Grotowski *via negativa*. In terms of the exercises, it demanded an emphasis on the elimination of the muscular blockage which inhibits free creative reaction, rather than a positive, methodical acquisition of physical skills. It also has an ethical application – what Grotowski terms "internal passivity." It is not a comfortable concept for the Western mind, which tends to prefer positive, intellect-guided action, but has direct parallels with the Taoist principle of *wu-wei*. "Non-action does not mean doing nothing and keeping silent. Let everything be allowed to do what it naturally does, so that its nature will be satisfied" (Needham 1956: 68–9).

This "internal passivity," which can appear such a negative stance to the Western mind, but which contains the possibility of true strength within Eastern mystical tradition, Grotowski has reaffirmed in his "Holiday" statement:

> But if one learns *how to do*, one doesn't reveal oneself; one only reveals the skill for doing. And if someone looks for means . . . he does it not to disarm himself, but to find asylum, a safe haven, where he could avoid the act which could be the answer . . . In the end one has to reject it all and not learn but unlearn, not to know how to do but how not to do and always face doing.
>
> (Ch. 23:218)

On a more practical level, but still intimately related to *via negativa*, is the emphasis on extreme and sustained physical action as a key to spontaneity. In relation to the exercises, this was connected with achievement:

> There are certain points of fatigue which break the control of the mind, control that blocks us. When we find the courage to do things that are impossible, we make the discovery that our body does not block us. We

do the impossible and the division within us between conception and the body's ability disappears.

(Grotowski 1968: 204–5)

Translated into the terms of paratheatre, this is a physical reality which is connected with one of the fundamental requirements of the work: disarmament. It is often misunderstood as an unnecessary spartan adjunct of the work, reminiscent of the early artistic severity and with overtones of masochism. On the contrary, it is one of the very few elements in the paratheatrical work that can justifiably be termed "technique."

> *July 25, 1977, 2:00 a.m.*
> *The Way, at first indifferent, has become hostile.*
> *Water scornfully invades and takes possession of*
> *every part of the body.*
> *The thread of human forms, like a lurching,*
> *drunken centipede, makes a hesitant path*
> *through the forest growth. From any and every*
> *angle it looks pathetic and uncomfortable and*
> *insignificant. From inside an individual body it*
> *is a massive experience. Robbed externally of all*
> *vision, the alternative perception is not completely*
> *reliable. The blackness pressing against the face*
> *and body has sharp edges and extrusions, skin-ripping*
> *electric neck-snapping sensations of pain which*
> *catapult without warning against the flesh. There is*
> *no way of preparing the organism against*
> *these assaults. To withdraw, to close up,*
> *to clench the muscles ever so slightly,*
> *detracts from the priority occupation: maintaining*
> *contact with the organism ahead. It is this which*
> *demands meditational concentration from every cell*
> *in the body.*

The Laboratory Theatre has been continuing its paratheatrical activities during the last couple of years – at La Biennale festival in Venice in autumn 1975, in France the following summer, and in Wroclaw in Poland from summer 1976 to summer 1977. The curiosity of the theatrical world as to the activities of the Institute has been temporarily appeased. But the commentators are now preoccupied with a far more practical question: for how long can the members of the theatre continue their rigorous, self-demanding search? The Laboratory Theatre is exceptional as an artistic institute in that its dedicated ensemble has remained virtually intact for eighteen years. Although they still possess an extraordinary fitness and vitality, they are almost all over forty, and the paratheatrical work is as demanding as their previous theatrical training, if not more so. And even beyond questions of physical necessity, for how long is it healthy for such an institute to remain creatively enclosed, to withhold the seeds of its work from a natural reproductive cycle?

Over the past few years, there has been a gradual move on the part of the actors towards independence – they now no longer necessarily conduct the paratheatrical work as a group, but may travel abroad alone or in smaller groups to undertake personal work sessions. Each actor has a personal project in the paratheatrical field, which is the product of his or her own research and preoccupations. In the practice of his or her project, the actor may have a small group of workers, permanent or temporary, professional members of the theatre, students, or members of the public working in their spare time. The state of these projects is and must be fluid. It is simply not possible to select any one actor and delineate in any permanent sense (as, generally, with a performance) the form which his or her project may take. But each individual has certain characteristics in his or her work that are recognizable, and which, to a certain extent, mold the structure of the project. This may be a fascination with the word, as is the case with Ludwik Flaszen (the theatre's literary adviser), or a preoccupation with the physical barriers of the body, as with Zygmunt Molik.

Simultaneously with these developments, there has been the emergence of younger, hitherto unknown members of the Laboratory Theatre, who are beginning to assume more responsibility. Not all of the newer members of the Institute are necessarily full-time professional employees. It is possible that for many years they have undertaken work at the theatre in addition, for example, to full-time studies on a completely unrelated subject at an academic institute elsewhere. This applies particularly in the case of the increasing number of young people who are being drawn into the ever-widening and intricate network of activities. One actor may gather around him or her a group of young people for a project: of these one or more will remain long enough to gain the experience necessary to lead work, and will themselves then select their own groups. But the process of expansion is a slow one; to the present there has been only a couple of these projects led independently by the "second-generation" paratheatrical workers.

One such project was the Mountain Project, led by Jacek Zmyslowski, with the collaboration of Irene Rycyk, Zbigniew Kozlowski, and others. In its entirety, the project covered a period of activity in and around Wroclaw from Autumn 1976 to the end of July 1977, and encompassed three distinct states: *Nocne Czuwanie* (*Night Vigil*), *Droga* (*The Way*), and *Gora Plomienia* (*Mountain of Flame*). The first of these – *Night Vigil* – was an open session of work conducted regularly during 1976 and 1977, in work rooms inside the familiar theatre buildings in Wroclaw. The number of participants in the *Night Vigil* varied from a few to several dozen, the majority of whom had responded to the following invitation printed on the posters for the project: "*Night Vigil* is taking place at monthly intervals from Autumn 1976 to Summer 1977. Anyone wishing to become an active participant is invited to write briefly – giving address or telephone number – to Jacek Zmyslowski, who will then suggest a date for a meeting."

Besides having intrinsic value as a paratheatrical experience for those taking part, the *Night Vigil* also served pragmatically as a means of assessing the participants' state of readiness to proceed to the later stages of the project. This in general operates subjectively for the participants as well as the organizers, and it is not often that there is conflict between the two. There is no element of normative assessment, in the way that a contribution to work may be measured. If the *Night Vigil* can be seen as an awakening, the awakened are recognized, and the sleepers, untouched, sleep on. A participant has described it thus: "*Night Vigil* is a synonym for the awakening of the other pole of life, usually hidden in night and sleep. Creating the possibility of contact with the unknown, it permits the participants to shake themselves free of everyday routines" (Kolankiewicz 1979).

> *July 25, 1977, 3:00 a.m.*
> *I am not really cold. Neither am I tired.*
> *I feel indefatigable.*
> *So when there is an unexpected halt, I am*
> *shocked to realize that we are stopping for*
> *the night. Paradoxically, after prior fears*
> *of incapacity in the face of physical*
> *endurance, I now feel like breaking down.*
> *Shelter is efficiently erected between the trees*
> *from the huge sheets of polythene. We crawl*
> *under the canopy and sit in a circle.*
> *Suddenly it is cold and wet and very weird,*
> *enclosed within the plastic membrane.*
> *The rain tattoo brings memory of childhood*
> *shelter.*
> *For a long time, the bodies shift and surge in*
> *a slow, blurred, amoebic dance, burrowing one*
> *into each other and the earth.*
> *Finally, there is peace and warmth. Of its own*

*accord the group has become a balance of
yielding and support.*

The Way involved a far greater depth of commitment – both in the degree
of organization required, and the amount of time and effort demanded of
the participants. These, who had either been selected subsequent to
participation in *Night Vigil* or on the basis of previous work with the
Laboratory Theatre, arrived in Wroclaw from within Poland or from
abroad, having been notified of the commencement of this part of the
project by telegram. They were then assigned a time and date at which
to attend the theatre.

On attendance, they found themselves part of a small group of about
eight people. The group spent several hours in a bare, candlelit room in
the theatre, being prepared for the journey ahead under the guidance of
two experienced "leaders." The preparation was of a strictly practical
nature, involving advice as to what to take (rucksack, sleeping-bag, one
change of shoes, jeans and underwear, a pullover and an adequate supply
of cigarettes); and in addition supplying the basic necessities (polythene
sheet, water-flask, minimal camping equipment for heating water,
enamel mug, and a plastic bag containing bread, butter, cheese, salt,
teabags, lemon and bacon-fat). Instructions of a more explicit nature –
either relating to a code of behavior or illuminating in any way what was
to be expected ahead – were absolutely minimal, silence to be observed
except in cases of real, practical necessity; the group to remain together;
eating and smoking to be restricted to specified occasions; and through
increased awareness, an effort to be made on the journey not to intrude
spatially in too insensitive a manner.

At some time during the afternoon the group for that day, together
with its leaders, was transported deep into the countryside outside
Wroclaw by van, and left to find their way on foot. At this stage no one
knew how long the journey would take, or had certain prior knowledge
of what to expect ahead. *The Way* involved at least one night spent in the
forest, regardless of weather, and the possibility of paratheatrical work
sessions in the countryside in addition to the journey itself. The entire
process of *The Way* could take up to forty-eight hours and was physically
demanding. In general, it was sometimes towards the end of the second
day that the group became aware of the Mountain on the curving
horizon.

The Mountain of Flame as a physical reality lies in a gently hilly area
northwest of Wroclaw. Its sides are deeply wooded, and it is surmounted
by an ancient castle, part in ruins. The main work areas in the castle were
two long rooms, one directly above the other. The lower room was more
intimate, with an open log fire and low ceiling. It was here that the

arriving group of participants, after changing their usually sodden garments, was received and fed before being led upstairs. The upper work room was massive and lofty, with rough stone walls, a wooden floor, and an archway at one end leading into a smaller area, where a log fire burned constantly. This small annex was exclusively a domestic area – its windows sealed off, it was lit only by log flames, and was bare except for a table in an embrasure, a huge pile of logs in one corner, and blankets entirely covering the floor. Here participants, in the customary and comfortable silence, ate and relaxed communally, or slept curled up in blankets on the floor. The practical requirements of both work and non-work activities were attended to unobtrusively by members of the central organizing group. Food appeared occasionally, and there was a constant supply of logs for the fire and hot water for tea.

All the "domestic" activities, such as eating and sleeping, were directed by the random pattern of the work periods – these were not controlled in any way by the organizing group but commenced spontaneously in the main room, at undetermined and irregular intervals. There was always the possibility for any participant to inaugurate, join or leave a work session. As the people seated in the annex became aware of the sounds of physical activity – running feet, dancing rhythms, perhaps drums – they were gradually drawn inside. There was an absolute vocal silence in the work room. All impulse – for expression, contact, physical endeavor, disarmament, exposure – was channeled into dynamic physical action, according to the needs of those taking part.

Considering the lack at any stage of a guiding code of behavior, combined with the anarchy of a completely unstructured form, there was at all times in the work room a remarkable cohesion of consciousness and awareness, which generally precluded intrusive action or discordant response. What is being here described is not conformity. On the contrary, it is rather a search, in the void, for the most truly individual response, stripped – by disposition, effort, and the prevailing conditions – of the many social and personality layers, of what Grotowski, in a theatrical context, has called the "life-mask." What is remarkable in the process is that a level of non-individual consciousness is almost invariably reached. The effect is of a vital and spontaneous cohesion within what is superficially a very narrow band of undisciplined human behavior – namely the basic physical activities of running, jumping, dancing, fighting, simply moving.

In addition, there was also the possibility for a group of people to leave the castle temporarily and work in the surrounding Polish countryside for several hours. This presented the framework for a very different state of being than that of the enclosed castle workshops (where the containment had created a density of awareness and experience) and in its very liberation was a sort of test, or initiation. Similarly, on the return, the perception of the almost claustrophobic environment of the mountain was heightened. Time within the castle transformed itself from its familiar patterns into a rhythmic and physiologically determined cycle of work, eating, and sleeping. Each day brought new faces to sit before the flames in the anteroom as others disappeared.

There was no predetermined period of time for an individual's sojourn upon the Mountain – it was decided for each individual by the leader of the project, Jacek Zymslowski. As the cycle of work came to a close for a participant, he or she was roused early in the morning and taken downstairs for a last meal together. Then he or she was led, with others in a group, to retrace the steps back out of the castle and down the Mountain, until he or she was picked up and transported back to Wroclaw by van.

> *July 25, 1977, 5:00 p.m.*
> *The Mountain came towards us through the mist*
> *like a living thing. As we climb upon its back*
> *I feel the edge of fear which is a feather-touch*
> *of physical pleasure down the belly.*
> *We are led into the old stone walls, which*
> *rise, living, from its trees.*
> *There, within the inner chambers, wait others.*
> *Moving among us they give us of their fire.*
> *Shadows imprinted against flame.*
> *Fire on flesh that is of my flesh.*

The Mountain Project was a significant development in the Laboratory Theatre's paratheatrical activity primarily because it decisively loosened the ties with the Institute's theatrical past. This project, for the first time, was planned and conducted by a member of the Institute not familiar to the public through theatrical activity. Jacek Zmyslowski was still in his twenties, and although involved for many years with Laboratory Theatre work, had not participated in any theatrical enterprise. There were more familiar faces from the Laboratory Theatre team on the Mountain, but they were present as participants. Perhaps most significant is the fact that the location in which the work took place was unconnected with theatre.

Location has always been a paramount concern in the organization of paratheatrical work. Practically, this is due to the fundamental require-ment of work security, of the need to create an environment into which no spectator may intrude and where each individual has the possibility of being a participant. But also there is the desire to find a meaningful space, almost magical, and certainly untouched by the patterns and rituals of our daily lives: "Maybe one must begin with some particular places; yes, I think that there is an urgent need to have a place where we do not hide ourselves and simple are, as we are, in all possible senses of the word" (Grotowski 1973:6; see also Ch. 23)

> *July 26, 1977, 3:00 a.m.*
> *There are many points of light/energy enclosed*
> *within the partially defined space. There is*
> *almost constant arhythmic motion. Occasionally,*
> *luminous moments ignite and explode. More*
> *rarely, silence and stillness dance against*
> *the watchful flame.*
> *I see the dance with an ache of remembered*
> *feeling.*
> *I recognize my need to join, knowing its*
> *inevitability, accepting its internal force.*
> *I sit, whole within my skin like a ripe fruit.*
> *I do not observe. I relax my resistance to*
> *the flows of energy around me, awaiting the*
> *birth-push.*
> *I know its power, the sweetness of opening*
> *to it: the intensity of going with it.*

It is not, to my mind, yet possible to identify precisely the terrain in which the Laboratory Theatre is now operating. It involves activities which border on many tangential disciplines, and thus far a distinctive vocabulary has not evolved to chart it. Although since 1975, a policy of commentary by participants of the work has been introduced and encouraged, there has been no particular commitment from the Laboratory Theatre itself to a verbal analysis of the work. And it must be recognized that any "objective" validity in an appraisal of the para-theatrical activities themselves (as opposed to an analysis of the limitations of *theatrical* activity) is defective, since a basic premise of the work is the absence of the spectator, or non-participant. The closest the Laboratory Theatre has reached towards a definition of its current activities can be seen on the latest posters. The familiar "Institute of Actor's Research" has been replaced by the following vague slogan: "The Laboratory Theatre is an institute involved in cultural investigation of the peripheral areas of art, and in particular of theatre."

But a healthy emphasis on action is still predominant in their work, characteristic of Grotowski's rejection in his earlier theatrical experiments of *a priori* aesthetic postulates. This is one of the main reasons I feel that this particular terrain may not be approached by any other route than that taken by the Laboratory Theatre, despite similarities to encounter work and other "self-growth" organized activity. Having been reached by the physical act of theatre, it lacks both the intellectual self-consciousness which is one of the most crippling elements of so much encounter work, and uniquely avoids the attitude that the activity constitutes a cure or treatment for psychic illness or inadequacy.

> *Seeking, through the organism, to test the models*
> *of our world, our existence, our experience of the*
> *world. But first wanting to break down and break*
> *through and explode those concepts which masquerade*
> *as form. Annihilating the form, so that there are*
> *no barriers left in what we aim to throw ourselves*
> *against. Annihilating the form, so that we may*
> *play with pure energy – children with building*
> *bricks.*
> *What we construct, imagine, dream, mold, is beyond*
> *definition and analysis – but what matters is that*
> *it is most truly our own.*
> *Like a blind man running, and touching no walls,*
> *I feel terror and ecstasy.*

ROUTE TO THE MOUNTAIN
A prose meditation on Grotowski as pilgrim

Ronald Grimes

One cannot with fidelity merely speak of Grotowski; one must speak with him. I have chosen to write a meditation rather than a report. Grotowski is in process, and his words, like his exercises, flow. Hence, to be faithful to him is not to imitate him but to transform him. His words are performative utterances – not things, but actions. Either we let an action die or we respond to it without repeating it; we "tell it forward," in other words.

The "other word" I would use is "pilgrimage". In "pilgrimage," Grotowski and I have a meeting of words. Pilgrimage is a process of taking leave of a bounded space, searching and researching for a way, ascending a mountain of first-seeing, and then making one's way home. A pilgrim is a person in motion, a person whose action originates in the deep roots of his own physical, cultural and spiritual home; who then proceeds to a far away place, often a mountain, in search of a shared adventure; and who descends finally to a new or renewed home-space. In short, he is en route to his roots.

A pilgrim is an ordinary person – student, actor, professor, sales-person. As pilgrims we are incidentally, not primarily, our roles. Grotowski as pilgrim is, incidentally, a director. His home-space is Polish and theatrical. Pilgrims leave home when the doors of perception no longer swing in and out, but rust shut. If one would be fully at home, one must sometimes move. Grotowski is on the move to a mountain, literally and metaphorically: Fire Mountain, June 1977.

Though a pilgrim is an ordinary person, he is proceeding through extraordinary space – in-between space, liminal, threshold space, boundary crossings, he is in paraordinary space. Grotowski calls his space "paratheatrical." It is parareligious as well, but whatever is in "para-" space is really outside the bounds of such carvings-up of reality. Yet "paraordinary" does not mean "supernatural." It means very-natural, very-ordinary, authentically simple and direct. At the center, at the pilgrimage site, is a mountain to be climbed, descended, and left. Once the mountain was a mere mountain; now it is becoming a set-aside (holy) place. But knowledge occurs only when a meeting on this special mountain enables the returning pilgrims to perceive even the mountain back home as very mountain of very mountain.

For the pilgrim the process is primary, the goal incidental. The goal is but a pretext for precipitating meetings and fellow travelings on the way to the mountain. It is not better to arrive than to be on the way. Nor is it better to be climbing up than to be climbing down. The pilgrim arrives at the *mons gaudium*, the hill of joyous first sight, from which he and his companions can see with their ears and hear with their eyes, that is, know with fully perceptive bodies. The vertical mountain conceals the taproot of reality and perception. To be on it is to see fully, which means, simply. The vertical root is only the upward glance of a horizontal route.

One cannot say how to prepare for a pilgrimage to Fire Mountain, for there are many way and many words. Be prepared for action. But we do not know what lies ahead. Along medieval pilgrimage routes bandits lay; they still do. Prepare for one kind of attack and another will bring you down before you can change your technique. By refusing to construct predefenses for some possible mishap, we become emptied and flexible enough to meet any contingency on the road.

The pilgrim is a serene adventurer who does not carry too much. Too much can break the rhythm of his stride, and the resulting sore feet create a clutching pilgrim who becomes a parasite on fellow travelers, hence the many beggars lining traditional pilgrimage ways. A cripple become beggar become thief – this is the fate of any hyper-prepared pilgrims and actors. Insofar as a defense is a rigid gesture to ward off would-be assailants, that automatized gesture will unwittingly also ward off the would-be sister or brother. To be ready for action in the world as a theatre of action is to suspend the playacting of daily life. On pilgrimages people who would not ordinarily meet because of the roles they play and occupy share their sandwiches and bedrolls. They are without rank or role. To repeat an action by imitation is to create a role or a stereotype. The stereotypes I create prevent me from improvising what the circumstances – the weather, the road, fellow travelers – call for.

A pilgrimage has a form though not the structure of a routinized ritual. Its form comes from the contact with the route itself. The form of a pilgrimage is makeshift, improvised, spontaneous. It is a response to, not an imposition on, the conditions of the road. So a pilgrimage is not a "work" in either a theatrical or a religious sense; it is an opus as in *magnum opus* or *opus dei*. It is a power surge.

A pilgrimage is not a race to a goal line. It is a co-creation, not a competition. Grotowski as a pilgrim is in "competition" only with his own weakness. To confuse pilgrimage with race-running is to cut oneself off from his own body and from other pilgrims. Pilgrims are away from home, and "out there" our race-running can only exhaust us into becoming mere hangers-on. Pilgrimage is running without racing.

In the history of religion pilgrimage sites are seldom located at the commercial and political centers. Furthermore, they are often composite shrines on the edges of things. Pilgrimage sites are cultural preserves located outside the cultural centres. Grotowski is in search of a preserve. The pilgrim leaves the commercial centers which are the domain of culture-as-artifice. The far away place, which is the domain of culture-as-primeval-site, is the space to which a pilgrim goes when art in pursuit of the art (artifice) becomes merely artificial. Grotowski thinks that culture is an event which occurs when one stands where he can see what is not yet born. It is the mountain from which one can see history making itself evident. Any acting which occurs must take the organic form of a response to the more primal action of the world itself. This primal action is not merely internal, though it is that too; it is living, and therefore, both interior and exterior.

Not every time is ripe for climbing Fire Mountain together. Grotowski knows the time is ripening. In wartime we speak of a "theatre of action." For Grotowski our time has broken the seams of the theatre. The action has shifted fields. It has shifted quite literally to the fields and forests. Grotowski is un-acting in preparation for an action of meeting which is making itself evident among us. A pilgrim is not a guru or a messiah, a priest or a rabbi. He is not to be followed but to be accompanied. One must not follow him, because he is following something else. When a pilgrim is elevated (and thereby degraded) by other pilgrims into a tour guide with a chauffeur's badge, he becomes a bus driver, and the holiday of pilgrimage becomes a mere vacation. Grotowskian pilgrims have been deeply into the Polish forest, literally and metaphorically. Pilgrims who are serious make temporary retreats and hermitages along the way. One who cannot close himself off cannot open himself up.

The strength of pilgrimages as ritual processes is that the theatre of the sacral deed does not perform by virtue of a priestly office. All are lay persons in the pilgrimage process. A difficulty is that lay people are easily distracted by the glut of holy souvenirs that clutter every pilgrimage site; medals, banners, holy water, blessed pictures. The active adventure of walking suddenly subsides at the foot of the holy mountain, and the pilgrim is severely tempted to lapse into passive holiness. Holiness is no longer an action done but a thing purchased, a quantity held.

Pilgrimages come to an end. Their death is implicit in their beginning. Theatre programs and holy relics are helpful only if they lead us to embrace the death of our actions. They are destructive if they become ways of trying to recapture the action. So I have two questions for those of us who will meet with Grotowski on Fire Mountain. First, can we converge there without carving up the trees into splinters, later to be peddled as slivers of the True Cross? And, when the mountain bursts its seams as the theatre did, can we say, "Yes, death, like life, cannot be unnecessary?"

27

THEATRE OF SOURCES

Jerzy Grotowski

This text is based on different extracts from Grotowski's explanations of the Theatre of Sources Project. The major fragments are based on Grotowski's text from 1981, the Polish version of which was edited by Leszek Kolankiewicz. The important fragments of explanation are from a talk given by Grotowski at York University in Toronto, in October 1980; the English version of this talk was prepared by Jenna Kumiega and Jerzy Grotowski. A number of fragments are based on other explanations from 1979 to 1982.

I

The really important question is the question about need. I am still asked for what aim I do something. It is as if these people asking suppose that you can put everything in perfect order in advance. It is a mechanical way of looking. In reality, an alive process, rather, resembles a tree: there is no matter of goal, but of the roots from which the tree is growing. The needs of our nature are the roots.

In childhood, in the time of the war, I was living among peasants in a village. There was a wild apple tree which had a very special shape. This apple tree was attracting me. I was climbing on this wild apple tree. I started to be almost possessed by the unreasonable temptation to do things as if I were the priest of this apple tree. I was almost doing some kind of Mass face to this tree.

It's clear for me that I felt my body to be weaker than the bodies of other children. Surely I was looking for compensation. And to climb on this tree was easier for me than on other trees. But also, it was the only wild tree there, and it stayed in my memory as something very important.

It was not even this apple tree which was important. What was important was compensation. And with all these doubtful motivations, maybe it was as if this tree were transporting me somewhere else.

Later when I began to know something about Taosim, I could better comprehend what I said before, that my dealings with the apple tree were transporting me somewhere else. In the Taoist tradition there exists a motif discriminating between what is natural and what is of source, *sourcial*; to be more precise I will say that what is natural is sending us toward what is sourcial. I will quote here from memory – as I keep it in mind from different translations – some significant text:

> The light of the nature sends back its brilliancy on the
> sourcial, the original.
> The imprint of the heart planes in the space; the brightness of
> the moon gleams in its purity.
> The boat of life reached its shore; the light of the sun shines
> dazzlingly.

Not important that my story was about the tree. And compensations should be accepted. Somebody can be transported by the light of the sun, somebody by the light of the moon, somebody "by the light of the nature." It is a question of the fact that "the light of nature" is not everything. "The light of the nature sends back its brilliancy on the sourcial, the original." When something like this happens to a human being, then – as they say in different traditions – "the imprint of the heart planes in the space." The adventure with the tree happened to me when I was probably nine years old.

The time I passed in the village was wartime. One day my mother set out to the city in order to find books, because she was convinced that some books can be nourishment. Then she brought two – *The Life of Jesus* by Renan and *A Search in Secret India* by Brunton. The book of Renan was forbidden by the Church, but my mother considered it an extremely important story about Jesus, and often repeated that for her it was the "fifth Gospel."

Mother was practicing the most ecumenical Catholicism. She still underlined that for her no one religion had a monopoly on truth. Her interest in the traditions of India was deep and stable. It was not by chance that she brought into the village for her children the book of Brunton. She repeated to me that intellectually (that is, because of her opinions), she felt herself to be Buddhist. She was also accepting persons whose attitudes were clearly not religious. It seemed logical enough, but during her confessions in the church it caused some funny discussions with the priest. Also because she emphasized in the time of confession that in her opinion, if humans have souls, then surely animals have also.

In the time when I was living among the peasants, the Church forbade reading the Gospels alone. The presence and interpretation of the priest was obligatory. Because I was asking to read the Gospels myself, I clashed with the old Catholic priest in the village school. He refused, of course. But his young assistant priest, in secret, gave me the Gospels, asking that his boss should know nothing about this, and that I should read it in conspiracy. In my pocket I carried this little book with its soft brown cover. I arrived to the farm where I was living, I put the ladder up to the loft, which was above a little wood shed for the pigs, I locked myself inside and I was reading. From above, I was listening to the grunting of the pigs. The light arrived through little holes in the thin wood wall. What I was perceiving when reading was not at all the story of the Divine Hero. It was rather the story of the Friend. I understood him as a friend of the neighbourhood horse who had only one eye and who was beaten by his owner. He was also the friend of me, and of everyone in the village who was in difficulties. Through these holes I had seen a very little hill with a couple of trees on it, and that became for me the image of Golgotha. All topography of the village became for me the topography of the Gospel story.

More or less two years later, I read a Polish translation of portions of the Zohar – it had a big impact on me, and some fragments, by the very fact of reading them often, I learned by heart. Later, interest was born in me for the Old Testament: Job, Ezekiel, Jakob . . . And Judaic tradition . . . Baal Shem Tov and the Hasidic patriarchs from the books of Buber. Still as a teenager, I read the Koran.

In the second book which my mother brought from the city was a report by Brunton about a man who was living on the side of Arunachala Mountain in India, and who in some way was projecting on this mountain the God-image. In his case it would be more precise to say the Godhead presence. His experience was oriented of course towards somewhere else than the mountain. This old man, who in our cultural context would probably be judged as a simpleton or even a crazy person (the Russians have the perfect word for this, *yorodiviy* – maybe we can translate this as holy fool), this old man was repeating that if one is investigating "Who am I?", then this question will send you somewhere back and your limited "I" will disappear, and you will find something else, *real*. Later I learned that this something else he was connecting with *hridayam*, etymologically: heart-is-this.

My first reaction when I read the report of Brunton was a fever. Later, I started to copy the conversations of this *yorodiviy* with his visitors. Then I discovered that I am not so much a changeling as I was supposing before. I discovered that somewhere in the world persons are living who are aware of and deeply involved in some strange, non-habitual possibility. It gave me a clear temptation, but at the same time put me more or less in contradiction with a conventional Catholic education. But it is well possible that all this I am saying is already some kind of rationalization, and that even if everything that happened under the influence of this report about the old man from Arunachala opened some horizon for me, at the same time, paradoxically, it was serving my need for self-importance, for development of a big ego. Anyway, from this time on I started to try, practically, to make this investigation: "Who-am-I?" which was not a mental investigation, but rather as if going more and more towards the source from which this feeling of "I" appears. The more this source seems to be approached, the less the "I" is. It is as if a river would turn and flow towards its source. And in the source, there is no longer a river?

In the same book by Brunton is a description of a meeting with some solitary Sufi hermit living in total isolation. He explained to the visitor that the normal stream of thoughts related to the "I"-feeling can be compared with a cart pulled by oxen into a long dark tunnel. He suggested: "Turn the cart back and you will find a light and the space." The event with the report of Brunton happened when I was maybe ten years old. Much later, I met the tradition of some other *yurodiviy*, also living in India, who was transcending any limitations of exclusive religion and who was at the same time behaving often in a totally crazy way. His craziness was full of meaning.

For the man from Arunachala, the Godhead, in reality, was totally impersonal. But when he personalized it and related it to his Mountain, it was Shiva, a male God. This second man, when personalizing, was calling it the Mother. I found this term very human and very natural, and at the same time, in a direct way, referring to something as the source.

When my mother moved to the village with my brother and me, my father didn't join us. He escaped from Poland after it was attacked by the German and Soviet invasions in 1939, in order to join the Polish army reorganized in France (for fighting against the Nazis) and after the defeat of France, in England. He was very strongly anti-Soviet, and after the war he didn't want to return to Poland, which was in the zone of Soviet influence. So, after 1939 I never saw him again. For him, Soviet and Russian imperialism were the same thing. In our family, for centuries there was a tradition of active fighting against the Tsarist effort to colonize Poland. My father hated even Dostoyevski, and this was strange from me: Dostoyevski with his novels became for me deeply important. In the wisdom of Father Zosima in *Brothers Karamozov* and the innocence of Prince Mishkin in *Idiot*, I found extraordinary images of *yurodiviy*.

I dedicated a thread of life to contact with such persons, direct contact, and without hiding that it was a matter of the conquest of knowledge, and not in some Romanesque way, like in the beautiful novels, but through real confrontation, when an actual transmission is received or stolen – as almost every true teacher is looking to be robbed by somebody of the next generation.

In wartime, we had seen many corpses, but what was really shocking to me was the image of cutting the throat of the calf in the farm where we were living. The calf had already had its throat cut but was still alive, running around, spreading blood. Why was I so shocked by this? I was eating meat without any resistance or doubt, so there was not this problem. It was rather that many people were saying that humans are killed because they are seen as enemies. This word referred to something devilish. In the case of butchering the calf it was clearly not a matter of an "enemy"; I myself participated in this strange game of nature because afterwards I was eating its body.

The other personalization of nature was a bull who was kept next to the barn. The cows was conducted to him to be mounted. The children from the village were observing this with great attention. Nothing in this was exciting for us, but rather mysterious and even very serious. I had a glimpse of nature as the Mother giving life and death. However, the light of nature is transporting somewhere else.

As a child I made many observations about people. Sometimes people arrived to our room to play cards. Then I hid under the table. I remarked that the legs of the people playing cards were communicating under the table in relation to many things that were not said at all above the table. But even more, I started to see the complete lack of sense of many human conversations. Somebody said, for example, that the cow has hooves, then somebody else was talking about his grandmother who had swollen legs, and then somebody else that in the concentration camps – before dying – the people are swollen because of starvation. In these conversations there was no consistent line, no true continuity. It was rather a kind of babbling.

Some years later I heard the expression: "Life is a dream." I should say that I never understood this sentence in the sense that we are dreaming and it is life and we wake up after the life and there is something else. I caught this sentence precisely in the spirit of my observations from the time under the table. Life is a dream in the sense that we are the prisoners of our babbling. Not only in conversations, but in the way of reacting, of thinking, in the way we are following some kind of internal monologues or dialogues, and it is a dream because this is just babbling.

It can seem very strange, but for me all this particular field of interest (which never stopped being a very special field of interest), from the very beginning was not a matter of any precise religion or even of different religions, but much more of something, I can say, technical. It was also not cut from the body or refusing the body. Because of my physical weakness I needed the body, I was craving organicity. It was rather the need to arrive to something that would give me the ground, the support – the confirmation from the "source". I am sure that inside me was some hidden fear of life, of my own weakness, some need for a powerful weapon, a need for some strong basis for my ego. But anyway it did not attach me to any local or exotic religion. In some way, it rather opened for me a completely natural doorway face to the different traditions, as if my motherland in this domain became very large. Something in this orientation, in the metaphoric sense, I can call "deeply anthropological," human. It was not the matter of heaven (after the life); it was the matter of *hic et nunc*.

II

So in some way, I began my own research as a young boy, almost alone, and I have continued it, now meeting – through life – different kinds of *yurodiviys*, some "normal," some bizarre, some mad. I have continued that work through the years but it has remained nevertheless almost private. One day, I found that it could be a more public activity as well – not in the sense of making a public show of it – but in the sense of not being able to hide that there is a kind of research with which I occupy myself. This research I began long before I ever started my work in the theatre and this had an influence on my theatrical way.

Now, given circumstances, it seems a natural time in my life simply to say publicly, "all right, this is my work." It was around 1977 that the occasion presented itself. I was given the opportunity both by the Laboratory Theatre and by certain international organizations and foundations to create an international program. I said to myself, "that's the moment," and I found the name *Theatre of Sources*.

It seems to me simplest to start from the information that this project is under realization by a transcultural group. Almost every one of the members of this group I found personally, most often in their own native milieus. On the whole, these were mainly traditional milieus representing traditions which in one way or another, at a minimum to some extent, were not unknown for me. Because of this factor, when I communicate with a respective member of the group, I can to some extent use the semantics of his tradition. What are these traditions? The transcultural group includes representatives of different Asiatic traditions, of traditions in origin African, American Indian, European, and Judaic. As you can remark, the key word is "tradition." Sometimes it is difficult to define whether it is cultural tradition or religious tradition, because in some milieus this kind of differentiation doesn't exist. It should just be taken for granted that every member of the transcultural group is more or less strongly rooted in his native background related to tradition and culture. By this fact itself, the group is some kind of Tower of Babel.

Sometimes we are working together, sometimes in minuscule groups of a few persons. In a few cases, communication within the group through spoken language is difficult, because some of us don't know any language that is understandable for a number of others. But it is not at all an obstacle for the group work. I will say already that in this investigation we are transcending the borderlines of one language, one tradition, one culture. Therefore it is possible to meet together on the terrain where what is important is what is done and not what is said or believed or supposed.

As a point of departure, we take for granted that every member of the transcultural group is related to his native culture and that he regularly renews the contact with his own milieu. I underline that each of the group members enters the work clearly for a limited period – for some months, for one year, for two years. Why? Because he should keep his settlement in his normal daily life; he should not cut himself off from it and become, let's say, some kind of professional of Theatre of Sources, which in any case is only a Project with a limited span of duration. The second reason is that it is favorable for the group member to keep some kind of autonomy face to me, that is, let's say, face to the person who is programming this work in a firm way.

III

Perhaps at this moment, it would be appropriate to turn to the subject of what we call the techniques of sources. The name Theatre of Sources is simply a code. It is possible to find another name, Apollinaire said that in our time everything should have a new name. I will try to decode this name, Theatre of Sources. For the present, I will leave out the word "theatre," and I will speak about the "sources." But be careful. I'm not talking about the sources of *theatre*. So what sources? It's very difficult to verbalize but in a certain trivial way one can give some examples. For instance, everybody knows that yoga exists. Yoga to some is a technique. In truth, yoga is an enormous bag within which there are many techniques, each different from one another. Whatever one describes it as, it is clear that yoga is a technique of sources. Many people in the West today are speaking about some of the Sufi techniques. When we focus that way, it is more or less clear what exactly we are talking about. What we are saying here is that there are "source" techniques known in our part of the world as Dervish techniques. Ethnographers who study the life and practices of North American Indians and those who study or are excited about some aspects of shamanism know that there exists what we can call techniques (proceedings).

We all know that there exists such a thing as a "walk of power." That's fine. Because thanks to this more or less confused knowledge, everybody knows that a technique of sources can be something in appearance very primary. Like, for instance, just walking. So, to speak again in an extremely trivial way, there are different techniques of sources. Other techniques – in zen buddhism. There are certain forms of this that are well known. Some involve simply sitting down. There are also techniques relating to the martial arts, the arts of the warrior, connected with zen for centuries. Here it is necessary to underline that the techniques of sources that interest us are not those most closely related to techniques of sitting meditation, but those that lead to activity, in action – for example, the martial arts techniques related to zen. Therefore, the techniques that interest us have two aspects: first, they are dramatic, and second, in the human way, they are ecological. Dramatic means related to the organism in action, to the drive, to the organicity; we can say they are performative. Ecological in the human way means that they are linked to the forces of life, to what we can call the living world, which orientation, in the most ordinary way, we can describe as to be not cut off (to be not blind and not deaf) face to what is outside of us. And I should underline that this aspect is the same whether we are in a natural environment or in an indoor space.

IV

Are the sources connected with "the body" or with "the soul"? It is very difficult to answer and to say where the body finishes and the psyche begins. Maybe in dealing with the question of sources it is better to say that there exists man [czlowiek] who precedes the differences. But anyway I am aware that all this kind of formulation can seem too foggy. Therefore, let us ask in this way: what happens when the daily-life techniques of the body which are habits in a definite cultural circle are suspended? These daily, habitual techniques of the body are – as analysed by Marcel Mauss – the first cultural differentiation. When they are suspended, what appears? Well, what first appears is deconditioning of perception. Habitually, an incredible quantity of stimuli are flowing into us, from outside something is "speaking" to us all the time, but we are programmed in such a way that our attention records exclusively those stimuli that are in agreement with our learned image of the world. In other words, all the time we tell ourselves the same story. Therefore, if the techniques of the body, daily, habitual, specific for a precise culture, are suspended, this suspension is by itself a deconditioning of perception. What it is – difficult to describe. Anyway, we do not then perceive and sense in the habitual way.

For me personally some hypothetical qualification is sufficient: we are simply going back to the state of the child. But not in the meaning of playing that we are children, and not in the sense that we become childish. When I talk about return to the state of the child, I have in the background of my mind some indefinable memory: plunging into the world full of colors, sounds, the dazzling world, unknown, amazing, the world in which we are carried by curiosity, by enchantment, experience of the mysterious, of the secret. We are drifting then in the stream of reality, but our movement, even if full of energy, is in point of fact a repose. We forgot about this state through the years of taming our body and with it our mind. It is necessary to refind this hypothetical child and his "ecstasies," which, long ago, we "abdicated," as Baudelaire said, if I well remember. It is something tangible, organic, primal.

All these conditionments, cultural, social, one can suspend also through working on the mind. This appears, for example, in some kind of yoga. Mircea Eliade called it "the techniques of deconditioning." But one or another orientation depends on personal preference. For me, the techniques of work on direct deconditioning of the mind are not proper for a transcultural project, and even to some extent seem risky, because they request a kind of manipulation in this unclear zone between the unconscious and consciousness, where one should dominate the process of ideation with all that precedes it. I know that there are people for whom this works very well, if they have the proper teacher and a very long perspective of time. But in the transcultural group with which I am working, the differences between individuals and among their habitual mind structures or, we can say, the structures of thinking, are enormous. Let me say that, for example, the Japanese have a concept of "emptiness" which is fundamentally different from what we associate with this word in Europe. Let's say, also, that the Hindus often call "consciousness" what in my cultural context would be called rather the "unconscious." Already on the verbal level enormous differences exist. It would require many very complicated translations and almost manipulations to arrive to some common territory of work on deconditioning the mind. In what are called the meditational techniques or contemplative techniques, there exists some kind of centering on Self which results in the restraint or even withdrawal of the senses from objects; as Patanjali said very well in the *Yoga Sutras*, the senses should be withdrawn in this way exactly as the turtle removes its paws. It can even happen that a yogin enters into some kind of, let's say, catalepsy or catatonia, but I don't mean this with a pathological connotation. We could say that his body is immobilized and his life processes slowed down, as in hibernation.

In our investigation the orientation is naturally performative, active, looking for and not at all cutting the contact with what is around us or face to us. Therefore, when I was looking for the members of the transcultural group, I was looking for persons who have a natural inclination toward performative behavior in the work, englobing the impulses of the body and accepting the awake senses; by this very fact I was looking for persons related, in one way or another, to pertinent kinds of traditional techniques.

The work on temporary suspension of the habitual, daily-life techniques of the body is a return to something as simple as the movement of the child. I don't think that it can be risky. But that is not the point. The point is that in this case reciprocal comprehension arrives very quickly because bodies, despite any difference of culture, are similar. Speaking about the temporary suspension of the habitual techniques of the body, I don't forget, however, that what is *not-bodily* is anyway deeply present in this process.

It is not a synthesis of techniques of sources that we are after. We search for sourcing techniques, those points that precede the differences. Let us say that there exist techniques of sources. But what we search for in this Project are the sources of the techniques of sources, and these sources must be extremely unsophisticated. Everything else developed afterwards, and differentiated itself according to social, cultural or religious contexts. But the primary thing should be something extremely simple and it should be something given to the human being. Given by whom? The answer depends on your preferences in the area of semantics. If your preferences are religious, you can say it's the seed of light received from God. If, on the other hand, your preferences are secular, you can say that it's printed on one's genetic code.

V

Theatre of Sources is an investigation about what the human being can do with his own solitude (next to the other, or to others). To some extent it can be said that around this is floating – in the most literal meaning – silence and solitude transformed into force. The primary thing that should precede the differences of traditions is simple, but demands palpable and, I would say, exterior actions in order to be touched. For example, they say you must find your inner silence. Of course. But if you cannot find your own inner silence, I don't think anyone else can do it for you. Silencing cannot be a philosophical postulate. It can appear only as something obvious from the context of the work, from circumstances. The context of work alone, the fact of where one is, the obviousness of being in the place as it is, suggests something: if we are in the natural

environment outside of the workroom, we should not turn the environment into garbage (it means not to leave traces behind you – the animals
know this), not smoking, not using flashlights, not making noise. In the
Theatre of Sources project we are not putting to ourselves the famous
demand, how to stop our mental river, this strange mixture of thoughts,
memories, daydreams, imaginations, feelings, fantasies. Looking on you
from outside, I cannot really know if, objectively, you stopped this river,
but I can know if you are silent. The *exterior* silence, if you are keeping
it, can draw you near toward *inner* silence, at a minimum in some
measure, after some time. It is not a matter of moving in an elevated way,
but rather of arriving to some kind of silence of movement, even if you
are running.

Through different kinds of action, it is possible to discover what is
noisiness or babbling of movement: this appears in the need always to
express something, to react with mimicry, to chatter with gestures – all
this is babbling. The word should appear when it is inevitable. Then it is
important. You can go through the forest at night and not hear anything,
neither the cry of a night bird, nor the whispering of the trees, because
you are still humming, hemming and hawing, smoking, lighting. There
exists a way of singing which doesn't disturb the singing of the birds at
all. But to arrive to this it is necessary to know silence: silence of words,
silence of movements. This silence gives the chance for important words
and ways of singing that don't disturb the language of the birds. One of
our colleagues in the transcultural group is Huichol. When he arrived in
Poland, he felt himself almost lost. But when in our work he heard the
dominating silence, he found himself more at home because his people
use words only when necessary.

The other matter is solitude *next to the others*. We are so much alone
in the crowd that we are looking for any illusion to surpass loneliness.
We meet, we act friendship that doesn't exist, we act desires that don't
actually exist. We think that we are with the others and that something
is happening, but often nothing happens – we are only trying to excite
our emotions. In the Theatre of Sources Project, the matter is of
something which surpasses the social game and which is in some way
coming back to the original. It is an extremely difficult battle, and it is
necessary to find the way not to get reciprocally jammed. This doesn't
mean that everyone in this work should be cold as a fish. It means that
everyone keeps a natural distance, simply in the meaning of space. It is
very well known that animals keep a protecting distance and only
humans, even when it is not necessary, sit one on the head of the other.
It is a matter of something which we can call the life space. Everyone
should concentrate on a proper battle and keep responsibility for
himself.

In this Project, a big part of the work is done not only in the natural environment, but in indoor spaces, and then all this interhuman aspect, the whole question of behavior next to the others, becomes not only fundamental but gives some lessons for daily life. The relationship that can be born from this kind of work has the nature of solidarity on the battlefield. It reminds me of a poem by Walt Whitman, which I read in my youth: it was an inscription on the grave of a soldier – "Bold, cautious, true and my loving comrade." Let's say that solitude next to somebody is not only the beginning of solidarity, but it is work *on individual*. Individual has value in itself, and this value precedes a pair of humans or a group.

VI

There's a very old expression which one finds in many different traditions: "Movement which is repose." It was in the early *Gnosis* (not *gnosticism*, which is very "baroque" or even "rococo" in its language, in its inventions of names and levels of reality) and in some particular transmission attributed to the not-public teachings of Jesus. But it is also in Tibetan yoga texts. The very same words. Also in yoga approaches in India it is said that we can be fully awake, vigilant, and also in repose: as if we were plunged into a sleep without confabulations. That movement which is repose is perhaps the crucial point where different techniques of sources begin. So we have two aspects: movement and repose. When we are moving, and when we are able to break through the techniques of the body of everyday life, then our movement becomes a movement of perception. One can say that our movement is seeing, hearing, sensing, our movement is perception.

All these things are quite simple. I mentioned before a "walk of power." Even in this term is some romanticism. . . . But in Theatre of Sources, one of the most ordinary actions is just a way of walking which, through rhythms different from the rhythms of habitual life, breaks the kind of walk which is directed towards an aim. Normally, you are never there where you are because in your mind you are already in the place where you are going, like in the train seeing only the consecutive stations, but if you change the rhythm (this is a very difficult thing to describe but it can be practiced), if for instance you change to an extremely slow rhythm, so slow that you are virtually standing still (and so that somebody watching might have the impression that he doesn't see anyone because you are almost immobile) then in the beginning you can be very irritated, questioning, vomiting the thoughts, but after a few moments, if you are really attentive, something does change. You begin to be where you are. It depends on individual temperament. Some have too much energy. In that case, one must begin with movement to burn off the energy, to set fire to the body, a kind of letting-go, but at the same time one must preserve the organicity of the movement and not its athleticisms. It's as if your animal body becomes master of the situation and starts to move – without obsession about what is dangerous or not. It may begin perhaps in jumping. Apparently you would never be able to jump that way. But you do it. It happens. And you don't look at the ground. You close your eyes and maybe even run among the trees but you don't run into them. It's nature and your body nature that is burning off. For your body is also nature. But when it's burnt off something happens. You feel as if everything is part of the great flow of things and your body begins to feel it and begins to move quietly, serenely, almost floating, as if your body were conducted by the flow. You can feel that it is the flow of all things around that carries you, but at the same time you feel that something is coming out of you too.

I remember a case of one teenager who wanted to make some money and because he knew how to climb well, he was employed in the forest gathering pine cones from the trees. It was easy for him because he could pass in the air from one tree to another. After some hours he remarked that the habitual babbling in him stopped. His body was in permanent movement and his hands were busy with the cones without interruption. He felt that now he was moving more fluidly, more softly, and at the same time that he gathered the cones more adroitly. Also, he didn't know anymore whether his head was up or down. He felt as if everything were translucent. It was as if he were plunging into a dream full of light, *without dreaming*. It was *without dreaming*, without memories, confabulations or reveries, and his memory was actually recording everything with perfect precision. In some moment he realized that his colleagues doing the same work also became totally silent. He asked one of them: "Is something strange happening with you?" And another: "What happened?" Then he said something like: "This gathering goes so lightly for me. It is as if I am . . . there. I have no words. It is awake."

This teenager, insofar as I know, was never before reading anything related to awakening or any such terminology. But let me say that in some manner and to some extent, he was in the movement which is repose. Because the movement which is repose can't be hallucinations or visions, miracles, or the feeling that you are the cosmos . . . but rather something incredibly simple. One day I observed somebody who arrived near to something similar washing the dishes. It was possible because he wanted to do it in such a way that nobody would know that he was doing this (for the others). He didn't know that I saw him or that anyone was watching him. A Hindu man who was beside me observed this activity and then he said, "That is the perfect karma yoga." Another time I looked on somebody who was walking back and forth. Walking, he started to lose his heaviness; he arrived to the way of walking of his four-year-old child. In his movement was directness, drive, and joy, the life of the child. In many traditions, we can find the notion of the child which is often confused with childishness. Or confused with playing at being childlike. But in fact, what it is all about is simply something very direct and immediate, and that is what is most touching in the child. This immediacy which is at the same time energetic and at the same time carries in itself joy. Perhaps the word joy is too much. Perhaps we should say only lack of anguish, lack of energetic depression. That's what it's all about. It's quite primal.

VII

In the group of Theatre of Sources a number of participants are allied to a technique of sources close to them, traditional for them. But a very important fact is that this is not shared. Though a colleague of mine is a Japanese Buddhist priest, he is nevertheless not doing something that is of his religion. He knows that that is not part of Theatre of Sources. He is studying zen buddhism but he knows that he won't be doing sitting meditation with any of the others in the group. He has a very full life and also practices the zen martial arts. He is a very good teacher of this, a specialist, but he never proposed to any of us to work with him on it. We don't "share" the techniques of sources. There is a Latin American Indian who has been with us for a long time. We began working with him long before the name Theatre of Sources was used. There is also a Hindu Bhakta. He is deeply rooted in his own tradition but is also keenly aware of the contemporary world. The three of them, the Latin American Indian, the Bhakta, and the Japanese priest work together but they do nothing that belongs to only one tradition. They look for some action, evident in its consequences for all three. That means it works for all three despite the differences of cultural context. The Project is oriented toward the kind of actions which "precede the differences," and for this reason englobe persons from traditions and techniques far from one another. This work can be explored and developed together even without special explanations or common language among the people, because its basis is formed by something ultimately, almost unimaginably, simple. The actions initiated by a Hindu are accepted as correct only if they work when done by non-Hindus, initiated by a Haitian only if they work when done by non-Haitians, initiated by a Japanese person only if they work when done by non-Japanese people.

Often an action begins as a childlike action, or from the almost infantile preferences of each one. It's like one wants to climb a tree but doesn't know why. Someone else has a preference for running but really to the point of letting go. Someone else searches only for a way of walking. Someone else has really a very particular idea that you can move without seeing. He puts a handkerchief over his eyes and moves. And he says, if the movement can see, then maybe I can see without eyes. The points of departure are mostly personal preferences but not the preferences of a particular tradition. Somebody makes several actions on the line of his preferences. Then he does it with someone from another tradition – often without even a language in common – and the first test is whether this thing works for someone who has been conditioned differently. If it works for the other people, we concentrate on that in our work. But the thing that appears after a long evolution is always something still more elementary. One could say that we arrive at something totally primary and simple.

In some periods, after a longer span of work with the transcultural group, we accept for a short period persons from outside. We try to confront them with different actions which we verify before in practice among ourselves. We simply ask the participants, the invited persons from outside, to imitate. In order to see if it works for them, they should do it immediately and not analyse it from the point of view of structure, for instance. The only way of doing this, therefore, is to ask them to imitate. That process is an amusing one in our contemporary world. In the current life, we all behave even too much in an imitative way. Most of our lives are only an imitation of other people's lives. That we accept. But if you ask someone simply to imitate the person who is guiding them in this action – "Do it!" – it is an enormous shock. But see how birds teach their young. It's really through imitation. By imitating without analysing, it's easy to find which actions give you this lack of anguish and this lack of energetic depression. Then you can make choices and the problem of imitation doesn't exist anymore. You must really work yourself in order to penetrate the thing.

In Poland, we are conducting the Project in an isolated place outside the city, with big simple buildings and indoor work spaces, and with a large natural environment around that has for us some kind of exceptional presence, where every path in the forest has for us a meaning and its own nature. In some actions the routes are directed toward the spots which for us seem to be charged as accumulators, striking, out of the ordinary. During the summer of 1980, when we conducted, day and night over three months, a practical seminar for 220 people from outside, the participants arrived in waves, as for some unusual "hunting," some kind of fullness – non-habitual in daily life. Our whole space, both indoor and outdoor, became the "theatre of events," in the same way it is said about a "theatre of war." In this sense, we can speak about Theatre of Sources.

VIII

The work in the intercultural group – according to the time and place (in Poland, in Haiti, in the reservation of the Huichols in Mexico, in Ife and Oshogbo in the Yoruba territory in Nigeria, in Bengal, India, and other places) – changed its human composition and the quantity of persons, and even to some extent the field of investigation. Some works are conducted with an extremely narrow circle of people. This started even before the official name of the project – Theatre of Sources – appeared. There exists only one basic rule – the human composition always includes persons from different cultures and traditions.

Everything that I said until now and which is connected with an aspect of silence, of solitude next to the other, and of some kind of relationship with what in dry language is called the natural environment – and without disturbing this environment! – can be seen in the perspective of this something that in the far past was called "the movement which is repose."

And all of that is the scope of the Project. But there exists also another line of work – only within the limits of the very narrow nucleus of the group (with not always the same persons); this other line of work tries to enter into much more particular – even if very initial – territories of investigation. One of these territories is work on archaic, initiatic texts of which the place and circumstances of arising are questionable, and which in some way relate to those, let's say, living experiences of the sources (someone will prefer to say: source). These texts are as if carrying in themselves the roots of what in Poland we call the Mediterranean Culture. We are studying these texts simply through singing them – through looking for the melodies which could carry them. Sometimes it is linked to an organic flow of movement. The level of this work – technically and in its substance – is very preliminary, but something special seems to be on the far horizon, even if this "something" we don't yet really recognize.

Mainly during expeditions, therefore in milieus where old techniques were born or developed or just surviving (but also in our transcultural, isolated place in Poland, together with traditional practitioners whom we found before and as individuals), this narrow group of persons encounter the components of traditional incantations and songs of the Hasidim, or the most simple forms of participation in performative elements linked to "grains of ritual" in Haitian voodoo or confrontations with Bauls, yogin-bards from Bengal in India.

I am speaking about that kind of participation which is an attempt at cognition in the most modest way. Cognition that in no way disturbs the happened event, cognition within the limits of elements which in practice become almost transparent for persons whose culture, language, mental and behavioral habits, traditions and mind structures are extremely different. For the present, in this time of preliminary investigations in the frame of the very narrow nucleus, we try to keep ourselves within the limits, I will say, of the minimum. We are dealing with and reacting face to the most elemental components in order to cognize initially, and not through verbalized observations (not verbalized even in thought), but through the most simple following in practice, even if often this "following" should be almost only inside the participant, without any visible exteriorization. But even in these cases, the streams of impulses are waking up and passing through the organisms if these ancient sourcing techniques are working more broadly than in the limits of only one tradition. Because this verifies itself in practice with the persons of another tradition, of another culture – or not.

Therefore, this other line of work is not concentrated only on "what precedes the differences." Here, some genuine, practical phenomena of traditions are approached directly, but – face to them – the members of the small nucleus group are consistently keeping just the first step of contact, careful to avoid becoming fascinated, as for example tourists could be fascinated, or pretending to get some illusory competence; the approach is modest, receptive, based on recognition of everyone's cultural and practical boundaries. All this is maybe just a premise for a field of work-possibility, remote in time; right now the point can be even a simple opportunity to meet some very special persons of tradition.

The other important topics of research with some members of the nucleus of the group are "the circulation of attention" and "the current 'glimpsed' by one when he is in movement."

I should underline some points in order to clarify hearsay and misunderstandings. My individual field work (which I started in 1956, and which is still under continuation), should not be confounded with the terrain of expeditions conducted with the narrow nucleus of the group in the frame of Theatre of Sources. I will give just some examples, related to India, Haiti and Mexico. For economy of time, I will not touch the topic of other traditional territories which were directly in the field of my interest. India: The expedition of the Theatre of Sources nucleus was concentrated mainly on Bengal; my individual studies also – and even more so – focused on South India (Kerala, Decan, Tamil Nadu), Central India, and North India, including traditional centers in the Himalayas. Haiti: the expedition was concentrated not only on a large area around Port-au-Prince, but on middle, and – especially – northwestern Haiti as well. The rumors that we concentrated on phenomena of so-called "voodoo trance of possession" are far from reality – in my individual investigations and in the expedition of the Theatre of Sources, the emphasis was clearly rather on witnessing some performative approaches and on possibilities for entering into direct contact with the strong human examples of the holders of ancient tradition. Mexico: my individual contacts were not related exclusively to the Huichol area. Also, contrary to the rumors about this point, I was not exploring the territories described by Artaud. In the expedition of the narrow Theatre of Sources nucleus among the Huichols, we were strictly avoiding any involvement in peyote use. (In this way we consciously marked a strong difference between our interests and those of foreign tourists sometimes trying to invade this reserve.) We concentrated on psycho-ecological aspects of Huichol culture: the notion of "sacred, charged spots," and on performative possibilities related to these kinds of places.

Three more points should be clarified: first, my experiments with so-called "shamanic approaches" were never done in Siberia. Second, the first step in the countries of the expeditions was to enter into contact with the people of the country and to find (or, if you prefer, to select) the local members of the narrow nucleus team. Third, the investigation described above of the very narrow nucleus team (with not always the same persons) is most often done not in open spaces, but in more traditional, constructed spaces.

IX

To end, I want to tell you a short little story. It seems to me instructive for two reasons: first, because there it appears that everything which is carrying a sense should be kept literally; second, because it seems very ordinary. Let's say that we have already received everything and in some way everything we desire is in our reach, but maybe we are not reaching it because it seems to us too simple. This is a little story about awakening. About this famous awakening that was the topic of great philosophers. About the awakening that Buddhism speaks of. The Gospels tell about awakening. At the same time everyone knows what it is to awake in the morning. But habitually, we think in a different way about this waking up, banal, and about the so-called spiritual, which we suppose requests "concentration of all spiritual powers in order that the ray of light can jet into the other reality . . ." But as a matter of fact it can be a very ordinary thing, and maybe it even means also – in some situations – literally to wake up, to awake. It is said about a man who initiated Buddhism in Tibet that for many years he was sitting facing the wall. Once it seemed to me bizarre. Now maybe I understand him a little better. And at present I will tell you this little story.

Let's say that you are looking for the "movement which is repose." You are looking for it persistently. You are working for a relatively long time: day, night, and next day. During this you sleep sometimes, but for very short moments because you request from yourself to be vigilant. Let's say that against all stubbornness nothing happens. In the beginning, it seems to you that you know what it is all about. After some time you start to have doubts. You look for how to dissolve these doubts in action. But still nothing happens, nothing is done. At the end you arrive to the point when you are already sure that nothing happens. You don't understand why. You know only that you are totally finished. You want simply to throw yourself, no matter where, just to sleep. You are not looking for a bed or for covering. You don't disrobe. Simply, you want to throw yourself down.

After some hours you awake. You have the impression that you were diving. And now – you emerged. When you were coming back from there, you had a fragment of a color-dream. But just before, you felt serenity and light. You felt something that was flowing from inside, as from source. You open your eyes and see what is really in front of you, for instance some wall of bricks or a plastic bag. But these bricks and this plastic bag are full of life, of light. Somewhere near by you hear voices. They are real voices. Simply, some people are quarreling. But these voices arrive to you as something harmonious. You feel that all your senses are working. But at the same time you feel as if everything is flowing as from some source. It is as if you turn on both flashing arrows in the car. Continually a double arrow is blinking. It flows from the middle and from the objects.

Such waking up is awakening. The difference between such awakening and banal awakening consists in the fact that we habitually prepare ourselves for going to sleep. We look for the bed, we cover it, we disrobe, we prepare an alarm clock, and when we wake up we are already thinking about what we should do next. In this way, we liquidate a time of awakening. In the little story I was telling, nothing was disturbing in the awakening. Why was it so full? Maybe because a moment before you were asleep you were not lying to yourself that you know something. Maybe because you lost all hope.

28

THE THEATRE OF SOURCES

Ronald Grimes

Jerzy Grotowski's work is divided into distinct phases: (1) the "poor theatre" phase (1959–1970), (2) the "paratheatrical" phase (1970–1975) and (3) the Theatre of Sources or "active culture" phase (1976–1982). Members of the Polish Theatre Laboratory Institute insist that the Theatre of Sources, which consists of explorations in "active culture," is not to be confused with the paratheatrical work, which was interpersonal in tone. Meeting what is "other," rather than meeting other people, is central to the latter phase. Whereas, in "Holiday; The Day That is Holy" (1973) Grotowski has said, "What matters is that, in this, first I should not be alone . . . ," in the Theatre of Sources one is "alone with others." Even though people work alongside one another in it, they are in solitude.

In both the paratheatrical phase and the Theatre of Sources, the forest, not a theatre, is the scene of action – action, not acting. But what is uncovered or discovered differs between the two projects. In the former, the goal was to disarm oneself in the presence of others. The search was for "bodily sincerity." In the latter, what is "other" than the interpersonal – call it nature, God, spirit, or do not name it at all – is the presence before which one searches out "the movement which is repose."

The paratheatrical work developed a bodily ethic of trust among one's "own kind of people." In the Tree of People, one of the paratheatrical projects, sincerity and trust were drawn beyond mere sincerity of words toward action that was revelatory. The paratheatrical work seemed to be a search for like-minded people and for ways of meeting that did not create audiences or depend on acting. "Meetings," not "performances," occurred.

In "The Art of the Beginner," Grotowski continued to articulate the interest in untraining that was present even in the work of his theatrical period. The article does not describe what is actually done in the Theatre of Sources any more than "Holiday" described the paratheatrical work; rather it sketches Grotowski's understanding of the process of reaching below the "techniques of sources" – that is, spiritual disciplines such as *zazen*, yoga, Sufi dancing or shamanic healing – to the "sources of the techniques of sources." By facilitating an interaction among representatives of old and young culture, he aims to incubate a sensibility nourished at the well from which springs meditation, celebration, and healing. He is searching for an original, precultural sense of beginning. This source or beginning is present here and now, not hidden away in some primitive culture. It is no lost golden age but is a capacity for a perpetual sense of discovery. Grotowski is not interested in imitating or syncretizing archaic disciplines but in finding simple actions to carry on the "work with oneself," the "opus-process." Grotowski refers to his project as a "journey to the East," but "East" does not mean that he intends to borrow either Asian or so-called "primitive" mystical techniques. It means rather that he wants to find out how any action begins. East is the direction of sunrise, of any culturally originative zone.

WORK WITH GROTOWSKI'S INTERNATIONAL STAFF

In the Theatre of Sources during the summer of 1980 in Poland, there were four groups: invited participants, a small group from India including a Baul, Grotowski's international staff, and part of a community of Haitians [*Saint Soleil*, led by Tiga (Jean-Claude Garoute) and Maud Robart]. No one, not even Grotowski, can describe everything that occurred during the Theatre of Sources. By design no person saw every action. Even though Grotowski "directed" the dozen or so staff people, each was typically accompanied only by a few invited participants. About fifteen people were in my group, only a few of whom were present for a given activity. Usually, one of Grotowski's staff led from two to fifteen of us. And eventually – by consultation, selection and decision – we each concentrated on working in only a few of the ways introduced to us. So any description is partial – the result of personal choice and limited perspective – and at best only illustrative. Therefore, I will describe only those actions in which I participated.

One action consisted of long walks during which participants paused at transitions of terrain or foliage, honored the sounds of animals, hugged trees, lay on the earth, crawled under dense pines, watched fish, ran through thickly entangled forest during the night, and walked under waterfalls. The ethics of participation required silence, lightfootedness, nonpollution, careful imitation of the guide, no movements disruptive of forest life or the group. One experiences a full range of emotions in the midst of such walking: loneliness, fear, elation, weariness, embarrassment, amazement, simplicity, boredom, disgust. My dominant response was a sense of attunement. I do not mean by this a sentiment of group kinship or nostalgia for unity with the forest; rather I mean a letting go of both feelings and thoughts as the center of awareness. You "just do" things. You respond – that is all. And it is enough. The staff clearly and overtly discouraged romantic attachment to "the beauties of nature." You lay on the earth quite simply; you do not imagine making love with it.

Another kind of action was a stylized step done clockwise around a tree to the rhythms of solid log drums. One might have called it a dance. We moved for very long periods, always in the daytime, always without innovating or improvising. The sense of monotony was profound. Some found it grounding; some found it boring. The sameness and repetitiveness of the step, like the simple monotony of the drums, provided meditative potentialities once the technique had been learned. The "dance" was neither freeform nor creative. While doing it, our feet replaced our eyes in feeling the ground before stepping.

Often, following this activity were several indoor sessions in which we were instructed to find and repeat some simple gesture to a slightly more complex beat. Again, the periods were quite long, so whatever interest there might have been in performing or displaying one's abilities withered. As with all the actions, they remained essentially uninterrupted, unnamed and unexplained. There was minimal group ideology, so entering, continuing or ending an event depended almost entirely on personal, unspoken motivations. We tested the actions as actions, not as concretions of some shared ideology, not as preludes to anything else.

Whirling was another of the actions. We whirled at a crossroads in the forest. Some fell, some vomited, some got up again. We whirled in one spot. We whirled while running in the woods. Sometimes we whirled in one direction; at other times we alternated directions. We had to attend to both centrifugal and centripetal forces while whirling and running in group. Clinging with one's eyes or attention had disastrous consequences. The whirling was not of the formal Sufi kind. It was more extroverted, rougher, exploratory.

Several of Grotowski's people taught a series of movements that I would call "spiritual exercises," provided "spiritual" connotes a way of being embodied with fullness rather than a way of exiting from the body.[1] Comparisons with tai chi and yoga were inevitable, but the movements were neither. Grotowski does not encourage the importation of techniques, especially those imbedded in long, rich cultural traditions. Rather staff persons coming from those traditions are encouraged to find some new action, which is then tested for its shareability with others.

Because of the complexity of describing gestural sequences, I will not recount individual movements in the series. Emphasis was on keeping our eyes open yet unfocused. Diffuse attention was always paid to vistas provided by one's posture, whether standing prone or upside down. The movements oriented us to the horizon surrounding us, to the sky and the earth. Vision was always to be outward, mobile and flowing – not introverted, static or choppy.

The exercises were for me like a generative grammar of the other actions of the Theatre of Sources. I felt they contained the kinesic seedbed out of which other events sprang as offshoots. The exercises I saw as a summary of the "gestural competence" of the project, in the way that *katas* constitute a grammar of karate competence.

The actions that comprised the forest work with Grotowski's international staff constitute a parashamanic form of hunting. The object of the hunt is not game for killing and eating, as it might be for a shaman; the object is the self/other nexus. The object is to become and encounter the subject – we hunted ourselves. When we ran after deer and were sought out in the night by the large birds and fowl, we were not hunting-culture shamans but postindustrial parashamans. Self-hunting could easily have become narcissistic had not introversion and interpersonal contact been so effectively discouraged. The self for which one hunted was not "unto itself" nor within but rather between persons and the environment. We hunted selves that were not turned in on, or blocked by, ourselves. The forest was not a ruse, not a hideout so people could have feelings or touch bodies. So Grotowski's phrase "work on oneself" can be a misleading one that is easy to misinterpret, especially by popular-therapy-oriented North Americans. "Work as oneself" is better – it does not play into the Esalen stereotype.

The hunting is symbolic insofar as no animals are killed, but quite concrete inasmuch as one's social self is drastically curtailed and one's body pushed to its limits and beyond. Perhaps another way to put the matter is to say that we were taught to hunt for an action – for the proper "verb" and "adverb". In shamanism one hunts for an animal or power. In parashamanism one hunts for the best way to hunt. The Theatre of Sources is a metahunt, the object of which is to deobjectify one's world. It is a hunt for a way of moving that allows earth, sky, foliage, animal and "other" to appear as subjects. The self that is hunted is not just my own private, ego-constituted self, but a selfhood that surrounds me. The effect of the work is centering but not centripetal. I find myself connected and balanced even as I trip and fall to the forest floor. But I also find that I am not the center of either social or cosmic attention. This point is regularly missed by those who hear phrases like "Song of Myself" or "working on myself," but do not actually participate in the actions led by Grotowski and his collaborators.

Shamans hunted animals who were their "tutelary spirits." Parashamans hunt *anima*, spirit. I do not mean *anima* in the Jungian sense of the feminine side of a man, but in the etymological sense of an animating surge that is our own and yet flows through us from among and around us. Describing the ethos of the hunting this way suggests both the continuity and difference between shamanism and parashamanism. Shamanic animism finds the world already alive, whereas parashamanism arises at a time in our history when our bodies have become puppetlike and mechanistic – reflecting a secularized, industrialized environment. The animistic world view finds *anima* unavoidable; it is "out there" pressing hard to come "in here." Whereas, a modern world view can barely locate *anima* at all. In the popular view, spirit is "in here," in the privacy of feeling and ego. But in the form pursued by the Theatre of Sources, *anima* is neither inside nor out. So things must be brought to life by doing "the work." The life of the forest, our bodies and cultures must be activated, animated. This is the meaning of Grotowski's term "active culture," of what I call "parashamanic animation."

WORK WITH THE HAITIAN COMMUNITY

In retrospect I interpreted my explorations with Grotowski's staff people as preparation for participation with the Haitians. While doing the activities, however, I did not view them as preparatory; I simply did them. The sequences of events, which differed for each participant, strongly affected people's experiences and interpretations, as well as their evaluations and capacities to integrate what occurred.

Grotowski's work is clearly phasic. To move from doing performances in which the action is not simulated but is actual self-revelation, to bringing part of a community of Haitians to Poland is a significant change. Grotowski studies under them, with them, and alongside them. He does not merely study them or direct them. The Laboratorium really is a laboratory; the term is not a euphemism. But there are no specimens in it. Or, if there are, Grotowski, as well as invited participants, is one of them. The study of others is a phase of self-study. Self-study is a phase of the study of others. This attitude, of course, bypasses the dualism that segregates the view of orthodox liturgics – "this work is only for us" – from that of conventional anthropology – "this work is only theirs."

However, the attitude is not syncretistic – a pinch of voodoo, a sprinkle of Polish Catholicism, a bit of comparative religion, a dash of Jung and a teaspoon of experimental theatre. Insisting on this is important. Shamanism and parashamanism are commonly syncretistic. But Grotowski is not borrowing from shamans so much as trying to locate the sources before the borrowing begins. The intention to borrow, like the one of inventing ritual, is self-defeating. And it differs considerably form the view that ritual can only be creatively discovered as we enter the ways of others in order better to find our own. What transpires in the Theatre of Sources is genuine ritual, though it is ritual experiment rather than ritual tradition. This is a truly modern form of ritual, dependent as it is on possibilities for travel, study, cultural interchange, and leisure.

I am tempted to speak of the Haitian work as "ritual contact," because of its cross-cultural emphasis, or as "initiation," because it was marked by a ritual beginning in which outsiders who were neophytes made their way toward the *poteau mitan*, the tree of the center. However, I think the neologism *sourcing* expresses the event better, since it suggests an action from or toward an originative zone in which contact is made across a chasm, in this case a religiocultural one.

We are not initiated into voodoo religion, which is a creative cultural synthesis of Yoruba, Christian, and Arawak symbols. No one taught us sorcery. Nor was debased voodoo theatrically performed for us, as is sometimes the case at nightclubs in Port-au-Prince. Nor did we observe voodoo possession rites for the purpose of documenting them in scholarly monographs or imitating them in theatres.

I would characterize what occurred as a "ritual greeting of the sources." Perhaps *re-sourcing* is also a good word for what we did. Since only a few intense days were spent together, considering it an initiation rite would be claiming far too much. So even though there were ritual elements such as meditative waiting, ritual painting, and burning of paintings, singing, dancing, veneration of the sun, and other actions for which I have no names, the overall character of what we did is best interpreted as a ritual introduction to, or greeting of, the sources.

Greeting and departing rites were prominent, deeply moving, never made routine. The Haitians found a new greeting for every person on each occasion of meeting. Each action of greeting seemed attuned to the specific person and the level of intimacy present at the moment. Warmth, joy, and lingering were typical, but laughter, irritation, and suspicion were permitted. One did not merely repeat a convention of greeting like handshaking or hugging but searched anew for the source of greeting. I take greeting as a metaphor for the whole of the event, because in our explorations no one was able either to forget his or her own culture or to ignore the others'. We and they expected to discover a mutual greeting that neither had brought to the ritual interface. We could neither retreat to gestural cliché, imitate, demand imitation or deny that we bore our cultures in the very marrow of our bones. We were thrown back on our cultural resources and yet had to find new resources among ourselves. A simple discovery made by many non-Haitians, one with immense ramifications, was how flexible and hard the Haitians' bodies were, and how soft and inflexible ours were.

I do not want to describe the details of our explorations with the

Haitians so much as indicate what conditions were present that facilitated the emergence of the ritual attitude of re-sourcing, or greeting the sources.

First, the environment differed significantly from that of either the ritual initiators or the ritual respondents. We were not in Haiti and not in a European or North American urban setting. A number of people remarked how odd it was to consider Haitians and voodoo in Poland. But this is precisely to the point: to dislocate the usual indigenous/outsider split. Prior to bringing the group to Poland, Grotowski had worked with them for extended periods in Haiti. And the move, which was, of course, temporary for the Haitians, was not arbitrary. They were not in Poland as part of a cultural zoo or ritual circus.

Even though the very old and very young stayed behind in Haiti, a significant portion of the community came, so it clearly was part of a society, not merely an assembly of individuals from the same country. There were both dislocation and solidarity. Most of the invited participants were dislocated linguistically and geographically, but we shared many of the same values that permeate Western, urban, literate, mobile, postindustrial societies. The Haitians, Grotowski and part of his international staff lived in a barn and shared shanties an hour or so away from Wroclaw, Poland. The Indians, the rest of the international staff and the invited participants usually stayed in two barns a few miles away. Most of the work took place in what Grotowski has called "the forest womb." Even though the Haitians were more native to forests than those in the invited group, much of the ritual contact with them was indoors in a barn that they had been allowed to convert into a sacred place. So they were literally removed from their own turf, but we were symbolically put in the position of walking on their holy ground, a large mat sewn with voodoo spirits on which we sat and danced.

A second condition for ritual re-sourcing was learning to see without looking. The Theatre of Sources project was able to a surprising degree to avoid the interpersonal highs and nostalgia for *communitas* that one has learned to associate with encounters and retreats in the North American human-potential movement. The success in doing so depended on being taught to keep our eyes open, usually toward the horizon, often in a circular pattern, and typically not focused on any one object such as a flower or rock. When we worked with the Haitians, we knew what was meant when they asked us to participate in a ritual by "seeing without looking, hearing without overhearing." If at first we thought this was for their benefit – they did not want us staring or analyzing – we later found it was also for ours. We were able to find without embarrassment our own ways of knowing what was going on. I say "knowing" rather than "explaining," because our way of understanding arose in the biblical sense of knowing as bodily engagement.

We do not recognize, I discovered, how much we paralyse ourselves by making eye contact too readily. Being prohibited from observing, we found that we saw more. We had to see with organs other than our eyes. Learning to do so is as useful for interpreting a ritual as for running in a pitch-black, foggy Polish forest.

A third condition was that of being relieved form the burden of having to believe, explain or perform. The Haitians did not have to perform rituals for us. We were not tourists, anthropologists nor a theatre audience with tickets. Nor were we voodoo initiates. These are the usual role definitions for seeing a ritual. No one was asked or expected to believe in what he or she did. Belief was an irrelevant consideration. And going native was impossible. We just did what we did – sing, dance, paint, hum, shout, imagine, be tired, jump, and a hundred other nameless actions. We were asked not to come with a view to profiting from or explaining what occurred. Although I am sure a myriad mixed motives characterized our group, we were invited to test and try only for ourselves. In short, the tone was experimental. We were allowed, even encouraged, to enter tentatively – with a questing, questioning attitude. The subjunctive mood of the event was acknowledged and even made central, but without any sense that what we were doing was imitation of something better or more real. In effect what transpires in such an environment is ritual modification and innovation for the more traditional participants, and the incubation of a ritual sensibility for the more secularized ones.

A fourth condition was gestural concentration. An axiom of much contemporary liturgies and social anthropology is that one should as a prerequisite know the language of the ritual, the Latin of a pre-Vatican II Mass or the Creole of voodoo, presumably for the purpose of knowing what the various gestures, postures, objects, and actions mean. There are occasions like this one, however, when not knowing the verbal language is a virtue. Not knowing is the prerequisite for knowing in another way. Learning the exegetical meaning of a symbol before internalizing the orectic, felt meaning can lead to reification and false objectivism.

We learned to sing songs we did not verbally understand and dance dances on a rug sewn with spirits we could not name. We would never have learned about our lips and feet what we did had we known "the meaning" too soon, because we would not have attended in such a concentrated way to nonverbal channels of communication.

A fifth condition was cultivated receptivity. Our ideologies, like our technology, are strongly activistic and therefore in cross-cultural contexts, often imperialistic. The Haitians gesturally followed us. Even though they were teachers and we learners, their way of instructing included following and responding to us. This was most obvious in singing, dancing, greeting, and departing.

Preparing for ritual contact demands training in bodily flexibility and in doing nothing. A crucial element in many rituals, not just voodoo, is diffusion of attention, intention, and action. Such times are not the occasion for boredom, preoccupation or planning – the three ways that people of Euro-American cultures typically respond. Ritual is misunderstood if defined as activity, especially if activity is restricted to its overtly active or intentional forms. Some of the most important ritual gestures are unintentional and receptive, rather than active, in tone. The cessation of an action has as much meaning as the initiation or sustaining of one. Monotony and repetition – so anathema to the Westernized, urbanized, and theatricalized sensibility – are necessary conditions for receiving a gesture, which is the most fruitful way ritual symbols emerge from their sources.

The final condition was the sense of the sources as both unitary and plural, both concrete and transcendent. The Haitian group was called Saint Soleil. For it the sun was a concrete manifestation of the unitary sacred. The many figures on the rug were symbolic embodiments of sacred plurality. No choice between monotheism and polytheism would have been necessary had we spoken of the matter at all. All that was necessary when the windows were opened during a particularly dramatic sunset was to be open to sun-being. Questions whether the sun is god, whether we are divine, whether the sacred is scattered or together, were of little importance. The lack of discussion of them had little to do with language differences but was a function of an ethic of silence so ritual re-sourcing could proceed. The source of cohesion between us and the Haitians was action, not theology. Of course, we did not constitute either a tradition or a society. At most we were a nascent community-event, so reflection and words were not so necessary. But the experiment did demonstrate that much verbal, interpretive latitude can be tolerated when a ritual greeting of the sources is made the ground of a meeting.

WORK WITH THE INDIAN GROUP

The people from India were in the process of becoming a group in Poland. Unlike the Haitians, they were not part of an already constituted community. Often they participated in the same way as we invited participants, though some of them had previously gone through the Theatre of Sources project. They also served as a support group for a young Baul from Bengal. The only direct work done with him was our sitting with spines erect listening to his sacred music and watching him dance. In addition, the Baul was a source of spontaneous outburst, affection, and humor – all qualities missing form the directed, structured phases of the project. He was a ritual clown, talking when silence was the rule, hugging when interpersonal gestures were being discouraged, moaning about the food when we were busy learning austerity, and refusing to run in the forest because it was too hard. In short, he gave voice and body to the desires we had to suspend. He inverted the extraordinary reality created in Poland, but the "ordinariness" he performed – and performed in this case is the right word – was itself astoundingly holy, vulnerable, and comical. His combination of virtuoso religious performance and deviance from the project ethic kept participants from taking the explorations with the unbearable, brooding seriousness that has sometimes been associated with the Polish Laboratory.

Before and after the project, the Indians were regularly interacting with invited participants – something neither the Haitians nor Grotowski's international staff did. So on the streets, in the trains, at the zoo, and in the restaurants they were a threshold group, filling the interstices of the project's structure and performing an important communication function. They were ferrymen, crossing rivers toward both shores: East and West, village and city, personal and political, highly educated and relatively uneducated, mystical and secular, leadership and followership, spontaneous joy and meditative quiet. Their informal work was utterly necessary for making the transition from the forest womb into the restive, bus- and train-filled streets of Polish cities.

But from there toward home, you walk, ride, and fly alone.

PART III

Objective Drama, 1983—86

29

INTRODUCTION

Objective Drama, 1983–86

Lisa Wolford

POLITICAL EXILE

Grotowski left Poland in 1982, during the period of martial law. (For further discussion of the Polish political context, see Taviani ch. 21.) Despite strong limitations on international travel due to the Polish political situation, Theatre of Sources allowed Grotowski a viable pretext to travel extensively. Yet he was faced with a difficult task at the onset of martial law: to ensure that if he were to refuse to return to Poland, his collaborators from the Laboratory Theatre would not pay the price of his exile through harassment from the martial law government or by being denied permission to work elsewhere. In a 1994 interview with Franco Quadri, Grotowski clarified that if he had still been working as a director in public theatre, he might have remained in Poland.

> I left Poland because of the martial law that was proclaimed there. For me personally, it was an inevitable decision, because in such a situation there is an enormous difference between directing (as the other stage directors were doing) a theatre that does performances for a *large national audience* – even if it is financed by a state considered as oppressive – and to direct (as I was doing in this period) an international, closed laboratory, still using the money of a country where martial law is in effect. I received political asylum in the United States.
>
> (1994:110)

When Grotowski left Poland, he made certain that each of his colleagues from the Laboratory Theatre was outside the country working on one project or another. Zbigniew Cynkutis, who had left much earlier, was in the United States with his wife and family. The remainder of the actors from the Laboratory Theatre (along with co-director Ludwik Flaszen) were in France, except for Cieslak, who went to Scandinavia; his exit had been most difficult to arrange. Grotowski traveled first to Italy, then to Haiti, still considering what course of action would be best for him.

Finally he arrived in the U.S.A., where he requested political asylum. While making this step, he asked André Gregory to travel to France in order to explain the situation to his colleagues. For their safety, they were informed that they should be aware of Grotowski's decision to request asylum and the possible repercussions for themselves if they individually chose to return to Poland. In the event that any of them wished to request asylum as well, they were told that contact had already been made with a lawyer in Paris who would arrange the details.

The members of the Laboratory Theatre either stayed outside the country for a longer time or returned to Poland immediately. The government chose to avoid any scandal that might ensue as a result of dissolving the Laboratory Theatre and continued business as usual, despite the fact that the group presented no public activities. The members of the Laboratory Theatre were in agreement that they would do neither public performances nor any open projects in Poland, as they did not wish to support the martial law government through presenting visible work. The group members continued to do individual work outside Poland, mainly independent workshops, productions, and teaching engagements, using the reputation of the Laboratory Theatre to continue their activities. In reality, the Laboratory Theatre ceased to exist at the end of 1982; the group, in agreement with Grotowski, chose to dissolve itself formally in 1984 in order not to prolong the fiction of its continued existence as a cohesive unit.

Such is the context of events behind Grotowski's emigration to the U.S.A. in 1982. He arrived first in New York, where he was aided by his dear friends Mercedes and André Gregory. During the 1982–83 academic year, Grotowski held a position at Columbia University. He began to develop plans for a program of research he called "Objective Drama," initially with the notion that this would be realized at New York University, in which aim he was assisted by Richard Schechner. Money to support the program was not forthcoming, however, and Grotowski accepted an invitation from the University of California-Irvine to conduct his research there, beginning with the 1983–84 academic year.

ART AND OBJECTIVITY

In a Rockefeller Foundation grant proposal written at the inception of the Focused Research Program in Objective Drama, Grotowski expresses concern that the ancient function of art as a cohesive and stabilizing force within a culture is being eroded by an ever-increasing dependence on modern technological methods of transmitting performative techniques. Grotowski observes that sophisticated technological means of recording artistic knowledge have replaced the traditional transmission of cultural heritage through "oral interpersonal handing down from one generation to another." As a result, many ancient performative/ritual practices, the subtleties of which cannot be adequately communicated except through direct personal interaction, are dying out or becoming distorted through partial transmission. Deprived of these traditional sources of knowledge, modern performance "can be an expression of the contemporary spirit but not of culturally traditional, inherent higher values." While contemporary performance can effectively communicate personal emotional and psychological states, "it is failing, by and large, to develop its function as a cohesive force expressing the shared human needs for values, identity and continuity. More and more these are made into a purely individual search [. . .] and society, as a result, fragments" (Focused Research Program in Objective Drama).

Grotowski's use of the term Objective Drama can be related to T.S. Eliot's concept of the "objective correlative." "The only way of expressing emotion in the form of art," writes Eliot, "is by finding an 'objective correlative'; in other words a set of objects, a situation, a chain of events which shall be the formula of that *particular* emotion, such that when the external facts, which must terminate in sensory experience, are given, the emotion is immediately evoked" (Eliot 1975:48). Eliot is concerned with the emotional response of a reader who encounters a literary work (or by extension, a spectator witnessing a performance), the effect on an observer in some way removed from the primary creative/ performative event. In Grotowski's research, by contrast, the effect of the action on the (occasional) spectator is rather secondary to the experience of the practitioner.

A further distinction can be made in that Grotowski's investigation is not specifically concerned with emotional response per se, but rather with the subtle psychophysical impact of the performative artifact on the practitioner, englobing the entirety of his or her body/mind/being. Grotowski seeks to determine the patterns of vocal vibration, the sequences of movement, etc., which in some sense serve as the specific "chain of events," to use Eliot's terminology, to open particular psychophysical processes, yet he clearly asserts that his intention is not to use such tools for manipulative purposes. "Each ritual carries within it its own content," Grotowski has said. "If I can identify the form, I will discover the content. But you cannot manipulate these elements. [. . .] This is not a manipulative investigation" (Drake 1983:5).

The term "objective art" can be found in the writings of Juliusz Osterwa, founder of Teatr Reduta, who uses these words in a diary from 1921. Zbigniew Osinski (who has written about the continuity between Teatr Reduta and the Laboratory Theatre), quotes from the diaries of Osterwa in order to elucidate Grotowski's concept of objective drama:

"Architecture [. . .] was an objective art – the most objective of arts [. . .]" (Ch. 39:384). Osterwa called for a theatre which could affect the spectator in a manner analogous to architecture, which he considered most noble because it enraptures both the connoisseur and the sensitive layperson, acting in such a way that the individual is not consciously aware of being influenced. This analysis of the power of architecture resonates strongly with a passage in "Tu es le fils de quelqu'un" in which Grotowski discusses objectivity in relation to the design of medieval cathedrals and Hindu temples (Ch. 30: pp. 298–99).

The use of architecture as an example of objective art can also be linked to the writings of G.I. Gurdjieff, who discusses a temple which he observed to induce a specific emotional/physiological state in all who entered (Gurdjieff 1973:184). Gurdjieff was also interested in other forms of what he called "objective art," including sculpture, writing, painting, acting, and most especially sacred dances. Osinski summarizes Gurdjieff's concept of objective art as follows: "Subjective art relies on a randomness or individual view of things and phenomena, and thus it is often governed by human caprice. 'Objective art,' on the other hand, has an extra- and supra-individual quality, and it can thereby reveal the laws of fate and the destiny of man" (Ch. 39:383–84). According to Gurdjieff, the art of traditional cultures is mathematically precise, reflecting a specific inner content. "In antiquity, that which is now called art served the aim of objective knowledge" (1973:32). Gurdjieff suggests that the performative artifacts of ancient civilizations "served the same purpose as is served today by books – the purpose of preserving and transmitting certain knowledge" (1973:183). Art of this nature, he asserts, is not intended to appeal to subjective or aesthetic faculties; it is meant to be understood as a language that is read by those who are familiar with its syntactic codes (1973:184). The knowledge encoded in such artifacts need not necessarily always be esoteric in nature, but, he says, can be something as simple and precise as "a recipe for good borscht."

GROTOWSKI IN ORANGE COUNTY (1983–86)

Objective Drama, like Grotowski's earlier work in Theatre of Sources, involved an investigation of apparently physical techniques and other performative/ritual elements related to various world cultures. The program employed (in different periods and for different durations) a number of "traditional practitioners" and "technical specialists," several of whom were artists trained in specific, non-Western performing practices: Tiga [Jean-Claude Garoute] and Maud Robart from Haiti, Jairo Cuesta from Colombia, I Wayan Lendra from Bali, Du Yee Chang from Korea, Wei Cheng Chen from Taiwan, along with others who arrived for shorter periods. In addition, Magda Zlotowska, who had previously collaborated with Grotowski, taught Motions, an extremely precise exercise which began to be developed during the Theatre of Sources period. Not all of these individuals were in residence at the same time. Tiga and Robart remained in California for the first year of the program, teaching the walk-dance *yanvalou*, as well as a number of Haitian ritual songs; these elements became one of the primary lines of investigation, and after the departure of Robart and Tiga were conducted by other practitioners. Other significant elements of work included Watching, a cycle of dynamic physical games which derived certain elements of its external structure from *Vigil*, a work developed by Jacek Zmyslowski during the paratheatrical period; an outdoor activity described as "Sculpting and Diving," which involved moving in adaptive relation to the terrain; and "Fire Action," a type of movement/dance done in relation to an outdoor fire, using the motion of the flames to create the rhythm, almost as a kind of music. These activities were led primarily by Cuesta.

Another central element of the work involved the development of acting propositions or "mystery plays" around a song related to an individual's childhood memory, most often associated with the person's family. Barbara Myerhoff observes that ethnic materials, related to the primary familial experiences of "first foods, care, language, songs, tales and the like," are "redolent with early, fundamental associations, and thus contain the possibility of carrying one back to earlier selves, overcoming time and change" (Myerhoff 1992:188–89). In the individual participants' work on "mystery plays," Grotowski asked that they find a song connected to childhood which had a particular importance for them. In the first stages of work with these songs, participants were simply asked to sing the song, trying to remember more completely both the song and the associations with which it was connected. Later, they began to create individual actions on the basis of these songs, sometimes connected to their memories of who first sang the song to them and the context of surrounding events. Gortowski notes that Du-Yee Chang's contribution to this line of work was particularly significant.

Occasionally, certain of these songs form childhood, initially explored by individuals, were taught to other group members in an experiment to see whether it was possible for a particular song to have impact beyond the context of one person's memory. Certain ancient songs were explored simultaneously by different participants (in one example, an American man working with a Gregorian chant juxtaposed his memory action to that of an Iranian working with a Sufi song). In such instances, participants not only tried to work in such a way that they did not disturb one another, but to arrive to some sort of harmony between them. In another experiment, Grotowski asked each participant to find two songs that could function practically for them in two opposite situations: when they needed to be more alert, as for example when falling asleep while driving, or when they wanted to sleep but were unable. Participants were instructed that they should not necessarily sing the song aloud, but silently to themselves, as a *retournelle*, and in this way explore the practical effects of the different songs in diverse situations.

Grotowski suggests that one of the most important contributors to his work during this period was James Slowiak, an Anglo-American, conventionally trained stage director who became his assistant and during the last year of Grotowski's full-time residence at Irvine (1985–86) was responsible as assistant director for the day-to-day work of preparing a scored performance structure with the members of the multicultural team. Slowiak was one of three artists who accompanied Grotowski on his relocation to Italy upon the establishment of the Workcenter of Jerzy Grotowski in 1986.

The California-based research was differentiated from the previous stage of Grotowski's activity in that the work of Theatre of Sources seemed to focus on "that which precedes the differences," while Objective Drama put attention to the developed forms of certain traditional techniques – not in order to synthesize these disparate practices into something Grotowski might describe as "the big soup," but rather to test the efficacy of precise technical elements when applied in a different context from that of their arising. Despite his interest in locating precise similarities underlying culturally specific techniques, Grotowski is by no means neglectful of the fact that genuine and significant differences exist. He warns against the danger of too easily assuming similarities among non-homogeneous things, as well as against "a pan-ecumenical spirit [. . .] which makes basic Western orientations seem identical to Oriental orientations. [. . .] 'It's the same thing, it's the same thing.' I'm sorry. Maybe it *should* be the same thing, but often that's not at all the case" (Grotowski 1996b:239; the quotation used in this text has been amended by Grotowski on the basis of the Price translation to correspond more closely with the original French language transcript of his lecture).

Grotowski is ruthless in his condemnation of the "stupidities" that arise in contemporary performances that attempt to simulate or appropriate ritual forms, stupidities stemming from misguided attempts to combine elements cannibalized from different cultural sources. Grotowski's work with traditional tools during this period was instead concerned with discovering the objective quality of specific technical elements, that which impacts directly on the perception and state of the practitioner. The term "ritual," as I understand its application in relation to Objective Drama, refers to undegenerated cultural traditions or techniques, often religious in origin, which exert a determinable and therefore objective effect on the practitioner. Grotowski's investigation in this period did not focus on social rituals or ceremonies in which the original objective capacity has been lost or obscured, nor was he overtly concerned with any of the wider applications popular culture has assigned to the term.

In a grant proposal written at the inception of the Objective Drama program, Grotowski said that one of the aims of his research was to discover a type of performance in which "poetry is not separated from the song, the song is not separated from the movement, the movement is not separated from the dance, the dance is not separated from the acting," a type of performance associated with very ancient ritual traditions. He posits that such forms of performance are rooted in the period "before the separation between art and rite, and between the spectacular and the participatory," a time before artistic creation was separated from its ritual function (Focused Research Program 1983). Grotowski calls this "art as a way of knowledge" (Sullivan 1983:42). He maintains that even within a program of closed research, working with skilled traditional practitioners, it would be impossible to create ritual in the same sense that we can create a theatrical performance. "Such a project," he wryly noted, "would require at least 1,000 years" (Sullivan 1983:42). Ritual, Grotowski clarifies, is a product of very long gestation and precise sociocultural circumstances developed in relation to a specific community. The techniques and patterns of Haitian voodoo, for example, could only arise in a community in which African rituals and belief systems were brought into contact with Euro-Christian iconography in the context of extreme colonialist oppression and slavery. On the other hand, Grotowski asserts that an individual or group cannot *improvise* ritual in its objectively efficacious sense, either for personal or artistic purposes.

Although the work conducted during the earliest period of Grotowski's residence in California was structured in such a way as to permit active participation by occasional visitors (usually members of the university community), Grotowski increasingly came to emphasize the need for artisanal competence in approaching the elements of traditional techniques that were the subject of his investigation. The renewed emphasis on craft, structure, and precision which characterize Grotowski's work and discourse during this period can be seen in some sense to represent a spiral development, returning toward certain aspects of professional work that were foregrounded in the earliest phase of his activity ("Theatre of Productions"), but now investigating these aspects in a different context.

Grotowski suggests that the first two years of his residence in California were spent preparing the ground, selecting and training a

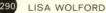

number of participants, creating the circumstances necessary for his delicate research. At the moment when the Theatre of Sources project was interrupted in 1982 as a result of the state of war in Poland, Grotowski had some idea of the vectors of investigation he wished to pursue, but on arriving in the United States he found it necessary to begin again from zero in practical terms. He had to find an amenable host institution and to create, against all predispositions of American artistic subsidy, a structure for closed research which would not result in any publicly accessible production. He had to locate and train collaborators with unusual skills and capacities – all before what he speaks of as "the real work" could even begin. While the technical specialists employed by the Objective Drama program were highly skilled practitioners of their respective techniques, their presence was temporary and changing. Also, the structure of the early phases of Objective Drama (open to active participation by students and occasional visitors) made it relatively difficult to achieve the level of precision and technical competence required for a rigorous investigation of the type Grotowski envisioned. By contrast, Grotowski acknowledges that during the third and final year of his full-time residence in California (1985–86), when he was working with a stable team of highly skilled practitioners in a context of closed research, he was able to conduct truly precise and systematic work which he regards as deeply valuable.

INSTRUMENTS OF KNOWLEDGE

"Tu es le fils de quelqu'un," one of Grotowski's richest and most significant texts, is based on a talk given in Florence in 1985 in relation to a two-month seminar of practical work held as a preamble for the founding of the Workcenter of Jerzy Grotowski in Pontedera, Italy. First published in English in the fall 1987 issue of *TDR*, the text was subsequently re-elaborated by Grotowski and appeared in the French review *Europe* in October 1989. The text offers clear, precise examples of the sort of techniques that were a focus of Grotowski's investigation in an intermediary period between the last two phases of his work, and clearly indicates his increasing emphasis on precision and craft. His discussion of *organon* and *yantra*, tools or instruments as precise as a surgeon's scalpel, is fundamental to understanding the work of this period. Grotowski's consideration of the work of the actor on the basis of an old song rooted in his or her familial memories, going toward the "origin" or beginning of the song, foreshadows the central emphasis on ancient vibratory songs that characterizes his subsequent research.

Jan Kott has written extensively on Grotowski's work, generally in a somewhat polemical tone (see especially Ch. 13, this volume). In prior years, he expressed a certain skepticism regarding what he interpreted as the metaphysical bases of Grotowski's performances and acting technique, and faulted his compatriot for the lack of overt political commitment in his art. Kott's response to Objective Drama, however, "Grotowski, or The Limit," takes a much warmer tone, laced with discernible affection for the former-guru-turned-Hasidic-rebbe whom Kott perceives Grotowski to be. Kott's imagistic descriptions of Objective Drama structures, particularly his evocation of *Main Action*, the central performance developed during the final year of Grotowski's full-time residence at UC-Irvine (1985–86), are remarkably vibrant testimonials that hover between prose and poetry, perception and dream.

The essay by Charles Marowitz, "Grotowski in Irvine: Breaking the silence," by contrast maintains an extremely aggressive and critical tone. The article was written in response to a conference held by Grotowski at UC-Irvine in 1988 following the initial distribution of Grotowski's text "Performer" (ch. 37), an early statement relating to the research conducted at the Pontedera Workcenter beginning in 1986. It is important to remember that Marowitz's essay was written during a liminal or tributary period of Grotowski's work, following Grotowski's relocation to Italy, and that it is a response to an intellectual dialogue around textual materials which have only an oblique relation to the practical work of either Objective Drama or Art as vehicle. The essay is significant in that it distills a strong current of critical response to the perceived esotericism of Grotowski's post-theatrical research. According to Marowitz, Grotowski's teaching, like his previous work, "is a fanatically proselytized tao leading to a cul-de-sac." J. Ndukaku Amankulor's text presents a different response to this conference, highlighting elements of correspondence between Grotowski's recent activity and traditional African performance practices.

Given that Objective Drama was for the most part closed to outside observers, Kott is among the only established scholars to witness and write about the practical work of the program. More detailed accounts, documenting the day-to-day activities and methods of Objective Drama, have been written by long-term participants and workleaders. The essay by Lendra, "Bali and Grotowski: some parallels in the Training Process," outlines certain practical and structural elements of the program, as well as examining a specific ethos he perceives to be characteristic of Grotowski's work. Lendra draws not only on his experience as a technical specialist in Objective Drama, but on his work as an actor–dancer in *kebyar* and *topeng* forms, examining similarities between Grotowski's California-based research and the values and practices of the Balinese traditions in which he was educated. Like my own essay, "Subjective Reflections on Objective Work" (which details a later period of the work at UC-Irvine), Lendra's text blends analytical reflection with practical description, striving to articulate a type of embodied knowledge that can arrive through extended practice of specific performative techniques. As Maurice Merleau-Ponty observes, "My body is the fabric into which all objects are woven and it is, at least in relation to the perceived world, the general instrument of my 'comprehension'" (Merleau-Ponty 1962:100).

CODA: THE FINAL YEARS OF THE IRVINE PROGRAM (1987—92)

Grotowski's Lessons in Directing

The Focused Research Program in Objective Drama provided a systematic base for Grotowski's research from 1983 to 1986. Officially, the program continued for six years after Grotowski's relocation to Italy, although his active participation grew increasingly rare. In 1987 and 1988, Grotowski held two-week sessions at UC-Irvine, working primarily with actors and directors from the university's M.F.A. programs. He was assisted by Slowiak, Robart and Pablo Jimenez, all of whom were employed by the Pontedera Workcenter at this time.

A five-month session conducted by Slowiak in 1989, which ended with two weeks of intensive work under Grotowski's direction, marks a significant shift in the aim and focus of the California-based research. While the name "Objective Drama" continued to be used for purposes of funding, the work of this period took a different turn, emphasizing issues pertaining to the actor's craft, the work of the stage director with the actors, and the ways in which specific meanings are created in the perception of the spectator. Grotowski was actively involved in the practical work of the sessions through 1990, analyzing the work of the young actors and directors and at times consulting individually with participants or intervening to offer indications on a fragment of work in progress (for further details, see Wolford 1996a). The program at Irvine concluded in the summer of 1992 with a two-month session directed by Slowiak and Cuesta which combined UC-Irvine students with members from the New World Performance Laboratory, an experimental theatre company based in northeast Ohio. During his two-week visit at the end of the session, Grotowski analyzed the performance structures developed over the prior months. (For a detailed account of the California-based work in these later years, as well as that of the New World Performance Laboratory, see Wolford 1994 and Wolford 1996b.)

Grotowski emphasizes that he considers his work-visits to UC-Irvine to be valuable and significant in their own right, but warns that it would be distortive to interpret this work by relying too heavily on the rhetoric and conceptualization of the "official" Objective Drama program, related to the activities conducted between 1983 and 1986. He advises that it would be more pertinent to consider the subsequent work at UC-Irvine as a separate activity, distinct from both the research conducted in California during the period of his full-time residence and from the activities of the Pontedera Workcenter. Grotowski suggests that the final sessions at UC-Irvine were oriented primarily toward lessons in theatre craft – the work of the stage director with the actor – "in the old, noble sense, as in the remote times of Stanislavsky."

30

TU ES LE FILS DE QUELQU'UN

Jerzy Grotowski

Each time we limit ourselves to certain terms, we are afloat in the world of ideas, of abstractions. We can then find some extremely revealing formulas, but they belong to the realm of thoughts and not to the realm of realities. I don't know if I have said, in the past, that theatre complements social reality. Perhaps I've said this. But for me theatre is not something that can be put in a box. How could I separate theatre from literature? For me, as for any good European, the relation between theatre and literature is extremely strong (which is not at all the case in certain types of classical Oriental theatre). Authors, the great authors of the past, were very important to me, even if I struggled with them. I stood face to face with Slowacki or Calderon and it was like Jacob's fight with the angel: "Tell me your secret!" But, to say the truth, your secret, what the hell? What counts is our secret, for us living today. But if I understand your secret, Calderon, I am going to understand my own. I don't speak with you as with an author whose work I will stage, but I speak with you as with my great-grandfather. That means I am in the process of speaking with my ancestors. And, of course, I am not in agreement with my ancestors. But at the same time, I can't deny them. They are my base; they are my source. It's a personal affair between them and me. And that was how I worked on dramatic literature and almost always with authors *of the past*: exactly because it was a matter of ancestors, of other generations.

One always finds some allies and one always finds some enemies to combat. You are faced with an extremely rigid social system; you must deal with it; you must refind your own freedom; you must refind your allies. Perhaps they are in the past. Therefore, I spoke with Mickiewicz. But I spoke with him about today's problems. And also about the social system in which I lived in Poland almost all my life. Voil'a, what was my attitude: *I work, not to make some discourse, but to enlarge the island of freedom which I bear; my obligation is not to make political declarations, but to make holes in the wall*. The things which were forbidden before me should be permitted after me; the doors which were closed and double- locked should be opened. I must resolve the problem of freedom and of tyranny through practical measures; that means that my activity should leave traces, examples *of freedom*. It's a whole other thing to lament about freedom: "Freedom is a good thing. You must fight for freedom" (and it's often the others who should do the fighting, etc.). It is necessary to accomplish the act; never to give up, but always to go one step further, one step further. That's it – the question of social activity through culture.

If one wishes to analyze it, one can easily see that romantic irrationalism appeared during the period when factories and railroads first developed. Obviously, this is complementary. The Futurists' error was exactly to create images of machines in the age of machines. When machines dominate, look instead for the living. All of life is a complex phenomenon of counterpoise. It's not a matter of having a conceptual image of that, but of asking yourself the question: This life that you are living, is it enough? Is it giving you happiness? Are you satisfied with the life around you? Art or culture or religion (in the sense of living sources; not in the sense of churches, often quite the opposite), all of that is a way of not being satisfied. No, such a life is not sufficient. So one does something, one proposes something, one accomplishes something which is the response to this deficiency. It's not a question of what's missing in one's image of society, but what's missing in the way of living the life.

II

Art is deeply rebellious. Bad artists *talk* about the rebellion, but true artists *do* the rebellion. They respond to the consecrated order by an act. Here there is a most dangerous and most important point. One can, in following this route, end up in a sort of rebellion that is not even exclusively verbal but anarchic, which is the refusal of our responsibilities. In the realm of art, this appears under the form of dilettantism: one is not credible in one's craft; one has no mastery; one has no capacities; one is truly a dilettante in the worst sense of the word – so one is rebelling. No, none of that. Art as rebellion is to create the *fait accompli* which pushes back the limits imposed by society or, in tyrannical systems, imposed by power. But you can't push back these limits if you are not credible. Your *fait accompli* is nothing but humbug if it is not *fait competent*. Yes! It is blasphemous! But it's precise. You know what you are doing, you have worked out your weapons, you have credibility, you have created a *fait accompli* which is of such mastery that even your adversaries cannot deny it. If you don't have this attitude of competence at your disposal in your rebellion, you will lose everything in the battle. Even if you are sincere. It's like, in the United States, the history of the counterculture of the sixties. This counterculture no longer exists, finished. It's not because of lack of sincerity and of very big values there. But it's because of a lack of competence, of precision, of lucidity. It's like the title of the old Swedish film, which in Polish is *She Danced for Just One Summer*. Yes, it was the sixties: they danced for just one summer; afterwards, they abandoned it all, without asking themselves if it had value or not. Big fireworks: one dances, one has ecstasy; and after remains nothing. Real rebellion in art is persistent, mastered, never dilettante. Art has always been the effort to confront oneself with the insufficiency, and by this very fact, art has always been complementary to social reality. Don't focalize on just one thing as limited as theatre. The theatre is all the phenomena around theatre, the whole culture. We can use the word theatre as much as we can abolish it.

III

Group improvisation. . . . First, one needs to see the banalities, the clichés which appear. There are banalities of work on improvisation, just as there are banalities of work on forms and structures. Here are some examples of clichés of group improvisation: to make "savages," to imitate trances, to overuse the arms and hands, to form processions, to carry someone in a procession, to play a scapegoat and his persecutors, to console a victim, to perform simplicity confused with irresponsible behavior, to present one's own clichés of behavior, social daily-life behavior, as if they were naturalness (so to speak, to conduct oneself as in a bistro). So in order to come to a valid improvisation, we should begin by eliminating all of those banalities plus several others. We should also avoid stomping the feet on the floor, falling and creeping on the ground and making monsters. Block all these practices! Then maybe something will appear: for example, it will appear that contact is not possible if you are not capable of refusing contact. It's the question of connection and of disconnection.

In actual societies, especially Occidental societies, the people so bloody trouble one another that they dream of a *positive* connection with the others. But in truth, they are not capable of such a connection. They are capable only of imposing themselves. Like when two persons do an improvisation, a third one clings to them and destroys everything. It's the reaction of the bulldog who, when he bites, can no longer open his jaws. That is your contact, your connection. Looking for connection, one should begin with disconnection. So I don't look anymore for contact with you; I took rather to utilize the common space in such a way that each one can proceed separately without disturbing the other. But if we should proceed without disturbing one another, and if I begin to sing and if you also begin to sing, it should not lead to disharmony. If it should not lead to disharmony, that means that when I sing I must hear you and that I, in some way, must harmonize my melody with your melody. But not only with you, since there is also a jet plane passing over the work building. And you, with your song, your melody, you are not alone: the fact is there. The sound of the engine is there. If you sing as if it is not, that means that you are not in harmony. You must find a sonic equilibrium with the jet plane and, against everything, anyway keep well your melody.

You see that in order to do all this one should be well trained in the movement, the song, the rhythm, etc., which means that in order to tackle the disconnection – without yet grappling with the connection – a real professional credibility is already necessary. But most often the people who practice so-called "improvisation" are plunged in dilettantism, the irresponsibility. For working on improvisation, one needs bloody competence. It is not goodwill which will save the work, but it is mastery. Obviously when mastery is here, appears the question of heart. Heart without mastery is shit. When mastery is here, we should cope with the heart and with the spirit.

IV

Why do the African hunter of the Kalahari, the French hunter of Saintonge, the Bengali hunter, or the Huichol hunter of Mexico all adopt – while they hunt – a certain position of the body in which the spine is slightly inclined, the knees slightly bent, a position held at the base of the body by the sacrum-pelvis complex? And why can this position lead to only one type of rhythmical movement? And what is the utility of this way of walking? There is a level of analysis which is very simple, very easy: if the weight of the body is on one leg, in the moment of displacing the other leg, you don't make noise, and also you displace in a continuous, slow way. Suddenly the animals cannot spot you.

But this is not the essential. The essential is that there exists a certain primary position of the human body. It's a position so ancient that maybe it was that, not only of *homo sapiens*, but of *homo erectus*, and which concerns in some way the appearance of the human species. A position which seems to fade out of sight in the night of the ages, linked to what the Tibetans sometimes call our "reptile" aspect. In the Afro-Caribbean culture, this position is connected more precisely to the grass-snake, and according to Hindu tradition derived from Tantra, you have a serpent asleep at the base of the spinal column.

You may say that all these are the prejudices of people from another epoch. But not necessarily of people from another tradition, because in Europe we also have had the image of a serpent which goes as far as the heart, not to mention the two serpents which constitute the caduceus of the physicians. It is probable that a brain specialist could even mention the reptile brain, this brain which is the oldest and which begins in the posterior part of the skull and descends the whole length of the spinal column. I speak of all this through images, without any scientific pretension. We have in our body an ancient body, a reptile body, one can say. On the other hand, one can almost imagine, observing the development of a human embryo, the apparition of a reptile in one of the primary phases. Let's say that this "reptile" which appeared in a very ancient phase of the embryo served as the basis for the formation of the "reptile brain."

I began to ask myself how all this is related to the primary energy, how – through diverse techniques elaborated in the traditions – access to the ancient body was looked for. I made several journeys, I read several books, I found several traces. Some of these traces are fascinating as phenomena; for example, in black Africa, the technique of the people of the Kalahari Desert which consists in "boiling of energy," as they say. They do this through an extremely precise dance. This dance, which is complicated and very long (it takes hours and hours), therefore could not be used by me as an instrument: first because it is too complex, second, because it is too much linked to the mind structure of the Kalahari people, third, for Westerners it would be almost impossible to keep going so long a time without losing psychological equilibrium. It is out of the question; but it is clear that in the case of the Kalahari it is the "reptile body" which is acting. Where does something similar exist? In the Zhar of Ethiopia, for example, and in the voodoo of the Yoruba in Africa, or even in certain techniques practiced in India. But all of this is extremely sophisticated and one cannot bring from it an instrument which is simple.

Now let's look at what happens with the *derivatives* of traditions. There exists in the Caribbean and particularly in Haiti a type of dance called *yanvalou*, which is applied, for example, at the time of the appearance of a *mystere*, of a divinity (under the influence of Christianity this dance is also called "the dance of penitence"). Here it is simpler, it is linked in a simple way to the "reptile body." This does not have anything strange: it can be said that it is clearly artistic. There is a precise step, tempo-rhythm, waves of the whole body and not only of the spinal column. And if you do this, for example, with the songs related to the Serpent Dhambhala, the way of singing and of emitting vibrations of the voice helps the movements of the body. So there we are truly in the presence of something which we can master artistically, really as an element of dance and song.

Well, let's look at this. If someone arrives from the outside and participates in this kind of work, it is like being confronted with a technique: very precise, artistic. We find ourselves face to the obligation to have competence. One should know how to dance and sing in a way that is organic and at the same time structured. For the moment, let's not talk about the reptile brain, let's talk only about this solely artistic aspect, that is, being both organic and at the same time structured. It is a test which makes it possible to discover immediately the dilettantism in people. For example, among the Occidentals (among the Orientals there are other tests for detecting dilettantism), because they are not in capacity, on the first attempt, to discover the difference between the steps and the dance, they beat the ground with their feet, believing they dance. Well, dance is what happens when your foot is in the air, and not when it touches the ground. It is just as with the songs. Because the Occidentals are products of notation systems, both in the sense of writing (musical notes) and of tape recordings, and because they are not related to oral transmission, the Occidentals therefore confuse song with melody. Anything that is possible to "notate," they are more or less able to sing. But anything belonging to the quality of the vibration, the resonance of the space, the resonating chambers in the body, the way in which exhalation carries the voice, all this they are not even able to grasp in the beginning. One can say metaphorically that a Westerner sings as if not catching the difference between the sound of a piano and the sound of a violin. The two resonating chambers are completely different, but the Westerner looks only for the melodic line without even grasping the differences in resonance. This obviously doesn't concern the great professionals, but the dilettantes. Through the foot which stomps the ground with a staccato rhythm and through the reconstruction of the melody without the (vocal) vibratory qualities, you can immediately recognize dilettantism. And then it is not the right moment to speak of the "reptile brain"; or the "ancient body." One must just resolve this first technical and artistic question. One is facing the basic problem of the song and of the dance. Afterwards, if the problem has been more or less resolved, one can begin to work on what rhythm really is, the waves of the "old body" in the actual body. At this point one can get lost in a sort of primitivism: one works on the body's instinctual elements *losing control of himself.*

In traditional societies, it is the structure of the ritual which keeps the necessary control, so there is not so much danger of losing control. In modern societies, this control structure is totally lacking and everyone must resolve this problem for himself. What problem? That of not provoking a kind of shipwreck or, in Western language, an inundation of unconscious content in which one could be drowned. This means that it is necessary to keep our quality of man [*czlowiek*], which in several traditional languages is linked to the vertical axis, "to stand." In certain languages, to say man one says "that which stands up." In modern psychology, one speaks of the axial man. There is something which looks, which watches, there is a quality of vigilance. In the Gospels, it is said again and again: Stay awake! Stay awake! Look what is happening. Look after you! Reptile brain or reptile body, it's your animal. It belongs to you, but it is the question of man which is to be resolved. See what is happening! Look after you! Then, something exists as the presence at the two extremities of the same register, two different poles: that of instinct and that of consciousness. Normally our everyday tepidity causes that we are between the two, and we are neither fully animal nor fully human, one is moved confusedly between the two. But in the true traditional techniques and in the true "performing arts," one holds these two extreme poles at the same time. It means "to be in the beginning," to be "*standing* in the beginning." The beginning is all of your original nature, present now, here. Your original nature with all of its aspects: divine or animal, instinctual, passionate. But at the same time you must keep watch with your consciousness. And the more you are "in the beginning," the more you must "be standing." It is the vigilant awareness which makes man [*czlowiek*]. It is this tension between the two poles which gives a contradictory and mysterious plenitude.

V

I have spoken to you about one element of work from among dozens and this small element is connected to the matter of the ancient body and of the awareness. As I have pointed out, the solution passes through a mastery of technical resources, I would even say artistic tools, and, therefore, through non-dilettantism. But it is when we are in non-dilettantism that the real abyss opens up: we are then, at the same time, face to the archaic (*arche*) and to the conscious. There is in this domain an instrument of work which I call *organon* or *yantra*. Organon, in Greek, designates an instrument. As does yantra in Sanskrit. In both cases it is a question of a very fine instrument. In the vocabulary of ancient Sanskrit to give an example of yantra, they say a surgeon's scalpel or an apparatus for astronomical observations. So a yantra is something which can reconnect with the laws of the universe, of nature, like an instrument for astronomical observations. In India, in ancient times, temples were constructed as yantra, that is, the building, the spatial arrangement, had to be an instrument which conducted from sensual excitement to affective void, from the erotic sculptures outside the building towards an empty center, making you void, making you vomit all your content. The same precision was worked out in the building of the cathedrals in the Middle Ages (here it was more linked to the questions of light and of sonority). In the realm of performing arts and in ritual arts, it is in truth the same: the *organons* or the *yantras*. These instruments are the outcome of very long practices. One should not only know how to make them, like certain kinds of dances and songs which have a specific effect on the executant, but must know how to utilize them in order not to degrade them, but in order to reach a totality, a fullness.

I have already given you an example of a yantra: the "reptile body," the dance and song which should be executed in a structured and organic manner, and at the same time kept up with alertness. In our craft, there is an extraordinary quantity of possible yantras. The problem here is not a lack of possibilities but – on the contrary – that there are too many of them, and that these instruments are so fine that we should gradually surpass the level of dilettantism and, after rising to that of competence, perceive what are the dangers and then "move toward the counter-dangers." But attention! There is a big difference between a yantra and a trick. With this type of yantra, can one make the artistic trade? No, something will not function. It's like asking yourself whether with the yantra for building a cathedral, you could build a good bordello. Agreed! It could have an interesting aspect, but something will not be in its place. It's a real problem. With Westerners, and particularly with Euro-Americans, it is even a burning problem. Stage directors and drama teachers who play the whore in arts sometimes take an interest in this type of research, because they ponder: maybe you could use all this for making a show. But no! The instrument is really fine. It is true that you must surpass the level of dilettantism, but once the level of non-dilettantism is attained, there will arise an essential and human question: that of your development as an individual. And this kind of thing can't be manipulated. Either there will emerge from it something fake or you will catch a number of pathological side-effects. Because from the standpoint of the circulation of energy, the yantras (organons) are instruments which are really potent.

VI

We are face to "instruments" which during the initial time concentrate in themselves all the technical and artistic aspects of work. During the initial time only, but this start is an indispensable condition without which nothing can function. So one loses, let's say, an enormous amount of time for this start and is confronted with all of the elements of *artistic* work. For example, one is confronted with the difference between improvisation as chaos and improvisation as readaptation to a structure, that is to say harmonic improvisation. Obviously, I am approaching these questions in a very incomplete manner, since all of this is very complex. In any case, what should be clearly made note of is that one cannot be a non-dilettante – have competence in such work – if one has the spirit of a tourist. By the spirit of a tourist, I mean that one replaces one proposition by another one without really accomplishing any of them.

In this field, one of the tests is a kind of individual ethnodrama, in which the starting point is an old song linked to the ethno-familial tradition of the person in question. One begins to work with this song as if, in it, were codified in potentiality (movement, action, rhythm . . .) a totality. It's like an ethnodrama in the collective traditional sense, but here, it is *one* person who performs, with *one* song and *alone*. So, immediately with modern people, there appears the following problem: you find something, a small structure around the song, then in parallel, you construct a new version, and parallel to that a third. This means that you always stay at the first level – superficial, let's say, as if the all-fresh proposal excited the nerves and gave us the illusion of something. This means that you are working going sideways – and not like someone digging a well. That's the difference between the dilettante and the non-dilettante. The dilettante may make something beautiful, more or less superficially, through this excitation of the nerves in the first improvisation. But it is to sculpt in smoke. It always disappears. The dilettante searches "sideways." In a certain manner, the numerous forms of contemporary industrial development obey this pattern, as for example Silicon Valley, the big American electronic complex; there are constructions alongside other constructions; the complex developed itself flatwise and in the end became ungovernable. This has nothing to do with the construction of cathedrals, that always have a keystone. It is exactly the plumb line that determines the value. But with an individual ethnodrama, it is a difficult thing to achieve, because you pass through crises. The first proposal: it works. After, you have to eliminate that which is not necessary and reconstruct it in a more compact manner. You go through periods of work that are "lifeless." It's a kind of crisis, of boredom. Many technical problems have to be solved: for example, the montage, like in film. You must rebuild, and rememorize the first proposition (the line of small physical actions), but eliminating all the actions that are not absolutely necessary. You must, therefore, make cuts, and then know how to join the different fragments. For instance, you can apply the following principle: line of physical actions – stop – elimination of a fragment – stop – line of physical actions. Like in cinema, the sequence in movement stops on a fixed image – we cut –

another fixed image marks the beginning of a new sequence in movement. This gives: physical action – stop – stop – physical action. But what must be done with the cut, with the hole? At the first stop you are, let's say, standing with your arms up and, at the second stop, sitting with your arms down. One of the solutions consists then in carrying out the passage from one position to the other as a technical demonstration of ability, almost a ballet, a game of ability. It is only one possibility among others. But in any case this requires much time to be done. You must also resolve this other problem: the stop should not be mechanical, but like a frozen waterfall: I mean that all the drive of the movement is there, but stopped. The same thing for that which concerns the stop starting the next fragment of action: still motionless, it must be already in the body, otherwise it does not work. Then you have the problem of the adjustment between the "audio" and the "visual." If at the moment of the cut you have a song, should the song be cut or not? You must decide: What is the river and what is the boat? If the river is the song and the physical actions the boat, then evidently the river must not be interrupted – so the song should not be broken but modulate the physical actions. But most often it is the contrary which is valid: the physical actions are the river and modulate the way of singing. You must know what you choose. And all this example about the montage concerns only the elimination of a fragment; but there is also the problem of insertions, when you take a fragment from another place in your proposition in order to insert it between two stops.

As I said before, this type of work passes through moments of crisis. You arrive at elements more and more compact. Then, your body must completely absorb all this and recover its organic reactions. You must turn back, toward the seed of the first proposition and find that which, from the point of view of this primary motivation, requires a new restructuring of the whole. So the work does not develop "to the side, to the side" but as with the plumb line and always through phases of organicity, of.crisis, of organicity, etc. We can say that each phase of spontaneity of life is always followed by a phase of technical absorption.

VII

You must face all the classical questions of the performing arts. For example: But who is the person who sings the song? Is it you? But if it is a song from your grandmother, is it still you? But if you are discovering in you your grandmother, through your body's impulses, then it's neither "you" nor "your grandmother who had sung": it's you exploring your grandmother who sings. Yet it can be that you go further back, toward some place, toward some time difficult to imagine, when for the first time someone sang this song. I'm speaking about a true traditional song, which is anonymous. We say: it's the people who sang. But among these people, there was someone who began. You have the song, you must ask yourself where this song began.

Perhaps it was the moment of tending a fire in the mountain on which someone was looking after animals. And to keep warm in front of this fire someone began to repeat the opening words. It wasn't a song yet, it was an incantation. A primary incantation that someone repeated. You look at the song and ask yourself: Where is this primary incantation? In which words? Maybe these words have already disappeared? Maybe the person in question had sung other words, or a phrase other than the one you sing, and maybe another person developed this first nucleus. But if you are capable of going with this song towards the beginning, it is no more your grandmother who sings, but someone from your lineage, from your country, from your village, from the place where the village was, the village of your parents, of your grandparents. In the way of singing itself the space is codified. One sings differently in the mountains and in the plains. In the mountains one sings from one high place to another, so the voice is thrown like an arc. You gradually refind the first incantations. You refind the landscape, the fire, the animals, maybe you began to sing because you had a fear of the solitude. Did you look for others? Did it happen in the mountains? If you were on a mountain, the others were on another mountain. Who was this person who sang thus? Was this person young or old? Finally, you will discover that you come from somewhere. As one says in a French expression, "Tu es le fils de quelqu'un" [You are someone's son]. You are not a vagabond, you come from somewhere, from some country, from some place, from some landscape. There were real people around you, near or far. It is you two hundred, three hundred, four hundred, or one thousand years ago, but it is you. Because he who began to sing the first words was someone's son, from somewhere, from some place, so, if you refind this, you are someone's son. If you do not refind it, you are not someone's son; you are cut off, sterile, barren.

VIII

This example shows how in starting with a small element – a song – one opens several problems of belonging, of *appearance* of the song, of incantation, of our human ties, of our lineage in time, all this appears, and along with this appears the classical question of your craft. What is it – the character? You? The one who first sang the song? But if you are the son of the one who first sang this song, yes, it is that which is the true trace of the character. You are from some time, from some place. It's not a matter of playing the role of somebody who you are not. So in all this work one goes always more toward the beginning, more "to stand in the beginning." And when you have the non-dilettantism, then it's the question of you – of man [*czlowiek*] – that opens up. With this question of man, it's like a big door opens: behind you, there's artistic credibility and in front of you something which does not demand technical competence, but competence of yourself. Hamlet, in speaking about his father the dead king, says, "He was a man." He says, "I shall not look upon his like again."

That is it, the true question: Are you man? You have an image of this in the gospel. On the road to Emmaus, two of Jesus's companions, scared, excited, desperate, walk towards this little village. A stranger joins them. They are very excited. They speak about the event: the death of Jesus. They are quarreling. The stranger says: "Why are you quarreling?" "But," they respond, "some frightful events have occurred. Didn't you hear?" And then they tell him. And which story do they tell? This story we know. The first sentence of this story (not in the canonical version, but in one translation from Greek), says: "He was a man." It's the first sentence that they had to say in order to describe their hero: "He was a man." This is the question which will present itself after that of non-dilettantism: "Are you man [*czlowiek*]?"

Translated by James Slowiak and the author.

© 1989 Jerzy Grotowski

GROTOWSKI, OR THE LIMIT

Jan Kott

A postcard I received a couple of months ago from Alexander Verlag, my German publisher, shows Jerzy Grotowski sitting side by side with Peter Brook. There is a blank wall behind them. They are sitting on chairs that have been placed together, or perhaps they are wooden benches. As in the waiting room of a railway station. But where? At what station? A large, bulging knapsack is lying at their feet. To which of the two does it belong? Brook is wearing a black suit and a turtleneck sweater. His head is slightly bent over, his immense forehead sloping back into the almost bald dome of his skull, with tufts of hair only along the sides. Grotowski is also wearing a black suit, but he has on an unbuttoned shirt and trousers with suspenders. His bare feet are thrust into sandals. For one moment one might think that Vladimir and Estragon have met again and are waiting for a new Godot.

Both Grotowski and Brook have traveled a lot. It might be better to say: they have wandered. Brook's travels, like everything else he has done, are well documented: descriptions, reports, photographs. Of Grotowski's wanderings – who for months would trek alone through the vast expanses of India – the only trace left is what he carries within him. Brook, in his travels to the ends of the earth, always insatiable for theatricality, was relentlessly searching in inaccessible villages of Africa and Asia for new ways to enrich the theatre: an undiscovered gesture or musical instrument or melody. Who can ever forget the ribbons, taken from the Kabuki, which entwine the lovers in *A Midsummer Night's Dream*; the arrows in the *Mahabharata*, suspended in midair, which may never have been released from the bent bow; or the bonfires that the old woman lights in the three corners of the world for Carmen and her last lover around their love bed? In Brook's productions fire, water, and sand are thrilling signs; these symbols never lose materiality. The red sand in the *Mahabharata* was actually brought from the banks of the Ganges. Like no other artist, Brook has turned ritual into theatre. Whereas Grotowski stubbornly and persistently tried to turn theatre back into ritual. Until he finally realized that for true believers such an attempt is sacrilege, pillage of the *sacrum*, and for nonbelievers a form of cheating, and that in Cieslak's self-flagellation in *The Constant Prince* martyrdom is mere acting.

In the postcard from Germany Brook has his hands on his knees and listens, eyes half-closed. I remember quite well how Brook listens. He is on the alert then, like a cat. Like a hungry cat. He says nothing, only from time to time he twists and folds the paper napkin in his hands. That crumpled napkin turns out to be a stage design. In the photograph Grotowski has his right hand raised, he's looking at Brook and talking. Brook always asks questions. Giorgio Strehler, with whom I worked on *The Tempest*, also asks questions, but he answers them himself and at great length. Then he asks another question, but he's interested only in his own answers. Conversation with Brook is difficult: the other person does all the talking. Conversation with Strehler is impossible: he does all the talking. Of the three, only Grotowski is a true conversationalist. Perhaps that is why the one final thing he wants to save from traditional theatre is the act of meeting. Reciprocally.

After many years I met Grotowski again in Santa Monica. He had changed considerably in comparison with the likeness on that German postcard. Over the years I have seen Grotowski alternatingly fat or thin as though his inner transformations were reflected in the bodily manifestation of his soul. In the photo Grotowski still had thick, dark hair falling into disarray over his ears and neck. Now his high forehead was prominent, his silvering hair blended with his already gray sideburns and sparse, scraggly goatee. He was wearing his usual dark suit, which was too big for him since he had lost so much weight, a white shirt, and an uncustomary old-fashioned dark tie with a thick knot. "He looks exactly like a civil servant from Galicia in the old Austro-Hungarian empire," said L.

Grotowski gave a talk about Haitian voodoo cult. About performing the ceremony, which is a trance that infects the participants. And about how the actor is able to control the trance. In the documentary film he showed, a white rooster's head was cut off, and his feathers floated in the air.

That was almost two years ago at the Getty Center in Santa Monica, where I had been invited for a year's residency along with nine art historians and ethnographers from America and Europe. I was the only theatre historian and perhaps that is why I was asked to arrange the talk for Grotowski. At that point he still spoke English with a very thick accent and the film he showed (perhaps owing to a faulty projector) kept breaking and flapping. Like the feathers of that white rooster. For years I have considered Grotowski a guru, having observed the trance he induces in his listeners, more by his personality, I think, than by anything he says. But that was always to an audience of theatre professionals. They came specifically "to sit at the feet of the great Grotowski." In contrast, my learned colleagues from the Getty Center had heard little or nothing of Grotowski. And when they displayed enthusiasm, it was for a sketch by Leonardo, unexpectedly discovered on the back of a well-known painting. Yet Grotowski was received enthusiastically by these art historians and ethnographers. As no one else either before him or after him that year. And there were excellent speakers among the lecturers in the series.

That evening Grotowski came to our place for Russian pierogis with cheese and potato filling. He ate with real gusto. I voiced my amazement: "You should be eating only lotus seeds." "Lotus seeds go wonderfully well with Polish vodka," he replied. For me that was a totally new Grotowski. I had never heard him make fun of himself before. He seemed to have opened up. He was lonely. For a long time now his friends and his actors have been scattered throughout the world. Or they are no longer living. Just like mine. As he was leaving, he gave me a book that he said he never parted with. It was a French translation of Martin Buber's *Tales of the Hasidim*. These tales are similar to the ones that Stanislaw Vincenz collected among the Hasidic Jews who lived on the upper Czeremosz River. "Good Lord," said one of those distant and later successors of the Baal Shem Tov, "save the Jews. If you can't save them all, at least save the ones who are your own personal chosen." It was strange, but that evening I had the impression that the former guru Grotowski, absorbed in eating Russian pierogis, was one of the Hasidim.

In May or June of the same year we were invited by Grotowski to his campus at Irvine. It is one of those Californian university campuses located in a thick forest where buildings and men pale to insignificance. The forest changes almost imperceptibly into open land. On the other side, the ocean is only a couple of miles away. On the edge of the campus, next to an old barn he had been given, Grotowski set up a circular Mongolian yurt built of bright wood. In that dark barn, in that bright yurt, in the nearby scrub, or along the seashore, for an entire year, day after day, sometimes well into the night, Grotowski kept training a new group of actors. There were seven young men and one woman. One young man was Mexican, one (I think) Balinese, the rest were from various countries of the two Americas. The young woman was Japanese. They came to Grotowski either on their own or at his initiative.

For that long night in Irvine, besides L. and me, Grotowski had also invited André Gregory and his wife [Mercedes] and two or three people from the campus. So the performers outnumbered the spectators. The yurt still smelled of fresh resin, the waxed floor was as shiny as in the Japanese Noh theatre. We took off our shoes and were seated on a wooden bench. The performance started with the young Mexican [Pablo Jimenez], who – Grotowski said – had absolute pitch. He began a song in which the same sequence of notes was repeated, then faded out and came back again. This singsong was accompanied by an equally monotonous dance step. The performer's knees rubbed against each other, and his toes were pointed in. At each step, given the position of his body, the performer's head and shoulders would bend down and then straighten up. This lasted a long time and suddenly tension mounted. As though that strange step had struck in each of our throats. Then the first dancer was joined by the others, all intoning the same monotonous singsong and executing the same rocking step. They resembled an uncoiling snake. There must have been something hypnotic in this snake, since the invited guests gradually joined in, repeating the nodding dance step and the chanting.

Later I asked Grotowski about the origin of this strange step so mortifying to the body. He said that it was a combination of the ritual rocking of the Hasidim and of the last of the meditative positions in Zen. Meditation requires tension of the body. And of the thinking process, which precedes action.

Then we were led out of the yurt several hundred feet into the scrub. On a small knoll facing us, two of the young men and the young woman were repeating the same bowing step once again, but standing in place. They would turn in succession to the four corners of the world, and then bow to the sky and the earth. To an outside observer it might have seemed that this dance was yet another secret ritual among the hundreds of strange cults that flourish in California, but it was only two young men from Latin America and a young Japanese woman standing on a small knoll while the sun was setting.

At one point three horses – two white and one black – passed in front of us. As though they had just stepped out of a Gauguin painting. Their front legs were fettered. The horses moved slowly, taking short steps, their heads bent down low in search of tufts of grass hard to find in the dry scrub. For an instant they blocked our view of the two young men and the woman, whose heads were bent low like the horses'. Later I asked Grotowski whether he had planned that moment of beauty. "No," he replied, "God is the only great director."

Then still later, at dusk, the seven men and the woman started to run in a huge circle in front of the yurt. They ran, now faster, now slower, changing step. They did not look at one another, but they all changed step simultaneously as though they were tied by an invisible thread. It lasted a very long time, but the longer this monotonous running, this abstract and empty ballet without music, lasted the more enchanting it became. Until it finally stopped. I asked Grotowski how he measured the length of the running time. "The running stopped," he said, "when it played itself out."

Late at night we were taken back to the barn. Again we were seated on the wooden bench along one of the walls. Grotowski was squatting in the right corner. The barn was dark, except for a dozen candles that flickered on a low table directly in front of us. The performers were now running close to the walls. They kept changing, but there were always only two: the pursuer and the pursued, a man and a woman or two men. They were naked, in white shrouds hanging loosely from their bodies, with skeleton bones drawn in thick, bold lines. In the light of the candles, whose flames swayed as though mown down by the wind from the onrushing bodies, enormous shadows moved along the walls of the barn.

The pursuit was a sequence that was repeated over and over again. And it always ended in a gesture signifying rape, murder or forgiveness. Twice, when the pursuer finally overtook his human prey, he covered it with a shroud, and twice after that the creature who had been hunted down or raped slowly lifted its head, still covered by the shroud, and froze in a half-seated position like Lazarus just risen from the dead, or, according to Grotowski's syncretism of myths and cultures, like an Egyptian mummy wrapped in white bandages slowly rising up out of a sarcophagus.

Early the next morning, as we were saying goodbye, I asked Grotowski whether he had any documentation about his work for the year – photographs, drawings, written accounts. "What for?" He seemed to be genuinely surprised. "The only lasting imprint is made on memory." Then he smiled. "You should know that best of all, Jan. You wrote about the body's memory."

That was the final year of Grotowski's work at Irvine. His new Centro di Lavoro is located in Pontedera, a small Tuscan village thirty or forty miles from Florence. There's not even a third-class restaurant in the village, so Grotowski's pupils – and there are about twenty of them – prepare their own meals. They will stay with Grotowski for three years. Shortly after the opening of this new school in the wilderness, Brook visited Grotowski. If they again sat side by side on a wooden bench, the wanderer's knapsack this time would have belonged to Brook. On this occasion Brook talked about Gordon Craig. He called Craig one of the greatest universal masters, since Craig's influence and legend have held sway throughout the entire century and embraced all aspects of theatre. Craig's legend has been spread by those who knew firsthand at least one of his very few productions and passed it on to their pupils, and so from one generation to the next of pupils of pupils. The Craig legend, which has lived on after him, comprises a vision of total theatre. This total theatre is – and Brook didn't stress this in his lecture – an impossible theatre, since its essence is not the word or the actor or the setting or the music. Perhaps it is only movement and light. I am not sure whether it was Brook who first compared Grotowski to Craig. But I think it is a revealing comparison. It says something about both of them.

Georges Banu was also present at that meeting in Pontedera. In a letter he wrote me, he said, "I saw Grotowski. What limitations he imposes! But what strength in those limitations. For the first time I experienced the limit of theatre."

I experienced that limit myself two years earlier in Irvine. At sunrise, in the scrub that almost creeps up to the threshold of Grotowski's yurt – the rattlesnakes hissed and the air quivered. Such quivering air I have seen once before in the Negev by the rose columns of Solomon.

Translated by Jadwiga Kosicka.

BALI AND GROTOWSKI
Some parallels in the training process

I Wayan Lendra

The Objective Drama project was a special research project conducted at the University of California-Irvine (UCI), formulated and directed by Jerzy Grotowski. The direction of the project was to isolate the performative expressions of several traditional cultures and introduce them to performers outside of their original cultural contexts. Once the technical aspects of a form were internalized, the effects of the relationships among performer, form, group, and environment were the subject of observation. A 1984 "Research and Development Report" described the project:

> "Objective Drama" is Jerzy Grotowski's term for those elements of the ancient rituals of various world cultures which have a precise, and therefore objective, impact on participants, quite apart from solely theological or symbolic significance. Mr. Grotowski's intention is to isolate and study such elements of performative movements, dances, songs, incantations, structures of language, rhythms, and uses of space. Those elements are sought by means of a distillation process from the complex through the simple and through the separation of elements one from the other.
>
> (Focused Research Program in Objective Drama)

Each cultural form was taught by an expert performer native to that culture. The traditional cultural forms included: Haitian voodoo ritual, dervish dances, Korean shamanistic dance and songs, Balinese incantation and mantra, hatha yoga, and Japanese karate. A number of exercises were also developed throughout the project. Literary texts such as the Gospel of Saint Thomas and some literature from Hinduism were used in the newly created songs.

Two traditional practitioners from Haiti, Maud [Robart] and Tiga [Jean-Claude Garoute], worked intensively with us for several months. They taught the movements and songs of Haitian voodoo accompanied by traditional drums. A karate master from Japan and a master performer of the Sufi dervish tradition taught for short periods. A number of new exercises were developed by "technical specialists" from traditional material Grotowski had worked on during his Theatre of Sources in Poland. In addition to all of these exercises, we worked intensively on our individual or group pieces called Mystery Plays, works that were not intended to be performed for the general public. Through Mystery Plays we explored our personal artistic possibilities, applying our insights and experience gained from the work and the creative energy generated by the exercises. This intensive work was directed by Grotowski. Mystery Plays were performed at marathon sessions – two days and two nights of work.

Four of us technical specialists worked with the project continuously: Du Yee Chang from Korea, Jairo Cuesta from Colombia, Wei-Cheng Chen from Taiwan, and myself from Bali, Indonesia. The four of us were accomplished artists in our own cultural traditions, with backgrounds in experimental modern theatre. We learned and recorded the materials of the traditional practitioners and helped Grotowski formulate new exercises. We then taught and guided participants in both the traditional forms and the new work. These participants included some students from UCI. Other participants, selected by audition, worked with us for set short periods of time. They came from different countries, many from cities and universities in the United States.

Throughout the three years of work, Grotowski's role was manifold. On the administrative side he was assisted by Marion Barnett. This allowed him to focus on his primary function as director of the research activities of the workplace. During the exercises Grotowski observed and made notes, taught, and commented. He intervened with either physical or verbal directions. The energy of his presence was an essential contribution to the working process.

The project took place on the southern edge of the campus of UCI, in an isolated area of rolling hills populated only with horses, cattle, and field rabbits. Our center of work was two buildings: an old historic building known as the barn, renovated into a studio theatre for the project, and a hexagonal, one-room, redwood structure called the yurt. Both buildings had wood floors and many windows that allowed in natural light. The color of the walls in the barn was light blue, while the yurt was natural wood. At night we used kerosene lanterns for light, although electricity was available. The hills behind our studios were as much a part of the workspace as the buildings, and much of our group work took place outdoors.

The work itself was very rigorous. It required not only physical dexterity and stamina, but mental perseverance. Grotowski imposed uncompromising discipline. We had to observe many requirements. Grotowski prescribed some rules which were difficult to perform, in the same way he chose participants, chose to work in nature, and isolated the essential elements of ancient performative rituals. In addition to all these, he proposed that we work long hours. Most of the time we worked between five and six days a week. Each exercise would last approximately two hours or longer depending on the development of the action. Our sessions, which usually began in the early evening, often extended for eight hours, sometimes through the entire night.

The work affected my perceptions on many levels simultaneously. There was a change of consciousness and awareness, a change of physical impulses and behavior, and an intensity which developed throughout the work. Generally I felt my body was awake even though I was working long hours almost every day. I was very much connected with myself and certainly with my native culture, Bali. There seemed to be a close similarity with the trance situations I had seen in Bali, or the trancelike quality of Balinese performing arts.

In the summer of 1984 I went back to Bali for a break from the project. During this visit I witnessed a calonarang performance, a trance dance drama featuring Barong (a mythical dragonlike figure of benevolent nature) and Rangda (an awesome masked figure of demonic quality), performed during the anniversary celebration of the temple, Bukit, in my village, Bitra. About twenty of my friends and relatives, men and women, went into trance. The following days I interviewed some of the performers, focusing on the specific question: whether they were aware of the spectators and surroundings during the trance. Each of them answered yes. They added that their bodies became sensitive and they felt a burning and itching sensation in different parts of the body, particularly in the chest. Their awareness became more acute than in normal everyday life. They said that if they were not totally alert they could hurt someone with the sharp *kris* (a dagger) they carried. Yet it was remarkable that they were not at all aware of stabbing their chests or cheeks with the sharp steel daggers, or of eating live chicks. During the violent moment of stabbing, the performers were carefully watched by assistants in case of an unexpected mistake.

Jane Belo, in *Trance in Bali* (recorded in the late 1930s and published in 1960), quoted trance performers who reported that during performance they "were in and out of trance" (1960:254). She reports that during the convulsions going in and out of trance, the performers were unaware of their beings and surroundings; the trancers I interviewed reported a similar state. She also writes that during the performance the trancers were often playful, stealing each other's chicks, eggs, or liquor and challenging each other in the action of stabbing. I also observed the childlike playfulness or behavior of the trancers in several different trance forms in Bali.

The point I am making here is that during the state of trance, the Balinese trancer experiences both a state of acute awareness, a state of the true self (*inget*), and a state of being unaware (*engsap*). In the state of inget the trancer is very much her- or himself and can be very playful, like a child, while in the state of engsap the connection with the surroundings is cut, during which time the stabbing may occur.

I am convinced that there are a number of similarities between Balinese trance performers, Grotowski's words concerning trance, and my experience in the project. Grotowski once said, referring to the Haitian trance tradition, that when a person is in trance he is "highly aware of the surroundings." During this time the person is deeply involved with what he is doing and at the same time is capable of sensing and incorporating the events in his environment without being affected by them. This may be similar to the state of being of a powerful actor, whose "presence" deeply affects the spectators as well as absorbs her surroundings. Her art is organic, a phenomenon generated not by her intention to "show," but by her honest and sincere motivation to "do" what she is doing.

My interest in this research in Bali was to relate it to my experience with Grotowski in California. From the beginning of the project I felt that there was something very Balinese about Grotowski's work, even though the nature of the theatrical exercises was not Balinese. I felt the project was more than a theatre project. I realized what Grotowski meant by "yes but not only" when he was asked in a 1983 interview for the *Los Angeles Times* if this was a theatre project.

The project certainly had a spiritual dimension even though Grotowski never referred to it as spiritual work. This is similar to the spiritual nature of the Balinese theatre that I have been doing since I was a child. Through the work of the project, Grotowski helped to deepen my insights into the spiritual nature of Balinese arts. He brought me back to my own sources. Through my research and knowledge of the Balinese performing arts and my interviews with religious practitioners in Bali, I found that there is a parallel between Grotowski's work and Balinese theatre in the training process as well as in its impact on the actor and the spectator.

To analyze and highlight Grotowski's work based on my interpretation as a direct participant and as a Balinese artist, I would first like to consider three elements basic to the Balinese way of life and art. The first is the intimate relationship between people and nature, which is similar to Grotowski's high regard for working in a natural setting. The second is the routine of religious rituals and custom, essential elements which have a close relationship with Grotowski's specific selection of traditional discipline and teaching methods applied in the project. And lastly, the way the Balinese people consider art, besides being an entertainment, as a medium of true inner expression, connecting the gods to their worshippers. This is similar to Grotowski's work, in the manner in which he examines how performative arts have the potential to generate higher awareness.

It is important to note that these three major elements are woven into Balinese daily life. The daily application of these elements throughout the stages of life allows a Balinese to express his respect for nature, to realize his humanity, and to shape him into a Balinese. As Belo accurately says in her book:

> The Balinese are people whose everyday behavior is measured, controlled, graceful, tranquil. Emotion is not easily expressed. Dignity and an adherence to the rules of decorum are customary. At the same time they show a susceptibility and a facility of going into states of trance, states in which there is an altered consciousness, and a behavior springing from a deep level of personality is manifested.
>
> (1960:1)

What do the traditional Balinese do that has inspired Belo to make such a statement? We should first examine the interrelationship between the essential nature of Balinese arts and the Balinese ways of life in relation to religion and nature.

Traditional Balinese arts, whether music, dance, theatre, painting, sculpture, or food offerings, always have a religious function as well as an entertainment or worldly function. The "essence of the true effort" in doing the arts serves as an offering to the gods and goddesses, while the "form and energy" generated from and stimulated by the arts or artists entertain, touch, and bring harmony to the spectators. Whether the art is sacred or secular, if it is true art coming from the deepest heart of the artist, the process of the making and the presentation of the arts in Bali always involve a religious commitment. Balinese consider the arts a tool for bringing out the expression of the inner spirit, our true nature. The artist's skill and the true and honest way of doing (*ngayah*) are the mediums for that expression. Because of this attitude, the arts should be handled with care and respect. This should be reflected in one's thoughts and actions.

Care and respect are performed not only to create a sense of humbleness necessary in the arts and in life, but because what is being cared for and respected has a definite meaning. Precise technical skills, for example, should be acquired through learning and through conforming to the traditional forms. These forms are difficult to master and, therefore, require a strong motivation and dedication. Even though they vary slightly from region to region and master to master, the basic forms – such as the *agem* (basic body positions) – are a physical structure that has a physical and psychological impact. In a precisely performed agem, the creation and flow of energy is nurtured (this will be further described below). Of course there are other technical elements involved in creating these effects of energy. These have an impact on the performer and the spectator: a heightening of awareness and a sense of well-being. A performer may say that she/he feels complete after ngayah, performing a true act.

However, the awakening of higher awareness cannot be fully accomplished only through the mastery of techniques. Observing religious and traditional ways of conduct constitutes the other half of the effort. In Bali, skilled activities, especially those that are going to be exposed to the public such as the performing arts, are always preceded by a presentation of an offering to the gods or the lower spirits. This is a form of protecting oneself against any unexpected danger. Making offerings is a form of contemplation which results in self-assurance, an alertness of the body and mind.

To the Balinese, life is wonderful, it is precious. The Balinese believe that an individual is a reincarnation of her or his ancestor, therefore life is a special thing to have and care for. Balinese also believe that we are not alone in this world. There are higher energies and spirits around us. These others cannot be seen, except occasionally by special eyes, heard by special ears, and understood by unsuppressed instincts. They are unknown to the brain, therefore they are a mystery. The mystery of the unknown and the belief in it create a wonder. This leads to our "humbleness," a state of being that is free, honest, and respectful. This is opposed to an "arrogant" manner – an attitude that a person "knows" is not considered refined and proper.

The Balinese believe that the higher energies (gods) and the lower energies (demons) exist in nature and in us. A Balinese *dalang* (puppeteer) told me: "Pray to your god inside you before you pray to the gods in the temples. If you cannot find it, try to find it while you pray to the gods in the temples." The Balinese believe that gods and other higher and lower energies live at the peak of the sacred mountains, in sacred spots, in sacred objects, in the ocean, in trees, and in animals. Each of these natural elements has its own life and energy. To the Balinese, their island is full of gods and both good and bad spirits. Their presence is felt instinctively and the vibrations of these energies are overwhelming. It is a magical place.

The Balinese built thousands of temples, shrines, and altars almost everywhere on the island. On this beautiful island, the view is wonderful during the day, while at night and during transitional times the place becomes awesome. The night belongs to the spirit world and to the gods, while the day belongs to the living and also to the ever-present gods. Life and death are one in Bali. Life is a beauty and death is a danger that creates a subtle undertone of fear. Yet, when death must come it is willingly accepted and even celebrated.

To avoid danger, the gods should be consulted and asked for their blessings whenever a person is doing any activity, especially a skilled activity. The lower spirits also have their place, and should be appeased. *Banten* – ornately decorated offerings of food, fruits, flowers, and incense – are usually presented to the gods for their blessing and to the lower spirits to assure that they will not disturb the activities. In the performing arts, the powers of gods or demons may be invoked if they are needed. If the actor is performing the character of a demon, the energy of the demon may be called. Similarly, the god may be invoked if an actor is performing a deity, or simply invited to witness and to bless the performance.

The banten physically acknowledges the existence of the gods and spirits of nature and expresses the spiritual commitment of the performer. If the believer does not do this preliminary ritual, she will have a feeling of guilt which leads to anxiety and perhaps incompetence. She may even fail. The Balinese are afraid of this state of imbalance, which could lead them to be disoriented (*paling*), and if prolonged, could lead to mental derangement (*buduh*).

RELIGIOUS PREPARATION IN TRAINING

When a group of children are chosen to become actors and dancers, an auspicious day from the Balinese calendar is selected for the very first rehearsal. Selecting a special day for the beginning of an activity is a common practice in Bali. The selection of the day is based on the cycle of the planets and the vibration of nature. This special time to start an activity is called *menausen*, which literally means "to mark with the auspicious day." On another special day soon after menausen, the children will undergo a ceremonial initiation called *meperascita*, which literally means "the purification of body and mind." The children may be taken to a temple to ask for a blessing from the gods. Preceding each rehearsal, small offerings (*banten canang*) are made and incense burned at the shrine for the god or guardian of the crossroads where the community center is located. The gamelan orchestra that accompanies the rehearsal, as well as the rehearsal space itself, are also given small offerings. Even though the degree of elaborateness and the frequency of this ritual differs from the village to village, or family to family, it is customary in Bali to observe this process properly. An unsuccessful activity would be blamed on the failure to observe the ritual routine, if only in its simplest form. The Balinese would say, "*Sing taen nang ngai canang kenkenan men bisa dueg*," which literally means, "Just a simple offering you never make, how can you be successful?"

Pasupati is the next ceremony that the children go through once they have achieved a satisfactory level of technical precision. The function of this ceremony is to transform raw materials – the costumes, headdresses, and masks – into powerful art objects by infusing them with spiritual energy. This process, carried out by a priest and blessed by the gods in the temple, transforms these ordinary materials into carriers of sacred power. The performers, who are also present at this ceremony, are further purified as well. In a parallel symbolic sense, the performer's art of dance or acting is transformed from raw learned technique into a spiritually internalized artistic expression. After this purification, the artists are united with the sacred objects and materials that will be used at the moment of their premiere performance and thereafter. From this time onward the performer is ready to seek *taksu*, the ultimate spiritual power that allows the performer to present his or her art in its truest form.

This process of religious ritual occurs not only in the performing arts, but in other skilled professions. To become a priest and/or a diviner, for example, one must go through several steps of ritual purification (*mewinten*) and adhere to an increasing number of behavioral restrictions that distinguish one from ordinary others. Only after these rituals are performed can a priest learn sacred texts such as mantras, sacred chants. The individual must also go through a ceremony called *mesakapan dewa*, a ritual "marriage" to the god of the temple in which he or she officiates as priest or acts as a diviner.

The main purpose of a purification ritual is to help the individual discover the meanings of her or his duties. It also creates a context for attention to appropriate behavior and respect for the occupation one has chosen. Consequently, a person establishes an identity that is valued by the community. This mental cleansing prepares the body and mind to concentrate fully, and through repeated practice it deepens one's dedication and insights. Ritual also generates alertness in the person, a higher awareness necessary in life and the arts. In Bali, this awareness is reinforced by beliefs; its meaning is nurtured by nature, and its continuity is assured through repetition and the training process. Proper traditional training is necessary for effective art, art that functions not only as entertainment, but as a means of uniting one's true self with the infinite power of nature.

In the Objective Drama project there were no religious practices. Even though we worked on exercises which derived from rituals of various traditions, Grotowski never referred to these exercises as religious. They were simply exercises that had special values. However, the manner in which this work was conducted and organized played an important role in the successful result and effect of the work. Like the religious practices that are part of the Balinese training process, the Objective Drama project was executed in a very distinct manner.

An important word which Grotowski used frequently was "alert"; participants should be alert. In order to be alert the first and most important basic rule is to be silent. This rule permeated every facet of the project. Participants were only allowed to speak when they really needed to express an idea related to the project, or when asked to discuss their reactions to specific activities. During breaks we generally did not speak. This was the time to absorb and internalize the experience. Grotowski called this a "silence of saturation." It was not meant to be a spiritual silence. Those who wished to discuss personal matters were asked to talk outside the project area. Due to the nature of the work, nobody did this. This requirement was unusually challenging, especially for newly arrived participants, as they had to abandon conventional socializing during and between the long hours of work.

Being silent allows many possibilities. Part of the work was to increase the awareness of being in an environment, to settle the mind through silent self-observation. This is closely related to the awareness and alertness resulting from the attentive and respectful manner seen in Balinese religious activities. By eliminating verbal dialog in the project we reduced the mechanical social interaction of ordinary life. This allowed us to develop an attunement to each other, the group, and the surroundings by sensing their presence or actions. It allowed us to suspend judgments about people and situations and just to be, do, and observe.

There were other specific requirements, such as: When you walked in the fields or in the woods, you were not allowed to pick up anything or to disturb nature. In Bali, an unnecessary action in nature (*usil*) is a degraded behavior strongly forbidden for Balinese children. In the project we were also told not to make noises with our feet or hum while walking in the field. Similarly, we could not make noises when walking in the work space. This type of requirement allowed participants to be self-observant. Occasionally Grotowski would spend a long time criticizing those who did not properly observe this way of working. To join the project, a participant had to learn exactly what to do and what not to do, a similar understanding held by believers in Balinese ritual, who know exactly what must be done in order to ensure the efficacy of the ritual.

Everything was neatly organized in the project. What needed to be prepared before a work session was clearly spelled out. Grotowski might ask Du Yee, Jairo, or me, during the first two hours, to discuss his plan for the rest of the session, while the others waited patiently and quietly. During this time some did warm-ups, some simply sat. In the meeting,

Grotowski specified what needed to be corrected, who would be correcting whom, where the work would take place, and approximately how long it would take. This was very specific and very orderly. Grotowski never discussed the whole plan of the session, for he did not want people to have expectations that could lead to mechanical work. He wanted to create an organic flow of events, and therefore rearranged the sequence of the work according to the need and flow of each session. He often said that the work should have "new life" at every session. The only exercise with a set time was the exercise called Motions. This exercise was always executed at sunset or sunrise. We should remember that Objective Drama was designed to test the impact of selected exercises. The participants were the "guinea pigs," therefore they were not informed of the direction or plan for each session. Probably Grotowski himself did not know what would need work. Even if he knew he did not tell because that would go against the principle of the experiment.

Because of the disciplined nature of the work, the lifestyle in the project was very different from that of normal life. Socialization and easygoing behavior did not take place. Alleviating one's social problems or complaining were discouraged. Doubt resulting from the rules of working was resolved by quitting the project or participating fully. But even participants who complied with the rules still faced other difficulties of commitment to the work.

This is similar to the commitment in the Balinese training process, except in Bali this commitment is not experienced as hard work, but as a religious commitment. But both the Balinese and Grotowski's style of commitment lead to the establishment of an identity. The religious nature of the traditional Balinese training is more pronounced than in the rigorous work of the Objective Drama project. In Bali commitment and dedication are internalized; dedication is shown in daily actions, diligent practices. No Balinese actor would practice eight hours a day, or work from early evening until early morning. A Balinese performer might work until early morning when performing but, even so, would not perform every day. Balinese actors might work hard and adhere to all kinds of rules and restrictions, but these rules and restrictions are tradition – everybody does the same. All are born into this tradition. There is no apparent pressure that an artist experiences, because her or his effort is supported by the society. Commitment and identity are molded by the traditional system, by the natural environment, and by religious beliefs.

Grotowski attempted to recreate this kind of tradition in the project by enforcing ways of working and by working in a natural setting. The experience of the work taught the participants the meaning of the work. Because the project was not intended to be lifelong, but only for three years, Grotowski had to conduct the work very intensely. In the project everything was condensed, distilled, and selected. This ranged from the selection of participants to the strictness of rules and the materials explored in the work.

Working in the evening and through the night with the illumination of only oil lamps, for example, may have seemed unnatural and mysterious to a new participant. But the practical intention of this setting was to make the body and the mind alert. Generally evening is the time most people rest. But if asked to do difficult exercises during these hours and in such a setting, most likely the participant will react organically, causing him or her to be alert and increasing the effectiveness of the work. Grotowski is very fond of the idea of "contradiction," an idea against conventional ways of living and understanding, but with the intention of provoking organic physical and mental responses on the part of participants.

The exercise called Motions, practiced at sunset or sunrise, also has a practical purpose embedded in the idea of contradiction. Sunset and sunrise are the times when ordinary nature is spectacular. Yet, during the Motions the participant is not allowed to respond emotionally to what she sees. She cannot say the sunset is beautiful, which people normally do; she simply observes what is out there. This is one of the contradictions seen in the Motions, a contradiction that creates alertness and awareness of physical impulses. Another important element of the training process in the project was that Grotowski never described the meaning of or the idea behind any exercise. In the same way, the Balinese (except specialists such as priests) would not know the meanings and symbolism of the elaborate religious rituals. If a Balinese is asked why he performs a religious ritual, the usual answer would be "*Nak mule keto*," meaning "That is the way it has been done." But he knows that he feels a sense of well-being after performing the ritual. Thus the ritual is efficacious. In the project one could only understand the ideas and values of the work by listening to Grotowski, by observing his way, by experiencing the exercises, and by relating them to one's own knowledge. Even so, the understanding was still an interpretation because the meaning of each exercise was not specifically described. Grotowski did not intend to give the meaning or the intended result of the exercises. He did not wish the participants to start working with an "idea." He thought that to work on a physical exercise with an idea would be misleading and deceiving, because the mind would be consciously searching for the result of the idea. The action would not be organic and the physical impulses would be blocked.

The rules and the technical precision and strategy of the different exercises were worked out in minute detail. In the workspace or at

Grotowski's apartment we often discussed and analyzed them – did they work or not? Changes or adjustments occurred based on re-evaluations. Once the criteria and rules were understood and became routine, specific corrections were given, mostly nonverbally. The understanding of the rules and the precision of the exercises were of primary importance. Grotowski and his assistants would always give corrections and criticism. The criticism, which was verbal, could be severe.

Because of the variety of both mental and physical demands encountered in the project, the work was not easy to follow. Grotowski was obviously aware of the difficulties. For this reason, he was very careful in selecting participants. He would look for a particular quality in a candidate. This was not based solely on technical ability, although technique had a value. It was based more on the "human quality" of the person. What Grotowski meant by "human quality" was a puzzle to me, but during our three years of working together, I came to understand. My interpretation is that he meant a person who is not arrogant, not pretentious, not overly nice, and not talkative; someone who is humble, simple, subtle but bright; a person who seems to have an interest in adventure and a curiosity for life. If this interpretation is correct, then I would definitely see a close relationship with the Balinese ideal of a novice performer.

The Balinese traditional theatre follows a formal structure, with characters that are well known to the people. Characters are divided into three different types: deities, humans, and demons. Actors are chosen for a role according to their personalities, human qualities, and physical types. The qualifications for the selection of a novice in Bali include a refined manner, respectfulness, and tolerance. Being humble is an important qualification because the responsibility of the artist is to become a medium. The artist must be able to invoke the character and allow that character to live through him or her. The spirit of the character would most likely enter the artist who has the qualifications mentioned.

PHYSICAL EXERCISES

Kinesthetic learning is the most important aspect of the learning process in both Balinese traditional training and in Grotowski's training. Verbal communication, describing what is being learned, is not a part of the training process. This is an ancient way in which a novice learns through the body directly rather than through a preliminary mental process. Grotowski says that "the body itself functions like a brain"; it can record and later recall movement patterns and emotion in a seemingly instinctive way when stimuli are given. Learning kinesthetically incorporates both the physical precision and the emotional quality of the action.

In Bali kinesthetic learning takes place in two distinct ways. In the first, the teacher moves the body of the young student, shaping and giving the flow of the direction of the movement. The body of the child is manipulated as a puppet is manipulated by a puppeteer. When the student is older and more accomplished, the teacher may offer corrections by a light touch or facial and body signals. The student also learns through observing and following the teacher, repeating the voice or movement sequence many times. Repetition is another basic principle of kinesthetic learning through which the body will internalize the physical experience. Repetition may lead to a mechanical quality, but a student is instructed to find the life of the action in each repetition.

In Objective Drama, this process of training was highly valued and consistently applied. Throughout the work, the exercises were communicated mostly nonverbally. When verbal direction was needed, the leader or teacher used only limited and precise words. As in Balinese training, the actions were learned through following the leader; the observation/ physical imitation/repetition formula was used. However, the Balinese puppet method of shaping the student's body was not applied because the project students were already adults. Using this method with adults is physically impractical and socially inappropriate.

THE MOTIONS

The Motions is a body-stretching exercise as well as training for mental endurance. The primary purpose of this exercise is to train the body to be sensitive and the mind to be alert. The Motions, executed in standing position, is a complex exercise, meditative in quality, slowly performed and physically strenuous. It was usually practiced outdoors on the hillside, in silence, and during transitional times, especially at sunset and at sunrise. The exercise always begins facing the sun. The original duration of the Motions was about one hour and a half, but later it was reduced to forty-five ·minutes. It is normally done in a group, in a diamond-shaped formation, in which four leaders stand at the four corners of the diamond. The participants find their places inside the diamond shape with appropriate distances from each other. They should be able to see the leaders at the four directions, just as the Balinese novice can clearly see the teacher and follow the action.

The exercise relates to seven directions: east, west, north, south, zenith, nadir, and center. There are three major movements, each of which is repeated at the four directions. There is also a very slow turning which is used to reach the four cardinal points. The slow turning, executed in place, may take from one to two minutes depending on which direction is being reached.

"Primal position," a basic body posture which appears to be one of the Motions' most important features, is similar to the basic stance of Balinese dance theatre called agem.[1] "Primal position' is executed standing. The feet are placed parallel, about one fist apart. The knees are slightly bent and the body weight rests on the balls of the feet, as if the performer is ready to move. The torso and the head and chin are gently pulled in, so that energy travels from the bottom of the spine up to the head. The torso and the head are tilted forward, which allows a slight contraction and pull at the bottom of the torso. The pelvic region is tucked in, the abdomen lifted, and the chest and the shoulders relaxed. The arms are straight, placed at either side of the body, and the base of each thumb touches slightly the section below the hips. The palms face backward, and the fingers, touching each other, are slightly curved in. The eyes see in a panoramic view. In this "primal position" the body should be alert and ready for action.

Grotowski's "primal position" is similar to the Balinese agem in the alignment of the torso and the head, and in the effect of the position on the body and mind. An exception is the male-style agem for a strong character, for which the legs are turned out and about one step diagonally apart. The pelvic region is slightly thrust out instead of tucked in as in the primary position. Because in Balinese dance the upper arms are generally raised in line with the shoulders, and the lower arms, with hyperextended hands and spread fingers, are bent forward at the elbows, the shoulders tend to be slightly contracted. However, the most important quality of both agem and the "primal position" is the alignment of the torso and the head, as well as the slight leaning forward of this line of the body. The tilt causes a pull and a contraction which generates energy. This energy flows upward to the head. Another essential result of both the Balinese basic stance and the "primal position," in my experience, is that it creates the feeling of lightness and readiness, an essential feeling of energy traveling upward, which triggers physical and mental sensitivity.

Another essential requirement of the Motions is that the eyes should see in a wide angle and the ears should hear all sounds at once. Grotowski usually said: "See that you are seeing and hear that you are hearing." Participants are instructed not to react to what they are seeing or hearing. Typically, when performing this slow and meditative exercise, our brain begins speaking – a variety of thoughts will come. If thoughts come we must not react to the thoughts or continue to develop them, but instead simply observe them and let them pass by in the same way we observe what we see and hear. While seeing and hearing, the body must be in the correct position and we must remember the sequence of the action. During this action, the body often slightly changes its position without our awareness. Because of this, Grotowski insisted that we strive always to be aware of the precision of the body position and make self-corrections from time to time.

The rules of this exercise seem to be simple, but to perform the Motions precisely – physically and mentally – is extremely difficult. The brain is occupied with monitoring the minute details of the physical action, thus freeing the inner mind, the subtler consciousness, to "come out" and merge with the environment. The inner consciousness can only do this when the brain is engaged in some directed thinking and so does not interfere. But the purpose of the physical precision of the movements is not just to keep the brain busy. When the movements are performed as designed, they help the body generate innate physical power. If the brain fails to watch the body, fails to observe the thoughts, and reacts emotionally to what is seen by the eyes and heard by the ears, the inner energy will not manifest itself.

The Motions is a complex exercise. Several elements of technique are performed at once. Really to see with panoramic vision is difficult. When you are able to see in a panoramic view, your perception cannot be as focused as when you see only one thing. In daily life we constantly focus, selecting from our perceptions what we want to see or hear. The brain is curious and will follow something of interest, almost automatically. But the requirement of the Motions is that you must not react to any one thing but must fully perceive all that there is to see and hear.

In my experience, when I see with panoramic vision and hear all sounds – both in performing Balinese dance/acting and in doing the Motions precisely – I become highly aware of my body; it absorbs what I see and hear. The surroundings become one with my body, and I feel as if my body is hollow and is being lifted. The more I see and hear, the more I sense my body. Especially in the Motions I feel the vibration of my energy throughout my body and I feel the pulses of my heart and in my feet. Sometimes I hear a high-pitched and continuous noise in my ears. Different parts of my body sometimes move by themselves. As I become aware of all these sensations, it seems that my attention to them diminishes the flow. When this happens, I proceed to correct my body positions. After each session of the Motions, I usually have the feeling of distilled energy and oneness in my body.

CONCLUSION

In my observation, the exercises practiced in Objective Drama have a single, most important purpose: the awakening of innate physical power.

This physical power, which the Hindu tradition refers to as the "sleeping energy" (*kundalini*) lies at the bottom of the spine. This innate energy can be awakened through a variety of physical and vocal exercises. Grotowski described what I call innate physical power as the "reptile brain," the spinal cord and brain stem, with the "sleeping energy" at the very bottom of the spine.[2] This unawakened energy source exists in every human being. Grotowski wanted to investigate and find a way to wake up this energy center which, when awakened, can increase our awareness, sensitivity, and perception. The awakened state is necessary not only in life but in the performing arts. For this reason Grotowski was interested in working on the undulating spinal movement of the Haitian voodoo ritual and the Hindu spinal movement exercise called kundalini, which I studied and practiced closely. Like the Motions, these two exercises have a powerful effect on the body.

In Bali, the study of gaining spiritual energy is still a strong tradition practiced by trancers and diviners. It is also practiced by dalangs, and by *pregina wayah*, highly accomplished artists, usually older performers. In the arts, this ability to awaken innate physical power and invoke this energy is a necessity. An artist who has this ability is considered to have *taksu*, an ultimate spiritual energy that helps the performer project the essence of his or her art.

The knowledge and ability to invoke taksu is not limited to artists. Dr. I Made Bandem, a Balinese and a scholar in Indonesian performing arts, told me that taksu can be referred to as "genuine creativity," an ability acquired through education, practice, and the experience of both worldly and spiritual insights. In Bali, highly competent spiritual practitioners such as priests, priestesses, diviners and traditional healers – especially those attached to specific temples – are also considered to have taksu. They can invoke innate physical power and receive signs and messages from nature. The diviners belonging to specific temples through their trance states deliver the messages of the gods or goddesses to the people. The messages are oracles which are followed by the people. The messages often contain requests for what is lacking and what needs to be done to restore the balance of life in the community. They can also contain prophecies or predictions which consequently alert the people and direct them to take necessary actions. This tradition remains alive in Bali – and is similar to what Grotowski is investigating.

SUBJECTIVE REFLECTIONS ON OBJECTIVE WORK

Lisa Wolford

I participated in the Objective Drama program at the University of California-Irvine from 1989 through the conclusion of the program in 1992. Objective Drama is the term used by Jerzy Grotowski to designate the phase of his research begun in 1983, following his emigration to the United States. A 1984 "Research and Development Report" for the program describes Grotowski's focus:

> Objective Drama is concerned with those elements of the ancient rituals of various world cultures which have a precise and therefore objective impact on participants, quite apart from solely theological or symbolic significance. Mr. Grotowski's intention is to isolate and study such elements of performative movements, dances, songs, incantation,

Plate 33.1 The University of California—Irvine Barn, site for Grotowski's Objective Drama research. (Photo: Richard Schechner.)

structures of language, rhythms and uses of space. Those elements are sought by means of a distillation process from the complex through the simple and through the separation of elements one from the other.

(Focused Research Program in Objective Drama 1984)

"Objective," therefore, can be understood to designate a type of performative technique which has a determinable effect on the participant's state of energy, analogous to the objective impact of undegenerated ritual. "Drama," in this context, refers not only to the enactment of scripted material (though this is one important aspect of the work), but to the performative impulse in all its forms.

Since 1985, Grotowski's research has been carried out primarily in Pontedera, Italy, under the auspices of the Centro per la Sperimentazione e la Ricerca Teatrale. Until 1992, Grotowski continued to teach at the University of California-Irvine, for approximately two weeks each summer. Later phases of the project at U.C.-Irvine (after 1986), while chronologically overlapping with Grotowski's subsequent phase of activity ("Art as vehicle"), are still classified within the parameters of Objective Drama research, and are recognized as a separate activity from the research of the Italian Workcenter.

When I participated in U.C.-Irvine's Objective Drama worksessions from 1989 to 1992, the bulk of instruction was administered by American director James Slowiak, Grotowski's assistant during the previous five years. Slowiak worked with the participants for five months prior to Grotowski's arrival, instructing us in the basic techniques of Objective Drama and preparing various "performance structures" for presentation to Grotowski. It is customary for Grotowski, in recent stages of his research, to allow great independence to trained assistants or "technical specialists" with whom he collaborates.

Participants worked for an average of nineteen to thirty hours per week under Slowiak's direction, including lengthy weekend sessions and occasional overnight marathons. During Grotowski's two-week residence the group met nightly, generally beginning at 7 p.m. and working till 3 or sometimes 5 a.m. While this is far less than the commitment required of participants at the Centro in Pontedera (minimum one-year commitment, six days a week, eight to fourteen hours per day), it seemed excessive to actors conditioned by American standards of training. No one who applied for admittance to the worksession was denied. At the time of Grotowski's arrival in May, our ensemble consisted of fourteen participants, all students or alumni of the University of California. The main body of our group work can be classified as follows: physical training, vocal work, individual actions, group activities, and the development of performance structures.

PHYSICAL TRAINING

Since the time of Grotowski's "Theatre of Productions" phase (1957–68), the director's work has been associated with an arduously challenging method of physical training. Slowiak explained that the training structure as we encountered it, which lasted for approximately thirty minutes and could be completed by any reasonably healthy and perseverant individual, had evolved from a more intensely demanding regimen. Throughout the course of the work, the genuine limitations of each participant were respected. While participants were expected to work towards the perfect accomplishment of each element of the training regimen, evaluation was consistently tempered by recognition of the individual's progress and stage of development.

With Slowiak's guidance, each participant developed six individual exercises. We were told that these should be difficult exercises, designed to recondition the body in a specific, tangible way. In designing a training regimen, we were instructed to consider our own areas of particular weakness. One actor's training would emphasize flexibility and equilibrium, while another's would be geared towards improving strength and speed. Slowiak coordinated each participant's training structure to assure a challenging, balanced regimen. He discouraged "cotton" exercises (fashionable aerobics, for example, or activities that the participant could easily perform), in addition to purely gymnastic choices that might lead to mechanical repetition. Along with the physical structure of the training, participants developed a precise flow of associations. Such associations might involve relation to a person or object in the room, an image, or a specific memory. Once the basic physical aspects of the training were mastered, participants devoted attention to interacting with the real or imaginary partner(s). While the external structure of the training was generally to remain unchanged, improvisation was encouraged in relation to the flow of associations.

VOCAL WORK

The significance of voice work in the context of Objective Drama is related not only to the process of actor training, but to what Grotowski calls the science of "yantra" and "organon". "The yantra is a very fine instrument." In the vocabulary of ancient Sanskrit to give an example of yantra, they say a surgeon's scalpel or apparatus for astronomical observations. So a yantra is something which can connect with the laws of the universe, or nature, like an instrument for astronomical observations" (Ch. 30:298). The process of distilling and determining the efficacy of such yantra and organon is at the root of Grotowski's more esoteric research:

> These instruments are the outcome of very long practices. One should not only know how to make them, like certain kinds of dances and songs which have a specific effect on the executant, but must know how to utilize them in order not to degrade them, but in order to reach a totality, a fullness.

(Ch. 30:299)

The types of degredation to which Grotowski refers include but are not limited to syncretic combination of traditional materials derived from different cultures, and external imitation of a technique by the participant rather than an attempt to locate the sound or movement pattern through exploration in his/her own body. One example of such inappropriate combination in the group's work drew immediate and harsh criticism from Grotowski. During the months prior to Grotowski's arrival, we had experimented with an undulating Haitian dance, the *yanvalou*, in conjunction with our vocal training. Under Slowiak's instruction, we had combined the dance with an American folk song, "Poor Wayfaring Stranger." Grotowski disapproved not only of our abysmal execution of the yanvalou, but of the arbitrary and illogical juxtaposition of Haitian movement and American song.

The traditional songs of various cultures provide rich material for the distillation of yantra and organon. Grotowski distinguishes between "songs of quality", those which are rooted in a culture's ethnic or religious traditions, and melodies of contemporary popular culture. A true song of quality, such as the incantations of Haitian ritual or the hymns of the Shaker movement, carries with it a specific pattern of vocal vibrations. This associated complex of vibrations, which cannot be conveyed by existing systems of musical notation, produces the creative response in the actor. Westerners "confuse song with melody," says Grotowski (Ch. 30:297). The dilettante is unable at first even to perceive these subtle vibratory patterns, or the way in which sound is produced through different resonators of the body.

As with any precise and delicate instrument, songs which function as yantra or organon must be handled respectfully. If a song of quality is co-opted by popular culture, as for example the English ballad "Greensleeves," the song eventually becomes desacralized and the original vibratory pattern distorted. Songs which were used in performance structures or as part of other actions were not to be sung inattentively or outside the context of the work.

This was particularly true of the Creole songs taught by Haitian ritualist Maud Robart. Participants were requested never to work with these songs save under Robart's supervision. The most basic reason, as the actors were explicitly told, was that they might begin to sing the songs incorrectly, creating patterns which would later be difficult to break. On another level, Robart's techniques and songs constitute some of the most sophisticated yantra of the Objective Drama program, and are capable of producing a profound inner effect on the participant. Participants who requested to audio tape Robart's songs were denied. Tape recording, we were instructed, cannot capture the vibratory pattern. When teaching a new song to the group, one leader (Robart, Slowiak, or a designated actor) would repeat the song until other participants learned it well enough to follow.

Songs were repeated until the song "arrived." Sometimes a song would arrive after only a dozen repetitions; at other times, we worked with a single melody for an hour or more. This required attention not only to tempo and melody, but to the use of appropriate resonators and the placement of the voice. Exercises described in *Towards a Poor Theatre*, devoted to opening different resonators of the body, were central to our group work. As with all aspects of the training, emphasis was placed on maintaining connection with an outside partner. Actors were not told to use the head or lower belly resonators, but were instead directed to converse with the ceiling or sing to the floor, then listen for the echo.

For each song integrated into the group's vocal training, a simple structure of movement was developed. This could involve a particular type of walking, running in a certain pattern, or even a simple swaying motion. These movement structures were not regarded as independent elements (i.e., dance or choreography), but rather were perceived to be in service to the song, aiding the actor to sing more freely. As with all training structures and group activities, vocal work was regarded in some sense as performance. Participants dressed in white clothing, with women in loose, flowing skirts. Preparation for vocal work involved a specific arrangement of the space and a particular type of lighting. We were consistently required to execute details of the song and movement structures with the same degree of professionalism and attention which would be accorded to public presentation.

The majority of songs incorporated into our group's vocal structure consisted of hymns from the American Shaker movement. Slowiak, who had some previous knowledge of these songs, intuitively recognized their potential in terms of yantra and organon. "This is something that's always been missing from the work," Slowiak mused, "genuine traditional material for Americans." Our encounter with the values encoded in the Shaker songs, such as simplicity, humility and impeccable attention to craft, provided us with a challenge which infused and richly inspired our way of working. While certain elements of Shaker tradition, as for example separation by gender, informed our development of movement structures, in no sense did we attempt to imitate or reconstruct authentic Shaker dance.

GROUP ACTIVITIES

In addition to our physical and vocal training regimens, participants worked with a number of structured physical activities. These group activities, which involved neither narrative nor dialogue, centered on the execution of specific objectives within a pre-determined physical structure. Certain of these activities stipulated execution of precisely structured forms, while others were loosely structured and allowed for improvisation within established parameters. An exercise called "The Motions," extensively documented by I Wayan Lendra (cf. Ch. 32) and Thomas Richards (1995), represents the most rigidly structured of such activities, while the game-like "Watching" illustrates a freer, more improvisational form.

"The purpose of the Watching, quite simply," Slowiak explained when first teaching the structure, "is to watch." In the context of this activity, however, watching is not to be equated with passive observation. The participant is required simultaneously to maintain active engagement and detached awareness. The Watching is structured in such a way as to bring every participant, regardless of physical condition, into confrontation with her own limits of attention and endurance. Watching is led by a select team trained in the execution of the structure. One leader designates the parameters of the worksite and instructs newcomers in the rules of the game: no verbalization, no touching, no collisions, no daily life activity, no imitation of animals and no crawling on hands and knees. The participants, positioned throughout the space by the leader, are told to follow along until they discover the structure of the game. They are instructed that they should not imitate the leaders, but rather should respond attentively to the various component activities demonstrated by the Watching team. Once the game has begun, participants should not stop for any reason. "It's very important that you not cut the flow of this activity," Slowiak emphasized. The structure involves various types of movement, most particularly running and dance. A section called "pulsations," for example, involves running back and forth from the periphery of the space to the center point, following the leader's rhythm. In another segment, "half-moons," participants describe arcs at various distances from the center-point, moving like spiders constructing a giant web. Watching culminates in a sequence of "connections/ disconnections": physical dialogue between pairs of participants. The meetings of connection/disconnection can occur only between two people, and should take place at a level which penetrates beyond the social mask.

INDIVIDUAL ACTIONS

Individual Action is a term used to describe a type of solo performance structure; this classification can be applied to a wide variety of performances, ranging from brief fragments with neither story nor discursive speech, to fully developed, scripted Actions. Early in the course of the worksessions, Slowiak assigned participants to construct a variety of fragmentary actions. The first such Action, which he described as a "companion action", required that each of us choose a literary, historical or mythological figure of our own gender about whom we could compile research. We were then assigned to develop a brief action suggested by some aspect of the character's life. Dialogue was pro- scribed, although we could, if desired, introduce text in the form of song. Any additional characters in the scenario could only be suggested by the response of the individual actor. Actors were discouraged from convey- ing situation in a clich´ed manner through use of objects or excessive mime. Witnesses were instructed to begin with two questions in their evaluation of such Actions: "Did you believe it?" and/or "Did you understand it?" Actions were judged to be successful insofar as they fulfilled either or both of these criteria. After participants had developed a draft or proposal, Slowiak created performance montage by juxtapos- ing the fragments of different participants, instructing actors to adjust their individual scores in response to the action of the partner. At times, such combinations seemed arbitrary; when "successful," however (i.e. when the combination appeared logical), the juxtaposition of such Actions created a larger storyline that synthesized individual fragments and suggested a coherent meaning to the perception of the observer.

In "Tu es le fils de quelqu'un," Grotowski discusses another variety of such structures, which he calls a sort of "individual ethno-drama" (Ch.30:300). This structure, which figures prominently in Objective Drama research, also features elements which foreshadow the transition to Grotowski's next phase of work, "Art as vehicle." One Action which demonstrated such possibilities was developed by an Iranian actor who had participated in the project during the previous five years. It was based on the Sufi fable, "Exile Occidental." While the narrative text was in English, the action featured Farsi songs and performative aspects of the dervish tradition.

The actor began in a seated position, his gaze moving sharply from left to right as he repeated the words "beginning, end." This motion carried him to his feet and into a slow, deliberate dance. He spoke of hunting with his brother in hostile lands, and having been imprisoned by men who denied his God. The actor guided witnesses on a magical journey to his father's house. A circle of black cloth on the floor became his prison, which he entered by means of a slow somersault. The hoopoe which visited him there was created by a swathe of fabric wound around the actor's arm, and a tower he later ascended was suggested by a white robe suspended from the ceiling. Upon reaching his Father's house, the hunter was told that he must for a time return to the Occidental prison. He was propelled, whirling, through the space, and collapsed again into his tiny cell. "May the Father deliver us from the captivity of nature," he whispered, directly addressing the witnesses. "Amen."

When Grotowski viewed this Action he praised it as an excellent example of art-as-meditation, a structure by means of which the actor might encounter his own cultural traditions in order to further his journey of personal development. While he criticized technical aspects of the performance, Grotowski encouraged him to continue exploring the possibilities of the structure.

Plate 33.2   The yurt, a small wooden building constructed for Grotowski's use at California/Irvine. (Photo: Richard Schechner.)

Plate 33.3   Inside the yurt. (Photo: Richard Schechner.)

PERFORMANCE STRUCTURES

Perhaps the most significant aspect of our group's work centered on the development of performance structures. Performance structures, which most closely correspond to a conventional Western understanding of theatre art, are developed Actions with a repeatable structure, involving narrative, characterization, *mise-en-scene* and montage, and, usually, scripted dialogue, either spoken or in the form of song. Slowiak directed participants in the development of two major performance structures, one based on *The Egyptian Book of the Dead* and another on *Indian Tales*, a collection of children's stories inspired by Native American folktales. The use of the term "performance structure," as opposed to scene, play, performance, etc., served to erase the distinction between rehearsal and presentation. Since the work of Objective Drama most frequently occurred without public witnesses, the specter of some future performance date was not allowed to dictate the pace of development of an Action. Work performed for presentation was not privileged over the

Plate 33.4 The fields adjoining the Objective Drama workspaces, designated a wildlife preserve. (Photo: Richard Schechner.)

daily effort of discovery. By the same token, the safeguard of "rehearsal" no longer existed as an excuse for lazy or half-hearted efforts.

Slowiak used the term "rendering" as interchangeable with "perform-ance structure." Rendering, as a verb, was used in place of the word improvisation, a somewhat suspect term in Grotowskian vocabulary. Slowiak linked the term rendering, in one sense, to a designer's sketch or working drawing, which conveys the basic parameters of a concept in unpolished form. He also evoked a secondary meaning of the word as illustrated in the process of rendering butter, the distillation of an object to its essence.

The process of rendering is governed by a number of rules: no improvised conversation, no random violence, no stomping on the floor, no imitation of animals, no crawling on hands and knees, no imitation of trance states and no processions, to name a few. These elements, deliberately proscribed from our work, characterize certain clichés of avant-garde and ritual theatre which have falsely been associated with the work of Grotowski.

When our group began work on performance structures, we were instructed that our primary task was to tell a story. Slowiak had distilled *The Egyptian Book of the Dead* to its simplest narrative form, and described for us the sequence of events essential to development of the storyline. A young man dies and his soul is separated from his body. The spirit of the young man enters the underworld, where his heart is weighed and he is judged to be righteous. He then progresses through a variety of challenges and temptations, aided by the spirit of his Guardian Brother, and is ultimately granted eternal life after reaching the palace of the Great Mother. Slowiak began by assigning each participant a number of roles and specific tasks which he or she was to perform. We were then given one hour to prepare our first version of the action.

During early stages of development, our actions were explored nonverbally, thus reversing the tendency to regard *mise-en-scene* as an illustration of text. When you find that verbalization is necessary, we were instructed, use song rather than extemporized dialogue. Only when a fragment of the Action arrived at a fairly developed structure was minimal dialogue introduced where necessary to clarify action and elucidate narrative.

It was not uncommon to spend hours or even days developing a fragment which comprised only moments of the eventual structure. The actor in this context is required not only to remember the basic outlines of an action (here I pick up the knife, here I cross to the corpse . . .), but to execute each task with precise attention to the details which characterize lived experience (Where is the tension in my hands as I hold the knife? I am old, but I am also exceedingly skilled in the use of this instrument. How am I changed by fighting its weight in my hand?). Stanislavsky's Method of Physical Actions, which stresses the importance of physical detail in discovering a character's inner life, is a fundamental component of this type of work. Vasily Toporkov's book *Stanislavsky in Rehearsal* was a required text for the worksession.

Despite this emphasis on the methods of Stanislavsky, the *Book of the Dead* rendering could by no means be regarded as an example of naturalistic theatre. Characters of the *Book of the Dead* are superhuman, sometimes divine animals, and can in no sense be encompassed or depicted within the limited parameters of naturalistic behavior. While developing this performance structure, we were discouraged from formulating our characters based on theological or mythological abstractions, an approach which would inevitably have led to vague and superficial characterization. Instead, we were directed to explore and discover our characters beginning with manifest elements of physical reality – a way of walking, a timbre of speech.

Certain fragments of the *Book of the Dead* structure resembled daily interaction more closely than did others. An exchange between the Traveler and the Keeper of the Scales, for example, grew from an image of dickering salespeople in a marketplace, though the objects of trade were sacred weapons awarded the Traveler in the course of his journey. Other Actions, by contrast, were highly stylized. When the Traveler crossed a river on his way to the East Side of the Sky, this barrier was suggested by a line of women performing an intricately synchronized score of individual actions. The Traveler's encounter with the Divine Crocodile and his subsequent rescue by the Guardian Brother also took the form of an elaborate dance, with the Guardian Brother in top hat and tails. Even episodes such as this, however, were underscored with personal associations. While on one level the actor depicting the Crocodile was directed to play the character as divine monster, at another she was told to work with the association of a mischievous sister terrorizing her younger brother.

The Book of the Dead rendering, in its most developed version, featured a broad range of theatrical spectacle, including lighting, costume, and minimal scenic elements. The responsibility to communicate a clear and coherent narrative, to perform an action as a testimonial before witnesses, figured prominently in our development process. In every conceivable sense, this work represented a realized and disciplined theatrical performance. Critics who suggest that Grotowski's recent research bears no relevance to theatre practice reveal their ignorance of the full range of experimentation conducted under his aegis.

GROTOWSKI'S SEMINAR

Grotowski's arrival in May signaled a transition into a very different sort of working process. Although Slowiak had attempted, throughout the course of the worksession, to defuse the notion that our five months of creative activity existed *only* as preparation for Grotowski's arrival, the final weeks of our preliminary work were characterized by a more focused intensity of purpose, as well as by anxiety and anticipation. For the duration of Grotowski's residence, the Irvine students were joined by a group of actors from Mexico City under the direction of Jaime Soriano and three actors from Brazil.

During the first night of Grotowski's attendance, participants presented their work on the *Book of the Dead* and *Indian Tales* performance structures, as well as other prepared actions and various songs from our vocal training structure. Grotowski offered no response at this time, but observed silently from his table in the corner. The following night's session, we were told, would consist of analysis. Participants arrived the next evening to find rows of stools set up inside the barn, an arrangement which came to signal a time for verbal or analytical response. Grotowski asked that participants refrain from taking notes, as he did not offer formulas, but rather sought to communicate a general understanding.

Descriptions of Jerzy Grotowski are many and varied; taken together, they comprise a colorful, contradictory array of fictions and projections which I would be loath to increase. One aspect of Grotowski's manner which does not, however, fully emerge in such descriptions is the man's extraordinary warmth and unparalleled ability to charm. During this first verbal session, it seemed he wished to welcome the group and put us at our ease. His harshest criticisms were softened by humor, his remarks punctuated with laughter and an engaging smile. In discussing our work on *Indian Tales*, Grotowski mentioned that he identified himself with the character of Old Man Coyote, the mischievous Master/Trickster. "I am Coyote Old Man," he quoted, speaking for the first time in English. "I am very old. I am so old," and here he paused and smiled, leaning forward as if inviting us to share some secret, his expansive voice echoing throughout the room, "that I know what was before after, and after before." Participants responded with joyous laughter, for the first time relaxing in the presence of this enigmatic man; we had been won, and in some fashion, also warned.

Grotowski began his analysis by speaking briefly about our work on the *Book of the Dead*, praising the fact that we had developed a precise and repeatable structure. This, he said, was in the best sense "not amateur." However, he continued, there is a difference between structure and life. While it is possible for the amateur to create life without structure, this would be like a vision sculpted in smoke, something which could not endure and could not be reconstructed. We had, in the *Book of the Dead* performance, discovered the structure, the vehicle for life, but not the way to infuse this structure with vibrancy. Only in our presentation of Shaker songs, Grotowski observed, did life break through.

Grotowski criticized the second of our performance structures, scenes from *Indian Tales*, because we had in this instance failed also at the level of conveying narrative. In constructing performance text, he observed, one could either begin with communicating story and then proceed to exploration of meaning, or begin with an idea of meaning and discover the way to present this in story form. Only as a third step, he indicated, should one's focus turn to depiction of the incidents or individual actions. Our presentation of *Indian Tales*, a montage of disparate vignettes without organized narrative structure, had inverted the logic of this process.

Grotowski commented specifically on the Action of a Jewish woman based on the memory of her grandmother which comprised one element of the *Indian Tales* structure. While he acknowledged that his attention had been held by the actor's characterization, Grotowski chided her for obscuring the narrative of the scene. In the original text, the episode in question is written as an exchange between two characters. The actor's choice to stage the episode as a one-person scene, without any clear physical or vocal attempt to delineate separate characters, made it impossible for the observer to follow the logic of the text. Grotowski observed that such a choice of staging was highly irresponsible. The actor, he stressed, is under obligation to make his/her work clear and comprehensible to the spectator. This does not mean, he qualified, that the actor should court the spectator of the marketplace, far from it. Rather, the actor's performance must be motivated by an impulse to communicate with something, some witness, outside the self, otherwise the work degenerates into self-indulgence.

Grotowski's observations on the responsibility of the actor to communicate led him to discuss a series of "so-called individual Actions" based on verses from the book *Indian Tales*. He noted that throughout these Actions participants generally did not direct attention outward, towards some partner, but instead remained focused on their internal processes. He wryly observed that the majority of participants' Actions had involved lying on the floor curled up in a fetal position. Embryos, he whispered in a tiny, high-pitched voice, slumping forward in his chair, embryos. . . . The laughter thus inspired softened his frank criticism of the work. If we had no more refined dramatic sense, might we at least pay attention to balancing the space? Nothing can happen in drama, he stressed, except in relation to the partner, to some other. In actions such as these, where is the partner, what is the story? For what, outside oneself, is the Action being done?

Returning to the *Book of the Dead* structure, Grotowski did not seem displeased with the dramaturgy, though here as well he made various comments regarding clarity. He cited an instance near the beginning of the Action in which the soul, or Traveler, is blinded by a black hood placed over his head. Slowiak intended this to represent a common element of near-death experience in which the dying person recalls moving rapidly through a black tunnel before emerging into a blaze of light. For Grotowski, this intention was not conveyed. What the witness saw was one actor getting a silly hat, an event that did not evoke the sense of movement through a tunnel. The first and most basic level on which meaning is created, Grotowski emphasized, is that of physical reality. One cannot ignore the presence of the actor's body as sign. Gender, age, physical appearance are all signifiers which the witness immediately registers, and which dominate his/her reading of an Action. An incident that occurred several days later during our work on this structure further illustrated Grotowski's point. At a certain moment in the *Book of the Dead* Action, the soul of the Traveler for the first time encounters the Guardian Brother face to face. The Brother, to simulate a physical resemblance to the Traveler, wore a long black wig and similar costume, comprised of a brief linen wrap. Traveler and Brother met and, hand in hand, surveyed the journey the Traveler had completed. Grotowski asked his assistant, Maud Robart, to describe what she observed in this action. Slowiak translated from Robart's French: "I see two men . . . in love . . . on a beach in California." This answer produced a spate of embarrassed laughter from the actors, and a wry, affirming nod from Grotowski.

While he encouraged us to grapple with issues of profound content, Grotowski simultaneously warned us against the dangers of sentimental, symbolic or "mumbo-jumbo" work. Various elements of our *Book of the Dead* structure were cited as evidence of our indulgence in such tendencies. First among these was the choice of lighting: dozens of white candles placed at intervals throughout the room. The primary purpose of the lighting, Grotowski mused, is to light. Our choice was ineffective in this sense, as witnesses frequently had difficulty discerning details of a given Action. Any use of lighting to create atmosphere or general mood was judged to be false and "symbolic." Grotowski pointed out that we could have utilized many alternatives other than candlelight, for example kerosene lanterns or even "good old electricity."

Grotowski warned that the use of natural elements – fire, water, earth – presents special dangers in the realm of symbolic action. Such elements immediately evoke a vast complex of emotional associations and must be utilized only in those situations where the introduction of the element in and of itself fulfils a precise function within the Action. He questioned our use of fire (to symbolize purification), earth (to symbolize rebirth) and water (to symbolize the Mother's compassionate love). He returned to this issue frequently throughout the course of the workshop, and on one occasion delivered a fierce diatribe against artists who use such elements in a manipulative or imprecise fashion. He remarked that he had, indeed, used natural elements in the sceneography of his own work, but that this choice had always been dictated by precise technical considerations. Other artists (and Slowiak's work with the group was included in this general condemnation) were held culpable for using such items merely to create an emotional response or general mood. Grotowski's first proposal for further work on the *Book of the Dead* structure was to do away with such symbolic factors, as well as with our cumbersome array of objects and suggestions of Egyptian costume. In addition, he proposed composition of a new Action based on the same narrative, in which Robart would present the story using traditional Haitian material.

WORK WITH THE *BOOK OF THE DEAD* STRUCTURE

Grotowski was careful that his experiments with the *Book of the Dead* structure not be interpreted as restaging another director's work. Rather, he wished to demonstrate various alternatives for further development of the presentation. Having discovered a repeatable score, Grotowski noted, we had allowed the vitality of the performance to die away, clinging instead to superficial forms and images. Grotowski insisted that we eliminate all inessential objects, as the work should not be about such items, but rather about characters and actions.

Our first evening of work with this structure focused on the opening moments of the performance text, the death of the protagonist and the separation of corpse from soul. Grotowski addressed the level of meaning created by choices of casting and costume. Why, he queried, if the Traveler is intended to represent the soul, is this character portrayed by the most definitively carnal actor in the room? Carnality, Grotowski emphasized, is not a matter of a body *per se*, but rather of the way in which one regards the body. Of itself the body is innocent; it is the human attitude which transforms corporeality into object by participating in the game of mirrors, seeing one's image in the eyes of the Other. The actor who portrayed the Traveler is an extraordinarily attractive young man, rather like Donatello's *David* in appearance. His brief costume, comprised of a white linen dishtowel, further emphasized the actor's physicality. The actor who played the corpse was, by contrast, dressed in black shirt and trousers, his body almost completely obscured. Grotowski pointed out that given these performers and this set of circumstances, the witness perceives the Travler not as soul, but as animal energy and vital force. He instructed the two actors to exchange roles and costumes, then asked witnesses what they received from this new set of signals. Observers concurred that the new actor's execution of the score conveyed greater vulnerability, due not only to the actor's less defined musculature, but to an elusive quality of innocence which characterized his manner and bearing.

During another session, Grotowski used an element of another actor's performance score to demonstrate the difference between action and gesture. The Keeper of the Scales must, in a certain moment, attract the attention of the sleeping Chorus so that they may judge the Traveler's worthiness. "Lift up your faces and look at him!" she commands. The actor had developed a set hand gesture intended both to indicate the Chorus to the Traveler and to elicit their response. Grotowski observed that this gesture did not emanate from inside the body, as with any true impulse, but rather began at the shoulder, weakly dissociating the arm from the body. Physical action, he clarified, combines impulse and intention. What do you want to do to your partner? How do you wish to make him/her react? Action emanates always from some intention towards the Other, made manifest through the body. The physical score is comprised of such actions/intentions, not of their manifestation through details of gesture.

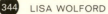

MAUD ROBART'S ACTION

Maud Robart, a long-time associate of Grotowski and a continuing leader in the Objective Drama program, constructed a very different sort of Action based on themes presented in the Egyptian *Book of the Dead*. A specialist in singing and traditional Haitian performative material, Robart has collaborated with Grotowski periodically since the Theatre of Sources phase. For her Action Robart selected those participants she judged most capable of quickly learning the yanvalou and complex Creole songs on which her work was based.

In the essay "Performer," Grotowski defines ritual as "performance, an accomplished action, an act" (Ch.37:374). Robart's performance structure beautifully illustrated ritual in this sense. Constructing a story using song and simple activities, Robart became the leader/participant of an unpretentious funeral rite. No attempt was made to pretend that the student-participants were Haitian villagers or experts in the material; rather, they appeared as themselves, or nearly so: apprentices following the lead of a trained practitioner. The story of the overall Action was clear, and the purpose of each component unambiguous. Objects were few (a white sheet, a suit of black clothing used to signify the corpse, and items that would be needed by the dead man in the next world) and were selected for their pragmatic, literal function, rather than to trigger emotional connotations. The Action was performed in full, direct lighting, and bore no trace of the clich´es of so-called ritual performance or corrupted voodoo. No one, including Robart, appeared to experience ecstatic trance.

LABORATORIO ARTE ESCENICO

The distinction between authentic ritual and action which utilizes only decorative ritualistic elements can be illustrated by comparing Robart's Action with another piece presented during the seminar, that of visiting director Jaime Soriano's Laboratorio Arte Escenico. This Action in its earliest form demonstrated numerous aspects of what Grotowski would call symbolic mumbo-jumbo: a character who appeared to be super-natural, a threshold between worlds, an action of throwing sticks that apparently signified divination. The space was vaguely defined, different areas suggested only by a decorative macramé hanging suspended from the roof beams. Actors alternated between naturalistic and highly stylized physicality, including one sequence directly copied from the Motions exercise. Despite the fact that the rendering was first presented in full daylight, a row of burning white candles created a barrier between the witnesses and the Action.

Three women, a grandmother, a mother, and a bizarre elfin child, engaged in a series of actions suggesting rituals of mourning. At one point the young girl, whom I understood to be some sort of demon figure, taunted the grandmother with a puppet constructed from a cloak and mask hung upon a stick. Soriano later explained that the puppet was intended to represent the recently deceased grandfather. While certain elements of the Action were visually engaging, others seemed arbitrary and failed to communicate any discernible narrative. Although I was able to follow about half of the Spanish text, I found the story largely incomprehensible. Grotowski sent the group back for private work, refusing to discuss the structure until he could find five witnesses who perceived relatively the same narrative.

The presentation, after two weeks of work, bore little resemblance to its original form. Characters developed into recognizable human types, and extraneous, decorative elements of ritual were removed. The Action was performed in full electric light, with economic scenic elements suggesting the interior of a house and a nearby grave. What emerged was an account of a Mexican family's response to the death of the father, evoking both the oppressive weight of tradition (the control of a patriarchal system which, even in the absence of an embodied representative, shadows women's lives and choices) and the deep connectedness which nourishes individuals' lives in the context of strongly felt familial bonds.

THE SHAKER STRUCTURE

The most exciting discovery of the worksession, in Grotowski's view, arrived by means of the student actors' work with Shaker songs. He recognized and responded to the group's particular regard for these songs, and acknowledged the value of the songs as traditional material, grown out of American soil and rooted in an Anglo-Protestant cultural heritage. Clearly, the Shaker songs held rich potential in terms of yantra and organon. Grotowski proposed that we develop some sort of narrative structure as a framework for these songs, concentrating attention on this as the main work of the seminar. The narrative frame, he advised, should be a simple, easily understood tale, something that could be conveyed without excessive dependence on spoken text. Ideally, we should find a story that would highlight the contrast between the Shaker way of life, drinking from the deep well of tradition, and the shallow sterility of modern culture. Perhaps we could be travelers, he suggested, who discover a barn once used by Shakers and sleep there for a night. While there we might find some traces of those who had erected the building and used it for their worship. Ultimately, this was the story we chose.

Our first rendering of the structure, which developed this tourist premise through improvised dialogue, triggered Grotowski's assertion that nothing good can come from improvisation. The text must be written, he advised. He suggested that we find an American equivalent to Ionesco, some masterful construction of contentless speech. Failing this, Slowiak and I compiled several pages of "Stupid American Dialogue" culled from plays by contemporary authors.

Once we had prepared the text for the Action, Grotowski began around-the-table work with a meticulousness alien to American sensibility. In our society's traditional rehearsal process, an actor is judged to be doing capable work if she/he can read the text in a manner that passes for natural speech. Grotowski found this insufficient. You must know what you are saying, he insisted, you must have some understanding of the text. Action must not illustrate dialogue. Most frequently, a character's words disguise his/her intentions from him/herself or others, or else communicate meaning on multiple levels. It would be wrong to assume that a line such as "Where's the bathroom?" (the opening line of the montage) refers only to a character's desire to exercise natural functions. Grotowski worked with the actor who delivered this line, suggesting that perhaps "bathroom" represented for her a place of sanctuary, a refuge from her intrusive companions. In her own mind then, perhaps the word "bathroom" should be substituted with "liberation" or some other grand, romantic conception of freedom. Grotowski insisted that the actor repeat the line, using a variety of images, until he as spectator could recognize the magnitude of this association for her character. The same process was repeated for each fragment of text. Once participants began to discover the potential Actions within their text, Grotowski shifted emphasis to creating relationships among characters. Here as well, he refused to settle for passive or ambiguous intentions. Each line was repeated until intentions were clear both for actor and observer. At the end of three hours, we had progressed through less than a page of text.

Of the Shaker songs selected for integration into this performance structure, several had pre-existing movement patterns which Grotowski judged workable. For the remaining songs, we attempted to discover appropriate structures of movement. After several days' work, the number of songs was reduced from five to three to allow for adequate development.

The performance opened with a group of tourists noisily entering the abandoned barn. One voice rose above another as each struggled to erect some verbal shield against the unfamiliar situation. "We gotta spend the night here?" one woman whined. "In the morning we can fix the bus," her companion reassured. "Who's gonna fix it," another screeched, "Gomer Pyle?" "What's that noise?" a woman asked, frightened by brief silence. "The wind under the door," her friend replied. Engaged in the meaningless rituals of their daily lives, the travelers for a time drowned out the quiet voices echoing within the ancient walls.

As the others settled down to sleep, one woman, unnoticed by her companions, paused in the center of the room. "Oh the . . . happy journey . . ." she whispered a broken fragment of melody. Slowly, tentatively, she explored the distant echo of a song, one phrase of which seemed to emanate from a high window, another from a wall, the next from a point near the floor. Another traveler, curious, moved to join her and together they discovered the remainder of the song. "Let all be awakened and up and be doing/That we may attain to our destined home." After a time a pair of women began marching briskly in a clockwise circle along the periphery of the space. Others joined, until all the women moved as a single unit, circling the men who turned with a precise marching step at the center. As the song built in strength, the brittle personae of the travelers crumbled away, revealing quiet figures who moved with a serene, ordered purpose – the Shakers who had come to inhabit their bodies.

The singers stopped in response to a signal from one leader. Confused and somewhat embarrassed, they stared at one another, hurriedly attempting to reconstruct the masks of their daily lives. Each mechanically repeated the words and actions which had engaged him/her upon first entering the space. Suddenly a man's clear voice cut forcefully through the din. "I will roar, roar, roar," he sang, the power of the melody transforming him into a resolute warrior. "Ye and I'll howl, howl, howl in my fury sayeth the Lord!" He began to run in a spiraling motion through the room. Others fell in behind him, following as he led them into an ever tightening spiral, then turned and signaled to a second leader at the far end of the line. Song and movement continued until a climax was reached, at which point the first leader silently commanded his warriors to stop. Immediately, a Shaker woman began another song, this one quickly recognized by other members of the group. "Come life, Shaker life, come life eternal," she sang, directing her words to the leader of the previous action. "Shake, shake out of me all that is carnal." The man responded as if compelled by her words, dancing in such a way as to cast off the bonds of sensuality which tied him to the transience of mortal life. The remaining Shakers quietly formed a chorus in one corner of the room, offering their song in support of their brother's attempt at transcendence.

When the Action had finished, the Shakers stood reflectively in their places. After a time, one woman responded, uncomprehendingly, to the echo of a distant voice. "Where's the . . . bathroom?" she asked, looking questioningly to the sister by her side. "They got a . . . bathroom?" a

Shaker brother replied, moving to find the source of the sound. In this manner the Shakers rediscovered the personae of the tourists, slowly dissolving in the habits of daily interaction. Someone announced that it was morning, time to go. The travelers gathered their belongings and resumed their previous patterns of relationship. As they left they were gentler, more subdued, slightly changed by their encounter with another people and another way of life.

CONCLUSIONS AND SYNTHESIS

Richard Schechner, in a discussion of Objective Drama which dates from the earliest phase of the work, suggests that this research might "synthesize Grotowski's multifaceted career – poor theatre, paratheatre, theatre of sources – into something that includes a reintegrative phase" (1985:106). Schechner voices misgivings regarding earlier stages of Grotowski's research, in which the participant goes through the separation or breakdown phase of initiation, but is "not then 'reconstructed,' either by being integrated into a society or by being given specific roles to play in a performance" (1985:255). Objective Drama, however, with its emphasis on the technical/performative aspect of traditional material and techniques, "supplies the constructive reintegrative phase of the process" (1985:257).

Clearly the work of Objective Drama, as evidenced both by Robart's and Slowiak's lines of research, focuses on instructing the participants in the pragmatic skills of the actor's craft. Participants are taught various forms of singing and dance, as well as an approach for constructing performance which owes much to Stanislavsky's Method of Physical Actions. Such skills are immediately applicable to the art and practice of theatre production. Any transference of the specific ritual material of Objective Drama, as for example employing the authentic yanvalou as a decorative element in a commercial production, would, however, be disastrous. Grotowski's approach to traditional performative material is neither cannibalistic nor syncretistic. By examining and comparing disparate elements of individual cultures' performative techniques, Grotowski seeks to discover certain irreducible common elements.

Grotowski insists that Objective Drama cannot be understood as a continuation of Theatre of Sources. He suggests that it is perhaps more appropriate to view this project in terms of a dialectic with Theatre of Participation and Theatre of Sources work. Grotowski's development, which has progressed in spiral rather than linear form, has returned to an emphasis on technical/performative aspects of craft. To anticipate that this would lead him once more toward the arena of public production would, however, be highly unlikely. "People were still asking the same questions after twenty years," Slowiak sighed, describing a lecture/ conference held in Irvine in 1988. "When are you going back to doing performances?" Slowiak paraphrased Grotowski's response as a denial that such an event would ever occur.

On various occasions, Grotowski has stated that he is in a stage of life in which he finds it appropriate to concentrate on sharing with artists of a younger generation the skills and knowledge resulting from his many years of research. The work of Objective Drama is, in some sense, most concerned with the training of leaders/technical specialists, persons with developed skills and areas of expertise who enter into long-term apprenticeship with Grotowski. Such leaders work directly with novice participants, preparing structures which are then presented to Grotowski for analysis. In addition to the feedback received during group sessions, Grotowski works extensively with each leader through one-on-one consultation. Many group leaders eventually go on to pursue independent careers in theatre. When asked what precisely he felt Grotowski endeavors to teach, Slowiak's response was simple and direct: "The skill of doing something well, not to be amateur, as most of us in this country have become."

GROTOWSKI IN IRVINE
Breaking the silence

Charles Marowitz

Over the past ten years, Jerzy Grotowski, one of the most pervasive and misunderstood influences of the sixties, had been quiescent. We had heard that he was conducting "researches" in Pontedera, Italy, and, for the past five years, had been spending the spring term at the University of California at Irvine. Like Solzhenitsyn and other emigres, he seemed to have been swallowed up by American academe, which is a little like disappearing down a beautifully furnished gopher-hole. In early May 1988, an invitation was dispatched to some sixty-five theatre people announcing that Mr Grotowski would be conducting a seminar. This was followed by a small printed booklet which included a short piece by Peter Brook and an essay by Grotowski himself (see Chs 37 and 38). These were the texts, we were informed, on which the seminar would be based.

On the appointed evening, Grotowski, bearded, smiling, dressed in a dark suit and a white shirt without a tie and looking a little like a defrocked rabbi, granted us an audience.

In response to a few initial questions, he proceeded to define ritual, or what he chose to call montage, as performance originating in the mind of the participants and performed for their sake – as opposed to false ritual, like voodoo or routinized ethnic dance and Gregorian chants, presented for touristic consumption minus the animating spirit which originally informed them. "Spectacle," in which he included most theatrical presentation, was disparagingly dismissed as the antithesis of true ritual.

Archetypes (the word had a hollow sixties clang to it) could not be created – only discovered – and the same was true of myths. It was a matter of returning to the true impulse of ritual – although in his restricted definition of the term, "ritual" seemed to refer only to original ethnic or anthropological manifestations. The whole notion of social rituals – ways in which people court one another, pursue their career, assert their identity, seek confirmation from their peers – were apparently excluded. Which begs the question: Why would one want to recreate the veracity of age-old rituals except to achieve some rarefied academic satisfaction; an endeavor as reactionary as it is futile?

Grotowski's answer to that would be: In order to perfect the skills involved in mastering those disciplines and then transferring them to the performing arts. An argument similar to that for studying Latin which, useless in itself, is supposed to sharpen the mind for other disciplines. But is the attempt to recreate rituals all that far removed from acrobatics, dance or tai chi, which are already used in conventional theatre-training for actors to sharpen their performance ability?

Like Castaneda, with whom he clearly identifies himself, Grotowski holds out the promise of a higher plane of artistic consciousness if only the student will divest himself of habitual functions. The problem is there is no body of work for him to interpret once he gets there. It is a satori divorced from the mundane concerns of the workaday world in which the terrestrial actor finds his material. It is a world in which Shakespeare, Chekhov, Ibsen, and Strindberg are beneath him.

The "rigor" that Grotowski constantly invokes sounds like a watered-down Artaudian concept. "Cruelty," wrote Artaud, "signifies rigor, implacable intention and decision, irreversible and absolute determination" – which is precisely how Grotowski refers to the pursuit of ritual. Artaud found a symbiosis between Balinese rituals, for example, and the living theatre, but Grotowski is constantly agitating for the mastery of skills which have no direct application to performance art. It is as if a teacher were to say to his pupil: I am going to turn you into an expert yogi-master and when I am done, you will be ready to tackle every great role in the Western repertoire. Grotowski's teaching, like his own previous work, is a fanatically proselytized tao leading into a cul-de-sac.

In the booklet distributed to participants beforehand, Grotowski aggrandizes "essence" as a desired good – as opposed to sociological attributes or consciously acquired skills. ("For example, conscience," writes Grotowski, "is something which belongs to essence; it is different from the moral code which just belongs to society.") Although if one traces the origin of moral codes and the laws which derive from them, it is virtually impossible not to find them directed by conscience. The whole conceit is a somewhat abstruse variation on the existentialist's old conundrum of Essence and Existence – just as Grotowski's notion of the I–I (the actor who acts and the same actor who "looks on") is little more than the old dialectical yo-yo about Subject and Object, the traditional notion of the actor's dual consciousness elegantly defined by Artaud in *The Theatre and its Double*, refloated by Michael Chekhov in the late thirties as "divided consciousness," exhaustively discussed by Brecht in his writings on the Epic Theatre, and an idea which has been kicking around esthetic discussions since Diderot's Paradox in the 18th century.

In almost every instance, Grotowski's tortuous definitions are merely semantic variations disguised as original concepts.

When it was charged that much of his advance essay was banal, Grotowski's reply was that "banalities" are often true (although some might argue that it is the untested, taken-for-granted nature of "truisms" which cause them to be labeled "banalities" in the first place). Justifying both his isolation and his arcane studies, he drew a parallel between the work of monks and religious faith. "The monastery," he said, "cannot exist without religion." But when religion is under assault and forced to defend its tenets in the parochial world, little of that penetrates the monastery walls where holy writ continues to be imperturbably worshipped. But even from an ecclesiastical standpoint, Grotowski's monastic parallel does not stand up. The rigor of monastic life involved an intensification of the practice of piety which is a tenet of the Catholic faith. It was supposed to serve as a living model for the emulation of the rest of the faithful. As such, monasteries were a very public showcase – not a private laboratory for the spiritual perfection of the few.

Just as Grotowski tends to diffuse relatively clear-cut terms such as "spectacle" and "ritual," so has the word "research" on his lips become a kind of wet fudge. It is unconscionable for Grotowski to refuse to define what the purpose of his researches are. "Pure research," which is how he characterizes his work, cannot consist of simply mucking about at random. Research consists of conducting a clearly organized set of controlled experiments into the nature of a given phenomenon, and a research of that kind always exists within a larger contextual body of experiential material with which it allegedly connects. It is distinct from problem-solving or technology because you don't know precisely what answers you are going to turn up, but it has to be based on a clear certainty of what the questions are. Otherwise, it loses its credibility as research. And if, as he admits, the experiments are intrinsically nontheatrical, why not present those findings to anthropologists and sociologists who are equipped to give him a relevant critique?

The grisly facts about Grotowski are that because of his penchant for performing for minuscule groups of between thirty and fifty, very few people have actually seen the Grotowski canon. There is no inscribed body of work which has come down from the sixties and early seventies to validate his aesthetic – only rumors, memories, and myths from that tiny minority which was fortunate enough to have squeezed into performances at Wroclaw or London or New York. I actually saw *Apocalypsis cum figuris* and *The Constant Prince* in Poland. They were striking demonstrations of charged physicality which were impressive despite the fact that one could grasp neither the language nor the historical milieu from which they sprang. Grotowski's insistence on the actor's physical purity of expression was so refreshingly different from the Western theatre's wallowing in behaviorism that it appeared like a glimpse from another world. Here was a director who had taken Artaud's Affective Athleticism and actually formulated it into a style of acting. It didn't matter that his themes were mawkish with Catholic symbolism or philosophically confused. The style was breathtaking – the actors, holy – the sounds, riveting – the atmosphere charged with medieval sanctity. Here was performance art which was the diametric opposite of "show business" and free from the leaden political clichés of "serious theatre."

In the sixties and seventies, in almost every European capital there were dozens of groups misapplying Grotowski's techniques – which was understandable, as most of the techniques were derived from besotted disciples who never entirely grasped them in the first place. The most atrocious were probably in England; the most commonplace in America – in the work of directors such as Tom O'Horgan, Richard Schechner, and Andrei Serban. Physicality and the supremacy of non-naturalistic sound and movement – the Artaudian ideal – soon began to pall. Drawing-room clichés were exchanged for avant-garde clichés, and before long, the new vernacular became as predictable as the political slogans of the New Drama.

As an "influence," Grotowski's dynamic corporeality came and went within a period of about ten years – leaving behind a dissatisfaction with pure kinetic expression which, eschewing language, never managed to create a physical vocabulary as rich as the linguistic one it had spurned. Vestiges of Grotowski simmered into Peter Brook's work, Joe Chaikin's Open Theater, even into straight and musty productions by stodgy bourgeois directors such as John Barton. In Denmark, Eugenio Barba, using the Grotowski franchise, actually marketed the master's wares, progressively revealing their paucity. The Grotowski touch, like Afghan coats, worry-beads and long hair, became part of the clichés of those heady times. Therefore, the recent seminar was an opportunity to discover what new territory Grotowski had begun to chart out for himself.

In public, Grotowski's preferred atmosphere is cowed silence. His method of conducting a seminar is to allow brief, usually leading questions, from which he can launch into long-winded, circuitous replies which, because they brook no interruption, allow contradictions and fallacies to go unchallenged. According to the dictionary, a "seminar" is a period in which students and professor "exchange results through reports and discussion – a meeting for giving and discussing informa- tion." For Grotowski, it is a span of time in which apprentices are immobilized so as to become better enlightened by the discourses of the master. In a period that ran for approximately three and one half hours, there was never one dialectical interchange. When a gushing female questioner asked when he might return to public performances, the master took it as an opportunity to extol the virtues of the meditative life and managed to suggest there was an overwhelming demand from a screeching multitude for him to return to the stage. An exhortation which could be heard only in the impenetrable interstices of Grotowski's own mind.

Continually, he insisted that he was not there to persuade or convert. His researches were *his* and he had no desire to impose them on others. It was not that members of his audience were resisting his ideas so much as trying to get him to justify the theories he had been expounding. This he never did, nor ever felt the need to do. The real significance lay in the fact that these were hidden findings; it was neither his business nor his inclination to justify them nor defend them against legitimate opposition. A seminar, his manner seemed to say, was a time for gratefully sopping up his theoretical manna. If it contained bits of stale popcorn or rancid weenies, these too were to be thought of as nourishment.

When the seminar started, the question had been put: What is the relationship between your ideas and the living theatre as we know it in our daily practice? the answer was honest and unmitigated. None! Grotowski's constant point of reference is Peter Brook, who was not only his champion in the sixties but is now one of his main sponsors. In Brook's introduction to the 1987 conference held in Florence (and reprinted in the advance booklet), he asks Grotowski "to make more clear to us how, and to what degree, his work on dramatic art takes a way which is inseparable from the necessity of a personal evolution for those who work around him. I would like him to throw some light on this."

The subtext of the question is blindingly clear: apart from the fact that you inspire and edify those uninitiated students and apprentices who have come to worship you as a great guru, what practical value does your work or your thinking have for the living theatre in whose name both are being espoused? The answer again is None! The greater answer, if Grotowski were to give it truthfully, is: The emoluments to my ego and the aura I have created about myself feel no compunction to contribute tangible, practical or even original contributions to the art of perform-ance. The intensity of my private contemplation, unchallenged by argument and unvalidated by proofs of logic or rational evidence, is sufficient unto itself.

Grotowski is on the second leg of a mystical journey through historical and anthropological research. It may be of interest to archivists, academics, or scholars, but it has nothing to say to contemporary practitioners of the theatre. And yet, here was a room made up of some of the leading directors, actors, and dramaturgs from

Southern California, sitting at the feet of the master and waiting for theoretical crumbs to roll off his metaphysical table. There was something unsightly and faintly undignified about it all. The need that theatre-people have for satori! The desire to be initiated into the arcane mysteries of art! To come with such a hunger only to be fobbed off with abstruse clich´es by a megalomaniac whose intellect is a ragbag of other men's ideas makes a mockery of the whole notion of enlightenment.

After the event, people's eyes were clouded and opaque, and that glazed look, that myopic unquestioning allegiance to an abstraction which allegedly embodies principles too rarefied to define, too hieratical to dispute, too mystical to sully with earthbound doubts of skepticism, is the very antithesis of art. It is nothing more nor less than esthetic fascism and deserves to be pelted with eggs, as the Socialists pelted Sir Oswald Mosley, or hauled up by its ankles, as the vigilantes did Il Duce.

35

JERZY GROTOWSKI'S DIVINATION CONSULTATION

Objective Drama seminar at U.C.-Irvine

J. Ndukaku Amankulor

Jerzy Grotowski's Objective Drama program is the next-to-latest phase of his personal search for meaning and philosophy in life through performance techniques. The project had its headquarters at the University of California-Irvine. On the evening of Tuesday, 17 May 1988, prominent theatre scholars and practitioners – mostly drawn from the California southland – were invited by Robert Cohen, chair of U.C.I.'s Drama Department, to what he called "a very special seminar on the progress of investigations of the Objective Drama program at Irvine and Art as vehicle in Pontedera, Italy."[1] This special seminar was to take place at the UCI Objective Drama Workspace, also called the UCI barn.

The prospective location for the seminar had some connotations that raised expectations for me. The traditional symbol of the barn as a space where farm harvests are gathered made it an unlikely place for a traditional theatrical performance to take place. But knowing Grotowski's penchant for ritual and his serious explorations of performance spaces, I was hoping that perhaps he would actually give some demonstrations or performances in the course of the seminar, even though he had stopped staging performances long ago. More people showed up at the barn than the space could accommodate and the seminar had to be relocated to a physics auditorium with a formal proscenium configuration. It was now doubly unlikely that Grotowski would present a performance. However, the seminar itself was a performative event, a unique as well as interesting experience, not just for the information given by Grotowski but because of his method and manner of communicating his information.

GROTOWSKI'S DIVINATION

The structure of the seminar was as follows: (1) Robert Cohen introduced Jerzy Grotowski; (2) Grotowski gave a brief reply and called for the selected respondents to ask their questions or make their comments; (3) the respondents asked their questions; (4) Grotowski answered, thus presenting the content of his seminar; (5) a few other participants asked questions.

Grotowski's seminar, as a performative event, followed the ritual structure of an African divination consultation. First, Cohen was a go-between, one known to both the diviner (Grotowski) and the client (participants at the seminar). In his introduction, Cohen paid glowing tribute to Grotowski and to the years of excitement and cooperation UCI shared with the Objective Drama project. The efficacy of divination depends very much on the effectiveness of the go-between as the one who interprets the diviner and his client to each other and thereafter withdraws to the background, leaving the parties face-to-face.

After he had been introduced by Cohen, Grotowski carefully laid out his pipe and smoking materials like a traditional African priest laying out his divination outfit, almost oblivious to the client before him. The interval seemed to magnify Grotowski's personality and to fill the auditorium with the aura of his power.

Grotowski's brief reply to Cohen's introduction encapsulated the theme of his comments for the rest of the evening. "Drama or performing arts," he said, "is a vehicle for my work." It was clear to me that performance was a means to an end for Grotowski.

In this second stage of the structure, the diviner in his awesome spirituality amplifies the tributes paid to him by making his client have full confidence in his supernatural powers, assuring him that he has come to the best. Thereafter the diviner invites the client to lay bare his heart (burden). The respondents and other questioners approached their task carefully, laying their burden of doubts before the guru and "with-drawing" for him to provide the answers. The usual academic debate that follows seminars became irrelevant as the participants sought to learn the answers from the master rather than debate with colleagues. As would be expected on such an occasion, Grotowski's responses did not necessarily clear up doubts harbored by respondents and questioners, but they were not challenged either. Such conflicts are not usual in ritual sessions because the individual consulting the diviner cannot question the divination process or verdict directly, no matter what the doubts.

By reversing the normal seminar process, Grotowski drew attention to the unusual nature of his presentation and the supremacy of his position in the event. Also by appearing to ignore the presence of the participants and concentrating on loading and smoking his pipe in a most casual manner, Grotowski generated an aura of spiritual superiority, thus reducing them to a position of dependence on himself as the one in control.

In phase three, as the client presents his problems, the diviner does not seem to concentrate on their magnitude. Instead he adopts a seemingly distant attitude in which he appears to be communing with more important but invisible presences. The four preselected respondents to Grotowski's seminar were made to ask questions cumulatively and he answered them as a unit, more or less. He appeared to pay no particular attention to the questions themselves, took no notes, but all the time paced casually to and from his position at a table which he occupied alone. His solitary occupation of the presentation stage coupled with his informal attitude helped to bolster his superiority. Although the respondents as well as other questioners later were not intimidated by Grotowski's presence, it was evident from their behavior that they were aware of being before an unusual and somewhat spiritual presence. As long as the seminar lasted, this attitude prevailed.

The diviner, in step four, takes the stage all by himself when he is aware of the problems he is called upon to solve. He invokes the invisible presences and communes with them to the utter amazement of his client. Thereafter, he makes his recommendations. Grotowski's performance at this fourth stage of his seminar structure continued to be dominated by his personal idiosyncracies – his smoking, pacing, stopping to be sure that he had not used the wrong English expression or to pick up the thread of a respondent's question. Yet the job of building his theories went on at the same time. It was easy to be disarmed by his statement that he was not trying to convert anybody and that his theories were unique to his own practice; it was difficult not to be seduced by the ritual and spiritual framework of these theories, which emphasized sharing, not selling.

In the fifth stage of the process, a divination ends with a client seeking further clarification on a few points. It is normally a short session, especially as the diviner has been through a major psychic and spiritual journey. Grotowski admitted only a few questions in this fifth stage of the process, but none invoked any controversy, in spite of whatever doubts the questioners might have had. However, when the seminar ended, informal debates among the participants about the import of Grotowski's ideas continued. Away from the presence of the theatre guru, disagreements were freely expressed, particularly on the life of the theatre without the traditional actor and the survival of ritual. It was evident that, for some, Grotowski's project was moving too far into the realm of pure ideas and too far out of the realm of theatre.

THE QUESTIONS

Leading questions or commentaries were presented by the preselected participants: Robert Cohen, Robert Benedetti, Charles Marowitz, and David McDonald. These people, specialists on the theory and practice of theatre, were earlier asked to be the initial respondents to the seminar. They had to ask their questions based on their previous knowledge of Grotowski's work and on the documentary material distributed to the participants beforehand.

Cohen asked whether as a "teacher of Performer," Grotowski was using Performer to train people or bring up responses. [. . .] Benedetti asked Grotowski to identify the process for finding specific actions in the Performer's search for a unity between the human being and God, the immanence of the divine, because he was troubled by that metaphoric identity. [. . .] Marowitz asked about the relationship between the existential idea and the theatre as we know it.

Grotowski's answers to the questions summarized his views on his continuing work. The following is a report on his "answers," put in the format of a report on the seminar he gave.

THE ANSWERS

Grotowski told his listeners that he was not, in working on the Objective Drama project, seeking to convince others to do the same thing. His work is unique to him in much the same way as Peter Brook's is to Brook. Nobody else can do the same thing or take the place of Brook in his experiments. [. . .] Grotowski stressed that he does not produce something for the mass performer but for the very trained or initiated Performer. "How do you reconcile this with ritual performance as communal act?" he asked rhetorically. This way of working gives an opportunity for others to learn the best ways of the art, not commercial art, but art as a noble tradition. "Don't improvise, please," Grotowski warned. This warning is paradoxical, he acknowledged, but the word "improvise" has become banal and associated with something fake. For this reason another word must be found. "'Reconstruction' is perhaps a purer word," Grotowski suggested, because "we can use an aspect of a song to reconstruct the personality and circumstances surrounding the song."

Referring to the concept of collage in his work, Grotowski became more philosophical and essentially spiritual. "God appears because his creation appears," he said. Grotowski perceives the inner elements of humanity not by sectarian means but still by a definite way of thinking. His work appears as either secular or sacred depending on the way it is received. "My terms are to help you understand what I am doing," he said, "not to convert you." He warned that any attempt to reach transcendent experience without discipline and preparation would be disastrous. The magic words become important in the effort to reach the essential grasp of consciousness or awareness, God or not God. "The higher connection is not possible if we are not in possession of higher skills," Grotowski told his listeners.

Grotowski's Objective Drama places much emphasis on ritual. He observes that theatre appeared from ritual and that the sources of theatre are complex, including the ritualized behavior of animals, games together with their rules, storytelling, and so on. The main dangers of theatre today are subjectivity and banality. Ritual has connotations, sometimes dangerous, as in voodoo. Ritual performance differs from ordinary acting because in ritual the Performer reaches toward the other, whereas in acting it is the self that is being expressed. Citing the example of monastic ritual, Grotowski referred to how Gregorian chants made the voice arise out of a rejected body, reaching towards a higher objectivity.

On performances and why he no longer gives public presentations of his work, Grotowski agreed that public performances are needed. "The monastery of the experiment cannot exist without the public performances existing," he said. He criticized the idea of contemporary Western performance which translates into selling instead of sharing. The old tradition of performance had the axis or the center-point. That axis is now no longer. He concluded by recommending that the new axis should be Work (with a capital letter) and such Work must be carried on without looking for the benefits.

Grotowski's evolution from the Poor Theatre through the Theatre of Sources into the Objective Drama project marks the stages from his conscious accessibility to the public through performances, to his relative withdrawal, to his monastic seclusion. In the monastery which his Workcenter represents, Grotowski retires to take stock of his encounter with the theatre of the past three decades. Today, he embodies the contradictions of the art which dies by that which keeps it alive, public performances. In Grotowski's theory, the conventional or classic performance exposes the performer as dilettante, an exhibitionist who caters to the superficial demands of performance, revealing those clichés and banalities that destroy the art. His move to a participatory theatre without banality involves working with people from a variety of cultural traditions in an effort to understand the ultimate significance of the primary energies deriving from cultural movements, and converting these to "find his own credibility," not imitating them to create a new synthesis.

OBSERVATIONS AND COMMENTS

The UCI seminar, like the talk given at Gabinetto Vieusseux (see ch. 30) and the excerpts from *Workcenter of Jerzy Grotowski* (see chs 37 and 38), authenticate the deepening of the artist's vision of the self. They demonstrate both Grotowski's competence and credibility in regard to theories of performance and, above all, his rebellion against dilettantism, banality, and clichés in conventional performance. The search which Theatre of Sources and Objective Drama represent are avenues through which Grotowski hopes to generate work on theatre that touches the world. The quality of performances designed for the public will depend on the quality of research that has gone into the work unknown to the public. Since nobody can give what he or she does not have, it goes without saying that productions not backed by significant research will turn out to be superficial. As the West African Pidgin English saying goes, "*Good soup na money mak'am*" (Good soup is made with money), so also the essence of a good performance flows from profound research. Of course there may be many kinds of good soup, but there is only one kind for Grotowski – the essential, not the synthetic or eclectic type.

Grotowski's contributions to 20th-century theatre have earned him enormous respect in the theatre world – both from those who endorse his present public-avoidance attitude and those who disapprove. However, one thing that most people appear to share about Grotowski's present philosophy of theatre, and this was evident at the UCI seminar, is a certain anxiety over its spiritual dimension. For Grotowski it is a personal spiritual quest for God or a similar being in an environment unpolluted by conventional secular manifestations, including the presence of an audience. In this regard, Grotowski's seminars become performances in themselves. They are extensions and continuations of his spiritual probe into the essence of humanity, of *be-ing*, as well as a demonstration of his role as "a teacher of Performer," a rebel conqueror of knowledge, a true teacher who makes the apprentice *do it*.

Grotowski's rhetoric has deepened into abstract spiritual concepts in his evolution towards understanding the knowledge which theatre or participatory performance gives and the techniques for achieving it. This is particularly so because this knowledge is not of sociological significance. It transcends the material world's contradiction and becomes a pure concept. The material contradiction Grotowski calls "body and essence" becomes "body of essence" when it is transcended. The "body of essence" thus describes the situation in which matter and spirit no longer fight each other and the body submits or yields to the total control of the spirit.

At the end of the UCI seminar, the question of the relevance of

Grotowski's performative research concepts to the practice of main-stream theatre remained unresolved. And the likelihood of it ever being resolved is bleak. But one thing was certain: Grotowski has carved an enviable artistic and intellectual niche for himself in contemporary 20th-century theatre and will continue to be a profound influence on the theory and practice of theatre in the twenty-first century. Grotowski's approach to performance through ritual techniques has drawn him irresistibly to non-Western traditions, bringing these traditions to our attention and contributing to our understanding of the varieties of world theatre. His laboratory or monastic approach to theatre is clearly a postmodern concept, especially in its confrontation of the modern tradition of theatre practice through techniques and traditions that are considered primitive and antithetical to it. Yet Grotowski's concern is not for the African or Asian societies from which he draws the bulk of his research material but for the contemporary Western civilization which he believes has excluded the sacred from the performing arts and therefore impoverished them both in terms of technique and the essential knowledge of humanity. He transcends the superficiality of contemporary themes in confronting contemporary society, preferring to use classical themes to focus attention on the essence of humanity, including social, material, and spiritual realities, and "creating a secular *sacrum* in the theatre" (Grotowski 1968:49), through which it could regain its function as a communal, collective art.

The idea of theatre as a communal collective and its intended purpose being sharing and not selling brought the traditional African theatre into a sharper focus for me in the context of Grotowski's seminar. His views emphasized the necessity for research into the performances of other cultures if the industrialized world is to appreciate their aesthetic and even spiritual value. Research in the indigenous performance traditions of Africa has convinced me that theatre is an indigenous African art form, but I could not help asking Grotowski, before he ended his presentation, to what extent he has been influenced by the rituals in African theatre. I could have given the answer to my own question, but I wanted to hear myself through Grotowski. He has been influenced by African perform-ance rituals among others, he answered in reply. Moreover, he has people of African descent in his workgroup as leaders helping to shape the process of his research. My question was also asked because I observed in Grotowski's approach to performance the same preparations evident before the public performances of initiation associations or cults. In an era when, according to Richard Schechner and Mady Schuman, the practices of these associations were seen by the colonial anthropologists as "savagery or a quaintness" (1976:165) of primitive religious practice, the associations themselves were also branded secret societies. But they were titular or communal associations, in fact only "secret" to the extent that aspects of their initiation rites were conducted away from the gaze of noninitiates. Male initiation rites in Africa such as the Igbo *mmonwu*, the Ibibio *ekpo*, the Mende *poro*, the Yoruba *egungun*, or the Chewa *nyau* are automatically open to all males of these ethnic groups after they undergo the necessary rites. It is during the period of seclusion or sequestration from the rest of the society that much of the artistic preparation is made and the cultural lessons taught to the neophytes. The men, women and children who constitute the audience are more than spectators; they are performers in a sense. For them the performance has aesthetic, sacred and cultural implications. They share in the spirit or essence of the performance in a manner that could be considered religious, but which is the demonstration of a certain fervor towards the totality of the initiation cult in all its cultural ramifications. Thus Grotowski channels his performance research along similar lines which enable the participants to understand and extend their capabilities without being superficial and the audience to appreciate the performance as genuine participants for whom it means something beyond superficial aesthetic pleasure.

It is unlikely that Grotowski will ever perform for conventional audiences again. Like the cult or initiation association rites, his performances may henceforth become outings or presentations of the initiate in an atmosphere of ritual ceremony. Outings or public performances of plays and dances are not a mandatory aspect of the traditional African initiation process, but they are used to maintain communal visibility and respect as well as to provide cultural entertainment and recreation. The performer is trained early in life to coordinate the activities of body and spirit and to transcend the former in total obedience to the latter. Thus in the Kalabari *Owu* performances of the Ijo ethnic group in Nigeria, the *teme* or spirit is said to displace the performer's *oju* or body and to possess it. Such possession performances are appreciated by spectators. Owu, the Water People, is a category of the second system of gods among the Kalabari (the first being the male and female principles responsible for creation and existence, respectively called *So* and *Tamunot*). These gods are said to be responsible for invention and human skills in people. They are patrons of today's performers who must appease them through the ancestors to achieve fantastic feats in their performances.

To what extent Grotowski's research will affect the practice of contemporary European and American theatre remains to be seen. His workshop participants are likely to propagate his techniques all over the world, yet they are unlikely to escape the fringe of mainstream theatre. First, economic pressures could prevent them from winning as much support as would be necessary to make the experiment succeed or to allow them to remain involved for as long as their "teacher of Performer." Second, Grotowski himself promises no assurance that his techniques will change the mainstream theatre. He refuses to convert anybody. I see Grotowski's appraisal of his influence on the theatre as an understatement. In terms of research and training, he will obviously be the Konstantin Stanislavsky of the twenty-first century and, along with the work of Peter Brook, Richard Schechner, and Eugenio Barba, among others, his techniques and theories are likely to endure for much longer. They are likely to become a strong osmotic force drawing the traditions of Western and non-Western cultures into the essence of a new theatre, not necessarily a synthesis of both. The contemporary elitist view of theatre based on industrial and economic factors will give way to an essential view of theatre as collective human institution.

If my views are optimistic it is because there is a greater enthusiasm for intercultural and interdisciplinary cooperation than before. Differences in ideology and the Cold War between the East and the West – like colonialism and neocolonialism – have permeated scholarship in all disciplines. The thawing in icy East–West relations will lead to new global priorities in social, economic, and cultural matters. Powerful ideas break cultural, economic, and political boundaries. Grotowski's theories and techniques for the postmodern theatre are among them.

PART IV
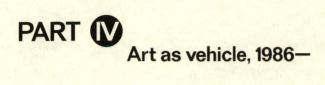
Art as vehicle, 1986—

36

INTRODUCTION

Art as vehicle, 1986—

Lisa Wolford

WORKCENTER OF JERZY GROTOWSKI

"Art as vehicle" is a practical work developed since 1986 at the Workcenter of Jerzy Grotowski, sponsored by the Centro per la Sperimentazione e la Ricerca Teatrale (CSRT) in Pontedera, Italy.[1] The Workcenter does not create public productions, nor is it an "acting school" in any conventional sense of the term. The artists accepted for residence at the Workcenter, selected either yearly or every two years from among hundreds of applicants throughout the world, must commit to a minimum of one year of intensive research, working six days a week, eight or more hours each day. The past and present members of the research groups represent a wide array of cultural backgrounds, and have included artists from Israel, India, Turkey, and Singapore, as well as from throughout Europe and the Americas.

From 1987 to 1993, the main activities of the Workcenter were conducted by two separate research teams, each following an independent line of investigation. The two groups (pragmatically referred to as "Upstairs" and "Downstairs" in reference to their use of different portions of the two-story workspace) were directed by Grotowski, though the day-to-day work was led by two of his collaborators, each of whom functioned as leader of the group under his or her authority. The group then referred to as "Downstairs Group," led by Thomas Richards (U.S.A.), focused on the development of performing structures around songs from African and Afro-Caribbean lines of tradition, also including fragments of very ancient texts. The exercise Motions was further developed here; physical training oriented toward fluidity and organicity of movement was also practiced. "Upstairs Group," led by Maud Robart (Haiti), concentrated on actions based on Haitian songs and texts with their roots in Egyptian and Middle Eastern culture. The group working under Robart's direction also reconstructed the "corporal" and "plastique" exercises from Grotowski's Laboratory Theatre. In 1993, the onset severe Italian financial crisis resulted in a drastic reduction of the resources allocated to subsidize the Workcenter. The remaining funds were sufficient to support only the work of Richards' group. Other expenses of the Workcenter, including housing that had previously been offered rent-free to accommodate participating artists, were also eliminated as a result of these funding cuts.

ART AS VEHICLE

According to Grotowski, the work of Art as vehicle focuses on "actions related to very ancient songs which traditionally served ritual purposes, and so can have a direct impact on – so to say – the head, the heart and the body of the doers, songs which can allow the passage from a vital energy to a more subtle one" (Thibaudat 1995:29). Designated by Grotowski as the final stage of his lifelong research, development of Art as vehicle at the Pontedera Workcenter has continued for approximately fifteen years thus far. The name by which Grotowski referred to this body of investigation is taken from a talk delivered by Peter Brook in 1987, "Grotowski, Art as a vehicle" (Ch. 38). Brook observes that Grotowski is looking for "something which existed in the past but has been forgotten over the centuries. This is that one of the vehicles which allows man to have access to another level of perception is to be found in the art of performance" (p. 381). Brook articulates Grotowski's concern with performance as a means, in a manner analogous to the way in which certain orders of monks have historically used music or the making of liqueurs to give form and structure to their inner search. In other contexts, Grotowski used the terms "ritual arts" or the "objectivity of ritual" to give some idea of the direction of his research. Grotowski clarified that the term Art as vehicle does not directly refer to all the activities of the Workcenter, but only to the work which directly deals with the process of energy transformation from "heavy but organic energies (linked to the forces of life, to instincts, to sensuality) [. . .] to a level of energy more subtle." In Art as vehicle, Richards became primary practitioner and Grotowski's essential collaborator, and has maintained responsibility for continuing this line of research following Grotowski's death.

Grotowski posited that performing arts can be viewed as a chain with many links. At one extreme, he placed the normal artistic theatre, the theatre of productions, oriented toward Art as Presentation; at the other end of the chain, he situated Art as vehicle. Grotowski articulated one of the differences between Art as Presentation and Art as vehicle in relation to the respective places of montage. "In performance," he clarified, "the seat of the montage is in the perception of the spectator;

in Art as vehicle, the seat of the montage is in the *doers*, in the artists who do" (1995:122).

To give an example of what he meant by the creation of montage in the perception of the spectator, Grotowski spoke about the work of Ryszard Cieslak in *The Constant Prince*. The actor's associations had nothing to do with a scenario of martyrdom, but were rather linked to a specific memory of love from his early adolescence. Everything constructed *around* Cieslak's line of actions, however – the logic of the Calderon/Slowacki text, the structure of the overall performance, the narrative elements and characters from the play, and the work of the other actors – suggested the story of a martyr; this, consequently, was the montage the spectators perceived. "That which the spectator caught was the intended montage," Grotowski explained, "while that which the actors did – that's another story" (1995:124). He further clarified that the creation of the montage in the spectator's perception is the duty of the director rather than the actor. "On the contrary," he continued, "when I speak of Art as vehicle, I refer to a montage whose seat is *not in the perception of the spectator but in the doers*. It is not that the doers agree between themselves about what the common montage will be, it is not that they share some common definition about what they will do. No, not verbal agreement, no spoken definition: it is necessary, through the very actions themselves to discover how to approach – step by step – toward the essential" (1995:124).

To explicate further this distinction between Art as Presentation and Art as vehicle, Grotowski drew an analogy to two different types of elevator.

> A performance is like a big elevator of which the actor is the operator. The spectators are in this elevator, the performance transports them from one form of event to another. If this elevator functions for the spectators, it means that the montage is well done.
>
> Art as vehicle is like a very primitive elevator: it's some kind of basket pulled by a cord, with which the doer lifts himself toward a more subtle energy, to descend with this to the instinctual body. This is the objectivity of the ritual. If Art as vehicle functions, this objectivity exists and the basket moves for those who do the Action.
>
> (1995:124–125)

Grotowski was acutely aware that a practice of this nature requires a precise structure. "One cannot work on oneself (to use the term of Stanislavsky), if one is not inside something which is structured and can be repeated, which has a beginning, a middle and an end, something in which every element has its logical place, technically necessary. All this determined from the point of view of that verticality toward the subtle and of its (the subtle) descent toward the density of the body. *The structure elaborated in details – the Action – is the key; if the structure is missing, all dissolves"* (1995:130; emphasis in original). In terms of its emphasis on precision, structure and performance craft, the work of Art as vehicle has much in common with that of artistic theatre. Grotowski observed that in respect to the need for a repeatable structure, each opus developed at the Workcenter should be even more precise than conventional performance. Yet he cautioned that, despite the fact that the two disparate practices share a common basis in the actor's craft, one should not overlook the distinctions between Art as vehicle and audience-directed performance: "It's not a matter of return toward Art as presentation; it is *the other extremity of the same chain*" (1995:121).

Grotowski maintained that a project such as Art as vehicle should not be entirely cut off from the outside world. "Anyway, things evolve. Now the Workcenter is much less isolated than someone might think," he asserted (Thibaudat 1995:30). The Workcenter hosts practical work exchanges (generally one to three days) involving observation and analysis with theatre companies who present examples of their own activities (both performance and training) and witness the structured opus and forms of training of the group under Richards' direction. The visiting companies do not work actively with artists from the Workcenter; the exchange is based on reciprocal observation of the creative work of the separate groups. More than 150 groups have visited the Pontedera Workcenter since Grotowski and his collaborators initiated this form of exchange. (At times, groups of individuals are also invited to witness the work.) The purpose of these encounters is not to change the orientation of the visiting artists, to convert them to a "Grotowskian" line of research beyond the boundaries of audience-directed theatre practice, but on the contrary, taking it as a given that these artists should continue in their own way. The exchanges address certain principles of craft that Grotowski maintained are valid at both extremities of the chain. "Art as vehicle poses in practice questions linked to craft as such, legitimate on either extremity of the chain of performing arts" (1995:133). He asserted that such exchange demonstrates one way in which this work, more or less isolated, can maintain an alive relation in the field of theatre (1995:132). He observed that both extremes of the chain of performing arts, Art as presentation and Art as vehicle, "belong to the same large family. A passage between them should be possible: of the technical discoveries, of the artisanal consciousness. . . . It is needed that all this can pass along, if we don't want to be completely cut off from the world" (1995:134).

The work of Art as vehicle continues at the Pontedera research centre, uninterrupted by Grotowski's death in January 1999 as a result of complications related to degenerative heart disease. During the final years of his life, Grotowski's health was precarious at best, and those who worked closely with him understood implicitly that they must be prepared to continue without him at a moment's notice. It had always been Grotowski's intention that the practice of Art as vehicle should survive his passing. From relatively early in the process of his apprenticeship Richards was given increasing autonomy and responsibility for leadership of the work. Along with Mario Biagini, an extraordinary Italian performer who participated in Art as vehicle since the inception of the program and ultimately became integral to the research, Richards continues to lead the creative activities of the Workcenter.

INSIDE THE "MONASTERY" (PONTEDERA, 1995)

"The secret of Casa Grotowski," I wrote to a friend shortly after arriving in Italy in the summer of 1995, "is that there is no secret." What I refer to in private conversation as Casa Grotowski, several kilometers distant from Pontedera, is the actual site of the Workcenter, though the sponsoring organization (CSRT) is based in the nearby city. The area surrounding Casa Grotowski is too small even to be described as a village, with only a few rambling houses and endless vineyards. No postal service comes out this far, and the people who live and work here must go to the next village to buy groceries or find a public telephone. A gravel road turns up a hill off the main road, leading past a large, two-story building that has been converted into a workspace for Grotowski and his collaborators. Horses graze inside a wood-fenced pasture, and the neighbors' children ride their bicycles up and down the path, shouting to one another in Italian. At the top of the hill is a row of small houses, in one of which lives Grotowski, the entirety of his small apartment piled from floor to ceiling with books in various languages. In another, Signora Rita, the elderly lady whom I've been told has lived here since she was a girl, tends to her roses and the flowers in her windowbox. She seems to have completely accepted the strange mix of foreigners who move in and out of the building next to hers, a three-bedroom apartment that has housed a number of Grotowski's collaborators over the past ten years. When I moved into one of the rooms, I was told by the young men living there that we have only one key to the front door, which was usually left unlocked. They showed me the hiding place where the key should be kept whenever the three of us happened to be away at the same time. "It's important to lock it when you leave," said W., who seemed unconcerned with thieves, but rather that the ever-persistent *Testimoni di Jehovah*, finding no one at home, might let themselves in and wait for somebody to return.

Grotowski invited me to stay for an extended period in Italy, working with him on various text-related projects and occasionally witnessing the work of the research team. I was grateful to be able to live near the worksite, both because it made transportation and communication easier in this group with few cars and no telephones, and more importantly because it allowed me to get a deeper sense of what life was like for the artists in residence at the Workcenter. After having lived at Casa Grotowski for several months, I had to laugh when I read an Italian director's description of one of the apartments near the worksite (a place where invited guests used to be taken for a verbal introduction before witnessing the practical work) as being like the kitchen of a monastery. Granted, P. and M. were probably better housekeepers than we are, but the image amuses me nonetheless as I wipe the coffee grounds from the stove and put the leftover meat in the freezer behind the Polish vodka. Grotowski may have joked to Jan Kott that such vodka goes very well with lotus seeds, but the people living in this house would make rather bohemian monks. Such austerity as there is about the life here – the extreme simplicity of the furniture, the reluctance to heat the rooms until winter has fully settled in, resulting in people being wrapped in sweaters, hats and woolen scarves even while indoors – things that outsiders may have tended to perceive as "spiritual asceticism," are in fact a direct result of straitened financial circumstances. Even the workleaders receive less money from the sponsoring organization than I was accustomed to making as a graduate assistant; the other members of the research team are not paid at all, and must cover the cost of their own room and board.

Zbigniew Osinski, writing about his visit to the Workcenter in the late 1980s, described the conditions of life and work as "modest." He was being polite. It might be more accurate to say that the artists who live and work at Casa Grotowski are, for the most part, poorer than the proverbial church mice. I remember coming downstairs to the kitchen one evening and finding bowls filled to overflowing with grapes and wild fruit. "Take," said P., enjoying the unaccustomed abundance. I later discovered that three of the men had made a pilgrimage through the nearby fields to gather what they could find. "This year," said P., "we take the grapes for fun. Last year, we were taking them because we needed the food." I understand that it wasn't always like this, that in years when fellowships and grants were more easily available from international cultural organizations, the participants here lived well. But the funding crisis that has menaced the art world as a whole has not spared Grotowski's Workcenter.

Perhaps because it's my nature to be susceptible to romanticisms such as the monastic image, or possibly because I'd assimilated many similar descriptions over the years, I had also internalized some concept of the Workcenter as "sanctified space." During the years when I was working in Objective Drama at U.C.-Irvine and later as part of James Slowiak and Jairo Cuesta's New World Performance Laboratory, the word "Ponte-dera" came to have an almost mythical significance. My colleagues and I regarded anyone who came from *there* with a touch of awe and wonder, almost reverence. The mythology related to Grotowski, which has always grown with amazing persistence and rapidity, found particularly fertile soil among those of us who aspired to something more concentrated, more intense than the way we were working in our own fragmented lives, where we tried to combine full-time rehearsal schedules with restaurant or office jobs. From seven thousand miles away, our image of the Workcenter was ornamented with all manner of paradisiacal illusions. Surely *there* the problems we struggled with, the lack of money and the pressures of time, didn't apply.

And so when I arrived at Casa Grotowski, when I unpacked my bags and settled in, I was surprised to discover the obvious truth that life is life and work is work and place, as T.S. Eliot wrote, "is always and only place," and in and of itself presents no escape, no easy solution. But in a strange way it delighted me when, after I'd been living in Italy for a month, I saw two of the so-called "monks" break into a perfectly mundane squabble in the kitchen which ended with one man storming off to his room and growling at the other to "Shut up!"

But behind the myth is also something real. Not in the sense of an elevated or pseudo-esoteric atmosphere, but in terms of a particular intensity of work, a purity of commitment. The first time I saw *Downstairs Action*, the performance structure developed by Richards in the late 1980s, I remember that for hours afterward I literally could not speak, could not form words, even in thought. The impact of the vibration in the doers' work on the ritual songs (call it emotional, physiological, as you will), the power of the actions developed around them, the concentrated intensity of performing – all these together *opened* something in me. And in a way that was not without pain, because it became a confrontation with my own limitations, both human and artistic. How to put words to this, how to translate this epiphany? Suddenly I was as the speechless tramp in Beckett's *Godot*, struggling to communicate a knowledge that overflowed meaning. Given the existence . . . *of this* – how to speak, what to say? Beyond this threshold, there is only silence.

DISCOURSES ON DISCOURSE

The handful of scholars invited to witness the work of the teams led respectively by Richards and Robart for the most part responded with a silence not dissimilar to my own, refraining from attempts to verbalize details of the performance structures. Ferdinando Taviani, who witnessed these two works in 1988, replied with a brief but evocative testimonial:

> I had the privilege, together with some tens of other persons subdivided into minuscule groups, to be invited to observe, for one evening, as a silent witness, the work of the group gathered around Grotowski. Two things appeared evident to me: the exceptional *quality* of that work, and – although it consists of physical actions, songs and stories – its profound extraneity from the spectator's gaze (that is not to say, of course, intolerance of every outside gaze). The first impression, I saw afterwards, was unanimously shared by all the other guests invited at different moments. It was not a judgment, but more a shared *astonishment*, to be faced with actions so rigorous as to assume an almost absolute character, free from psychologisms, which some attribute to classical art and others to symbolism. The second impression, on the other hand, the extraneity from any spectator, was not shared by all. It can be said, in fact, that the work developed around Grotowski could function, should its creators so desire, as a performance *sui generis*, of a quality that would not fear comparison. The fact remains, however, that it is not about a new type of performance that Grotowski writes when he indicates, in "Performer," the horizon within which his empirical research moves.
>
> (1988:270)

"Performer," based on a conference given by Grotowski in 1987, is among the most lyrical and complex of his published statements. Grotowski's use of the term Performer (capitalized and always in the singular) differs from the meaning given to the word in common parlance. Performer, in Grotowski's sense, "is a state of being." "He is not a man who plays another. He is a doer, a priest, a warrior: he is outside aesthetic genres." Taviani, who was present at the two-day conference by Grotowski of which "Performer" is a distilled and partial record, observes that in constructing this text, Grotowski found a way to capture in the written word a characteristic of oral discourse, able to communicate *between the words* (1988:265).

Taviani traces the evolution of the text, which he describes as a "discourse on discourse," observing that it was originally constructed from notes taken by Georges Banu during the course of Grotowski's conference and subsequently re-elaborated by Grotowski. Taviani draws attention to the final fragment of the text, which was not part of the actual meeting but was added by Grotowski at a later time; it is a passage taken from Meister Eckhart which "cites, or better mounts in words, a page that has a complete sense, but that Eckhart historically never wrote" (1988:267). Treating Eckhart's sermons in a similar manner to the way in which he approached textual montage during his work as a stage director, Grotowski constructed the final fragment of his text, "the inner man," by weaving together passages from two separate sermons by the German mystic.

Osinski, one of the foremost authorities on Grotowski's life's work, was also among the first scholars invited to witness and write about the practical activities of the Pontedera Workcenter. In "Grotowski Blazes the Trails: From Objective Drama to Art as vehicle," he positions Grotowski's final work within the scope of the director's lifelong research, examining aspects of continuity which link this program to earlier phases of Grotowski's activity. Drawing on a wide range of published materials by and about Grotowski, as well as his own personal observations during a ten-day sojourn in Pontedera, Osinski describes the overall structure of the Workcenter's activities and examines Art as vehicle from a philosophical as well as a historical perspective.

The essay by Halina Filipowicz, "Where is Gurutowski?" likewise examines the arc of Grotowski's developing research, considering his significance as cultural icon and opening possibilities for interpreting his practice and discourse in relation to deconstructionism and other strands of postmodernist thought. She further explores the volatility and liminal positioning of Grotowski's later praxis, which she perceives to be balanced on a thin cusp between theatrical and spiritual traditions.

My own essay, "*Action*: The Unrepresentable Origin," describes the performance structure developed at the Workcenter and initially presented to witnesses in the summer of 1995. Richards, who is both the creator and primary doer of *Action*, acknowledges that this structure is different on the level of montage from the opus developed with his group five years before (*Downstairs Action*), because now some window exists, allowing the possible interpretation of a person witnessing from outside. Still, it would be misleading to regard *Action* as a theatre performance in any conventional sense of the term.

Through his dual experience as leader and doer, Richards has gained a genuine knowledge of the delicate process of energy transformation at the heart of the current praxis. In Chapter 42, a condensed version of an interview I conducted with Richards in August 1995, he articulates his inner process as doer and workleader in an extraordinarily evocative way, witnessing to the lived experience of what he describes as "a vertical journey toward the subtle." Richards also discusses the relation of the Workcenter's activities to more common forms of theatre practice, analysing the importance of the actor's craft as a foundation for his work and that of his colleagues. He speaks of *Action* in relation to what he imagines might be "the edge-point of performance," a performative structure that can accept the look of the witness, but is not dependent on that look.

PERFORMER

Jerzy Grotowski

Performer, with a capital letter, is a man of action. He is not somebody who plays another. He is a doer, a priest, a warrior: he is outside aesthetic genres. Ritual is performance, an accomplished action, an act. Degenerated ritual is a show. I don't look to discover something new but something forgotten. Something so old that all distinctions between aesthetic genres are no longer of use.

I am a *teacher of Performer* (I speak in the singular: *of Performer*). A teacher – as in the crafts – is someone through whom the teaching is passing; the teaching should be received, but the manner for the apprentice to rediscover it can only be personal. And how does the teacher himself come to know the teaching? By initiation, or by theft. *Performer* is a state of being. A man of knowledge, we can speak of him in reference to Castaneda's novels, if we like romanticisms. I prefer to think of Pierre de Combas. Or even of this Don Juan whom Nietzsche described: a rebel face to whom knowledge stands as duty; even if others don't curse him, he feels to be a changeling, an outsider. In Hindu tradition they speak of *vratias* (the rebel hordes). *Vratia* is someone who is on the way to conquer knowledge. A man of knowledge [*czlowiek poznania*] has at his disposal *the doing* and not ideas or theories. The true teacher – what does he do for the apprentice? He says: *do it*. The apprentice fights to understand, to reduce the unknown to the known, to avoid doing. By the very fact that he wants to understand, he resists. He can understand only after he *does it*. He *does it* or not. Knowledge is a matter of doing.

Danger and chance

When I use the term: warrior, maybe you will refer it to Castaneda, but all scriptures speak of the warrior. You can find him in the Hindu tradition as well as in the African one. He is somebody who is conscious of his own mortality. If it's necessary to confront corpses, he confronts them, but if it's not necessary to kill, he doesn't kill. Among the Indians of the New World it was said that between two battles, *the warrior has a tender heart, like a young girl*. To conquer knowledge he fights, because the pulsation of life becomes stronger and more articulated in moments of great intensity, of danger. Danger and chance go together. One has no class if not face to the danger. In a time of challenge appears the rhythmization of human impulses. Ritual is a time of great intensity; provoked intensity; life then becomes rhythm. *Performer* knows to link body impulses to the song. (The stream of life should be articulated in forms.) The witnesses then enter into states of intensity because, so to say, they feel presence. And this is thanks to *Performer*, who is a bridge between the witness and this something. In this sense, *Performer* is *pontifex*, maker of bridges.

Essence: etymologically, it's a question of being, of *be-ing*. Essence interests me because nothing in it is sociological. It is what you did not receive from others, what did not come from outside, what is not learned. For example, conscience is something which belongs to essence; it is different from the moral code which belongs to society. If you break the moral code you feel guilty, and it is society which speaks in you. But if you do an act against conscience, you feel remorse – this is between you and yourself, and not between you and society. Because almost everything we possess is sociological, essence seems to be a little thing, but it is ours. In the seventies, in Sudan, there were still young warriors in the villages Kau. For the warrior with organicity in full, the body and essence can enter into osmosis: it seems impossible to dissociate them. But it is not a permanent state; it lasts not long. In Zeami's words, it's *the flower of youth*. However, with age, it's possible to pass from the *body-and-essence* to the *body of essence*. And that in outcome of difficult evolution, personal transmutation, which is in some way the task of everyone. The key question is: What is your process? Are you faithful to it or do you fight against your process? The process is something like the destiny of each one, his own destiny, which develops inside time (or which just unfolds – and that is all). So: *What is the quality of submission* to your own destiny? One can catch the process if what one does is in keeping with himself, if he *doesn't hate what he does*. The process is linked to essence and virtually leads to the *body of essence*. When the warrior is in the short period of osmosis *body-and-essence*, he should catch his process. Adjusted to process, the body becomes non-resistant, nearly transparent. Everything is in lightness, in evidence. With *Performer*, performing can become near process.

The I—I

It can be read in ancient texts: *We are two. The bird who picks and the bird who looks on. The one will die, the one will live.* Busy with picking, drunk with life inside time, we forgot to *make live* the part in us which looks on. So, there is the danger to exist only inside time, and in no way outside time. To feel looked upon by this other part of yourself (the part which is as if outside time) gives another dimension. There is an I–I. The second I is quasi virtual; it is not – in you – the look of the others, nor any judgment; it's like an immobile look: a silent presence, like the sun which illuminates the things – and that's all. The process can be accomplished only in the context of this still presence. I–I: in experience, the couple doesn't appear as separate, but as full, unique.

In the way of *Performer* – he perceives essence during its osmosis with the body, and then works the process; he develops the I–I. The looking presence of the teacher can sometimes function as a mirror of the connection I–I (this junction is not yet traced). When the channel I–I is traced, the teacher can disappear and *Performer* continue toward the *body of essence*; that which can be – for someone – as if seen in the photo of Gurdjieff, old, sitting on a bench in Paris. From the photo of the young warrior of Kau to that of Gurdjieff is the passage from the *body-and-essence* to the *body of essence*.

I–I does not mean to be cut in two but to be double. The question is to be passive in action and active in seeing (reversing the habit). Passive: to be receptive. Active: to be present. To nourish the life of the I–I, *Performer* must develop not an organism-mass, an organism of muscles, athletic, but an organism-channel through which the energies circulate, the energies transform, the subtle is touched.

Performer should ground his work in a precise structure – making efforts, because persistence and respect for details are the rigor which allow to become present the I–I. The things to be done must be precise. *Don't improvise, please*! It is necessary to find the actions, simple, yet taking care that they are mastered and that they endure. If not, they will not be simple, but banal.

What I recall

One access to the creative way consists of discovering in yourself an ancient corporality to which you are bound by a strong ancestral relation. So you are neither in the character nor in the non-character. Starting from details you can discover in you somebody other – your grandfather, your mother. A photo, a memory of wrinkles, the distant echo of a color of the voice enable to reconstruct a corporality. First, the corporality of somebody known, and then more and more distant, the corporality of the unknown one, the ancestor. Is it literally the same? Maybe not literally – but yet as it might have been. You can arrive very far back, as if your memory awakes. That is a phenomenon of reminiscence, as if you recall *Performer* of the primal ritual. Each time I discover something, I have the feeling it is what I recall. Discoveries are behind us and we must journey back to reach them. With the breakthrough – as in the return of an exile – can one touch something which is no longer linked to beginnings but – if I dare say – *to the beginning*? I believe so. Is essence the hidden background of the memory? I don't know at all. When I work near essence, I have the impression that memory actualizes. When essence is activated, it is as if strong potentialities are activated. The reminiscence is perhaps one of these potentialities.

The inner man

I quote:

> Between the inner man and the outer man there is the same infinite difference as between the heaven and the earth.
>
> When I was in my first cause, I had not God, I was cause of me. There, nobody asked me to where I tended, nor what I was doing; nobody was there to question me. What I wanted, I was it, and what I was, I wanted; I was free from God and from anything.
>
> When I came out (flowed out) all creatures spoke of God. If someone asked me: – brother Eckhart, when did you come out of the home? – I was still there just a moment ago, I was myself, I wanted me myself and knew me myself, to make the man (which here below I am). That is why I am unborn, and by my mode unborn, I cannot die. What I am by my birth will die and vanish, because it is given to time and will decay with time. But in my birth also were born all creatures. They all feel the need to ascend from their life to their essence.
>
> When I return, this breakthrough is much more noble than my coming out. In the breakthrough – there, I am above all creatures, neither God, nor creature; but I am what I was, what I should remain now and forever. When I arrive – there, nobody asks me where I come from nor where I have been. There I am what I was, I do not increase nor diminish, because I am – there, an immobile cause, which makes move all things.

Note (which accompanied the text "Performer" in the booklet published by the Workcenter in Pontedera, Italy): One version of this text – based on a conference by Grotowski – was published in May 1987 by *Art-Press* in Paris, with the following gloss by Georges Banu: "What I propose here is neither a recording, nor a summary, but notes carefully taken, as close as possible to the formulas of Grotowski. It should be read as indications of a trajectory and not as the terms of a program, nor a document – finished, written, closed." The text has been reworked and extended by Grotowski for the present publication. To identify *Performer* with the participants of the Workcenter would be an abuse of the term. The matter is rather of that case of apprenticeship which, in all the activity of "teacher of *Performer*" occurs vary rarely.

Translated by Thomas Richards
© 1990 Jerzy Grotowski

38

GROTOWSKI, ART AS A VEHICLE

Peter Brook

Nothing is as joyous as a paradox, and speaking about Grotowski and his work immediately places us in front of an immense paradox. Grotowski, as I have known him for more than twenty years, is a deeply simple man, who carries out research which is profoundly pure. How is it possible, then, that over the years, the result of this simplicity has been to create both complications and confusion? Through personal contact with his work I have gained an intimate knowledge of its value; a work initiated in Poland by an exceptional man in collaboration with a very small number of persons, which, thanks to the 20th-century systems of travel and communications, has passed very rapidly into the books, the reviews, the interviews and the work of small groups all over the world. Unfortunately, this ultra-rapid diffusion has not always gone through qualified people, and around the name of Grotowski – like a rolling stone – have come to attach themselves, to graft themselves, all kinds of confusions, excrescences and misunderstandings.

I heard some years ago there was a flight controller at a Paris airport who, when he went home at the end of his working day, held Grotowski workshops. Perhaps he was a very well-qualified person who communicated something essential to two or three people. But I am afraid it is more likely that he was someone who felt that he was a specialist in Grotowski's work simply because he had seen a Polish plane in the sky.

So what is the result, today, of all these years of confusion? What we need to make clear to ourselves is this: what precise, concrete relationship exists between Grotowski's work – and the theatre? There was a time when the answer seemed obvious. The Wroclaw actors did productions which created a shock across the world because of their quality. So they clearly belonged to theatre. Their performances were like a lamp, a lighthouse, demonstrating that in any theatre it is possible to reach a higher standard, a deeper and more intense one, on condition that the actors reach a level of dedication, sincerity, seriousness, and understanding of their own means, which doesn't exist at the mediocre level of normal productions. Unfortunately, it was just at this point that the first confusion set in. Theatre groups who shared a desire to go towards a theatre of different intensity began to follow Grotowski's footsteps without realizing that if they did not possess his quality of understanding, then all the work that they did, instead of taking them towards the ideal, brought the ideal down to their own level, which was precisely the level they were in revolt against.

The second stage of Grotowski's work became more mysterious and more complex. Grotowski stopped giving public performances and, while following a pathway which was still simple, logical, and direct, he gave the impression of making an extraordinary change of direction. A question began to be asked: if there are no longer any productions, what has this new work got to do with the theatre?

If you look at this new work closely, you can see that it was the old direction that continued to develop, to evolve, to become richer and richer, both important and necessary. However, seen from far off, it appeared more and more obscure. This is the price new research has to pay. It is fragile, it must be protected. It cannot be both a research in-depth and yet something which is open to all. The curiosity of the idle would be its ruin. None the less, I believe that there are certain moments – like our meeting here today – when it is necessary to allow a powerful gust of wind to blow away the shadows, opening up some insight into the Grotowski mystery. So let us take a close look at what we really wish to know.

First of all, let's take the point of view of theatre. Theatre is an abstract word and to be concrete needs a vehicle. The vehicle which is the strongest in all the forms of theatre is the human being. This individual, this human being, is always an unknown quantity. And it is an absolute necessity that somewhere there should exist exceptional conditions in which this strange unknown being – the actor – can be explored.

Now, if I mention a happy coincidence, it is no digression. As I was coming in here, I said hello to an old friend who is the son of one of our greatest masters, Gordon Craig. I say one of our greatest masters, because there are few people who have had such a direct, long-lasting influence on the entire theatre of our century as Gordon Craig. But this influence has passed through events and writings which only a very small number of people have read or seen, but as these were truly extraordinary, created an influence which has gone right round the world. The theatre world is extremely intuitive, and its great quality is that it is capable of catching what is in the air. Such influences, when they are really strong, penetrate quickly and go a long way. That's why I believe that although Grotowski's work at Pontedera seems remote and con-cealist, it concerns theatre everywhere. It is a laboratory where experiences can mature that are impossible to accomplish without a laboratory.

And the fact that we, as the Centre International de Creations Theatrale in Paris, feel a kinship with Grotowski's Centre is due to the fact that we are absolutely convinced that there is a living, permanent relationship between research work without a public and the nourishment that this can give to public performance.

I believe that there is another aspect that would be interesting to deal with today. Right from the first moment when one begins to explore the possibilities of the human being, one must face up squarely to the fact that this investigation is a spiritual search. I use an explosive word, which is very simple, but which creates many misunderstandings. I mean "spiritual" in the sense that, as one goes towards the interiority of man, one passes from the known to the unknown, and that as the work of Grotowski's successive groups has gradually become more essential, thanks to his own personal evolution, the inner points that have been touched upon have become further and further from any normal possibility of definition. It may thus be said that in another epoch, this work would have been like the natural evolution of a spiritual opening. The spiritual traditions of the whole history of mankind have always needed to develop their own specific forms, for nothing is worse than a spirituality that is vague or generalized. On the contrary, in the great traditions one can see, for example, how monks, looking for a solid support for their inner search, discovered the need to make pottery or liqueurs. Others turned to music as a vehicle. It seems to me that Grotowski is showing us something which existed in the past but has been forgotten over the centuries. That is that one of the vehicles which allows man to have access to another level of perception is to be found in the art of performance. For this, there is one condition: the individual must be talented. It is clear that if a man wants to search for God, and enters into a monastery where all the work is based on music, but doesn't love music and has no musical "ear," then he has come to the wrong address. On the other hand, there are many people in the world who are attracted by acting. This is a function which is very natural for human beings. Mankind is divided into two groups: those who want to act and have no talent, and those who possess a real talent. Often those who possess this talent haven't got the faintest idea of what this means; they can't explain it by themselves; they simply know that they feel an "attraction." With this attraction, the persons who dream of becoming actors can, in a perfectly natural way, go straight towards the world of the theatre. But in certain cases they may also feel something else. They may feel that this gift, all this love, is an opening towards another understanding; and they may feel that they can't find this understanding except through personal work with a master.

This seems to be the point that Grotowski has reached and it is the reason why I would like to ask my friend, our friend Grotowski, to make more clear to us how and to what degree his work on dramatic art is inseparable from having around him people whose real need is for a personal inner evolution. I would like him to throw some light on this. As far as I am concerned, I am convinced that his activity in the realm of "art as vehicle" is not only of great value, but that no one else can imitate his way, or do it for him. For this reason, I would draw one simple conclusion: nobody can speak for him. Let him speak for himself.

Translation revised by the author, September 1995.

39

GROTOWSKI BLAZES THE TRAILS
From Objective Drama to Art as vehicle

Zbigniew Osinski

I

Apocalypsis cum figuris was the last premiere of the Teatr Laboratorium in Wroclaw. Since 1968, Jerzy Grotowski has not directed another theatre production. Nothing indicates that he ever will. This has to be made very clear.

The past twenty-one years constitute a period longer than Grotowski's entire work in the theatre, even if we add his training as actor and director. He spent eighteen years in the theatre, including eleven years (1957–68) as a director. We must take note of these facts to avoid misunderstanding.

Grotowski's work since 1985 represents the closure of a thirty-year creative journey – the achievement and crowning of a lifetime. This is the fourth period of his work. The first, the "Theatre of Productions," lasted from either 1957 (the year of his directorial debut, Ionesco's *The Chairs*, at the Stary Teatr in Cracow) or 1959 (the founding of the Teatr Trzynastu Rzedow in Opole, which later evolved into the Teatr Laboratorium) until 1969. The second period was the "Theatre of Participation" (known as "Active Culture" or "Paratheatre," 1969–78), the third the "Theatre of Sources" (1976–82). The fourth period, "Art as vehicle," corresponds to the work he has been doing in Italy. The short interim period after the Theatre of Sources, when he was working in California, is known, to use his term, as "Objective Drama."

It is possible to associate this term Objective Drama with Jung's "objective unconscious" or T.S. Eliot's "objective correlative," but it would be more profitable to link it to the distinction between objective art and subjective art made by G.I. Gurdjieff (1877–1949) (see Gordon 1978; Bennett 1973). Subjective art relies on a randomness or individual view of things and phenomena, and thus it is often governed by human caprice. "Objective Art," on the other hand, has an extra- and supra-individual quality, and it can thereby reveal the laws of fate and the destiny of man.

The term Objective Art appeared in 1921, completely independently of Gurdjieff, in a notebook (the so-called "Kievan Diary") of Juliusz Osterwa (1885–1947), one of the foremost Polish actors and directors and a co-founder, with Mieczyslaw Limanowski, of the Teatr Reduta (1919–39). Osterwa thought that "Architecture [. . .] was an objective art – the most objective of the arts. Then comes music. Then painting, then the word . . . and literature." He thus postulated: "Suppose theatre is like architecture. [. . .] Architecture is the most refined . . . moves the experts and the observer to a state of rapture – while it affects everyone in such a way that they are not even conscious of it." Grotowski recently showed me these notes of Osterwa.

On 11 August 1982, his forty-ninth birthday, Grotowski completed the final stage of the Theatre of Sources in Ostrowina near Olesnica. The next day, while martial law was still in effect, he left Poland. After a short stay in Italy and Haiti he settled in the United States. Associated at first with Columbia University as a professor of drama, in 1983–84 he became a professor in the School of Fine Arts at the University of California-Irvine (UCI). While at Irvine he launched the Objective Drama program subsidized by UCI, the Rockefeller Foundation, and the National Endowment for the Arts.

In 1985 he started in Italy what he now calls Art as vehicle.

Grotowski's current work is the logical outcome of all the previous stages of his creative development: of the theatrical phase that ended with the production of *Apocalypsis cum figuris*; of the Theatre of Participation with its apex at the Research University of the Theatre of Nations in Wroclaw (July–August 1975); and of the Theatre of Sources which encompassed transcultural experiments (conducted mainly in Brzezinka and Ostrowina near Olesnica) as well as his research expeditions to places where archaic rites are still alive: Haiti (voodoo), Bengal (the tradition of the Bauls who are both yogis and artists), Nigeria (the Yoruba), and Mexico (the Huichol).

Objective Drama focused on the discovery – within the individual and through the individual – of certain elements of techniques, or "performative elements" (movement, voice, rhythm, sound, use of space). In all likelihood, these elements were already present when art was not yet separated from other spheres of life and before there was a division into artistic genres and categories. In his first interview on this subject, published in the *Los Angeles Times*, Grotowski defined the goal of his explorations:

> To re-evoke a very ancient form of art where ritual and artistic creation
> were seamless. Where poetry was song, song was incantation, movement
> was dance. Pre-differentiation Art, if you will, which was extremely
> powerful in its impact. By touching that, without concern for philosoph-
> ical or theological motivation, each of us could find his own connection.
> (quoted in Drake 1983)

In another interview he said:

> One might say – but it is only a metaphor – that we are trying to go back
> before the Tower of Babel, and discover what was before. First to discover
> differences, and then to discover what was before the differences.
>
> We can hope to rediscover a very old form of art, art as a *way of
> knowledge*. But we live *after* the tower of Babel, and the attempt will not
> be to form a new synthesis. We cannot say: 'Now we will create a new
> form of ritual.' Maybe it is possible to do this, but one has to have 1,000
> years.
>
> Nor is the intention to discover new ways of manipulating the
> consciousness of people. To do this [. . .] is to bring something very high
> down to something very low. The effect of our work must be indirect. The
> intention is just to rediscover some very simple things that everyone in his
> own frame can be nourished by.
>
> (in Sullivan 1983)

Some ritual and liturgical techniques have been known to produce certain
energetic results in those who practice them. Grotowski: "These
techniques involve extremely precise, almost physical actions. [. . .] A
precise moving or incantation gets a precise result" (in Sullivan 1983).

The performative elements distinguished by Grotowski – always
quite simple – seem largely universal. He certainly does not want to
attach to them any philosophical or theological labels since, as he says, "it is
precisely by not labeling religious or philosophical content that we might
touch a transcultural nerve" (in Drake 1983). This is exactly why the
performative fragments have an "objective" character in the sense I
discussed at the beginning. Grotowski has called them *organons* or
yantras.

In Greek, "organon" means: (1) organ; (2) instrument. In ancient
Sanskrit, the word "yantra" also has two meanings: (1) a medical
scalpel; (2) an astronomer's observational device. In the second of these
meanings – as an instrument of astronomical observation – yantra is
directly connected with the universe and with nature, while in both cases
it refers to extremely delicate instruments. In ancient India, temples were
built as yantras – that is, as instruments of transformation or of energetic

passage from stimulation to tranquility, to "peace." A similar "instrumentalization" plays a role in the structure of the cathedrals of the Middle Ages: it refers both to the entire structure and to each specific detail in it.

And this is precisely what Grotowski is aiming for today in the field of the performing arts: genuine mastery, supreme competence. The focus is on the particulars, on the detail.

While working in California, Grotowski strove for a separation of certain performative fragments from others through a process of "distillation." The method of analysing and distilling "fragments" naturally demanded precision and discipline. Objective Drama, of course, was not Grotowski's return to the theatre but rather a resumption of his work on professional precision and discipline – the antitheses of which are dilettantism, incompetence, and amateurish execution. Yet the approach differed radically from that in the Theatre of Productions. At that time his attention had been focused on the acting process, on the human act [*akt ludzki*] of the actor for whom only afterwards a structure or a "harness of form" was found. In Objective Drama, the situation was the exact opposite: work on form released a desired process from the participants. But form itself did not determine everything – only what seemed to be non-material – and it could therefore release the quality of lived experience and the quality of human presence. Objective Drama was thus a selective examination of a few instruments.

Common to both the Art as vehicle and the Theatre of Productions is the "total act" [*akt calkowity*], the "utter act" [*czyn totalny*], and the "total man" [*czlowiek calkowity*], as Grotowski understands them. However, the path to this is not identical, as Grotowski's programmatic statement "Performer" attests. The "dialectic of spontaneity and discipline" is expressed through a symbiosis of ritual and creativity, structure and process, each of which nourishes the other.

The period between 1983 and 1985 separates the Theatre of Sources from the very different, artisanlike work on Art as vehicle. Objective Drama was clearly more of an interim period than a preparation for the current work that developed only afterwards in Italy.

In 1984 and early 1985, the Centro per la Sperimentazione e la Ricerca Teatrale in Pontedera initiated the idea of the Centro di Lavoro di Jerzy Grotowski (Workcenter of Jerzy Grotowski). The prologue to this work was a seminar in the villa dei Marchesi Frescobaldi (near Florence) between 12 June and 12 August 1985. The opening of the Workcenter was announced at a conference on 15 July 1985 in the Gabinetto Vieusseux in Florence. Since August 1986 the research program of the Workcenter has been conducted in Tuscany. It is supported by the Centro per la Sperimentazione e la Ricerca Teatrale, the Region of Tuscany, American foundations, and private donors.

Associated with the center are the University of California-Irvine and Peter Brook's Centre International de Creations Theatrales in Paris.

The work on Art as vehicle corresponds to a reclusive phase in Grotowski's life, and one should take this quite literally. He lives and works in a village several kilometers from Pontedera. This seclusion by choice, however, does not mean a refuge from the world or escapist posturing. On the contrary: it is a special calling (a lay one in this particular instance), an expression of the striving for a transformation of man's mode of existence in this world:

> Intentional, chosen, and mobilizing solitude has nothing to do with isolation or alienation [. . .] since it is rooted in the affairs of the world and society, in spiritual and transcendental values as well as material ones. [. . .] It values everything that aims at a creative development of man.
>
> (Osinska 1988:14)

This solitude comes from the deepest human need to free oneself from constraints and limitations in order to be fully able, in silence, to focus on the work that needs to be done. Therefore, it is an active and creative state, in which exploration and knowledge do not mean the ability to describe the world in theoretical terms, but rather a constant preference for action, to which everything else is subordinated. A respect for silence and concentration is naturally connected with

> a desire to reach the deepest layers of human existence – the depths of one's inner, spiritual environment, where creative silence reigns and where the experience of *sacrum* occurs. [. . .] Solitude also symbolizes bonds with people, since the more profoundly we experience our existence and open ourselves up to spiritual values, the stronger are our relationships with other people.
>
> (Osinska 1988:8–9)

At the same time I want to emphasize that Grotowski's is not a hermitage in the religious (denominational or sectarian) sense. This seeming hermitage is no more than a very special artistic studio, and its basic goal is unconditional integrity, and not proselytization.

II

A Tuscan village. There are four of us: Barbara Schwerin von Krosigk from West Berlin, author of the first book in German on Grotowski (1986); another German woman, Catherine Seyfert, whom I had met in Poland (at the turn of the decade she took part in the Theatre of Participation and was later one of Grotowski's instructors in the Theatre of Sources); an Italian director from Bergamo, Renzo Vescovi; and myself. We walk up a hill. On the right, we pass an old red barn converted into a workspace. Further along the country road fields stretch out to the right and the horizon encloses the Apennine mountain range. On the left, low houses. Before the last of them, just next to the roadside, Grotowski greets us and invites us inside. We enter a kitchen that serves as a common room: a place to meet, to talk, to receive visitors.

As it turns out, more people live in the house. Each has a separate room. Grotowski lives in a neighboring house and his two-room apartment is filled primarily with books. Seventeen participants in this work have rented rooms in the village, down the hill, or in nearby towns. They are divided into two parallel teams, and several of the members of both teams work in yet a third. During my visit, work began each day punctually at noon and ended around 10:00 p.m. One works ten hours a day and more – as much as is necessary. Often it is fifteen or sixteen hours a day.

Most of the activities take place in two converted rooms of an old farmhouse. In each of the rooms, wooden tiles have been laid on the stone floor. Next door to the work rooms are a dressing room, a bathroom, and a small kitchen where one can eat and drink during the breaks between sessions.

The conditions of life and work are very modest. The participants themselves cover the cost of their room and board. The group is composed of about twenty people, all brought up and educated in Western culture. They have come from Argentina, Belgium, Denmark, France, Greece, Holland, Mexico, Norway, Poland, and Italy. There is also a French woman born in a Laotian family and a Canadian of American Indian descent. They are young people, and with one exception there is no one here who has been with Grotowski in the previous stages of his work. This exception is one of his main collaborators, Maud Robart. She worked with Grotowski in Haiti from 1978, and together with a group of Haitians she participated in his work in Poland. She was also at Irvine. His other main collaborator is Thomas Richards of the United States, whose father's ancestors came from Jamaica.

The work takes place in three groups. Twice I saw the work of two of the groups. Each group always uses the same room and is always composed of the same people. The first group has four men and one woman. Their work takes place in the downstairs room, and it is led by Richards, with whom Grotowski has worked regularly since 1985. The second group, led by Robart, is made up of two men and six women.

Grotowski does not lead the work of the groups himself and seldom interferes directly. Instead, he works with his main collaborators, the leaders of the respective subgroups. This is practical work. During the work of a group he may appear in a room at any given moment. He sits down in a chair as an observer, from time to time jots something down in his notebook. At times, he also leads an analysis in the group.

Work always begins punctually, to the minute. The participants wear white clothing. Their shoes are removed at the entrance to the room – only because the wooden tile is fragile, not for some symbolic reason.

Sometimes work begins with a very special walk-dance executed with the spine and knees slightly bent, while the hips remain motionless. The students walk one behind the other for a very long time. Often this walk-dance is also accompanied by a song, and the manner of singing releases the vibratory qualities of the voice, which in turn assists the movement of the body. Accuracy and precision are crucial. The steps must be exact, the body is "flowing" the entire time, and, as in Stanislavsky training, the precise structure of tempo and rhythm is observed. I call this step the "serpentine." I learn from Grotowski that it is an ancient form of dance movement, linked to the "reptile brain," and that Haitians may associate it with the earliest ancestor of man, the serpent Dhamballa. In Haiti this walk-dance is called *yanvalou*.

The physical training constitutes the permanent part of the program. Each of the participants always performs nine exercises assigned to him or her. Each has a different set of exercises, aimed at helping the participant to overcome a particular physical block or limitation and to develop the proficiencies that he or she is lacking. Beyond the nine main exercises, the physical training consists of a dance, though it does not resemble any of the dances I know. Each of the participants has worked out his or her individual form of the dance.

Much of the program focuses on details. Fundamental to this work is that here technique is paramount and everything is highly structured. This is already evident in the physical training itself, but even more so in the creative activities proper, which are called "Action" [*Akcja*]. In its emphasis on technique and structure, Art as vehicle differs from the Theatre of Participation and the Theatre of Sources, while resembling (but only in this one respect) Grotowski's purely theatrical practice.

So far, the door of the room has been left open. Now the windows are covered, the lights are put out, the door is closed, everything necessary for the Action is prepared. Every day the ritual is evoked anew. Always the same and yet each time not just the same. This ritual is appearance, is reappearance, and not just a theatre creation, or an imitation or reconstruction of any of the familiar rituals. (After all, here, the words "Action" or "Actions" are used instead of "ritual.") Nor is it a synthesis of rituals which, in Grotowski's opinion, would be impossible in practice. In the widely publicized attempts to create "syntheses of ritual" (in Germany and the United States, for example), the alleged syntheses are nothing but the effect of "verbal manipulations, which seek a combination of distinct elements by virtue of their superficial similarity" (Grotowski 1987:107).

Grotowski's work, on the other hand, has elements related concomitantly to several traditions which are archetypal. These elements are set into a composition. The conscious development of a frame structure of the Action is also present, and so is a strict composition whose sense, significance, and possible narrative motifs have a common coordinate in the consciousness of the doers. In a theatre performance, on the other hand, the common coordinate is called forth in the consciousness of the spectators. Grotowski defines the technical difference between a theatre production and a ritual in relation to "the place of montage." In the production, the spectators' minds are the place of the montage. In the ritual, the montage takes place in the minds of the doers.

The connection with old initiation practices is very subtle, and the basic duty of each doer is to do everything well. This should be understood in a tangible, almost physical, sense. The body must respond properly and precisely, and must not pump up emotions and expression. Therefore, Grotowski would not ask anyone, "Do you believe?" but "You must do well what you do, with understanding."

In an interview for *Zycie Warszawy* shortly after my ten-day stay at the Grotowski Workcenter, I said:

> Here one can see a fulfilment of everything that was part of Grotowski's earlier work. One works on technique and on the precision of detail. Never, in any theatre in the world, did I see anything so spiritual, so pure. No, I will never describe this as theatre, as I once described the Teatr Laboratorium's *Akropolis* and *The Constant Prince*. [. . .] If I described what I saw, what I experienced at Pontedera, as a production, I would feel disgraced. Maybe someone else would be able to live with his conscience if he did so. I couldn't.

> (in Stepien 1988:3)

Still, it is possible to describe the basic elements of this work. They are songs, physical actions (in Stanislavsky's sense), dances, structural elements of movement, texts, and narrative motifs so old that they are anonymous.

The Action is evoked and accomplished each day in its totality. Sometimes it is executed every few days if the technical work on details or the search for some elements from scratch take up too much time. The theatre functions in relation to the spectators who come to see a production. Here, the logic and clarity of the Actions are essential and – through these Actions – the process of participants bringing them to life. There is no place for spectators as such.

The door opens. The windows are uncovered. The lights are turned on. After a longer break, the sustained, arduous work on specific details continues. One works through to the end.

We leave the room for a nearby hill from which the surrounding area, the sculpturing and architectonics of the terrain, can be seen perfectly. Out in the open, in complete silence and concentration, an intricate sequence of positions and body stretches called the Motions are executed. These positions and movements are always aimed in the six directions: east, west, north, south, zenith and nadir. If they are executed in an open space, their first direction is east (toward the rising sun) or west (toward the setting sun). Physically, these Motions are difficult; for beginners, they are sometimes mixed with pain. For example, certain balancing positions – one leg stretched and completely straightened at the knee, raised parallel to the earth, while the other is bent at the knee – are held for long periods of time. A preoccupation with the greatest precision possible is apparent everywhere. Everyone executes the positions and body movements in unison, in precisely the same rhythm.

After nearly an hour of the Motions we make our way downwards. The work is over.

The work – and this is important – takes place in almost complete silence. Speech is limited to that which is absolutely necessary.

Later, at night, Grotowski continues to work with his main collaborators.

Will the sequence of activities be precisely the same the next day? Perhaps only some part will be extended? And will this go on each day – for weeks, for months, for years?

This, no doubt, is very hard work. For Grotowski's collaborators it must be painstaking, perhaps even tedious. One must always counter the crisis of fatigue, the temptation of mechanization ("I already know," "I already know how"). It is necessary to take up the challenge. To wrestle with oneself as if against oneself – against one's own weariness and weakness.

III

The significance of Grotowski's text, "Performer," may be compared only to that of his book, *Towards a Poor Theatre* (1968). "Performer" is an unusually restrained pronouncement; it has not a single superfluous word. Its precision and exactitude make "Performer" a difficult text that requires effort on the part of the reader or listener. One can treat it as a programmatic text. However, I would prefer to speak of it as a kind of testimony.

Throughout his life, almost since childhood, Grotowski has steered his explorations in two directions: on the one hand, the personal, internal, and esoteric, for himself and possibly several other people; and on the other hand, the external, public, and exoteric. The first current has always constituted the foundation of his work, concealed from the outside observer. It is, at the same time, closely connected with rigorous discipline and technique. It is hardly a coincidence that Grotowski's explorations have always had a technical character: they have been an in-depth probing of techniques. Art as vehicle is no different in this respect. The center's official document states:

> The aim of the Workcenter of Jerzy Grotowski is to transmit to several persons of the younger generation the conclusions – practical, technical, methodological and creative – linked with the work that Grotowski has developed during the last 30 years.
>
> Candidates are persons with artistic experience – in some cases beginners – who are active in the field of performing arts, and who possess not only a specific interest, but also the creative capacities and determination needed for work based on rigor and precision. However, this is in no way a school. Rather it is a creative institute for continuous education aimed at self-responsible, adult artists. Here, Dramatic Art is a vehicle for individual development; the activities consist mainly of creative work, in Grotowski's terms.
>
> During the first years, about 200 young professionals from Europe and America have taken part in the activities of the Workcenter; the time span of their participation has varied from several days to many months. This is one of the characteristic aspects of the way the Workcenter functions.
>
> The rudimentary aspects are the following:
> Relation: precision/organicity
> Relation: tradition/individual work
> Relation: ritual/drama
> Dance and rhythm
> Singing
> Vibration of the voice
> Body resonators and spatial resonance
> Respiration
> Awareness of space and reacting to its constituent elements
> Improvisation: the impulses/the vigilant mind
> Improvisation within a structure
> Montage of physical actions
> Montage with regard to the role
> Search for a precise line and a logic of impulses and physical actions: the score

> The group involved in the program for long-term participation (from several months to a few years) numbers between 10 and 20 people, working simultaneously during the same period.
>
> (Workcenter of Jerzy Grotowski: 1988:25)

Grotowski's work is not easy to verbalize. The danger of vulgarization and possible distortions always exists. Art as vehicle encompasses polarity and duality, joined once again in a state of complete unity. This further increases the difficulty of description and interpretation.

Let me reiterate: the center is almost like an artistic–creative hermitage. This means, among other things, that no public demonstrations are organized here. Only the participants systematically working here and the visitors invited by Grotowski can know this work. The visitors are not spectators, however, as in the theatre, but *witnesses*. The witnesses are simply to attest to what they have seen and felt and, when necessary, to give a reliable testimony.

It is impossible to anticipate what will happen at the center in the future. It is certain, however, that theatre productions oriented toward a spectator will never take place here.

For theatre people to draw conclusions from Grotowski's present experience is just their own business, a matter of their own responsibility. Peter Brook said that from time immemorial there have been centers that are not unlike the one conducted by Grotowski at present (Ch. 38). (They have been called, I would add, mysteries [*misteria*], centers for work on oneself, etc.) It is for this reason that Brook speaks, in this case, of art as a vehicle. A truly creative theatre cannot exist without such a base; it has always drawn on explorations carried on in silence and seclusion. And if one delves into history deeply enough, it may turn out that much of the most creative inspiration has sprung from isolation, from the realm where, to quote Grotowski, "silence and solitude, most literally conceived are the two most important conditions for one's work on oneself" (1987:110).

The work conducted near Pontedera should be placed in a larger context of sources, cultural roots, and traditions. This work is closely linked with ancient rituals and the "art of performing" in the traditional, archaic sense. Analogies to the ancient mysteries are also clear. Grotowski's work might in fact be seen as part of the "great mysteriosophical movement in the West, which at the beginning of our era embraced gnosticism, hermeticism, Greco-Egyptian alchemy, and the tradition of the mysteries" (Eliade 1984:217). Yet Grotowski searches for something that existed even earlier. He is concerned with uncovering not "something new but something forgotten." He is speaking here about the relation "I–I," about a search for Self in self, about a discovering of Self with oneself and (through self in Self) of one's forebears. "You are someone's son," as Grotowski has said (Ch. 30). It is not that you have come from nowhere and belong to no one. It has always been like that with Grotowski, including the time when he was working on the Objective Drama project in California. What is at stake in Art as vehicle, however, is, as Grotowski says, something much more radical: "Can one touch something which is no longer linked to the beginnings but – if I dare say – to *the beginning*?' (Ch. 37:377).

For Grotowski, only a direct relationship to tradition exists, one that can be compared to stargazing. In 1970, he had this to say to the participants in the Latin American Festival in Colombia:

> Tradition is truly active if it is like the air we breathe without thinking about it. If you must force yourself to accept tradition, if you must make spasmodic efforts to search for it and, having found it, to hold it up ostentatiously, then the tradition is no longer alive inside you. There is no point to do that which has ceased to be alive because it will not be true.
>
> (1972:118)

Art as vehicle situates itself within tradition thus conceived. The relationship with tradition is direct and thus alive, since only a living tradition can actually exert an influence. What is affected, conceived through "spasmodic effort," and "forced," is dead.

In ancient Greece, Beauty, Truth, and Good were one. The aesthetic function ("the beautiful") did not exist independently until art was emancipated, the consequence of which was its gradual degeneration and degradation. Already in Grotowski's theatrical period, the aesthetic aspect was not the most important in his productions. But critics isolated this aspect from among others and separated it from an entire complex by bringing their perceptions of other theatres to the work of the Teatr Laboratorium. They thus reduced its work to an aesthetic. Of course, people always see what they want to see and what they are capable of seeing. But such a perceptual limitation has by no means trivial consequences. When two people see the same thing, then it is not the same thing at all. It is necessary to remember this when dealing with the published evidence of the reception of the work of Grotowski and the Teatr Laboratorium.

In the interview for *Zycie Warszawy*, I said:

> I think that there, in that Tuscan village, emerges something similar to what the Eleusinian mysteries were, for example, in the life of ancient Greece. It is apparent that the social and cultural context is completely different now than it was a thousand years ago. Man too is different, and

yet the question arises: what do we have in common with those people?
[. . .]

I am not claiming that what Grotowski does with his group is the
Eleusinian mysteries, but that in our culture it can serve a similar function.
After all, the ancient mysteries were not for the crowds either, and yet
through the ages they have proved an important and creative inspiration.
All textbooks of theatre history discuss the significance of the mysteries
for the theatre, even though the mysteries themselves were not theatre.
[. . .]

I am also aware that in Grotowski's present research, which strives to
tap the hidden and forgotten knowledge of thousands of years ago, what
is at stake is not a performance or its evaluation. I would like to be well
understood: by no means do I deny a need for the theatre. I myself attend
and respect it, and I have more than respect for several of its representatives. But for Grotowski, the game is played for different stakes. Surely
the highest possible. [. . .]

And does it have to take place among a crowd? With applause, with
television, the press, away from peace and quiet?

(in Stepien 1988:3)

My response to this last question today is the same as after my return
from Italy: Such places cannot be open nowadays. If they were,
television crews and newspaper reporters from across the globe would
find their way there immediately. But if this were to happen, a murder
would be committed against what emerges there in the daily labor, effort,
and struggle.

IV

In addition to the work described above, the center also organizes
seminars and workshops. On 13 and 14 February 1987, about thirty
invited guests from many countries attended a closed theoretical seminar.
Grotowski informed them about his work and shared his reflections. A
month later (on 14 March), at a meeting in the Medici Riccardi Palace
in Florence, Grotowski, accompanied by Peter Brook, spoke publicly for
the first time about the work of the center that bears his name. Over 200
people participated.

In July 1987, the Centre d'Aide Technique et de Formation Theatrales
in Brussels organized a month-long meeting between the Workcenter and
young theatre troupes from all over northern Europe. The meeting took
place at the Chateau de l'Ermitage in France, near the Belgian border. It
consisted of demonstrations of the work, its analysis, and three
workshops for actors and directors. Each of the workshops lasted ten

days. A conference with Grotowski was held in the Palace Hotel in the center of Brussels.

After a seminar in February 1987, the well-known French critic and theatre historian Georges Banu wrote in the Paris *Art-Press* in May 1987:

> Grotowski intends to closet himself not alone with books – like Craig, but – alone with others. After turning the Western theatrical world upside down at the beginning of the century, Craig retired to Florence in the '30s, where he created the Arena Goldoni; and Grotowski finds his tower only 20 kilometers away, at the academy of Pontedera. There he convened some friends of his, in order to talk in the context of a family-like security, and to avoid the social game. [. . .] He is a voice from beyond the theatre, a voice which incarnates this supreme demand, whose vocation is not to save an art, but rather to help a being to accomplish himself.
>
> (Banu 1987:40–41)

Such *trailblazing* appears to be essential to the significance of the Art as vehicle in a broader context. After all, the trailblazing – and not the founding of a creative sect or the closing up into a special group of people – has been central to each period of Grotowski's creative work both in the theatre and outside the theatre. Grotowski would probably agree with Osterwa, who in October 1919, wrote: "If we don't get there, then others, who will come after us, will; we will perhaps have shown them which way the road lies" (Osterwa 1968:52).

At the very heart of Grotowski's explorations lies a conviction about the existence of cultural generalities or cultural universals. This means that in a great many cultures certain elements are common, and thus they must have preceded cultural differentiation. In Grotowski's words, "sources – something quite simple – are given to each individual" – "they are something given at the beginning":

> One could say that human nature is the same everywhere despite the cultural differentiation of people. A sociologist might think this theory about human nature an entirely backward view, but to dismiss it completely would seem racist to me. [. . .] When we talk about sources, one might rather say: man precedes difference.
>
> (Grotowski 1987:108)

For the Grotowski of Objective Drama, it was the "performative fragments" that were universal. They revealed "man [who] precedes difference." And thus the job was to uncover those "performative fragments" in action, to see how they remain alive, to draw them out, to "purify" them, and finally to "preserve" them and to mobilize them in a different context.

With Grotowski, the ancient opposition between *imitatio* and *creatio* is annulled. We know that the ancients, the Greeks of the classical age, for example, did not believe art to be creation, and the value of art did not consist of creatio. On the contrary, its value lay in the fact that it corresponded to a set of fixed rules, the eternal forms of the cosmos. The ancients believed that art should uncover and expose these forms, and not create them. At the same time, the function of art was seen as imitation, mimesis, conceived of not as a slavish repetition of reality but as the free enunciation of the artist about it. Clearly, the task was still *imitatio*.

It is only since the Renaissance that art in the West has been defined as *creatio*. The modern age considers creativity to be *the* characteristic that distinguishes art from other human activities: "There is no art without creation, and wherever there is creation, there is art as well" (Tatarkiewicz 1989:267). The modern belief, which identifies art with creation, is supported by yet another conviction: that art has the right and obligation to produce new forms. Thus novelty should be one of the greatest virtues of a work of art. For the avant-garde, novelty becomes the fundamental value. From this belief springs the morbid race to be always ahead, which in the West very often bears all the marks of a cultural pathology.

For the ancients, of course, novelty was not a virtue. They even believed that an eagerness for new forms was only an obstacle in their search for the perfect forms, which they considered the true function of art.

Grotowski has never been a modern artist. Even during the theatrical period, Ludwik Flaszen, Grotowski's closest collaborator, saw the creative work in the Teatr Laboratorium as being much nearer to the "rear-guard" than to the "avant-garde" – a statement that was not simply an intellectual provocation, as his speech, "After the Avant-garde," was interpreted at the time. Here are the closing lines of the speech which Flaszen delivered on 25 February 1967, at the International Congress of Young Writers in Paris:

> Our work may be understood as an effort to restore the ancient values of the theatre. We are not moderns, but traditionalists through and through. [. . .] It just so happens that the most startling things are those which have already been. The deeper the well of time that separates us from them, the more they strike us as novelty.

> (1983:364)

Grotowski himself was strikingly consistent in the matter of his alleged avant-gardism. Yet for whatever reasons, the people writing about him did not see or did not want to see his consistency. Here is the very characteristic final paragraph from his speech on 22 August 1969, published separately eleven years later as "A Reply to Stanislavsky":

> I do not think that my work in the theatre may be described as a new method. It can be called a method, but it is a very narrow term. Neither do I believe that it is something new. That kind of exploration most often took place outside the theatre, though inside some theatres as well. What I have in mind is a way of life and cognition. It is a very old way. How it is articulated depends on period and society. I am not sure whether those who painted on the walls of the Trois Frères cave sought merely to exorcise their fear. Perhaps [. . .] but not only. And I think that the painting was not the goal. The painting was the way. In this regard I feel much closer to that cave painter than to artists who think that they create the avant-garde of the new theatre.
>
> (Grotowski 1980:119)

Among avant-garde artists and would-be avant-gardists, Grotowski has always been different. He was and is a changeling [*odmieniec*]. This is the root of the paradox of his situation. He has been declared the "Pope of the world's theatrical avant-garde." Granted, he has been a modern artist in one sense: he blazed the trails, he cleared the way. But as is clearly evident today, those routes were mapped out, above all, for himself alone and according to his own standards. Others who attempted to hike the mountain trail forged by Grotowski broke their necks. He has always remained alone.

When speaking of Art as vehicle, the best and safest recourse is to focus on technique and mastery, on craft and competency. One can also evoke the "sacred dances" of Gurdjieff and the "physical actions" of Stanislavsky. I would, however, like to quote from the Polish poet Cyprian Norwid, who, in *Promethidion* (1850), thus envisioned the art of the future:

> the apostle's highest craft,
> the angel's humblest prayer.

Today, when I think of what I had the privilege to see in Pontedera over half a year ago, I feel particularly close to this image of the poet: the hermit and the outsider who conceives of art as both the humblest prayer and the highest craft, and of aesthetics as a living and positive asceticism.

Translated by Halina Filipowicz and Anna Heron.
Edited by Halina Filipowicz.

Plate 39.1 Motions at the Workcenter of Jerzy Grotowski. Mario Biagini, Przemyslaw Wasilkowski and Thomas Richards. (Photo: Alan Volut.)

Plate 39.2 Motions. (Photo: Alan Volut.)

Plate 39.3   Motions at the Workcenter of Jerzy Grotowski. (Photo: Alain Volut.)

Plate 39.4   Motions. (Photo: Alain Volut.)

Plate 39.5   Motions at the Workcenter of Jerzy Grotowski. (Photo: Alain Volut.)

Plate 39.6   Motions. (Photo: Alan Volut.)

WHERE IS *GURUTOWSKI*?

Halina Filipowicz

In 1986, Kazimierz Braun, a distinguished Polish director, confronted his readers in Poland and the United States with a compelling question: "Where is Grotowski?" (1986, 1986a).

It was not impossible to view Braun's essay as a planned provocation that disparaged Grotowski (see Burzynski 1989). Braun presented him, or so the argument went, as a has-been who left no trace in the collective cultural memory or the current theatre practice. It remains an open question why Braun felt it necessary at the time to indulge (in the English version of the article) in a political insinuation, or why he turned his reservations about misguided criticism into an attack (in the Polish version) on the "incompetence" of theatre scholarship. This is an issue that must be left, at least for the present, hanging.

But behind Braun's "Where is Grotowski?" I could not help hearing a less strident tone. His question reverberated with the elegiac sense of an ending and the pervasive sense of exile from the time when the guru from Poland commanded the attention of the world. Braun's question may well have been: "Where is *Gurutowski*?"[1] And so his essay seemed less an uneasy confession of aversion than a testimony of cultural as well as personal deprivation:

> Where are the candles flickering on a low table, moving shadows on his concentrated and inspired face when he teaches, preaches, prophesies? Where is the fire flaring up high on the mountain, behind his head, as an aureole, while he sits looking at the sacred dance of his tribe? Where are the words about brotherhood? About [the] elements? About the mystery?
>
> (1986:240)

In the 1970s, *Gurutowski* filled a need of many who heard about him from enigmatic reports, who went on pilgrimages to Poland's new holy place, Wroclaw, who tried to recapture their experience in eager testimonials. But it has been difficult to keep up with Grotowski's evolution, as if his real name were *Growtowski*. Anyone's foothold in the vast reaches of his vision has been precarious from the start. He eludes even his most loyal followers, as Zbigniew Osinski found out when he published an important essay on convention and anticonvention in the Laboratory Theatre. New publications by Grotowski, cautions Osinski in the final footnote, make it necessary "to reinterpret" some of the issues raised in the article (1972:47).

The exasperating elusiveness of Grotowski is, most obviously, a matter of language. We will do well to remember that Grotowski has always been adept at multilingual communication. I do not mean his command of foreign languages but rather his proficiency in different kinds of discourse. If his public statements must be approached cautiously, it is because he is among those artists who, deliberately or not, use an official language to conceal rather than reveal their ideas. As his predilection for such verbal masks as "active culture" and "objective drama" shows only too well, his language as a public figure and as an artist are two quite different things, often at odds with one another. He says only what he believes needs to be said at a given moment – not merely to secure funding for his work but, more importantly, to protect a creative process that is far from completion as well as articulation.

These strategies of evasion are further complicated by publications which turn to Grotowski for legitimation. What are we to make of Andrzej Bonarski's interview with Grotowski, which is copyrighted by the latter rather than the former (Bonarski 1979:44)? What are we to make of Osinski's article, "Grotowski Blazes the Trails: From Objective Drama to Art as vehicle," which sometimes refers us to the source, sometimes masks quotations by cunning cannibalization (Ch. 39)? It is only fair to add that Osinski's article has been scrutinized by Grotowski for terminology and turns of speech. The question "Who owns the text?" becomes a particularly thorny one when a text in question concerns Grotowski. Braun reproachfully described the "servility" of Grotowski's explicators (1986:231). "Deference" may be a more elegant word, but it still will not cut through layers of coded words and strategies of mystification, which obscure Grotowski's official language.

New complications arise when Grotowski's work is regarded within an orientation to theatre praxis. To be sure, Peter Brook, in his memorable "Preface" to *Towards a Poor Theatre*, conceded: "For Grotowski acting is a vehicle" (1968:13). He hinted at a mystical interpretation ("A way of life is a way to life"), but he did not pursue it further lest he should appear an exponent of a vicious dogma (1968:13). In "Grotowski: Art as a Vehicle," Brook seems to take up where he left off in 1968. Armed with hedges ("I use an explosive word [. . .] which creates many misunderstandings"), he tells us that Grotowski's explorations are "a spiritual search" grounded in "the need of the beyond" (Ch. 38; Peter Brook has deleted the latter phrase from the version of his article that appears in this volume). However, Brook's position in "Grotowski: Art as a Vehicle" is ultimately that of a theatre practitioner speaking to other theatre practitioners: yes, Grotowski's current work is more unusual than before, but the theatre may still hope to find something for itself in his laboratory. Such a conclusion decenters the claim about the spiritual search. If Grotowski's new work indeed falls within the long tradition of mysticism – and this is what Brook seems to imply – then its potential for serving the theatre's practical needs of the moment is really beside the point (for a similar conclusion, see Kolankiewicz 1989a:138).

While Brook was beating about the bush, Jan Blonski and Jan Kott wasted no time. Grotowski's Laboratory Institute in Wroclaw, argued Blonski in 1976, had as much in common with the theatre as the experience of Jacob Boehme, a German mystic, had with shoemaking (1981:123). Kott reported that Grotowski gave him a French translation of Martin Buber's *The Tales of the Hasidim*. This is the book, Grotowski told Kott, with which he never parts. Over a plate of pierogi later that evening, "the former guru," noted Kott, looked like one of the Hasidim (Ch. 31:306). Blonski's and Kott's essays are separated by almost fifteen years. Could it be that Grotowski's current investigations represent not a turn in a radically new direction but rather a continuation of his lifetime project? It is not irrelevant to point out that in one of his most recent programmatic texts, "Performer," Grotowski quotes extensively from two sermons by Meister Eckhart, a medieval German mystic accused of heretical teaching and censured by the Catholic Church (see ch. 37). It certainly would not be too much to say that Grotowski's work has always situated itself among twentieth-century versions of Pascal's wager, which put the stakes not on metaphysics and faith, but on a precarious hope that individual life is not meaningless in the vast universe that surrounds us.

Grotowski is not an artist in the conventional sense of the word. When commentators such as Brook view his explorations with an eye to their application in the theatre, they deny what is, I believe, central to Grotowski's work: an expansion of what can be thought, not what can be done. He works – has always worked – on the margins of knowledge, constantly interrogating our assumptions about cultural authority, constantly thinking beyond the limits. He is a man of the margins who has turned his marginal and ex-centric position to his advantage. Born in a country along the edges of European culture, he has always situated himself on the borders of artistic centers in every possible way. He did his theatre work in Opole and Wroclaw rather than Warsaw or Cracow. Later, he defied national boundaries. He eventually settled in a secluded Italian village. That he is now a stateless person can be seen as a metaphor of the modern sense of existential homelessness. But it can also be seen as an apt allegory for Grotowski's transgression of the conceptual demarcations of modern culture.

Sanford Schwartz might be describing Grotowski when he speaks of the crucial "exchange between tradition and innovation" in Eliot and Pound who viewed "artistic creativity" as a difficult balancing between "the recovery of past experience and the invention of a new voice for modernity" (1985:134). Pound searched continually, Schwartz argues, "for the right relationship between recollection and renewal, between fidelity to tradition and the will to creative innovation" (1985:136). If Grotowski's work has always resisted domestication or integration into the artistic and intellectual mainstream, it is precisely because he is not an avant-gardist but an innovator. Avant-gardists throw the past to the wind and replace it with the new. Innovators make the past new for a new age, to paraphrase Pound. The project of the avant-gardist offers ever new tricks and devices which can be duplicated, imitated, proliferated by the many acolytes who throng around him or her. The project of the innovator creates new meanings out of the broken shards of the past.

Osinski (in "Grotowski Blazes the Trails") agrees that Grotowski, as an innovator, is a bearer of tradition (see also Gerould 1980 and Puzyna 1980). But Osinski and other scholars as well propose a premodernist reading of *a postmodern thinker*. Osinski's central metaphor of blazing the trails implies a determined course forward and glosses over contradictions and waverings. He writes about Grotowski on the assumption that his work is always organically unified, that the antithetical tendencies within it are eventually reconciled in a harmonious whole. It is not surprising, then, that Osinski finds it difficult to deal with those aspects of Grotowski's work which are not easily assimilated on the assumption of unity. And so he tells us that Grotowski's work defies verbalization. But Grotowski seeks to disrupt the very conceptual model of unity by which he is judged. Concomitantly, Grotowski is aware, I am sure, that "in a culture that has lost established principles of order, chaos and dogma are the two extremes to which the mind is prey" (Schwartz 1985:133).

Perhaps, then, rather than lament the "incompetence" of theatre scholarship or the inability of the current linguistic practice to keep pace with Grotowski, we should adopt new critical approaches that would correspond to his own disruption of the ruling paradigm. The lessons of deconstruction and feminist criticism may be useful in examining – from different angles – creative tensions and productive interactions between the contradictory elements in Grotowski's work. Feminism, through its deconstructive strategies for displacing "male" readings of texts, may help us understand the concept of the "author" in the writings by and about Grotowski. Deconstruction may allow us to unravel the central contradiction in his work: like the literary and philosophical texts of the Western culture, it contains both what may be called metaphysics and the putting in question of metaphysics. Does Grotowski's lifetime project involve the invention of forms that would change the way in which we order reality? Or does it seek the recovery of alternative forms of awareness – from the past, from non-Western cultures – that might allow us to renew a world fragmented, unstable, incomplete?

The village near Pontedera, where Grotowski now works, is in Dante's Tuscany. Mandelstam, in a late poem, celebrates the "universal hills" of his beloved Dante's region. "For Dante," writes Mandelstam elsewhere, "time is the content of history understood as a single synchronic act; and vice-versa: the contents of history are the joint containing of time by associations, competitors, and co-discoverers" (1979:420). In the universal hills of Tuscany, Grotowski has joined fellow outsiders, conspirators, and investigators. He has subverted the provincialism of geography as well as the "provincialism of time" (Pound 1973:168). The ungraspable reach of Grotowski's vision obliterates the lines that divide languages, peoples, and cultures. As he works across the confines of space and time, does he construct a new, encompassing tradition that would answer to the needs of the dispossessed modern age? Or does he create a common inheritance that would defy both space and time?

ACTION, THE UNREPRESENTABLE ORIGIN

Lisa Wolford

Action is a performative opus with a consciously crafted, repeatable score developed at the Workcenter of Jerzy Grotowski in Pontedera, Italy, by workleader Thomas Richards and his group of actors/doers, a stable team of performing artists who commit to a minimum of one year of intensive practical research. One could say that *Action*, the central opus of the investigation conducted by Grotowski and Richards in the field of Art as vehicle, is analogous to a theatrical performance in its structure and precision of details, its use of performative means (song, movement, physical action in the sense described by Stanislavsky (see Toporkov 1979)), and its basis in the craft of acting. Yet the structure is not intended for public performance, even though invited guests periodically witness *Action*. The essential aim of the work, its primary purpose, is not to create meaning in the perception of an outside observer, but rather to facilitate a special process that can occur within practitioners performing with and around certain songs taken from African and Afro-Caribbean ritual traditions.[1] The performing structure functions as an objective support to assist the doer in what Grotowski terms an "itinerary in verticality:"

> Verticality – we can see this phenomenon in categories of energy: heavy but organic energies (linked to the forces of life, to instincts, to sensuality) and other energies, more subtle. The question of verticality means to pass from a so-called coarse level – in a certain sense, one could say an "everyday level" – to a level of energy more subtle or even toward the *higher connection*. At this point to say more about it wouldn't be right. I simply indicate the passage, the direction. There, there is another passage as well: if one approaches the *higher connection* – that means, if we are speaking in terms of energy, if one approaches the much more subtle energy – then there is also the question of descending, while at the same time bringing this subtle something into the more common reality, which is linked to the "density" of the body. The point is not to renounce part of our nature – all should retain its natural place: the body, the heart, the head,

something that is "under our feet" and something that is "over the head."
All like a vertical line, and this verticality should be held taut between
organicity and the awareness. Awareness means the consciousness which
is not linked to language (the machine for thinking), but to Presence.

(1995:125)

At the time I witnessed *Action* – five times during July and August 1995
– the performance team consisted of Richards, Mario Biagini, Jerome
Bidaux, Nhandan Chirco, and Przemyslaw Wasilkowski.[2] It is important
to remember that Grotowski is not the director of *Action* (insofar as
"director" is an appropriate term); rather, he functions as Richards'
teacher and, in his own words, as an "advising ancestor" to the group. It
would be more appropriate to regard Richards, leader of the day-to-day
activities of the research team, as the creator of the opus, as it was he who
assembled the performance and textual montage, in addition to serving
as primary performer and teacher for the group members.

When visitors arrive to witness *Action*, they are led into a room in the
upstairs portion of the Workcenter building, adjacent to the workspace.
Mario Biagini gives a brief introduction to prepare the witnesses for what
they are about to see. Biagini is fluent in various languages, including
French, English, and Italian, and addresses the visitors in whatever
language they best understand. What you are about to see, he tells us, is
Action. He counsels that it is better if we do not try to make some story
from this *Action*; if we are looking for an analogy, he suggests, it is more
like poetry than narrative prose. He requests that the witnesses not try to
participate in the songs by singing along with the doers, clapping, or
moving in their chairs in the rhythm of the songs. Just watch, he
proposes, and listen.

Biagini tells us that *Action* includes some fragments of text in English,
translated from a very old source, so old that no one knows for certain
where it originated or who its author (or authors) might have been. He
explains that the text was translated literally from Coptic, word for word.
(In a meeting afterwards with the group that witnessed *Action* that
evening, Grotowski clarified that it was Biagini himself who made the
translation, and that they chose to remain as close to the Coptic version
as possible rather than render the text in proper English because the
person(s) at the source of the text had very precise reasons for choosing
the words and formulations they did. "We have no right to interpret.")
Biagini gives each visitor a sheet of paper with a transcription of this
text.[3] He allows time for us to read the fragments thoroughly, then
collects the papers. After receiving some signal that the others are ready
to begin, he leads the witnesses toward the workspace.

The room where *Action* is done not a performance space in the conventional sense of the term. Nor is it "ritual space," in the sense of mystical or elevated atmosphere. It is simply a room, a place where people once went about their business in ordinary ways. It is a large, open space, approximately 40 × 25 feet, with white stucco walls and reddish wood tiling covering a portion of the floor. (The tile was added during the renovation of the workspace.) At the far end of the room is an arched passage, opening on to other rooms we cannot see. A number of folding chairs are positioned in an area near the doorway, always precisely enough for the number of people witnessing the structure on a given evening; I have never seen the room prepared for more than six visitors. The threshold between the wooden tile and the simple concrete divides the main work floor from the place where the visitors are seated. The visitors are placed at an angle near one wall in the area between the tiled space and the door – a place where we will not be in the way.

The room was not structurally altered to accommodate *Action*. And yet, the separation of the tiled floor from the place where we are sitting, the white walls and the arched door at the far end of the space, conspire to create something faintly resembling a stage. The primary source of illumination is ordinary electric ceiling lights, though four white candles burn in clay bowls arranged at intervals near the far portion of the space. The work room is liminal space, space set apart for a specific purpose, charged with a particular quality of concentration. The space, which is also laminated with the particular expectations and behavioral codes of Workcenter culture, requests a type of silent attention, alertness and anticipation – a response I noted not only in myself, but in the other visitors.

A Sufi master once said that the worst form of lying is to speak as if one knows about what one does not know. Lying destroys memory in essence. I cannot understand *fully* what is *Action*, because it is a practice that finds its primary meaning among those who do; as an outside observer, I have only partial access to what and how it means. Further, I have only partial recall of details – some songs, some fragments are omitted in my telling, as in my memory. Another witness would tell this differently, and the doers differently still.

But I want to tell you a story. It is a story that unfolds like a dream, or like memory, with its strange eddies and currents, fragmented in some moments, dilated in others, still others altogether washed away.

At the beginning of *Action* the door to the space opens and the doers file silently into the room. There are five of them, four men and one woman, the men dressed in dark blue pants and simple white shirts (except for Richards, who is all in white) and the woman in a full-skirted dress, mid-calf length, with a yellow background and flower print. They seat themselves on a low wall or ledge running along the back portion of the room, the men on one side, the woman on the other. Bidaux crosses to the arched doorway at the far side of the room and seats himself on the ground with his back to the visitors. He raises his right hand high in the air, one finger pointing, shaking as if with age, and begins to speak forcefully. His actions immediately communicate a sense of "character," of someone other than himself. In this instant I understood something almost parodic, a slightly exaggerated figure of a fanatical prophet speaking to his fold. He tells about coming from the place of origin, about being one of the elected people, about how he can be recognized as such.

Bidaux begins a sequence that in some way suggests the stages of life. He rolls quickly backward from his seated position in the door frame, ending on his back near one of the lit candles with his legs curled up toward his head, like an infant playing with its feet. He explores his surroundings with the curiosity of a toddler, repeating a fragment of the text he had spoken before about original light. He examines the candle, bringing his face and body close to it as if trying to understand the relation between this flame and the origin of which he speaks. He touches the flame and pulls his hand back as if startled to find himself burnt. He looks at the flame for an instant – almost resentful, almost as if betrayed. The temptation becomes too strong, and the child again reaches toward the flame. This time the candle goes out.

The actor rises, now a young man, a warrior at the height of his physical power. He assumes a martial pose, each muscle taut with anticipation, standing as if with a drawn sword poised above his head. A portion of the text recurs, this time spoken more aggressively, with arrogant self-assurance. He speaks of his privileged birthright as one of the elect. Advancing toward the center of the space, he strikes down with a forceful blow that extinguishes the second candle.

Bidaux crosses toward the third candle as a figure of decrepit age, a very different sort of old man from the "prophet" of the opening sequence, weak and without authority. Some fragment of the first text is spoken again, but now with an undertone of darkness, almost despair. He lowers himself to the ground, his final exhalation extinguishing the third candle. The natural cycle of life ends in the grave.

Bidaux moves to the center of the space in the strange, loping gait of a powerful animal. With a mixture of interrogation and amused disdain, the creature examines some small thing it sees below, as if trying to decide whether to annihilate it. This Sphinx is Guardian of the Threshold, pitiless keeper of the gate to the afterworld. It raises first one giant paw and then another, carefully placing them to either side of its potential victim – the soul or phantom of the man whose life was depicted in the previous three fragments. The Guardian smiles threateningly and asks the man from where he came. Bidaux alternates between the character of the Sphinx and that of its phantom-prey, enacting the dialogue between them. The Sphinx crouches on its haunches, the trunk of its body arched upward, powerful and superior; the man cowers on his back, looking up at the hovering Guardian. He struggles to answer its questions correctly, knowing that the very fact of his afterlife hangs in balance. The text is almost the same as that of the first sequence, repeated this time from beginning to end, but now it becomes a trial, an act of judgment, with the Sphinx as judge and executioner. The man gains courage as the interrogation continues, telling of his origin in the Light. The Guardian laughs in disbelief, demanding that he give some sign of his identity, some proof of his claim. The man describes the sign by which he should be recognized. The Guardian shakes its head, clicking its tongue doubtfully, and extinguishes the last candle with a cold finality. No afterlife for the solicitor. Thus ends the portion of *Action* I consider as the prolog.

From the rear of the space a song is heard – I have never heard singing like this before. It is begun by Richards, who sings with a fluctuation of vibration so alive, so extreme, that the song becomes in some sense tangibly present in the space. I understand in a way I never could before what Grotowski means when he speaks of "vibratory qualities which are so tangible that in a certain way they become the meaning of the song" (1995:126). The resonance is spatial, concrete; it strikes my skin in a particular way. There is something . . . almost inhuman about it, not like anything I ever imagined a human voice could do. As if not only words and melody but even the singer himself comes to be *aspirated* by the song. Not that the words or melody are made any less precise – exactly the opposite – but this powerful fluctuation of resonance – physical as well as audible – the living presence of the song, fully unearthed and embodied, is so alien to my perception, so unique, that it is as if I experience *song* for the first time.

I understand this as a song of emergence. Invocation. In the beginning. The voices of the others become secondarily discernible under that of Richards. They cross to the wood-tiled floor where Bidaux joins them. Richards is the last to move toward the tiled space, as if allowing the song to carry him, as if he rides it down – not in any externalized sense of demonstrating "journey," but rather as if the body impulses connected with the song suggest the way of moving, as if it is the song-body which crosses the space.

Silence. The doers acknowledge one another's presence – simply, without sentimentality, just by looking at each other. Really looking, as if each seeks to determine the state of his or her colleagues in that moment. Chirco clears away the clay bowls containing the extinguished candles, which are used only in the opening fragment.

The second song is a warrior song, aggressive, *tamasic*, a call and response between Richards and the group of men. I understand it as a summoning of force, charged with the power and violence of Creation. Chirco stands in the center of the room and begins a fragment in which her body dilates, not from the hips but from the chest and into the shoulders, as if something in the center of her body opens, twisting, growing. There is something volcanic and elemental in her movement, like the earth pulsing fire from within itself. She stands firmly rooted, legs apart. Richards lies on the floor behind her and passes between her legs, sliding quickly on his back, emerging from under the hem of her dress with a cane in his hand.

In contrast to the life cycle of the actor in the prolog, who progresses from infancy to death in age, Richards is born as an old man, crippled and frail. In the moment after birth he stands silent with the cane in his hand, as if becoming accustomed to the limitations and confines of the aged body: what is it, how does it function? His reactions are those of a man of seventy or more. He looks at his surroundings, at his colleagues, and then enters into connection with Biagini, whose gaze appears radiant with welcome and recognition. The power of light that surrounds Biagini is a palpable force, a tangible quality of incandescence – and all this light pours out toward Richards, as if Biagini had been waiting only for him. As if he knew that his purpose, his task, was to help this other.

The two doers approach each other and speak a fragment of text – antiphonous, chanted, incantatory. A text that I understand to speak about the coming-down-to-earth, awake, with full awareness. About a gift that is offered and ignored, or refused. About people who come into life in a drunken stupor, and seek to leave it in the same way.

Richards begins another song, this one softer, in some way more subtle than the warrior song that preceded it – as if this song resonates in a slightly higher place inside the body. As the song continues, Biagini comes close to Richards, bending down so that his head is near Richards' chest. The fragment is striking not only for the physical image it creates (Biagini is by far the taller man, towering above the others in the work team), but for something that passes between them, some current that travels from the heart of one into the body of the other. Externally, it is a simple fragment and could even be understood in a technical sense – as if Biagini were actively listening for a precise sonic resonance emanating from a specific point in Richards' body. I have an association (my own image, nothing indicated or illustrated by the doers in the space) of a bird bathing in a spring of living water. Nothing in this fragment is recognizably mimetic; my attention is captured by a moment of connection, an alive relation.

The next song, again begun by Richards, is much darker in aspect. Its tone and resonance are strikingly low, with a quality almost like weeping – a repeated, broken cry that rises from the depths of the body (all within a precisely elaborated melodic structure, nothing improvised). Richard struggles to remain upright but is eventually pressed to the ground by the weight of vibration. When the song ends, it hangs for a moment in the air; Richards slowly stands, using the cane to pull himself up.

Silence. The actor from the opening sequence lies down at Richards' feet, his hands folded on his chest in the position of a corpse. Richards stands above the corpse and gazes at it, then begins to sing a song of mourning. The song is multilayered, an intricate weaving of voices and parts accompanied by a complex pattern of clapping (not in unison, but with each doer following a precise and different rhythm). This strikes me as one of the most powerful and "tribal" of the songs, in the sense that it seems to function as a channel that focuses the energies of the group or community in a very specific way. Of the various strands of melody, Biagini's rises as dominant (something very high, both in pitch and in quality, song-as-bird, striving to ascend). Biagini begins to lead the younger doers, three of them working together in a corner of the space; in a sense, it is as if he becomes a weaver, drawing the threads of energy from each and channeling them through himself.

While the others are thus occupied, the "corpse" rises, catches Richards' attention, and begins to lead him out of the space. The risen one is a demon/trickster, almost serpent, hypnotically luring Richards in a way that is both seductive and menacing. And Richards follows, almost painfully open, gazing at the Enticer with trusting vulnerability. He continues his line of melody in the song but forgets his companions – and for some moments they are forgetful of him as well, caught up in the intricacy of their intertwining melodies. The Enticer reaches the door of the room, ready to open it and lead Richards out; his smile is victorious, threatening. Just as Richards prepares to step through the doorway, something changes in him. It is as if some other force appears, something as primal and terrible as the wrath of an avenging angel, or some fearsome being from the Afro-Caribbean tradition in which these songs were formed. The quality of the song changes, as if something very powerful and dominating appears. Richards' face becomes contorted, his eyes wide, one side of his lip curled upward. His left leg stiffens, jutting out in front of him. He advances with leg and cane together like a weapon toward the Enticer, who now cowers by the door. Relentlessly, methodically, Richards drives him back toward the central space. As Bidaux rejoins the other doers, the character of the Enticer dissolves – simply, almost invisibly, as if the actor had laid aside some mask.

For Richards, the transformation does not occur so quickly. When he arrives among the others he seems still to be conducted by the menacing power, stalking his companions and confronting each in turn. It is as if the force that inhabits his body, once summoned, is a devouring fire that attempts to destroy or consume everything in its path. The song ends abruptly, and Richards stops, lame leg outstretched. He freezes, facing Biagini as if challenging him, testing him. Silence. Connection.

Biagini as doer looks to Richards with what seems to me an abdication of all defenses, absolute trust. He begins a song I think of as a reconciling force, a healing song, song of the open heart. The song gives form to a spirit of forgiveness, a subtle radiance that permeates the room. Richards' threatening aspect dissipates. For a moment he appears again as the old man, frail and warm. Biagini takes the cane from his hand. Richards' body straightens abruptly, becoming that of a young man. The two doers face one another, mirroring the connection in the fragment after Richards' birth, and speak/sing together another fragment of text, this one about the importance of looking for Origin in the time when one is alive, because at the point of death it will no longer be possible.

Richards has moved from old age to the full force of youth. He explores his newfound range of movement, dancing in a way that is fluid and free, fully alive. There is a special lightness in this dance, like the joy of a young animal that runs for the sheer pleasure of moving. He begins a song I think of as related to a journey or passage for a young person alone. The power of this young warrior is in no way like that of the swordsman from the opening fragment – it is without anger, without arrogance. The other doers keep a supporting vocal line beneath Richards' song, responding to him, receptive to his play. From all this vitality, all this overflowing of the life force, something begins to rise, to surge upward, and Richards as leader carries the others with him on this wave.

Following this passage with its quality of joy, I perceive the next fragment as presenting a new and necessary challenge, a further threshold. Richards, in the center of the space, maintains a complex melody line; the others, around him like the points of a compass, keep a repetitive, sonorous chant with a deep, almost cavernous resonance. The chant carries them progressively toward the floor, so that each crouches low, as if pulled down by the weight of vibration. (There is no heaviness in the doers, no sense of collapsing under this weight or surrendering to it; their stances are active, oriented toward the floor, and the sound that almost seems to emanate from it.) I understand this as an incantation giving thanks. My perception (or projection, as you will) is that within the context of the incantation Richards confronts something unseen, that the numinous force the sound evokes, what it praises, makes itself present to Richards (or within him) in a form that is not only benevolent, but embraces also a terrible and destroying aspect. This is something Richards must face alone; the others cannot help him. I perceive some kind of battle within him, a struggle to accept, to keep himself open. His voice breaks. He seems almost at the point of surrendering. And then out of this struggle a deep praise emerges, not easily won, a praise of something higher. This acceptance, this surrender, releases a force of light. The doers stand swiftly, in one decisive movement. Something is tangibly different among them, some quality of joy. The song ascends.

The next song is begun by Wasilkowski, who in the frame of *Action* seems almost like an adolescent. This is the first moment in which his voice can be heard alone; it is as if each night he discovers anew some authority in the song, as if each time is the first occasion on which he ventures to make himself heard among the others. He looks to Richards, almost hesitant, and Richards, the young man, guides this adolescent as leader and teacher. The song takes time to be fully born, the others joining slowly. The four men stand together. This passage of the adolescent, his acceptance into the community of men, is something among themselves.

Detached, a little apart, Chirco begins to move in the serpentine rhythm of *yanvalou*,[4] walking with the hem of her yellow skirt raised slightly, bending forward from the waist with the fabric lifted in her hands. I remember having been told years ago that the stepping of yanvalou is a way of looking or perceiving with the foot, letting the foot first test and sense the ground before it comes down with weight. But Chirco seems to move as if not on the ground but above it, almost gliding, like a skater on ice. As if she is walking on clouds, not fully corporeal. Richards begins a song that is high and subtle, softer in tone and quality than anything he has yet been heard to sing, in praise of female godforce. The other men join softly. Chirco continues the walk-dance, approaching them as if in some way it is she who is evoked and summoned by the song. As she makes a half-circle toward the men, Biagini welcomes her from a distance and joins the yanvalou, moving first beside and then behind her. The others join also, forming a line behind Chirco – except for Richards, who remains for a time in the center of the space, rapt in the song, with his attention seemingly directed toward some memory or line of associations known only to himself. The song concludes, and the yanvalou continues in silence. As the line passes him, Richards begins to move alongside it, keeping step with the others but remaining in some way detached. The movement seems to function differently in him, as if he carries it toward some memory that he follows to its source. The memory, the actions, the flow of life inside this walk-dance, become in some sense more prominent than the yanvalou itself, until the stream of life devours the way of moving, though without ever compromising the precision of the form.

Still maintaining the yanvalou, Richards disconnects from the others and moves in the opposite direction, clockwise as they continue counterclockwise. The movement finishes and Richards begins to sing a fragment of an earlier song – the one he sang in the moment when the old man became a young man. (Does the song itself function as a spell of sorts, assisting/enabling the journey back?) Biagini comes near him, and the two sing and play together, the melody now transformed into something like a kind of laughter, a complicity between them. And now Richards is a little boy, and Biagini relates to him as brother, guiding and watching over him. (It is important to realize that Biagini never assumes or changes "character"; his function throughout is to support and assist Richards, responding in whatever way is needed in a given moment.)

Richards, now a little child, begins a lullaby, a soft Creole song. He does not sing straight through from beginning to end, but allows the song to appear in fragments, like something carried to the surface of memory, punctuated by breaks of silence. His voice cracks from time to time as he searches for the high, reedy voice of the child he was some thirty years before. Biagini takes him by the hand and leads him toward a bundle wrapped in red cloth, like a child's birthday present. (Richards had put the bundle there in the beginning of *Action*; Chirco later placed a white metal basin full of water beside it.) Richards sits on the floor and unwraps the bundle, revealing a dried gourd that he shakes as a rattle. (Is it a ritual rattle? A toy rattle?) His reactions are those of an infant, almost too young for speech. Richards finds within his body the impulses of the child-body, the infant-body, and along with this comes the sound of the child. He does not "perform child" in the sense that term might normally be understood; rather, what the witness perceives is a physical act of re/membering, a search for the exact details of his own child-body in a particular circumstance.

Once the physicality of the child is fully discovered, Richards begins to speak, alternating between the inarticulate sounds of the infant and a clearly spoken text, though keeping always something of the child-voice in his way of speaking. Shaking the rattle, looking at neither the witness nor the other doers but at something I believe is fully precise and clear to him, he speaks about the "littl'uns" entering the place of Origin. It seems that a part of his attention is directed deeply within himself – on one level following the line of the child-actions and on another level tracing something deeper, more elusive. If we are as these "littl'uns," he asks, will we also enter the Kinghood? His foot touches the water in the basin, almost as if by accident, almost as if the actions might be connected with some memory of bathing as a child. But it is as if the touch of the water wakens some knowledge in him; the answer comes not from outside, but from within himself. Richards continues with a very special text – paradoxical, impossible to comprehend in a linear way – about the conditions that must prevail within the human being in order to enter this special "place". He describes a condition in which the greatest differences are cast into doubt: high confounded with low, male with female, inner with outer. All this said through the child-voice, the child-body, but with a wisdom that combines the child's simplicity with something other. Throughout, he continues playing with the gourd-rattle, sometimes shaking it, sometimes fondling it. The sensuality with which the child handles the toy makes it seem in some moments symbolic, almost Freudian, but then it appears again simply as a toy.

As I listen to the words, I recognize the limits of my own awareness; I do not understand, concretely, how to arrive at the "place" of which the text speaks – not in the sense of knowing what should be accomplished, what must be done. But I fully believe that Richards does. And one night, witnessing *Action*, I felt certain that if I listened to him closely enough, if I were only able to follow with the whole of my attention, then I too would understand.

In another portion of the space, Biagini and the others begin a new song, something light and vibrant with complex strands of melody intertwined, accompanied by a pattern of rhythmic clapping. The three men stand together; Richards, still maintaining the impulses of the child-body, crawls toward them. He seems fascinated by their actions, looking up at them and shaking the rattle in accompaniment with their song. Chirco clears away the objects on the floor. Richards looks at her in a way that suggests he perceives her as his mother, as if trying to draw her attention. She finishes her task and goes toward him, the four doers making a kind of turning wheel with Richards seated in the center as their axis. I sense something gathering, something building through the song, something collecting and at a certain instant ready to explode (not in violence but in joy) and then . . . release.

Richards stands. Connection with Biagini. Through this, some affirmation arrives: the third and final portion of the journey is accomplished. Biagini begins a very special song, something I perceive as a kind of benediction, absolute blessing. I do not understand the words but feel that some precise, essential message is communicated between them. And then a line of actions begins to develop from inside Biagini's body, something that pulls him slightly away from the connection with Richards. It is an action of rising and falling, rising again. And through all this the song continues, Richards joining at a certain point. The song soars, descends, finds at last some safe place of landing, some fullness of completion. When it is finished Richards moves away slightly and sits on the floor, still holding his rattle, one leg outstretched. The *Action* seems finished.

Epilog: Bidaux rises, crossing toward Richards to offer some challenging, half-taunting question about how life will end. When Richards does not respond, Bidaux crosses toward the witnesses, as if to answer the question for himself. Looking over the heads of the witnesses, he goes through a sequence that suggests the age and withering of the body; he stands a little apart from his actions, as if commenting on the character/situation he portrays. The words of the text, in which Beginning and End are conjoined, are undermined by this demonstration of an accelerated process of decay. The actor lies on the red-tiled floor, each of his limbs abruptly pulled out in turn until he assumes the position of a crucified Christ, his body jerking as the nails pierce first one hand and then the other, then his feet. As the sequence unfolds he continues with a text that speaks of blessing, of evading death. The juxtaposition of text and actions renders the whole ambivalent, dubious. The words he speaks are attributed to Jesus, and yet, the actor seems to ask, if this is the way his life ended, what good did such wisdom do him? Bidaux sits, facing forward, looking at his "wounded" hands. His face is twisted in an ironic smile – a small sound of laughter, followed by a single syllable of rejection: "No." Refusal of this way, of this fate, refusal of all that has gone before (even the whole of *Action*). And then the answer arrives: the same words, the exact same text, evoking the union of End and Beginning, repeated by Richards and the others as incantation. Simply, without pretension, without any externalized doings. Still seated on the floor with the toy in his hand, Richards gazes at Bidaux, and in his psalmody the sense of the text is inverted, becomes an affirmation. Not sentimental, not even emotional. In some way almost cold. Knowledge. Certainty. When the words end, Richards stands. The five doers exit the room together, simply, quickly, efficiently. *Now* it is finished.

This is the place where language collapses, falls in on itself, the place where the Word becomes silent and dances itself into being. I cannot say in language what is *Action*; I think it would be monumental hubris to pretend that I could grasp in a matter of days, of hours seated in this room, the mystery that these people have discovered/created, some of them over a span of nearly a decade. In the text "Performer," written during the earliest phase of his current research, Grotowski asserts that "Knowledge is a matter of doing" (Ch. 37:374). In no instance is this more clear or more important to remember than in relation to the process of energy transformation that constitutes the essential aspect of Art as vehicle. It is a knowledge born in and through the body, pervading the cells, an active becoming that I as a passive witness cannot fully share. Something is available to me, insofar as I am both willing and able to open my perception, to make myself receptive to this, but these others, these doers, know *differently* what it is they do and how it means.

The song is a seed of light that finds its rootedness in the heart of the doer, radiating outward, upward, burning away the dead matter and leaving behind it a visible trace – in the body, yes, but not only, and not even primarily, in the body. To some extent I perceive and respond to the presence of the song-as-force, the song-as-living-entity, but my perception is not the same as that of the doer, who takes the song into himself and allows it to rise through his body, voice, and being. What I as detached observer can comprehend of this process is partial and by its nature secondary. I am witness to a living phenomenon that finds its meaning in the life/experience of those who *do*; what I see are the visible traces of this and not, as in conventional performance, a series of signs created so that someone looking from outside might perceive them.

Narrative is so loosely drawn in *Action* that what the witness makes of it is likely to have as much to do with her own associations and projections as with any meaning put there by its creators. As Richards suggests, the story/nonstory of *Action* is present in potential, something that "can almost be understood like an awake dream, or like a dream of awakening – by someone who's watching, all around that which is the essence of this work, around this 'inner' aspect related to the transformation of the energy" (from unedited version of Ch. 42). The "inner" aspect Richards refers to carries us toward the boundary of the ineffable, the unrepresentable origin where words and concepts falter. To formulate it in language presents enormous dangers of misrepresentation. Perhaps this "inner" aspect of the work can be spoken around, approached indirectly – in a way that lies in ambush beneath and between words – using metaphor and personal imagery (what Barba calls the "seeds of active silence" 1986:17); it can be disguised as a discussion of structure or technique – but only by one who knows, in body and being, the fullness of the lived process. I am not such a one.

In speaking of *Action*, I can describe only what is visibly or otherwise tangibly available to me – what meaning I assemble from these fragments, the primary purpose and function of which precede and remain independent of my interpretation. I can speak about images, structural elements, a story I saw or dreamed. But it is important to remember that this story is not the essential element: it is only a way of seeing. Important also to remember that what I record is *my* story, *my* way of seeing, only this.

During the earliest stages of Art as vehicle, Grotowski used the word "doers" (as in noh drama) to refer to the artists engaged in the practical work of research. Presumably, the word was intended in part to emphasize a distinction between "perform" or "act", in the sense of accomplishing some action, and the mimetic connotation that is also attached to these words. In *Action*, however, one could say that the research team includes those who work more as actors and more as doers, or even that a particular member of the team alternates between or synthesizes elements from both registers. The distinction I point to between actors and doers should by no means be understood as a judgment of superior/inferior quality, but rather as different orientations, different means of approach, here coexisting within a single performative structure. Certainly, the prior training of most members is rooted in the actor's craft, which provides the necessary basis and foundation for the current research.

Grotowski has said that performing arts can be viewed as a type of continuum, a chain with many links (1995:118). At one extremity of the chain, he places the work of public performance, the normal artistic theatre; at the other, he positions the more isolated work of Art as vehicle, which he subtly links to ancient Mysteries. During the early years of Art as vehicle, the rhetoric surrounding the work tended to emphasize aspects that differentiated Art as vehicle, the relatively isolated and unfamiliar aspect of the chain, from Art as Presentation, the normal artistic theatre.

Zbigniew Osinski, one of the few scholars to write about this initial phase of work based on first-hand observation, emphasizes the reclusive aspects of the project, the necessity for solitude. Such places cannot be open nowadays. If they were,

> television crews and newspaper reporters from across the globe would find their way here immediately. But if this were to happen, a murder would be committed against what emerges there in the daily labor, effort, and struggle.
>
> (Ch. 38:395)

Osinski witnessed the work of Art as vehicle in a very early stage, during a period when the performance structure was very rarely presented to outsiders. "Only the participants systematically working here and the visitors invited by Grotowski can know this work" (p. 393). He sagely observed, however, that it was impossible to anticipate what form this work would take in the future.

It is natural – indeed, highly desirable – that over the course of a decade, a rigorous and systematically pursued program of research should evolve, changing its form and structure to a considerable degree. This is precisely what has happened in the ongoing activity of the Pontedera Workcenter, all without compromising the connection with the essential nucleus of research: the process of energy transformation that can occur within the doer performing with and around the ancient vibratory songs. One aspect of evolution in the outer form of the Workcenter's activity can be seen in the increased accessibility of the work to groups of invited witnesses, most frequently young theatre ensembles that arrive for brief periods of work exchange. More than eighty groups have thus far taken part in this form of exchange. "Now the Workcenter is much less isolated than someone might think," Grotowski noted in a recent interview (Thibaudat 1995:36).

Concurrent with this development (though I do not believe the relationship is causal or direct), one can now perceive in *Action* what Richards describes as a more consciously constructed "window" through which someone looking from outside might view and understand the performing structure. It is as if, having discovered what can exist at the far extremity of the long chain of performing arts, Richards (and probably Grotowski as well), without ever losing his rootedness in this mysterious soil, has begun to re-emphasize elements of continuity that link this work to the work of artistic theatre. Not to conflate, not to deny the differences – merely to assert that there is also commonality, that both extremities "belong to the same large family" (Grotowski 1995:134). It seems to have become important to Grotowski and Richards, following an initial period of necessary seclusion during which they established a solid foundation for their work, to create conditions for dialogue with their colleagues in the craft, to test the degree and ways in which their work can be made accessible to fellow artists without compromising the integrity of the inner process that is the essence of this work. In a recent meeting in Pontedera, Grotowski referred to the members of the research team as "Thomas and his group of actors." Grotowski is extremely precise in matters of language, never hesitating to coin new terms or break the rules of the tongue in which he is speaking in order to arrive at a more exact meaning. His use of the words "actors" should not be overlooked.

On first witnessing *Action*, I was surprised to find the work so *theatrical* in some sequences. From the very first fragment, when Bidaux sits in the frame of the doorway speaking text in what I understood as a blasphemous image of some "prophet," all preconceptions of what I was about to see were completely destabilized. Only once did I view the presentation in the company of others who were not directly connected with the work (as current or former participants of the research team); the response of the invited witnesses echoed my own surprise. Those of us who had seen one or another version of *Downstairs Action*, the opus from five years before, came to the presentation with no expectation of receiving anything that could be remotely understood as character or narrative. Based on what I had read and what I remembered of the earlier structure, I arrived with the preconception that the work of Art as vehicle was purely in opposition to anything related to narrative or mimesis. I believed that what I was about to see was the elusive, impossible form of performance that theorists theorize can't exist, the "nonrepresentable origin of representation" (Derrida 1978:234). It is. And it is not.

Certain elements of *Action* are clearly intended to convey a specific meaning to a person observing the structure from outside. The work of one of the actors in the group (Bidaux) could even be described as presentational, standing a little apart from the character he portrays and directly addressing the witnesses. From beginning to end of the structure, it is possible to discern (or project) a story of sorts. I perceived this virtual narrative as an "objective correlative" for the inner itinerary, a structure that not only benefits someone watching from outside, but serves as a support for the doers pursuing this vertical journey. The "objective correlative" can be traced precisely in the juxtaposition of the framing sequences – prolog and epilog – to the actions developed around the songs. In the first sequence, the witness perceives a being who experiences a natural process of age and decay, moving from child to warrior to old man. The riddle of the three stages of life ends with the man groveling in the dirt, awaiting the judgment of a highly skeptical Sphinx.

Juxtaposed with this sequence is the journey of one who is born old and progressively attains the state of the child. The process that enables the central figure of *Action* to move from old man to child is what I perceive as the correlative or analogy for the vertical itinerary at the heart of Art as vehicle. Not illustration, not equivalent, but rather *concretization by analogy*. Any fool can descend into the graveyard of things; to reverse the process is not so simple.

This virtual narrative is not, however, the substance of *Action*. The story functions more as a container – transparent, open – within which the process of energy transformation can occur. In a discussion with a group of witnesses who viewed *Action* together with me on one occasion, Richards mentioned that what can be perceived as story in the structure (what I read as the juxtaposition of the natural process from birth to decay with the reverse process, passing from old man to child) is a relatively new development. He noted that in some respects the construction of the acting score was still a work in progress and that certain elements of this acting line had been discovered fairly recently. The work involving the vibratory songs, however, has extended over more than a decade, with the roots of this exploration tracing back to earlier stages of Grotowski's research.

Grotowski notes that in the work of Art as vehicle, "the elements of the Action are the instruments to work on the body, the heart and the head of the doers" (1995:122). The performance structure – precise, repeatable, objectified in its details – is developed with an aim to facilitate this process. Narrative, insofar as it exists, is secondary to a logical order of arrangement in the cycle of the songs and is oriented toward the impact of the respective songs as tools for passing from the coarse to the subtle. "From the point of view of verticality toward the subtle and the descent of the subtle to a level of more ordinary reality," Grotowski observes, "there exists the necessity of a 'logical' structure: a specific song cannot locate itself either a little before or a little after in respect to the other songs – its place must be evident" (1995:128). The order of the songs is discovered by the leader and the doers in practice, step-by-step. The development of the acting score, the precise sequence of details, goes hand-in-hand with this process, but the primary emphasis remains always on discovering what can best serve the doers in the transformation of energy. This itinerary in verticality constitutes the axis of the structure, its essential aim and goal; all other elements of the work find their place in relation to this axis.

For the occasional witnesses, however, the presence of the "window" Richards describes – a means by which they can comprehend a (virtual) story – seems to serve an important function. One group of witnesses with whom I viewed *Action* responded very positively to the presence of a few recognizably theatrical sequences. Is it possible that the presence of something that is in one sense familiar, in one sense recognizable, helps the witness to be open to what is unfamiliar, unknown? That the internal chatter ("I don't understand") can be quieted at the moment when the witness sees something through which she can comprehend certain elements of the structure, a point of orientation that allows her to navigate into the unfamiliar territories of perception toward which *Action* carries her? The story/nonstory of *Action* is not the essential element, but as a "window" it allows the witness to perceive.

The work as actors and doers in the same performative structure does not create contradiction, but rather evokes simultaneously the two extremities of the vast chain of performing arts. *Action* encompasses both, though not in equal measure (Bidaux as thesis, Biagini antithesis, and Richards . . . *not* synthesis, but rather arrival at something beyond?).[5] In a strangely metaphoric way, I understand the outer structure of *Action*, the visible score, to be in some sense similar to the skin of a living creature – alive in itself, and within which a living process is in motion. On the level of the acting score, certain elements can be perceived as a form of representation; the riddle of the Sphinx, for example, or the citation of Christ's crucifixion, communicates to witnesses by means of allusion to a received body of knowledge which is the heritage of what Grotowski describes as the Western cradle. The actor who performs these fragments conveys precise meaning: the citation of the crucifixion could not possibly be understood as anything other than what it is, a blasphemous reference to the Christ story. I recognize these fragments as theatre – and very good theatre at that.

But there is also something else present in this structure – another register, more mysterious, almost unknown. The work of the doers – the process of energy transformation that comprises the essential element of Art as vehicle and thus of *Action* – is nonmimetic, nonrepresentational, in the sense that it is not something that exists in order to be seen, nor does it take as a point of reference something outside itself of which it is an imitation or copy. The living process that appears inside the frame of the external score has many levels; beneath/within the outer structure of the virtual narrative, the journey made by Richards as the old man becoming child, is something *other*, dependent on neither the story nor the gaze by which that story is received. It takes life between doer, action, and song, and requires only this: the well-honed tool, and the one with the knowledge and capacity to use it. It is not repetition, not (re)presentation, but something more akin to Grace, alive in every moment. This is *Action*.

Plate 41.1 Action (1995) — Nhandan Chirco and Thomas Richards. (Photo by Alain Volut.)

Plate 41.2   Action (1995) — Thomas Richards. (Photo by Alain Volut.)

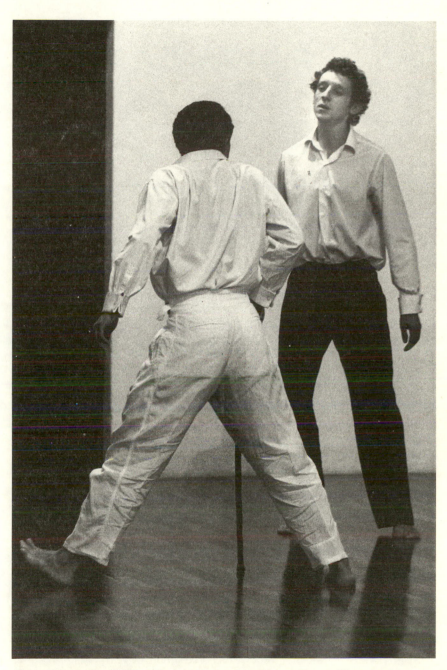

Plate 41.3   Action (1995) — Thomas Richards and Mario Biagini. (Photo by Alain Volut.)

Plate 41.4   Action (1995) — Thomas Richards. (Photo by Alain Volut.)

Plate 41.5   Action (1995) — Thomas Richards and Mario Biagini. (Photo by Alain Volut.)

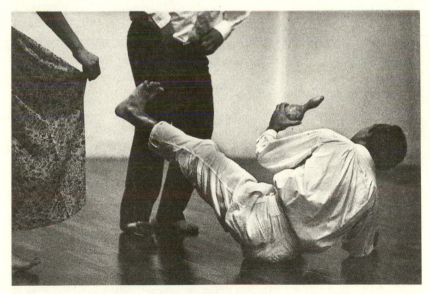

Plate 41.6   Action (1995) — Thomas Richards. (Photo by Alain Volut.)

THE EDGE-POINT OF PERFORMANCE
(Fragments)

Interviewer: Lisa Wolford

Thomas Richards

LISA WOLFORD: During one conference Grotowski talked about what he calls "actual work" (the current work here in Italy)[1] as "having two chiefs." More recently, he has begun to say that you are the true creator of the recent performance structure [*Action*] and that he is more an "advising ancestor" to you. Could you talk about how you and he have worked together practically, and how the dynamics of your work together have changed over the years?

THOMAS RICHARDS: There are many different steps that led me toward the work of Grotowski. The first was a work-encounter with Ryszard Cieslak which took place at Yale University when I was in my senior year as an undergraduate.[2] This relatively brief work-encounter – two weeks – turned my head around totally; through Cieslak I began to perceive the practical possibilities in the art of the actor from a whole other angle. He had extraordinary presence, it was flowing from him. And this charged human warmth going with all of his mastery led me to seek out Grotowski. It's funny, but just a few days after I started to look for information concerning Grotowski's whereabouts, the head of our Theatre Studies Department announced that Grotowski himself was going to arrive at Yale to conduct a selection of students to participate in his Focused Research Program in Objective Drama at the University of California-Irvine.

While at Yale, Grotowski gave a lecture/conference. Many under-graduates interested in theatre were present, and also many professors and students from the graduate school. I was struck by the way in which Grotowski answered our questions. There was a specific quality of silence before each of his responses which was not at all artificial. It was as if he was really thinking, taking the time needed; the habitual rhythm of normal life questions and immediate answers had been broken and in that dynamic silence, something passed. After the conference, I ran to my job (I was working in a Japanese restaurant) filled with some sort of excitement. I was laughing a little.

I passed the selection and worked that summer at U.C. Irvine in the seminar which lasted two weeks. I found the work extremely interesting. Grotowski was working with different practitioners from around the world, among them Tiga (Jean-Claude) Garoute and Maud Robart from Haiti. When I heard the songs of Haiti, the traditional songs, it was like hearing the voice of my grandmother, whom I've never heard sing before. My grandmother's line comes from the Caribbean (my family, through my father and his parents, comes from Jamaica). And during these two weeks when I heard these songs, it was like . . . touching in me something that had really never been touched up to that point. It's hard to explain, but even the melodies, this kind of sound and its vibration – which in that moment gave me the feeling I was hearing a tree sing – was shocking. It was the way that Grotowski was dealing with these songs: testing around them and through them something which seemed to me very ancient and at the same time very new; looking through them – as if – in their background might be hidden something comparable to Greek or rather Egyptian antique Mysteries; discovering in their melodies and rhythms a coded potentiality of organic presence for the human being, almost an organic score – all this opened for me the door toward an unknown possibility which before I did not even suppose existed.

After that two-week seminar, I worked with Grotowski, still as a participant, in a two-month workshop he held a year later in Italy.[3] Grotowski was trying to teach the actors present the basic elements of performance craft. He criticized me strongly for my dilettantism. His attacks were so persistent and accurate that finally I couldn't bear it. I left the work after only one month. I went on a journey – at the Odin Theatre, I saw the documentaries of the Polish Laboratory Theatre's performances. I was completely blown away. Really, in the work of Grotowski I was seeing something like an awakening of a potential, almost like a hidden, unconscious potential in the human being which became like a river flowing through a person, and at the same time this river was entering a structure, a theatre piece, so precise – and these two aspects were meeting on such a high level. All of this pulled me like a magnet to the telephone to contact Grotowski again, and ask if I could work with him the following year at his research program at U.C. Irvine. I was accepted on the condition that I would stay one year.

When I arrived at California in October of 1985, I consider that, of the nine actors on the team, I was really on the lowest level in terms of craft. An extraordinary Korean actor, Du Yee Chang, was in the group. In fact, most of the actors were already in some way masters of some traditional performative practice. It was difficult for me in the beginning. I often thought I was about to be kicked out of the group. I could not create any fragments on the level needed to be included in the Action which we were creating. (At Irvine, between October 1985 and June 1986, we created an Action, meaning a precise performative structure, an opus, which was called *Main Action*.)

That year, the day-to-day work was led by Jim Slowiak, who worked as Grotowski's assistant director. One day, when we had already created the initial structure of *Main Action*, Grotowski came to see it. After a short time, he stopped us and began working practically with one of the actors on a small fragment. This was the first time I had ever seen Grotowski working directly with an actor. I was at the same time fascinated and terrified. He entered the space like a volcano and began giving indications to the actor – again, again, asking him to repeat his score, driving the actor without any hesitation, like a rider guiding a horse in some way; the actor was immediately jumping to another level of quality in his work. The force with which Grotowski entered and demanded and pushed this actor, pushed not in a negative sense but in the sense of request, made this person immediately and deeply engage. I watched, and something in me said, "Ah! There is something." And in that moment, within me, my way of fighting to discover something from the work changed. Really I thought, "If I could work with him directly. . ." I began to mobilize in another way.

A short time later, Grotowski was seeing a draft of *Main Action*, and I had a small fragment in which I was walking, carrying an object for another actor. Grotowski stopped us. He said there was something in my work, in what I had done. For me this was strange because I was just walking. He said, no, there was organicity, the seeds of organicity in me in that moment. He asked what my association was, what I was thinking as I walked, for whom I was walking. . . . As he questioned me, a memory came up about a time in my youth when I was carrying an object for my father in the hospital. I wrote down the memory in my notebook.

This was the turning point in his relationship with me. It was as if he had seen in me some possibility, and from that moment on he began to work with me directly – first I joined a separate mini-team which had already been working individually with Grotowski, Jairo Cuesta and Pablo Jimenez. Grotowski worked with us to create the central motif of *Main Action*, and then, on our line of actions, which would later become the principal line. I entered into a relationship with him which was . . . before, in some way, it was as if in the work I didn't exist. And then, from that moment on, through his eyes and his attention, I really began to exist. We would work together almost every day, in the team of three or two, or with me alone, many hours – even ten, twelve hours a day. Then he would invite me to a restaurant, and we would go and speak for another two or three hours. It was as if he was looking to find the way to unearth in me this possibility that he was sensing, what he had called organicity.

My mother is white; my father is black. Half of my heritage comes from the European culture, and half from the African. Though my skin is a lighter color, in my physicality there is something of my father's line, the African line. I grew up in New York City educated in a Western way, and this African line in the body, related to its fluidity of movement, its continuity of movement, the flow of vitality through the movement – which I would later discover to be a rich and creative channel for me – had to a great extent been blocked, not yet discovered. Grotowski began to look to unblock this through practical work and also through conversations with me, in order that I might begin to accept in the working situation this resource in the body.

Soon, I began to totally accept this. And then, in certain fragments of *Main Action*, especially the ones on which he had worked directly with me, it became as if my body began to conduct me – absolutely by itself – in a flow of movement which was coming from inside, a stream of impulses running through the body. It was a discovery that was flowing like a river. I was a little detached, watching it. My mind was no longer manipulating my body, telling it, "Go here, go there;" now my body was conducting me. Even the source of the impulses seemed not to be muscular. I was like the rider on the horse, not telling the horse where and how to go, but just watching the horse fly, and in some way guiding it – here, here – but guiding it without manipulating, just in some way directing it. This stream of life in the body began to flow strongly, and the totality of *Main Action* became for me the discovery of this African aspect, and the aspect of organicity. The story of *Main Action*, if you looked at it from the outside as spectator, was the initiation of a young man, a "native boy." We saw him (meaning me, I was in that role in *Main Action*) go through certain tests, which he was confronted with by other members of the group.

The following year,[4] when Grotowski transfered his work to Italy, he asked me to become his assistant. In Italy, what is now the central aspect of the work began to become clear as the performing on the basis of ancient vibratory songs coming from the African and Afro-Caribbean line.

From this field, the Haitian songs were worked on at Irvine in the

Objective Drama project, and at the beginning of the work in Italy, Grotowski put into my hands the responsibility for these songs. My level of working on them, in 1986, was rather elementary. Grotowski had made big efforts before we moved from California to Italy in order that I might really learn these songs and the way of singing them. A month before we left, he put me alone in a room with I Wayan Lendra from Bali, who was conducting the work on the songs at that moment, and had Lendra sing them with me for hours. I had to repeat and repeat and repeat them. "No, again, not like that, wrong vibration of voice. . . No, again." I must say, Lendra was very frustrated with me. I remember him sitting down one day when we were working – it was after maybe six or seven hours of singing, and Lendra sat against the wall in total defeat and said, "Do you really think Grotowski thinks you can sing!?" I said, "Uh. . . I dunno." We kept trying.

So, in 1986 when we moved to Italy, my level of singing was rather elementary. Over the following nine years, however, I worked on these songs with Grotowski: first on the Haitian songs, then West African, then African and Afro-Caribbean (but not Haitian), and then on an entire line of some African and Afro-Caribbean ancient vibratory songs. I worked with Grotowski on the development of performing structures with and around these songs, and – which is the main issue – on a process that can happen, let's say, inside the human being through all this work. I began to receive from him a practical knowledge about this. And step by step, what was elementary in my capacity nine years ago has developed to a certain level of knowing how to work with these tools – because these songs really are tools, or rather can be tools for the human being to make a work on himself. They can become tools that help the organism in a process of what we can call a transformation of energy.

I know that the word energy is in circulation today, and that to a certain extent it has become banal. In spite of this, Grotowski feels that the banality of this word is rather positive for our vocabulary because it diminishes the danger of too much "mumbo jumbo" mystical terminology. He underlines, however, that we use the word "energy" not in the meaning of big, crude quantities of force (or strictly speaking, the magnitude of available force), which would rather be related to vitality in a quasi-biological meaning of tonus. When speaking about energy, we are speaking about the *qualities* and not the quantity of energy. We are not speaking about being energetic. We are speaking in terms of qualities of energy, and the transformation from one quality of energy (coarse) to another (subtle).

In my intimate language, for myself, I am calling this the "inner action." Of course the totality of our work is related to many different aspects of the performing arts, and acting is one of the most important. But the songs of tradition do organize our work in some way being a kind of axis. When a doer begins to sing a song of tradition, and begins to initiate something of the inner process, the song and the melody will start to descend in the body. The melody is precise. The rhythm is precise. The person who is singing begins to let the song descend into the organism, and the sonic vibration begins to change. The syllables and the melody of these songs begin to touch and activate something I perceive to be like energy seats in the organism. An energy seat seems to me to be something like a center of energy inside the organism. These centers can become activated. In my perception, one energy center exists around what's called the solar plexus, around the area of the stomach. It relates to vitality, as if the life force is seated there. In some moment it's as if this begins to open, and is as if receiving through the stream of life impulses in the body related to the songs – the melody is precise, the rhythm is precise, but it's like some force is collecting in the plexus. And then through this place, this very strong energy which is collecting can find its way, as if entering a channel in the organism, toward a seat slightly above it, for me related to what in my intimate world is "heart." Here, what is in the vital pool begins to flow upward into this other resource and transform itself into a quality of energy which is more subtle. When I say subtle I mean more light, more luminous. Its flow now is different, its way to touch the body is different – these energy pools can be perceived as touching the body. From this pool related, let's say, to the "heart," something becomes open which is permitting some passage upward, and it's as if there begins to be touched a level of energy around the head, in front of the head, behind it. I don't mean this to be a general formula which should be the same for everyone. But in someone's perception it can be all connected, like a river which is flowing from the vitality to this very subtle energy someone might perceive as being behind the head and above, even above, touching something that is no longer just related to the physical frame, but is as if above the physical frame. As if some source, when touched, begins to be activated, and something like a very subtle rain is descending and washing every cell of the body. This journey from one quality of energy, dense and vital, up and up toward a very subtle quality of energy, and then that subtle something descending back into the basic physicality. . . It's as if these songs were made or discovered hundreds or thousands of years ago for waking up some kind of energy (or energies) in the human being and for dealing with it.

The energy transformation – all this process – I perceive as the "inner action." But I should clarify terminology, because if not, it can be confusing what I mean when I use the word "action" in different domains. In our present terminology, the word Action with a capital letter refers to the totality of a performing structure. When in italics *Action*, it often functions for us as a title to indicate a specific opus – for example, the performing structure developed during our last year of work in Irvine was called *Main Action*, the performing structure we developed five years ago, which is documented in the film by Mercedes Gregory, was called *Downstairs Action*, and the performing structure you have seen now, we are calling simply *Action*. So these are the titles of separate structures, each a different opus. The word action with a small a, often in plural, refers only to the basic beats of acting, one can say the tangible elements of behavior, for example, little actions or physical actions in the sense relatively similar to Stanislavsky's terminology.

These terms you should see as distinct from what I mean by "inner action." This appeared for me as doer; it's a very personal term which I use when referring to the process of energy transformation in performing with and around these ancient vibratory songs.

So, the first years in Italy, all of the group work was centered on the basic elements of performing craft, on acting. But – concurrently – Grotowski worked also with me alone, and it was not the same program as with the group. In the first year, it was the two of us alone in the room, and we created two Actions, meaning precise performative structures, with myself as the only doer. The next period in Italy, Grotowski said, "Now, Thomas, you begin to look to pass something which is appearing in your work to your colleagues." So I began to lead a work-group, and to create a performing structure with four other actors which might become for them the discovery of this transformation of energy – not in words but in practice – on the ground of the ancient vibratory songs. Grotowski put more responsibility in my hands. I should now be in the Action we were to create as a doer, and also be its creator – with the other group members. Grotowski was passing a critical period with his health (heart problems), and he felt that it was necessary as quickly as possible that I learn not only how to do, but also how to pass that practical doing to someone else. The result of that phase of work is *Downstairs Action* (called thus simply because our group was working downstairs in our building).

From that point on it developed naturally; the more that my practical knowledge of the work grew, the more Grotowski took some distance. Because if he were always present in the workspace, I might just use him as a continual reference point, and thus, to a certain extent, remain passive and not learn how to confront obstacles alone. Once, when Grotowski was at a conference and someone asked him in a rather polemical way, "What good are you? I understand that often you leave the work to be done by your assistants, and that actually you are even not systematically present in the workroom. Why?" Grotowski said, "When a watch works, don't fix it."

LW: I think the way you speak about what you call "inner action" is perhaps the clearest way of distinguishing between "Art as vehicle" and the theatre of public performance. For me, this is an even more essential distinction than when Grotowski gives an example of the difference between the two kinds of work as being in the seat of montage, that in performance-oriented theatre the montage is in the mind of the spectator, and in this work the montage is among those who are doing.

TR: I would like to avoid saying or implying that some inner process, which I consider very special, can be in one place of work and not in another. When I speak of this "inner" aspect, I don't use it as a basis for distinction between "Art as vehicle" and public performance. So far I have simply been witnessing my personal experience as a long-term doer in this work.

Here, in this work with Grotowski, I have approached the "inner action" with certain specific tools: performing actions based on ancient vibratory songs. These songs have developed over a long period of time, and as I look to understand their nature through doing, it seems to me that they were simply not made for doing a "public performance" as we can conceive of this term now. But surely in the past, something inner related to the songs arrived to articulate itself in many different, complex performance situations, which probably appeared as different forms of events in different times and places. In such events, I suppose that – for some individuals who were doing – the experience of energy was in some way the essential.

In our work, we are not looking to make what might be conceived of now as a "public performance," but I also don't want to say that this type of inner process cannot exist in an event which someone might consider to be a kind of theatre. It could. And here, actually there are many occasions when people arrive to see our work; we have performed in the presence of witnesses many times. Numerous groups of individuals have seen our performative opus. And theatre groups have often come to visit the Workcenter to make exchanges with us. In the case of theatre groups, they see our work, we see their work, and after, we discuss and analyze together the practical questions related to theatre craft that have arisen from the exchange. So, when witnesses see our work, to a certain extent they are in what we can call a theatrical situation: they observe, without active participation, the artistic opus of someone else. In the case of what they're watching in our work, they're observing a group of actors working in a precise performative structure with some tools related to tradition we can say, with very ancient vibratory songs, and – I suppose – something of this, what for me I am calling the "inner action," is happening in the people who do. The others are observing. So, is it theatre? Is it not theatre? On a certain level, you can say, yes, they are witnessing something, they are seeing something done.

So I don't feel that this type of "inner action" can be present and alive and accomplished only when no one is watching, or only in an event that we call by a name other than theatre. But in our work the essential is that this inner stream – which is not just inner in reality – is not lost. So, in relation to inviting people to see our work, we're simply going as is needed. Can witnesses be there? Can witnesses watch and this inner stream be still lived, really?

LW: When speaking about the "exchanges of work" with the theatre groups, Grotowski talks about things that can be passed along in terms of technique and precision at the level of craft. This is clearly what the visiting groups can gain from seeing your work. I'm wondering what you and your collaborators gain from these dialogues with the visiting groups.

TR: Our basis is the craft of the actor. The people involved here are almost exclusively actors. The elements of our work are not only related to the very special ancient songs, but also to the creation of lines of little beats of human behavior, lines of performing details, an acting score with its specific tempo-rhythms, to the discovery and structuring of points of contact between acting partners, to the work on organic but structured flow of impulses, to forms of movement; it deals with the "living word" (the approach of texts). It's oriented toward the creation of a comprehensible performing structure through the montage of series of basic little reactions and actions, and finally – which from the point of view of acting seems fundamental – it's looking for the development of the ability to repeat a performing score hundreds of times and each time maintaining its precision and truly alive process. Our basic elements are the same as the basic elements of acting. And on one level, the level of craft, the work is the same for the actor in public theatre and the person who is doing this work. It's in some way the same field. So, when we invite a theatre group to see our work, we are tested. It's a test for us on the level of craft. They might tell us, "no, no, this is not done, this is not clear, or not yet accomplished." They might criticize in a way that can objectify for us our work on the level of craft. Are we in self-delusion, entering into amateurism with the desire of so-called inner discoveries? Or is the level of craft in our work honestly accomplished? They can sometimes put to us very good questions.

Also we can receive from them something which might concern the quality of our work in relation to another aspect. For someone who is sitting witnessing a doer in the process of the "inner action," there can happen the phenomenon of induction, to utilize Grotowski's term. If you have an electrical wire with current flowing in it, and you take another electrical wire without current in it and put it nearby, because there is current in this first wire, there can also appear in the second wire close to it the traces of an electrical current. This is the phenomenon of induction, and it can also happen when someone is witnessing the performing structure in which the doers are going toward this "inner action," this transformation of energy. Inside themselves as they're watching, witnesses might begin to perceive something of what is happening in the doers. When a visiting theatre group comes and watches our performing opus, and after in the analysis someone says for example, "Ah, when performing, you were singing. And I don't know what exactly happened, but it was almost like a movement inside me – inside my body? I was just sitting, watching." We can see, ah, there was induction. But it's not the objective of our performing opus to produce induction. If it became our objective, I feel we would immediately lose this something "inner." So that's another aspect through which, through a special kind of reflection, we can better see ourselves and our work, to objectify what we're doing.

There's another aspect still, which seems to me to be a true human need which I notice in myself: that one receives from one's colleagues in the same craft a simple recognition – "ah, yes, there in what you're doing, is something." It seems really quite simple, but this, coming from the companions of your craft, other actors, or even other people who visit the work, can give some kind of meaning, it can give some kind of fuel to continue.

LW: How can an acting score, a sequence of an acting score, serve as a support for the "inner action?"

TR: The two lines can happen simultaneously and in some complex way go together. The first condition is the technical precision and elaboration of the acting score: everything related to the flow of small actions and impulses, as well as the precision of the songs and the articulation of their rhythms, the logics of behavior, your personal associations – everything – should be totally and practically absorbed by the doers. Only then might the two lines, acting score and "inner action," begin to be approached simultaneously.

Let's take a hypothetical example: we start to work on an ancient song which is a funeral song, and this song is also a very potent tool because of the vibratory qualities which are coded in it. We start by singing the song in rehearsal, first working on it technically, so that the melody is precise and sung in tune by the whole group following the leader of the song. The rhythm is becoming exact and the words of the song are pronounced in total synchronization with the leader. Then, we begin to work not only technically: while singing, the leader begins to go toward the "inner action." The transformation of the energy is happening, it's working. We stop. Then we begin to gradually develop the acting lines. We see that this song is a funeral song, so we approach it, as one possiblilty, like actors working on the situation of a funeral. (This is only one hypothetical possibility which has nothing to do with the fragment of the funeral in our present performing structure.) I imagine, for example, that I am faced to the coffin. There is a line of people before the coffin and I am waiting to be able to look in. I watch the others before me who, one by one, look into the coffin. I arrive closer. Who is in the coffin? It's my grandmother. What does the face of my grandmother look like in the coffin? And now a precise memory comes back to me from the funeral of my grandmother. I remember the image of someone in my family who is whispering something. I start to work on this as an actor. I gently let the corporeality of that person come into me. How did he stand at the coffin? What was the exact angle of his spine? How old is that person? What is his relationship to my grandmother? I let myself remember through doing the small actions of that person faced to the coffin. What is his reaction as he sees her face – which now becomes my reaction. It's as if what I wanted to say to her in life and never said, I wish to say to her now, in this last moment. It comes into my mouth. I hesitate. I whisper it to her. Then, someone is behind me – did they hear me say that thing? I turn to see if they heard. . . . So, we begin, thus, to construct these detailed series of small impulses and actions around the circumstance of the funeral: we create our acting score. We eliminate what is not really needed. We memorize this score. Now we go through the score, but all the time as we do, this funeral song is happening. Imagine, that through the years, you already have some experience with this "inner action;" you have been looking for it, and for the practical knowledge of how these songs can work with it – and now (even if not without blind alleys), you know how the two processes can go together almost like one thing. You start the song, you start your line of actions. At first, you're probably more concentrated on your acting score. But you are singing also and another part of your attention is with the melody; for some seconds maybe on its tuning. And then, not technical thinking, you let the vibratory qualities descend in you as you're following your line of actions. And because your acting score naturally begins to have its way of contacting certain associations, awakening something in you from your life and memories, the song begins to enter that and do something with it. It can begin to let that resource of life which is collecting go up, to rise. Now, as doer, my attention goes with this inner ascending of energy. I let my primary attention go with that. In some way, I let my "I" go with that, the "where I am" with that, and let the score of actions go almost by itself. The acting score has already been dominated, memorized, and the body – and not just – is doing the line of actions. But you are going with this vertical journey toward the subtle. The two things begin to happen simultaneously, as if you have your horizontal score, related to your line of actions, related to the contact with your partners, the order of actions – and something like a vertical score which is related to this "inner action," your vertical itinerary, what quality of energy is with you now.

LW: In witnesing both *Downstairs Action* and the performance structure I've seen recently [*Action*], my attention is drawn by different dynamics of partnership, how the primary axis of relationship changes in the two works. In *Downstairs Action*, your primary partner was the actress who in one moment had a fragment as a young girl and in another as an old woman. You had very long sequences juxtaposed together. But in *Action*, I focus on a working relationship between you and a doer I remember even in the other structure [*Downstairs Action*], from many years ago. I focus specifically on how this doer acts as a support for your journey. In *Action*, I see this as the primary axis of connection in the structure. In the discussion the other night with the group that had just observed *Action*, you spoke of the ascending of energy as something that happens between you and him, because the two of you have experienced over many years the possibility of how these special songs with the actions related to them can be a support in this process. The newer members of the group are at an earlier stage in their work with this possibility. Is this partnership an additional support for what you are calling the "inner action?"

TR: In the meeting the other night I was speaking about a working relationship, in *Action*, with Mario Biagini. Mario has been at the Workcenter almost from its beginnings in Italy. The more I have been leading the work with the group members, the more he has been helping, almost like a younger brother, a brother, assisting and supporting in an extraordinary way. As doers in the actual performing structure, *Action*, in some way we both work in a kind of tandem. Mario really knows something deep and practical about how these ancient songs, and the doings around and with them, can work on the human being.

In *Action* you will see moments of contact between us in which we are both singing – and performing – and the "inner action" starts to happen. When we are in this kind of contact, what is happening is not like when an actor might have some mental image which he projects onto his partner – for example, that he sees his real brother projected onto his acting partner and reacts as if faced to his real brother in a specific circumstance. But, in these moments of connection with Mario, it is that I expect something from him and he expects something from me, something related to our vertical scores. If I am the leader of the song in that moment, he orients himself to my process in such a way that it becomes two people going on this journey, not just one. Or when he is the leader of a particular song, in that moment I orient myself around his process. And in some way, there is an induction which happens in me – through following him – which in me then becomes active. Meaning, the leader initiates the process, the "inner action," and the other follows and then is also fully going inside himself while keeping the acting score and the song. This can create a strong energy reservoir between the two people, and what we can call the transformation of energy can seem to be no longer existing just in one or in the other, but in both and between. This is something which has been appearing rather recently in the work. In the beginning, when one is working toward this ascending, this transformation of energy, the perception of it might be more related to something inside, and almost be as if this something is tight around you. It's as if this river is finding its way through knots, untying and untying. And now in the work, in perception, it can be not necessarily just close around you, but all around you – not just inside but also around in a very ample way, around the physical frame. This can also englobe your partner and his doing, englobe his inside and his outside. And it can be said that it is almost the space between them which is ascending in quality of energy, and something subtle descending into it, into them.

LW: One thing that strikes me strongly, both in the way that you're speaking and in the times I've seen you working, is something I understand not as a dividing of attention, but a doubling of attention. How you can put one part of the attention to the acting score, for example, and yet another part to what is even further beneath or within. It's clear that this kind of attention can only be the result of very long work. Some of the people you're working with now have been here either less than one year, or for a little over a year and a half. Is their task at this point simply to catch the songs, the possibilities of the songs, or are they in some way trying to work with this layered attention as well?

TR: When we first arrived in Italy, when I was working alone with Grotowski, we created a structure, *Pool Action*, with myself as the one doer. It was called *Pool Action* because there was a small plastic pool for children in which I had one fragment of my score. The *Pool Action* was related to a cycle of songs – I would be singing and simultaneously doing in the whole space a very dynamic physical score related to organic movement, and also this "inner action," which was at an initial level in that moment. At its initial level, the "inner action" can be extremely absorbing for the doer, the danger can be to go entirely into this, losing external attention – because it's incredibly fascinating for the person discovering it, it's totally unknown. You can let your attention be totally overwhelmed, so much that you can forget what is around you, what is outside of you, your score, etc. I remember one day in rehearsal of *Pool Action*, in which the only object in the space was this small pool for children; I arrived, and found now many objects in the space – there were chairs, there were many shoes, there were brooms leaned against chairs, many obstacles – and Grotowski said to me, "Now you do the same structure, with the same songs and score, and in every moment adjust to all the objects in the space, never breaking either your inner process or your physical score." So at the same time I had to keep this stream related to the inner life, the transformation of the energy, and keep the dynamic flow of the physical score, and be jumping over the chairs, adjusting to the new situation. It was the teacher putting the apprentice into a trap – either be attentive or fall down! So it was needed to find the way to go deeply toward the "inner action" rooted in the songs, and also know clearly what's around, what's happening, the two lines of attention which in our work go hand in hand.

Now, with the new members of the group, the question is first to learn the melodies, the tempo-rhythms, the sonic vibrations, to learn the syllables of the words precisely, their pronunciation. To be able to sing in tune – oh, my goodness, we spend hours and hours working to sing in tune! And then after, if the person is ready in some way, then we look for them to discover what the song can do to them as they sing, and of course, after, there is the whole question of developing the performing structure, the line of actions, the elements of acting. But really, we go very quickly toward the inner possibilities related to the work on and around the songs, without pushing, but generally we go rather swiftly toward that. This is the stage they're at – on one level to look, basically through induction, to discover something, while singing in total synchronization with the leader, and also continually adjusting the voice in order to adapt to the changes of the vibratory qualities in the song led by the leader. And then in other rehearsals, outside of the rehearsals on *Action*, I work with them on certain songs with one of them leading and myself silent, helping them step by step to touch some hidden possibilities.

So, in this work, there is no pushing toward the "inner action." It's not something that you can demand of someone. It's something that can (or not) unfold in its own time. The process of development for each actor in the group has its own wave and character.

LW: During the meeting several nights ago, people who had just witnessed *Action* were speaking of the work very much in terms of theatre. Some of the people who witnessed *Action* at this time had also seen *Apocalypsis cum figuris* or another production of Grotowski's theatrical period, and one of them said that in some way he was perhaps more affected by *Action*. I have been told, for a very long time, that it is not a good thing to look for a story in the actual work. Even on this particular evening, when people arrived to witness *Action*, Mario Biagini gave an introduction saying it's better to think of the structure in terms of poetry than as narrative prose. And yet – in the meeting, you spoke of a window through which a person looking at this from the outside might have a way to see. And I did find myself assembling a narrative.

TR: On the level of montage, *Action* is different than the *Downstairs Action* filmed by Mercedes Gregory, which we were doing five years ago. *Downstairs Action* was constructed without any consideration for someone who might be in the room watching. The space was a wine-room without any chairs or designated place for spectators. We never even thought from which angle a visitor might witness that opus. The montage was made entirely for the people doing. There was no place for any story. The montage was the structured sequences of the songs with precise actions, with points of contact and spatial relationships that were giving the possibility to help the transformation of the quality of energy of the doers.

In the structure of *Action*, however, there is some window. There are more elements which can be read by someone watching as being something similar to "character." Some very simple story? – which somebody watching from the beginning to the end may perceive? For example, the other night in the meeting, when you were speaking about *Action*, you clearly articulated this (as perceived by you) story. Maybe it is, in a very discreet, a not exposed way, there in potential. But maybe it's not just a story, rather some way of looking, of questioning, which can be perceived almost as a story. And it is still a work in progress. And it *should be* a work in progress.

What exists now in *Action* it seems to me is something very complex. I see beginning to appear from this research something which, for me, is like the primary act of performing. It's like the performative structure which can embrace the look of the witness without depending on that look. Even when it is done with no one watching it, its process can be accomplished. The value for the people doing is not in the fact that they're being watched, but in the essence of what they're doing. And that, for them, is some substantial nourishment.

Grotowski, when speaking about our work now, often refers to some similarity with the tradition of the Bauls which is still surviving in Bengal. Many years ago, he told me a story, as a tale, like a grandfather speaking to a young boy. He was not giving me books to read about the Bauls; he just spoke to me about them. He said that some time ago (in his story he was speaking about four generations, because he met Bauls of four generations) there was a tradition in India of singers/performers. And these singers/performers had songs which they were singing that were very old or linked to a very old tradition. With these songs, they made a work on themselves related to something "inner." Periodically, they would be isolated, some young people and their teacher. The young ones were learning this technique of singing, related to a kind of yoga, from this older, more experienced person. They were working in a very closed and isolated way for months and months with their teacher. And then the Bauls would go from village to village, two or three or more of them together. When they would arrive at a village and come to a square, they would begin to sing. A group of peasants would come around them, and the Bauls would do something that was like performing, but it's not just that they were doing theatre – they did have some precise doings with these songs, some way of behavior with these songs, which was artistically on a high level – but what they were doing really was related to the work with their teacher, to this something "inner." So they found the way to travel, to go to a village, and make something like a performance, which was in reality the continuation of this work on themselves. They would be doing their performing and someone who would see might say, "Ah, this is incredible singing," and appreciate it as a work of art. And another among the spectators, who was an ex-Baul, someone who in his youth had been a Baul and knew something about the inner process, or even, someone who simply had some receptivity for this "yoga," would follow through a kind of induction, inside, and in that way, either remember or intuit this something "inner." Often, in some special and discreet way the Bauls were singing for this particular spectator in the village – for example, the old Baul who was now in the village working as a peasant. The Bauls were in the frame of an artistic event which was being appreciated in one way or another by the spectators, and then, by one or two other ex-Bauls, who were perceiving their inner process, and in some way, inside, were also going with them. After, the Bauls would go to another village, and then to another, moving for months and months.

This became for me a precious story which in some way is like a dream, a secret, behind the work we're doing now. These Bauls would travel and then after some time of doing this so-called performance – doing their inner work, which was accepting and embracing the fact that people were looking at it – they would return to their teacher and continue the work in isolation; and again, go toward the villages, and again back to their teacher. This story became, as I was leading the work, like. . . in the back of the mind, as something behind me, related to a dream deep in me.

What I see appearing in the work now is something related to this dream. We are performing. *Action* is in some way a performance. It can be seen. But is it just for – to be seen? No. Because the moment it's – just for to be seen, just for this, it would lose the contact with its original intention, with the reason for doing. *Action* is on that edge-point, which is like what I can imagine, from my orientation, as "primary performance." It's finding its value in the act of doing, and that act of doing exists in a structure which accepts the fact that someone is there watching, and also that there is not someone watching.

LW: In *Action*, one of your collaborators is very clearly working in a different way to the others, much more in a way that is familiar as acting, with a predominance of clearly articulated forms intended to communicate certain meanings to a spectator. Both you and Grotowski say that this actor is working differently to the other members of the group in two of his fragments related to text. Grotowski makes reference to the paradox of putting sugar in the consommé, even though consommé isn't meant to be sweet. I'm wondering how you work differently with this artist than with your other collaborators? How do you interweave this register, which is recognizably more "theatrical," with the other elements of your opus?

TR: There are many different ways that someone can approach acting. For example, we can find big differences between acting "as Stanislavsky" and "as Meyerhold." "As Meyerhold" means to look rather from the angle of composition. You can see certain actors who are naturally oriented in this way. Another approach is rather "as Stanislavski," where the arrival to the structure comes more from the actor's life of associations, through the way that the role is step by step uniting with his own life. Of course, there are many other possibilities between these two apparently opposite ways. And someone from an Oriental theatre tradition, for example, might have yet another way to approach the creation of a structure. When working with an actor, I look simply to discover that person's natural approach.

With the actor in our group whom you speak of, his process was clearly to start from composition. He received ancient texts suggesting strong possibilities in this domain, and he started from composition based on the content and structure of these texts. So it's some kind of dramaturgy. He first created the acting propositions for these frag-ments of text, and then these propositions were edited by us and put in juxtaposition with almost the totality of our performing structure. His text-actions are very much related on the one hand to a meaning of those very ancient, "inner" oriented sayings, but on the other hand, and it's contradictory, to the blasphematory meaning (in respect to those "inner" oriented sayings) intended by this actor to be conveyed to someone watching *Action*. We were looking to juxtapose these text-actions with the totality of our opus, because it was for us an experiment to see in what way the two orientations might work together. Our perception was that they did work together, and that even this contradiction between them was alive. As Grotowski describes it, when you create a consommé, to add a little bit of sugar in the last moment gives a special contradiction in the taste, almost imperceptible, but in some way strengthening the stuff. So, in the totality of our performing structure, these two text-actions are like the sugar in the consommé.

The other night in the meeting the aspect of blasphemy which is present in those text-actions was not touched. Those two fragments are not only more theatrical in the classical meaning of this word, but they are also in some way "against" – they cut in the opposite direction of all the flow, all this inner process, which we are looking for in *Action*. The sugar in the consommé, cutting against. This aspect of blasphemy or "against" is extremely important, and we can lose the consciousness of its importance when we, from the culture in which we grow up, learn a morality based on "good and bad." Good conduct/ bad conduct. Good things to say/wrong things to say. In every human being is contradiction. In every human being there are two sides. Every time when someone in our group is trying to approach the "inner action," there is the fight inside between "yes" and "no," which exists both in the doer, and in the partner. We have right hand; we have left hand. We have "yes;" we have "no." A part of us wants this transformation from vital to more subtle to succeed, and a part, no. And there is always a fight in the doer between these two aspects. So for us the fact that in these two text-actions is an "against" is totally natural, because this "against" exists in us. To blaspheme can be a liberatory act, because in that moment we exteriorize our "left hand."

LW: What you've said makes me think very strongly about the complementarity between your way of speaking in your book *At Work with Grotowski on Physical Actions* and the essay by Grotowski printed in appendix in the same volume. I think it's necessary, for a full understanding of the work, to have both kinds of knowledge. But it's clear that one way of speaking can serve in one time and place, and another in a different time and place. I want to ask whether, in the practical work, your way of communicating verbally with your collaborators is similar to your way of speaking in your book, focusing on the level of craft rather than directly on the transformation of energy?

TR: First, it's important to say that when working we speak very little. Of course we use words when necessary, but it is not at all discursive explanation; rather, a shortened language, some "emergency call," indicating a possibility, a block, etc. If longer conversation is needed, we approach the point either in the group or individually during an interval in the practical work, or at the end of that day's session. Secondly, by principle – not to put the cart before the horse – when working, we don't talk at all about energy or the "inner action." This is only an attempt here in words to indicate some process, which is a practical process experienced by someone (and not in a way which is identical for everyone). But when you're looking to transmit in doing, as we are, we don't speak about energy at all. It's just day to day work on the performing and the songs. Songs: precision of the melody, how the body should be kept while singing, where decontracted – there's a specific knowledge of how to keep the body, and how to allow the songs to let the body come alive and the impulses in the body go with the song, to discover what is blocking in someone's way of standing, for example. The work is a very precise technical level of craft, and not at all speaking about qualities of energy. That's something to be discovered in practice. Then you will know: ah, this exists! A doorway opens in you, and you touch something and something touches you. And ah, it exists! You might then think that's the end – that's it, I've discovered it. And then a year later, you see that it wasn't the end. There's a whole other territory that's now open. And then, year after year, it's like you see that what is possible to be growing and extending through some inner channel is almost endless. It seems, there's no point of arrival. But in the work we never speak about it, really – unless it's inevitable for some exceptional reason.

Also: we have *never* spoken during the process of work about "energy seats." If in this interview I have been speaking about my perception of something as "energy seats," it is just because I am trying here to witness in words some personal perception as a doer in this work. And I am aware that somebody else can have another topography of perception, or even no perception of this kind at all. In everything, there is *no* exclusive right way for everyone, *no* exclusive possibility. The other reason why we keep a rule not to mix the topic of "energy seats" with our work terminology was discussed by Grotowski:

> In our work we avoid as much as possible to verbalize the questions of the centers of energy which we can locate in the body. I mean it when I say "which we can locate in the body" because it is not so clean-cut. Do they belong to the biological domain or to one that is more complex? The best known are the centers according to the yoga tradition, those called *chakra*s. It is clear that one can in a precise way discover the presence of centers of energy in the body: from those that are most closely linked to biological survival, then sexual impulses, etc., to centers that are more and more complex (or, should one say, more subtle?). And if this is felt as a corporal topography, one can clearly draw up a map. But here there is a new danger: if one starts to manipulate the centers (centers in the sense close to the Hindu *chakra*s), one begins to transform a natural process into a kind of *engineering*, which is a catastrophe. It becomes a form, a cliché. Why do I say "like" the *chakra*s? Because the tradition of the centers exists in different cultures. Let's say that in the Chinese culture it is more or less linked to the same tradition as in India. But it existed also in the West, in Europe. In the text of Gichtel from the seventeenth century one can find for example drawings that from this point of view are very instructive. If all this is verbalized, there is also a danger of manipulating the sensations which one can artificially create in different places of the body. So we prefer a less fixed terminology, even if in precise work one can discover here something very precise and fixed.[5]

But I'd be interested, Lisa; you said that my way of speaking is very different from Grotowski's. What's different?

LW: In Grotowski's essay he speaks very explicitly about energy transformation – in this essay more explicitly than I've ever heard him. In your book, your writing, all this is lying in ambush; it's never addressed directly. Someone who's receptive can, in reading your text together with Grotowski's, see what's present as subtext in your work, but I get the sense that these things aren't meant to be spoken of directly because that obstructs the process.

TR: What we find in the book *At Work with Grotowski on Physical Actions*, and this seems to me fundamental, is that my text and Grotowski's essay are speaking about two different periods of work. My text is speaking about the first years of our work together, when he was trying to pass on the fundamental elements of acting craft, from which we would then take off into the next step of the work, which is what he speaks about in his text, "From the Theatre Company to Art as vehicle." So in his essay printed in appendix in my book he's speaking about the work after these first years. Thus the way of speaking is different. Also, in my book, I was writing mainly about the elements of our work which could have a practical use for an actor. Everything I was touching upon was focused toward that; I was thinking how what I have learned from Grotowski might help someone who finds themselves in the situation of a young actor in the theatre.

LW: I have a question in terms of the different periods of Grotowski's work, between what is referred to as Objective Drama[6] and the current work,[7] in relation to traditional materials. One of the significant aspects of Objective Drama involved people working with material connected to their own cultural traditions. The songs that are the center of the work now are in some way related to your cultural tradition – in some way, one could make a case for this. Are these considerations relevant to the current work, that there be some kind of cultural connection with the material?

TR: The majority of the songs we are working on here come from traditions (or can we say a tradition?) that exist in the Afro-Caribbean and African area, a line that Grotowski intuits has something in common with ancient Egypt or even maybe hypothetical roots preceding it. Grotowski speaks of some large "cradle of tradition," including ancient Egypt, the land of Israel, Greece, and ancient Syria, as the cradle of the Occident.

Now, as a theoretical supposition, you can agree with this or disagree. For me, the essential that I see in practice is that these tools, these songs, can work independently of nationality or race. Certain songs coming from the African and Afro-Caribbean tradition, certain songs which can become tools for the "inner action," can work just as well for a girl or boy from the USA, India, or France. What's possible through the work with and around these songs is appealing to the human being – appealing meaning calling something in the human being, allowing some process in the human being – rather than someone of a particular nationality, race or sex. This is evident to me from the practical research we've made – that the objective impact of the proper work on and around such a song can be the same on persons from different cultures.

On the one hand, we can say the Afro-Caribbean line is my tradition – my father is black, his family came from Jamaica, so his line was from Africa. But my mother is from Texas. Her line is from England and from France. So, is it really my tradition? On one level, deep down, let's say even "genetically," yes. But on the other hand, I see that it can work for an Italian, who, in a very deep way begins to touch something of the "inner action" in connection with these songs. So the process that can be discovered through a specific work is in some way transcending one particular culture. But attention! What I've said just now can lead us to the thought, "Ah! This means that we can go take a little from Tibet and a little from Greece, or China, or the Caribbean, and we can make a mixture of all this and have a beautiful multicultural soup. . ." In that way we make a disaster. No, on one side, the question is the authenticity of your penetration into a given tradition. Do you really take the time and have a genuine capacity and involvement necessary to discover what is transcultural in a tradition? On the other side, we should not just mix elements from different cultures, but rather test how the ways of doing which appeared in one context or another have a practical objective impact:

— are they working only within the limits of their own ethnic or cultural environment?
— do they have a practical objective impact in more than one traditional territory?
— can this practical impact work also outside the original place (or places) of development?

Also, a crucial element is that you learn *to do* from someone who knows. I happened to find the way to reconnect my so-called African line of tradition from a Polish man with a white beard, in California and Italy. It seems absurd, but it's working. Grotowski had worked with practitioners from that African-Caribbean tradition – and not only from that tradition. He worked with practitioners from many cultures, in depth. And then he looked, really, to transmit what he knew, practically, not just theoretically, and not in an easy way. There exists another level. We can say, yes, someone might discover what is transcultural in the tradition. Because it seems to me a thread does exist. Underneath and between every deep and alive tradition is something technically similar, even if the forms are different, or the departing points toward arrival are different.

This question is very tricky because we can begin to mask our inertia with changes of form. For example, we have the good thought or good idea – a so-called "high idea" – that we want to touch something high, and we just exchange the forms of one tradition which we claim is dead with different forms from far places, and now claim it to be alive simply because of the change of form. It's not the change of form that makes something living. So the question is to see the individual, every time. What's blocking one isn't what's blocking another. Someone can be looking toward the techniques of another tradition for a very true and deep reason and it works, and another person can be looking in another tradition just for the act of escaping. And what might be needed is to push that person to face what they're running from – no, don't escape! And in another person, you see that the act of entering some other culture's techniques is helping them in their inner growth. Each individual case is different and should be treated differently.

LW: You said that a few of the songs you are working with now came to you through the Haitian practitioners working with Grotowski in California. Are all of the songs passed to you through oral transmission, or have you discovered them in different ways?

TR: The only person whom I learned the "inner action" from, was Grotowski; and this seems to me fundamental. I learned songs from the two practitioners from Haiti – it was very precious – but the "inner action" I did not learn from them. So, in California, I learned Haitian songs directly from practitioners of that tradition, and also from some other members of the Objective Drama Program who were in different moments leading these songs. But still, it was only on the level of melody, rhythm, and vocal resonance even if it was from voice direct. In that moment, also, I was singing really as a student, a music student – in reality, I was manipulating my voice a lot with my head. And because of this "student aspect," the way I learned the melodies linked them at the time to a certain artificial way that my voice was being controlled by my mind.

But even before the work with Grotowski, I had learned other songs from a practitioner of an African line who was not in the Objective Drama Program. In my personal studies, I had learned some songs of the West African tradition from this practitioner. I had also learned –

from other sources – several Caribbean and African songs. So, in some way when I arrived to Grotowski, I was a storehouse of certain songs from what we can call this extended line of tradition. But only melodies and words. The melodies and words should be precise, of course, for these songs to work, but it's *not just that* which is needed to help this "inner action" begin to come alive.

So, on one level, the way I learned these African and Haitian songs we can say was through "oral transmission," or "voice direct;" but what does "oral transmission" really mean? In a culture in which the tradition is living, "oral transmission" is something that passes to a person through years and years, and very gradually. The child already begins to learn the songs and the living impulses that support the songs while in its mother's arms, and also, the child gradually absorbs practical knowledge through being/playing in and around the context of the events in which possibly certain adults are entering deeply into the process related to the songs. But it seems to me that "oral transmission" does not stop here. After, if the youth is showing some very special aptitude or connection with this process through the songs, maybe he might be accepted by some older person with a specific knowledge, who then begins the long work of transmission related to the practical workings of these traditional tools. This is what we might imagine oral transmission to be, in a society in which the given tradition is still really living. It takes years and years; it's a question of time, of gradual and deep immersion, and eventually, of the capacity of doing of the individual.

It's also even possible that a culture has potent tools of tradition within it, but has almost totally lost the capacity of working practically with them. So, how to arrive? It seems important for someone in this situation to realize that oral transmission is not at all just to listen to a living voice for two months or one year, and learn melodies perfectly from that living voice, and then to claim that the work is authentically "traditional," defending it with the term "oral transmission." It is also not even guaranteed that someone who has grown up in and around an area of a living tradition has received a true oral transmission, even if in appearance it seems that they "hold the keys." It's thus easy for our mind to utilize this term "oral transmission" as a label, like some sort of diploma related to tradition, and in this way not have to deal with really looking to perceive, to question the authenticity, the quality of a given individual's capacity of doing, and the integrity of their work. And thus, through easy labels, a part in us which really might be awakening through all this work can just remain asleep.

So, in the work with Grotowski in the succeeding years, it was he who was teaching me not just to sing melodies, but to discover this potential which can exist through a specific work on these songs of tradition. And it was a very complex and gradual process. It was through him that I was receiving the teaching.

One day, in the beginning of my apprenticeship when we were already in Italy, I was in his house and we were speaking. We had been analyzing the fact that something was blocking me in my process related to the songs. And as I went to the bathroom – on my way, I began to sing softly. It was an African melody, this time one that I had learned just from an ethnological record! Just from a record! Grotowski suddenly called from the kitchen, "Stop, stop! Come back! What were you just singing? There was something special in your sonic vibration. What was that?" I said what it was, and how I had learned it. Much to my surprise he said, "Let's go to work." I said, "But. . . it's not orthodox, I just learned it from a record." He said quietly, "Please Thomas . . . don't be ashamed." We began to work on this melody – and on other special songs I had learned in this way. And these songs, because I had learned them when I was alone, just between myself and them, with the simple need that was drawing me to them, without someone, even competent, over me onto whom I could project the image of "music teacher," led them to be a little more free in me. These songs were not so much linked to my speaking mind or my "good student." So Grotowski began the work of teacher with me on these songs, the work of oral transmission. He began to work from them, and it was really through this work that I began to have some take off toward the "inner action," and only after could I go back and also sing the songs which I had learned from the practitioners, without this "good student" conducting, but with some other particular knowledge connected to the process involved in the singing which I had learned from Grotowski. And this possibility has arrived step by step through ten years of work together. So the way in which I learned was extremely complex. We can say that the full oral transmission came step by step. I received the melodies in one or another place in one or another way. But the "inner action" and a way of doing related to the songs – what one might even consider to be the purpose of oral transmission – I received from a teacher in another place and another time. And then that was developed, so that the two could then go together.

LW: In your book, you speak in a way that is very cruel with your younger self in terms of certain life expectations you had. I can imagine nothing further from this vision you discuss than the life you have now. It seems to me necessary that there be an environment separated from all calculation for what takes place here, and that one of the things that could destroy this work would be any tendency to become a thing for sale. In this sense, the work you're doing is very far from the notion of theatre-as-industry. How do you see this affecting your life and work in the future? Can you create the space for this work? Also, how do you look now on this vision of your younger self?

TR: I see that at a certain age in me there became a separation between what I *thought* was valuable in life and what I deeply felt was valuable in life. I'm sure, to a certain extent, this happens in everyone. For me, this separation was accentuating itself around the age of nine or ten. I remember when I was about nine years old, I had a very special game I played with my brother, which indicates to me now the direction in which I wanted to take off in that moment. My brother would be upstairs in his room. I was looking for contact with him. I would go upstairs very quietly into his room and start making a sound: tick tock tick tock tick. . . . And I'd start to move in a very odd way, almost dancing around his room. He would say to me, "Tick Tock, please clean my room." And I would say "Yes, yes, tick tock, tick tock. . . ." And I would start to clean his room – make his bed, clean the floor, do everything – and then he would give me a raisin. I'd open my mouth and he'd put a raisin inside. And I would go on "tick tock tick tock" and continue dancing around the room.

My parents were horrified by this game. I think they thought it was the most oppressive game that could be for their child – and they told us immediately to stop. On one level, I can see that they were right. But on another level, I see that in that moment when I was Tick Tock for my brother, and when I was doing these things for him, I experienced an extraordinary freedom and joy. I was doing *for him*, he was my brother, and everything made sense. I don't know why. It was not filtered through my mind, that this was right or this was wrong. It was just working. And I was dancing – so free! And doing the things perfectly, much more perfectly than when I was doing for myself when I cleaned my own room. Some nourishment was coming from him. He gave me some food. But it was not just the food of the raisin, it was the connection, what was passing from him to me in that moment. So I can see that in that moment in my life, it was like I was looking for my teacher. I was looking for the relationship where someone says to you, "Do it." And from the freedom by way of that older person who says, "Do it," you enter in action – "okay, I do it." And you do it. And from that can come an extraordinary freedom.

This is very tricky, because the person who's saying "do it" should not be looking just to serve themselves, manipulate you, etc. All this should be very far from any cult atmosphere. If this person is a true teacher, and is looking to pass to you a real knowledge, there can be established the relationship of teacher to apprentice, of older one to younger, of "do it" to "yes," and this can become extremely liberating for the apprentice. As a young child, around the age of nine, I can see that on one level I was ready to begin the work that I'm doing now. But my life of course took another turn. A "good student aspect" and other layers came into my personality, other ideas about what has value, and what not; what is achievement and what should be appreciated. These began to form on top of that. Afterwards, in the work with Grotowski, I was never remembering this game of Tick Tock – until recently. But, the work with him was like re-entering a stream, a river that was broken back at the age of nine – a stream related much more to what in me was not an idea of achievement, but the way that what was in me wanted to achieve itself. Not just for me. No. You do – why? It's for something else. And from that "for something else," some possibility is liberated, some channel opens.

About the future, and about the necessity of protecting the work, I don't necessarily agree that this work is something which should be protected and isolated. Right now, it finds its funding through Grotowski; he was a stage director who was known all over the world, and after, he could continue his research, in some way leaving public performance behind, and still maintain a relationship with funding sources to create the possibility to continue. For the future, I don't know what will happen, but I see that what's essential is to continue the work as a development, not as a development of forms, but of this way that it's nourishing us, to develop and not lose that. Who knows what form it will take in the future? I don't know. I see that now the structure of *Action* is embracing the presence of someone looking, in a way that *Downstairs Action* we created five years ago was not. I see that this aspect is present now, and still the essence of the work is in priority. About the future, what's crucial is to not lose what we're doing: this performing, this *Action*, finds its value in the doing and not simply in being seen. Then this, in some moment, is seen – but not dependent upon that look. In some moment, not seen. Maybe in some moment, only with its teacher. Or maybe in some moment traveling. Maybe seen. Maybe again hidden. So the form it will take in the future, I don't know.

But of course we should confront the necessity of finding the financial sources to support this type of art, and here all of the dangers will present themselves. How to continue and not just shift into an echo of what was done? How to continue, and to really continue. But also, we need to eat. We need to have a place to stay. So to find this line where what is the true research is developing, is going forward, is passing to another, developing in you and in your doing, not lost and not dying – How? We will see.

I don't at all look back on my desires to be a famous actor as something negative, something low – not at all. Yes, in some way we need to conquer the acceptance of our milieu and our peers. You never know what's operating in a person. It might have been the accomplishment of that need which would have freed me to make another step and touch yet something different. But, in my case, it happened to leave that and look for something else. And it was okay. For another person, it can be totally different.

What seems to me fundamental is that I feel in myself, and what I can imagine might be in others, the need for two aspects of development. One in respect to some inner ripening. That when you're thirty, in your inner ripening you have something you didn't have when you were twenty. When you're fifty, you have something you didn't have when you were thirty. And when you're sixty, seventy, you have something you didn't have when you were fifty; that life is in some way this inner ripening. And at the same time, outer ripening: that something necessary for the individual to accomplish as his task in life, face to his milieu, face to his society, his family, is also accomplishing itself. That these two aspects can have their ripening hand in hand. Maybe in one moment one is most important for someone, and then another becomes most important. Or for someone else, first this and then that. But that these inner and outer ripenings go hand in hand towards some kind of. . . what I can only intuit now as accomplishment of both these aspects, which I can perceive in certain older persons as some extremely special fullness of presence, quite difficult to articulate in words, but nevertheless, you perceive.

Pontedera, August 1995.

EXODUCTION
Shape-shifter, shaman, trickster, artist, adept, director, leader, Grotowski

Richard Schechner

Note: I wrote this piece while Grotowski was alive. Except for one detail I have not changed it, and have kept references to him in the present tense. RS

He's a fox, eagle, snake, mole. A shape-shifter, elusive, extremely powerful in the way he holds people close or keeps them at a distance, in either case dazzling them with his aura. His presence is scary to some, mysterious to others. His public appearances are largely just that, and have been for a quarter of a century or more: apparitions, well controlled, with carefully calibrated doses of wisdom and evasion, insight and repetition. Like the songs, dances, and rituals he and his colleagues have harvested from many cultures, Grotowski mixes humility and arrogance, certainty and skepticism, simplicity and pomp. In Catholic Poland he said he was an atheist, but no one who knows his work believes that. But exactly what his religious beliefs are is not easy to say. Those who know him best, have worked with him the longest, have shared whole days and weeks, say he can be witty, warm, friendly, and downright snugly.

I remember his forty-ninth birthday, 11 August in 1982, at André and Chiquita Gregory's Central Park West apartment. There were people there, but not a big crowd; 11 August is also Carol Martin's birthday, so we were celebrating together, drinking, eating. The Grot put away a lot of vodka and champagne, me less, Carol champagne only. Suddenly, Grotowski began singing, "Fucky birthday to you, fucky birthday to you, fucky birthday, fucky birthday, fucky birthday to you!" Then he seized a champagne bottle, gave it a shake, and began squirting the bubbly all over us. I responded in kind. Soon many of the party began splashing each other, singing, and laughing.

This, too, is Jerzy Grotowski, and why not?

I suppose it is nothing unusual for a person to have many aspects,

Plate 43.1 Jerzy Grotowski, 1995. (Photo: Romano Martinis.)

many faces, many presences, many characters (as in the theatre). This multiplicity of roles is something Grotowski finds in Gurdjieff, a researcher of the mind–body–spirit with many affinities to Grotowski. "We are all continuously playing a character, a role; it is what Jung defined as persona" (Grotowski 1996a:100). And in that nearly undecipherable concept, presence, Grotowski's mastery is most manifest. More than any of his actors, including the great, tragic Ryszard Cieslak, Grotowski was and continues to be a presence. Exactly what that means, how it works, and what consequences it has for theatre and beyond, is the subject of this writing.

The basic bio-data of Grotowski's early life, until he entered theatre school in 1951, are well known, but skimpy (see Osinski 1986:13–14 and Kumiega 1985:4). As Kumiega summarizes it:

> Grotowski was born in Rzeszow, near the Eastern border of Poland, on 11 August 1933. His father worked in forestry and his mother was a schoolteacher. His only brother, three years his senior, was to become a professor of theoretical physics. [. . .] At the outbreak of the Second World War, at the age of six, Grotowski settled with his mother and brother in the small village of Nienadowka, about twenty kilometres north of Rzeszow (his father having left Poland to settle in Paraguay, where he lived until his death in 1968). The small Grotowski family spent the entire occupation in these rural surroundings. [. . .] In 1950 the family moved again, to Cracow, where Grotowski completed his secondary education (although he had earlier missed a year due to a serious illness). In July

> 1951 he applied for admission to the Acting Department of the State
> Theatre School in Cracow .
>
> (1985:4)

No other work in English gives us more.[1]

The Grotowski the world knows begins in Opole with the establishment in 1959 of the Theatre of 13 Rows. Begins, in fact, when Grotowski
can ration what is known. Osinski gives some account of Grotowski's
earlier theatre work, his activism during student days, his lectures on
"Oriental philosophy," and his 1956 trip to "Central Asia" (Osinski
1986:18). But these accounts are bloodless facts, not a life.[2]

What about boy Grotowski's experiences just before and during
World War Two? What were the formative incidents of his childhood? I
discussed this period of his life with Grotowski in 1996. I did not tape
record that meeting, so what follows are paraphrases of what he told me.
In the years before World War Two, the economic situation of the
Grotowski family "descended to the level of the Polish peasant." During
the war, Grotowski and his mother lived in a very small village near a
forest. His father went to Paris to join the Polish exile army. Jerzy would
never see him again. After the war, his father emigrated to Argentina and
then to Paraguay where he died in 1968, working first on the docks and
then later for the British consulate. He said he would not live in a Poland
dominated by the USSR. "He was a sculptor and a forest ranger,"
Grotowski told me. But it is Grotowski's mother who formed the young
artist's mind and work. He always speaks of her with deep love and
respect.

> Mother was a very wise woman. She worked as a schoolteacher when she
> could. But she also worked cleaning houses, doing manual labor – what-
> ever it took to provide for her small family [Jerzy and his older brother,
> Kazimierz]. She always kept books of different religions on the shelf
> [where young Jerzy would have easy access to them]. Christian, Jewish,
> Hindu, Buddhist. She would say that these were all different but also
> really all the same, they are all speaking about the same essential truths.
> [. . .]
>
> Once during the war the Germans gave people soap. But my mother
> said not to use it, that the soap was made from Jewish bodies. But we had
> actually very little information about what was going on. There was talk,
> we heard talk.

More than talk. Grotowski told me he saw corpses in the forest. The
Germans entered houses in the village, he heard shots. He was a boy of
six when the war began, twelve when it ended. *Akropolis*, ostensibly
about Auschwitz, is also about what Grotowski felt, saw, and reacted to

during the war, including reading classic texts in the midst of a world that ignored or brutally parodied what these books said and meant.

The genocidal Nazi occupation segued into the complicated oppression–permission–oppression dance of the Communist years, climaxing in the Solidarity movement, martial law, and finally the collapse of Communism. After the imposition of martial law in December 1981, Grotowski avoided Poland for nearly a decade. He returned in April 1991 to accept an honorary doctorate from Wroclaw University and to share his recent work with young people and old friends by screening Mercedes Gregory's film of *Downstairs Action*. In December 1996 and February–March 1997, Grotowski traveled to Warsaw and Wroclaw to discuss his Art as vehicle work and to receive two awards, the Konrad Swinarski Prize and the Grand Prize of the Polish Culture Foundation. But despite these trips, since Theatre of Sources, Grotowski has mostly worked outside of Poland. Some have wondered why Grotowski did not get himself involved directly and deeply in Solidarity. In fact, the young Grotowski was politically active during the "Polish October" of the mid-1950s. But by the time he joined the theatre of 13 Rows in Opole in 1959, this direct involvement in politics subsided. In truth, Grotowski was no more a political person in the Solidarity sense than he was a theatre person in the Broadway sense. He eschewed actions that bounnd him to groups beyond his own circle; when he interacted outside that circle, it was entirely on his own terms, dictating how questions were to be put to him, the hours of meeting, the people he would meet with. To his Workcenter in Pontedera stream those wanting to learn more about what he did. At the Workcenter they participate in carefully regulated encounters.

We are not likely to find out what the young Grotowski was thinking from 1945 into the mid-1950s. His tracks before the emergence as a brilliant young auteur-director are covered or destroyed by the war, its aftermath, the Russian occupation, and the Cold War. The man himself is not eager to open his life history. Like G.I. Gurdjieff – a figure resembling Grotowski in key ways, and about whom I will write later – Grotowski journeys into Central Asia, India, and China where he meets "remarkable people," acquires esoteric knowledge, practices yoga, develops his opinions about human life. Several times later in life, Grotowski leaves his colleagues, steps out of sight, journeys into Asia or across America. When he re-emerges in New York, Warsaw, or Wroclaw he is changed, but the process that led to the changes are not spelled out. His is a life constructed, an auto-biography written with doings and results rather than words and explanations.

Grotowski plays his cards very close to his chest. Nor do I feel right in getting too personal about him. Does he have a sex life? If so, where are his lovers, present or former? Are the categories "straight," "gay," "bisexual," or something else? Does it matter in relation to his work? Was it appropriate for me to reveal his fucky birthday caper? To what degree ought what is private about a well-known person be left alone? Why am I worried? Why should Grotowski so thoroughly control what gets out about him? Is this control central to his work? The control steers all enquiries about the man to his work, giving the impression, which amazingly may be the truth, that the work is all there is of the man. Like a noh master, Grotowski lives a strictly bounded life, measuring carefully even his journeys, his times out. But if his private life and innermost creative processes remain more or less secret, "the Grotowski work," if I may be permitted to term it as such, has been very widely disseminated. This is all the more amazing because Grotowski is not the author and director of his own plays (as Brecht was), nor an author, actor, director, and teacher of actors (as Stanislavsky was), nor even the director of enormously popular productions, as Brook is.

The Grotowski work is fundamentally spiritual. People say Grotowski "left theatre," but the fact is he was never "in theatre." Even in his early stage productions, theatre was his path, not his destination. Ready to enter university, Grotowski had three possibilities: theatre training, Indian-Hindu studies, medical school ("not to heal the sick," he told me, "but to become a psychiatrist who would help healthy persons develop their insights into life"). He chose theatre because he concluded that there he would encounter the least censorship and mind control. Censors read words, the scripts submitted to them. They were not concerned with staging. Censors cared about what was put before the public, what could be quoted and circulated, not what happened during workshops or rehearsals. So it was the nonverbal aspects of theatre that Grotowski developed most intensely. It was the pre-public or non-public part of theatre, the long process of preparation, where Grotowski took the greatest risks, exposed himself and his co-workers to each other. And he gathered around him in the Laboratory Theatre individuals like himself.

> To the outer world [Grotowski told me in 1996] the Lab presented an image of unity and solidity. But the people themselves were very "risky" and often marginal, highly charged, risk-taking. The Lab was an incredibly anarchic group. The work often verged on chaos. Intense. Much passion and fighting within. This was natural because that kind of work, at that time, in that Polish society, would of course attract people who were risk-takers, who would go to the edge, to the extreme.

The Lab's public performances played to minuscule audiences. The pieces were gestural and musical, uttered and sung rather than spoken, personal to the point of intimacy, but not easily decipherable for a large public. Word texts drawn from classics were broken into fragments, remolded into a montage of soundscapes and complex vocalizations, hard to follow, unlikely to draw either large crowds or the censor's fire.

But underneath these public shows, Grotowski and his "colleagues" (a term he favored, a kind of non-Communist "comrades") used theatre to pursue spiritual, mystical, and yogic interests. Grotowski himself would not use the word "spiritual," he would more probably mock the idea. But I don't know what other word encompasses his quest, his methods, his journeys, and his vocabulary in interviews and writings. His is not an obscurantist mysticism, but one connected to the ancient tradition of gnosis and the Hasidic figure of the exiled, wandering Shekhinah: a search for "scattered truth," sparks hidden in far-away places, barely discernible, in need of gathering, re-assembling, re-connecting. Grotowski's goal was, and is, to approach – yet not grasp, hold, possess, or in any way squeeze to death – a definite and particular kind of spiritual knowledge. This knowledge, though concrete and expressible in terms of sound and movement, is ineffable, not translatable into words. That is why it so often takes the shape of song, "action" or "motions." The more ordinarily theatrical aspects of the Grotowski work have been codified by Eugenio Barba, the earliest and most loyal disseminator of the work, and probably Grotowski's most theoretically inclined disciple. In 1991, Barba (with Nicola Savarese) published *A Dictionary of Theatre Anthropology*, a book whose theorems are not Grotowski's as such but are closely related, fruits of the same tree. What Grotowski will permit to be written down about his recent way of working, the Art as vehicle phase, is in Thomas Richards' *At Work with Grotowski on Physical Actions* (1995). Many entries in this *Sourcebook* tell what it was like to participate or witness this or that Grotowski project. But for all this telling, little is known of the interior processes of Grotowski's mind. Nor will he leave behind a set of textbooks and a biography, as Stanislavsky did; or reproducible theatre works, as Brecht did. Grotowski's processes are much more coherent than Artaud's, and he has trained, or at least deeply touched, many persons. But his legacy is to some degree equivalent to Artaud's: elusive but strong, open to many interpretations, a "story" maybe even more than a "system." Like a rock thrown into a lake, Grotowski will disappear. He will be known only through the ripples.

THE ORAL TRADITION

Grotowski transmits what he knows by means of an oral tradition. His deepest ways of working cannot be reduced to written discourse. His "way" is the actual work process itself. This process is not shared with many people simultaneously. At any given time, Grotowski works with less than a dozen persons, and those he really shares with may be only one or two. Visitors come and go to Pontedera, but not in large numbers. Earlier, the Laboratory Theatre was a small enterprise in terms of numbers, its working methods sealed off from the public, and even the spectators numbered less than 100 for any given performance. Only in the 1970s, during the paratheatrical phase, did Grotowski open his work to a large number of people. And even then, what he judged the "real" work of the paratheatrical period was conducted by a small, closed group, those Grotowski considered the "guides" of the rest.

Grotowski thinks in action, or in active reflection, a one-to-one intense process. This method has not changed much through the various periods of his work, from the "Theatre of Productions" through "Paratheatre" and "Theatre of Sources," and on to "Objective Drama" and "Art as vehicle." What unites all these periods, despite their diverse objectives, different styles, and fluctuations in the number of people participating, is Grotowski's insistence that what he has to offer can be acquired only through direct contact, person-to-person interaction, Martin Buber's "ich und du": the oral tradition.

Grotowski has written no book. Most of what is published under his name are records of meetings or interviews. Of the fourteen items in *Towards a Poor Theatre*, only four were written by Grotowski. I am certain that if the sources of these four were looked into further, they would also be found to originate in talks or workshops. Of the five great forces in European theatre in the twentieth century – Stanislavsky, Meyerhold, Brecht, Artaud, and Grotowski – Grotowski is the least writerly. He distrusts words as such, privileging inwardly focused bodymind work, psychophysical work, direct personal contact that operates on the psyche (which in its original Greek meant "soul") "like a scalpel," as he on more than one occasion has remarked, cutting through the ephemeral and getting at – revealing and releasing – the essential. Here again the notion of "spiritual" enters in its etymological sense as "breath": utterance, voice, song. Of course, the assumption that there is an essential needs to be examined critically. But for the moment, take Grotowski at face value.

Many teachers, from Buddha and Socrates to Jesus and the Sufi masters, lived the oral tradition, even if subsequently their teachings were written down.[3] In *Meetings with Remarkable Men*, Gurdjieff tells how his "whole future destiny" depended on his recognition of how the oral tradition can bring forward in time materials from very far back. He writes that in the ruins of what had been ancient Babylon were found tablets with the story of Gilgamesh engraved on them.

> When I realized that here was that same legend which I had so often heard as a child from my father, and particularly when I read in this text the twenty-first song of the legend in almost the same form of exposition as in the songs and tales of my father, I experienced such an inner excitement that it was as if my whole future destiny depended on all this. And I was struck by the fact, at first inexplicable to me, that this legend had been handed down by ashokhs [Asian and Balkans, local bards] from generation to generation for thousands of years, and yet had reached our day almost unchanged.
>
> (1963:36)

Gurdjieff depended on "orature"[4] rather than literature to disseminate his work. He instructed that his own core text, *Beelzebub's Tales to His Grandson*, be read aloud to students.

Grotowski believes various existing oral traditions link back to ancient practices. He both sent colleagues out to search for and brought "masters" in who could perform elements of these traditions. This was the work especially during Theatre of Sources and Objective Drama. What was sought were archetypal or "essential patterns" of movement, gesture, utterance, and song. Not only were these essential patterns learned by his core group, they were used as tools to activate inner, intimate processes. The meeting of the essential patterns and the inner processes led to *Downstairs Action* and *Action*, the two performances thus far emanating from the Art as vehicle phase of the Grotowski work.[5] Searching for the essential relates to Grotowski's travels to Central Asia, China, and India. The conviction that the essential patterns brought forward in time by oral traditions will converge with materials uncovered within individual performers by means of a rigorous inner process relates to the Hindu belief in the identification of Brahman (the ultimate universal Self) with atman (the individual Self). Each person, if properly trained, can experience the identicality of atman and Brahman. When trained, touched, found, liberated, experienced (which is the right word? no word is right), all boundaries between the individual and the ultimate evaporate. Different religions have different terms for this: moksha, enlightenment, ecstasy, rapture, nirvana – words differ as the emphasis changes, from achieving the all to merging with the divine to reaching the end of the path that is no-path.

At the intersection of the most intimate-personal with the most objective-archetypal, Grotowski's doers construct actions which are presumed to be the distilled essence of what is abiding, ancient, and true, in human life. Warning against "self-indulgence," as he has done throughout his career, Grotowski caustically denies that people can find the essential without undergoing the most rigorous and committed training. The atman is not easily or casually accessed. What is essential can be researched only by means of a disciplined process joining what is learned from those who know to what is found inside the individual self. This self, as I have noted, is the Hindu atman–Brahman impersonal Self, not the ego-driven narcissistic self of daily life. What I am outlining here is Grotowski's process as I understand it, and the assumptions upon which that process is founded. I must put aside for now the question of whether such deep patterns or archetypes exist.

Grotowski lives and works within the oral tradition. That's one of the reasons why he's hard to pin down. One finds Grotowski not in a collection of texts, a film vault, or anywhere other than in the people he engaged with, poured himself into. And these persons changed or died, even as they passed on "the work" as they received it and interpreted it. At each phase of his professional career, Grotowski deeply engaged only a few persons, often confiding mostly in one key figure designated at the time to receive the teachings. In the Theatre of Productions it was for a time Zbigniew Cynkutis, then it was Ryszard Cieslak. During Paratheatre it was Jacek Zmyslowski until his death in 1982. At present, for Art as vehicle, it is Thomas Richards, of whom Grotowski writes:

> The nature of my work with Thomas Richards has the character of "transmission"; in the traditional sense – in the course of an apprenticeship, through efforts and trials, the apprentice conquers the knowledge, practical and precise, from another person, his teacher. A period of real apprenticeship is long and I have worked with Thomas Richards for eight years now [1993].
>
> (Richards 1995:x)

This is the way of the oral tradition.

Among those working with Grotowski there was conflict concerning who was the chosen one. I remember speaking to Cynkutis in 1985, about two years before he crashed himself to death in an automobile accident that some say was suicidal. Cynkutis spoke excitedly about the Drugie Studio Wroclawskie (the Second Studio of Wroclaw–Grotowski's Laboratory Theatre being the "first studio"). Drugie Studio was located at Rynek-Ratusz 27, the former home of the Laboratory Theatre. Cynkutis intended the work to carry on Grotowski's Theatre of Productions tradition. Standing in the freezing cold on the small balcony of his Wroclaw flat, watching the traffic scoot by below us through a gray icy drizzle, Cynkutis insisted that he was Grotowski's chosen one, the rightful heir to the methods and aura of the Laboratory Theatre.

On 11 February 1986, Cynkutis hand-wrote me a letter in English detailing just how he intended to continue Grotowski's work:

After three months of rehearsals with the Polish and international group we have inaugurated a sequel of premieres of the project *Phaedra–Seneca*. If I were to evaluate what has happened due to this opening I would have to stress the crossing of the barrier of psychological fear. For me and my colleagues, for many people of the Wroclaw artistic center the period of speculations and uncertainty finished. The speculations oscillated among respectful and emotional desires for mummification of a myth, turning the former building of Grotowski's theatre into a museum and a monument of his theatrical achievements.

There is a thing existing: in the same building, however, with a totally changed function of the interior, the next generation of actors presents their work every evening. Again people under the age of 25 search for their own way of expressing those feelings which brings present reality, without destroying others' achievements.

I serve them as old boat in which they can pass over all the litter of routines and habits which very easily cling to each new enterprise. I serve them with my knowledge, I discipline them to go further, not to rest where someone else has already used his energy. Hence I am neither a good and beloved daddy, nor a romantic leader pointing to a certain direction. I am a difficult witness and I stimulate them to an escape from that which is worthless [*sic*]. I convince them with the discipline of work, sincerity of demands, and knowledge of undertaking certain tasks by using already known tools. [. . .]

I wish you could see what we have been doing. However, I expect the most interesting phase after two or three years of work when my activity will stimulate an initiative of a young director, and he himself, taking the theatrical basis and tradition will create in this place a new and important act. I believe in it – that is why I decided to direct the Second Studio of Wroclaw.

The car wreck prevented Cynkutis from experiencing "the most interesting phase." After his death in 1987, the Drugie Studio continued on and still existed in 1995 (according to an article in the Polish journal *Notalnik Teatralny*). But people tell me that the work is "wretched," not a continuation of what Cynkutis wanted, no less Grotowski.

Many of Grotowski's closest associates have had bad luck. Cieslak, Zymslowski, and Chiquita (Mercedes) Gregory were taken by cancer, Cynkutis in the car wreck. Antoni Jaholkowski and Stanislaw Scierski also died young. Of these I knew Cieslak and Gregory best. In the years before his death in 1990, I detected in Cieslak a broken heart caused by Grotowski's decision to end the Theatre of Productions. I remember five minutes with Cieslak, in 1976, on a grassy slope outside Warsaw, in the midst of the only Grotowski paratheatrical event I ever took part in.

Cieslak and I were alone. I addressed him with words to the effect that, "Grotowski is one of the great theatrical directors, and you one of the great actors. But now you are not acting anymore, you are not exploring roles like the Constant Prince or the Simpleton of *Apocalypsis cum figuris*. You are running around in the countryside leading amateurs who crave God knows what kind of experiences. How do you feel about that?" Cieslak fixed me with his immense, heavy, powerfully sad brown eyes. "I have given myself to Grotowski, and I will follow him wherever he goes." End of query, but not the end of the story.

Cieslak did not follow Grotowski, exactly. He taught many work-shops, he acted, he tried directing. The last role I saw him play was the blind king Dhritarashtra in Peter Brook's *The Mahabharata*. Dhritarash-tra's open yet unseeing eyes belied the tragedy of Cieslak's later life. This actor was equipped for Grotowski only. Not even Brook could replace the Polish master. Once deprived of Grotowski-as-director, Cieslak smoked and drank himself to death. His final job, before lung cancer choked him, was as leader of the "Cieslak Studio" at the undergraduate drama department, Tisch School of the Arts, NYU. The announcement for that studio read:

> Ryszard Cieslak, co-founder with Jerzy Grotowski of the Polish Labo-ratory Theatre, will remain with us for another year to form a one-year ensemble track/studio that will focus on the variety of training techniques that gave rise to the Grotowski/Cieslak as the Master Teacher [sic], but will also involve teachers of the Polish Mime Tradition, acrobatics, third-world music and dance (African, Brazilian, Asian), vocal training, and magic technique. The ensemble will most likely develop and show a project or series of projects in late spring 1991.

"Master Teacher" was a joint being, a Grotowski-in-Cieslak, designating the closest relationship, that of "transmission," from Grotowski to his disciple. This is why Cieslak was listed as a co-founder of the Laboratory Theatre although he did not join until October 1961 at the start of the Lab's third year. It was absolutely necessary for NYU and Cieslak to claim the originary moment, the singular foundation point.

Similarly, when the Lab disbanded in 1984, the statement published in Wroclaw's *Gazeta Robotnicza* (see p. 169) was signed by Cieslak and three other "founding members." No lie was told in either case because by the 1980s the oral tradition had fused Cieslak with Grotowski. The myths of the oral tradition are stronger than the written record. According to that record, only Ludwik Flaszen, Rena Mirecka, and Zygmunt Molik were in the Laboratory Theatre from beginning to end, 1959–84. Grotowski himself was not among the signers. In their statement they wrote, "Each of us remembers that our origins lie in the common source whose name is Jerzy Grotowski, Grotowski's theatre. [. . .] After twenty-five years, we still feel close to one another, just as it was in the beginning, regardless of where we are now – but we have also changed." What matter that Cieslak trod that path for twenty-three years, not twenty-five? And why did Cieslak sign the statement and Grotowski not? Cieslak signed as himself and as a stand-in: over time no one was more closely identified with Grotowski than Cieslak.

Grotowski did not sign for two reasons. Pragmatically, having claimed political asylum in the United States, and not wishing to endanger his colleagues still in Poland, Grotowski was extremely careful regarding direct contact with them. He mainly communicated with them through Flaszen who was living in Paris, as he still does. But Grotowski did not sign also because his spirit inhabited the entire project, the unnamed first cause, too necessary, powerful, and obvious to have his name written down with the others. As in his productions, he was all-present by means of his absence, like God.

CONTROL

Grotowski suffers from heart and other ailments that put him up against death. Conscious of his frailty, he studiously oversees his realm and his inheritance. Having no fortune in money or goods, he need write no complicated will. But how to measure and distribute his knowledge and authority is another matter. Is the Grotowski work heritable, and if so, who will inherit it? At the present phase of his life's work, a period which appears to be ultimate, Grotowski is intensely concerned with how and to whom what he knows will be passed on. His relationship to Richards turns on this matter of transmission. Speaking of the oral tradition and Gurdjieff, a spiritual leader Grotowski says was only "somewhat important" to him, but in whose life and practices I find many compelling parallels, Grotowski reveals much about his own work:

> It is a terrible business, because there is, on the one hand, the danger of freezing the thing, of putting it in a refrigerator in order to keep it impeccable, and, on the other hand, if one does not freeze it, there is the danger of dilution caused by facility. [. . .] The burning question is: Who, today, is going to assure the continuity of the research? Very subtle, very delicate and very difficult.
>
> (Grotowski 1996a:101)

Here I recall Gurdjieff's last words, spoken on 27 October 1949, to Jeanne de Salzmann – the closest of his collaborators and his chosen heir:

> The essential thing, the first thing, is to prepare a nucleus of people
> capable of responding to the demand which will arise. . . . So long as there
> is no responsible nucleus, the action of the ideas will not go beyond a
> certain threshold. That will take time. . . a lot of time, even.
>
> (Moore 1991:315)

Which leads me to a dark side of Grotowski, his need to control. This
need is driven by his double sense of himself as immanently mortal and
as the source of powerful, useful knowledge. Because there is much
more about him than by him, Grotowski tries to control what materials are
disseminated. This *Sourcebook* is a case in point. Before releasing texts
and interviews with him, Grotowski wanted to go over the table of
contents of the book. He and Richards wanted to make certain that
everything they wrote or said was exactly how they wanted it to be, even
if upon occasion this went against standard grammar and word usage. On
almost every item, Wolford, I, and Grotowski agreed. But on Philip
Winterbottom Jr.'s "Two Years Before the Master" (1991), we did not.
The article in *TDR* is a cutdown version (I did most of the editing) of a
100-page journal Winterbottom kept of his participation in the Objective
Drama project in Irvine, from January 1984 to April 1985. In his journal,
Winterbottom speaks not only about working with Grotowski, but about
how he reacted emotionally to his teacher.

> The more he uses me the more fulfilled I feel. I fear my own failure in this
> project; that fear is always with me. [. . .] When Jerzy met me tonight, all
> my fears were put to sleep by his beautiful, childlike, brotherly smile. I
> gushed.
>
> (1991:142, 145, 146).

Most of what *TDR* published of Winterbottom's journal was not this
personal. Nor was Winterbottom critical of Grotowski, far from it: I think
he was in love with Grotowski, a hopeless yearning because Winterbottom clearly recognized that for Grotowski "the bottom line was
always the work" (1991:154). Grotowski was vehement in his opposition
to including selections from Winterbottom's diary. Winterbottom's
account was inaccurate, we were told. Good enough, but other accounts
of Grotowski's work, especially of the paratheatrical events, some
included in this *Sourcebook*, are subjective and "inaccurate." And
Winterbottom was hardly an outsider with just a casual experience of
Objective Drama. He was a full participant in the work. I think
Grotowski was queasy about Winterbottom's adoration, the love pro-
fessed by the acolyte for the master. The choice was stark: use the
Winterbottom and lose Grotowski. If Wolford and I decided to publish
"Two Years Before the Master" in this *Sourcebook*, we would get not one

iota of cooperation from Grotowski or those in his inner circle. I did not cave in immediately. I asked the opinion of three persons who knew Grotowski's work well. One did not reply. Another, who was not in Objective Drama, liked Winterbottom's piece. The third person, a participant in Objective Drama, condemned the article as being inaccurate and sentimental. Wolford, who was in Objective Drama, also said that Winterbottom's journal did not give an accurate description of the work. I agreed to drop the Winterbottom. But was I doing so in the interest of "accuracy" or because of Grotowski's threat? Finally, I didn't want to sacrifice the *Sourcebook* on the altar of my authority as editor. Anyone interested can get *TDR* and read the Winterbottom.

The Winterbottom incident is indicative of Grotowski's lion-like determination to keep a tight hand on what is known about him, what is published under his imprimatur, who gains access to his presence, the work at Pontedera, the film that Chiquita Gregory made of the Art as vehicle work as it was in the 1980s. But to say that Grotowski controls his work is not to say that the work is closed. By 1996, more than 150 groups had seen the operation at Pontedera. But they witness what happens on Grotowski's terms. There are no places available to the general public on a first-come, first-served basis. Has Grotowski absorbed the Polish and Soviet penchant for controlled history? Or the opposite, having experienced what can happen in a totalitarian state, will he always be fearful of the damage information can do, how fragile his reputation and situation? His need for control goes beyond responding to outside pressures or models. It is part of the traditions he follows: the hierarchical Roman Catholic Church (Polish edition), the Indian guru–shishya relationship, the Hasidic rebbe, surrounded by adherents hanging on his every word, arguing and interpreting, guarding him from intrusions.

SOURCES NEAR AND FAR

Grotowski's own oral tradition is linked to other oral traditions. The near tradition is that of experiments within twentieth-century European theatre and dance: Stanislavsky, Meyerhold, Vakhtangov, Eisenstein, and Okhlopkov; Dalcroze, Appia and others who worked at Hellerau in the years just before World War One; Artaud. But the closest theatrical link is Juliusz Osterwa's Reduta theatre in Poland between the World Wars. The far traditions are more complicated. They include ancient gnosis and hermetics[6] as well as the closely related work of Gurdjieff. And Hasidism, especially Buber's interpretation of it. There is also an American connection, itself a transformation of German–Jewish intellectual life and its coalescence with American utopian tendencies to form "new age" practices. Here gestalt therapist Fritz Perls comes to the fore. No one doing scholarship on Grotowski (in English) has gone deeply enough into these various theatrical, mystical, and intellectual sources, linking them to each other and to Grotowski. What I write concerning Grotowski's sources, I offer as a step along the way.

STANISLAVSKY, MEYERHOLD, OSTERWA

Grotowski takes from Stanislavsky the axiom that continuous actor training is fundamental, and that this training is before anything else "work on oneself." Grotowski: "This expression – this formula, 'work on oneself' – is one that Stanislavsky always repeated and it is from him that I take it" (1996a:89). What changes over the years is how Grotowski interprets not only the work but the self; how the "actor" as a someone who presents a character for an audience recedes, to be replaced by "performer," or "doer," a person using techniques drawn from theatre and elsewhere but for purposes that are trans-theatrical. During the Theatre of Productions phase, Grotowski explored the tensions between the actor, the space, and the audience.

Spectators were deployed through environmental theatre spaces the better to witness the actors in their celebrations and agonies (in the ancient Greek sense). The scenography, far from fostering empathy or audience participation, radically separated spectators from performers. Witnesses peered over a fence at the immolated Constant Prince, sat at Faustus' banquet table, watched the inmates construct their own crematorium in *Akropolis*. But these spectators were never brought into the work directly, and the physical proximity generated a metaphysical distance. Grotowski's actors were so intense, so much into what they were doing, that even when a whisker away from you, they were in another world. Only with the starkly simple space of *Apocalypsis cum figuris*, the Laboratory's last work to which a general public was admitted, did spectators emerge as participants. During the New York performances attendees sat on the floor at the edges of a large room – the Washington Square Methodist Church, cleared of all furniture. The actors performed in the center, at the same level as those watching. Lighting was one huge fresnel lying on the floor like a fallen sun. At a point in *Apocalypsis*'s life, Grotowski began to invite some spectators to stay after the show. When the rest of the public left, the Laboratory's actors and the visitors began mutual performative explorations. In this way, Grotowski segued from the Theatre of Productions to Paratheatre. In my view, this transformation was stimulated by Grotowski's encounter with American youth culture, gestalt therapy, and new age religions. But I am getting ahead of the story.

The questions Grotowski confronted in every production before *Apocalypsis* concerned the following: for whom were the performances made; how could a textual–gestural montage be constructed; and how could the spaces of performance contain and express the overall life of the event? In answering these questions, Grotowski followed and then superseded Stanislavsky. Stanislavsky always put the actor at the center. He accepted the proscenium stage space and playwrights' texts as given. Grotowski, aware of what Meyerhold, Vakhtangov, and Okhlopkov attempted, took from these experimenters without abandoning Stanislavsky's core quest: the work of the actor on himself. Stanislavsky's "method of physical actions," developed in the 1930s, was probably influenced by Meyerhold's bio-mechanical work of the 1920s. Meyerhold emphasized dancelike acrobatic movements performed with the efficiency of (the then admired) assembly line. Grotowski's adaptation of Stanislavsky and Meyerhold, reshaped by other influences still to be discussed, were the "association exercises" and "plastiques" (movement work). These were freer than Meyerhold's bio-mechanics, more set than Stanislavsky's or Vakhtangov's acting etudes. The exercises consisted of specific movements – rotations, lifts, and stretches of limbs, torso, head, face, and eyes – which took on intensity, rhythm, and emotional coloring from whatever "associations" – feelings, memories, near-dreams – a person might have while executing the movements.[7]

But even while still making productions for a public, however tiny, Grotowski was aiming at targets other than theatre. *Towards a Poor Theatre* is full of allusions to the spiritual path. Theatre was his means, not an end. The goal was not political, as with Brecht; nor artistic, as with Stanislavsky; nor revolutionary, as with Artaud. Grotowski's goal was spiritual: the search for and education of each performer's soul. The contradiction, power, and beauty of the Laboratory Theatre's work in the 1950s and 1960s came from Polish circumstances. Grotowski and his group had to make theatre, that's what the government subsidized them to do. So that is what he and his colleagues in Opole and later Wroclaw did. But, as already noted, Grotowski chose theatre over medicine and Hindu studies because the rehearsal process offered him a chance to work in relative freedom, behind closed doors. This suited him just fine: his interests ran to the esoteric and hermetic anyway. Grotowski told me in Copenhagen:

> Because theatre was at that time the only possibility where I would not be censored. Censors could squelch playtexts, they could censor the final dress rehearsal. But most of the real work in theatre takes place during rehearsals; and gestures and music and such did not have "meaning" the

censors could grasp, could censor. The censors didn't enter the rehearsals. They only came in when a performance was ready for the public. So theatre was a place where one could work more or less freely, for a long time in preparation.

A very shrewd appraisal. A strong argument for emphasizing process over product. But there is more to it, of course. With Grotowski there are always layers of significance, double or quadruple meanings, contradictions.

In making a "theatre laboratory," Grotowski consciously emulated Neils Bohr, the nuclear physicist his brother once worked with. But the experiments of this theatre laboratory had more in common with Grotowski's closest Polish predecessor, Osterwa. Osterwa believed that acting was a "calling," that actors play *vis-à-vis* spectators but never for spectators. Kazimierz Braun traces the importance of Osterwa's Reduta to Grotowski:

> Who was Osterwa? An actor, a director, a teacher, a reformer. [. . .] Reduta [. . .] was a theatre, but at the same time it was an acting workshop and a school. All events of life and artistic activity were communal, with a common kitchen and money. Specialists of varying skills were called to rehearsals as advisors and teachers. Actors and spectators met after performances to discuss the work. All this was based on Osterwa's belief that the theatre is a process, an inter-human process artistically conditioned.
>
> Osterwa's approach to the theatre was based on the contention that its mission is above all spiritual, educational, and moral. Work in the theatre should be based on the individual ethics of actors and directors, of all the people involved in creating theatre, including the spectators. [. . .]
>
> Osterwa experimented with special methods of rehearsal. He was among the first in Europe to introduce actor training separate from rehearsals. He also experimented with audience participation. He used to bring actors and spectators into close contact, even merging them. [. . .] Osterwa's most acclaimed production was *The Constant Prince*. [. . .] Osterwa himself playing the title role made this play a ritual of sacrifice, obviously (as Grotowski did later on) comparing the Constant Prince to Jesus Christ. Osterwa's production of *The Constant Prince* was in the open air, lit – partially – by open fire. [. . .]
>
> Grotowski took much from Osterwa: the idea of the actor sacrificing her/himself for the spectators, his pattern of comparing the studio/theatre to a monastery, his attempts to include spectators into the theatrical action. Even on the simply external level, however significant, Grotowski took an old Reduta trade mark [a graphic emblem] for "Laboratory Theatre".

(1986:235–36)

Grotowski followed and absorbed Osterwa; was like his predecessor and went beyond him; made a new theatre under Reduta's old sign.

DALCROZE AND GURDJIEFF

More intriguing, because less well known, are the parallels between Grotowski's researches and Emile Jaques-Dalcroze, Martin Buber, and Gurdjieff. These and many others including Shaw, Appia, Stanislavsky, and Nijinsky participated in or saw work at Hellerau, near Dresden. The Hellerau project lasted only from 1911 to 1914, before being snuffed out by World War One. Hellerau looked back to Wagner's *Gesamtkunstwerk* and forward to the Bauhaus and Black Mountain College. At Hellerau, the idea of art, health, and education converged. Dalcroze's eurhythmics were reshaped under Adolph Appia's influence into an integrated dance–music–theatre art. Buber participated in theatre at Hellerau;[8] and the physical plant was entrancing enough to induce Gurdjieff to seek it in 1922 for his headquarters. But the link joining Dalcroze, Gurdjieff, and Grotowski is more than real estate.

At Hellerau – a radiant meadow – what was Dalcroze's work? Hellerau was more than a theatre, it was a model community for living in harmony with nature and art. In the theatre building, the whole space was designed. Spectators and performers illuminated by diffused lighting watched and enacted movements expressing not narration but feelings. Dalcroze worked not with individuals, but with groups, crowds. The goal was an integration of music, dance, theatre, lighting, and scenography. Dalcroze said that "only an intimate understanding of the synergies and conflicting forces of our bodies can provide the clue to this future art of expressing emotion through a crowd; while music will achieve the miracle of guiding the latters' movements – grouping, separating, rousing, depressing, in short, 'orchestrating' it, according to the dictates of natural eurhythmics" (1976 [1921]:x). Dalcroze did not investigate Buber's "ich und du," the intimate dyad so important to Grotowski. Nor did Dalcroze go as far as Gurdjieff and Grotowski: asserting that "objective" movement and song is truth embodied, felt, and performed. But Dalcroze's work is an important step along the way.

To Gurdjieff dance – sacred movement – was the core of the received wisdom of the oral tradition. Gurdjieff described himself as a "dancing master," aligning himself with Sufi masters whose whirling dances embodied their understanding of the world.[9] Throughout most of his life as a teacher, Gurdjieff staged dances, sometimes for large paying publics, as in Paris in 1923 and New York in 1924, sometimes privately for patrons or disciples. Movement, Gurdjieff taught, brings people close to the truth of things. According to James Moore:

The interface between Dalcroze eurhythmics and Gurdjieff's Sacred Dance dates from the Tblisi period when Jeanne [de] Salzmann put her Dalcroze pupils at Gurdjieff's disposition for the demonstration at the Opera House on 22 June 1919. In winter 1921, when Gurdjieff came to Hellerau more or less under the patronage of Dalcroze, he evidently presented a programme of sorts [. . .] Jessmin Howarth and Rose Mary Nott – Dalcroze students who abandoned eurhythmics and attached themselves to Gurdjieff around this time – later became respected teachers of Gurdjieff's dances. When Gurdjieff first arrived in Paris in July 1922, he established himself in the Institut Jaques-Dalcroze in the Rue de Vaugirard.

(1991:362)

Moore says the "question of direct personal contact between Gurdjieff and Dalcroze is clouded." But whether or not the two men ever personally interacted, they were linked by Jeanne de Salzmann who, more than putting her dancers at Gurdjieff's "disposal," became Gurdjieff's closest disciple, the heir to his knowledge, the receiver of the oral tradition. In the body of de Salzmann, Dalcroze and Gurdjieff met. But what about Grotowski?

When Grotowski first met Peter Brook, a Gurdjievian of the highest rank, the Englishman thought the Pole

was the emissary of a lost branch of Gurdjieff's school which survived in Poland after the emigration of Gurdjieff and his primary teachers to the West during the Russian revolution. Grotowski speculates that Brook's conclusion was based on certain pronounced similarities between Grotowski's objectives and rhetoric and the specialized terminology of Gurdjievian teaching, as well as Gurdjieff's focus on embodied practice as a means for self-remembering. [. . .] What might have come as a surprise to Brook, however, was that Grotowski [. . .] had never so much as heard the name of the Armenian master before that day.

(Wolford 1996c:225)

Grotowski repeats the denial in a 1991 interview (Grotowski 1996a). Is trickster Grotowski to be believed? Grotowski's journeys as a young man took him to many of the regions Gurdjieff explored at the turn of the century: interior central Asia, China, India, Tibet – threading the ancient silk-route into areas where Sufis danced, where Buddhism, Lamaism, Hinduism, and Islam feed each other. Even at the start of the Theatre of 13 Rows, Grotowski, like Gurdjieff, worked from a close inner circle, transmitting knowledge directly by means of dance, song, utterance, and intimate encounter. Granted that Grotowski was barely thirty when he met Brook, could it be that in his pursuit of esoteric knowledge – his research into old forms of Christianity, his studies of the Tao, Vedism, yoga, Sufism, gnosis, and shamanism – Grotowski never heard the name "Gurdjieff"?

Or maybe it is that once Grotowski learned of Gurdjieff, and saw how close the intention of their work was, he drew certain elements from him. In discussing Objective Drama in the 1980s, Grotowski uses terms very much like those Gurdjieff employed discussing the objective laws of art. "In real art," Gurdjieff said, "there is nothing accidental. It is mathematics. Everything in it can be calculated, everything can be known beforehand. [. . .] It will always, and with mathematical certainty, produce one and the same impression. [. . .] This is real, objective art" (Ouspensky 1949:26–27). Ouspensky asked Gurdjieff if this art exists now? "Of course. The great Sphinx in Egypt is such a work of art." But in our own day? Gurdjieff told of what he saw "in the desert at the foot of the Hindu Kush," an ancient god or devil. "[T]his figure contained many things, a big, complete and complex system of cosmology. And slowly, step by step, we began to decipher this system. [. . .] In the whole statue there was nothing accidental, nothing without meaning" (1949:27). Gurdjieff's desire to produce his own "objective art" led him to synthesize what he called The Movements from different sources. According to Ouspensky, "We began rhythmic exercises to music, dervish dances, different kinds of mental exercises, the study of different ways of breathing, and so on" (1949:372). Over time Gurdjieff put these together into a "ballet" or "revue" which as performed in Tiflis, Paris, and New York "there entered [. . .] dances, exercises, and the ceremonies of various dervishes [mostly Mevlevi] as well as many little known Eastern dances" (1949:382). Michel de Salzmann, Jeanne's son and a leading Gurdjievian, writes that Gurdjieff's "aim was to show the forgotten principles of an objective 'science of movements' and to demonstrate its specific role in the work of spiritual development" (1987:139). The Movements also show Dalcroze entering the work via Jeanne de Salzmann. Moreover, The Movements are similar to Grotowski's Motions, a basic exercise developed during the Objective Drama phase. In Motions, as in Movements, the physical details are very precisely codified, repeated in exactly the same way.

Having neither done nor witnessed The Movements or Motions, I won't presume to compare the two. However, photographs and descriptions indicate what I feel is more than a coincidence. The similarities can be explained two ways. Either Grotowski took something from Gurdjieff or both Gs drew from the same sources. Whichever, what interests me is the underlying drive of the work. Speeth says The Movements "are a kind of meditation in action that also has the properties of an art form and a language" (1989:83,88). This could just as well be said of *Downstairs*

Action and *Action*. Grotowski, in an interview published in *Encounters with Gurdjieff*, observes:

> The Movements: they are something fundamental. Gurdjieff is rooted in a very ancient tradition, and at the same time he is contemporary. He knew, with a true competence, how to act in agreement with the modern world. It is a very rare case. [. . .] From the moment I began to read about Gurdjieff's work, the practical comparisons not only had to corroborate but also to touch me, it is obvious. It would be difficult to analyze: which details, which elements? Because there is also a danger of asking oneself: "From where comes this element, and from where another?" What is important is not that they come from somewhere, but that they work. This criterion, is it clear? This means: There is an element which works, and it is corroborated here and there. In the case of Gurdjieff, the impact is of something both very ancient and contemporary. Both the tradition and the research are strong. And at the same time there is there a manner of posing some ultimate questions. Here we are no longer in the technical data, but in the depths of ideas, with all the dangers that this brings.
>
> (1996a:93–94)

Isn't Grotowski describing himself as much as Gurdjieff? The convergences are just as clear when he talks about his 1990s work at Pontedera:

> At present my work is very much linked to ancient song, to "vibratory" song. In a period of my "Laboratory Theatre," for example in *The Constant Prince*, the research was focused less on song, though in a certain way it was already a sung action. I have always considered it very strange to want to work on voice or song, or even pronounced words, while cutting them off from corporeal reactions. The two aspects are very much linked; they pass through each other. [. . .] At my Workcenter in Pontedera, in Italy, as far as technical elements are concerned, everything is as it is in the performing arts; we work on song, on the vibratory qualities of song, on impulses and physical actions, on forms of movement; and even narrative motifs may appear. All this is filtered and structured up to the point of creating an accomplished structure, an Action, as precise and repeatable as a stage production. Nevertheless it is not a production. One can call it art as a vehicle or even the objectivity of the ritual. [. . .] When I refer to ritual, I speak of its objectivity: that is to say that the elements of the Action are, through their direct impact, the instruments of the work on the body, the heart, and head of the "doers".
>
> (Grotowski 1996a:87–88)

Ironically, Grotowski the stage director goes out of his way to deny the theatre while Gurdjieff the spiritual master behaved so often as an impresario.

What tethers the Gs to each other, finally, is their search for gnosis, an ancient religious practice of the interior Middle East, Central Asia, Iran, Afghanistan.

SUFIS AND HASIDS

Gnosis is a Greek word meaning, roughly, "knowing." It is cognate with the English "know" as well as with Sanskrit jnana, the yoga of wisdom or knowing. Gnosis is an "underground," sometimes heretical, tradition in Judaism, Christianity, and Islam. Gnosis is affined with Sufism and the hermetic religion of Egypt and Greece. The precise sources of gnosis are disputed. Some say Egyptian, some Hebrew, some Iranian. Probably all these, mixing effervescently during the two millennia before Christ. Gnosis has long been resistant to orthodoxy, whether Jewish, Christian, or Islamic. In some manifestations – the teachings of Mani (216–77), for example – gnosis was condemned as heresy. The Egyptian-Greco root of gnosis is Hermes Trismegistos, "thrice great Hermes," who proclaimed, "He who knows himself, knows all." Such knowledge can be tragic, ask Sophocles' Oedipus. This "self" is not personality, but the identicality of Brahman and atman: that which in each is All. This impersonal self Oedipus sees after he stabs out his eyes. Such blindsight Krishna gives to Arjuna in the *Bhagavad-Gita*.

> KRISHNA:
> But you cannot see me
> with your own eye;
> I will give you the eye to see
> the majesty of my yoga.
> SANJAYA:
> The brightness of a thousand suns
> burning together in the sky
> is the light of that great self.
> And Arjuna saw the whole universe
> converged into one body. [. . .]
> ARJUNA:
> O, God! [. . .]
> You are the imperishable.
> Beginning, middle, and end
> you do not know.
> Your arms, numberless.
> Your eyes the sun and moon,

> your mouth flaming fire
> burning up all that is.[10]

Arjuna has the courage to ask: "Who are you in this terrifying being I see?" "I am time, that which swallows all," says Krishna.

Gnosis knows that atman–Brahman is an absolute that can be experienced but not reduced to discourse. Gnosis is expressed in metaphors and practices. Gnosis is an upward journey along the path of the chakras, the ancient yogic wheels of energy within each human, from the lowest center at the base of the spine upwards to the high center in the skull. Gnosis is the scattered sparks of original fire, embers that can be gathered into larger and brighter centers of light. It was in search of these miraculous embers, these "sources," that Gurdjieff and Grotowski undertook their journeys geographical, mystical, and theatrical.

In the 1991 interview previously cited, Grotowski talks about how his work

> is like a kind of elevator, but an elevator as in very ancient times, in the so-called primitive societies: a big basket with a rope by means of which the person who is inside, by his own effort, has to move himself from one level to another. The question of verticality means to pass from a so-called coarse level – in a certain sense one could say an "everyday" level – to a level of energy much more subtle or even toward the *higher connection* [Grotowski's italics]. At this point to say more about it wouldn't be right.
>
> (1996a:88–89)

But he does say more about it. Grotowski describes how in *Action*, songs are the way of rising toward the subtle and of making the subtle descend "to the level of the more ordinary." These songs are "very ancient [. . .] linked to the ritual approach, because that is the material of our work" (1996a:90–91).

Grotowski knows that different cultures, at different periods, have different terms for the same system. He finds analogous theories and practices of the upward and downward flow of energy in Gurdjieff, in the theory of chakras, in India, China, and Europe. Still he resists "naming," reducing to discourse.

> In general, one can say that we try not to freeze language. An "intentional" language is used, i.e., one which functions only between the people who are working. There, where one approaches the more complex issues, the so-called inner work, I avoid as much as possible any verbalization.
>
> (1996a:92)

Then, exasperated by the interviewer's insistence, "But if you are pushing me toward the language of religions then . . . O.K. . . . I let myself go" (1996a:105). In a burst of references, Grotowski ranges over fables, expressions, figures, metaphors: Jacob's ladder, Kali, the Shekhinah, jnana, gnosis. "In the traditions, there exist several versions about the two currents of the world: the descending and the ascending. This can take quasi-gnostic forms of explanation [. . .]but it also exists in the sciences. The appearance of life and consciousness would be like a small countercurrent because, in the scientific sense the world has been created through entropy and in entropy. A kind of an opposite process is the appearance of life" (1996a:105–6). There the interview abruptly ends.

When Mevlevi Sufi dervishes dance, the right palm faces upwards receiving divine solar energy, the left down transmitting the energy into the earth, the people. As in gnosis, the work is to gather energy, focus it, and redirect it. Work similar to that of Hasids seeking the Shekhinah or yogins training their serpent kundalini up the ladder of chakras. Each are part of the "small countercurrent" acting against universal entropy. Sufis can be of any religion, or (as Grotowski) none. They are "hidden more deeply than the practitioner of any secret school. Yet individual Sufis are known in their thousands . . . in the lands of the Arabs, the Turks, the Persians, Afghans, Indians, Malays" (Shah 1971:18). Sufi knowledge is various and complex[11], reaching back and into Toth/Hermes[12], gnosis, Hebrew, Egyptian, Greek, and Islamic sources. Sufism is an embodied practice, existing in its dances and songs. The ceremonies of the Mevlevi Order founded in the thirteenth century in Konya (today's Turkey) by Mevlana Celaleddin Rumi, poet and mystic, were closely studied by Gurdjieff.

> In 1920 Gurdjieff led his Institute into exile in Turkey, and studied the techniques of the Rufai and Mevlevi rituals. [. . .] Later his troupe travelled across Europe and the U.S.A., always incorporating some elements of the Whirling Dervish movements combined with other dervish dancing from Central Asia, Christian Assyrian ritual, and folk and country dances from Turkey and Transcaspia. The male members of his company were generally attired exactly like the Whirling Dervishes.
>
> (Halman and And 1983:73–74)

Dervishes, The Movements, Motions, *Downstairs Action*, *Action* are linked by the kind of movement used, the sources of that movement, and by purpose and function. Not to reduce Grotowski to Sufism, but to indicate Sufism as another strong presence within the Grotowski-body (not his own so much as those he has trained most intently: Cynkutis, Cieslak, Richards).

If Sufism (and all it refers to and synthesizes) is a key ingredient in Grotowski's work, his way of working is Hasidic. To find Sufis, yogins, and other Asian knowers, Grotowski had to travel. Hasids were all around him in Poland, even as they went up in the smoke of the Holocaust (a vanishing represented in *Akropolis*). Modern Hasidism arose in Eastern Europe in the mid-eighteenth century among followers of Yisrael ben Eliezer, the Baal Shem Tov ("Master of the Good Name") known by his acronym, Besht. Before Besht was Shabbetai Tsevi who, in 1665, during a period of Jewish suffering unequalled in Europe before the Holocaust, proclaimed himself Messiah and "was venerated as 'our lord and king' from Cairo to Hamburg, from Salonika to Amsterdam from Morocco to Yemen, from Poland to Persia" (Werblowsky 1987:193). Then when in 1666, imprisoned by the Ottomans and told to convert or die by torture, Shabbetai traded yamulka for turban, a great disillusionment gripped Jewish communities, preparing the way for Besht and Hasidism. Hasids rejected Shabbetai. Instead they emphasized practices connected to the Kaballah and the Zohar. As in gnosis, but in terms that affirm Jewish monism (as opposed to gnostic dualism), Hasids believe that God "contracted" himself "away from the world which vacated the space in which the cosmos was going to be created from the divine light of the godhead, the first exile of God" (Dan 1987:207). Or as Martin Buber puts it:

> The Kabbalistic teaching, which Hasidism built into its own system, [. . .] teaches that the firestream of creative grace poured itself out over "the vessels," the first created primal forms, in all its fullness; but the vessels could not stand it, they "broke into pieces" – and the stream flashed forth into the infinity of "sparks," the "shells" grew round them, want, defilement, evil came into the world. But He does not leave it to lie alone in the abyss of its struggles; his Glory itself descends to the world, following the sparks of his creative passion; His Shekhinah goes into it, goes into "Exile," lives in it; she lives with the sorrowful, suffering, created things in the midst of their defilements – eager to redeem them.
>
> (1948:105–06)

> God's Shekhinah descended from sphere to sphere, wandered from world to world, enveloped itself with shell upon shell, until it was in its furthest exile – in us. In our world God's fate is being accomplished.
>
> (1948:64–67)

Hasids seek the Shekhinah, whom the Greeks called Sophia, the light of wisdom, in order to break through the "shells" and gather her "sparks." In Grotowski's terms, this search for the Shekhinah is his "Theatre of Sources," his "Objective Drama," his "Art as vehicle."

Grotowski says that Buber – "the last great Hasid" – affected him more than Gurdjieff. "I knew about the Zohar from the time I was ten years old," Grotowski told me, "and Buber from about age eighteen." But what kind of impact did Buber–Hasidism have? Certainly Grotowski's method of working with those he once called actors and now calls "performer" or "doer" has the quality of "ich und du," an intimate dialogue, unique and unrepeatable. But there is more. Hasids worship God directly, stressing the "mystical contact with God through *devegut*, usually attained while praying but also achieved when a person is working for his livelihood or engaged in any other physical activity" (Dan 1987:207). Hasids believe in the "zaddik," the righteous person, of whom there are precious few.

> [I]n every generation there are some righteous persons who can and should, by their outstanding mystical worship, correct the sins and transgressions of lesser-endowed people. [. . .] This theory demands that the *Tsaddiq* be in constant movement between good and evil, heaven and earth. [. . .] He has to be close to the evil that he is to correct, subjecting himself to the process of a "fall".
>
> (Dan 1987:208)

Grotowski's "primal elevator," the rising up, the falling down; the persistent theme of seeking-and-sacrificing in *The Constant Prince*, *Akropolis, Apocalypsis cum figuris*, reconfigured but not abandoned in the various phases of "cultural research" from the paratheatrical experiments to the "Art as vehicle", show strong Hasidic affinities.

But it is not in the philosophical systems that Hasidism and Grotowski most closely approach each other. It is in Grotowski's style of leadership, his relationship to his inner circle and they to the wider world. Rebbe Grotowski is the center from whom all radiates. His authority is unquestioned, yet gossiped about. Stories about him abound. His aura surrounds, protects, and illuminates him. The core of what he has to teach cannot be put into words. He is always seeking.

> The Baalshem himself belongs to those central figures in the history of religion who have done their work by living in a certain way, that is to say, not starting out from a teaching but aiming towards a teaching, who have lived in such a way that their life acted as a teaching, as a teaching not yet translated into words.
>
> (Buber 1948:2)

To see those who serve Grotowski accomplish their work, is to witness a Hasidic community and its rebbe. Grotowski answers his disciples' love not sanctimoniously or sentimentally, but in typical Hasidic fashion: paradoxically, with wit, demanding unremitting hard work, radiating light and energy. This is, as Buber points out, like Zen. "In both [Zen and Hasidism], man reveres human truth, not in the form of a possession, but in the form of a movement, not as a fire that burns upon the hearth, but, speaking the language of our time, like the electric spark, which is kindled by contact" (1948:194).

Grotowski is Hasidic (and not that only) in another way: the "place" of women in his work. Yes there were a few strong women performers in Grotowski's projects, notably Rena Mirecka in the Theatre of Productions and Haitian Maud Robart in Objective Drama. But the principals have always been men. At least two other women have been very important to Grotowski, but not in the work itself. Carla Pollastrelli runs the Pontedera Workcenter. And until cancer took her in 1992, Mercedes Gregory was a very close friend and the film documenter of *Downstairs Action*. Grotowski speaks of Chiquita (as she was known), and her husband André Gregory, as "my family." But generally women have been a tiny minority as performers and absent as inheritors. Here Grotowski diverges radically from Gurdjieff, whose heir was Jeanne de Salzmann. Grotowski's "structural sexism" stems from his belief in archetypal differences between the genders and his almost reverential regard for his mother. This attitude fits the Hasidic treatment of women and their view of the Shekhinah. But there is also more than a small dose of Polish Catholicism in Grotowski's treatment of women. In his artistic work, women are cast along the polar opposition of the Virgin Mary or Mary Magdalene.

THE AMERICAN CONNECTION

The Grotowski who left America in 1969 after performances of the Laboratory Theatre was one man, the person who returned in 1970 to deliver the lectures that were to become "Holiday" was another. In between was his third trip to India and a bi-coastal hitch-hike across the U.S.A. Leaving New York was a pudgy, pale Polish intellectual wearing a black suit, eyes shielded by dark glasses even indoors, short hair neatly combed, clean-shaven cheeks smooth as a baby's. Returning was a skinny man in jeans and shoulder bag, a wispy scraggly beard streaming from his face, eyes visible through thick but clear lenses, silky hair cascading down over his shoulders. This Grotowski seemed both a hippy and an ageless Chinese sage. Whatever happened to him was more than a meeting in an ashram or a few hours in a Haight Ashbury haberdashery. I believe Grotowski's encounter with American youth culture was decisive. After all, Grotowski had previously immersed himself in Asian cultures, but the America he met on the road was new to him.

What did Grotowski see, do, and take into himself during his American trek? What happened to him on the road is not known, but surely he drank in the extraordinary energies of the sixties epoch. In

California especially he came into contact with various strong currents: hippies in full flower, the ideas of Carlos Castaneda and Barbara Myerhoff (both of whom he met[13]), Native American cultures, especially the shamanic practices of northwest Mexico (of great importance, in the 1930s and after, to Artaud), and the widely radiating influence of the Esalen Institute which, like Hellerau more than a half-century earlier, conflated art, religion, science, and "spiritual work."

Grotowski absorbed stuff from the then emerging "human potential movement," the incipient "new age." Grotowski says he did not visit Esalen or meet gestalt therapists Fritz or Laura Perls (man and wife) either there or in San Francisco. But Esalen's links to Eastern religions and practices (yoga, zen, massage, meditation, music, dance), its program of mindbody integration, and the strong, charismatic persons at work there in the late 1960s and early 1970s, like the Gurdjieff work, strongly coincided with Grotowski's interests and research.

Esalen and the "human potential movement" centered there were historically linked to theatre through Fritz and Laura Perls and through the founder of psychodrama, Jacob Moreno. In the 1920s, before becoming a psychoanalyst, Fritz Perls studied theatre in Berlin with Max Reinhardt. Throughout his career, Perls "was keenly interested in integrating movement and dance into his active therapy as a means of self-expression" (Gainese 1979:112). As a co-founder of Gestalt Therapy, Perls co-authored with Ralph F. Hefferline and poet–playwright Paul Goodman the influential *Gestalt Therapy: Excitement and Growth in the Human Personality* (1951). New York-based Goodman worked with the Living Theater in the 1950s and 1960s. Perls also worked briefly with the Living. The Perls were affected by Buber as well. At the very least, in the 1920s when the Perls were living in Frankfurt, Laura Perls attended Buber's lectures. Buber, of course, was active earlier at Hellerau, collaborating on productions and writing about theatre. At Esalen and elsewhere, Fritz Perls' therapy sessions, performed in front of audiences of several hundred, were very theatrical, employing methods of direct confrontation (the famous Perls "hot-seat") and intense one-on-one dialogue. Up the coast, Perls conducted a series of Gestalt Therapy sessions for Anna Halprin's San Francisco Dancers' Workshop. From the mid-1960s on, Halprin was moving away from "art dance" to events very close to what Grotowski would research during his Paratheatre, Theatre of Sources, Objective Drama, and Art as vehicle periods. Halprin was interested in uncovering or inventing rituals and enacting links to archetypal, traditional knowledge. She was also deeply committed to healing, on both the individual and community levels. As a choreographer, Halprin relied more on movement and song than on spoken words. She worked intimately with people on very private material which she helped them connect to archetypes through gesture, movement, song, and dance[14]. I do not say that Grotowski knew Halprin or Perls–but that the California *zeitgeist* of the late 1960s and early 1970s must have struck Grotowski. What he had been working on more or less privately, almost in secret, was public culture in California.

Grotowski did meet Carlos Castaneda. In his "Don Juan" books of "Yaqui knowledge" Castaneda farmed the ground between field research and fiction (and reaped a fortune)[15]. I have some first-hand knowledge of the Yaquis, at least those who live close to Tucson[16], and the people and practices Castaneda writes about are not them. What Castaneda did was weave together into a single fabric various strands of traditional lore, both Native American and Asian. The veracity of his field data aside, the underlying theme of Castaneda's work is that traditional and ancient ways of knowing are at hand, if only one knows how and with whom to look. This knowledge – powerful, oral, dangerous, beautiful – was literally right across the Mexican border from ultra-modern California. But what the Yaqui shaman Don Juan had to offer was accessible only through initiation, after enduring many ordeals. Intentionally or not, Castaneda kicked off a full-scale culture tourist industry: "I know a shaman who can teach you" (for a price). Grotowski detests this kind of "dilettantism." But that did not stop him from traveling to Mexico (as Artaud did in the 1930s). Grotowski also, I think, detected in Castaneda a kernel of experienced truth. Castaneda's Don Juan – whoever he was, literal, dreamed up, or hodge-podge – was a "remarkable man" in the Gurdjievian and Grotowskian sense: someone to learn from. And Grotowski recognized many of the Hindu and Sufi sources which Castaneda, in his later books, represents as Yaqui.

The sources of the American human potential movement and of new age shamanism include exiles from the Frankfurt School, Buberian ich–du neo-Hasids, Timothy Leary's and Allan Watts' psychedelic flower-power children, persons seeking Asian and Native American ways of knowing (from yoga to Zen to Castaneda), and innovators in psycho-analysis such as Moreno and the Perls. These forces flowed together under the aegis of the peculiarly Californian penchant for hybridity. The human potential movement and new age shamanism took so strongly in the 1960s and early 1970s because America then seemed open to change. The African American Freedom Movement and the student movement against the Vietnam War shared strategies, persons, and long-term goals. By sitting-in, marching, demonstrating, and living out their values, adherents of the Movements (a poignant coincidence of nomenclature) acted from a moral and ethical base, effectively challenging both official authority and mainstream culture. Rarely in American history have intellectuals, students, artists, and ordinary persons of different colors, classes, and ethnicities acted in such concert. It was a period of utopian hopes. Hitch-hiking across this America, ending in California, what must Grotowski – a man from monolithic Communist Poland – have felt and thought? In turning in his dark suit for blue-jeans, his suitcase for a backpack, his clean-shaved face for a beard, his fat for lean, the man was making a statement.

Grotowski is not someone whose "sources" can be pinned down to a simple "from this comes that." He accumulates knowledge, integrates what he learns, and engages in a continuous process of research. No simple causal chain can be forged to explain his work or personality. But in my view his journey across America, the people he met, the youth culture he saw and most probably participated in, the interactions he might have had with the human potential movement, all strengthened changes that were inherent in his European program – the connections to Gurdjieff, Dalcroze, Sufis, and Hasidism. In fact, American culture of that epoch was itself fed by this European stream. The flight of especially Jewish intellectuals and artists from Nazism carried to America one packet of seeds of the human potential movement; the other packet came from across the Pacific Ocean. Working bi-coastally, connections soon were made between the two linking Asian, Native American, and European ideas and practices. Not surprisingly, the Pacific theatre of World War Two, the occupation of Japan, the Korean War, and the Vietnam War fed American interest in what was to become known as the "Pacific Rim." The politics of anti-Communism dictated that in the 1950s and 1960s China be excluded from this interest. The Chinese connection began in earnest after Nixon's fabled 1972 trip to Beijing.

What Grotowski saw in late 1960s–early 1970s' America, confirmed tendencies already operating in his own work: An expanded sense of theatre, the bridge from "productions" to "sources"; an emphasis on process over product; a systematic research into traditional performance practices; reliance on dance and song instead of spoken dialogue; a possibility of integrating the performance knowledge of diverse cultures. In changing his appearance, Grotowski allied himself with a utopian youth culture which believed young people could change the world by changing themselves, that "inner trips" were as transformational as outward journeys. Of course Grotowski interpreted what he saw in his own terms. He rejected what he felt was "self-indulgent," or soft-headed. But he took away with him the idea that performance, rather than theatre, was the path he ought to tread. A poster of Grotowski appeared somewhat later, in 1979 on the occasion of the Laboratory Theatre's twentieth anniversary. Grotowski is depicted as two persons, walking towards each other, both coming and going from us. He is bone-thin, long-haired, in blue-jean jacket and shoulder-bag, on the road. The

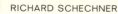

Grotowski of this period, with his wispy beard and faint smile, looks more like Bob Dylan than a European theatre director.

GROTOWSKI'S SIGNIFICANCE, GROTOWSKI'S DEFICIENCY

Grotowski is significant because he continues the main work of Stanislavsky and Meyerhold: focusing theatrical art on the actor rather than the playwright; because he helps performers connect their own bodymind experiences and memories with the more "objective" elements of theatrical expression – movements, dances, and songs – of "ancient" or "traditional" cultures (the quotation marks will be explained later); because he follows a process of montage whereby the performers rigorously stitch these ancient and traditional bits of performance into coherent wholes; because his work as embodied in designated successors and in a complex and far-reaching web of persons and groups disseminates his wisdom and practice: Grotowski's influence will grow over the coming years.

Grotowski has researched, used, and articulated a coherent and deeply thought-out system of acting, actor training, *mise-en-scene*, scenography, and textual montage. Granted, he has not worked exclusively on these problems since the late 1960s, but his ideas have thoroughly permeated theatre practice in and beyond the West. Grotowski knows European theatre history and, though he has not said so explicitly, tendencies in his work indicate that he seeks an important place for himself in that history. A number of Grotowski-influenced groups and a much greater number of Grotowski-influenced individuals are working in the theatre. These "offshoots" have come in waves, emanating from the different periods of Grotowski's work. Of these, only a few can be mentioned here. From the Theatre of Productions there is, of course, Barba and his Odin Teatret; but also The Performance Group and André Gregory's Manhattan Project. From Paratheatre and Theatre of Sources there is Gardzienice, and the work of Nicholas Nuñez and Helena Guardia in Mexico. From Objective Drama there is the New World Performance Laboratory.

Grotowski's work has affected fields other than theatre: dance, performance art, and healing. Grotowski's practice since the Theatre of Productions – mostly everything he has been doing after 1970 – has taken him into research whose ramifications are not yet clear. The early phase of this work, Paratheatre, will probably prove to be relatively unimportant (except for those wishing to understand Grotowski's trajectory and those whose lives were changed by their experiences). But the later phases, especially Objective Drama and Art as vehicle, have drawn Grotowski once again towards theatre-as-theatre. Art as vehicle nearly closes the circle – spiral or gyre would be better figures – with the Theatre of Productions. In *Downstairs Action* and *Action* there is scenic montage, roles, and at least the hint of a narrative.

Action is not a regularly scheduled performance playing to a paying public. It is shown to invited audiences, mostly people closely associated with Grotowski, invited groups of young performers, and scholars. I won't describe *Action* here: Lisa Wolford does so in Chapter 41 of this book. To those who know Grotowski's "poor theatre" work, *Action* will come as no surprise. Song, dance, chant: intensity bottled in a tightly confined space admitting only a few spectators; no stage as such, but movement throughout the space; spectators–witnesses "confronted" but not asked to participate. The performers are well trained and highly disciplined in body and voice. Even more impressively, they embody and communicate to each other and to the witnesses a spiritual actuality, a believed-in reality far surpassing Stanislavsky's "as if." Yet these players are not in trance, not possessed. Quite the opposite, they have found themselves. When Wolford wrote about it, she ended not with description, but rapture.

> I cannot say in language what is *Action*; I think it would be monumental hubris to pretend that I could grasp in a matter of days, of hours seated in this room, the mystery that these people have discovered/created, some of them over a span of many years. [. . .] The song is a seed of light that finds its rootedness in the heart of the doer, radiating outward, upward, burning away the dead matter and leaving behind it a visible trace – in the body, yes, but not only and not even primarily in the body. To some extent I perceive and respond to the presence of the song-as-force, the song-as-living-entity, but my perception is not the same as that of the doer who takes the song into himself and allows it to rise through his body, voice, and being.
>
> (Ch.41:418–19)

Decisive as *Action* is, possibly Grotowski's concrete living legacy, I doubt that what Wolford saw is final or definitive – or could be. Because of Grotowski's restless, relentless research, if time allows (and Grotowski's health is precarious) *Action* is another step along an endless way.

For all this, there are deficiencies in Grotowski's work, and in the assumptions that drive that work. These ought to be aired and discussed. His method – derived from gnostic and hermetic sources and modeled to some degree on Hasidic and Gurdjievian closed-circle communities – forecloses open discussion. As in the Hindu guru–shishya relationship, knowledge is transferred from teacher to learner with scant chance for disclosure, debate, and challenge. Although at one time called a

Laboratory, then the Grotowski Workcenter, and now the Grotowski–Richards Workcenter, there is little of the scientific method of proposal, experiment, and consensual search for provisional truth. The scientific method may be followed by Grotowski and those resident at the Workcenter. Or it may be the way of a particular group of Grotowski-ites. But there is no open debate between different Grotowski-influenced individuals and groups; no discussions open to the scholarly or general public. Grotowski assumes that there are "truths" existing to be "discovered" or "recovered." As with Gurdjieff, these truths are objective. Furthermore, there is a single person, or a small coterie, who are closer to these truths than others. As in the line of transmission of a Japanese noh family, the head of the family possesses the "secrets" and hands them on to his designated heir, at this moment, Thomas Richards.

Furthermore, the whole notion of "truth," "ancient," "objective," and "traditional" can be challenged. Grotowski's fundamental belief is in a kind of archeology of performance, whereby the modern layer, present practices, can be scraped away, or dug down under, so that, older, more authentic, deeper layers of performance can be recovered and practiced. Flying against today's call for cultural specificity, the denial of "universal" human cultural traits, Grotowski's method, from Theatre of Sources onward, has been to sift through practices from different cultures for what is similar among them, searching for the "first," the "original," the "essential," and the "universal." His belief is that performance practices which have survived over time carry, or actually are, "deep" or "ancient" human trans-cultural truths. These truths then "meet" what is most intimate and personal in individual performers. Grotowski is clear about his goal:

> To re-evoke a very ancient form of art where ritual and artistic creation were seamless. Where poetry was song, song was incantation, movement was dance. [. . .] One might say – but it is only a metaphor – that we are trying to go back before the Tower of Babel, and discover what was before. First to discover differences, and then to discover what was before the difference.

> (in Sullivan 1983)

In order to "go back" Grotowski creates a liminal time/space whose physical and experiential references are to the work itself; that is, to what Grotowski chooses to instill. He assumes that the ancient practices are superior to the modern; that through careful research and workshop the ancient practices can be recovered or reconstructed; and that, in his own version of Jung's theory of archetypes, properly trained actors can find in their individual and collective memories – the actual performance work done together – elements parallel to, or even identical with, these ancient practices. Thus that which is most objective is also most intimate; the Brahman is identical to the atman.

In Art as vehicle, Grotowski both distances himself from the avant-garde he was such a defining part of in the 1960s, and makes clear his strong links with that movement:

> When I speak of "theatre company," I mean the theatre of ensemble, the long-term work of a group. Work which is not linked in any particular way to the concepts of the avant-garde and which constitutes the basis for professional theatre of our century. [. . .] In Art as vehicle, from the point of view of technical elements, everything is almost like in the performing arts; we work on song, on impulses, on forms of movement, even textual motifs appear. And all is reduced to the strictly necessary, until a structure appears, a structure as precise and worked out as in a performance: the *Action*.
>
> (Grotowski 1995:115, 122)

And what this structure approaches is "the essential": "It is necessary, through the very actions themselves to discover how to approach – step by step – toward the essential" (1995:125). The step by step work is disciplined, precise, repeatable. This insistence on precision and hard work has always distinguished Grotowski from those he scornfully dismisses as "dilettantes" or "self-indulgent." For Grotowski, what are universal are doable acts of the body which can be learned without knowing the ideologies and histories they are part of or represent. Or to put it another way, Grotowski assumes that culture is often a "shell" in the Hasidic sense, concealing the "sparks" of essential human life. These sparks are present in certain songs, dances, chants, and other practices that it is his work to recover.

This formulation does not satisfy me. I cannot recognize wisdom that exists before or behind cultures and genres, in the "original" times, in the "old practices." Why, for Grotowski, does old equal good? The old is nearer to the beginning, a version of Eden. And, in a Darwinian mode, what survives is fit and strong. Finally, the old is like fine wine, refined and deeply flavored. But how far back can one take this argument? Did Lucy or whoever the first human was dance/sing/perform in a purer and finer way than anyone since? And were the "first humans", whoever they might have been, without culture, without ways of doing/being particular to their group, tribe, selves? This idea of the truth that is behind phenomena – a version of Platonism – is reformulated into Eugenio Barba's "pre-expressive decided body" existing behind and before any particular genre of performance[17]. Does Grotowski's search for the universal, for the essential, cover up a desire to get hold of powers and resources thought to reside in exotic (for Westerners) others, those who lived earlier, elsewhere, or on the margins? What happens to the African or Asian "sources" of *Action*? Is *Action* universal or is it a cultural appropriation? And to whom is *Action* addressed? Is it only for those who do it, for the select few invited to see it? How would *Action* play in the source cultures from which its parts were "distilled"?

There are no final words. As long as Grotowski lives and works he will change. In the Theatre of Productions, he was interested most in Buberian dialogue, and its difficulty of accomplishment. The actors sometimes achieved – along with bodily and vocal skills rarely if ever seen on European stages – a lucidity and transparency of soul (if I may be permitted the word). Their ich und du was experienced by many of us who witnessed those performances. Then in Paratheatre Grotowski tried, briefly but intensely, to open his work to all who were interested – on the American model, it seems. This failed: there were too many hangers-on, persons who wanted "good feelings" and results, but who could not endure focused work under strict discipline long enough to get anywhere. In Theatre of Sources, Grotowski sought and found persons who in their bodies contained and expressed performance knowledge. These masters of traditional performance served as teachers and examples. This tendency to seek, join with, and learn from "the others" was systematized in Objective Drama. In his most recent work, Art as vehicle, Grotowski seems closer to Gurdjieff than Buber, to a singularity rather than a dialogue. It appears as if he desires to distill himself, to simplify, to enter into and become one with an ultimate tonic tone.

NOTES

1 GENERAL INTRODUCTION

1   Kumiega 1985 and Osinski 1986 provide the most complete studies of the theatrical period of Grotowski's career. Osinski is particularly attentive to the growth of public attention directed toward Grotowski's work and incorporates extensive citations from newspaper criticism and scholarly analysis, both from Poland and throughout Europe. For a more concise introduction to the theatrical period of Grotowski's work, see *The Theatre Event* by Timothy Wiles and the chapter by Kumiega in *The Director and the Stage: From Naturalism to Grotowski*, edited by Edward Braun.

2   See Grotowski 1968 and the special issue of *Mascara* edited by Edgar Ceballos (1993) for collections of Grotowski's most significant texts setting forth his theories of performance and *mise-en-scene*. For a consideration of how Grotowski's theories were incorporated into other forms of contemporary experimental production, see especially Schechner 1973.

3   Grotowski made this observation at a meeting in La Rotta, Italy, on 9 August 1995, with a small group that had witnessed the work of the Pontedera research team the evening before.

4   Grotowski studied directing for one year at the State Institute of Theatre Art in Moscow; he worked with a number of actors and directors who had been associated with the Moscow Art Theatre, though his closest professional relationship was with Yuri Zavadsky (see Kumiega 1985:4).

5   Grotowski's most explicit discussion of this process is included in his text, "From Poor Theatre to Art as vehicle," printed in appendix to Richards 1995.

6   I should caution the reader that I heard Vassiliev's remarks via double translation, from Russian to Portuguese and subsequently from Portuguese to English. Consequently, while the quotations and paraphrases I have made from his observations correspond accurately to the notes I took during the symposium, I cannot be certain that the meanings rendered in this complex process of linguistic transition correspond precisely to Vassiliev's words, though I hope I have not strayed far from his intent.

2 INTRODUCTION TO PART I

1   Barba, twenty-three years old at the time, had been working with Grotowski (as assistant and observer) for more than three years. An Italian by birth, Barba was soon to leave the Laboratory Theatre for Norway and then Denmark where he would gain international recognition on his own for the Odin Theatre, the International School of Theatre Anthropology (ISTA), and many books, including *Alla Ricerca del Teatro Perduto* (1965), the first full-length study of Grotowski's work. The best and most complete documentation of Grotowski's

psychophysical exercises for actors are the films of this work in the Odin's archives and available for rental.

2 Not that there were no places of ritual performances inside Poland. The work of the Gardzienice Theatre Association has affinities to Grotowski's Theatre of Sources. Gardzienice, founded in 1977 and led from the start by Wlodzimierz Staniewski, "seeks to rescue what remains of indigenous culture in the ethnically and religiously heterogeneous territories of southeastern Poland. [. . .] Gardzienice's methods, however, are not those of folklorists and anthropologists. [. . .] Folk materials recorded during expeditions are filtered and distilled through the group's experiences and sensibilities and juxtaposed with literary and dramatic texts such as Rabelais's *Gargantua and Pantagruel* and Adam Mickiewicz's *Forefather's Eve*" (Filipowicz 1987:137). In my 1986 interview with Staniewski, I asked him about his relationship to Grotowski, with whom he worked from 1971 to 1976. Staniewski replied:

> When people ask me this question I feel they want a connection to be there, whether it exists or not. Ask Grot about it – he should say what he thinks about this whole history. He should say how much he gave me, how much I gave him. [. . .] As you know, in 1976 at the climax of Grotowski's paratheatrical work, I left his laboratory to do very profane theatre. [. . .] For me it was very important to make something with its own performative architecture, possessing more than changing ceremonies and rituals.
>
> (in Filipowicz 1987:159)

For more on Gardzienice see Filipowicz 1983 and 1987 and Allain 1995.

3 The *Akropolis* film, though widely known and powerful, doesn't come close to the stage production in intensity or effect. The reasons are multiple. The studio audience for the film appears to be ill at ease; the space itself is too large and too neutral for the production. Peter Brook's introduction, though praising and interesting in its own way, is more a barrier than a bridge.

4 In Witold Filler's *Contemporary Polish Theatre*, published in Warsaw in 1977, the chapter on the avant-garde asserts "the three names which immediately come to mind are Jerzy Grotowski, Jozef Szajna and Tadeusz Kantor" (1977:61). Szajna's *Replika*, which was still being performed in the early 1970s when I saw it in his Warsaw Studio Theatre, has much in common with *Akropolis*. Szajna is an Auschwitz survivor and his experiences – and the ways they are refracted in terms of scenic environment, actors' movements, and overall feeling – is similar in *Replika* and *Akropolis*. The great difference is that Grotowski emphasizes the intense and personal work of the actor, while Szajna embeds the actors in a total mechanistic design. In a mimeographed handout distributed in New York in 1969 when he felt that too much focus was on him and not enough on his collaborators, Grotowski praised Szajna's work on *Akropolis*. "Not for nothing was designer Jozef Szajna billed as realizer. As soon as Auschwitz was seen to be our central theme, I immediately thought of him, not only because he is a brilliant man of the theatre but also because he had been a prisoner in Auschwitz. His contribution to the production was not that of an ordinary designer. He suggested various props and costumes which we used, in the course of creation, like musical instruments on which we invented our own chords." But as Grotowski's biographers rewrote his artistic history, Szajna's contribution was devalued to zero. There is no mention of him in either Osinski's or Kumiega's books on Grotowski.

5 Juliusz Osterwa (1885-1947), the founder-director in 1919 of Reduta, a Polish experimental theatre that has influenced Grotowski in several key ways – in terms of ongoing workshop, the spiritual dimension of theatre work, and the need for absolute dedication to the work. See my Exoduction in this *Sourcebook*

for more on the relationship between Grotowski and Osterwa, as well as Osinski (1990).

7 *THEATRE LABORATORY 13 RZEDOW*

1   Grotowski uses the word archetype in a very precise and explanatory sense. For Jung, the archetype could not be grasped consciously by the individual. The collective unconscious was a supra-individual psyche. On these points, Grotowski disagrees with Jung.

11 INTRODUCTION: THE LABORATORY THEATRE IN NEW YORK, 1969

1   The plastiques are documented in videos distributed by Eugenio Barba's Odin Teatret. These are not abstract or gymnastic, but movements with an "accent" or particular objective. According to a journal kept by NYU workshop participants Tom Crawley and Jerry Mayer (ms, 1967) the plastique movements are done "with a personal association, a partner [. . .] an object. [. . .] You aren't doing the exercises to be technically exact, you do these exercises to express something personal about yourself" (1967, Nov. 8:3–4). Crawley and Mayer speak of Grotowski's insistence that the exercises combine "technique" – a specific way of moving – and "spontaneity," the "accent" of the movement, its personalization. The association exercises actually segue from the plastiques. After mastering the techniques, the performer brings to the movement specific "associations," or images, moods, emotional tones. The movements remain basically the same, but they are inflected by the associations. According to Crawley and Mayer:

> Mr. Grotowski told us that we would do the plastic exercises again, and that he wanted us to work with personal associations, that we *must not imitate* the instructor, we mustn't imitate the elements of his exercise, we must take these elements and use them to express ourselves [. . .] with our own personal images and experiences." (1967, Nov. 8:8)

In 1969–70, Crawley played Duncan in The Performance Group's production of *Makbeth* which I directed. Mayer was a member of André Gregory's Manhattan Project.

21 IN MEMORY OF RYSZARD CIESLAK

1   A "stochastic," non-directional or "casual" process is almost synonymous with "creative" process.
2   André Gregory discussed this project with me in Livorno in December 1982. In the early 1970s, Gregory was the director and guiding force of the experimental Manhattan Project group. He had left the work abruptly and set off along his own crisis-torn path, leaving behind him other actors who no longer had anyone to work with. He was to describe his travels, his experiences, his breaking away and going back, in the film *My Dinner with André*, written and performed together with Wally Shawn, and directed by Louis Malle, in which two friends sitting in an elegant Manhattan restaurant are talking – or rather, André is talking, while Wally almost exclusively listens. The whole film consists of a conversation, which is most often a monologue, but the unexpected surprises

and *coups de theatre* hold the viewer's attention. It is a unique piece of its genre. The script is published by Grove Press.

3 Directed by Torgeir Wethal, produced by Odin Teatret Films for Programmi Sperimentali della Televisionie Italiana (in two parts, running time for each part 50 minutes). Two actors from the Odin Teatret took part in the film as Cieslak's students.

4 The film was presented as an 'audiovisual reconstruction of the performance,' based on a 16 mm feature, shot by an unknown camera operator with a fixed camera, and synchronized later at the Department of Theatre and Performance Studies at the University of Rome in 1974, under the supervision of Ryszard Cieslak. The soundtrack was taped in Oslo in 1965, a couple of years after the film was made. During the editing of the film, there was no need to integrate or correct the soundtrack, which matched up with the images perfectly, despite the time lapse between the film and the recording. The only points where there was not perfect correspondence between sound and image were on those occasions when the filming was interrupted to change the reel – and when that happens, the gap is immediately obvious, as it should be in a restored work. There is a better-quality film (because it was made specifically) of the last 10–15 minutes of the production, made by Norwegian Television, in the archives of the Odin Teatret.

22 INTRODUCTION TO PART II

1 Spychalski went on to become artistic director of Le Groupe de la Veillee in Montreal. Le Groupe was founded by Gabriel Arcand, but Spychalski has been its leader since 1982.

2 Elizabeth Albahaca, Antoni Jaholkowski, Zbigniew Kozlowski, Zygmunt Molik, Teresa Nawrot, Andrzej Paluchiewicz, Irena Rycyk, and Jacek Zymslowski.

3 I suspect what Grotowski read was from a grant proposal. Theatre of Sources was funded by the Rockefeller Foundation, the National University of Mexico, and the Milan Center for Theatre Research.

28 THE THEATRE OF SOURCES

1 Editor's note: the exercises Grimes describes are an early version of what later came to be known as Motions.

32 BALI AND GROTOWSKI

1 In Balinese theatre, in addition to physical positions and their execution (*wiraga*), such as agem, there are two other elements that complete the effectiveness of acting work onstage. These are: *wirasa*, the feeling of what is being performed; and *wirama*, the musicality of the acting. For the purpose of this article, discussion of these two elements is not necessary.

2 Editor's note: For a full discussion of the "three brain" concept-reptilian, old mammalian, and new mammalian – and their relation to trance and other kinds of performance, see Turner (1983, reprinted in Turner 1986). Possibly Grotowski was aware of Turner's writing on this subject.

35 JERZY GROTOWSKI'S DIVINATION CONSULTATION

1   Editor's note: From 1986 to 1992, Grotowski maintained dual residence between U.C.-Irvine, where he functioned as a visiting professor and continued the work of Objective Drama on a part-time basis, and Pontedera, Italy. Grotowski's text "Performer," published and distributed by the Centro per la Sperimentazione e la Ricerca Teatrale in Pontedera, might more appropriately be considered in relation to his later research.

36 INTRODUCTION TO PART IV

1   In 1996, the name of the site for Grotowski's current research was changed; it is now called the Workcenter of Jerzy Grotowski and Thomas Richards.

40 WHERE IS *GURUTOWSKI*?

1   The appellation *Gurutowski* was first used by Patricia Pekmezian in a report from a conference which Grotowski held in Brussels in July 1987. See Jean-Pierre Thibaudat, "'Comme au couvent.' La comedienne Patricia Pekmezian a participe au stage (intensif) que Grotowski a anime cet ete dans un chateau italien. Elle raconte," *Liberation* (1 March 1988): 35–36.

41 *ACTION*: THE UNREPRESENTABLE ORIGIN

1   The majority of songs used in *Action* are derived from West African and African diaspora traditions, including a small number of Haitian songs. *Action* also includes one song by a contemporary Greek composer. This choice is in some sense anomalous, given Grotowski's preference for working with ancient materials which become quasi-anonymous through being transmitted orally from one generation to the next, yet Grotowski maintains that the song in question has the type of "objective" or psychophysiological impact he associates with songs intended to function as tools in ritual/performative practices. Grotowski suggests that examples of such tools, what he elsewhere describes as *yantra* and *organon*, can be found not only in African rituals, but in embodied practices connected with Islamic, Buddhist, Hindu, Christian, and Judaic traditions, among others.

2   Mario Biagini arrived at the Workcenter shortly after it was founded and has participated in the work of Art as vehicle since 1986. He has become a key member of the research team and functions, in some sense, as an assistant workleader. Chirco and Wasilkowski both joined the research team in January 1994. Three other participants (two women and one man) also joined the group at that time, but left the work after fulfilling their initial one-year commitment. Bidaux joined the group in January 1995, though it was understood from the beginning that he would be unable to complete the customary one-year residency due to prior artistic/professional commitments.

3   In accordance with Grotowski's stipulation, my description of *Action* does not include direct quotations from the textual source materials used in the opus – quotations for which I would, at any rate, have to rely entirely on memory, since Biagini's translation was not made available to me for consultation, except on two brief occasions when I examined the text in the company of other witnesses prior to presentations of the structure. In relation to those sections of the

performance structure that foreground text, I have attempted to paraphrase, as closely as possible, my understanding of the source materials.

4 The yanvalou is a kind of walking-dance used in certain types of Haitian ritual practice. It is characteristically performed for a relatively long duration by a group of dancers moving in a line. The dancer's body is angled forward slightly from the hips, and the knees are bent. The stepping pattern of yanvalou calls for the dancer to touch the ground once with the flat of the foot, almost as if caressing the ground, then lift the foot before placing it down again and transferring the body's weight, alternating right and left feet in a gentle, repetitive motion. With each step, the dancer's upper body moves in a soft, almost serpentine wave, the impulse of the movement coming from the base of the spine.

5 Bidaux completed his period of residence at the Workcenter shortly after the presentations I describe. Subsequently, Biagini began to perform the text-based fragments previously executed by Bidaux. I never had a chance to witness the structure once this change was made, and I am curious as to how the shifting of Biagini's role alters the distinction I here elaborate between actors and doers. Does Biagini now alternate between the two registers in his own performance? Does he present the "blasphemous" fragments previously done by Bidaux in the extraordinarily transparent style (performance-without-mimesis) that character-izes the rest of his score? Or has the entire tenor of his performance altered with the addition of these more compositional/representational fragments?

42 THE EDGE-POINT OF PERFORMANCE (Fragments)

1 1995.
2 1984.
3 1985.
4 1986.
5 From Jerzy Grotowski's interview in *Les dossiers* H 1992, Paris (l'Age d'Homme et Bruno de Panafieu), pp. 102–103. Grotowski has reviewed the English translation of this quotation.
6 In residence at the University of California, Irvine (1983–1986).
7 In the Workcenter of Jerzy Grotowski in Pontedera, Italy (1986 on).

43 EXODUCTION

1 Zbigniew Osinski's *Grotowski wytycza trasy: studia i szkice* (1993) is said to have more information concerning Grotowski's early years, including inter-views with friends, associates, family, and so on. Not reading Polish, I can't say.

2 Osinski's *Grotowski and His Laboratory* as it appears in English is abridged. Maybe translators Lillian Vallee and Robert Findlay left out a bunch of stuff about Grotowski's early life. But I doubt it. Grotowski wants to shape what is known about him. He is not eager to lead people to sources he cannot monitor.

3 In the Judaeo-Christian portion of Western intellectual history there are two traditions of transmission, one written and one oral. The written tradition goes back to the "Five Books of Moses," at the center of which are the Ten Commandments, the original "set in stone" document. In this tradition, the core meaning of the universe is written, what remains for succeeding generations is "exegesis" and "interpretation." Nothing new can be added to or taken from the core originary texts. However, through brilliant, shrewd, cunning, and dis-putatious exegesis, these originary texts can be interpreted to mean just about whatever the Talmudists want them to mean. The law is inscribed, but the

practices that stem from the law is open to argument. Not only Talmudic Judaism but Roman Catholic Christianity is heir to this written tradition. And, in our own day, in the field of cultural studies, the dominant Talmudic figure is Jacques Derrida, a French Algerian Jew well versed in word play, exegetic strategies, and interpretation; and a person whose core belief, like Kafka's, another out-of-place Jew, is in the inscribed "text," now far expanded beyond mere words on parchment or stone. The second Judaeo-Christian tradition is the oral "Jesusism." Jesus wrote nothing, carried no tablets of stone down from the mountain.

The opposite of Moses, Jesus preached on a gentle slope, the Mount of Olives. All that we know of Jesus' teachings comes from what his disciples remembered of his utterances. Jesus operated wholly within the oral tradition, gathering around him disciples who also became disseminators. Jesus honors no texts, reveres no Torah as the "book," but rather is passionate about the "Word," something very different, something uttered, spoken, practiced. Jesus did not interpret, he changed. The Mosaic law is distinct and specific, "Honor thy Father and Mother, Take No Other Gods Before Me, Do Not Murder," and so on. And the Five Books, however scholars regard them historically, are written as if they are history: in this place, between these people, who lived this long, such and such happened. Jesus and his followers operate very differently. Jesus speaks in parables, teaches through example, presents his very body, life, and death as mysteries. Jesus is the Messiah because of the miracles he performs, the promises he makes, the sacrifice of his life, and his resurrection.

Ironically, Hasidic Judaism owes much to Jesusism. Even as Jesusism was systematically Hebraicized and Romanized into the regimented, hierarchical, text-based Church, strong currents of Jesusism persisted, in the spontaneous worship of miracle-makers (often sanctified by the Church in its need to coopt any and every species of local worship); in the underground traditions of gnosis and hermetics; and in the continued need for ordinary people, poor people, to believe that life had something better to offer than what they were experiencing daily. On the Jewish side, as the Jews of Europe gained and lost their place, being pushed ever further eastward after the expulsion from Spain in 1492, followed by expulsions from almost every other Western European country, Mosaic faith in the text was shaken. In Eastern Europe, Poland especially, surrounded by hostile, often ecstatic and superstitious Catholics, Jews, victims of pogroms and other horrors, fought fire with fire, inventing their own kind of ecstatic worship, Hasidism. Hasidism carried in its heart both Mosaic tendencies – the passion for learning, the argumentative style – as well as anti-structural inclinations: the celebration of good deeds done against the letter of the law but in keeping with its essence, its true meanings, and more than a little yearning for the Messiah (still to come).

4 Ngugi wa Thiongo's term for the oral tradition, especially as it has flourished in African cultures. See especially Ngugi wa Thiongo's *Decolonizing the Mind* (1987) and Okpewho's *African Oral Literature* (1992).

5 Grotowski considers *Downstairs Action* and *Action* as separate pieces. They each have their own songs, textual materials, and narrative. Other people think of the two as a single, developing work, much as *Apocalypsis* went through several incarnations in the 1960s. But if *Downstairs Action* and *Action* are not cognate, why give them such similar titles? In the late 1980s, Chiquita Gregory made a movie of *Downstairs Action*. But this film is not distributed; Grotowski allows it to be shown only when he is present to explicate it. There is no film of *Action*, though rumor has it that Grotowski and Richards are looking for the right person to make one. Nor is *Action* a regular performance playing to a regular paying public.

6 During our conversation in Copenhagen in May 1996, Grotowski told me that

he felt influenced by gnosis, but not by gnosticism which he said was very different. Checking Gilles Quispel's article in the *Encyclopedia of Religion*, I found how right Grotowski was in making the distinction. "Ever since the congress on the origins of gnosticism held in Messina, Italy, in 1966, scholars have made a distinction between gnosis and gnosticism. *Gnosticism* is a modern term, not attested in antiquity. [. . .] Today gnosticism is defined as a religion in its own right" (1987:567). Ancient gnosis is related to Egyptian Coptic (Christian) religion; and to sources still earlier in Egypt related to the teachings of Hermes Trismegistos – "three times great Hermes" – a being identified with the Egyptian god, Toth. Current scholars believe that gnostics are also related to Hellenic-Jewish practices and thought, especially in Alexandria, a city where Egyptian, Greek, and Jewish cultures intermixed during antiquity.

7   I do not know of any film or video records of these exercises as Grotowski's actors practiced them in the 1950s and 1960s. But the videotapes on actor training which Eugenio Barba made later at the Odin Theatre in Holstebro, Denmark, follow closely Grotowski's exercises. As one who learned the association exercises from Grotowski and Ryszard Cieslak in 1967, I can attest to the similarities between them and what Barba recorded on film.

8   According to Maurice Friedman, Buber joined with Emil Straus, Jakob Hegner, and Paul Claudel to found the Hellerau Dramatic Union. "Buber took an active part in the preparation of the festival of plays that celebrated the opening of the Hellerau Playhouse" in 1913 (1969:16). During this period, and specifically for work at Hellerau, Buber wrote several essays about the theatre.

9   As Ouspensky put it:

> Imagine that in the study of the movements of the heavenly bodies, let us say the planets of the solar system, a special mechanism is constructed to give a visual representation of the laws of these movements and to remind us of them. In this mechanism each planet, which is represented by a sphere of appropriate size, is placed at a certain distance from a central sphere representing the sun. The mechanism is set in motion and all the spheres begin to rotate and to move along prescribed paths, reproducing in a visual form the laws which govern the movements of the planets. This mechanism reminds you of all you know about the solar system. There is something like this in the rhythm of certain dances. In the strictly defined movements and combinations of the dancers, certain laws are visually reproduced which are intelligible to those who know them. Such dances are called "sacred dances". In the course of my travels in the East I have many times witnessed such dances being performed during sacred services in various ancient temples.
>
> (1949:16)

In *Meetings with Remarkable Men* Gurdjieff himself wrote about dances he saw in a monastery in "central Asia." These movements were regulated by an apparatus of ball joints "at least four thousand five hundred years old" (1963:162):

> When all the balls are placed as designated, the form and extent of the given posture are fully defined, and the young pupils stand for hours before the apparatuses, regulated in this way, and learn to sense and remember this posture. Many years pass before these young future priestesses are allowed to dance in the temple, where only elderly and experienced priestesses may dance. Everyone in the monastery knows the alphabet of these postures and when, in the evening in the main hall of the temple, the priestesses perform the dances indicated for the ritual of that day, the brethren may read in these dances one or another truth which men have placed there thousands of years before. These dances correspond precisely to our books. Just as is now done on paper, so, once, certain information about long past events was recorded in dances and

transmitted from century to century to people of subsequent generations. And these dances are called sacred.

(1963:162–63)

10 My "translation" of this *Gita* passage, chapter 11, is adapted from the translations of Barbara Stoller Miller (1986) and R.C. Zaehner (1973). To hear the Sanskrit is something else again.

11 As Shah writes with a wink:

> According to one Persian scholar, Sufism is a Christian aberration. A professor at Oxford thinks that it is influenced by the Hindu *Vedanta*. An Arab-American professor speaks of it as a reaction against intellectualism in Islam. A professor of Semitic literature claims traces of Central Asian Shamanism. A German will have us find it in Christianity plus Buddhism. Two very great English Orientalists put their money on a strong Neoplatonic influence; yet, one of them will concede that it was perhaps independently generated. An Arab, publishing his opinions through an American university, assures his readers that Neoplatonism (which he invokes as a Sufic ingredient) is itself Greek plus Persian. One of the greatest Spanish Arabists, while claiming an initiation of Christian monasticism, plumps for Manichaeism as a Sufi source. Another academician of no less repute finds Gnosticism among the Sufis; while the English professor who is the translator of a Sufistic book prefers to think of it as "a little Persian sect." But another translator finds the mystical tradition of the Sufis "in the Koran itself." [And Professor R.A. Nicholson writes] "Although the numerous definitions of Sufism which occur in Arabic and Persian books on the subject are historically interesting, their chief importance lies in showing that Sufism is undefinable" [1914:25].

(Shah 1971:41)

12 Hermes Trismegistos as the Greeks called him was also the god Toth to the Egyptians. The Arabs called him Idris. According to Shah, quoting the Spanish-Arab historian Said of Toledo (d. 1069):

> Sages affirm that all antediluvian sciences originate with the first Hermes, who lived in Sa'id, in Upper Egypt. The Jews call him Enoch and the Moslem's Idris. He was the first who spoke of the material of the superior world and of planetary movements. He built temples to worship God [. . .] medicine and poetry were his functions.

(in Shah 1971:220)

13 Grotowski met Castaneda during his first trip to California. He met Myerhoff later. Myerhoff's fieldwork among the Huichol of Mexico was a most important source of Castaneda's writings. Castaneda and Myerhoff were graduate student classmates in the anthropology department of the University of Southern California. Castaneda's Yaquis, if they are anybody, are likely to be the Huichols Myerhoff writes about in her *The Peyote Hunt* (1974). Through Myerhoff and me Grotowski became familiar with the writings and work of Victor Turner, though the two of them never met.

14 For an overview/retrospective of Halprin's work, see her *Moving Toward Life* (1995).

15 Within four years, Castaneda published three popular, influential books: *The Teachings of Don Juan: A Yaqui Way of Knowledge* (1968), *A Separate Reality* (1971), and *Journey to Ixtlan* (1972).

16 See my "Waehma: Space, time, identity, and theatre at New Pascua, Arizona" in *The Future of Ritual* (1993). I have discussed the Yaquis with anthropologists who have lived with them in Mexico. Unanimously, they believe Castaneda's books to be fictional constructions, probably helped along by some pretty hefty swallows of peyote or some such. Of course, as Myerhoff and others show,

ingesting peyote, under proper guidance, is exactly what the Huichol and other Native American peoples do.

17   Barba, of course, is one of Grotowski's earliest followers. Over more than thirty-five years, the two men have remained very close. For a full explication of Barba's ideas concerning pre-expressivity and the decided body, see Barba and Savarese *A Dictionary of Theatre Anthropology* (1991).

BIBLIOGRAPHY AND REFERENCES CITED

Allain, Paul (1995) "Coming Home: The New Ecology of the Gardzienice Theatre Association of Poland," *TDR* 39, 1:93–121.

Auslander, Philip (1995) "Just Be Yourself: Logocentrism and difference in performance theory," in Phillip Zarrilli (ed.) *Acting (Re)Considered*, Worlds of Performance series, New York: Routledge, 59–67.

Banu, Georges (1978) "Grotowski a l'academie de Pontedera," *Art-Press* no. 114:40–41.

Barba, Eugenio (1978) "Il parco e la reserva," in Ferdinando Taviani (ed.) *Il libro dell'Odin*, Milan: Feltrinelli.

—— (1986) *Beyond the Floating Islands*, New York: PAJ Publications.

—— (1995) *The Paper Canoe*, New York: Routledge.

Barba, Eugenio and Nicola Savarese (1991) *The Secret Art of the Performer*, ed. Richard Gough, London: Routledge.

Beacham, Richard C. (1987) *Adolph Appia*, Cambridge: Cambridge University Press.

Belo, Jane (1960) *Trance in Bali*, New York: Columbia University Press.

Ben Chaim, Daphna (1984) *Distance in the Theatre: The Aesthetics of Audience Response*, Ann Arbor: UMI Research Press.

Bennett, John G. (1973) *Gurdjieff: Making a New World*, London: Turnstone Books.

Bennett, Susan (1990) *Theatre Audiences: A Theory of Production and Reception*, New York: Routledge.

Bharucha, Rustom (1993) *Theatre and the World*, New York: Routledge.

Birringer, Johannes (1991) *Theatre, Theory, Postmodernism*, Bloomington: Indiana University Press.

Blau, Herbert (1990a) *The Audience*, Baltimore: Johns Hopkins University Press.

—— 1990b "Universals of Performance," in Richard Schechner and Willa Appel (eds) *By Means of Performance*, London: Cambridge University Press.

Blonski, Jan (1981) "Znaki, teatr, swietosc: 1976," in *Romans z tekstem*, Cracow: Wydawnictwo Literackie. (English translation by Edward Rothert: "Signs, Theatre, Holiness," in Stefan Morawski (ed.) *Polish Art Studies: Studies in Art History*, Wroclaw: Zaklwd Narodowy im.)

Bonarski, Andrzej (1975) "Rozmowa z Grotowskim," *Kultura* (30 March): 12–13.

—— (1979) *Ziarno*, Warsaw: Czytelnik.

Braun, Kazimierz (1986) "Where Is Grotowski?" *TDR* 30, 3:226–40.

—— (1986a) "Gdzie jest Grotowski?" *Odra* 11:15–25.

Brook, Peter (1968) "Preface," in Jerzy Grotowski *Towards a Poor Theatre*, New York: Simon and Schuster.

Buber, Martin (1947) *Between Man and Man*, London: Kegan Paul.

—— (1948) *Hasidism*, New York: Philosophical Library.

—— (1970) [1922] *I and Thou*, New York: Charles Scribner's Sons.

Burszynski, Tadeusz (1975) "Grotowski's Exit from the Theatre", *Theatre in Poland (July) 15–16*.

Burzynski, Tadeusz and Zbigniew Osinski (1979) *Grotowski's Laboratory*, Warsaw: Interpress.

——— (1989) "Grotowski – wielkosc nieurojona," in Janusz Degler and Zbigniew Osinski (eds) *Jerzy Grotowski: Teksty z lat 1965–1969*, Wroclaw: Centraly Program Badan Podstawowych, 182–88.

Castaneda, Carlos (1968) *The Teachings of Don Juan: A Yaqui Way of Knowledge*, New York: Ballantine Books.

——— (1971) *A Separate Reality*, New York: Simon and Schuster.

——— (1972) *Journey to Ixtlan*, New York: Simon and Schuster.

Crawley, Thomas and Jerry Mayer (1967) (Untitled journal of Grotowski's 1967 NYU workshop).

Croyden, Margaret (1975) "New Theatre Rule: No Watching Allowed," *Vogue* (New York) December: 196–97.

——— (1993) *In the Shadow of the Flame*, New York: Continuum Press.

Dalcroze (also known as Jaques–Dalcroze), Emile (1976) [1921] *Rhythm, Music, and Education*, New York: Arno Press.

Dan, Joseph (1987) "Hasidism," in Mircea Eliade (gen. ed.) *The Encyclopedia of Religion*, vol. 6:203–11, New York: Macmillan.

De Angulo, Jaime (1953) *Indian Tales*, New York: Hill and Wang.

Derrida, Jacques (1978) "The Theatre of Cruelty and the Closure of Representation," in *Writing and Difference*, trans. Alan Bass, Chicago: University of Chicago Press 232–50.

Drake, Sylvia (1983) "Grotowski to Set Scene at U.C. Irvine," *Los Angeles Times* 29 September 1, 5.

Eliade, Mircea (1984) "Jaga", in *Niesmiertelnosc*, trans. Boleslaw Baranowski, Warsaw: Panstwowe Wydawnictwo Naukowe.

Eliot, T.S. (1975) "Hamlet," in *Selected Prose of T.S. Eliot*, ed. Frank Kermode, New York: Harcourt, Brace and Jovanovich.

Filipowicz, Halina (1983) "Expedition into Culture," *TDR* 27, 1:54–71.

——— (1987) "Gardzienice: A Polish expedition to Baltimore," *TDR* 31, 1:137–63.

Filler, Witold (1977) *Contemporary Polish Theatre*, Warsaw: Interpress.

Findlay, Robert (1982) "Grotowski's *l'homme pur*: Towards demystification," *Theatre Perspectives* no. 2.

——— (1986) "1976–1986: A necessary afterword," in Zbigniew Osinski *Grotowski and His Laboratory*, trans. and ed. Lillian Vallee and Robert Findlay, New York: PAJ Publications.

Flaszen, Ludwik (n.d.) "Documents on the Laboratory Theatre 13 Rzedow," *International Theatre Institute*.

——— (1962) Interview with Eugenio Barba.

——— (1983) *Teatr skazany na magie*, ed. Henryk Chlystowski, Cracow: Wydawnicto Literackie.

Focused Research Program in Objective Drama (1983) *Rockefeller Foundation Grant Proposal* (unpublished manuscript on file at UCI Foundation Relations Office).

——— 1984 "Report to the Rockefeller Foundation" (unpublished manuscript on file at UCI Foundation Relations Office).

——— 1985 "Research and Development Report" (Unpublished manuscript on file at UCI Foundation Relations Office).

Furlong, Gary and James Harrison (1985) "In Search of Impulse: Zygmunt Molik and the Polish Theatre Lab," *Theatrum: A Theatre Journal* (Summer): 11–31.

Gainese, TK (1979) *Fritz Perls Here and Now*. TK: Celestial Arts.

Gerould, Daniel (1980) "Jerzy Grotowski's Theatrical and Paratheatrical Activities as Cosmic Drama: Roots and continuities in the Polish Romantic tradition," *World Literature Today* no. 3:381–83.

Gordon, Mel (1978) "The Theatre of the Miraculous," 22, no. 2 (T78):32–44.

Grotowski, Jerzy (1961) "The Ancestors," *Wspolczesnosc* (November).
—— (1968) *Towards a Poor Theatre*, New York: Simon and Schuster.
—— (1972) "Co bylo (Kolumbia – lato 1970 – Festiwal Ameryki Lacinskiej)" *Dialog* 17, no. 10:110–18.
—— (1973) "Holiday," 17, no. 2 (T58): 113–35.
—— (1978) "The Art of the Beginner," *International Theatre Information* (Spring/Summer):7–11.
—— (1979) "Exercises," originally published in *Dialog* (unpublished translation from French and Italian by James Slowiak).
—— (1980) "Odpowiedz Stanislawskiemu," *Dialog* 25, no. 5: 111–19.
—— (1987) "Teatr Zrodel," *Zeszyty Literackie* 5, no. 19: 102–15.
—— (1990) "Ensemble since Stanislavsky," lecture, U.C.-Irvine 27 May.
—— (1995) "From the Theatre Company to Art as vehicle," in Thomas Richards, *At Work with Grotowski*, London: Routledge, 115–35.
—— (1996a) "A Kind of Volcano," in Jacob Needleman and George Baker, *Gurdjieff: Essays and Reflections on the Man and His Teachings*, New York: Continuum, 87–106.
—— (1996b) "Orient/Occident," trans. Maureen Schaeffer Price, in Patrice Pavis (ed.) *The Intercultural Performance Reader*, New York and London: Routledge.
—— (1999) 'I do not put on a play to teach others what I already know.' *The Drama Review* 43, 2:12–13.
Gurdjieff, G.I. (1963) *Meetings with Remarkable Men*, New York: E.P. Dutton.
—— (1973) *Views from the Real World*, New York: Dutton.
Halman, Talat Sait and Metin And (1983) *Mevlana Celaleddin Rumi and the Whirling Dervishes*, Istanbul: Dart publications.
Halprin, Anna (1995) *Moving toward Life*, Middletown: Wesleyan University Press.
Kelera, Jozef (1974) "Grotowski w mowie pozornie zaleznej," *Odra* 14 (May):35–44.
Kolankiewicz, Leszek (1979) *On the Road to Active Culture*, trans. Boleslaw Taborski, Wroclaw: Instytut Laboratorium.
—— (1989a) "'Dramat Obiektywny' Grotowskiego (1)," *Dialog* no. 5: 126–39.
—— (1989b) "'Dramat Obiektywny' Grotowskiego (2)," *Dialog* no. 6: 143–54.
Kott, Jan. (1989) "Grotowski albo granica," *Dialog* no. 5: 146–49.
Kumiega, Jenna (1985) *The Theatre of Grotowski*, New York: Methuen.
Lendra, I Wayan (1991) "The Motions: A detailed description," *TDR* 35, 1:129–38.
Mandelstam, Osip (1979) "Conversation about Dante," in *The Complete Critical Prose and Letters*, trans. Jane Gary Harris and Constance Link, Ann Arbor: Ardis, 397–442.
Marranca, Bonnie and Gautam Dasgupta (eds) (1991) *Interculturalism and Perform ance*, New York: PAJ Publications.
Merleau-Ponty, Maurice (1962) *Phenomenology of Perception*, trans. Colin Smith, London: Routledge and Kegan Paul.
Molinari, Renata (1982) "Aspetti del rapporto attore-spettore attraverso le esperienze parateatrali del Teatr Laborotorium di Wroclaw," *Conjunto* 10: 17–23.
Moore, James (1991) *Gurdjieff: The Anatomy of a Myth*, Rockport, MA: Element.
Myerhoff, Barbara (1974) *The Peyote Hunt*, Ithaca: Cornell University Press.
—— (1990) "The Transformation of Consciousness in Ritual Performances: Some Thoughts and Questions," in Richard Schechner and Willa Appel (eds) *By Means of Ritual*, Oxford: Oxford University Press.
—— (1992) *Remembered Lives: The Work of Ritual, Storytelling, and Growing Older*, ed. and introduction Marc Kaminsky, Ann Arbor: University of Michigan Press.
Needham, J. (1956) *Science and Civilization in China*, Cambridge: Cambridge University Press.
Needleman, Jacob and George Baker (eds) (1996) *Gurdjieff: Essays and Reflections on the Man and His Teaching*, New York: Continuum.

Ngugi wa Thiongo (1987) *Decolonizing the Mind*, Heinemann, NH: James Currey.

Nicholson, R.A. (1914) *The Mysteries of Islam*, London.

Okpewho, Isadore (1992) *African Oral Literature*, Bloomington: Indiana University Press.

Osinska, Krystyna (1988) *Pustelnicy dzis: Samotnosc z wyboru ludzi swieckich*, Warsaw: Instytut Wydawniczy PAX.

Osinski, Zbigniew (1972) "Konwencja y antykonwencza w Teatrze Laboratorium," *Teksty* no. 3:33–47.

—— (1986) *Grotowski and His Laboratory*, trans. Robert Findlay and Lillian Vallee, New York: PAJ Publications.

—— (1990) "La tradizione di Reduta in Grotowski e nel Teatro Laboratorio," *Teatro e Storia* 5, no. 2:259–300.

—— (1993) *Grotowski wytycza trasy: Studia i szkice*, Warsaw: Wydawr Pusty Oblok.

Osterwa, Juliusz (1968) *Listy Juliusza Osterwy*, Warsaw: Panstwowy Instytut Wydawniczy.

Ouspensky, P.D. (1949) *In Search of the Miraculous*, New York: Harcourt Brace.

Perls, Frederick, S., Ralph F. Hefferline, and Paul Goodman (1969) [1951] *Gestalt Therapy: Excitement and Growth in the Human Personality*, New York: Julian Press.

Pound, Ezra (1973) "Provincionalism the Enemy," in *Selected Prose 1909–1965*, ed. William Cookson, London: Faber and Faber, 159–73.

Puzyna, Konstanty (1980) "Grotowski i dramat romantyczny," *Dialog* no. 3:107–11. For an English translation by Jacob Conrad, see "Grotowski and Polish Romantic Drama," *Theatre Three* (Spring 1988):45–50.

Quadri, Franco (1994) "Interview with Jerzy Grotowski," *Patologo* 17: 109–12.

Rasmussen, Iben Nagel (1979) "Le Mute del Passate," *Scena* 3–4: 49.

Richards, Thomas (1995) *At Work with Grotowski on Physical Actions*, New York: Routledge.

Ronen, Dan (1978) "A Workshop with Ryszard Cieslak," *TDR* 22 (December): 67–76.

Salzmann, Michel de (1987) "Gurdjieff, G.I." in Mircea Eliade (gen. ed.) *Encyclopedia of Religion*, vol. 6:139–40, New York: Macmillan.

Schechner, Richard (1982) "The Decline and Fall of the American Avant-garde," in *The End of Humanism: Writings on Performance*, New York: PAJ Publications.

—— (1983) *Performative Circumstances from the Avant Garde to Ramlila*, Calcutta: Seagull Books.

—— (1985) *Between Theatre and Anthropology*, Philadelphia: University of Pennsylvania Press.

—— (1993) *The Future of Ritual*, New York: Routledge.

Schechner, Richard and Mady Schuman (1976) *Ritual, Play, and Performance*, New York: The Seabury Press.

Schechner, Richard and Willa Appel (eds) (1990) *By Means of Performance*, London: Cambridge University Press.

Schwartz, Sanford (1985) *The Matrix of Modernism: Pound, Eliot and Early Twentieth-century Thought*, Princeton: Princeton University Press.

Schwerin von Krosigk, Barbara (1986) *"Der Nackte Schauspieler": Die Entwicklung der Schauspielertheorie Jerzy Grotowskis*, Berlin: Publica.

Shah, Idries (1971) *The Sufis*, Garden City: Double Day Anchor.

Shawn, Wallace and André Gregory (1981) *My Dinner with André*, New York: Grove Press.

Speeth, Kathleen Riordan (1989) *The Gurdjieff Work*, New York: G.P. Putnam's Sons.

Stepien, Joanna (1988) "Gdzie jest Grotowski" [an interview with Zbigniew Osinski], *Zycie Warszawy* [*Kultura i Zycie* supplement] 45 (27 May): 3.

Sullivan, Dan (1983) "A Prophet of the Far Out," *Los Angeles Times* 2 October:1, 42.

Tatarkiewicz, Wladyslaw (1989) *Historia estetyki*, vol. 2, Warsaw: Arkady.

Taviani, Ferdinando (1988) "Commento a il Performer," *Teatro e Storia* 3, no. 2:259–72.

Thibaudat, Jean-Pierre (1989) "Gurutowski," *Liberation* March 1:35–36.

—— (1995) "Grotowski, un vehicle du theatre," *Liberation* March 1:35–36.

Tiezzi, Federico (1988) "Pas de viande dans un restaurant de poisson: Il grado zero della scrittura," *Patologo* 11:210–13.

Toporkov, Vasily Osipovich (1979) *Stanislavsky in Rehearsal*, trans. Christine Edwards, New York: Theatre Arts Books.

Turner, Victor (1982) *From Ritual to Theatre*, New York: PAJ Publications.

—— (1983) "Body, Brain, and Culture," *Zygon* 18, no.3:221–46.

—— (1986) *The Anthropology of Performance*, New York: PAJ Publications.

Werblowsky, R.J. Zwi (1987) "Shabbetai Tsevi," in Mircea Eliade (gen. ed.) *The Encyclopedia of Religion*, vol. 13:192–94, New York: Macmillan.

Winterbottom, Philip (1991) 'Two Years before the Master," *TDR* 35, no. 1:140–54.

Wolford, Lisa (1994) "Re/Membering Home and Heritage: The New World Performance Laboratory," *TDR* 38, no. 3:128–51.

—— (1996a) *Grotowski's Objective Drama Research*, Mississippi: University Press of Mississippi.

—— (1996b) "*Ta-wil* of Action: The New World Performance Laboratory's Persian Cycle," *New Theatre Quarterly* 46:156–76.

—— (1996c) "The Occupation o the Saint: Grotowski's Art as vehicle," Doctoral dissertation; Northwestern University.

Workcenter of Jerzy Grotowski (1988) "Introduction," *Workcenter of Jerzy Grotowski*, Pontedera, Italy: Centro per la sperimentazione e la Ricerca Teatrale.

INDEX